Greenwich Readers : 5

An Introductory Reader in Developmental Psychology

An Introductory Reader in Developmental Psychology

edited by

JAMES D. DEMETRE

SENIOR LECTURER IN PSYCHOLOGY
UNIVERSITY OF GREENWICH

Greenwich University Press

Selection, arrangement, preface and section introductions are
© Greenwich University Press 1995

First published in 1995 by
Greenwich University Press
Unit 42
Dartford Trade Park
Hawley Road
Dartford
Kent DA1 1PF
United Kingdom

British Library Cataloguing-in-Publication Data
A CIP catalogue record for this book is available from the British Library

ISBN 1 874529 36 1

Designed and produced for Greenwich University Press by
Angela Allwright and Kirsten Brown.

Printed in Great Britain by The Bath Press, Avon.

Every effort has been made to trace all the copyright holders, but if any have been inadvertently overlooked the publishers will be pleased to make the necessary arrangements at the earliest opportunity.

Contents

Preface

The field of developmental psychology

Developmental psychology has undergone a number of transformations in the last half-century and is currently more diverse in its subject matter, theoretical underpinnings, and research methodology than at any time in the past. Modern developmental psychologists study as diverse a range of phenomena as is to be found in the whole of psychology, and an indicative list of current topics receiving serious attention could include:-

the contribution of friendships to children's social and intellectual development;

the identification of brain pathologies associated with children's learning difficulties;

the effects of media and information technology on children's social and intellectual development;

newborn infants' visual and auditory capacities;

the origins of different personality attributes;

the contributions of parent-child relationships to social development;

the contribution of cultural patterns to intellectual development;

the influence of childhood experiences on subsequent psychiatric problems.

Developmental psychologists who specialise in any one of the above areas are likely to have a very different profile of knowledge, technical research skills, and theoretical orientations from those who specialise in 'neighbouring' areas of developmental psychology. Indeed, some developmental psychologists are better equipped through their training and interests to communicate with investigators in another discipline, such as neurophysiology, psychiatry, or sociology, than with other developmental psychologists.

'Getting into' the field

The diversity of coverage within the subject can be both a source of delight and frustration to the new student. Textbooks on developmental psychology provide useful maps of key concerns, issues, theoretical orientations and empirical evidence currently dominating the field, but generally provide little insight into how a given topic becomes important, how arguments and evidence are marshalled by investigators, or how conclusions are reached. It is my belief that it is these aspects of any discipline that students have the greatest difficulty in mastering. The implicit model governing university education for undergraduate students seems to be that learning itself is an implicit affair: given time, exposure, and sufficient motivation students will 'crack' the 'deep structure' of a discipline. This putative, inductive learning process of somehow extracting underlying principles from particular facts does not seem to be the means by which scientists learn about the world (see Medawar, 1969), and seems a very hit-or-miss method to use in education.

My intention in compiling this Reader is to provide a guided tour of how researchers pinpoint a given research problem, how they create "hypotheses" or reasoned guesses as to a likely answer or range of answers to a given question, and how they set about gathering evidence and marshalling arguments for a given conclusion. This book is intended for students new to psychology (first and second years), though I strongly suspect that more advanced students would also stand to benefit from it, as would students and trainees in education, nursing, psychiatry and paediatrics.

The reporting of research

Before proceeding it is important to say something about the structure of the 'research paper'. Most of the published research conducted by psychologists is ultimately reported in the fairly standardised form of the 'scientific article'. This routinely comprises four major sections: the Introduction, telling readers about the background to the research question and providing arguments as to likely answers (hypotheses); the Method, reporting the details of exactly how the research was undertaken; the Results, informing the readers of the actual outcome of the research; and the Discussion, offering an interpretation of the findings reported in the Results, relating these to any hypotheses proffered in the Introduction, and making suggestions for possible 'fruitful' avenues of research to be pursued. Many of the articles reproduced in this volume conform to this standard format and I would like to make two main points relating to this.

First, it is important as a new student to read an article at least twice: on the first reading, focus on the main content of the article and attempt to make some general sense of "what it is about", what was found by the researchers, etc. On the second, slower reading, make an attempt to "get into the minds" of the authors, paying close attention to the structure of arguments and rationale used in their introductory section; envision undertaking the study yourself from the details furnished in the Method section; focus on the type of evidence produced in the Results section; and examine closely how the evidence is related to the hypotheses in the Discussion. It is precisely through this examination of the *structure*, as well as the content of research articles in developmental psychology, that you gain insights into the motivations and reasoning that influence investigators and consequently insights into the character of the field as a whole. By concentrating on the structure of research articles it is also likely to improve the standard of your own writing in psychology.

Second, and in contrast to the first point made above, the research article in many ways perpetrates a convenient mythology as to the process of investigation: in many cases, the research process is not motivated by beautifully crafted and elegant hypotheses leading inexorably to a specific study with a single interpretation. The intellectual biographies of eminent researchers make it clear that 'intuitions', 'gut feelings' and plain luck make incalculable contributions to the whole enterprise (for particularly interesting instances, see Bruner, 1983; Crick, 1988; Medawar, 1979, 1982, Watson, 1968). These are not openly discussed in research articles, neither are the equally important influences of *Zeitgeist* (intellectual and cultural climate) and preferences of funding agencies for particular kinds of research (see Rose and Rose, 1969). Nevertheless, the structure of research articles does provide insight into the accepted canons of the discipline and demonstrates how investigators ultimately have to frame their enquiry.

Data and statistics

Most research articles in developmental psychology contain copious amounts of quantitative data in the form of descriptive and inferential statistics. It is beyond the scope of this volume to elucidate fully the use of statistical analysis in psychological research, but readers are referred to Clegg (1988) for a gentle introduction to this topic. The final chapter of the present volume contains a brief statistical primer: readers lacking an elementary education in statistics may wish to read this chapter in its entirety, others may simply wish to consult sections relating to statistical terms encountered in the main articles. A few of the articles make reference to more advanced statistical tests which most readers will not encounter until their final year of study.

For our current purposes my advice is not to be put off by the statistics. If you do not understand what $p < .05$ means, do not worry about this, unless it is a requirement that you understand inferential statistics! It is likely that most psychology students will have received some instruction in inferential statistics before the end of their first year of university study. Irrespective of whether or not you understand inferential statistics, pay attention to the main descriptive statistics: the means (arithmetic averages) are presented typically either in the form of numerical values in a table, or in the form of bar charts.

A good strategy for dealing with the statistics is to attempt in the first instance to understand the reported findings as much as possible without paying undue attention to the statistics; then read the primer at leisure, and then reread the original articles.

Coverage

A number of conflicting considerations entered into the compilation of this volume. On the one hand, it is desirable to include 'landmark' studies and articles representing key areas and debates in the field; on the other hand, it is equally desirable that articles be accessible to the new student and not be too abstruse. Predictably under the circumstances I have opted for a compromise: work relating to major developmental theorists such as Piaget, Bowlby, Vygotsky, Chomsky and Erikson has been included, but as far as possible, the selections were made with readability in mind. Articles reporting studies that are cited frequently in textbooks feature very strongly here.

Other goals informing my selections have been either more implicit or only partially realised. One such goal was to show how researchers in developmental psychology can take a theoretical issue or a piece of 'pure' research and use it to address a practical problem. This is illustrated in the section *Cognitive Development in Childhood*, where Demetre & Gaffin explore the implications of the classic study by Hughes and Donaldson in attempting to understand road accidents to children. Similarly, in the following section, *Social Relationships in Childhood*, the article by Bierman, Miller and

Stabb takes on board research into the influences of friendship on development in order to devise intervention programmes for peer-rejected boys.

The choice of topics for this volume was also the result of multidimensional compromises. The content parallels a first-year course that I teach at the University of Greenwich. The overriding factor informing topic selection is a notion of what currently constitutes 'core areas' in developmental psychology. Years of acquaintance with the primary research journals and textbooks provides one with a sense of what students are expected to know. This, together with limitations of space, has led to the exclusion of some topical research areas (e.g., influences of media on children; influences of information technology and computer games on children; the effects of environmental toxins on intellectual development) as well as areas of long-standing debate (e.g., the development of gender roles; temperament and personality development; childhood precursors of psychiatric problems). Students are advised to read this volume in conjunction with a key textbook in developmental psychology; the texts by Cole & Cole (1993) and Smith & Cowie (1991) are especially recommended.

References

Bruner, J. (1983) *In Search of Mind: Essays in Autobiography*. New York: Harper and Row.

Clegg, F. (1988) *Simple Statistics*. Cambridge: Cambridge University Press.

Cole, M. & Cole, S. R. (1993) *The Development of Children*. San Francisco: Freeman/Scientific American Books (2nd edition).

Crick, F. (1988) *What Mad Pursuit: A Personal View of Scientific Discovery*. Harmondsworth: Penguin.

Medawar, P. B. (1969) *Induction and Intuition in Scientific Thought*. London: Methuen.

Medawar, P. B. (1979) *Advice to a Young Scientist*. New York: Harper and Row.

Medawar, P. B. (1982) *Pluto's Republic*. Oxford: Oxford University Press.

Rose, H. & Rose, S. (1969) *Science and Society*. Harmondsworth: Penguin.

Smith, P. & Cowie, H. (1991) *Understanding Children's Development*. Oxford: Blackwell (2nd edition).

Watson, J. D. (1968) *The Double Helix*. Harmondsworth: Penguin.

Publisher's note

The contents of the readings in this anthology have been reproduced as they appear in the publications from which they are taken. In the majority of cases footnotes and bibliographic material are included, the exceptions being where they are of excessive length. Photographs have not been reproduced.

Early Experience

A number of writers in psychology and biology have assigned a paramount role to experiences occurring in the opening years of life. Traditionally, three main arguments have been proposed in support of the view that the earliest experiences are the most crucial in shaping the development of the individual.

One of the most contested arguments relates to 'critical' or 'sensitive' periods in development. According to this view, experiences occurring at a relatively specific time (usually early) in development have a durable impact on an individual because the organism is purportedly in some optimal state of 'readiness'. This view is particularly associated with the biologist, Konrad Lorenz, and with Sigmund Freud, the originator of psychoanalysis. The view has been echoed by John Bowlby in his theory of infant social attachments: if the human infant does not experience a durable relationship with a caregiver by the age of two or three years, then the child's social and emotional development will be forever compromised.

A second argument relates to the developmental plasticity of the brain. While it is now recognised that the brain continues to develop and change thoughout the lifespan, it is nevertheless the case that both the rate and character of early brain development suggest that it may be particularly affected by experiences. Some authors argue that experiences can 'set' the patterning of neural circuits early in life when the brain is particularly maleable, and that once set, such neural circuits become relatively difficult to alter. Thus, there are two sides to this argument: in early development, the brain has an excess capacity to be 'programmed' by experiences, and hence, skills and abilities may more readily be acquired in early life; once this period of heightened plasticity is over, changes to pre-existing circuits and the creation of new circuits are both more difficult to accomplish.

A third argument relates to 'unlearning'. Simply stated, early experience is argued to have a disproportionate impact on development because patterns of behaviour derived from early experience need to be dismantled systematically or unlearned before later experiences can have an impact. For example, a young child who grows up experiencing hostility from adults will learn to avoid adults and will also develop various associated emotions and coping strategies. If this child were then placed in a new environment peopled by benevolent adults, the effects of the earlier experiences will (for a time at least) interfere with the acquisition of new expectations and modes of behaviour more appropriate to the child's new circumstances.

While each of the arguments presented above can be debated at length, there is a dearth of evidence relating to the primacy of early experience. Ideally, one would look to evidence from systematically controlled experiments to establish whether indeed the timing of various kinds of experience is crucial or advantageous. However, on both ethical and pragmatic grounds such evidence is unlikely to be forthcoming. Researchers have instead focused on 'natural experiments' — individuals who for reasons unintended by the researchers have 'missed out' on 'normal' experiences in early life.

The first article by Ann Clarke provides a brief review of various strands of evidence relating to the issue of early experience. The following two papers by David Skuse attempt to make some systematic sense of the different outcomes characterising individuals who have experienced sensory and/or social deprivation in early childhood. The case material provided by Skuse is particularly interesting in that the reader has the opportunity to construct his/her own interpretation of what factors can compensate for a poverty of early experience, and the implications this has for a theory of the contribution of early experience.

1.   Early Experience and The Life Path
Ann M. Clarke

In the early 1950s my husband and I were appointed to an institution for the mentally retarded, a large, very old-fashioned establishment run on a minimum budget, housing some 1,400 people of various ages and degrees of handicap. John Bowlby's monograph had just been published, reinforcing an ancient view concerning the crucial importance of early experience for later development. Imagine our surprise, then to discover, at first accidentally, and later in controlled studies, that among a large group of mildly retarded adolescents and young adults, substantial improvements in cognitive and social functioning were revealed, and these were correlated with the degree of early social disadvantage — the worse the history, the better the outcome. We began to believe that there might be much more resilience and potential for change than the published evidence suggested, and cautiously stated this from 1958 onwards, becoming much more confident by 1968. However, it was not until 1976 that sufficient hard data from a variety of fields were available for us to mount a major challenge to the widely held belief that the effects of severe and prolonged environmental disadvantage in the early years were irreversible. Early experience *per se* does not, unless reinforced, possess crucially formative, long-term effects.

As I wrote, in *Early Experience: Myth and Evidence* (1976) 'We have assembled a body of information which suggests a reformulation; this should not be interpreted literally as a counter-balance, which might be an equal and opposite extreme, but rather an attempt to achieve a balanced view'. We emphasised the essential methodological point that 'unless it can be positively shown that there was a significant discontinuity between early and late environmental circumstances, no conclusions can legitimately be drawn concerning the effect of the former' (p.271), a point endorsed by Bronfenbrenner (1979) who stated that 'the enduring developmental effects of a setting cannot be effectively assessed within that setting' (p. 286). We ourselves warned that one of the ways in which the effects of early experience can be perpetuated is via transactional processes. A given effect in the child acts upon the environment, producing in turn a reinforcing feedback. We also hypothesised that adverse early experience might lead to overt recovery, but with later possibly increased vulnerability to stress.

This lecture will attempt to recapitulate and to up-date the findings of our book, a decade later almost to the day. It must be first stated that there is now a much better understanding of development than formerly. Research suggests several interacting processes, the headlines of which can be stated as follows: as I have indicated elsewhere (Clarke, 1984; Clarke, Clarke and Berg, 1985) many human differences have at least some hereditary components. This genetic or constitutional trajectory unfolds at

Ann M. Clarke: 'Early Experience and the Life Path' (The Sixth Vernon-Wall Lecture delivered at the University of Nottingham, September 1986). Reproduced by permission of the author and the British Psychological Society. © British Psychological Society 1987.

different rates — a down-to-earth example is the adolescent growth spurt, lasting a few years. Then there is a social trajectory, determined within broad limits by accident of birth, and alterable by chance events or by design. It also unfolds at different rates, depending on the child's familial and later widening social interactions. Lastly, there is the effect of children on parents, siblings, teachers and others, and the latter's reactions which, in feed-back cycles, can reinforce or alter behaviour. This Transactional Model (Sameroff and Chandler, 1975; Sameroff, 1975) enjoys increasing recognition. Studies of child abuse represent an empirically supported example of transactional processes. Abused children tend to differ from their siblings prior to maltreatment; they may be 'difficult' or physically or mentally handicapped or deviant in some other way (Belsky, 1978). If parental resources or competence are marginal, tragedy may be an outcome. Transactions are also indicated in the work of Brophy and Good (1974), among others; pupils tend to create their own learning environments, differing in the amounts of teacher attention they seek, and thus eliciting differential responses as well as differences in teacher ratings, even within fairly homogeneous ability groups. Or again, in my reassessment of Trasler's (1960) study of fostering breakdown, it emerged that the vast majority of unsuccessful first placements were known to have occurred with foster parents found to be unsuitable in a variety ways. It is assumed that disturbed children elicited adverse responses from foster parents whose competence was probably marginal. Child maladjustment was thus reinforced by further adversity, an early example of transactional effects (Clarke, 1968).

Inter-personal transactions continue throughout childhood, and, indeed, the life span. Such findings underline the immensely complex picture of development, and endorse our view that this is potentially somewhat open-ended.

These fairly new concepts owe much to the investigations of Chess and Thomas, the initiators of the New York Longitudinal Study over twenty-five years ago. Emerging from this research was a very important theoretical notion, namely 'goodness of fit'. They write that 'When the organism's capacities, motivations and style of behaving and the demands and expectations of the environment are in accord, goodness of fit results. Such consonance between organism and environment potentiates optimal positive development. Should there be dissonance . . . there is poorness of fit, which leads to maladaptive functioning and distorted development . . . There is no implication in the concept of goodness of fit that stress and conflict are absent . . . (these) are essential aspects of the developmental process . . . It is rather excessive stress due to poorness of fit that results in behaviour problems' (Chess and Thomas, 1984, p.21). Differences between child and parental temperaments are prime causes of poorness of fit.

Rescue from severe adversity

Case histories can be highly selective, and it is necessary to check that processes of recovery revealed when children are rescued from the severest adversity exhibit in exaggerated form the same phenomena which are less marked in studies in which changes in less deprived children are recorded. The following examples include those which meet these criteria.

One well documented study is by Koluchova (1972, 1976 and personal communications, 1981, 1986). Monozygotic twin boys, born in 1960, were taken into care when their mother died shortly thereafter. Development was entirely normal, and after a year a maternal aunt looked after them for six months. The father, a simple man, remarried and moved to another town. The stepmother, who proved to be a sadistic psychopath, conceived a pathological hatred of the boys who were banished for most of the time to a cellar or to an unheated closet. They were malnourished, neglected and cruelly chastised. At the age of seven, some five and a half years after exposure to these conditions, the father brought one of the boys to a paediatrician asking for a certificate that his son was unfit to enter primary school. Because the child looked as if he was aged three, hardly walked and appeared severely mentally retarded, the doctor agreed, but insisted on kindergarten attendance and an investigation of family circumstances. It gradually became clear that criminal neglect was involved.

The children were without speech upon discovery, but communicated by means of gestures; the IQs on non-verbal measures were in the 40s. After treatment for rickets they were placed in a school for the mentally retarded, but to cut a long story short, soon graduated to a normal school where they were placed in a class with younger children. At the age of nine they were adopted into the home of two unmarried middle-aged ladies with some experience of deprived children. IQs and emotional development improved markedly, so that by age eleven, the former were in the 90s, by fourteen around 100, and as adults 115.

In time, because of hard work, they skipped a class in order to be with children nearer their own age, and at around fifteen moved to a vocational school ultimately specialising in 'electro-technology'. They were regarded as entirely normal emotionally, scholastically and intellectually. Now aged 25 all goes well and one is shortly to be married.

Case histories like these have been excellently reviewed by Skuse (1984a and b). In the first paper the author has provided an important addition to the literature in describing the later development of two sisters rescued as young children from an extraordinary family. One girl appears to have recovered completely, while the other remains handicapped, shows autistic features and is microcephalic, like her mentally retarded mother, later diagnosed as schizophrenic. In the second paper, Skuse has reviewed the whole field of extreme deprivation, concluding that 'in the absence of genetic or congenital anomalies, or a history of gross malnourishment, victims of such deprivation have an excellent prognosis. Some subtle deficits in social adjustment may persist . . . most human characteristics, with the possible exception of language, are strongly 'canalised' . . . and hence virtually resistant to obliteration by even the most dire early environments' (p.567). This statement coincides with my own view, except the point about gross malnourishment. Isabelle (Davis, 1947), the Koluchova twins and a case now to be described, were all severely malnourished yet made extraordinary recoveries.

The case of Adam, summarised by Clarke (1984) and extensively by the investigator (Thompson, 1986) is a further indication of the potentiality for recovery of severely deprived, malnourished children.

This Colombian child was abandoned at four months, and received into a reformatory for girls. Thompson visited him there and described his condition as appalling. His main diet was a watery vegetable soup and porridge, and he remained in a bleak, bare, windowless room in perpetual darkness unless the door was open. Removed at sixteen months to a missionary orphanage he weighed only 12 pounds, 12 ounces and appeared developmentally to function at a three-month level. He was diagnosed as a mentally retarded spastic. He improved rapidly, both physically and mentally and was adopted at 32 months by a North American family. There were initially very severe problems but now in his teens the boy is above average in ability and is regarded as a normal schoolboy, in fact, doing very well (Thompson, personal communications).

At this point it might be possible to rest my case, that, provided there is a significant environmental shift, early adversity does not predetermine a disastrous life path. However, it is necessary to check this out with studies of more 'typical' deprived groups. By now there are a large number of well designed studies which could be mentioned. I will concentrate on just a few.

It will be appropriate now to consider some further examples of intervention studies, so I must first say what I mean by intervention. This term can be interpreted widely as involving any systematic attempt to alter the course of development from either its established or predicted path. It may aim to produce 'desirable' behaviour or prevent the continuation or emergence of the 'undesirable'; it may be short- or long-term. Intervention studies are of intrinsic interest, but their wider significance are expressed in general terms by the late Walter Dearborn 'If you want to understand something, try to change it' (Bronfenbrenner, 1977). There are, of course, a variety of forms of intervention, but here only three will be considered, each primarily, though not exclusively, within the cognitive domain. I will start with two studies of children who were adopted rather late, these being examples of *total* intervention.

Total intervention: late adoption

If we are right in arguing that early experience by itself, unless reinforced subsequently, possesses no crucial long-term effects, what about later intervention? Can later intervention have as large immediate effects as earlier, and are these any more or any less persistent? These questions are difficult to answer, since there is a dearth of later intervention studies, although some, such as those by Davis (1947) and Koluchova (1972, 1976) already noted, represent major developmental increments at relatively late ages after major ecological change.

Among studies of groups, the work of Kadushin (1970) is among the finest. He reported on a group of healthy children, typically coming from large families in substandard circumstances, often below poverty level and suffering physical neglect. Natural parents showed a picture of promiscuity, mental deficiency, alcoholism, imprisonment and psychosis. At an average age of 3½ the children had been legally removed from their homes, and after an average of 2-3 changes of foster homes were placed for adoption at an average age of just over 7, and followed up at an average of almost 14 years. Adoptive parents were older than natural parents and of a considerably higher socioeconomic level. Outcome was far better than might have been predicted (1) from social history; (2) after several foster changes; and (3) following very late adoption.

Kadushin looked deeply into the social and emotional adjustment of the children to their new parents, as well as the outcome in terms of school achievement. He offered two factors as being of probable relevance to the resilience of these late adopted children. First, the security of the home, and the relationships within it; second, he believed that the wider social context was significant. These children had experienced a number of changes from a situation that offered little in meeting their needs for affection, acceptance, support, encouragement and understanding to ones which involved these essentials. From severely deprived problem homes, their context had become respectable, status-conscious middle class. The child 'now receives messages which proclaim his acceptability, and support, reinforce and strengthen whatever components, however limited, of self-acceptance he has been able to develop as a result of whatever small amount of affection he received in his former home. The effect of positive parent-child relationships within the home are now buttressed by social relationships outside the home rather than vitiated by the contradiction between the acceptance of the lower-class child in the lower-class home and his rejection by the community' (p.222).

A further example of a rare follow-up of late-adopted (as opposed to fostered) children has been conducted in Scotland. Until recently an appropriate belief in hereditary influences, coupled with an inappropriate belief in the overwhelming importance of the early environment, led adoption agencies to be wary of offering children, whose ancestry was not relatively impeccable, until they became old enough to show signs of normal development. By this time they would appear unsuitable to many adopting parents who wished a closely matched substitute for the natural child they could not have, and who also believed in the critical importance of the early years. It would take an exceptionally determined research worker to undertake the task of seeking and studying late adopted children as adults.

This has been accomplished by Triselitis and Russell (1984) who report on two samples of adults with adverse early environments. Of these 44 had been adopted late and 40 reared in children's residential homes. There were considerable problems in tracing the late adopted sample, and in fact 33 out of 91 could not be found. A straight-forward comparison of outcome for the two samples could not be made because of differences in potentially potent background variables.

The adopted children experienced on average 3.5 moves before adoption at a mean age of $3\frac{1}{2}$ (range 2 to 8). They had all been taken into care at an average age of $2\frac{1}{2}$ and early histories were very adverse. Unsurprisingly, some 40% displayed moderate to severe emotional and behavioural problems prior to adoption.

As adults, a third of the adopted children were classified as professional, and less than a quarter were in unskilled occupations. A small number had been referred for psychiatric help as children, and some 27% had appeared as adults before the court, of whom around half had been convicted for minor offences. In general, outcome was regarded as highly creditable, considering that, as infants, they had been regarded as so seriously at risk either for subnormality, criminality or other social problems as to be ineligible for *early* adoption, in consequence of which they had experienced several transitions as young children. The adult status of the institutional children was also far more satisfactory than might be expected from parental history, early adversity and rearing in care.

Studies such as these indicate that if children experience a complete ecological change from adverse circumstances, it is likely that most will adapt to new environments within the constraints of their constitutional dispositions.

Early intervention — preschool programmes

The notion of early intervention to change the course of human development by manipulation of the social context arose in modern times from the work of the Iowa Group, Stoddard, Skeels, Skodak, Wellman and others. They flourished in the 1930s and continued to publish until the 1960s. They were strongly humanitarian but their methodology was by no means water-tight. To their credit they recognised that there was a degree of plasticity in human development. Nevertheless on methodological grounds they were devastatingly criticised by McNemar (1940) and others subsequently (e.g. Clarke, Clarke and Berg, 1985). Skeels' final monograph (1966) referred to the countless number of deprived children who were sound constitutionally, but whose low level of functioning could be dramatically improved by appropriate intervention.

This view was ready-made for the wave of optimism in the USA for the making of a Great Society in the 1960s. Head Start programmes were designed in haste to lift the disadvantaged from low functioning, to ease their entry to normal school and to break the cycle. It seemed that anything termed 'intervention' was thought to have dramatic effects. When these failed to occur, or having occurred, 'washed out' a counter-reaction set in. Thus Zigler (Zigler and Valentine, 1979) an adviser to successive Presidents, and one-time enthusiast for Head Start, writes 'in retrospect it is hard to believe that so much confidence could have been placed in one isolated year of intervention in one "magic period" in a child's life' (p.13) . . . 'It is now my view that such tokenistic programs are worse than no programs at all. The danger . . . is not so much that they damage children as that they give the appearance that something useful is being done, and thus become the substitute for more meaningful efforts' (p.365).

During the last decade a self-appointed group of eminent researchers formed a Consortium for Longitudinal Studies, pooling data from twelve very special early intervention projects. Their aim was to establish whether there were longer-term effects of such programmes than were apparent in earlier and briefer evaluations of Head Start (Lazar, Hubbell, Murray, Rosche and Royce, 1977).

On follow-up in adolescence, although the previously very significant effects on IQ had vanished, there were important reductions in special class placement and, to a lesser extent, retention in grade. As noted, these were no ordinary preschool programmes and in some cases they had been initiated before Head Start had been set up.

Among the more remarkable of the Consortium findings it seemed that neither type nor duration of programme, presence or absence of language goals, training or non-training of teachers produced differential effects. It did not matter what was done nor when it was done nor for how long, within the broad limits of a high quality preschool programme. As long as something good was done, a chain of events was set in motion (Lazar and Darlington, 1978). Nevertheless, the levels achieved were modest. As Ramey (1982) put it in a commentary 'that these results obtained in spite of the efforts of some of our leading scientists and educators, testifies to the difficult and complex set of conditions associated with lower socioeconomic status in this country' (p.149).

Royce, Lazar and Darlington (1983) have provided a more recent report of the outcome of the special preschool programmes evaluated by the Consortium. A further follow-up has taken place in 1980. They indicate that 'steady, small program-control differences were found throughout elementary school and junior high school and continued to the end of high school. Progressively higher percentages of control children failed to meet school requirements at each grade level . . .' (p.713). At seventh grade the difference between the two sets of groups amount to 8.6% for special educational placements and 11.8% for meeting school requirements for the median project.

After controlling for variables such as gender, ethnicity and initial background factors, the oldest samples showed a 15.1% difference between programme and control children for high school graduation.

The subjects of three projects, the members of which were 19-22 years of age, were interviewed in detail. Those with preschool attendance were found to have higher occupational aspirations and expectations, and expected to attain their occupational choices.

No differences were, however, found in employment status, earnings, hours worked or type of job between programme and control young adults. Indirect links, however, were established via school competence measures, school graduation and through 'commitment to achievement'. School success was a key intervening factor. Especially those who had never been retained in grade were more likely to be employed.

In speculating about the processes involved, the authors consider that the effects could be explained by an ongoing series of success exchanges or transactions — a flow of events initiated at preschool. However, these implications 'need to be tempered by limits on generalizability. While the families and various curricula are typical of Head Start, our sample of programs was not a sample of Head Start sites ... the Consortium programs differ from most early childhood programs because they were research and demonstration studies with monitoring and documentation ... high quality programs using many approaches can be effective' (p.717-718). This warning about possible lack of generalizability is important, for many have wrongly assumed that the Consortium programmes represented ordinary Head Start designs. Similar cautions have been expressed by Woodhead (1985).

This warning is repeated by Evans (1985), 'it is hazardous', he writes, 'to generalize broadly from findings about model demonstration programs (whatever their patterns) to localized, unsponsored programs of early intervention' (p.197). This author conducted an 11-year follow-up on the long-term outcome for low income, minority high school students who had experienced two different approaches to preschool education, as well as comparing those with and those without preschool experience. In the former case no differences were found in achievement tests between those who had followed a highly structured programme and those who had been exposed to an ordinary Head Start programme. Nor were significant differences found for programme versus control children on any standardised achievement measure during high school, nor on the Quality of Life Scale.

'Such findings', writes the author 'seem especially likely in the absence of powerful and sustained follow-through procedures. Even then there is little reason to suspect cumulative advantages from preschool education in the absence of a sustained family effort . . .' (p.201). Evans concludes that 'few (if any) serious students of early education expect that a year or two of preschool, however well accommodated, will solve the educational problem usually associated with the low income minority experience . . . model demonstration projects have claimed modest long-term achievement advantages . . . This study, perhaps more typical of field projects in the public sector, cannot' (p.202).

Since this lecture is concerned primarily with possible long-term outcomes, scant attention is paid to immediate effects of particular forms of early intervention. However, an interesting British study by Jowett and Sylva (1986) contrasting the early school behaviour of working class children half of whom had attended LEA nursery classes, and half of whom were play group graduates, showed greater gains by the former in several important areas (e.g. play activities of high complexity, self-initiated writing). Whether such differences might be maintained via a continuing transactional process remains an open question, for the follow-up after school entry must have been no more than nine months.

The largest and best designed study included in the Consortium group is undoubtedly the Perry preschool project, with a follow-up of 123 disadvantaged black children to age 19 (Schweinhart and Weikart, 1980; 1981; and Berrueta-Clement, Schweinhart, Barnett, Epstein and Weikart, 1984). These were randomly allocated to preschool or no preschool conditions at the ages of three or four, with the former being exposed to one- or two-year programmes by a group of exceptionally dedicated teachers and researchers. Their parents were of low socio-economic status, and children's initial Stanford-Binet IQs lay between 60-90. (Note, however, that Schweinhart and Weikart, 1980, gives the range as 70-85). Preschool attendance lasted for 2½ hours per day with an additional 1½ hours weekly visit to the home by a teacher.

The earlier follow-up reports have been considerably amplified and endorsed by the age 19 (1984) study. Although there was often considerable overlap on the reported variables by the ex-preschool and ex-no-preschool groups. Many findings were statistically significant. For example, the Preschool Group differed from the No-preschool Group in per cent of years in special education, 16% vs 28%, respectively; for High School graduation, 67% vs 49%; for college or vocational training, 38% vs 21%; for employment, 59% vs 32%; and ever detained or arrested 16% vs 28% (pp.2 and 26). IQ differences had, as usual, washed out.

Evidence is advanced to suggest that this high quality programme had direct effects on both children and parents, which in each led to an ongoing transactional sequence in

10

which effects, both direct and indirect, in turn become causes of further effects, reinforced both by the home and by achievements in the school, the reactions of teachers and others.

Later educational intervention

As noted, the findings of the Consortium and of the Perry Preschool project (which was the largest to be included in the analysis) suggest that the later effects were due to an ongoing transactional process in which family support for educational achievement played an important part among these impoverished working class families. Corroboration has come from work in England in which intervention at a later age has been shown to be effective.

Recently a group of psychologists have called attention to an important variation among homes which can, at least to some extent, be harnessed as an educational resource: parental teaching. Starting with the solidly based correlations between academic attainment and social status, Hewison and Tizard (1980) aimed to discover whether differences *within* a working class population could be related to differences in home background. Among many factors studied, the most powerful predictor of reading ability was whether or not the mothers had spontaneously undertaken coaching at home by listening to their children reading, unbeknown to the schools.

The next important question was, of course, whether parental coaching could be shown to be a causal influence by indicating that an advantage accruing to some pupils by virtue of their parents' initiative could be reproduced in families where this had not occurred naturally. With the cooperation of the Heads and teachers in six primary and junior schools in the London borough of Haringey two types of intervention were employed for a two-year period (Tizard, Schofield and Hewison, 1982). In one experimental condition teachers invited parents to hear their children read, books were supplied and regular checks made; in another condition an additional teacher was employed in the school to accelerate reading skills. Allocation to experimental or carefully designated control conditions was on a random basis, and the scoring of the standardized reading tests was done by experienced teachers unconnected with the intervention.

The results indicated that after two years of intervention the children, by now aged 8-9 years, had made highly significant gains in the home intervention condition in one school, and significant, albeit smaller gains, in another. By contrast no significant improvement in reading was shown between the extra-teacher groups versus controls in either school. Finally, one year after intervention had ceased the children were tested again; the difference between the home intervention group and the controls was still highly significant in one school but not in the other, although intervention children had better reading scores in both.

In commenting on the results and their interpretation, the authors point out that about half of the children in all classes would be expected to be given reading practice at home regardless of the intervention, so the differences are likely to be an underestimate of the effect. Further that in this project, unlike several others, no detailed instructions in the techniques to be used by parents were given.

By now in England the method of 'paired reading' initiated by Morgan and Lyon (1979) has become a standard technique for remedial instruction. There is a focus on *a*) affording a means whereby correct reading responses may be acquired, and *b*) increasing the probability of their performance through reinforcement. Thus the parent receives a good deal of *instruction* on how to help a child to read, followed by home visits to ensure that the method is being used appropriately. There is a large literature on paired reading and there seems no doubt that the technique results in substantial gains after relatively short periods of instruction (5 weeks to 12 months). However, in the published literature there has been an absence of comparison between various methods of parental involvement in children's reading. A recent paper by Lindsay, Evans and Jones (1985) contrasts Paired Reading with Relaxed Reading, the latter involving a much simpler procedure of parental instruction. In both conditions children made substantial gains, but there was no significant difference between them, leading the authors to advocate Relaxed Reading as the preferred choice. They do, however, suggest that a fairly structured approach to parental teaching is important.

Relative and absolute changes in reading attainment are not necessarily confined to the school years. Rodgers (1986), using the cohort from the MRC National Survey of Health and Development, has argued that a substantial improvement in reading scores occurred between the ages of 15 and 26, and in particular indicated that the prevalence of illiteracy/semi-literacy fell substantially between these ages. He maintains that early adulthood is not a period of stagnation intellectually and that several features of individual life histories may be involved.

Education in general is, of course, itself a form of intervention to which the whole population is exposed up to at least the age of sixteen. Indeed, it is the only social service which is compulsory for all. Moreover, differences between schools represent differences in the forms of intervention. Recently there has been a considerable output of sophisticated research implicating schools and individual teacher strategies in differentially influencing the well-being and general progress of pupils. Rutter (1983) indicates that, holding constant pupil intelligence and family background, the quality of schools may make a difference of as much as one standard deviation in achievement. Out of school measures such as truancy and delinquency are also related to the general ethos of schools.

Commentary

This review has up-dated the findings outlined in our book a decade ago, adding further evidence. Some objections to our formulations will be considered in this concluding discussion.

Obviously, the notion of critical periods in development, which entered psychology from embryology (where it is certainly correct) via ethology (where it has been somewhat modified) is challenged by these findings. We are far from being alone in our critique. Connolly, for example, as long ago as 1972 suggested that the term 'sensitive period' was more appropriate and we have no quarrel with that; it should be emphasized, however, that there is unlikely to be one 'sensitive period'. Rather there may be many, each for a different process and at different stages of development.

In the United States, from the early 1970s onwards, Jerome Kagan, initially unaware of our own researches, independently arrived at conclusions closely similar to our own. In the monumental edited volume on constancy and change, he has summarised his position as follows: 'The view that emerges from this work is that humans have a capacity for change across the whole life span. It questions the traditional idea that the experiences of the early years, which have a demonstrated contemporaneous effect, necessarily constrain the characteristics of adolescence and adulthood . . . many individuals retain a great capacity for change, and the consequences of the events of early childhood are continually transformed by later experiences, making the course of human development more open than many have believed' (Brim and Kagan, 1980, p.1)

What then is the role of early experience, is it unimportant, a notion some critics have put into our mouths? Far from it. For most children in normal circumstances early experience represents a foundation for the next stage of development. But the shape and form of what is to come depends on whether there are continuities or discontinuities in the micro- and macro- environment as well as upon the unfolding of the biological trajectory. We can suggest a very crude 'wedge' model reflecting at the thick end the sensitivity to environment which appears to be a feature of the young human. This tails off to the thin end which may well be very much later in life, even in old age. But, as noted, there is a dearth of studies on the effects of radical environmental change after adolescence. Certainly up to this period there is no indication that increasing age exercises any obvious constraints upon responsiveness. The 'wedge' may be little more than the crudest of approximations to describing the potentiality of the human for responding to changing circumstances at different periods of the life span. There appears to be a degree of plasticity, a potential responsiveness to changing conditions. But, as always, individual differences obtrude, reflecting different ranges of reaction, presumably constitutional in origin, which limit the amount of change which can occur. Part of this is the 'self-righting tendency' of Waddington (1957, 1966) who suggests that the human is programmed to produce normal developmental outcomes under all but the most adverse circumstances.

If indeed, as we suspect, increasing age does impose greater and greater limitations upon responsiveness, there may be a combination of different reasons for this. Factors intrinsic to the aging process, forced or chosen life paths, the unlearning of deeply ingrained modes of reaction, all these may be relevant.

A number of important reviews of the early experience literature have been published in recent years, very few of which have appeared to disagree with our interpretation of the evidence. Sroufe (1977, 1979), however, suggests that it cannot be assumed that early experience will be cancelled out by later experience: 'lasting consequences of early inadequate experience may be subtle and complex, taking the form of increased vulnerability to stress, for example, or becoming manifest only when the individual attempts to establish intimate adult relationships or engage in parenting' (1979, p.840). As already noted, we had anticipated the possibility of increased vulnerability to later stress in our 1968 paper, and we certainly do not disagree with Sroufe's quoted comments, but these are not testable hypotheses unless, to repeat the point, a clear environmental discontinuity after the early years has been demonstrated, enabling an uncontaminated assessment of early experience to be made.

Hunt's (1979) wide-ranging review recognizes the critical periods are less 'critical' than sensitive, and that early losses can be made good, or early gains subsequently lost. Other reviews are entirely congruent with our findings. For example Rutter (1980) concludes that 'the residual effects of early experiences on adult behaviour tend to be quite slight, both because of the maturational changes that take place during middle and later childhood, and because of the effects of beneficial and adverse experiences during all the years after infancy . . .' (p.811). This point has been more recently illustrated by Quinton and Rutter (1985). They showed that among young adults who had experienced early adversity, outcome in terms of adequacy of parenting was related to events occurring after the early years. Factors such as positive school experiences, the supportiveness of spouses and lack of socio-economic stress were related to a good outcome. Once again, adverse early experiences did not necessarily foreclose the future, unless continued in school, marriage and material stresses.

Wachs and Gruen (1982) in their review of the field agree that later experiences should be considered as well as early ones, but strongly disagree with the notion that *equivalent* effects may come from later as well as earlier experiences. 'Rather we would stress that early experiences have a greater *probability* of having a more dramatic and longer lasting impact upon the organism than later experience' (p.4). Some aspects of this area thus remain the subject of controversy. At the very least, however, there can be no doubt whatever that the effects of early experience *per se* are far from being as crucial as has until lately been widely accepted. We ourselves would go further than this, but underline what at the moment seems to be a growing consensus in this field.

It appears to be important to emphasise the transactional nature of development. Extremes, whether of temperament or cognitive ability, are particularly likely to elicit reinforcement from the environment. The unusually aggressive child encourages counteractive aggression from peer; the difficult, maladjusted child may well ensure less than optimal handling by teachers — or even child abuse from parents or foster parents; and the attractive, equable individual may equally be reinforced for 'good' behaviour by continuing adult approval. The gifted child seeks the company of adults and older children, while the less able may well be rejected and become the victim of failure experiences.

These are the sort of mechanisms by which the effects of early experience may indirectly be perpetuated; but a radical change, with more appropriate handling by adults, or indeed the converse, can break this ongoing, and sometimes cumulative, cycle of events and set for the child a new and different life path.

References

Belsky, J. (1978) 'Three theoretical models of child abuse'. *Child Abuse and Neglect*, 2, 37-49.

Berrueta-Clement, J.R., Schweinhart, L.J., Barnett, W.S., Epstein, A.S. and Weikart, D.P. (1984) *Changed lives: the effects of the Perry Preschool Program through age 19*. Ypsilanti, Mich.: High/Scope Press.

Brim, O. and Kagan, J. (eds.) (1980) *Constancy and change in human development*. Cambridge, Mass.: Harvard Educational Press.

Bronfenbrenner, U. (1977) 'Towards an experimental ecology of human development.' *American Psychologist*, 32, 513-531.

Bronfenbrenner, U. (1979) *The ecology of human development*. Cambridge, Mass.: Harvard University Press.

Brophy, J.E. and Good, T.L. (1974) *Teacher-student relationships: causes and consequences*. New York: Holt, Rinehart and Winston.

Chess, S. and Thomas, A. (1984) *Origins and evolution of behaviour disorders: from infancy to adult life*. New York: Brunner/Mazel.

Clarke, A.D.B. (1968) 'Learning and human development: the 42nd Maudsley Lecture.' *British Journal of Psychiatry*, 114, 161-177.

Clarke, A.D.B., Clarke, A.M. and Reiman, S. (1958) 'Cognitive and social changes in the feebleminded: three further studies.' *British Journal of Psychology*, 49, 144-157.

Clarke, A.M. (1984) 'Early experience and cognitive development.' *Review of Research in Education*, 11, 125-157.

Clarke, A.M. and Clarke, A.D.B. (eds.) (1976) *Early experience: myth and evidence*. London: Open Books; New York: Free Press.

Clarke, A.M., Clarke, A.D.B. and Berg, J.M. (eds.) (1985) *Mental deficiency: the changing outlook*. London: Methuen; New York: Free Press.

Connolly, K. (1972) 'Learning and the concept of critical periods in infancy.' *Developmental Medicine and Child Neurology*, 14, 705-714.

Davis, K. (1947) 'Final note on a case of extreme isolation.' *American Journal of Sociology*, 45, 554-565.

Evans, E.D. (1985) 'Longitudinal follow-up assessment of differential preschool experience for low income minority group children.' *Journal of Educational Research*, 78, 197-202.

Hewison, J. and Tizard, J. (1980) 'Parental involvement and reading attainment.' *British Journal of Educational Psychology*, 50, 209-215.

Hunt, J. McV. (1979) 'Psychological development: early experience.' *Annual Review of Psychology*, 30, 103-143.

Jowett, S. and Sylva, K. (1986) 'Does kind of preschool matter?' *Educational Research*, 28, 21-31.

Kadushin, A. (1970) *Adopting older children*. New York: Columbia University Press.

Koluchova, J. (1972) 'Severe deprivation in twins: a case study.' *Journal of Child Psychology and Psychiatry*, 13, 107-114.

Koluchova, J. (1976) 'A report on the further development of twins after severe and prolonged deprivation.' In A.M. Clarke and A.D.B. Clarke (eds.) *Early experience: myth and evidence*. London: Open Books; New York: Free Press.

Lazar, I. and Darlington, R.B. (1978) *Lasting effects after preschool*. Washington, D.C.: U.S. Department of Health, Education and Welfare No. (OHDS) 79-30178.

Lazar, I., Hubbell, V.R., Murray, H., Rosche, M. and Royce, J. (1977) *The persistence of preschool effects: a long-term follow-up of fourteen infant and preschool experiments*. Washington, D.C.: The Consortium on Developmental Continuity, Education Commission of the States, DHEW Publication No. (OHDS) 78-30130.

Lindsay, G., Evans, A. and Jones, B. (1985) 'Paired Reading versus Relaxed Reading: a comparison.' *British Journal of Educational Psychology*, 55, 304-309.

McNemar, Q. (1940) 'A critical examination of the University of Iowa studies of environmental influence upon the IQ.' *Psychological Bulletin*, 37, 63-92.

Morgan, R. and Lyon, E. (1979) ' 'Paired Reading' — a preliminary report on a technique for parental tuition of reading-retarded children.' *Journal of Child Psychology and Psychiatry*, 20. 151-160.

Quinton, D. and Rutter, M. (1985) 'Parenting behaviour of mothers raised 'In care'.' In A.R. Nicol (ed.), *Longitudinal studies in child psychology and psychiatry: practical lessons from research experience*. Chichester: John Wiley.

Ramey, C. (1982) 'Commentary on 'Lasting effects of early education: a report from the Consortium for Longitudinal Studies' ' (Lazar, I. and Darlington, R.) *Monographs of the Society for Research in Child Development*, 47, Nos.2-3.

Rodgers, B. (1986) 'Change in the reading attainment of adults: a longitudinal study.' *British Journal of Developmental Psychology*, 4, 1-17.

Royce, J.M., Lazar, I. and Darlington, R.B. (1983) 'Minority families, early education and later life chances.' *American Journal of Orthopsychiatry*, 53, 706-720.

Rutter, M. (1980) 'The long-term effects of early experience.' *Developmental Medicine and Child Neurology*, 22. 800-815.

Rutter, M. (1983) 'School effects on pupil progress: research findings and policy implications.' *Child Development*, 54. 1-29.

Sameroff, A.J. (1975) Early influences on development: fact or fancy? *Merrill-Palmer Quarterly*, 21, 267-294.

Sameroff, A.J. and Chandler, M.J. (1975) 'Reproductive risk and the continuum of caretaking casualty.' In F.D. Horowitz, M. Hetherington, S. Scarr-Salapatek and G. Siegel (eds.), *Review of Child Development Research*, 4, 187-244. Chicago: University of Chicago Press.

Schweinhart, L.J. and Weikart, D.P . (1980) *Young children grow up: the effects of the Perry Preschool Program on youths through age 15*. Ypsilanti, Mich: High/Scope Press.

Schweinhart, L.J. and Weikart, D.P. (1981) 'Perry preschool effects nine years later: what do they mean?' In M.J. Begab, H.C. Haywood and H.L. Garber (eds.), *Psychosocial influences on retarded performance*, vol.2. Baltimore: University Park Press.

Skeels, H.M. (1966) 'Adult status of children with contrasting early life experiences.' *Monographs of the Society for Research on Child Development*, 31 (3), no.105.

Skuse, D. (1984a) 'Extreme deprivation in early childhood — I. Diverse outcomes for three siblings from an extraordinary family.' *Journal of Child Psychology and Psychiatry*, 25, 523-541.

Skuse, D. (1984b) 'Extreme deprivation in early childhood — II. Theoretical issues and a comparative review.' *Journal of Child Psychology and Psychiatry*, 25, 543-572.

Sroufe, L.A. (1977) 'Early experience: evidence and myth.' *Contemporary Psychology*, 22, 878-880.

Sroufe, L.A. (1979) 'The coherence of individual development.' *American Psychologist*, 34, 834-841.

Thompson, A. (1986) 'Adam — a severely deprived Colombian orphan.' *Journal of Child Psychology and Psychiatry*, 27, 689-695.

Tizard, J., Schofield, W.N. and Hewison, J. (1982) 'Collaboration between teachers and parents in assisting children's reading.' *British Journal of Educational Psychology,* 52, 1-15.

Trasler, G. (1960) *In place of parents: a study of foster care.* London: Routledge and Kegan Paul.

Triseliotis, J. and Russell, J. (1984) *Hard to place: the outcome of late adoptions and residential care.* London: Heinemann.

Wachs, T.D. and Gruen, G.E. (1982) *Early experience and human development.* New York and London: Plenum Press.

Waddington, C.H. (1957) *The strategy of genes.* London: Allen and Unwin,.

Waddington, C.H. (1966) *Principles of development and differentiation.* New York: Macmillan.

Woodhead, M. (1985) 'Pre-school education has long-term effects: but can they be generalised?' *Oxford Review of Education,* 11, 133-155.

Zigler, E. and Valentine, J. (eds.) (1979) *Project Head Start: a legacy of the war on poverty.* New York: Free Press.

2. Extreme Deprivation in Early Childhood — I. Diverse Outcomes for Three Siblings from an Extraordinary Family

David Skuse

Introduction

In the autumn of 1977 a little girl of almost 9 yr was referred to the children's department of a post-graduate teaching hospital. Over the previous year Mary had exhibited increasingly disruptive behaviour in the small children's home where she had lived for 6 yr with her sister, Louise, who was 14 months her elder. When their early history was investigated further it transpired that these children had spent their early lives in a remarkably deprived environment on account of their having a mother (Patricia) who was not only mentally retarded and microcephalic but may additionally have been suffering from a severe psychiatric disorder. Enquiries also led to an elder brother being traced to a distant children's home. Joseph has lived in care nearly all his life; he is an albino who is severely mentally retarded and autistic. On discovery the girls lacked all speech and social skills yet, following their removal into more propitious circumstances, Louise seemed to have made a near complete recovery from her early experiences. In contrast, Mary continued to exhibit social, emotional and cognitive problems which may have derived from that time.

Previous accounts of severe deprivation in early childhood have tended to report either that some progress was made in rehabilitating the victims but that ultimately their attainments were strictly limited (e.g. Davis, 1947; Curtiss, 1977) or that considerable gains were rapidly achieved and sustained (e.g. Davis, 1947; Skeels, 1966; Koluchova, 1976; Douglas and Sutton, 1978). Mary and Louise appear to be unique in that in no other case were the courses of development of children brought up in the same restrictive environment, so disparate. This paper details accounts of the early lives and developmental histories of Joseph, Louise and Mary. Clinical findings are discussed and some tentative conclusions drawn. A broader theoretical analysis of the retardation and recovery of severely deprived children, together with some wider implications in the context of developmental psychology, is presented in a companion paper (Skuse, 1984).

Note: Names, geographical locations and identifying details have, where appropriate, been altered to protect the family.

David Skuse: 'Extreme Deprivation in Early Childhood — I. Diverse Outcomes for Three Siblings from an Extraordinary Family'. *THE JOURNAL OF CHILD PSYCHOLOGY AND PSYCHIATRY* (1984) Vol 25. No. 4, pp. 523-541. © 1984 Association for Child Psychology and Psychiatry.

Maternal background

The children's mother is a native of a cluster of islands in the Indian Ocean, born in a small seaside resort on the main island of the group about 40 yr ago. She was the only legitimate child amongst her mother's four living offspring; the others, all healthy adults, are married with families of their own. Her father died when she was 6 yr of age. Patricia was educated from 6 to 12 yr at one of the best primary schools on the island. Her first child, Melanie, was born illegitimately in 1961 — being left at the age of 2 yr in the care of her maternal grandmother (now deceased) when Patricia came to England to find employment. Melanie is working as a salesgirl in her home town and educational reports suggest she is of normal intelligence with a 'pleasant personality'.

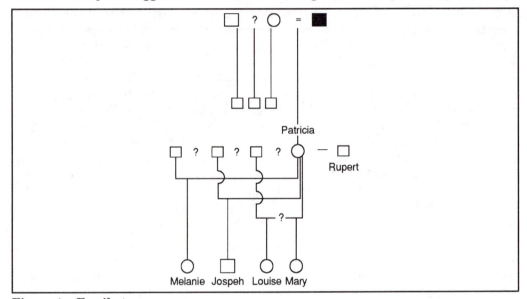

Figure 1   Family tree

Early developmental history

Joseph

On her arrival in England Patricia took a job as a kitchen maid in London and was, by accounts of those who knew her at the time, an attractive, sociable woman, well dressed and with many friends. In May 1966 her second child, Joseph, was born in hospital, a normal delivery after an uneventful pregnancy. He is an albino and this seems to have rendered him unacceptable to her; she is black, as was Joseph's putative father. Nothing can be determined about this man apart from the fact he was once employed as a hotel porter and came from the same island community as Patricia.

Joseph was cared for initially in a day nursery of unknown quality, whilst a private arrangement was made for him to be fostered by an elderly lady in a distant town who had successfully undertaken long-term fosterings in the past. He lived with her from the age of 8 months. Although his motor milestones were only moderately delayed, she recalls having found him in other respects an extremely unusual child. He persistently avoided her gaze and rarely smiled for long, showing no obvious pleasure in her affectionate overtures. Early babbling was very limited and he did not express any gestured communications.

Patricia soon ceased contact with this foster mother, who came to realise that long-term care for Joseph by herself would be impracticable. She contacted a charitable organisation soon after the boy came to her, but it was 18 months before a suitable placement could be found in one of the organisation's children's homes. Meanwhile he was taken regularly to the local child health centre and to the paediatric clinic of a nearby general hospital. At 1 yr 10 months he had a DQ of 55 on the Griffiths Mental Developmental Scale (Griffiths, 1954). Individual scores were not uniformly retarded: on the locomotor scale most items were passed at the 18-month level, eye and hand items to 14 months, performance skills to 12 months, personal-social items to 11 months and hearing and speech to the 10th month level only. The medical officer who performed this assessment commented at the time that it was difficult to say how much of Joseph's retardation could be due to past and current social, emotional and perceptual deprivation, but he had the impression that the boy was in any event 'mentally subnormal'.

Joseph was first admitted to the children's home at 2 yr 4 months. Accounts of his state at that time emphasise those elements of retarded development already recognised: very withdrawn, many mannerisms, still drinking from a bottle, eating baby food and in nappies. His preferred activity was to lie in his cot. Reports also speak of his 'poor physical condition', with widespread impetigo. Continual head banging and rocking, followed later by self-mutilation, led to his admission into hospital in 1972 for control of such behaviour by medication. Following discharge he began at a school for the severely mentally retarded. The closure of this residential placement precipitated a move to another of the organisation's homes, this time for the mentally handicapped, where he has remained from 1977 to this day.

When assessed by the author and his colleagues at the age of 12.2, Joseph was found to be severely mentally retarded with marked autistic features, in respect of social behaviour, language handicap and stereotyped interests. His overall nonverbal mental age was 3.9, and even this level of performance was limited to a few items on the Merrill-Palmer Scale (Stutsman, 1948). He was even more profoundly handicapped in language-related functions, with no meaningful expressions, and verbal comprehension at a 12-month level. An EEG in January 1972 indicated bilateral temporal lobe dysfunction, but when repeated in May 1979 the result was equivocal; other tests have found a normal chromosomal pattern and no evidence of underlying metabolic disturbance. None of Joseph's sisters are aware they have a brother.

Louise and Mary

Early in 1967 Patricia became pregnant once more and in September Louise was born in hospital, after a normal pregnancy and delivery. The infant was breast fed for 1½ months with no special difficulties. She sat at 1 and walked at 2 yr. Analysis of the children's and mother's blood groups indicates Louise is unlikely to share the same father as Joseph, although a quantitative account of this probability is unfortunately not possible. No information about the man can be discovered.

So far as is known, Patricia lived alone up until this time. She stopped work following the birth of Louise and, unable to continue paying her rent, was threatened with eviction. Then a chance meeting in a park with an old friend and neighbour led to an offer to go and stay with him in the single room he rented. The man's name was Rupert, a labourer, and he and Patricia have been together ever since. At the time of this encounter she was already pregnant with Mary who, serum typing suggests, may have had the same father as Louise. Her pregnancy was uneventful, without antenatal care. It had progressed 38 weeks when, in the early hours one November morning of 1968, Patricia went into labour at home. By the time the ambulance arrived Mary had been born in her mother's bed. On admission to hospital she was slightly hypothermic and cyanosed, but she rapidly recovered in an incubator. Head circumference was 33.8 cm (50th percentile) (Egan *et al.*, 1969), birth weight 2.44 kg (25th percentile). Absence of the nails of the right second, third and fourth toes was noted, but she was otherwise thought to be a normal child and returned home within 72 hours. Mary was bottle fed with no particular problems. She seemed a quiet baby and was, like her sister, developmentally a little slow; she sat at 1 and walked at 2 yr of age.

It is not clear how much time Rupert spent in the room where his adopted family lived for the next year or so, but he has claimed the children were well cared for physically. He also reported that Patricia was not the same lively character he had known four years previously. She began to neglect her appearance, talked less and had seemed withdrawn and irritable since Mary's birth. Yet when the family were evicted in February 1971 and moved temporarily into an insalubrious block of council flats, Patricia maintained their new home in 'apple pie order'.

Social Services kept a wary eye on the inhabitants of these dwellings and in March 1971 a comment was made by a GP, whom they had asked to visit, that "Louise and Mary were very strange creatures indeed". Aged 3.6 and 2.4 yr respectively, they "took no notice of anything or anyone except to scamper up and sniff strangers, grunting and snuffling like animals". Both still sucked dummies and as no attempt had been made to toilet train them they remained in nappies. Neither child had any constructive play, objects being merely picked up, smelt, then felt. Mary had no speech whatsoever and made no hearing responses. Her vocalisation seemed limited to a few high-pitched sounds. Patricia commented that she was not concerned the children did not speak as they were still 'only babies', but she did apparently talk to them a little in patois.

The family were moved again in mid-1971 to the third floor of a now demolished pre-war construction, described as a 'ghetto' by someone who knew it well. The flats had a play group attached and Patricia was encouraged to send the girls there, but she was most reluctant to do so. They did not attend at all for 3 months, and even then went on a sporadic mornings-only basis rather than regularly. In the autumn something came to light which, by Rupert's account, had been going on ever since the children became mobile, although very much against his wishes. The health visitor found Mary and Louise tied on leashes to the bed, a measure their mother had taken partly because she insisted on keeping the flat spotlessly clean and partly because she was worried that they would fall off the balcony. If she considered them too noisy or active they were put onto a mattress and covered with a blanket. This discovery led to their referral to a medical officer at the Borough Child Health Department and a detailed account is available of their status of development at that time.

First developmental assessment — November 1971

Louise was said to have made 'tremendous strides' in the 3 months she had been attending the play group, where both girls received 'excellent handling'. At 4.2 yr she was well developed in terms of motor skills but needed great encouragement to play other than in a very rudimentary way. Socially reponsive, she had formed a warm attachment to a particular helper in this group. She used quite a lot of echoed words and phrases, was said to be fond of singing and could comprehend simple gestured commands. Head circumference was above the 50th percentile, vision and hearing were normal and no physical abnormalities were found.

Mary (3 yr), on the other hand, was initially totally unresponsive and related only to her regular helper. She also had a variety of odd behaviours. For instance, when given a drink she insisted on manipulating the helper's hand so that the latter should hold the cup for her. She always returned to her chair when removed from it and when distressed rocked violently and beat her leg up and down. She sniffed at food and would eat a biscuit only after her apparent suspicions have been allayed by persuasion. There was little indication that Mary understood words or situations and she vocalised almost continuously, rather like a baby of 9 or 12 months. Hearing and vision seemed to be normal. Motor skills were now good but she was said to have been 'very stiff' on starting at the play group. Mary showed no spontaneous play and did not give the impression of being a normal child. Physical examination revealed more stigmata than had been found at birth. Her head circumference was now below the third percentile and she had a fattened occiput. A partial syndactyly existed of the second and third toes on both feet and they lacked distal phalanges. A pale area of skin was noted in the midline of her forehead.

Over the next few months the local Social Services department kept an eye on the family and visited the home on a fairly regular basis, although Patricia's unpredictable behaviour made entrance impossible as many times as not. She was described as presenting an odd appearance; of very small stature, she walked with an anxious shuffle, talked in clipped sentences and sat on the edge of her chair turning away frequently as if she did not wish to answer questions. She made little or no eye contact. An NSPCC officer, to whom the author has spoken, well remembers her having "screaming fits" and meeting "a tirade of anger" when she suggested that the children should not be tethered. Her relationship with the girls was said to be one of "stunned stupor". She refused to accept the suggestion that she should receive psychiatric help. For a further year social workers made frequent visits to the home, almost always finding one or both of the children tied with the leashes that allowed them to take only four or five steps, despite the fact that the balcony had now been covered in a wire mesh guard. Rupert often seemed to be supporting Patricia in her worries about the danger of allowing freedom. Over the period of September 1971 to August 1972 she became even more uncommunicative and suspicious, and constantly fidgeted with her hands. In April 1972 she attacked Rupert with a knife when he tried to untie the children. She also remained resolute in her refusal to allow them to be assessed by a paediatrician for fear they would be taken away; some appointments were made but she never kept them. Then in August 1972, on a day when the social worker found Mary tied yet again to a bedpost covered by a sheet, an interim care order was invoked. They were removed to a privately run children's home and a full care order subsequently obtained. Patricia was distraught at losing the girls; when later asked whether she wished to visit them she seemed strange, sad and rather evasive. She insisted she would wait for them to come home, even though she was told they would not be allowed to live with her again.

Second developmental assessment — August 1972

This event took place at a university centre specialising in developmental assessment 9 months after the previous report. Louise, now aged 4 yr 11 months, was a well-grown and more lively girl than her sister, although she still had practically no comprehensible expressive language except to say "yes" and "no" (which she often got the wrong way round) and "Hello". Echolalia and jargon speech persisted but were not used for social communication. She responded to spoken instructions only if these were accompanied by gestures and her receptive capacity was considered to be at the 2½ yr level. Her play continued to lack symbolic features. Louise's social skills were appropriate to a 2 yr 9 month child, and reliable toilet training had been accomplished during the day only. Her tolerance of frustration was poor and transient temper tantrums could be easily provoked, but she was usually an active and happy child who began to form an attachment to her house mother and related reasonably well to the other children in her new home.

At the same assessment Mary (3.9 yr) was described as very miserable and withdrawn. She clung to her mother, who had been persuaded to accompany the girls, "rather like a baby monkey after examination". Initially she smelt and mouthed objects, patted furniture and felt around the room. Resisting engagement with strangers or toys, she avoided eye contact, and when left alone rocked persistently back and forth. Mary's vocalisations were usually cries and moans and she intermittently ground her teeth. Temper tantrums and screaming could be provoked by trivial incidents. She appeared to recognise her own name but had no obvious understanding of spoken or gestured commands, Neither did she appreciate shape when faced with a puzzle, but her fine motor skills were thought to be normal, as was her gait. Mary enjoyed listening to music and would occasionally dance to it with rhythmical movements.

Mary's social skills were seriously delayed. She did not join in mealtimes but scavenged, and habitually crammed food into her mouth with her hands apparently oblivious of taste, eating at 'every available opportunity'. Pica was a great problem. Enuresis and soiling were a daily occurrence; she showed a keen interest in her own excreta. At night she slept poorly and wandered in search of food, apparently lacking normal childhood fears (such as being alone in the dark).

Later development of the girls

The children's home in which the sisters were placed catered for 12 boys and girls between 2 and 8 yr, under the care of a house mother and her assistants. Louise made rapid progress in respect of socialisation and language, encouraged by regular speech therapy. Within a few months she was using her characteristically unintelligible speech with the phrasing and intonation of natural language, to perform clear social functions; she now comprehended simple oral instructions and appreciated verbal praise. An increasing proportion of symbolic features was seen in her spontaneous play and she greatly enjoyed rough-and-tumble activities. Her drawing skills were age appropriate by 5 yr 2 months when she began half time at the local primary school, going full-time from September 1973. Initially disruptive, for her moods were labile and she became easily frustrated and upset, she was an inquisitive child and rapidly settled in. She grew to love going to school and soon made one special friend.

One year after being taken into care Louise was talking in simple sentences with verbs. Some difficulties persisted in comprehension and she was still occasionally echolalic, but her articulation had much improved with speech therapy. At 5 yr 9 months Louise's social skills were found to be only 9-15 months below age level and her height, weight and head circumference were on the 50th percentile. She seemed pleasant, cooperative and friendly to all who had dealings with her.

In contrast, Mary remained distant and aloof, lacking social responses and failing to initiate interactions with adults or children. A home movie of the residents evoked 'rapt attention' in Louise but was of practically no interest to her sister, who viewed it on the same occasion. In fact, the girls had very little to do with one another. Mary did often smile and laugh, but that seemed to be in response more to her internal than to the external world. She barely responded to verbal or gestured commands and was said to have a 'remote stare'; however, she did not appear to avoid eye contact deliberately. After a trial period in late 1972 Mary was considered an unsuitable candidate for speech therapy. The only activities about which she showed any real enthusiasm were dancing to music, stereotypic rocking, and bath time, when she loved to play with the bubbles and would, if not restrained, eat the soap. Gradual progress was made with respect to toilet training, and after 1 yr she no longer handled her faeces. Pica was a continuing concern for a little while longer.

At 4½ yr of age it seemed unlikely that Mary would be an appropriate candidate for normal school. However, some progress was being made. In the summer, 12 months after coming into care, she made her first spontaneous attempt to communicate, she tried to attract attention by touching an adult's arm and now her smile seemed occasionally appropriate, even social. She also began to point in order to make her needs known, came to understand a few simple verbal instructions and vocalised tunefully now and again. Mary did not as yet engage in any representational or symbolic play but she concentrated for relatively long periods completing jigsaws; using shape rather than picture clues, she could do them equally well upside down. Her main talents were, it seemed, limited to motor skills, both fine and gross coordination being excellent, but she frequently crawled rather than walked. In January 1974, aged 5 yr 2 months, she began to attend the local ESN(M) school.

Over the next few years Louise's social and academic adjustment proceeded in most respects at a far more rapid pace than her sister's (Figs. 2 and 3, Tables 1 and 2). Several detailed assessments were made of Mary's development through this period. They indicated that the main area of retardation was that of language acquisition. Mary was 5 yr 9 months old before she began to echo words in a one-to-one situation with an adult, and even at that stage she did not speak spontaneously. A little symbolic play, in a sense of using one play object to stand for another, was first noted 3 months later. She seemed by then to understand the concepts 'in', 'under' and 'on', and could draw a man with the skill of a child aged about 4 yr.

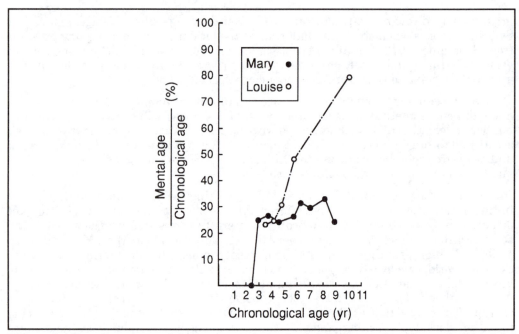

Figure 2 Development of language comprehension from the time of the girls' discovery

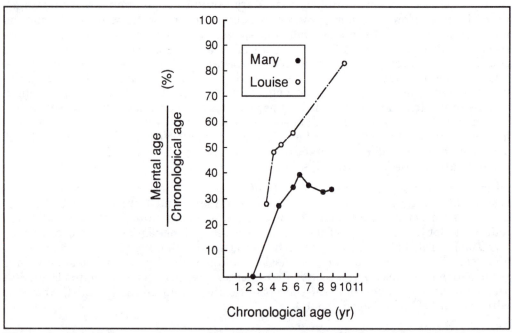

Figure 3 Development of expression of language from the time of the girls' discovery

Table 1 Development assessment of Mary (mental ages)

Chronological age	Language		Vision and fine movements	Social behaviour and play	Posture and large movements
	Comprehension	Expression			
2.4	*	*	*	*	2.0 (RE)
3.0	*	<1.0 (CJ)	1.0 (RE)	1.0 (RE)	3.0 (CJ)
3.9	*	1.0 (CJ)	1.6 (RE)	1.6 (RE)	3.9 (CJ)
4.7	1.3 (CJ)†	1.0 (CJ)	3.1-3.2 (G)	3.4(G)	4.10 (G)
5.9	2.0 (CJ)	1.6 (RE)	3.0-3.6 (RE)	3.6 (CJ)	
6.3	2.6 (CJ)	2.0 (CJ)	4.8-5.0 (G)	3.9 (G)	6.2 (G)
7.0	2.6 (CJ)	2.0 (CJ)	3.0-7.0 (CJ)	‡	7.0 (CJ)
8.2	2.8 (R)	1.11 (R)	2.6-8.6 (McC)	4.0 (RE)	'Excellent' (CJ)
8.11	3.0 (R)	2.2 (R)	WISC (perf. score) 94‡	‡	

* Unmeasurable
†CJ, contemporaneous clinical judgement; RE, retrospective estimation from written accounts; G, Griffiths Scale of Developmental Abilities; R, Reynell Developmental Language Scale; McC, McCarthy Scales of Children's Abilities; WISC, Wechsler Intelligence Scale for Children
‡ See test.

Table 2 Development assessment of Louise (mental ages)

Chronological age	Language		Vision and fine movements	Social behaviour and play	Posture and large movements
	Comprehension	Expression			
3.6	1.0 (RE)*	0.9 (RE)	1.6 (RE)	†	<3.0 (RE)
4.2	2.0 (RE)	1.0 (RE)	2.0 (RE)	2.0 (RE)	
4.10	2.6 (CJ)	1.6 (RE)	2.6 (RE)	2.9 (CJ)	4.10 (CJ)
5.9	3.3 (CJ)	2.9 (CJ)	4.6 (CJ)	4.6-5.0(CJ)	
10.1	WISC (verb) 77	8.0 (CJ)	WISC (perf. score) 80	‡	'Age appropriate' (CJ)
	Neale (A) 6.8 (C) 8.5				

* RE, retrospective estimation from written accounts; CJ, contemporaneous clinical judgement; Neale, Neale Analysis of Reading Ability: (A) accuracy; (C) comprehension; WISC, Wechsler Intelligence Scale for Children
† Unmeasurable
‡ See text.

When engaged in playful activities Mary preferred to be alone. But she was not an unpopular child amongst her peer group; other children would play with her but she invariably took the role of passive participant, cast by them as 'the baby'. However, even when functioning at her best, at 7 yr of age she could not be tolerated in the local youth club or the Brownies because normal social reciprocity was lacking. Social contact meant, for her, physical contact; she was happy to engage in rough-and-tumble play and to stroke the faces or hair of other people in an inquisitive fashion. A personality trait which both intrigued and exasperated her caretakers was her 'obsessionality'; she was excessively tidy, one psychologist commenting after an assessment that Mary absolutely insisted on cleaning up the room before leaving, having lined up all the chairs and put the test materials neatly away in their cases. Mary was also subject to episodic insistence on neatness and sameness in other situations; when travelling by car she 'had to have' her bag by her on the seat or would throw a tantrum, and when 'dressing up' she invariably chose the same two items of clothing.

In view of persisting oddities in Mary's social manner and the increasing disparity between her verbal and non-verbal skills, transfer to an autistic unit was realised at 7 yr 5 months. One year later, after further intermittent speech therapy, she could name a wide range of objects and recognise about 50 words on flash cards, but there was no evidence she could read an unfamiliar book with much understanding. Despite this, her ability to comprehend remained slightly in advance of expressive language skills, as shown in Figs. 2 and 3. A talent for mimicry enabled her to make a good attempt at copying someone reading aloud, but her usual vocalisations were confined to a characteristic 'mumbo-jumbo' expressed in strange gutteral monotones rather like the speech of a deaf child. Auditory tests confirmed she did not suffer hearing impairment, although she found difficulty differentiating words of a similar sound, whether these were written or spoken (e.g. hat/hot). In terms of Mary's ability to complete a (limited) range of performance tasks her gains were much more impressive. In fact, the consultant in developmental paediatrics who had kept her under regular review throughout the previous 5 yr came to believe she might, at age 8 yr, be of potentially normal intellectual abilities (Table 1). Besides a remarkable facility at completing tasks such as object assembly (WISC) (Wechsler, 1949) and the Seguin Formboard (Merrill-Palmer Scale, Stutsman, 1948), Mary could now maintain good attention throughout testing and seemed to understand all spoken instructions, although with complex problems she tried to elicit help by pulling the examiner's hand whilst crying or whining. Considerable progress had also been made in terms of social responsiveness, at least in the ambience of the testing room, where she appeared amicable, affectionate and sustained excellent eye contact. Regrettably, Mary's behaviour on subsequent occasions was to prove less compliant.

Later adjustment difficulties

At Christmas 1976, after Louise had protested for a long time that she wanted to see Uncle Rupert again, he was invited to visit. He brought toys, and the children were delighted to see him. Mary in particular was very upset and clinging when it was time for him to go. Rupert returned to see them regularly at weekends over the next few months, and from the summer of 1977 the children began to go home overnight on occasions. This was the first contact they had had with their mother for nearly 5 yr and she was by this time under the care of a consultant psychiatrist, very withdrawn, virtually mute and thought to be suffering from schizophrenia. Louise seemed relatively unaffected by the resumption of contact with her family, but Mary's behaviour, which had started to deteriorate at the beginning of the year, became a lot worse by the autumn. At first her concentration failed, although her cognitive abilities in general were unaffected. Then bizarre and disturbing patterns of behaviour began, with rages 2 or 3 times a day for no obvious causes. She started to hide or rip her clothes and tore large quantities of paper into tiny pieces. She hurled objects (especially her shoes) at other children, smashed windows and mirrors, scattered talcum powder and stole food. Pica, which had not been seen for many years, was again prominent. Relationships with her peers that had been steadily improving until then became unpleasant and unpredictable; she often kicked them, squeezed them and broke their possessions. Mary also had a persisting tendency to self-injury, and was observed in the last few months of her stay in the children's home to hit her head with a plate, and to scratch and bite herself. She lost interest in playing with her toys, and no longer showed any enthusiasm for lessons in writing and reading. Then she began to run away from the children's home, often wearing very little clothing, and each time it was a major operation to find her. Having been dry day and night for over 2 yr she again became enuretic. By the winter of 1977 it was clear she could no longer be contained within that informal residential placement and care was transferred to a unit for mentally retarded children set in the grounds of a large mental hospital in the country.

Further investigations

Mary has subsequently been investigated for the possibility that a metabolic disorder underlies her psychopathology, but none has been found. In 1978 X-rays taken of her skull and chest were normal, although the bone age appeared 4 months delayed. Whilst microcephalic, she does not share her mother's small stature, being on the 50th percentile for height and the 25th percentile for weight at 19 yr. Both girls have had an EEG: Mary's tracing showed no focal or paroxysmal abnormalities, but the rhythm was poorly developed for her age (10.6). Surprisingly, Louise's (11.5) record demonstrated a moderate abnormality over the anterior part of the head, with an excess of intermediate, slow- and fast-rate activity. The changes were thought to be of long standing and not necessarily indicative of any specific underlying disorder.

Louise now has a very special place in the affections of the lady who runs the children's home in which she has lived for the past 9 yr. One striking characteristic of her personality is a well-developed mischievous, but not malicious, sense of humour. When assessed by the author and his colleagues at 10.1 her social behaviour was essentially normal, although she did lack reserve. She also exhibited some remarkable lacunae in her general knowledge; for example, so far from knowing why it is that criminals are locked up, she did not even know what criminals are! Her development of cognitive skills is chronicled in Table 2 and Figs. 2 and 3. The results show her to be functioning at a borderline normal level. There are no significant differences between verbal and non-verbal skills. However, her scores on the sub-tests of the WISC were extremely varied. She performed least well on items eliciting information, vocabulary and picture arrangement. Reading accuracy was close to that predicted by IQ but her comprehension was less good, and she suffered occasional minor articulatory difficulties. On the Vernon Graded Word Spelling Tests (Vernon, 1977) she scored in keeping with her overall IQ. Louise has been educated throughout at normal schools, commencing at the local comprehensive establishment in 1979, where she is making good progress and has gained many friends.

Patricia was first persuaded by her social worker to be assessed by a consultant psychiatrist in 1976. Physical examination revealed her height to be just below the third percentile by British norms, those for her small island community being unavailable. Her head circumference was correspondingly more than two standard deviations below the mean. She had bilateral epicanthic folds but no other congenital stigmata. Psychological testing on the WAIS (Wechsler, 1955) showed her full-scale IQ to be only 55. Whilst inclined to become tense and miserable when asked about her children, Patricia has not appeared clinically depressed since coming under psychiatric care, nor has there been any clear schizophrenic symptomatology. A social worker who has known her since 1976 comments that she can intermittently function well and seems quite happy when her cohabitee is at home; she shops and cooks for them both. At other times she tends to neglect her appearance and remain within the house, refusing to speak and suspicious of visitors. The question of whether a true personality change followed Mary's birth cannot now be resolved. Medical opinion as to which psychiatric condition she currently suffers from seems to be divided. However, there does not appear to have been any consistent trend towards deteriorations in her personality or cognitive faculties since the first appraisal was made in 1971. Recent investigations have shown her chromosomes to be grossly normal, syphilitic serology is negative and metabolic disturbances, including phenylketonuria, have been excluded. Patricia's EEG and EMI scans are normal.

Discussion

The period of deprivation suffered by Mary and Louise was not great by comparison with certain other cases reported in the literature. Isabelle (Mason, 1942) was 6½ yr old when found, the Koluchova twins (Koluchova, 1972) were nearly 7 yr and Genie (Curtiss, 1977) had experienced isolation for over 13 yr. Mary was 2.4 and Louise 3.6 yr at discovery, yet in terms of their appearance and behaviour at that first assessment they were remarkably similar, both to each other and to other well documented cases such as the Koluchova twins (1972, 1976). At this early stage each girl was said to exhibit 'autistic tendencies', and it would have proved too difficult to predict which, if either, would recover from her experiences. But after only 6 months in the playgroup, which they attended irregularly for 2 hr a day, that picture had changed dramatically. Louise was clearly making rapid progress in all aspects of her development, whereas Mary did not give the impression of being a normal child.

Louise's recovery of cognitive skills is documented in Table 2, and Figs. 2 and 3. In terms of language her pattern of accelerated attainment is in keeping with Mason's (1942) and Koluchova's (1972, 1976) accounts of speech development in their subjects. Recovery was aided, no doubt, by the consistent speech therapy she received. Acquisition of comprehension proceeded more rapidly than the facility to express herself

(Table 2, Figs. 2 and 3), an observation which accords with the findings of these and other authors (e.g. Curtiss, 1977; Douglas and Sutton, 1978). Visuomotor abilities were also rapidly gained, at a somewhat faster rate than language (Table 2). Finally, social behaviour and play were first manifested by Louise within a few months of her starting at the playgroup. She formed strong attachments to key individuals, both in her early childhood (to Rupert, and to a playgroup assistant) and later to the house mother of her new home. Over the greater part of a decade this child has demonstrated a consistent trend towards recuperation in virtually all aspects of cognitive functioning, emotional adjustment and social relationships. It is arguable that those minor peculiarities which persist, for example, in terms of articulatory difficulties and relative social disinhibition are legacies of both her original environment and later upbringing in a group home. Nonetheless, Louise presents as someone with excellent potential for normal development and adjustment. The account of her recovery from that dire state in which she was found resonates with optimism.

Joseph remained with his mother for only 8 months, cared for in large measure at a day nursery. During the subsequent 20 months he was placed with an experienced and kindly foster mother who, however, did not (contemporaneous accounts suggest) provide an adequately stimulating environment for this difficult child. It may be that he too suffered from relative emotional and perceptual deprivation in early childhood, but he has additionally always given the impression of being a mentally handicapped individual. No sustained improvement in his faculties followed removal at the age of 2.4 yr to more favourable circumstances, and he presents today as not only severely retarded but also autistic in his social behaviour, language handicaps and stereotyped interests. Decreased mental ability occurs no more frequently in albinos than amongst people with normal pigmentation (Witkop, 1971), although a recent report is of interest in this respect. Rogawski *et al.* (1978) present an account of two unrelated tyrosinase-positive albino boys, one of whom was negroid. They were both mentally retarded (IQ less than 50) and suffered from childhood autism. The authors suggest that, as the random concurrence of autism and albinism amongst the black population is 1 in 33,000,000, these observed coincidences reflect an underlying genetic linkage. Certainly, the occurrence in a single family of one definite recessive condition (albinism in Joseph) and another different, possibly recessive, condition (mental retardation with microcephaly in Mary) raises the possibility of parental consanguinity (Carter, personal communication). Contemporaneous reports indicate that Mary's father was West Indian and hence this was not a possibility in her case, but Joseph's father did come from the same small island group as Patricia. It seems only reasonable to conclude that this child never suffered deprivation to such a degree as to engender his current mental state, but that he is the victim of genetically determined disorders.

The course of Mary's development since discovery presents a variety of puzzling aspects. Very shortly after she was found, at the time of her first medical assessment, she was thought to be stigmatised by virtue of congenital anomalies (e.g. microcephaly, partial syndactyly of digits) and that mental retardation was very likely to be her destiny, with a persistent deficit comparable to that suffered by Anna (Davis, 1940). Anna's mother was, like Patricia, mentally retarded, with a full-scale IQ on the Stanford-Binet of less than 50. Yet Mary did not go on to present a straightforward picture of global handicap;

in fact, certain visuospatial and performance skills developed as rapidly as those of her sister (Table 1), the main areas of disability being those of language and social relationships. These various strands may be considered separately and in relation to one another.

Mary does not suffer from a recognisable syndrome of multiple congenital malformations. She does, however, possess a head circumference of more than two standard deviations below the mean, as does her mother. A deviation of this degree is often taken as representing significant microcephaly (e.g. Martin, 1970; Avery *et al.*, 1972), but the coincidence of the condition in mother and daughter is an extremely unusual one. Microcephaly may be genetically determined, but when it is, it is usually inherited as a recessive or sex-linked phenomenon (Warkany and St. J. Dignan, 1974). That explanation would not seem to accord with our observations, but a recent report (Haslam and Smith, 1979) described four families with an autosomal dominant trait and the authors suggest this form of microcephaly is more common than previously recorded. At least one former account (Hanhart, 1958) of 'recessive' microcephaly in an isolated mountain community also stated that a maternal heterozygote may possess a significantly reduced head circumference. It is noteworthy that Mary was born with a head of normal dimensions. Microcephaly may apparently be determined by genetic or congenital factors even with this finding (e.g. Sylvester, 1959; Streissguth *et al.*, 1970). It cannot be absolutely certain whether Mary suffered a significant prenatal or perinatal insult. Although possible intrauterine infections such as rubella (Chess, 1971, 1977) or congenital cytomegalovirus (Stubbs, 1978) cannot now be excluded, other potential contributory conditions such as maternal phenylketonuria (Fisch and Anderson, 1971) and congenital syphilis (Rutter and Lockyer, 1967) have been.

The development of Mary's performance skills is chronicled in Table 1. Both girls showed a rapid and sustained rate of acquisition, even though these abilities had been seriously retarded at the time of their discovery. Comparison may be made between the highest level achieved by these sisters and reports of other severely deprived children (e.g. Mason, 1942; Koluchova, 1972; Curtiss, 1977; Douglas and Sutton, 1978). Substantial gains were made in all cases, but it is of additional interest that not only were their performance skills less retarded than language at the earliest assessment but in most cases (the exception is Davis' 1940 account of Anna) their eventual level of attainment equalled or even exceeded verbal ability. This finding is compatible with the well-established observation that psychosocial deprivation usually has a more profound effect on verbal than on visuospatial skills (e.g. Rutter and Mittler, 1972; Rutter and Madge, 1976). However, Mary did not perform equally well on all tests of non-verbal abilities. For example, those that were completed at or above age level included object assembly (WISC), the Seguin Formboard and drawing. She was considerably less successful at picture arrangement (WISC) and conceptual or block building (McCarthy Scales of Children's Abilities) (McCarthy, 1972). Mary, then, was handicapped not only by retardation of language development, but the pattern of her relatively greater achievements in terms of non-verbal cognitive skills was very uneven. This uneven pattern was, incidentally, similar to that displayed by Louise, who also performed worst on the picture arrangement sub-test, a little better on block design and relatively well with object assembly (WISC).

Besides displaying a peculiar pattern of achievement on visuomotor tasks, performing best on those items which are least verbally loaded (Cohen, 1959; Maxwell, 1959), Mary showed oddities in several other areas of functioning. Firstly, in the quality of her spoken language, and concomitantly in her play; secondly, in her social relationships; thirdly, in terms of a certain insistence on sameness; fourthly, in relation to stereotypes of motor behaviour; fifthly, she has shown frequent outbursts of destructive, seemingly randomly directed, bizarre behaviour associated on occasion with self-injury.

Table 1 and Figs. 2 and 3 review the development of comprehension and expression of Mary's spoken language from the time of her discovery until our latest available reports. In both of these faculties her accomplishments are far less striking than those of Louise. The question arises, why should there be such a discrepancy in the developmental histories of these children, after discovery? It seems highly unlikely that the duration of deprivation alone could be responsible, although it is possible that the children's mother lapsed into virtual mutism only after Mary's birth and that Louise had some significant verbal stimulation during her first 14 months. In this connection it is of interest that linguistic competence was achieved by the twins described by Koluchova (1972) and those reported by Douglas and Sutton (1978), all of whom spent the first year or so of their lives in a 'normally stimulating' environment. In contrast, Genie (Curtiss, 1977) also passed her first 20 months in such circumstances and did not achieve useful expressive speech, whereas Isabelle (Mason, 1942) had no such early verbal stimulation but subsequently recovered completely. Mary's level of comprehension at the time of our latest reports was somewhat greater than her expressive language. In fact, she could understand virtually all simple instructions, both singly and when two were combined in one statement. However, her speech was not only very limited but also had a strange quality. Her voice was deep, unnatural and expressionless, her words poorly articulated and she said practically nothing spontaneously. Despite repeated trials of speech therapy, her vocabulary never expanded beyond 100 or so nonmetaphorical items. She rarely used gesture (other than pointing) or mime, and never expressed social greetings or people's names. Such deviance is not at all typical of children with speech delay due to a lack of adequate stimulation or appropriate experience in early life (Rutter, 1972, 1977). Neither is it entirely in keeping with the language deficit of childhood autism, although there are features which suggest this may be a more likely explanation for her disability than developmental receptive dysphasia (see Bartak et al., 1975, 1977). Firstly, the impairment was severe and extended beyond verbal communication. Mary's play was very limited in scope, with symbolism not progressing beyond, for example, dressing and undressing dolls. Even her use of constructional toys never showed creative representational features. Secondly, the form of her language was deviant, with recurrent echolalia and some stereotyped utterances, but these were not marked and she never expressed pronominal reversal. Her unusual phonology would be more in keeping with a dysphasic picture (Menyuk, 1978).

Mary's main distinction from that group of children with developmental dysphasia must be on behavioural grounds. Her social relationships were distorted, but not grossly abnormal; she had appropriate gaze and a social smile, and attracted attention from adults by gesture. Stereotypies of motor activity, usually involving her feet, were noted;

for example, she frequently put her right foot on her left cheek. Much of this behaviour would be comparable to that seen in mildly autistic children, although the overall severity of Mary's disorder is less than in Kanner's classical (1943, 1946) descriptions.

Mary and her half brother Joseph both have marked cognitive and psychosocial disabilities, characterised by autistic features. But Mary has normal (non-verbal) intelligence, whereas Joseph is globally severely retarded. Both children suffered a period of relative deprivation in early childhood, although in neither case was this sufficient to account for their current state. The boy's psychological disorder is associated with oculocutaneous albinism and the girl's with microcephaly and congenital anomalies of her limbs. Their mother is mentally retarded, microcephalic and mentally disturbed, particularly in terms of emotional functioning. Attempting to arrive at a satisfactory explication of these findings presents a considerable dilemma. Other families have been described in which there is more than one autistic sibling (e.g. Verhees, 1976; Sloan, 1978), but Mary and Joseph almost certainly did not share the same father. As it seems highly improbable that their common autistic tendencies are coincidental, the implication is that inheritance occurred in a complex non-Mendelian fashion.

Folstein and Rutter (1978) have concluded that many cases of autism appear to result from a combination of brain damage and an inherited cognitive abnormality. They remark on the importance in this respect of biological hazards in the prenatal and perinatal period. Associations have also been reported between autistic symptoms and genetically determined conditions such as phenylketonuria (see Coleman, 1976). The autistic handicaps suffered by Joseph and Mary suggest they had in common an inherited predisposition to this condition and that the overt expression of autistic symptoms was precipitated by additional organic abnormalities, which were themselves congenital.

A study of this extraordinary family has presented many puzzling aspects, but some general conclusions may yet be drawn; conclusions which tend to uphold current theories about the relevance of early experience to later development (e.g. Kagan, 1979; Rutter, 1980). Firstly, more evidence is adduced by the development of Mary and Louise to disconfirm the concept of a sensitive period (e.g. Clarke and Clarke, 1976) in the early years of childhood for the development of intellect, language and personality. Secondly, it is shown that placement in a nuclear family is not necessary for substantial gains to be made in intellectual, emotional or social functioning. Louise has spent the last decade in a small children's home, albeit with a consistent primary caretaker. Yet she has made advances in both verbal and non-verbal skills, as well as social and emotional achievements, comparable to those shown by Isabelle or the Koluchova twins, all of whom were rehabilitated in small family groups. Thirdly, the structure of formal educational experience received after removal from deprived circumstances may not be a crucial factor in the development of intellect in a child who is not constitutionally disadvantaged. A caretaker's qualities of emotional availability, sensitive responsivity, encouragement and provision of perceptual stimulation, which have been shown to be important for an infant's development (Moore, 1968; Clarke-Stewart, 1973; Bradley and Caldwell, 1976), are also the salient influences bearing on later learning and maturation in these deprived children. Fourthly, we have an excellent example in Mary's history of how stresses may interact to potentiate each other and how one, probably congenital, vulnerability may predispose to later difficulties (see Rutter, 1981). Her failure to develop language was associated with problems in forming social relationships and rendered her a less than fully integrated member of the children's home. Later, when she became disturbed by the reunion with her mother and stepfather, she was unable to express her distress in socially acceptable terms. Disruptive behaviour led to her becoming increasingly alienated from peers and caregivers, and ultimately to her exclusion by them.

Summary

An unusual family is described which has been studied for several years. Accounts are given of the later development of two sisters who had suffered severe social and emotional deprivation in infancy. One girl appears to have completely recovered. The other remains handicapped, mainly in language skills, and shows a variety of autistic features. She is also microcephalic as is their mother. The development of a half brother who was raised elsewhere is recounted. He is an albino, severely mentally retarded and autistic. The later discrepancies in development of these children are discussed, with reference to former case studies of extreme deprivation in early childhood.

Acknowledgements

I would like to thank those doctors, social and child care workers and lay persons who have shown care and concern for these children and their mother over many years and who gave so freely of information and advice in the preparation of this paper. Unfortunately, it is not possible to mention individuals, but I would reserve especial gratitude to Professor Michael Rutter for his particular guidance and support.

References

Avery, G.B., Meneses, L. and Lodge, A. (1972) 'The clinical significant of "measurement microcephaly" '. *Am. J. dis. Child* 123, 214-217.

Bartak, L., Rutter, M. and Cox, A, (1975) 'A comparative study of infantile autism and specific developmental receptive language disorder — I. The children.' *Br. J. Psychiat.* 126, 127-145.

Bartak, L., Rutter, M. and Cox, A. (1977) 'A comparative study of infantile autism and specific receptive language disorder — III. Discriminant function analysis.' *J. Autism Child Schizo.* 7, 383-396.

Bradley, R.H. and Caldwell, B.M. (1976) 'Early home environment and changes in mental test performance in children from 6 to 36 months.' *Dev. Psychol.* 12, 93-97.

Chess, S, (1971) 'Autism in children with congenital rubella.' *J. Autism Child Schizo.* 1, 33-47.

Chess, S. (1977) 'Follow-up report on autism in congenital rubella.' *J. Autism Child Schizo.* 7, 69-81.

Clarke, A. M. and Clarke, A. D. B. (1976) *Early Experience: Myth and Evidence*. Open Books, London.

Clarke-Stewart, K.A. (1973) 'Interactions between mothers and their young children: characteristics and consequences.' *Mongr. Soc. Res. Child Dev.* 38, No. 153.

Cohen, J. (1959) 'The factorial structure of the W.I.S.C. at age 7-6, 10-6, and 13-16.' *J. consult. Psychol.* 23, 285-299.

Coleman, M. (1976) 'Introduction.' In *The Autistic Syndromes* (Edited by Coleman, M.), pp. 1-20. North-Holland, Amsterdam.

Curtiss, S. (1977) *Genie: a Psycholinguistic Study of a Modern-day 'Wild Child'.* Academic Press, London.

Davis, K. (1940) 'Extreme social isolation of a child.' *Am. J. Sociol.* 45, 554-565.

Davis, K. (1947) 'Final note on a case of extreme isolation.' *Am. J. Sociol.* 52, 432-437.

Douglas, J.E. and Sutton, A. (1978) 'The development of speech and mental processes in a pair of twins: a case study.' *J. Child Psychol. Psychiat.* 19, 49-56.

Egan, D.F., Illingworth, R.S. and MacKeith, R.C. (1969) *Clinics in developmental Medicine, No. 30. Developmental Screening 0-5 Years*, p. 3. Heinemann/S.I.M.P., London.

Fisch, R.O. and Anderson, J.A. (1971) 'Maternal phenylketonuria.' In *Phenylketonuria and Some Other Inborn Errors of Amino Acid Metabolism* (Edited by Bickel, H., Hudson, F.P. and Woolf, L.I.), pp. 73-80. Georg Thieme Verlag, Stuttgart.

Folstein, S. and Rutter, M. (1978) 'A twin study of individuals with infantile autisim.' In *Autism: a Reappraisal of Concepts and Treatment* (Edited by Rutter, M. and Schopler, E.), pp. 219-242. Plenum Press, New York.

Griffiths, R. (1954) *The Abilities of Babies.* University of London Press, London.

Hanhart, E. (1958) 'Veber einfache Rezessivität bei Mikrocephalia vera, spuria et combinata und das herdweise Vorkommen der Mikrocephalia vera in Schweizer Isolaten.' *Acta genet. Med. Gemellol.* 7, 445-524.

Haslam, R.H.A. and Smith, D.W. (1979) 'Autosomal dominant microcephaly.' *J. Pediatr.* 95, 701-705.

Kagagn, J. (1979) 'The form of early development.' *Archs gen. Pscychiat.* 36, 1047-1054.

Kanner, L. (1943) 'Autistic disturbance of affective contact.' *Nerv. Child* 2, 217-250.

Kanner, L. (1946) 'Irrelevant and metaphorical language in early infantile autism.' *Am. J. Psychiat.* 103, 242-245.

Koluchova, J. (1972) 'Severe deprivation in twins: a case study.' *J. Child Psychol. Psychiat.* 13, 107-114.

Koluchova, J. (1976) 'The further development of twins after severe and prolonged deprivation: a second report.' *J. Child Psychol. Psychiat.* 17, 181-188.

McCarthy, D. (1972) *McCarthy Scales of Children's Abilities.* The Psychological Corporation, New York.

Martin, H.P. (1970) 'Microcephaly and mental retardation.' *Am. J. Dis. Child.* 119, 128-131.

Mason, M.K. (1942) 'Learning to speak after six and one half years of silence.' *J. Speech Hear. Disord.* 7, 295-304.

Maxwell, A.E. (1959) 'A factor analysis of the Wechsler Intelligence Scale for Children.' *Brit. J. educ. Psychol.* 29, 237-241.

Menyuk, P. (1978) 'Linguistic problems in children with developmental dysphasia.' In *Developmental Dysphasia* (edited by Wyke, M.A.), pp. 135-158. Academic Press, London.

Moore, T. (1986) 'Language and intelligence: a longitudinal study of the first eight years. Part II: Environmental correlates of mental growth.' *Hum. Dev.* 11, 1-24.

Neale, M.D. (1958) *Neale Analysis of Reading Ability* (Manual). Macmillan, London.

Reynell, J. (1969) *Reynell Developmental Language Scales,* experimental edition (Manual). National Foundation for Educational Research, Windsor.

Rogawski, M.A., Funderburk, S.J. and Lederbaum, S.D. (1978) 'Oculocutaneous albinism and mental disorder: a report of two autistic boys.' *Hum. Hered.* 28, 81-85.

Rutter, M. (1972) 'Psychiatric causes of language retardation.' In *Clinics in Developmental Medicine, No. 43. The Child Delayed Speech* (Edited by Rutter, M. and Martin, J.A.M.), pp. 147-160. Heinemann/S.I.M.P., London.

Rutter, M. (1977) 'Infantile autism and other child psychoses.' In *Child Psychiatry: Modern Approaches* (Edited by Rutter, M. and Hersov, L.), pp. 717-747. Blackwell Scientific, Oxford.

Rutter, M. (1978) 'Protective factors in children's responses to stress and disadvantage.' In *Primary Prevention of Psychopathology* (Edited by Kent, M.W. and Rolf, J.E.), Vol. 3, pp. 49-74. University Press of New England, Hanover, NH.

Rutter, M. (1980) 'The long term effects of early experience.' *Dev. Med. Child Neurol.* 22, 800-815.

Rutter, M. (1981) *Maternal Deprivation Reassessed,* second edn. Penguin, Harmondsworth.

Rutter, M. and Lockyer, L. (1967) 'A five to fifteen year follow-up of infantile psychosis (1). Description of sample.' *Br. J. Psychiat.* 113, 1169-1182.

Rutter, M. and Madge, N. (1976) *Cycles of Disadvantage: a Review of Research.* Heinemann Educational, London.

Rutter, M. and Mittler, P. (1972) 'Environmental influences on language development.' In *Clinics in Developmental Medicine, No. 43. The Child with Delayed Speech* (Edited by Rutter, M. and Martin, J.A.M.), pp. 52-67. Heinemann/S.I.M.P., London.

Skeels, H.M. (1966) 'Adult status of children with contrasting early life experiences.' *Monogr. Soc. Res. Child Dev.* 31, No. 3.

Skuse, D. (1984) 'Extreme deprivation in early childhood — II. Theoretical issues and a comparative review.' *J. Child Psychol. Psychiat.* 25, 543-572.

Sloan, J.L. (1978) 'Differential development of autistic symptoms in a pair of fraternal twins.' *J. Autism Child Schizo.* 8, 191-202.

Stanford-Binet Intelligence Scale, third revision (1973) George G. Harrap & Co., London.

Streissguth, A.P. Vanderbeer, B.B. and Shephard, T.H. (1970) 'Mental development of children with congenital rubella syndrome.' *Am. J. Obstet. Gynecol.* 108, 391-399.

Stubbs, E.G. (1978) 'Autistic symptoms in a child with congenital cytomegalovirus infection.' *J. Autism Child Schizo.* 8, 37-43.

Stutsman, R. (1948) 'A guide for administering the Merill-Palmer Scale of Mental Tests.' In *Mental Measurement of Preschool Children.* N.F.E.R., Windsor.

Sylvester, P.E. (1959) 'Cerebral atrophy in microcephalic cousins.' *Archs Dis. Child.* 34, 325-330.

Verhees, B. (1976) 'A pair of classically early infantile autistic siblings.' *J. Autism Child Schizo*, 6, 53-60.

Vernon, P.E. (1977) *Graded Word Spelling Test* (Manual). Hodder & Stoughton, London.

Warkany, J. and St. J. Dignan, P. (1973) 'Congenital malformations: microcephaly.' In *Mental Retardation and Developmental Disabilities* (Edited by Wortis, J.), Vol. 5, pp. 113-135. Brunner/Mazel, New York.

Wechsler, D. (1949) *Wechsler Intelligence Scale for Children* (Manual). The Psychological Corporation, New York.

Wechsler, D. (1955) *Wechsler Adult Intelligence Scale* (Manual). The Psychological Corporation, New York.

Witkop, C.J. (1971) Albinism. In *Advanced in Human Genetics* (Edited by Harris, H. and Hirschhorn, K.), Vol. 2, pp. 61-142. Plenum Press, New York.

3.

Extreme Deprivation in Early Childhood — II. Theoretical Issues and a Comparative Review

David Skuse

Introduction

It has often been suggested (e.g. Clarke, 1972) that a careful analysis of the sequelae of severe deprivation in early childhood could serve as an excellent experimental paradigm when considering the vexed question of how developmental disorders arise within the context of maturational processes. Indeed, over many centuries this very experience has been rendered both by nature and, on occasions, by design.

One of the earliest accounts of children reared in conditions of extreme isolation as an experimental measure was by Herodotus, who reported that, in the 7th century B.C. the Egyptian king Psammetichos had two children raised by shepherds who never spoke to them, in order to see what language they would develop (Carter, 1962). In our own times two infants were studied for more than a year in conditions of minimal perceptual and social stimulation (Dennis, 1941). There are also a number of relatively recent reports concerning children who have spent their early years in conditions of exceptional impoverishment and deprivation as the result of deliberate action by nefarious, ignorant or incompetent caretakers (Davis, 1940; Mason, 1942; Koluchova, 1972, 1976; Curtiss, 1977; Douglas and Sutton, 1978). A companion article (Skuse, 1984) presents detailed case histories for another pair of children and discusses the clinical implications of those findings. Certain features are common to both recent victims and their historical counterparts. First, they are initially lacking basic attributes such as speech and social skills, which are ubiquitous except in severely retarded and dysphasic children or those with autistic features. Secondly removal from the impoverished conditions is often followed by a remarkable and usually relatively rapid development of their cognitive and other faculties (see also Curtiss, 1981a).

Three main issues are addressed by these observations: firstly, what minimal experiences during childhood are sufficient and necessary for normal psychological development? Secondly, are there critical periods in development during which inadequate or absent exposure to certain experiences may have permanent sequelae? Thirdly, if the evidence does not support the notion of critical periods, what are the minimal compensatory influences necessary to alleviate psychological handicaps that have resulted from an adverse early environment? Variability in outcome after extreme deprivation must relate to congenital and experiential influences on development. Although it is no longer contentious to assert that all human behaviour is a function of

David Skuse: 'Extreme Deprivation in Early Childhood — II. Theoretical Issues and a Comparative Review'. *THE JOURNAL OF CHILD PSYCHOLOGY AND PSYCHIATRY* (1984), Vol. 25, No. 4. pp. 543-572. © 1984 Association for Child Psychology and Psychiatry.

both heredity and environment (e.g. Anastasi, 1958; Shields, 1980), just how that environment and an individual constitution interact and transact remains a matter for debate.

A number of specific questions are also posed by consideration of children who spent their lives in circumstances far removed from the 'average expectable environment' (Hartmann, 1958). To answer these we need first to look at similarities and differences between subjects *at discovery*, in terms of their behaviour and in terms of their mental faculties. For instance, how do they perceive the world? What social responses do they manifest? Do they speak or understand speech? What emotions do they express? Do those findings suggest that some of our psychological attributes are more susceptible to the vicissitudes of an impoverished upbringing than others? Having taken cognizance of that situation, we may turn our attention to evidence of *recovery* and the circumstances in which recovery takes place. How quickly is each faculty gained and what is its course of development? How is that course dependent on the stimulation provided and what intensity of intervention is necessary to optimise the rate of recovery?

Finally, what is the *outcome* after a suitable follow-up period? To what extent is normal psychological development attained, in quality and degree, taking each mental attribute separately? Is it possible to predict outcome at discovery? If not, how soon may such prediction be made? Is the crucial prognostic factor the rate of recovery and, if so, how may this 'rate' be measured? If there is evidence of incomplete recovery in some areas does this imply constitutional limitations on growth, a truly critical phase for normal development or inadequate intervention and compensation during the follow-up period?

Commenting on Koluchova's 1972 paper about the discovery and subsequent development of severely deprived twins, Clarke (1972) asserts that the gratifying results of their education underlines the inadequacy of theories which stress the overriding importance of early experience for later growth. This concept of 'critical periods' evolved partly through the influence of purely psychoanalytic theories (e.g. Freud, 1905, 1915; Klein, 1932), partly from early ethological observations (e.g. Lorenz, 1935; but see Hinde, 1963) and partly from Bowlby's (1958, 1969) synthesis of these diverse conceptualisations. Those who believed in 'superenvironmentalism' held that early trauma or deprivation would have irreversible effects on later development, but compelling evidence against the notion has been assembled by Clarke and Clarke (1976) among others (e.g. Rutter, 1981), and even its original proponents have by now modified their views (e.g. Bowlby, 1979). However, it is regrettable that in most debates on these aspects of early deprivation and disadvantage the evidence has not been judged with sufficient percipience.

For example, with regard to variability in outcome, no satisfactory distinction has been drawn between different aspects of development which may be affected by an adverse environment (Sroufe, 1977). Additionally, discussions about the role of deprivation in development have usually failed not only to separate the quality of deprivation from its psychological consequences but also neglected to draw apart the particular aspects of deprivation (perceptual, social, emotional, linguistic, nutritional, etc.) from their sequelae. Such distinctions may have been considered unduly contrived, but they nevertheless seem to provide a useful framework. Of course, the model is complicated by the fact that different psychological variables interact. For example, cognitive influences underlie the development of all aspects of behaviour, affect and social interactions, besides there being "no behaviour pattern, however intellectual, which does not involve affective factors as motives" (Piaget and Inhelder, 1969).

This paper aims to illustrate and explore these issues by reference to six well-documented accounts of severe deprivation. The reports concern children brought up in what were nominally home environments rather than institutions. Detailed information is presented about the circumstances both before and after removal from adversity, and about outcome at follow-up. These six are the most full descriptions available in the English language of psychological and physical consequences of such an upbringing: Davis (1940, 1947); Mason (1942); Koluchova (1972, 1976); Curtiss (1977); Douglas and Sutton (1978); Skuse (1984). Important work has, of course, been published on the effects of impoverished institutional environments. Skeels (1966) reviews the outcome of 13 children initially in an understimulating orphanage but transferred before 3 yr of age to a home for the mentally retarded from which they were adopted. A remarkably favourable prognosis was found at follow-up assessments over the subsequent 30 yr. Their outcome contrasted dramatically with a comparison group who remained in the original orphanage and who were likewise followed into adult life. The scientific validity of Skeel's conclusions has, however, been heavily criticised in a recent publication by Longstreth (1981), but however incisive in pointing out the weaknesses of Skeel's study, Longstreth does not seriously undermine the main claim that infants from a very poor background made a substantial and lasting recovery when transferred to a more satisfactory environment. Dennis (1973) reported on a similarly deprived foundling home in Beirut, Lebanon, where he found a temporary, apparently environmentally induced, developmental retardation maximal between 3 and 12 months of age. These valuable reports will not be discussed in detail because insufficient data are available about individual characteristics of the children and because the circumstances of their upbringing were so different from the main group.

Case histories

Briefly, the facts of each case are as follows:

Anna (*Davis*, 1940, 1947)

On 6 February 1938 the *New York Times* reported that a girl of more than 5 yr had been found tied to an old chair in a storage room on the second floor of her farm home 17 miles from a small Pennsylvania city. She had apparently been there since babyhood. The child, Anna, was wedged into the chair which was tilted backwards to rest upon a coal bucket, her spindly arms tied above her head. She was unable to talk or move, and was dressed in a dirty shirt and napkin. Her hands, arms and legs were just bones, with skin drawn over them so frail she could not use them. She had never had enough nourishment. Anna never grew normally and the chair on which she lay, half reclining and half sitting, was so small she had to double her legs partly under her. Immediately following her discovery Anna was removed to a children's home, where she was noted to be completely apathetic and lay in a limp supine position, immobile, expressionless and indifferent to everything. She was believed to be deaf, possibly blind.

Isabelle (*Mason*, 1942; *Davis,* 1947)

Born apparently 1 month later than Anna, a girl, who has been given the pseudonym Isabelle, was discovered in November 1938. At the time she was approximately 6½ yr old. She was an illegitimate child and had been kept in seclusion for that reason. Her mother was a deaf mute and it seemed that she and Isabelle had spent most of their time together in a dark room shut away from the family who had rejected them. Lack of sunshine and inadequacy of diet had caused Isabelle to become rachitic and her legs were "so bowed that as she stood erect the soles of her shoes came nearly flat together, and she got about with a skittering gait". Isabelle's mother eventually escaped with her child after nearly 7 yr seclusion and the girl was brought to the Children's Hospital in Columbus, Ohio on 16 November 1938 for orthopaedic surgery and physiotherapy. Her behaviour towards strangers, especially men, was found to be that of a "wild animal". She manifested much fear and hostility and, in lieu of speech, made only a strange croaking sound.

Koluchova twins (*Koluchova*, 1972, 1976)

Jarmila Koluchova reported in 1972 the case record of monozygotic male twins, who were born on 4 September 1960. Their mother died shortly after giving birth and for 11 months they lived in a children's home. They then spent 6 months with a maternal aunt but were subsequently taken to live with their father and stepmother. For 5½ yr, until their discovery at the age of 7, the twins lived under most abnormal conditions, in a quiet street of family houses in Czechoslovakia. Because of the actions of their stepmother, who had her own children whom she actively preferred, the boys grew up in almost total isolation, never being allowed out of the house but living in a small unheated closet. They were often locked up for long periods in the cellar, sleeping on the floor on a plastic sheet, and they were cruelly chastised. When discovered at the age of 7 they could barely walk. They showed reactions of surprise and horror to objects and activities normally very familiar to children of that age, such as moving mechanical toys, a TV set or traffic in the street. Their spontaneous speech was very poor, as was their play.

Genie (*Curtiss*, 1977)

One of the most extraordinary cases of severe deprivation yet reported is that of Genie, who was born in U.S.A. in April 1957. She was found at the age of 13 yr 7 months, a painfully thin child who appeared 6 or 7 yr old. From the age of 20 months she had been confined to a small room under conditions of extreme physical restraint. In this room she received minimal care from a mother who was herself rapidly losing her sight. Genie was physically punished by her father if she made any sound. Most of the time she was kept harnessed into an infant's potty-chair; but at night she was confined in a home-made sleeping bag fashioned like a strait jacket and lay in an infant's crib covered with wire mesh. She was fed only infant food. Genie's father was convinced that she would die; he was positive that she would not live past the age of 12 and promised that the mother could seek help for the child if she did so. But when the age of 12 had come and gone and she survived, the father reneged on his promise. It was not until Genie was 13½ yr old that her mother managed to get away, leaving home and husband, to seek help for the child. At this time Genie could not stand erect and could walk only with difficulty, shuffling her feet and swaying from side to side. Having been beaten for making any noise she had learned to suppress almost all vocalisation save a whimper. She salivated copiously, spitting onto anything at hand, and was incontinent of urine and faeces. Curtiss comments "Genie was unsocialised, primitive, hardly human".

Alice and Beth

[Douglas and Sutton (1978) report another pair of deprived twin girls.]

For the first 3 months of their lives their mother was working to support herself and they had no contact with her at all. She had separated from her husband, an itinerant musician, whilst pregnant. They were initially looked after by friends and then some distant relatives took charge and planned to adopt them, but their own marriage broke up. The twins were then taken into care for a few weeks, after which an aunt and uncle looked after them for the remainder of their first year. During that same year their mother returned to her husband for a time, became pregnant, and left him again after 3 months. Soon after that she moved with the twins into a council house, but it was damp, infested with mice and due for demolition. She suffered from depression badly enough to require medical treatment. It seems the girls received very little stimulation and, although they learned to walk at the normal time, they were very slow in learning to talk. When nearly 5 and due to move to infants school they still could not talk intelligibly, except to each other in a private language incomprehensible to others.

May and Louisa (Skuse, 1984)

In the autumn of 1977 a little girl of almost 9 yr was referred to the Children's Department at a large postgraduate teaching hospital. Over the previous year Mary had exhibited increasingly disruptive behaviour in the small children's home where she had lived for the previous 6 yr with her sister Louise, who was 14 months her elder. When their early history was investigated further it transpired that these children had spent their early lives in a remarkably deprived environment on account of their having a mother (Patricia) who was not only mentally retarded and microcephalic but may additionally have been suffering from a serious psychiatric disorder. When discovered in March 1971 by the Social Services the comment was made that "Louise and Mary are very strange creatures indeed". Aged 3 yr 6 months and 2 yr 4 months respectively, they took no notice of anything or anyone except to scamper up and sniff strangers, grunting and snuffling like animals. They both still sucked dummies and no attempt had been made to toilet train them, so they remained in nappies. Neither child had any constructive play but picked up objects and handled then smelt and felt them. Mary had no speech whatsoever and made no hearing responses. Her vocalisation seemed limited to a few high pitched sounds. Later that year something came to light which had not been noticed by the authorities before but had apparently been going on daily ever since the children became mobile. The health visitor found them tied on leashes to the bed, a measure their mother had taken partly because she insisted on keeping the flat spotlessly clean and partly because she was worried they would fall off the balcony. If they became too noisy or active the children were put onto a mattress and covered with a blanket. They were subsequently removed from her and taken into care.

Presentation of data

Tables 1-6 illustrate in schematic form the information available about these six cases of extreme deprivation. The structure of each table is arranged so that individuals whose outcome was relatively poor (Anna, Genie and Mary) may be readily contrasted with those who had a good prognosis (Isabelle, the Koluchova twins, Alice and Beth, and Louise).

Genetic, prenatal and perinatal influences

Table 1 presents information about potential genetic, prenatal and perinatal influences upon these children. When we consider the aetiology of their developmental problems, the issues seem daunting. Genetic, congenital and later environmental influences interact in processes of great complexity, but a useful initial step is to consider the role of constitutional factors separately. For example, we need to know not only if either parent suffered from an autosomal dominant or sex-linked condition but whether they were consanguinous, with an increased risk of producing a child homozygous for a recessive condition. Also, whether either suffered significant mental retardation of presumed constitutional aetiology. Evidence indicates that mental handicap in the close relatives of those with mild-to-moderate retardation is quite commonly encountered (Akesson, 1962; Heber *et al.*, 1968). This is not, of course, to assume that such a well-described association is due wholly to genetic influences. As Clarke and Clarke (1974) point out, most mildly retarded children have parents from the lower social classes. The proportion of low-social-class children with low IQ is excessively large; therefore such mild retardation may be due at least partly to adverse social factors.

Table 1 provides information about the parents of the six families under consideration. In no case is either parent known to have suffered from a recognisable congenital syndrome associated with mental handicap, although at least two mothers (Davis, 1940; Skuse, 1984) were moderately mentally retarded.

Prenatal and perinatal complications are infrequently reported. In most cases we do not know whether antenatal care was provided, although the evidence suggests it was not. However, the relevance of such complications to developmental disabilities is not always direct. Leaving on one side the impact of major pre- and perinatal insults, which do not seem to have occurred in these cases, the apparent importance for intellectual outcome of minor adversities such as heavy smoking (Butler and Goldstein, 1973) or poor maternal nutrition (Broman *et al.*, 1975) in pregnancy may be mediated mainly by general associations with suboptimal social and economic circumstances of upbringing (Sameroff and Chandler, 1975). Low birth weight does, however, seem to show a small association with IQ quite apart from the stronger associations with social class (Davie *et al.*, 1972). Illegitimacy (the case for several of these children) has been shown to be related to disturbances in later behaviour and with learning difficulties (Crellin *et al.*, 1971; Herzog and Sudia, 1973).

Table 1   Genetic, prenatal and perinatal influences

Name	Date of birth	Illegitimate	Parental characteristics		Antenatal care	Birth in hospital or clinic	Birth trauma
			Mother	Father			
Anna (Davis, 1940)	1.3.32	yes	IQ(S-B)50	not known	not known	yes	no
Genie (Curtiss, 1977)	?.4.57	no	few details reported		not known	yes	caesarean exchange transfusion
Mary (Skuse, 1984)	24.11.68	yes	micro-cephalic (IQ (WAIS) 55	not known	no	no	no
Isabelle (Mason, 1942)	?.4.32	yes	uneducated severely deaf	not known	none	not known	not known
Koluchova twins (MZ boys) P.M. J.M. (1972)	4.9.60	no	normal intelligence	below average	not known	not known	mother died shortly after birth
Douglas and Sutton twins (?Z) Alice, Beth (1978)	7.2.69	no	few details reported; below average intellects		not known	yes	no / forceps delivery
Louise (Skuse, 1984)	30.9.67	yes	micro-cephalic IQ(WAIS) 55	not known	not known	yes	no

*S-B, Stanford-Binet Intelligence Scale; WAIS, Wechsler Adult Intelligence Scale.

Early environmental stimuli and influences

Early environmental stimuli and influences are shown in Table 2.

Nutrition

The time of most rapid brain growth in man is from the last trimester of pregnancy until about 17 months of age, and is fastest towards the time of birth (Dobbing, 1975). Severe undernutrition of children in the first year of life is associated with decreased brain weight, less brain protein and RNA and fewer brain cells in the cerebrum (Winick et al., 1970), leading to failure of growth of head circumference as well as stunting of height (Cravioto et al., 1966). It is alleged that social skills may be reduced (Waterlow, 1974) as well as intellectual level (Hertzig et al., 1972). Eichenwald and Fry (1969), reviewing the evidence linking nutrition and learning in animals and man, conclude that, although the intellectual and emotional development of the individual may be permanently and profoundly affected, it is not possible to state whether this outcome is due mainly to the malnutrition or whether intimately related influences, such as an inadequate social and emotional environment, make the significant contribution. Richardson (1977) adds that a further complicating factor is due to the fact that malnutrition seems to be an interactive variable, with different effects depending on the overall ecological context, especially after the incident of severe malnutrition. Of the children reviewed in Table 2, four were definitely severely malnourished. Despite this, the outcome for the Koluchova twins and Isabelle was good, whereas Anna and Genie exhibited profound handicaps. There is no evidence that Mary and Louise were malnourished.

Table 2   Early environmental stimuli and influences

Name	Date of birth	Severe malnourish-ment	Maltreat-ment*	Longest period in normal environ-ment	Consistent social contacts†	Language	
						Spoken	Gesture
Anna (Davis, 1940)	1.3.32	yes	N.R.E	birth-6 months	M, S	minimal	minimal
Genie (Curtiss, 1977)	?.4.57	yes	N.R.E.A	birth-1.8 yr	M, F, S	minimal	minimal
Mary (Skuse, 1984)	24.11.68	no	R.E.	none	M, S, F	limited	limited
Isabelle (Mason, 1942)	?.4.32	yes	E.	none	M (Mute)	minimal	siginificant stimulation
Koluchova twins (MZ boys) P.M. J.M. (1972)	4.9.60	yes	N.A.E.	birth - 1.6 yr	M, F, S (4)	minimal	minimal
Douglas and Sutton twins (?Z) Alice Beth (1978)	2.2.69	no	E	birth - 1.0 yr	M F (from 4 yr)	limited	limited
Louise (Skuse, 1984)	30.9.67	no	R.E.	? birth-1.2 yr	M S (from 1.2 yr) F	limited	limited

* N, gross neglect; R, physical restraint; A, physical abuse/chastisement; E, impoverished environment with minimum stimulation
†M, mother; F, father (inc. cohabitee); S, sib(s).

Maltreatment

Table 2 also reviews the evidence for maltreatment of the children, and the various forms of abuse they suffered are indicated. 'Gross neglect' refers to reports of deliberate failure to attend to normal child care practices, e.g. leaving the child unattended for long periods, failing to wash and change clothes and bedding, failure to encourage motoric development skills and the absence of any attempt by the child's caretaker to establish a social relationship. The employment of physical restraint means that for a significant period (at least several hours) of each day the child was tied and its movements severely restricted by the use of a leash or other device. Physical abuse and chastisement were certainly experienced by the Koluchova twins and by Genie to an extraordinary degree. The twins were regularly beaten by their father with a rubber hose until they lay flat on the ground unable to move. Genie's father hit her with a large piece of wood which he kept in the corner of her room and used whenever she made any sounds. We do not have any clear evidence of similar atrocities in the other cases reported.

Development of perception

One feature common to all cases, with the possible exception of the twins reported by Douglas and Sutton, was that they suffered a very restricted perceptual environment. Perception may be defined both in terms of the ability to respond to a stimulus and as an ability to distinguish between stimuli and respond differentially. All sensory modalities may be affected by the experience of extreme deprivation, as evidenced by the cases reviewed, although the precise determining influences for such disabilities are difficult to establish. There has been considerable research in the past decade into the development of an infant's auditory and visual perception (see Cohen and Salapatek, 1975), and it will not be possible to give more than a brief account here.

Visual perception. Anna was thought to be possibly blind when first discovered. She had been kept confined within one room from birth and received minimal visual stimulation. The impression of blindness was given by her failure to maintain eye contact; she could not fix visual attention on any object. An ability to visually fixate normally occurs at 1 week of age, and some preference may be shown for complex large stimuli (Fantz and Fagan, 1975). It has even been claimed that facial gestures may be imitated by normal infants less than 3 weeks old (Meltzoff and Moore, 1977). On removal from her deprived circumstances Anna did, however, rapidly develop this faculty and, within 2 weeks, fixation of her visual attention was more readily induced (Davis, 1940). She also began to demonstrate some sense of colour recognition: she preferred a green pencil to a yellow one. Colour discrimination can be observed in normal infants at as early as 2-4 months of age (Bornstein, 1976; Bornstein *et al.*, 1976). It is unclear what factors might have led to this child's visual behaviour at discovery, but the rapid development of visual fixation in blind persons who later recover their sight has been described (e.g. Gregory and Wallace, 1963). Genie is reported to have been kept in a room in which the furthest object she could see was 10 ft away. On removal she was found to be short-sighted to exactly this degree, but Curtiss does not present any further information about the course of her condition in a normal environment. Commenting on Koluchova's (1972) paper, Clarke (1972) states "the failure of the twins to understand the meaning of pictures and their relation to reality is itself a testimony to the length and severity of their deprivation". The inability to recognise two-dimensional representations is not reported in other cases; reviewing Koluchova's original report, her statement seems ambiguous, but it suggests that the twins' *vocabulary* could not be assessed by means of pictures. We cannot conclude that because they did not name pictures they could not understand their meaning, although such a conclusion would seem to be congruent with Hebb's (1949) views about perceptual development. An experiment by Hochberg and Brooks (1962) illustrates the point; they raised their son to the age of 19 months in the absence of two-dimensional representations of objects, yet his recognition of such objects, including photographs, is reported to have been excellent subsequently.

Auditory perception. All the cases reported were brought up in conditions of abnormal auditory stimulation, although we lack exact information about the quality of experiences which were available except in the case of Genie, where, we are informed, virtually the only sound she heard for 13 yr was from an adjoining bathroom. In the case of Isabelle her sole companion was a deaf mute mother and Anna, Isabelle and Mary were all thought to be deaf when first discovered, although there does not seem to have been such concern about the twins described by Douglas and Sutton, or Genie or Louise. Anna initially showed a peculiar pattern of hearing responses in that she would, for example, turn her head towards a ticking clock, yet neither clapping hands nor speech produced a reaction. This behaviour is reminiscent of Bonnaterre's (1800) account of the Wild Boy of Aveyron, who would not flinch at a pistol shot yet showed immediate interest in the sound of a cracking nut, and such differential responsiveness is well recognised among autistic children (Wing, 1976). Establishment of normal hearing responses was, however, remarkably rapid in all cases. For example, Isabelle was within 1 week listening attentively to vocal sounds and she made her first imitative vocal responses less than 2 weeks after discovery. Given the importance of engaging her attention in order to teach vocal language for communication, it is remarkable, and most significant, that she is said to have expressed "joy in successful performance", although she was not at first inclined to repeat is spontaneously.

Psychological variables may affect abilities relating to attention. They may serve either to enhance it (e.g. Levy and Hobbes, 1979) or to impair it (e.g. Hansley and Busse, 1969; Tizard and Rees, 1975), but the precise determining factors are not known (Taylor, 1980). The rapidity with which selective concentration for both auditory and visual stimuli became established in these deprived children carries implications for an understanding of how this essential but elusive facility develops, pointing toward the relative importance of current *vis-à-vis* past environmental stimuli and the limitations set by congenital factors. One crucial piece of evidence in this enquiry is the final degree of attentional competence achieved. Details are not given in any of the case accounts where early attentional problems have been commented upon, but no long-standing deficits are reported by Davis (1947) or Koluchova (1976).

Other senses. There has been relatively little research into the importance of environmental influences upon the development of discrimination in the senses of taste and olfaction, of cutaneous and kinesthetic sensation and the appreciation of pain (e.g. Cowart, 1981). For instance, there is scarcely a mention of them in Pick and Pick's major

(1970) review of sensory and perceptual development. The range of perceptual experience was seriously restricted in most of the cases reported. For example, Anna was fed for nearly 6 yr on diet which consisted almost solely of milk and oatmeal and in her early days in care showed no taste preference at all, although this became rapidly established on a normal diet. Curtiss (1977) provides some illuminating detail. Even after many years of severe deprivation Genie showed an intense need for, and delight in, acquiring new experiences, as evidenced by her eager exploration by touch, smell and examination of the meat at a local store. Her enthusiasm was in marked contrast to initial observations made of the mysterious alleged isolate Caspar Hauser (Anon., 1834): "As he appeared to be also suffering from hunger and thirst, a small piece of meat was handed to him; but scarcely had the first morsel touched his lips when he shuddered, the muscles of his face were seized with convulsive spasms, and he spat it out with great abhorrence".

Attachment

Harlow's well-known studies of mother surrogates with infant rhesus monkeys (reviewed by Rajecki *et al.*, 1978) have pointed to the importance of tactile contact for the processes of attachment and the devastating effect total social isolation in early life has upon subsequent social, sexual and parenting behaviour. An inanimate surrogate is in the long term a very unsatisfactory substitute for a genuinely sensitive and responsive mother. When infant monkeys without access to parental figures are raised in the social milieu of their peer group a qualitative difference in attachment behaviour results, but untoward long-term consequences seem to be relatively few. These researches have been well reviewed by Ruppenthal *et al.* (1976). That close peer relations may also have an ameliorating influence on humans is suggested by Freud and Dann's (1951) account of six young children brought up in a stable group by multiple caretakers in a concentration camp. Their long-term outcome has been described by Goldberger (1972). The vicissitudes suffered by the children reviewed in Table 2 must indeed have been terrible, but perhaps the consequences of those experiences would be diminished for the two sets of twins who always had each other for comfort and communication. In fact, it is now regarded as highly unlikely that Bowlby's erstwhile (1969) belief in monotropy is correct (Rutter, 1981; Chapter 2) and, although a hierarchy may exist amongst attachment figures, there are unlikely to be qualitative differences. It is important to note that the children under review were not 'deprived' simply in the sense that they had multiple caretakers or no adult attachment figures at all. The relationship with their primary caregiver was often distorted, and characterised not only by neglect (for example, Anna's mother neither bathed or caressed her) but also by the transmission of punishments and pain rather than affection and attention aimed at reducing distress. In this connection Mary's clinging behaviour to her mother when brought to a clinic, aged 2 yr 10 months, seems relevant. It was described at the time as resembling that of a maltreated baby monkey and is suggestive of the anxious insecure attachments seen in abused animals (for discussion see Rajecki *et al.*, 1978). Data on human subjects are few, but the evidence points to anxiety being an influence which serves to intensify attachment behaviour regardless of the source of that anxiety (Rutter, 1980).

Social development

When we consider the experience of psychosocial deprivation in relation to its detrimental influence upon the ability to socialise successfully with adults and peers, it is difficult to draw any firm conclusions about cause and effect. The social behaviour on discovery of these deprived children is reviewed in Table 3. There is a remarkable contrast in the findings reported. This may be in part a function of their differing ages and levels of social maturity, but it must also reflect the form and extent of adversities suffered in earlier life. Beth and Alice (Douglas and Sutton, 1978) were not maltreated in the sense this term applies to the other cases, and were 'friendly and amenable to adults' on discovery. Genie, who had suffered tremendous hardship and deprivation for over 12 yr, was reportedly "intensely eager for human contact and attention" when taken into care, whereas Anna, at almost 6 yr, was profoundly withdrawn and apathetic and failed to show significant improvement for several months until moved into the intimate environment of a foster family. Isabelle initially shared the wariness of strangers typical of an infant late in the first year of life; she had not been physically abused. During the first few days away from her depriving environment (remaining with her mother) her social responses were said to be those of a child of 6 months. Nevertheless, in under 2 yr she was reported as having made tremendous progress in social adjustment. Mary and Louise demonstrated prosocial behaviour of a sort when first seen (aged 3 yr 6 months and 2 yr 4 months), but it was characterised by their "scampering up and sniffing strangers, grunting and snuffling like animals". Ten months later, following their admission to a play group, Louise was said to be socially responsive and to have formed a warm attachment to one particular helper. Mary (a less regular attender) related less intensely, responded solely to one woman and failed to integrate with the group. However, Mary's aloofness and withdrawal did gradually abate; at the age of 13 she was found to be moderately socially responsive and physically affectionate to her main caregivers, with good eye contact. It would be tempting to conclude that this latent period in the development of Mary's attachment behaviour indicated the course of her recovery from an earlier state, determined largely by extreme social deprivation, in which those systems designated to facilitate attachment (Bowlby, 1969) failed to operate. However, there is evidence that she had many years before formed some affectional bonds. That bonding (Ainsworth, 1973; Sroufe and Waters, 1977) is suggested by her strong reaction to an unexpected visit by her mother's cohabitee, Rupert, nearly $4\frac{1}{2}$ yr after their last meeting. Mary was upset and clinging at his departure (Skuse, 1984). This observation would be in keeping with the abundant evidence that infants usually develop their first attachment to a specific person at about 6-12 months of age (Ainsworth, 1973) and that the figure is likely to be the one with whom they have had most active interaction (Rutter, 1980). It is now appreciated that fathers have a potentially important part to play in the fostering of many aspects of social, emotional and cognitive development (e.g. Lamb, 1981; Parke, 1979). What minimal early stimulation these little girls received is likely to have been provided by Rupert. Recalling Mary's behaviour at the time of entry to the children's home, when she rocked silently by herself, we might now speculate whether this represented her profound yet inarticulate response to that earlier separation. Her behaviour is reminiscent of Robertson and Robertson's (1971) account of an infant's silent despair and detachment, observed in similar circumstances. Rocking is known to occur in normal children when abandoned or distressed, in institutions for the mentally handicapped (Berkson and Davenport, 1962) and in infant chimpanzees who appear to 'comfort' themselves by squatting on their haunches with their heads bowed, rocking backwards and forwards when lonely or frightened (Davenport and Menzel, 1963).

As discussed earlier, most work which has tested hypotheses about how social attachments are formed, and their significance for the development of later relationships, has been based on children brought up in institutions from a very early age. For instance, Tizard and Hodges (1978) comment that although the first bonds may be formed as late as 4-6 yr of age, fully normal social development does appear to be dependent on early *selective* social bonding; in their sample the children had been subject to multiple (up to 50) caretakers in their early years. Ainsworth *et al.* (1973, 1978) suggested that 'sensitive responsiveness' by the caregiver is the one quality in any interaction likely to foster a secure attachment. Sensitive responsiveness did not characterise the early relationships of those extremely deprived children under discussion, and we must conclude that any attachments as did exist were relatively insecure. Bowlby's (1969) attachment theory proposes that insecure infants "living in a constant state of anxious attachment" due to multiple separations or abuse grow into adults who manifest various neurotic traits, including 'overdependency' and 'compulsive reliance'. Unfortunately, we do not have any information about whether or not, in the cases reviewed, early attachments developed to inanimate objects or 'transitional objects' in Winnicott's (1951) terms. Both psychoanalytic theory and direct observation of institutionalised behaviour (Provence and Lipton, 1962) indicate that children who have failed to form a pre-eminent human attachment do not show this evocative tendency.

Relationship with peers is thought to be one of the aspects of socialisation most vulnerable to distortion and inadequacies of early attachment (e.g. Waters *et al.*, 1979; Easterbrooks and Lamb, 1979). Limited information is available about peer relationships after extreme deprivation. Anna was never integrated into her peer group, remaining on the outside, a follower rather than a leader, yet she 'conformed to group socialisation' and even tried to help other children in difficulties. Isabelle is said to have functioned as normally as other children at her school but no details are given about her social adaptation. Genie remained sufficiently odd in her manner as to preclude acceptance. The Koluchova twins were reported (in 1976) to have a strong mutual emotional bond without striking abnormalities in their social contacts with others; relationships within their foster family were particularly good. Louise was a well-socialised child 10 yr after being received into care; she had excellent relationships with adults and other children and was a popular figure with them, although at school she had only one close friend. Mary, on the other hand, was never wholly integrated, being persistently more difficult than her sister in many respects, even before the onset of later disturbances. Her failure to develop good expressive language was a great handicap to fitting in with normal children; it may be that she was also temperamentally less appealing or tractable.

Table 3   Characteristics of extremely deprived children at discovery

Name	Date of birth	Age at discovery	Physical stigmata at discovery	Motor retardation (degree)	Speech Comprehension	Speech Expression	Formal psychometric assessment	Emotional expression and social behaviour
Anna (Davis, 1940)	1.3.32	5.11	cachetic	+++	nil	nil	S-B <2.6	profoundly withdrawn; completely apathetic
Genie (Curtiss, 1977)	?.4.57	13.7	cachetic dwarfed	++	PPVT* 1.6	echoes single words	LIPS (wide scatter on sub-tests) 4.9 VSM 1.05	alert and curious; eager for social contact; silent tantrums
Mary (Skuse, 1984)	24.11.68	2.4	microcephalic syndactyly	+	nil	nil	CJ (non-verbal skills) nil	withdrawn; gaze avoidance; temper tantrums
Isabelle (Mason, 1942)	?.4.32	6.6	rachitic	++	simple gestures only	simple gestures only	S-B 1.7 VSM 2.6	withdrawn; fearful and hostile towards strangers
Koluchova twins (MZ boys) P.M. and J.M. (1972)	4.9.60	6.11	rachitic	++	(RE) 2 years	(RE) 1.6	CJ (non-verbal skills) 3.0	timid and mistrustful
Douglas and Sutton twins (?Z) Alice and Beth (1978)	2.2.69	4.11	no	none	RDLS (at 5.4) Alice 3.4 Beth 3.8	unintelligible	S-B 3.7	friendly; amenable to adults
Louise (Skuse, 1984)	30.9.67	3.6	no	+	CJ 1.0	CJ <1.0	CJ (non-verbal skills) <1.6	affectionate; happy; temper tantrums

*CJ, Contemporaneous clinical judgement; RE, retrospective estimation (from written reports); S-B, Stanford-Binet Intelligence Scale; RDLS, Reynell Developmental Language Scale; VSM, Vineland Social Maturity Scale; LIPS, Leiter International Performance Scale; PPVT, Peabody Vocabulary Test.

Emotional development

The development of temperament and the expression of emotion have not received a great deal of attention in the literature on the long-term effects of deprivation in early childhood. Rutter (1981) commented that an important research strategy in this area should consider the significance of individual differences in relationship to variations in response to a depriving experience and its sequelae. Much attention has been directed in recent years towards understanding such differences, conceptualised in terms of temperamental attributes (see Dunn, 1980). The former tendency of authors reviewing literature on early deprivation has been to focus upon effects on cognitive development. Sroufe (1977), in a pertinent criticism, asserts "data on recovery in intellectual functioning are not adequate for fully assessing the issue of continuity or the impact of early experience on personality structure". Kessen et al. (1970) have also pointed out the need for improved recording of affective and emotional development in infants as a basis from which to understand individual differences and continuities. The problem, which they acknowledge, is that appropriate conceptual systems do not yet exist. Hence the selection and measurement of variables is made extremely difficult by a paucity of standard measures. Recent work has, however, elicited evidence for a developmental shift in older children's understanding of emotional concepts (Harris et al., 1981).

Language

All children reviewed had very limited language abilities at discovery. Table 3 records their initial competence in expressive speech and comprehension and Table 2 presents a limited account of the degree of stimulation they formerly received, both in terms of gesture and spoken language. Reviewing the evidence for relevant early environmental influences, Clarke and Clarke (1976) comment there is now unequivocal evidence that an environment which improves in middle or even late childhood can lead to major gains in speech capacity. Kagan et al. (1978) concur with their formulation, adding that persistent defects imply a persistence of adverse experiences, although to this must be appended the rider that we assume there is no underlying brain pathology. Certainly language skills are rapidly acquired by many of the children represented in Table 5. Isabelle, the Koluchova and Douglas and Sutton twins and Louise reached virtually age-appropriate levels within a few years, despite the variety of ages at which they were removed from their formerly understimulating circumstances. In his discussion of the Koluchova case, Clarke (1972) suggests that the fact that the twins spent their first 18 months in a nutritionally normal environment may be of importance, for the foundations of perceptual and linguistic development may be laid down at this time. It is, perhaps, significant that the Koluchova twins were not the only children to experience a relatively well nourished period at the outset of their lives, as Table 2 indicates. The evidence for a direct link between malnutrition and the development of language is tenuous (Klein et al., 1977), but the evidence suggests that, although poor nutrition alone is unlikely to have been a sufficient cause of Anna and Genie's condition, it could nevertheless have played a significant role in restricting their potential cognitive capacities, particularly, perhaps, of verbal intelligence (Evans et al., 1980). The evidence provided. for example, by Winick et al. (1975) in their study of formerly malnourished Korean children adopted into American homes is also in favour of that hypothesis. In these case reports the account of Isabelle seems to confound the thesis, for she was never in a nutritionally normal environment before her discovery at 6½ yr yet went on to excellent linguistic achievement.

Table 4   Sequence of events after discovery

Name	Date of birth	Age of discovery	Removed from mother†	Placement after discovery†	Formal education began
Anna (Davis, 1940)	1.3.32	5.11	yes at 5.11	5.11 (I) 6.8 (FH)	7.5
Genie (Curtiss, 1977)	?.4.57	13.7	yes at 13.7	13.7 (H) 14.3 (FH)	13.11
Mary (Skuse, 1984)	24.11.68	2.4	yes at 3.9	2.9 (NG) 4.9 (CH)	5.2
Isabelle (Mason, 1942)	?.4.32	6.6	no	6.6 (H)	6.6
Koluchova twins (MZ boys) P.M. and J.M. (1972)	4.9.60	6.11	yes at 7.3	6.11 (NG 7.3 (H) 8.10 (FH)	9.0
Douglas and Sutton twins (?Z) Alice and Beth (1978)	2.2.69	4.11	no	4.0 (NG at home with mother	5.0
Louise (Skuse, 1984)	30.9.67	3.6	yes at 4.11	3.11 (NG) 4.11 (CH)	5.1

* See text for details
†H, hospital; I, other institution; NG, nursery group; FH, foster home; CH, children's home.

A great deal of research has been published in the past decade on the importance of 'prelinguistic behaviour' in the context of the infant's earliest environment (e.g. Brazelton *et al.*, 1974; Stern, 1974; Schaffer *et al.*, 1977). Its relationship to the development of initial speech acts is not clear. However, a prelinguistic period in a normally stimulating environment may be of crucial importance for later speech acquisition. Psychosocial deprivation has been reported as impairing preverbal vocalisation and babble (Provence and Lipton, 1962), but we do not have any reliable account of these phenomena in the children reviewed here. It seems unlikely that Dennis' (1941) experiment in which twin boys were raised deliberately in conditions of 'restricted practice and minimum social stimulation' to the age of 14 months could or would be repeated nowadays, but it is notable that those boys did exhibit a wide range of preverbal sounds. The data are not available on which to make a definitive judgement. Only Mary and Isabelle suffered a persistently abnormal upbringing from birth and, although Mary remained severely handicapped at the age of 9 yr, Isabelle gained language rapidly. The stimulation she received by gesture and interaction with her mute mother prior to discovery is almost certainly of significance in that respect.

Table 5   **Latest available reports on the children's developmental level (cognition)**

Name	Date of birth	Age at discovery	Language		Formal tests of cognition	
			Comprehension	Expression	Performance	Verbal
Anna (Davis, 1940)	1.3.32	5.11	(C.A. 10.3) RE 2.6	(C.A. 10.3) RE 2.6	(C.A. 8.1) M-P 1.7	(C.A. 8.1)
Genie (Curtiss, 1977)	?.4.57	13.7	(C.A. 16.10) ITPA Auditory Reception 5.0	(C.A. 16.10) ITPA Verbal Expression 3.8	(C.A. 17.9) RCPM 11.0 FGPT 11.0	(C.A. 18.9) PPVT 5.10
Mary (Skuse, 1984)	24.11.68	2.4	(C.A. 13.0) RDLS 4.0	(C.A. 13.0) RDLS 3.5	(C.A. 8.11) WISC 94	
Isabelle (Mason, 1942)	?.4.32	6.6	(C.A. 8.2) reported as age appropriate		(C.A. 8.2) reported as of normal intelligence	
Koluchova twins (MZ boys) P.M.	4.9.60	6.11	(C.A. 10.0) RE 9.0	(C.A. 10.0) RE 9.0	(C.A. 10.0) WISC 85	(C.A. 10.0) WISC 97
J.M. (1972)	4.9.60	6.11	(C.A. 10.0) RE 9.0	(C.A. 10.0) RE 9.0	(C.A. 10.0) WISC 86	(C.A. 10.0) WISC 94
Douglas and Sutton twins Alice	2.2.69	4.11	(C.A. 6.4) RDLS < 6.0	(C.A. 6.4) RDLS 6.0	(C.A. 6.4) WPPSI 108	(C.A. 6.4) WPPSI 102
Beth (1978)	2.2.69	4.11	(C.A. 6.4) RDLS 5.1	(C.A. 6.4) RDLS 5.3	(C.A. 6.4) WPPSI 92	(C.A. 6.4) WPPSI 85
Louise (Skuse, 1984)	30.9.67	3.6	(C.A. 14.5) age appropriate (SR)	(C.A. 14.5)	(C.A. 10.1) WISC 80	(C.A. 10.1) WISC 77

*ITPA, Illinois test of Psycholinguistic Abilities; M-P, Merrill-Palmer Scale of Mental Abilities; WISC, Wechsler Intelligence Scale for Children; WPPSI, Wechsler Preschool and Primary Scale of Intelligence; FGPT, Figure Ground Perception Test; C.A., chronological age at assessment; RCPM, Ravens Coloured Progressive Matrices; PPVT, Peabody Picture Vocabulary Test; RDLS, Reynell Developmental Language Scale; RE, retrospective estimation from written reports; SR, school report.

Besides the lack of deliberate stimulation offered by caretakers, the children's failure to develop language development may be due in part to the lack of opportunities they had to explore and act on their environment (Piaget, 1967; Furth, 1970). Following a longitudinal study of preschool children, White (1977) said that restrictions upon locomobility in the newly crawling child are likely to interfere in both linguistic and intellectual development. His findings may be relevant in that Anna, Genie and Mary and Louise were all physically restrained to a greater or lesser extent (Table 2). However, contrary evidence exists. Swaddling or restraint upon a cradleboard, as practised by most societies in the north temperate, mediterranean and middle-eastern areas until a few centuries ago, has no retarding effect on the attainment of motor milestones. Neither does it seem to have other long-term sequelae, at least in a population which habitually employs this child-rearing technique (Dennis, 1940; Chisholm, 1978). It therefore seems unlikely that restriction of movement as such is sufficient to retard development. A similar conclusion was reached by Dennis (1960) in his study of institutionally reared children in Iran.

Genie was not brought out of her hopeless social conditions until 13 yr 7 months and she failed to develop any useful conversational speech, although she did gain enormously in comprehension over the following 5 yr. Lenneberg (1967) may have been correct when he suggested that language acquisition must occur during the first 12 yr if it is to proceed normally, and Genie's history is often taken as pointing in favour of his hypothesis (e.g. Rutter, 1981, Ch. 9; Curtiss, 1981b). We do have good evidence that after unilateral brain damage children may switch cerebral dominance for various functions relatively easily, at least until puberty intervenes. Curtiss (1977) concludes, after a detailed account of her painstaking assessment of Genie's linguistic abilities, that the child is a 'holistic' right-hemisphere thinker in respect of both verbal and non-verbal tasks. She believes this may be a direct result of Genie's not acquiring language during the 'critical period'. It seems a pity, therefore, that nowhere does she produce evidence to confirm that the left hemisphere of that unfortunate girl is functioning normally from a neurophysiological point of view.

Development of play

Language development may be correlated with the development of spontaneous play; in Piaget's (1967) terms both are aspects of the same semiotic ability and as such play may be considered a cognitive activity which contributes to the infant's knowledge of his relationship to the world about him (Rosenblatt, 1977). We may follow, through the development of play, the process by which the child learns that events, objects and ultimately symbols have an existence, function and purpose outside himself. This process is reflected in the three major achievements of play: initially functional, later representational and eventually truly symbolic (Rosenblatt, 1977). Functional or sensorimotor play consists of no more than manipulation of objects with reference to their immediate attractive and inherent properties. Representational play involves using toys as if they were the corresponding real objects; for example, where a miniature tea set is manipulated to simulate the child's real life experience of a tea party. Symbolic play implies that the child is using an object in the play scene to stand for something else; its original meaning has been transcended, as, for example, where the child employs a ruler as an aeroplane. Such play normally starts around the age of 24 months and is well established by 30 months. Mary and Louise showed no play when first seen, although Louise made relatively good progress in her nursery group and within 18 months was using functional and occasionally representational skills. Mary, on the other hand, was 4½ yr old when she began to display even the rudiments of functional play, 2 yr after discovery, and it was a further 2 yr before representational play became established. Louise had reached this stage at 5 yr. For both girls the achievement was coincident with their having achieved a language comprehension age-equivalent of 2½ yr. Normally, the transformations of category which underlie symbolic play are appearing by the age of 2 yr (Ross, 1977), although not infrequently they may be seen considerably earlier (Zelazo and Kearsley, 1976). The close relationship between the development of a capacity for using symbolic function and associations and the onset of representational play has been described by several workers (Sinclair, 1971; Lowe, 1975; Rosenblatt, 1977), and it is well known that autistic children suffer a severe handicap in both areas (Rutter, 1977). Even so, children suffering from a developmental dysphasia may play with some representational features (Egan, 1975). In normal children a correlation seems to exist between language comprehension (but not expression) and symbolic play (Largo and Howard, 1979).

We have little information about the play of other severely deprived children. Anna's freedom of movement and the range of objects available for her tactile exploration were certainly very limited. This was also true for Genie, whose 'toys' consisted of empty cheese cartons and two plastic raincoats. We do not know what toys were available to Isabelle, but the evidence suggests that they were few, if any. The Koluchova twins had only a handful of building bricks. Koluchova (1972) reports that the twins' spontaneous play was very primitive (functional/sensorimotor), but imitative (representational) play soon developed. Anna, just 1 yr after discovery, was said to "hardly play, when alone". Isabelle, on the other hand, enjoyed undressing a doll very shortly after first being brought into hospital. Within a few months she was drawing and colouring with crayons and over the next 2 yr play is said to have become "highly imaginative". Genie showed little in the way of play for several years. A little sensorimotor activity with toys or other materials plus an inclination to hoard is all that was observed, until 4½ yr after discovery she first engaged in an acting fantasy with Susan Curtiss. A comparison may be drawn with the experiments reviewed by Sackett (1965), who reported that rearing infant monkeys under conditions of social isolation and perceptual impoverishment produces animals who show little inclination to activity or exploration.

Perceptuomotor skills

The development of Mary and Louise's performance skills is chronicled in Tables 1 and 2 of the companion paper (Skuse, 1984). Both showed a rapid and steady improvement, even though at the time of discovery they had been seriously retarded. Comparable psychological test findings are provided by Koluchova, and the rate and extent of the twins' achievements (1972, 1976) are similar in the two studies. Table 5 reveals the latest available reports on the performance of these and other children. Substantial gains had been made by many, it being clear that not only were these performance skills less retarded than language at the earliest assessment but that in most cases (with the exception of Anna) the eventual level of performance equalled or exceeded verbal abilities. That finding is compatible with the well-established observation that psychosocial deprivation usually has a more profound effect upon verbal than visuospatial skills (see Rutter and Mittler, 1972; Rutter and Madge, 1976). Moreover, subsequent enrichment of the environment seems to be of slightly more benefit to verbal tasks, from the evidence of children who were raised from infancy in relatively depriving circumstances such as institutions (Tizard and Hodges, 1978).

Considering the effects of early environmental influences, studies have tended to focus upon IQ. A distinction between development of verbal and performance skills or achievement measures is often omitted, even in assessments of normal children such as those who have been subject to early intervention programmes (see Clarke and Clarke, 1982). Recently an increasing use of these distinctions, among others, has been commensurate with a change in the conceptualisation of 'intelligence', from a global and static quantity to a dynamic system of many abilities and developing processes (e.g. McCall, 1977; Wohlwill, 1980). Attempts to evaluate what constitutes a good stimulating early environment have also been paying closer attention to the role played by children themselves in influencing developmental processes. For instance, the relationship with a caregiver is advantageously viewed using a transactional rather than a main effect model (e.g. Emde, 1981). In this sense important environmental events may initiate new and sometimes progressive cycles which possess only indirect connections to the original stimulus, this rendering the evaluation of outcome an exceedingly complex undertaking. However, long-term changes do appear to result from continuing long-term processes (Clarke and Clarke, 1981).

Implications of findings

Adverse early life experiences may, but not necessarily, have serious lasting effects on development in some circumstances (Rutter, 1981, Ch. 9). Individuals possess a good deal of resilience to such events and circumstances; it is not possible to draw simple correlations between cause and effect in most cases. Furthermore, there is an increasing tendency to see the child as part of a social system, with which he is in a mutually modifying relationship (Berger, 1973). His mother's role is no longer considered to be so pivotal as earlier conceptualisations, rooted in psychoanalytic theory, would have it. Rutter (1981, Ch. 7) has suggested that the global concept of maternal deprivation is too heterogeneous and its effects too varied to be of continuing value. There is now a need to focus instead on the particularities of specific early experiences in order to understand better the various mechanisms by which they operate.

Not only must variation in outcome relate to the specific deprivations and distortions of early experience, but the vulnerability of the individual to such adversity will itself vary. Certain factors, as discussed, may exacerbate the chances of a handicap ensuing. Others may protect the child. It would be of great benefit, with regard not only to our understanding of developmental processes but also with respect to our potential for helping children who have been subject to such circumstances, if we could identify the nature of protective factors and uncover individual sources of resilience. Such sources may themselves be rooted largely in genetic determinants. Little has yet been written on the concept of 'canalisation' of mental development. This term, as used by Scarr-Salapatek (1976), is adapted from a model proposed by an animal geneticist (Waddington, 1957, 1977). Waddington was speaking of a constitutional mechanism by which the number of alternative phenotypes within a range of environments, some of which may be adverse or atypical, is restricted. McCall (1979) has suggested the tendency of mental development to 'self-righting' is stronger in infancy than in later childhood. Hypotheses based on these ideas about the aetiology of continuities and discontinuities in human growth patterns are likely to generate increasing interest as

Table 6   Latest available reports on the children's developmental level

Name	Date of birth	Age at discovery	Motor skills	Social and self-help skills	Emotional expression	Final report
Anna (Davis, 1947)	1.3.32	3.11	(C.A. 10.3) walks well but runs clumsily	(C.A. 8.1) VSM 1.11	pleasant disposition excitable (C.A. 10.3)	died of jaundice (liver failure) 10.5
Genie (Curtiss, 1977)	?.4.57	13.7	(C.A. 14.3) good	(C.A. 18.0) some progress but lazy and socially disinhibited	Affectionate; happiness; sadness; temper tantrums (C.A. 18.0)	few normal or appropriate acts of communication at 18.0
Mary (Skuse, 1984)	24.11.68	2.4	(C.A. 13.0) agile and well coordinated	(C.A. 13.0) good, but impulsive	socially repsonsive; affectionate; tempter tantrums (C.A. 13.0)	attends ESN(S) schools; lives CH for mentally handicapped (C.A. 13.0)
Isabelle (Davis, 1947)	?.4.32	6.6	(C.A. 8.2) good	(C.A. 8.2) good	sense of humour; negativism; affectionate (C.A. 8.4)	At 14.0 well established in normal school
Koluchova twins (MZ boys) P.M. and J.M. (1976)	4.9.60	6.11	(C.A. 9.0) good	(C.A. 14.0) good	labile disposition (C.A. 14.0) deep emotional bonds to foster mother (C.A. 14.0)	At 14.0 well established in foster family; attending normal school
Douglas and Sutton twins (?Z) Alice and Beth (1978)	2.2.69	4.11	(C.A. 12.6) age appropriate	(C.A. 12.6) age appropriate	good sense of humour, full range of emotional expression; close ties to family (C.A. 12.6)	normal infant, then delicate school (9-11yr); at 13.3 Alice in comprehensive Beth in secondary delicate school; mother remarried
Louise (Skuse, 1984)	30.9.67	3.6	(C.A. 4.10) good athlete, poor fine motor skills	(C.A. 13.0) excellent	affectionate; humorous; close bonds to housemother; sociable and popular (C.A. 14.0)	attends normal school; lives on at original CH (C.A. 14.0)

VSM, Vineland Social Maturity Scale; CH, children's home; ESN(S), educationally subnormal (severe); C.A., chronological age at assessment.

life-span models for predicting developmental change become more sophisticated (Emde, 1981).

How may the findings from a comparative study of extreme deprivation in early childhood further our understanding of these issues? Firstly, is there a characteristic clinical picture of the victims of such deprivation at discovery? The evidence suggests certain behavioural features are almost ubiquitous: motor retardation, absent or very rudimentary vocal and symbolic language, grossly retarded perceptuomotor skills, paucity of emotional expression, lack of attachment behaviour and social withdrawal. The combination of these features is unlikely to be found in any other condition except, perhaps, in the conjunction of profound mental retardation with childhood autism. Of course, the additional signs of malnourishment and deficiency disease should make the differential diagnosis relatively straightforward, but in the absence of these latter features it is of the utmost importance that the possibility of environmentally induced handicap be excluded (see Koluchova, 1976). Global deprivation does not, however, lead to uniform retardation in all aspects of mental and physical development. The disentangling of proximate influences is complicated by the fact that although duration of deprivation is one readily quantifiable independent variable, degree of deprivation is the other. Quantitative assessment of that degree must be an approximation and, furthermore, these variables must interact.

Language is undoubtedly the most vulnerable cognitive faculty; it has been profoundly retarded at first in all cases reviewed, even where other features of mental development are apparently unaffected (e.g. Douglas and Sutton, 1978). Expressive speech is most seriously retarded at discovery, and develops less rapidly than comprehension after placement in a normal environment. Perceptuomotor skills are relatively resilient to lack of stimulation, as is gross motor development, but the opportunity for practising these potential skills must be relatively more accessible, even in the most impoverished and unstimulating settings.

The exact features presented by a victim of extreme deprivation at discovery do not seem to have substantial prognostic implications. There is, however, a tendency for those who also suffered serious general malnourishment (Anna, Genie) to have poor outcomes. This evidence would be in accord with Winick *et al.* 's (1975) findings that a group of Korean adoptees with a history of very inadequate nutrition failed at follow-up to achieve an intellectual performance or scholastic attainment equal to their formerly well-nourished companions. That group was also significantly shorter, an observation which recalls Genie's reported dwarfism.

Certain overt congenital anomalies (e.g. microcephaly), which are associated with mental retardation amongst the population at large, e.g. Warkany and St. J. Dignan (1973), must also indicate a relatively bad prognosis; cf. Mary in Skuse (1984).

Complete absence of comprehensive and expressive speech at discovery seems ominous, especially where there is a large discrepancy between non-verbal and verbal abilities (e.g. Anna, Genie, Mary). In view of the fact that initial social behaviour was highly variable between cases, correlation with later social adjustment is necessarily weak. Nevertheless, there are indications that the early combination of profound language deficit, and apathy or withdrawal from social contact, means that the child will have especial difficulties developing a normal range and quality of relationships in later life (cf. Anna, Mary).

Following removal from deprivation, the evidence suggests that if recovery of normal ability in a particular faculty is going to occur, rapid progress is the rule; for instance, in the realm of perception the fact that normal vision was achieved by Anna (Davis, 1940, 1947) within a few months, or the extraordinary rapidity with which Isabelle (Mason, 1942; Davis, 1947) came to understand the meaning and function of spoken language. In the sphere of social adjustment attachment behaviour was a differentiating feature, indicating those children who were later going to be relatively easily integrated into close relationships with caretakers and peers. Formation of an early focus of attachment onto one special adult seems to have been the decisive characteristic, and the contrast between Mary and Louise's behaviour (Skuse, 1984) in their first nursery group is a good example of this. The urge to make a single loving relationship was also commented on by Skeels (1966), who described such behaviour in the orphans who were 'fostered' by a ward of girls at an institution for the mentally retarded prior to adoption. He asserts "this highly stimulating emotional impact was observed to be the unique characteristic and one of the main contributions of the experimental setting" (p. 17). It is also noteworthy that the greater part of the orphan's gains in IQ had been made whilst still in that setting, and major increases beyond these values were achieved only in 'superior' adoptive homes.

There is good evidence from the cases reviewed that if normal language is going to be achieved, progress is virtually exponential and occurs at much the same rate as the acquisition of visuospatial skills (e.g. Koluchova, 1972). Where a discrepancy in recovery of these abilities is noted (e.g. Skuse, 1984) the outcome is likely to be poor, and it may well be that there exist constitutional limitations on achievement. One is reminded of Itard's valiant but ultimately unsuccessful efforts to teach Victor, the Wild Boy of Aveyron, vocal speech (Itard, 1801, 1806). Despite Lane's (1977) assertions to the contrary, it does not seem likely that his failure was entirely due to inadequate techniques of therapy. Genie, for example, was subject to highly skilled education by Susan Curtiss for over 4 yr but developed few normal or appropriate acts of communication. We do not know whether this is a testimony to her extraordinarily long period of deprivation or to some organic dysfunction of the left cerebral hemisphere, or to a combination of these factors.

Koluchova (1976) comments "in spite of the fact that the twins had scarcely spoken at all until the age of 7 [their] development was quickest after their ninth year when they came to their foster family, which provided them with all the prerequisites both in the development of speech and for the whole personality". Although they did subsequently attend speech training, this seems to have been with the aim of improving pronunciation and articulation rather than instilling a desire to communicate by vocal language. Similarly, Isabelle received nearly 2 yr of intensive speech therapy from a team of therapists under the direction of Marie Mason, who capitalized on her motivation. This contrast, between the child who is eager to attract adult attention and understanding and the child who is apathetic and disinterested in such contact, is most strikingly shown in the comparison between Louise and Mary. Both girls did receive speech therapy soon after discovery, though when little progress was made with Mary it was abandoned. Her relative lack of social communication and language had been reminiscent of autism at the age of 9 yr but 4 yr later a remarkable transformation had taken place. Mary had made tremendous progress in both areas and such 'autistic' features had vanished. Despite having been placed in a variety of children's homes over that period, she received some consistent intensive speech therapy which, reports suggest, was successful in engaging an emergent change in social attitudes. This observation is in itself important in that it suggests further progress may be made with children several years after removal from deprivation even in cases where the obstacle to success was thought to consist of genetic or congenital anomalies.

However, in general, intensity of intervention does not seem to be of singular value in bringing about recovery from the vicissitudes of extreme deprivation in early childhood. It seems that qualitative rather than quantitative influences are paramount, and Koluchova's (1976) conclusions are apposite: "the most effective and integrative curative factor is (the) foster mother and the whole environment of (the) family" (p. 185).

There remains the question of eventual attainments and adjustments so far as records allow. Of course, tremendous and rapid achievements were made by Louise, the Koluchova twins and Isabelle in all areas of ability, but is there evidence that subtle deficits remain? Taking the cases as a whole, a diversity does indeed exist, and is summarised as Tables 5 and 6. Cognitive attainments are considerable in the group with superior outcome.

Personality and social adjustment problems have also been described as long term consequences of early deprivation. Unfortunately we do not as yet know the adult status of most children discussed in this review but, so far as they have been followed-up, no gross disorders exist in those with good intellectual growth. In Skeel's (1966) account, where adoptees had been followed into adult life, the findings were also most encouraging. Dennis (1973), on the other hand, confines his remarks on the effects of early institutional rearing almost entirely to intellectual development. There is, in addition, the important work of Tizard and Hodges (1978), who reported that 8-yr-old children who were adopted late, after initial care in an institutional environmental with multiple caretakers, were often attention seeking, disobedient, restless and unpopular at school, even though no such problems existed at home. The implication is that early adversity may well have far reaching but situation-specific sequelae. Koluchova (1976) recounts that at 14 yr of age the twin boys, 7 yr after discovery, had no psychopathological symptoms or eccentricities of personality. One could infer that their exceptionally close mutual emotional bond has had some protective value and may well have facilitated integration to the scholastic environment. In a recent correspondence Koluchova (quoted by Clarke, personal communication) provides further information about the twins' adolescent development that sustains the earlier optimism of her published accounts. By 20 yr of age they had completed a quite demanding apprentice by school training in the maintenance of office machinery. They are now described by Koluchova as having above-average intelligence. Also, emotional and social development is said to be very satisfactory, good relationships having been sustained with their foster mother and her relatives, and their adopted sisters.

We have little information about Isabelle's later life except that, 8 yr after discovery, she "participated in all school activities as normally as other children" (Davis, 1947). Louise certainly did behave in a relatively disinhibited manner when last assessed at 13 yr, but at school she is described as "reserved". Of course, it cannot be certain to what extent those social eccentricities were a result of upbringing in a group home rather than a legacy of earliest experiences. An intriguing comparison may be made between the emergent sexuality of Genie (Curtiss, 1977) and of her historical counterpart Victor (Lane, 1977), for in both cases attempts to protract intensive education through adolescence were curtailed by compulsive masturbation. Such gross social disinhibition is likely to reflect something more than a failure to have inculcated social mores because of language handicap. A potential area of interest, not commented on by any of the above authors, is the isolated child's awareness of gender identity and how such sexual knowledge develops during recovery. However, Koluchova's latest (Clarke, personal communication) account records that the boys' relationships with girls have developed in a normal way, and that they have, in fact, both recently experienced their first love affairs.

Conclusions

Extreme deprivation in early childhood is a condition of great theoretical and practical importance. Clinically it is essential that such children are recognised and differentiated from cases of global mental retardation, so that appropriate environmental manipulation and educational experience may commence as soon as possible. Fortunately the evidence reviewed suggests that, in the absence of genetic or congenital anomalies or a history of gross malnourishment, victims of such deprivation have an excellent prognosis. Some subtle deficits in social adjustment may persist. Theoretical observations include the implication that most human characteristics, with the possible exception of language, are strongly 'canalised' [in Scarr-Salapatek's (1976) conception] and hence virtually resistant to obliteration by even the most dire early environments. On removal to a favourable situation, the remarkable and rapid progress made by those with good potential seems allied to the total experience of living in a stimulating home and forming emotional bonds to a caring adult. We may hypothesise that a caretaker's qualities of emotional availability, sensitive responsivity, encouragement and provision of perceptual stimulation shown to be important for normal infants' development (Moore, 1968; Bradley and Caldwell, 1976; Clarke-Stewart, 1977) are also the salient influences bearing on later learning and maturation in these unfortunate children.

Summary

Five previously published and one novel case history of children who suffered extreme deprivation in early childhood are reviewed. Aspects of cognitive, emotional and social development are subject to critical appraisal and three main issues, central to theories about the origins of developmental disorders, are addressed. Firstly, what minimal experiences during childhood are sufficient and necessary for normal psychological development? Secondly, are there critical periods in development during which inadequate exposure to certain experiences has long-lasting or permanent sequelae? Thirdly, what minimal compensatory influences are necessary to alleviate psychological handicaps resulting from an adverse early environment?

Acknowledgments

I wish to thank Professor Michael Rutter for his many helpful comments during the preparation of this manuscript. Also Jo Douglas and Andrew Sutton for updating and amplifying the case histories formerly described by them, and Professor Alan Clarke for so kindly making available additional information on the Koluchova twins. And finally, my secretary Jenny Smith for her patient and persistent assistance.

References

Ainsworth, M. (1973) 'The development of infant mother attachment.' In *Review of Child Development Research* (Edited by Caldwell, B.M. and Riccuiti, H.N.), Vol. III, Ch. 1, pp. 1-94. University of Chicago Press, Chicago, IL.

Ainsworth, M. Blehar, M., Waters, C. and Wall, S. (1978) *Patterns of Attachment: a Psychological Study of the Strange Situation.* Lawrence Erlbaum Associates, Hillsdale, NJ.

Akesson, H.O. (1962) 'Empirical risk figures in mental deficiency.' *Acta genet. Statist. med.* 12, 28-32.

Anon, (1834) Caspar Hauser. *The Penny Magazine of the Society for the Diffusion of Useful Knowledge*, Vol. III, p. 47.

Anastasi, A. (1958) 'Heredity, environment and the question "How?" ' *Psychol. Rev.* 65, 197-208.

Berger, M. (1973) 'Early experiences and other environmental factors — an overview.' In *Handbook of Abnormal Psychology* (Edited by Eysenck, H.J.), 2nd edn., pp. 604-644. Pitman, London.

Berkson, G. and Davenport, R.K. (1962) 'Stereotyped movements of mental defectives.' *Am. J. mental Defic.* 66, 849-852 .

Bonnaterre, P.J. (1800) 'Historical notice on the Sauvage de L'Aveyron.' Translated in *The Wild Boy of Aveyron* (Lane, H.), pp. 33-48. George Allen & Unwin, London.

Bornstein, M.H. (1976) 'Infants are trichromats.' *J. exp. Child Psychol.* 21, 425-445.

Bornstein, M.H., Kessen, W. and Weiskopf, S. (1976) 'The categories of hue in infancy.' *Science,* 191, 201-202.

Bowlby, J. (1958) 'The nature of the child's tie to his mother.' *Int. Psychoanal.* 39, 350-373.

Bowlby, J. (1969) *Attachment and Loss. Vol. 1. Attachment.* Penguin Books, Harmondsworth.

Bowlby, J. (1979) *The Making and Breaking of Affectional Bonds.* Tavistock Publications, London.

Bradley, R.H. and Caldwell, B.M. (1976) 'Early home environment and changes in mental test performance in children from 6-30 months.' *Devl Psychol.* 12, 93-97.

Brazelton, T.B., Koslowski, B. and Nain, M. (1974) 'The origins of reciprocity: the early mother-infant interaction.' *In The Effect of the Infant on its Caregiver* (Edited by Lewis, M. and Rosenblum, L.A.), pp. 49-76. John Wiley & Sons, New York.

Broman, S.H., Nichols, P.L. and Kennedy, W.A. (1975) *Preschool IQ: Prenatal and Early Developmental Correlates.* John Wiley & Sons, New York.

Butler, N. and Goldstein, H. (1973) 'Smoking in pregnancy and subsequent child development.' *Am. J. Dis. Child.* 66, 471-494.

Carter, H. (1962) *The Histories of Herodotus and Helicarnassus* (translated and edited by Carter, H.). Oxford University Press, London.

Chisholm, J.S. (1978) 'Swaddling, cradleboards and the development of children.' *Early Hum. Dev.* 213, 255-275.

Clarke, A.D.B. (1972) 'Commentary on Koluchova's "Severe deprivation in twins: a case study".' *J. Child Psychol. Psychiat.* 13, 103-106.

Clarke, A.M. and Clarke, A.D.B. (1974) *Mental Deficiency: the Changing Outlook* (3rd edn.). Methuen, London.

Clarke, A.M. and Clarke, A.D.B. (1976) *Early Experience. Myth and Evidence.* Open Books, London.

Clarke, A.D.B. and Clarke, A.M. (1981) 'Sleeper effects in development: fact or artifact?' *Dev. Rev.* 1, 344-360.

Clarke, A.M. and Clarke, A.D.B. (1982) 'Intervention and sleeper effects: a reply to Victoria Seitz.' *Dev. Rev.* 2, 76-86.

Clarke-Stewart, A. (1977) *Child Care in the Family: a Review of Research and some Propositions for Policy.* Academic Press, New York.

Cohen, L.B. and Salapatek, P. (eds.) (1975) *Infant Perception: From Sensation to Cognition. Vol. 1: Basic Visual Processes, Vol. 2.: Perceptions of Space, Speech and Sound.* Academic Press, New York.

Cowart, B.J. (1981) 'Development of taste perception in humans: sensitivity and preference throughout the life span.' *Psychol. Bull. 90,* 43-73.

Cravioto, J., DeLicardie, E.R. and Birch, H.G. (1966) 'Nutrition, growth and neurointegrative development: an experimental and ecologic study.' *Pediatrics* 38, 319-372.

Crellin, E., Pringle, M.L.K. and West, P. (1971) *Born Illegitimate: Social and Educational Implications.* National Foundation for Educational Research, Windsor.

Curtiss, S. (1977) *Genie: a Psycholinguistic Study of a Modern-day 'Wild Child'.* Academic Press, London.

Curtiss, S. (1981a) 'Feral children.' In *Mental Retardation and Developmental Disabilities,* (Edited by Wortis, J.), Vol. XII, pp. 129-161. Brunner/Mazel, New York.

Curtiss, S. (1981b) 'Dissociations between language and cognition: cases and implications.' *J Aut. Desl Dis.* 11, 15-30.

Davenport, R.K. and Menzel, E.W. (1963) 'Stereotyped behaviour in an infant chimpanzee.' *Archs gen. Psychiat.* 8, 99-104 .

Davies, R., Butler, N. and Goldstein, H. (1972) *From Birth to Seven: a Report of the National Child Development Study.* Longman, London.

Davis, K. (1940) 'Extreme social isolation of a child.' *Am. J. Sociol.* 45, 554-565.

Davis, K. (1947) 'Final note on a case of extreme isolation.' *Am. J. Sociol.* 52, 432-437.

Dennis, W. (1940) 'The effect of cradling practices upon the onset of walking in Hopi children.' *J. genet. Psychol.* 56, 77-86.

Dennis, W. (1941) 'Infant development under conditions of restricted practice and of minimal social stimulation.' *Genet. Psychol. Monogr. 23,* 143-189.

Dennis, W. (1960) 'Causes of retardation in institutional children: Iran.' *J. genet. Psychol.* 96, 47-59.

Dennis, W. (1973) *Children of the Creche.* Appleton-Century-Crofts, New York.

Dobbing, J. (1975) 'Prenatal nutrition and neurological development.' In *Brain Mechanisms in Mental Retardation* (Edited by Buchwald, N.A. and Brazier, M.A.B.), pp. 401-420. Academic Press, New York.

Doll, E.A. (1965) *Vineland Social Maturity Scale: Manual of Directions* (revised edn.). American Guidance Service Inc., Minneapolis.

Douglas, J.E. and Sutton, A. (1978) 'The development of speech and mental processes in a pair of twins: a case study.' *J. Child Psychol. Psychiat* 19, 49-56.

Dunn, J. (1980) 'Individual differences in temperament.' In *Scientific Foundations of Developmental Psychiatry* (Edited by Rutter, M.), pp. 101-109. Heinemann Medical, London.

Dunn, L.M. (1959) *Peabody Picture Vocabulary Test.* American Guidance Service, Minneapolis, MN.

Easterbrooks, M.A. and Lamb, M.E. (1979) 'The relationship between quality of infant-mother attachment and infant competence in initial encounters with peers.' *Child Dev. 50,* 380-387.

Egan, D. (1975) 'Delayed milestones.' *Br. J. Hosp. Med.* 13, 623-629.

Eichenwald, H.F. and Fry, P.C. (1969) 'Nutrition and learning.' *Science* 163, 644-648.

Emde, R.N. (1981) 'Changing models of infancy and the nature of early development: remodelling the foundation'. *J. Am. Psychoanal. Ass.* 29, 179-219.

Evans, D., Bowie, M.D., Hansen, J.D.L., Moodie, A.D. and Van Der Spuy, H.I.J. (1980) 'Intellectual development and nutrition.' *J. Pediat.* 97, 358-363.

Fantz, R.L. and Fagan, J.F. (1975) 'Visual attention to size and sex of pattern details by term and preterm infants during the first 6 months.' *Child Dev.* 16, 3-18.

Freud, S. (1905) 'Three essays on the theory of sexuality.' In *The Standard Edition of the Complete Psychological Works of Sigmund Freud,* Vol. VII (1953), pp. 125-245. Hogarth Press and the Institute of Psycho-Analysis, London.

Freud, S. (1915) 'Instincts and their vicissitudes.' In *The Standard Edition of the Complete Psychological Works of Sigmund Freud,* Vol. XIV (1957), pp. 109-140. Hogarth Press and the Institute of Psycho-Analysis, London.

Freud, S. and Dann, S. (1951) 'An experiment in group upbringing.' *Psychoanal. Study Child* 6, 127-168.

Furth, H.G. (1970) 'On language and knowing in Piaget's developmental theory.' *Human Dev.* 13, 241-257.

Goldberger, A. (1972) 'Follow-up notes on the children from Bulldog Bank.' Unpublished notes, London.

Gregory, R. L. and Wallace, J. G. (1963) 'Recovery from early blindness — a case study.' *Exp. Psychol. Soc. Monogr.,* No. 2.

Hansley, C. and Busse, T.V. (1969) 'Perceptual exploration in negro children.' *Dev. Psychol 1,* 446-448.

Harris, P.L., Olthof, T. and Terwogt, M.M. (1981) 'Children's knowledge of emotion.' *J. Child Psychol. Psychiat.* 22, 247-262.

Hartmann. H. (1958) *Ego Psychology and the Problem of Adaptation.* Imago Publishing Co., London.

Hebb, D.O. (1949) *The Organisation of Behavior.* John Wiley & Sons, New York.

Heber, R., Dever, A. and Conry, J. (1968) 'The influence of environmental and genetic variables on intellectual development.' In *Behavioural Research in Mental Retardation* (Edited by Prehm, H.J., Hamerlynck, L.A. and Crosson, J.E.). University of Oregon, Eugene, OR.

Hertzig, M.E., Birch, H.G., Richardson, S.A. and Tizard, J. (1972) 'Intellectual levels of school children severely malnourished during the first two years of life.' *Pediatrics* 49, 814-824.

Herzog, E. and Sudia, C.E. (1973) 'Children in fatherless families.' In *Review of Children Development Research* (Edited by Caldwell, B.M. and Riccuiti, H. N.), Vol. III, pp. 141-232, University of Chicago Press, Chicago, IL.

Hinde, R.A. (1963) 'The nature of imprinting.' In *Determinants of Infant Behaviour* (Edited by Foss, B. M.), Vol. 11, pp. 227-233. Methuen, London.

Hochberg, J. and Brooks, V. (1962) 'Pictorial recognition as an unlearned ability: a study of one child's performance.' *Am. J. Psychol.* 75, 624-628.

Itard, J. (1801, 1806) In *Wolf Children* and *The Wild Boy of Aveyron* (Edited by Malson, L., translated by White, J.), pp 91-179. N.L.B., London, 1972.

Kagan, J., Kearsley, R. and Zelazo, P. (1978) *Infancy: Its Place in Human Development.* Harvard University Press, Cambridge, MA.

Kessen, W., Haith, M.M. and Salapatek, P.H. (1970) 'Infancy.' In *Carmichael's Manual of Child Psychology* (Edited by Mussen, P.H.), Vol. 1, 3rd edn., pp. 287-446. John Wiley & Sons, New York.

Klein, M. (1932) *The Psychoanalysis of Children.* Hogarth Press, London.

Klein, R.E., Irwin, M., Engle, P.L. and Yarborough, L. (1977) 'Malnutrition and mental development in rural Guatemala.' In *Advances in Cross Cultural Psychology* (Edited by Warren, N.), pp. 91-119. Academic Press, New York.

Koluchova, J. (1972) 'Severe deprivation in twins: a case study.' *J. Child Psychol. Psychiat.* 13, 107-114.

Koluchova, J. (1976) 'The further development of twins after severe and prolonged deprivation: a second report.' *J. Child Psychol. Psychiat.* 17, 181-188.

Lamb, M.E. (1981) *The Role of the Father in Child Development,* 2nd edn. John Wiley & Sons, New York.

Lane, H. (1977) *The Wild Boy of Aveyron.* George Allen & Unwin, London.

Largo, R.H. and Howard, J.A. (1979) 'Developmental progression in play behaviour of children between nine and thirty months 1: Spontaneous play and imitation.' *Devl Med. Child Neurol.* 21, 299-310.

Leiter, R.G. and Arthur, G. (1955) *Leiter International Performance Scale*. C. H. Stoelting, New York.

Lenneberg, E. (1967) *Biological Foundations of Language*. John Wiley & Sons, New York.

Levy, F. and Hobbes, G. (1979) 'The influences of social class and sex on sustained attention (vigilance) and motor inhibition in children.' *Aust. N.Z. J. Psychiat.* 13, 228-231.

Longstreth, L.E. (1981) 'Revisiting Skeels final study: a critique.' *Devl Psychol.* 17, 620-625.

Lorenz, K. (1935) 'Der Kumpan in der Unwelt des Vogels.' *J.f. Ornith.* 83, 137-313, 289-413.

Lowe, M. (1975) 'Trends in the development of representational play in infants from 1-3 years — an observational study.' *J. Child Psychol. Psychiat.* 16, 33-59.

McCall, R.B. (1977) 'Challenges to a science of developmental psychology.' *Child Dev.* 48, 333-344.

McCall, R.B. (1979) 'The development of intellectual functioning in infancy and the prediction of later IQ.' In *Handbook of Infant Development* (Edited by Osofsky, J.D.), pp. 707-741. John Wiley & Sons, New York.

McCarthy, J.J. and Kirk, S.A. (1963) *Illinois Test of Psycholinguistic Abilities*. University of Illinois Press, Urbana, IL.

Mason, M.K. (1942) 'Learning to speak after six and one half years of silence.' *J. Speech Hear. Disord.* 7, 295-304.

Meltzoff, A.N. and Moore, M.K. (1977) 'Imitation of facial and manual gestures by human neonates.' *Science* 198, 75-78.

Moore, T. (1968) 'Language and intelligence: a longitudinal study of the first 8 years — II. Environmental correlates of mental growth.' *Hum. Dev.* 11, 1-24.

Parke, R.D (1979) 'Perspectives on father and infant interaction.' In *Handbook of Infant Development* (Edited by Osofsky, J.D.), pp. 544-590. John Wiley & Sons, New York.

Piaget, J. (1967) *Play Dreams and Imitation in Children*. Routledge & Kegan Paul, London.

Piaget, J . and Inhelder, B . (1969) *The Psychology of the Child*. Basic Books, New York.

Pick, H. L. and Pick, A.D. (1970) 'Sensory and perceptual development.' In *Carmichael's Manual of Child Psychology* (Edited by Mussen, P.H.), Vol. 1, 3rd edn., pp. 773-848. John Wiley & Sons, New York.

Provence, S. and Lipton, R.C. (1962) *Infants in Institutions: a Comparison of their Development with Family-reared Infants during the First Year of Life*. International University Press, New York.

Rajecki, D.W., Lamb, M.E. and Obmascher, P. (1978) 'Toward a general theory of infantile attachment: a comparative review of aspects of the social bond.' *Behav. Brain Sci.* 3, 417-464.

Raven, J.C . (1965) *Guide to Using the Coloured Progressive Matrices*. Lewis, London .

Reynell, J. (1969) *Developmental Language Scales,* experimental edn. (Manual). National Foundation for Educational Research, Windsor.

Richardson, S.A. (1977) 'Malnutrition and mental development: an ecological perspective.' In *Research to Practice in Mental Retardation: Biomedical Aspects* (Edited by Mittler, P.), Vol. III. pp. 297-309. University Park, Baltimore. MD.

Robertson, J. and Robertson, J. (1971) 'Young children in brief separation: a fresh look.' *Psychoanal. Study Child* 26, 264-315.

Rosenblatt, D. (1977) 'Developmental trends in infant play.' In *Clinics in Developmental Medicine, No. 62. Biology of Play* (Edited by Tizard, B. and Harvey, D.), pp. 33-44. SIMP/Heinemann, London

Ross, G. (1977) 'A study of conceptualistation in children.' PhD Dissertation Harvard University (cited in Kagan *et al .,* 1978) .

Ruppenthal, G.C., Arling, G.C., Harlow, H.F., Sackett, G.P. and Suomi, S.J. (1976) 'A 10-year perspective of motherless-mother monkey behavior.' *J. abnorm. Psychol.* 85, 341-349.

Russo, M. and Vignolo, L. (1967) 'Visual figure-ground discrimination in patients with unilateral cerebral disease.' *Cortex* 3, 113-127.

Rutter, M. (1977) 'Infantile autism and other child psychoses.' In *Child Psychiatry. Modern Approaches* (Edited by Rutter, M. and Hersov, L.), pp. 717-747. Blackwell Scientific, London.

Rutter, M. (1980) 'Attachment and the development of social relationships.' In *Scientific Foundations of Developmental Psychiatry* (Edited by Rutter, M.), pp. 267-279. Heinemann Medical, London.

Rutter, M.L. (1981) *Maternal Deprivation Reassessed,* 2nd edn. Penguin Books, Harmondsworth.

Rutter, M. and Hersov, L. (1977) *Child Psychiatry: Modern Approaches.* Blackwell Scientific, London.

Rutter, M. and Madge, N. (1976) 'Intellectual performance and scholastic attainment.' In *Cycles of Disadvantage* (Edited by Rutter, M. and Madge, N.), pp. 80-139. Heinemann Educational, London .

Rutter, M.L. and Mittler, P. (1972) 'Environmental influences on language development.' In *Clinics in Developmental Medicine, No. 43. The Child with Delayed Speech* (Edited by Rutter, M. and Martin, J.A.M.), pp. 52-67. SIMP/Heinemann, London.

Sackett, G.P. (1965) 'Effects of early rearing conditions upon the behaviour of rhesus monkeys' *(Macaca mulatta). Child Dev.* 36, 855-868.

Sameroff, A.J. and Chandler, M.J. (1975) 'Reproductive risk and the continuum of caretaking causalty.' In *Review of Child Development* (Edited by Horowitz, F.D.), Vol. IV, pp. 187-244. University of Chicago Press, Chicago, IL.

Scarr-Salapatek, S. (1976) 'An evolutionary perspective on infant intelligence: species patterns and individual variations.' In *Origins of Intelligence* (Edited by Lewis, M.), pp. 165-197. Plenum, New York .

Schaffer, H.R., Collis, G.M. and Parson, G. (1977) 'Vocal interchange and visual regard in verbal and preverbal children.' In *Studies in Mother-Infant Interaction* (Edited by Schaffer, H.R.), pp. 291-324. Academic Press, London.

Shields, J. (1977) 'Polygenic influences.' In *Child Psychiatry: Modern Approaches* (Edited by Rutter, M. and Hersov, L.), pp. 22-46. Blackwell Scientific, London.

Shields, J. (1980) 'Genetics and mental development.' In *Scientific Foundations of Developmental Psychiatry* (Edited by Rutter, M.), pp. 8-24. Heinemann Medical, London.

Sinclair, H. (1971) 'Sensorimotor action patterns and a condition for the acquisition of syntax.' In *Language Acquisition: Models and Methods* (Edited by Huxley, R. and Ingram, E.), pp. 121-135. Academic Press, New York.

Skeels, H.M. (1966) 'Adult status of children with contrasting early life experiences: a follow-up study.' *Mongr. Soc. Res. Child Dev.* 31, No. 103, 3.

Skuse, D.H. (1984) 'Extreme deprivation in early childhood — I. Diverse outcomes for three siblings from an extraordinary family.' *J. Child Psychol. Psychiat.* 25, 523-541.

Sroufe, L.A. (1977) 'Early experience — evidence and myth.' Review of *Early Experience: Myth and Evidence* 1976 (Edited by Clarke, A.M. and Clarke, A.D.B., Free Press, New York). *Contemp. Psychol.* 22, 878-880.

Sroufe, L.A. and Waters, E. (1977) 'Attachment as an organisational construct.' *Child Dev.* 48, 1184-1199

Stanford-Binet (1973) *Intelligence Scale (3rd) Revision.* George G. Harrap & Co., London.

Stern, D.N. (1974) 'Mother and infant at play: the dyadic interaction involving facial, vocal and gaze behaviours.' In *The Effect of the Infant on its Caregiver* (Edited by Lewis, M. and Rosenblum, L.), pp. 187-213. John Wiley & Sons, New York.

Stutsman, R. (1948) 'A guide for administering the Merrill-Palmer scale of mental tests.' In *Mental Measurement of Preschool Children.* N.F.E.R., Windsor.

Taylor, E. (1980) 'Development of attention.' In *Scientific Foundations of Developmental Psychiatry* (Edited by Rutter, M.), pp. 185-197. Heinemann Medical, London.

Tizard, B. and Hodges, J. (1978) 'The effect of early institutional rearing on the development of eight-year-old children.' *J. Child Psychol. Psychiat* 19, 99-118.

Tizard. B. and Rees, J. (1975) 'The effect of early institutional rearing on the behaviour problems and affectional relationships of four-year-old children.' *J. Child Psychol. Psychiat* 16, 61-74.

Waddington, C.H. (1957) *The Strategy of the Genes.* George Allen & Unwin, London.

Waddington, C.H. (1977) *Tools for Thought.* Jonathan Cape, London.

Warkany, J. and St. J. Dignan, P. (1973) 'Congenital malformations: microcephaly.' In *Mental Retardation and Developmental Disabilities* (Edited by Wortis, J.), Vol. V, pp. 113-135. Brunner/Mazel, New York.

Waterlow, J.C. (1974) 'Some aspects of childhood malnutrition as a public health problem.' *Br. Med. J.* IV, 88-90.

Waters, E., Wippman, J. and Sroufe. L.A. (1979) 'Attachment, positive affect and competence in the peer group: two studies in construct validation.' *Child Dev.* 50, 821-829.

Wechsler, D. (1949) *The Wechsler Intelligence Scale for Children (Manual).* The Psychological Corporation, New York.

Wechsler, D. (1967) *Wechsler Preschool and Primary Scale of Intelligence.* Psychological Corporation, New York.

White, B.L. (1977) 'Early stimulation and behavioural development.' In *Genetics, Environment and Intelligence* (Edited by Oliverio, A.), pp. 337-369. Elsevier, Amsterdam.

Wing, L. (1976) *Early Childhood Autism: Clinical, Educational and Social Aspects,* 2nd edn. Pergamon Press, Oxford .

Winick, M., Rosso, P. and Waterflow, J. (1970) 'Cellular growth of cerebrum, cerebellum and brain stem in normal and marasmic children.' *Exp. Neurol.* 26, 393-400.

Winick, M., Meyer, K.K. and Harris, R.C. (1975) 'Malnutrition and environmental enrichment by early adoption.' *Science* 190, 1173- 1175.

Winnicott, D.W. (1951) 'Transitional objects and transitional phenomena.' Reprinted in *Through Paediatrics to Psycho-Analysis* (Winnicott, D.W.), pp. 229-242. Hogarth Press, London, 1978

Wohlwill, J.F. (1980) 'Cognitive development in childhood.' In *Constancy and Change in Human Development* (Edited by Brim, O.G. and Kagan, J.), pp. 359-444. Harvard University Press, Cambridge, MA.

Zelazo, P.R. and Kearsley, R.B. (1976) 'Functional play: evidence for a cognitive metamorphosis in the year old infant.' Unpublished manuscript (cited in Kagan *et al.,* 1978).

Perception and Cognition in Infancy

The last twenty years have witnessed a proliferation of experimental studies of infants' perceptual and cognitive abilities. Psychologists and philosophers have long debated the nature of the newborn human: whether there are innate, biologically specified ways of organising sensations and understanding the world, or whether this is constructed by the infant from experience. The relatively recent spate of experimental studies of infants owes much to two influences. First and foremost, to Jean Piaget, the Swiss psychologist and biologist, who put forward an elaborate theory of cognitive development which had at its core the notion that infants and children construct concepts from their experiences. Second, to an enboldened willingness to measure changes in infants' rates of response to stimuli as an index of underlying mental processes.

The utilisation of such measures goes back to Robert Fantz, an American psychologist, who in the 1950s and 1960s attempted to understand the development of visual preferences in infants, and to Lewis Lipsitt and Hanus Papousek who were interested in the applicability of operant learning principles to infants. The first two articles appearing in this section, by DeCasper and Fifer and by Rovee-Collier *et al.*, provide graphic examples of what can be learned about newborn infants' and somewhat older infants' capacities respectively through the use of operant learning methods.

The remaining three articles are now considered to be 'modern classics', each calling into question an aspect of Piaget's theory of sensorimotor intelligence. Piaget proposed that infants progress through six stages of development between birth and approximately two years of age. According to the theory, it is only from Stage 4 (around 9 – 12 months of age) that infants acquire the ability to perceive equivalencies across sensory modalities (e.g., an object explored only tactually is recognised as the same when it is explored only visually). The simple and elegant study by Meltzoff and Borton claims that this capacity has a much earlier and different origin from that proposed by Piaget.

Similarly, the 'object concept', or the notion that objects continue to exist when not perceived, was believed by Piaget to clearly surface in Stage 4 of the sensorimotor period. Through the use of very different methodologies, the studies by Hood and Willatts, and by Baillargeon converge in suggesting that this capacity is present much earlier in infancy.

4. Of Human Bonding: Newborns Prefer Their Mothers' Voices

Anthony J. DeCasper and William P. Fifer

Abstract. *By sucking on a nonnutritive nipple in different ways, a newborn human could produce either its mother's voice or the voice of another female. Infants learned how to produce the mother's voice and produced it more often than the other voice. The neonate's preference for the maternal voice suggests that the period shortly after birth may be important for initiating infant bonding to the mother.*

Human responsiveness to sound begins in the third trimester of life and by birth reaches sophisticated levels [1], especially with respect to speech[2]. Early auditory competency probably subserves a variety of developmental functions such as language acquisition[1,3] and mother-infant bonding[4,5]. Mother-infant bonding would best be served by (and may even require) the ability of a newborn to discriminate its mother's voice from that of other females. However, evidence for differential sensitivity to or discrimination of the maternal voice is available only for older infants for whom the bonding process is well advanced.[6]. Therefore, the role of maternal voice discrimination in formation of the mother-infant bond is unclear. If the newborn's sensitivities to speech subserves bonding, discrimination of and preference for the maternal voice should be evident near birth. We now report that a newborn infant younger than 3 days of age can not only discriminate its mother's voice but also will work to produce her voice in preference to the voice of another female.

The subjects were ten Caucasian neonates (five male and five female)[7]. Shortly after delivery we tape-recorded the voices of mothers of infants selected for testing as they read Dr. Seuss's *To Think That I Saw It On Mulberry Street*. Recordings were edited to provide 25 minutes of uninterrupted prose, and testing of whether infants would differentially produce their mothers' voices began within 24 hours of recording. Sessions began by coaxing the infant to a state of quiet alertness[8]. The infant was then placed supine in its basinette, earphones were secured over its ears, and a nonnutritive nipple was placed in its mouth. An assistant held the nipple loosely in place; she was unaware of the experimental condition of the individual infant and could neither hear the tapes nor be seen by the infant. The nipple was connected, by way of a pressure transducer, to the solid-state programming and recording equipment. The infants were then allowed 2 minutes to adjust to the situation. Sucking activity was recorded during the next 5 minutes, but voices were never presented. This baseline period was used to determine the median interburst interval (IBI) or time elapsing between the end of one burst of sucking and the beginning of the next[9]. A burst was defined as a series of individual sucks separated from one another by less than 2 seconds. Testing with the voices began after the baseline had been established.

Anthony J. DeCasper and William P. Fifer: 'Of Human Bonding: Newborns Prefer Their Mothers' Voices.' *SCIENCE* (1980), Vol. 208, pp. 1174-1176. © American Association for the Advancement of Science.

Figure 1

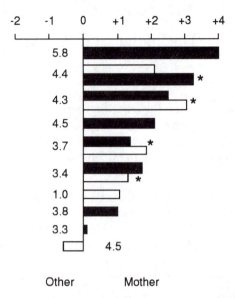

For each subject, signed difference scores between the median IBI's without vocal feedback (baseline) and with differential vocal feedback (session 1). Differences of the four reversal sessions (*) are based on medians with differential feedback in sessions 1 and 2. Positive values indicate a preference for the maternal voice and negative values a preference for the nonmaternal voice. Filled bars indicate that the mother's voice followed IBI's of less than the baseline median; open bars indicate that her voice followed intervals equal to or greater than the median. Median IBI's of the baseline (in seconds) are shown opposite the bars.

For five randomly selected infants, sucking burst terminating IBI's equal to or greater than the baseline median (t) produced only his or her mother's voice (IBI $\geq t$), and bursts terminating intervals less than the median produced only the voice of another infant's mother[10]. Thus, only one of the voices was presented , stereophonically, with the first suck of a burst and remained on until the burst ended, that is, until 2 seconds elapsed without a suck. For the other five infants, the conditions were reversed. Testing lasted 20 minutes.

A preference for the maternal voice was indicated if the infant produced it more often than the nonmaternal voice. However, unequal frequencies not indicative of preference for the maternal voice *per se* could result either because short (or long) IBI's were easier to produce or because the acoustic qualities of a particular voice, such as pitch or intensity, rendered it a more effective form of feedback. The effects of response requirements and voice characteristics were controlled (i) by requiring half the infants to respond after short IBI's to produce the mother's voice and half to respond after long ones and (ii) by having each maternal voice also serve as the nonmaternal voice for another infant.

Preference for the mother's voice was shown by the increase in the proportion of IBI's capable of producing her voice; the median IBI's shifted from their baseline values in a direction that produced the maternal voice more than half the time. Eight of the ten medians were shifted in a direction of the maternal voice (mean= 1.90 seconds, a 34 percent increase) (sign test, $P = .02$), one shifted in the direction that produced the nonmaternal voice more often, and one median did not change from its baseline value (Fig. 1).

If these infants were working to gain access to their mother's voice, reversing the response requirements should result in a reversal of their IBI's. Four infants, two from each condition, who produced their mother's voice more often in session 1 were able to complete a second session 24 hours later, in which the response requirements were reversed[11]. Differential feedback in session 2 began immediately after the 2-minute adjustment period. The criterion time remained equal to the baseline median of the first session. For all four infants, the median IBI's shifted toward the new criterion values and away from those which previously produced the maternal voice. The average magnitude of the difference between the medians of the first and reversal sessions was 1.95 seconds.

Figure 2

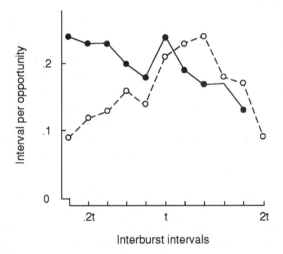

Interburst interval per opportunity when the maternal voice followed intervals less than the baseline median (solid line) and intervals equal to or greater than the median (dashed line). The IBI's are represented on the abscissa by the lower bound of interval classes equal to one-fifth the baseline median (t).

Apparently the infant learned to gain access to the mother's voice. Since specific temporal properties of sucking were required to produce the maternal voice, we sought evidence for the acquisition of temporally differentiated responding. Temporal discrimination within each condition was ascertained by constructing the function for IBI per opportunity: IBI's were collected into classes equal to one-fifth the baseline median, and the frequency of each class was divided by the total frequency of classes having equal and larger values[12]. When IBI's less than the baseline median were required, the likelihood of terminating interburst intervals was highest for classes less than the median (Fig. 2), whereas when longer intervals were required, the probability of terminating an IBI was maximal for intervals slightly longer than the median. Feedback from the maternal voice effectively differentiated the temporal character of responding that produced it: the probability of terminating IBI's was highest when termination resulted in the maternal voice.

Repeating the experiment with 16 female neonates and a different discrimination procedure confirmed their preference for the maternal voice[13]. The discriminative stimuli were a 400-Hz tone of 4 seconds duration (tone) and a 4-second period of silence (no tone). Each IBI contained an alternating sequence of tone-no-tone periods, and each stimulus was equally likely to begin a sequence. For eight infants, a sucking burst initiated during a tone period turned off the tone and produced the Dr. Seuss story read by the infant's mother, whereas sucking bursts during a no-tone period produced the nonmaternal voice. The elicited voice remained until the sucking burst ended, at which time the tone-no-tone alternation began anew. The discriminative stimuli were reversed for the other eight neonates. Testing with the voices began immediately after the 2-minute adjustment period and lasted 20 minutes. Each maternal voice also served as a nonmaternal voice.

During the first third of the testing session, the infants were as likely to suck during a stimulus period correlated with the maternal voice as during one correlated with the nonmaternal voice (Table 1). However, in the last third of the session the infants sucked during stimulus periods associated with their mother's voice approximately 24 percent more often than during those associated with the nonmaternal voice, a significant increase [$F(1, 14) = 8.97$, $P < .01$]. Thus, at the beginning of testing there was no indication of stimulus discrimination or voice preference. By the end of the 20-minute session, feedback from the maternal voice produced clear evidence of an auditory discrimination; the probability of sucking during tone and no-tone periods was greater when sucking produced the maternal voice.

The infants in these studies lived in a group nursery; their general care and night feedings were handled by a number of female nursery personnel. They were fed in their mothers' rooms by their mothers at 9:30 a.m. and at 1:30, 5:00, and 8:30 p.m. At most, they had 12 hours of postnatal contact with their mothers before testing. Similarly reared infants prefer the human voice to other acoustically complex stimuli[14]. But, as our data show, newborns reared in group nurseries that allow minimal maternal contact can also discriminate between their mothers and other speakers and, moreover, will work to produce their mothers' voices in preference to those of other females. Thus, within the first 3 days of postnatal development, newborns prefer the human voice, discriminate between speakers, and demonstrate a preference for their mothers' voices with only limited maternal exposure.

The neonate's capacity to rapidly acquire a stimulus discrimination that controls behavior[15] could provide the means by which limited postnatal experience with the mother results in preference for her voice. The early preference demonstrated here is possible because newborns have auditory competencies adequate for discriminating individual speakers: they are sensitive to rhythmicity[16], intonation[17], frequency variation[1, 13], and phonetic components of speech[18]. Their general sensory competency may enable other maternal cues, such as her odor[19] and the manner in which she handles her infant[20], to serve as supporting bases for discrimination and vocal preference. Prenatal (intrauterine) auditory experience may also be a factor. Although the significance and nature of intrauterine auditory experience in humans is not known, perceptual preferences and proximity-seeking responses of some infrahuman infants are profoundly affected by auditory experience before birth[21].

Table 1 **Mean ($\overline{X}$) and standard deviation (S.D.) of the relative frequency of sucking during a stimulus associated with the maternal voice divided by the relative frequency of sucking during a stimulus associated with the nonmaternal voice. A ratio of 1.0 indicates no preference.**

Stimulus associated with maternal voice	First third		Last third	
	$\overline{X}$	S.D.	$\overline{X}$	S.D.
Tone	0.97	.33	1.26	.33
No tone	1.04	.31	1.22	.19
Combined	1.00	.32	1.24	.27

References and Notes

1. Eisenberg, R.B. (1976) *Auditory Competence in Early Life: The Roots of Communicative Behavior.* University Park Press, Baltimore.

2. Eimas, P.D. (1975) in *Infant Perception: From Sensation to Cognition,* Cohen L.B. and Salapatek, P.(Eds). Vol. 2, p. 193. Academic Press, New York.

3. Friedlander, B. (1970) *Merrill-Palmer Q.* 16, 7.

4. Bell, R. (1974) in *The Effect of the Infant on Its Caregiver,* Lewis, M. and Rosenblum, L.A., (Eds). Wiley, New York, p. 1; Brazelton, T.B., Tronick, E., Abramson, L., Als, H., Wise, S. (1975), *Ciba Found. Symp.* 33, 137.

5. Klaus, M.H. and Kennel, J.H. (1976) *Maternal Infant Bonding.* Mosby, St. Louis. DeChateau P. (1977) *Birth Family J.* 41, 10.

6. Miles, M. and Melvish, E., *Nature (London)* 252, 123 (1974); Mehler, J., Bertoncini, J., Baurière, M., Jassik-Gershenfeld. (1978), *Perception* 7, 491.

7. The infants were randomly selected from those meeting the following criteria: i) gestation, full term; (ii) delivery, uncomplicated; (iii) birth weight, between 2500 and 3850 grams; and (iv) APGAR score, at least eight at 1 and 5 minutes after birth. If circumsized, males were not observed until at least 12 hours afterward. Informed written consent was obtained from the mother, and she was invited to observe the testing procedure. Testing sessions began between 2.5 and 3.5 hours after the 6 a.m. or 12 p.m. feeding. All infants were bottle-fed.

8. Wolff, P.H. (1966), *Psychol. Issues* 5, 1. The infants were held in front of the experimenter's face, spoken to, and then presented with the nonnutritive nipple. Infants failing to fixate visually on the experimenter's face or to suck on the nipple were returned to the nursery.

Once begun, a session was terminated only if the infant cried or stopped sucking for two consecutive minutes. The intitial sessions of two infants were terminated because they cried for 2 minutes. Their data are not reported. Thus, the results are based on 10 of 12 infants meeting the behavioral criteria for entering and remaining in the study.

9. With quiet and alert newborns, nonnutritive sucking typically occurs as bursts of individual sucks, each separated by a second or so, while the bursts themselves are separated by several seconds or more. Interburst intervals tend to be unimodally distributed with modal values differing among infants. [Kaye, K. (1977), in *Studies in Mother-Infant Interaction*, Schaffer, H.R., Ed. Academic Press, New York]. A suck was said to occur when the negative pressure exerted on the nipple reached 20 mm-Hg. This value is almost always exceeded during nonnutritive sucking by healthy infants, but is virtually never produced by nonsucking mouth movement.

10. The tape reels revolved continuously, and one or the other of the voices was electronically switched to the earphones when the response threshold was met. Because the thresholds were detected electronically, voice onset occurred at the moment the negative pressure reached 20 mm-Hg.

11. Two infants were not tested a second time, because we could not gain access to the testing room, which served as an auxillary nursery and as an isolation room. The sessions of two infants who cried were terminated. Two other infants were tested a second time, but in their first session one had shown no preference and the other had shown only a slight preference for the nonmaternal voice. Their performance may have been affected by inconsistent feedback. Because their peak sucking pressures were near the threshold of the apparatus, very similar sucks would sometimes produce feedback and sometimes not, and sometimes feedback would be terminated in the midst of a sucking burst. Consequently, second session performances of these two infants, which were much like their initial performances, were uninterpretable.

12. Anger, D. (1956), *J. Exp. Psychol.* 52, 145.

13. Three other infants began testing with the voices, but their sessions were terminated because they cried. Their data are not included. This study is part of a doctoral thesis submitted by W.P.F.

14. Butterfield, E. and Siperstein, G. (1972) in *Oral Sensation and Perception: The Mouth of the Infant*, Bosma, J., (Ed). Thomas, Springfield, Ill.

15. Siqueland, E.R. and Lipsitt, L.P. (1966) *J. Exp. Child. Psychol.* 3, 356; Kron, R.E. (1967) in *Recent Advances in Biological Psychiatry*, Wortis, J., (Ed), Plenum, New York, p. 295.

16. Condon, W.S. and Sander, L.W. (1974) *Science* 183 , 99.

17. Eisenberg, R.B., Cousins, D.B., Rupp, N. (1966) *J. Aud. Res.* 7, 245; Morse, P.A. (1972), *J. Exp. Child. Psychol.* 14, 477.

18. Butterfield, E.C. and Cairns, G.F. (1974) in *Language Perspectives: Acquisition, Retardation and Intervention*, Schiefelbusch, R.L. and Lloyd, L.L., (Eds), University Park Press, Baltimore, p. 75; DeCasper, A.J., Butterfield, E.C., Cairns G.F, paper presented at the fourth biennial conference on Human Development, Nashville, April 1976.

19. MacFarlane, A. (1975), *Ciba Found. Symp.* 33, 103.

20. Burns, P., Sander, L.W., Stechler, G., Julia, H. (1972) *J. Am. Acad. Child Psychiatry* 11, 427; Thoman E.B., Korner A.F., Bearon-Williams L. (1977) *Child Dev.* 48, 563.

21. Gottlieb, G. (1971) *Development of Species Identification in Birds: An Inquiry into the Prenatal Determinants of Perception.* Univ. of Chicago Press, Chicago; Hess E.H. (1973) *Imprinting.* Van Nostrand-Reinhold, New York.

22. Supported by Research Council grant 920. We thank the infants, their mothers, and the staff of Moses Cane Hospital, where this work was performed, and A. Carstens for helping conduct the research.

5. Reactivation of Infant Memory

Carolyn K. Rovee-Collier, Margaret W. Sullivan, Mary Enright, Debora Lucas and Jeffrey W. Fagen

Abstract. *Three-month-old infants learned to activate a crib mobile by means of operant footkicks. Retention of the conditioned response was assessed during a cued recall test with the nonmoving mobile. Although forgetting is typically complete after an 8-day retention interval, infants who received a reactivation treatment — a brief exposure to the reinforcer 24 hours before retention testing — showed no forgetting after retention intervals of either 2 or 4 weeks. Further, the forgetting function after a reactivation treatment did not differ from the original forgetting function. These experiments demonstrate that (i) "reactivation" or "reinstatement" is an effective mechanism by which early experiences can continue to influence behavior over lengthy intervals and (ii) memory deficits in young infants are best viewed as retrieval deficits.*

The pervasive influences of early experiences on later behavior have been extensively documented, as have early memory deficits or "infantile amnesia" [1]. Considered jointly, these phenomena pose a major paradox for students of development: How can the effects of early experiences persist into adolescence and adulthood if they are forgotten during infancy and early childhood? Campbell and Jaynes[2] proposed a resolution to this paradox in terms of reinstatement, a mechanism that maintains a memory which would otherwise be forgotten through occasional reencounters with the original training conditions over the period of development. Any given reencounter, however, would be insufficient to promote new learning in organisms lacking the early experience. Spear[3] attributed the efficacy of reinstatement procedures to improved retrieval produced by the reactivation of a sufficient number (or kind) of existing but otherwise inaccessible attributes of the target memory. He hypothesized that reexposure to stimuli from the original training context, which had been stored as attributes of the memory, could prime or arouse other attributes that represented the original experience, increasing their accessibility and, thus, the probability of their retrieval.

"Reinstatement" or "reactivation" has been demonstrated in young and adult rats[2, 4, 5] and in grade-school children[6]. We now report that a reactivation treatment can alleviate forgetting in 3-month-old infants after a retention interval as long as 4 weeks and that the forgetting function after a reactivation treatment is similar to the function after original training.

Our procedures were modeled after those of animal memory studies in which the experimenter trains a specific response in a distinctive context and later returns the subject to that context to see if the response is still produced. Because the retrieval cues

Carolyn K. Rovee-Collier, Margaret W. Sullivan, Mary Enright, Debora Lucas, Jeffrey W. Fagen: 'Reactivation of Infant Memory'. *SCIENCE* (1980), Vol. 208, pp. 1159-1161. © American Association for the Advancement of Science.

are contextual and response production is assessed before reinforcement is reintroduced, the procedure is analogous to a test of cued recall[3].

In our studies, footkicks of 3-month-olds were reinforced by movement of an overhead crib mobile. The infant controlled both the intensity and frequency of the mobile movement by means of a ribbon connecting the ankle with the hook from which the mobile hung. This procedure, "mobile conjugate reinforcement," produces rapid acquisition and high, stable response rates attributable to the contingency and not to behavioral arousal[7]. During nonreinforcement phases (baseline, retention tests, extinction), the mobile remained in view but was hung from a second mobile stand with no ribbon attachment and could not be activated by kicks.

Infants received three procedurally identical sessions in their home cribs. The first two were training sessions, spaced by 24 hours; the third followed a lengthy retention interval. Each session consisted of a 9-minute reinforcement phase preceded and followed by a 3-minute nonreinforcement period. In session 1, the initial 3-minute period defined the baseline; in sessions 2 and 3, it was a long-term retention test of the effects of prior training. Total footkicks during this test (B) were expressed as a fraction of the infant's total kicks during the 3-minute nonreinforcement phase at the conclusion of the preceding session (A), which was an immediate retention test. The ratio B/A indexed the extent of an infant's forgetting from one session to the next. Ratios of ≥ 1.00 indicated no forgetting, and < 1.00 indicated fractional loss.[8]

A reactivation treatment was administered 24 hours before session 3. It consisted of a 3-minute exposure to the reinforcer (mobile movement) in a context identical to that of session 2 except that (i) the ribbon was not connected to the ankle but was draped over the side of the crib, where it was drawn and released by the experimenter at a rate corresponding to each infant's mean response rate during the final 3 minutes of acquisition in session 2; and (ii) the infant was in a reclining seat, which minimized footkicks and altered the topography of those which did occur.[9] These changes, as well as the brevity of the reminder, precluded the opportunity for new learning or practice during a reactivation treatment. Footkicks were recorded by the experimenter and, independently, by a second observer present for at least a third of the sessions and naive with respect to group assignment and session number. Pearson product-moment reliability coefficients were $> .95$ for all studies reported here.

In study 1, retention of conditioned footkicks was assessed 2 weeks after training. Infants [mean ($\overline{X}$) age = 88.4 days, standard error (S.E.) = 3.3] were tested in three groups of six each: (i) a reactivation group received a 3-minute reminder 13 days after session 2 (24 hours before session 3); (ii) a no-reactivation group received training but no reactivation treatment prior to session 3; and (iii) a familiarization/reactivation control group received a procedure identical to that of the reactivation group except that infants in this group were removed from their cribs during the reinforcement phases of sessions 1 and 2 and thus had no training before session 3. The rates at which their reminders occurred were matched to those of the reactivation group.

Infants in this control group showed no change in response rate either within or across sessions (all t's < 1). Thus, infants of this age do not simply become more active over the 2-week interval, and their footkicking during the session 3 cued recall test is not a result of either elicited familiarity reactions or the reactivation treatment *per se*. The acquisition curve of this group in session 3, when reinforcement was introduced for the first time, was indistinguishable from the session-1 learning curves of the other two groups. An analysis of variance with repeated measures over sessions and blocks confirmed that response rates of the reactivation and no-reactivation groups did not differ during training (Fig. 1A). A 2 by 2 analysis of variance over retention ratios yielded a significant group-by-sessions interaction: Although 24-hour retention ratios did not differ, the 14-day retention ratio of the reactivation group significantly exceeded that of the no-reactivation group ($P < .01$), whose ratio reflected a return to baseline performance of session 1 (Fig. 1B). The retention ratio of the reactivation group was as high as in the 24-hour measure. Thus, both prior training and a reminder are prerequisite for reactivation.

Figure 1

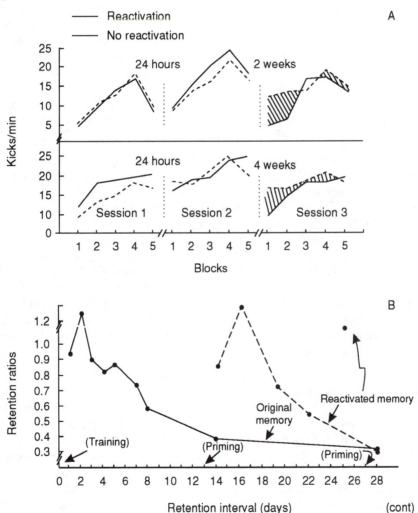

85

(A) Mean kicks per minute during training (sessions 1 and 2) and an identical session (session 3) occurring either 2 or 4 weeks after the completion of session 2. Blocks 1 and 5 are nonreinforcement phases; performance during long-term retention tests (block 1, session 2 or 3) is expressed as a fraction of the infant's performance during immediate retention tests (block 5, session 1 or 2, respectively). The reactivation group received a reminder 24 hours before the 2- or 4-week session; the facilitating or priming effect of the reactivation treatment is indicated by the hatched area, session 3. (B) Retention ratios after 2 days of training (solid line) or 2 days of training plus a tractivation treatment (broken line); priming occurred 13 days after training for all points connected by broken lines or 27 days after training for the single data point at the 28-day retention interval. Each data point represents at least five infants.

In study 2, we repeated the procedure with 18 infants ($\overline{X}$ age = 76.9 days, S.E. = 2.0) but doubled the length of the retention interval. The reactivation group ($N = 9$) received a reminder 27 days after training, and retention was assessed the next day. A significant group-by-sessions interaction ($P < .03$) again confirmed the superior retention of the reactivation group in session 3 relative to that of the no-reactivation group ($N = 9$), which received no reminder during the retention interval (Fig. 1B). As before, the groups had not differed during training (Fig. 1A) or in 24-hour retention performance. The 28-day ratio of the no-reactivation group reflected performance equivalent to their session-1 baseline level. The retention ratio (.96) of the reactivation group is remarkable in view of the relatively young age of the infants during training and the relatively large portion of their lives that 4 weeks constitutes.

In study 3, we determined the course of forgetting following a reactivation treatment. Twenty infants ($\overline{X}$ age = 90.0 days, S.E. = 1.3) received a reactivation treatment 13 days after training as described for study 1; however, session 3 now occurred 3, 6, 9, or 15 days ($N = 5$ per interval) after the reminder. This corresponded to 16, 19, 22 or 28 days, respectively, after the completion of training. The session-3 retention ratios, along with those of the six infants tested 1 day after a reactivation treatment in study 1, were compared with retention ratios describing the original forgetting function. [We had previously obtained this function from 69 infants in a number of different experiments[10] carried out according to the same procedure as that used with the no-reactivation groups of this report.] At least five infants per retention interval contributed data 1, 2, 3, 4, 5, 7, 8, or 14 days after training (Fig. 1B). The no-reactivation group of study 2, tested after a 28-day retention interval, was also a control group for the reactivation group tested 15 days after the reminder (28 days after training).

Figure 1B is a composite of retention ratios of all groups tested after 2 days of training only ("original memory" function) or after 2 days of training plus a reactivation treatment ("priming") given either 13 (studies 1 and 3) or 27 (study 2) days after training ("reactivated memory" function). A one-way analysis of variance over all data points except that of the study-2 reactivation group indicated that ratios differed reliably as a function of retention interval ($P < .025$) and provided the error term for individual comparisons between means (Duncan's multiple range test). The latter indicated that the apparent increase above 1.00 in retention ratios in each function (Fig. 1B) was reliable; also ratios of groups tested 8 (original memory function) and 19 (reactivated memory function) days after training did not differ from ratios of no-reactivation groups tested after retention intervals of 14 and 28 days, respectively. Regression analyses indicated that retention was a linear decreasing function of time since either training ($P < .005$) or priming ($P < .005$). Although the linear model provided a relatively poor fit in each instance, the intercepts and slopes of the two functions did not differ (t's < 1). Thus, forgetting of a reactivated memory following the same temporal course as forgetting of the original experience.

Our findings confirm Campbell and Jaynes'[2] proposition that reinstatement is a potent mechanism through which experiences of early infancy can continue to influence behavior. An infant's reencounters with contextual aspects of prior training or an earlier experience can prime or recycle the remaining memory attributes and enhance access to them, alleviating forgetting which otherwise appeared complete weeks earlier. Moreover, a reencounter with the original context can maintain access to the target memory with the same efficacy as original training. Our findings also implicate reinstatement as the mechanism which, during infancy, facilitates the acquisition of the vast amount of learning characteristic of that period of development.

More generally, our findings support a distinction between availability and accessibility of information in memory and imply that failures to observe retention in infants should be discussed in terms of retrieval failures rather than memory deficits[3, 4]. We think that procedures that improve accessibility to important retrieval cues will radically alter current views of infant memory[11] and that conditioning procedures, which permit a direct assessment of retention in infants, offer a promising means by which to bridge the gap between human and animal memory research.

References and Notes

1. Beach, F.A. and Jaynes, J. (1954) *Psychol. Bull.* 51, 239; Schachtel, E.G. (1947) *Psychiatry* 10, 1.

2. Campbell, B.A. and Jaynes, J. (1966), *Psychol. Rev.* 73, 478.

3. Spear, N.E. (1973), *ibid*, 80, 163.

4. ——— and Parsons, P.J. (1976) in *Processes of Animal Memory*, D.L. Medin, W.A. Roberts, R.T. Davis, Eds. Erlbaum, Hillsdale, N.J. p. 135.

5. Mactutus, C.F., Riccio, D.C., Ferek, J.M. (1979) *Science* 204, 1319.

6. Hoving, K.L., Coates, L., Bertucci, M., Riccio, D.C. (1972) *Dev. Psychol.* 6, 426.

7. Rovee-Collier, C.K. and Gekoski, M.J. (1979) *Adv. Child Dev. Behav.* 13, 195.

8. Because operant levels are typically doubled or tripled during acquisition, retention ratios of .30 to .40 usually indicate performance at operant level. A 3-minute period of nonreinforcement at the conclusion of initial training sessions does not typically extinguish responding in infants 11 to 13 weeks of age.

9. During the reactivation treatment, infants produced responses at a rate of 0 to 2 kicks per minute; operant levels are typically 8 to 11 kicks per minute. In the infant seat, infants rarely exhibit the vertical leg thrusts characteristic of conditioned responding; rather, their movements seem to be postural adjustments or horizontal squirming.

10. Rovee, C.K. and Fagen, J.W. (1976) *J. Exp. Child Psychol.* 21; 1 Sullivan, M.W., Rovee-Collier, C.K., Tynes, D.M. (1979) *Child Dev.* 50, 152; M.J. Gekoski, paper presented at the meeting of the Eastern Psychological Association, Hartford, Conn., 9 to 12 April 1980.

11. Cohen, L.B. and Gelber, E.R. (1975) in *Infant Perception: From Sensation to Cognition,* L.B. Cohen and P. Salapatek, Eds. Academic Press, New York, vol. 1, p. 347; Kagan, J. (1979) *The Sciences* 19, 6; Ramsay, D.S. and Campos, J.J. (1978) *Dev. Psychol.* 14, 79.

12. Study 1 of this research formed a portion of a dissertation submitted by M.W.S. to Rutgers University in partial fulfillment of the requirements for the Ph.D. J. Davis and L. O'Brien assisted in the data collection. Supported by NIMH grant 32307 to C.K.R.-C.

6.   Intermodal Matching by Human Neonates

Andrew N. Meltzoff and Richard W. Borton

Normal human adults judge two identical objects to have the same shape even when they are perceived through different modalities, such as touch and vision. The ontogenesis of man's capacity to recognise such intermodal matches has long been debated. One hypothesis is that humans begin life with independent sense modalities and that simultaneous tactual and visual exploration of shapes is needed to learn to correlate the separate tactual and visual sense impressions of them[1-3]. A second hypothesis is that the detection of shape invariants across different modalities is a fundamental characteristic of man's perceptual-cognitive system, available without the need for learned correlations[4-7]. Recent research has shown that 6-12-month-old infants can recognise certain tactual-visual matches[8-11]. However, such data cannot help resolve the classic theoretical debate. Infants of this age repeatedly reach out and touch objects they see, and such simultaneous bimodal exploration presumably offers ample opportunity for learning to correlate tactual and visual sense impressions. The experiments reported here show that humans can recognise intermodal matches without the benefit of months of experience in simultaneous tactual-visual exploration. We demonstrate that 29-day-old infants can recognise which of two visually perceived shapes matches one they previously explored tactually, thus supporting the second hypothesis listed above.

For our assessment of intermodal matching, we adapted a paradigm used to test infant memory[12]. We began with a brief familiarisation period during which the infant tactually explored an object. Next, the infant was shown a pair of visual shapes, only one of which matched the tactual stimulus. Visual fixation to the matching versus non-matching shape was then recorded. Three experimenters were used to ensure objectivity of the results. One experimenter selected the tactual shape and the left-right positioning of the visual shapes. This experimenter was not involved with testing the infant. A second experimenter administered the tactual stimulus. He was not informed about the left-right positioning of the visual shapes. A third experimenter observed the infant's visual fixations through a 0.64-cm peephole in the centre of the rear wall of the testing chamber. He was unaware of both the tactual shape used and the left-right positioning of the visual shapes. Corneal reflections of the test objects were visible to this scorer, but the shapes of the objects were not resolvable. He scored the infant as fixating the left object when the left reflection was visible in either of the infant's pupils, and as fixating the right object when the right reflection was visible[13]. These fixations were recorded on a Rustrack event recorder. Inter-observer agreement was high when assessed in both experiments (0.93, experiment 1; 0.98, experiment 2).

Thirty-two full-term infants ranging from 26 to 33 days old (mean 29.4 d) served as subjects in experiment 1. As infants of this age will not explore objects manually, the tactual stimuli were constructed by modifying pacifiers so that small, hard-rubber shapes could be mounted on them (Fig. 1). The matching shapes used for the visual test were constructed from dense Styrofoam and painted bright orange (diameter 6.4 cm). The experiment started with a 90-s tactual familiarisation period during which infants orally explored one of the tactual stimuli. This stimulus was then removed and the infant presented with both visual shapes for a 20-s visual test. Care was taken to ensure that the tactual stimulus was administered and removed without the infant seeing it. The shape used for tactual familiarisation, the left-right positioning of the visual objects, and the sex of the infants were counterbalanced. Thus, half the infants were tactually familiarised with the sphere and half with the sphere-with-nubs; half the infants in each of these groups were shown the familiar shape on the left and half on the right; half the infants within each of these subgroups were male and half female.

The results clearly demonstrate that infants under 1 month of age are capable of intermodal matching (Table 1). Of the 32 infants, 24 fixated the shape matching the tactual stimulus longer than the non-matching shape. These results were significantly different from chance ($P < 0.01$; binomial test). The mean per cent of total fixation time directed to the matching shape was 71.8%, as compared with the chance level of 50% ($t = 3.07$; $P < 0.01$). There were no significant differences due to sex of the infant, familiarisation object or method of feeding (breast or bottle), nor were there significant preferences for fixating the right versus left side or for fixating the sphere versus sphere-with-nubs.

Table 1   **Numbers of infants who looked longer at the object matching one they had explored tactually, compared with those who looked longer at the non-matching object**

	n	Looked longer at matching shape	Looked longer at non-matching shape	P (binomial test, two-tailed)
Expt 1	32	24	8	0.01
Expt 2	32	22	10	0.05

Studies using paired-comparison paradigms usually report a preference for the novel stimulus. The present findings are not incompatible with this, as there are several important procedural differences between the present experiments and those previously reported. For example, the present experiments (1) used infants younger than typically tested with the paired-comparison technique, (2) assessed tactual-visual rather than visual-visual matching, (3) used three-dimensional forms rather than two-dimensional patterns, (4) used a 90-s tactual familiarisation period. These differences may interact to influence the direction of infant visual preference.

A second experiment checked whether different experimenters using a different sample of infants could replicate the previous effects. A new group of 32 full-term infants 27–31 days old (mean 29.4 d) served as subjects. The procedure was identical to that used in experiment 1 and the effects were replicated (Table 1). Of the 32 infants, 22 fixated the matching shape longer than the non-matching one ($P = 0.05$). The mean per cent of total fixation time directed to the matching shape was 67.1% ($t = 2.14$; $P < 0.05$).

Figure 1

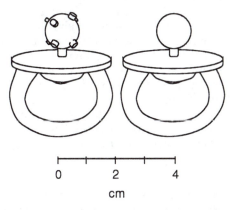

The tactual objects. The tactual shapes were 1.2 cm in diameter. They were moulded from G.E. RTV-620A silicone rubber and fixed to a threaded nylon rod (6–32) that was bolted to the pacifier backing. The sphere-with-nubs was administered so that four of the nubs were orientated towards the base of the infant's mouth and four towards the roof. The nubs on the sphere were 2 mm high x 3 mm wide. The tactual stimuli were administered while the infant sat in an infant chair with his back to the visual objects. They were administered without the infant seeing them by having the experimenter hide them in his cupped hand while he was bringing the objects to and from the infant's mouth. The tactual familiarisation period started as soon as the infant began sucking on the tactual shape. Ten seconds before the end of the familiarisation period, the room lights were extinguished and the infant's seat was swivelled around so that he faced the visual objects. When the familiarisation period ended, the experimenter removed the tactual object, centred the infant's head midway between the visual objects, and only then switched on the light illuminating the visual objects. As soon as the infant made his first fixation to either object, the visual test period began, and the experimenter removed his hands from the infant. The centres of the visual objects were 28 cm apart and 32 cm from the infant's eyes. They were displayed in a three-sided black cardboard chamber 71 cm high x 112 cm wide x 52 cm deep, and each suspended from the ceiling of this chamber by a thin black rod (diameter 0.64 cm). Illumination for the visual objects was provided by an incandescent bulb directly above and behind the infant's head, yielding a luminance of approximately 0.86 log cd m^{-2} at the objects and -0.14 log cd m^{-2} at the background midway between the objects. The visual sphere-with-nubs was orientated so that four of the nubs directly faced the infant. Each nub on the visual object was 1.1 cm long and 1.2 cm in diameter and fashioned from a section of wooden doweling with the edge rounded.

These experiments used a successive, intermodal matching task. The tactual object was no longer in the perceptual world at the time the infants were presented with the visual test. Positive results from such a task indicate that neonates can (1) tactually discriminate between the shapes presented, (2) visually discriminate between them, (3) store some representation of the tactually perceived shape, and (4) relate a subsequent visual perception to the stored representation of the tactually perceived shape. The last point has implications for our current theories of infancy.

A basic assumption of piagetian theory[3] is that infants begin life with independent sense modalities that gradually become intercoordinated with development. Our findings, however, show that neonates are already able to detect tactual-visual correspondences, thereby demonstrating an impressive degree of intermodal unity. Thus, whatever develops in the first year of life, it is apparently not the *de novo* coordination of functionally independent sense modalities. A more general implication of the present research is that human neonates are not limited to processing bits of sense-specific information such as retinal images or tactual sensations. If neonates were restricted to registering such sensory elements they could not succeed on these intermodal matching tasks. Obviously, these initial experiments do not isolate the exact nature of the information perceived as invariant across the different modalities. However, they suggest that neonates are capable of using and storing surprisingly abstract information about objects in their world. This information must be abstract enough, at least, to allow recognition of objects across changes in size and modality of perception.

This research was supported by grants from the Spencer Foundation, the University of Washington Graduate School Research Fund and the Johnson & Johnson Baby Products Company. We thank C. Harris, V. Johnson, R. Carlson and C. Marsh for help in the research, and Drs G. Sackett, L. Lipsitt, D. Teller, V. Dobson, D. Holm, K. Barnard and B. Mackoff for helpful advice.

References

1. Locke, J (1690) *An Essay Concerning Human Understanding.* Basset, London.

2. Berkeley, G (1709) *An Essay Toward a New Theory of Vision.* Pepyat, Dublin.

3. Piaget, J (1952) *The Origins of Intelligence.* Norton, New York; *The Construction of Reality* Basic, New York. (1954); *Play, Dreams and Imitation in Childhood.* (Norton, New York, (1962).

4. Gibson, J.J (1966) *The Senses Considered as Perceptual Systems.* Houghton Mifflin, New York.

5. Gibson, E.J (1969) *Principles of Perceptual Learning and Development.* Appleton-Century Crofts, New York.

6. Bower, T.G.R. (1974) *Development in Infancy.* Freeman, San Francisco.

7. Meltzoff, A.N. & Moore, M.K. (1977) *Science* 195, 75-78.

8. Bryant, P.E., Jones, P., Claxton, V. & Perkins, G.M. (1972) *Nature* 240, 303-304.

9. Bryant, P.E. (1974) *Perception and Understanding in Children.* Methuen, London.

10. Gottfried, A.W., Rose, S.A. & Bridger, W.H. (1977) *Child Dev.* 48, 118-123.

11. Ruff, H.A. & Kohler, C.J. (1978) *Infant Behav. Dev.* 1, 259-264.

12. Fagan, J.F. (1970) *J. exp. Child Psychol,* 9, 217-226.

13. Fantz, R.L., Fagan, J.P. & Miranda, S.B. (1975) in *Infant Perception: From Sensation to Cognition,* (eds Cohen, L.G. & Salapatek, P.) 249-345. Academic, New York.

7. Reaching in the Dark to an Object's Remembered Position: Evidence for Object Permanence in 5-Month-Old Infants

Bruce Hood and Peter Willatts

Five-month-old infants were restrained from reaching for an object that was presented to the side within reaching distance. The room lights were switched off, the object was removed and the infant's hands were released. Significantly more reaches were directed towards the object's previously seen location than to a corresponding control location where no object had been presented. This finding supports the claim of Bower & Wishart that young infants show a form of object permanence, and challenges the Piagetian view that young infants are unable to represent objects that are no longer perceptually available.

According to Piaget (1955), young infants are unable to distinguish between their actions on an object and the object itself. An object only exists while it is perceived or is acted upon and, until the capacity for mental representation has developed, the infant cannot understand that objects may continue to exist after they have disappeared. This lack of a concept of object permanence is revealed by the failure of infants in sensorimotor Stage 3 to search for an object that has been hidden. However, the onset of search behaviour in Stage 4 was not interpreted by Piaget as indicating that mental representation had developed. He argued that only a new organization for action schemes had appeared that supported goal-directed, means-ends behaviour. Representation did not develop until the end of the sensorimotor period when infants search for objects that have undergone a series of invisible displacements. This sequence of search behaviour has been reported in several studies, and there is general agreement that search begins between 7 and 8 months (Corman & Escalona, 1969: Scofield & Uzgiris, 1959: Miller *et al.*, 1970; Gratch & Landers, 1971: Uzgiris, 1973: Willatts, 1984: Wishart & Bower, 1984).

There are two reports that infants as young as 5 months will search in certain conditions. Brown (1973, cited by Bower, 1974) reported that 5-month-olds searched behind a screen, but did not search for an object hidden beneath a cup. Rader *et al*, (1979) showed that 5-month-olds could find an object hidden beneath a small rigid cover, but did not retrieve the object from beneath a larger cloth. However, the status of these observations has been questioned by Willatts (1984) who found that younger infants did not search in the same way as older infants. Most of the 6-month-olds in his study produced a form of 'transitional' search in which a cover was picked up without any apparent intention of finding the hidden object. Intentional search appeared later (between 7 and 8 months), and was indicated by the infant's behaviour with the cover,

Bruce Hood and Peter Willatts: 'Reaching in the Dark to an Object's Remembered Position: Evidence for Object Permanence in 5-Month-Old Infants.' *BRITISH JOURNAL OF DEVELOPMENTAL PSYCHOLOGY* (1986), 4, pp. 57-65. © 1986 The British Psychological Society.

direction of gaze and the speed with which the hidden object was retrieved. Neither Brown nor Rader *et al*, reported on search behaviour in sufficient detail to indicate whether transitional or intentional search had been observed. If the infants in those studies produced transitional search, then it could be accounted for by Stage 3 behaviours, and their findings would not conflict with Piaget's own observations.

A different approach has been used in another study that does challenge the Piagetian account of object concept development. Bower & Wishart (1972) tested a group of 5-month-old infants on a standard search task: none was able to retrieve the hidden object. They were then presented with an object suspended on a string and within reaching distance. The room lights were extinguished, and the infant was left in darkness for up to three minutes. The infants' behaviour was recorded by means of an infra-red TV system, and it was reported that all of them reached out to grasp the object in the dark. The reaching was accurate, even after a period of distress lasting up to 90 seconds. This result was replicated in a second study (Wishart *et al.*, 1978).

Reaching for objects in the dark implies that some form of object permanence is understood by young infants but that the method by which an object disappears may be important for the perception of permanence. Permanence may be perceived when the object vanishes in darkness, but not when it is covered by another object. Bower (1982) has suggested that the problem for infants with the standard search task is not the lack of object permanence but the failure to understand that objects can maintain their identity while coming into contact with each other. The infant fails to search, not because he or she is unable to recall the object, but because the object has combined with another and been transformed into something new.

Two criticisms of the Bower & Wishart study were made by Haith & Campos (1977). Firstly, they suggested that the infant may have been already reaching when the lights went out. Secondly, infants who had previously handled the object may have engaged in 'tactile groping' to continue this activity in darkness. Piaget (1955, observation 17) observed this behaviour in Stage 3, and this too may occur without representation. These criticisms were later answered by Wishart (1979). In relation to the first point, the infants were restrained from reaching by their mother and could not have been in the act of reaching. With regard to tactile groping, none of the infants was allowed to touch the object prior to the lights going out, and the behaviour in the dark cannot be compared with Piaget's observations.

A further criticism of the Bower & Wishart study is that there is nothing in their procedure which distinguishes between accidental and intentional contacts with the object. Infants sitting in darkness may produce arm movements regardless of whether they remember the object. In our own pilot work we frequently observed infants making 'exploratory' arm movements in darkness when no object had been presented in the light. The photograph of an accurate reach in the Bower & Wishart paper shows that the object was located at the midline and apparently close to the infant. Almost any movement of a hand across the midline would have had a reasonable chance of making contact with either the object or the string. In addition, Bower & Wishart also noted that some infants reached directly even after a period of distress lasting up to 90 seconds. This observation must be treated with caution because distressed infants might produce disorganized arm movements that would increase the likelihood of accidental contacts. A similar criticism has also been made by Harris (1983).

These criticisms cast doubt on the claim of Bower & Wishart that young infants showed object permanence when they reached for an object in the dark. In order to examine this claim more carefully, we carried out a study that included a number of modifications to the Bower & Wishart procedure. These were designed to reveal whether reaching in darkness was intentional or accidental. Firstly, the object was removed after the room lights were switched off. This was done to prevent the infant accidentally brushing up against the object and then reaching for it. The possibility that the object might be grasped as the consequence of some form of 'tactile groping' was therefore avoided. Instead of recording whether the infant grasped the object, we observed whether the infant reached towards the location where the object had been presented on that trial. Secondly, the position of the object was varied to assess whether reaching was directed to the object's current seen location. This allowed a comparison to be made of the number of reaches to the position where the object had been presented on the trial, and to a corresponding control position where no object had been presented. In addition, control trials were included on which no object was presented at either location. Thirdly, a shorter trial duration of 25 seconds was used instead of the three minutes allowed by Bower & Wishart. This was intended to reduce the occurrence of distress and the incidence of accidental reaching that might have been produced by prolonged trial durations.

Method

Subjects

Thirteen full-term infants were tested at 5 months of age (mean = 21 weeks 4 days, SD = 4 days). A further 13 infants were dropped from the study because of distress that occurred before sufficient trials had been completed. Infants were recruited by notices placed in local newspapers.

Apparatus

The stimulus object was a green Christmas tree bauble surrounded with tinsel and mounted on the end of a short wooden rod. Testing was carried out in a room from which all external sources of light were excluded by means of door seals and light-proof window blinds. Infants were seated in a standard commercial infant chair with their mothers positioned directly behind. Two infra-red light sources were constructed by placing 100 watt tungsten bulbs in light-tight boxes with apertures covered by Kodak 87C Wratten gelatin filters. These cut out all wavelengths below 800 nm, and transmitted all wavelengths above 1000 nm. These infra-red sources were placed on either side of the infant, and were aimed at a white screen placed about 1.5 metres in front of the infant. With the lamps full on, a dim red glow was just visible from the infra-red sources but this could not be seen because they pointed away from the infant. The whole scene was illuminated by the infra-red radiation reflected from the screen, but the room was in total darkness and nothing at all was visible when the lights were switched off. A Hitachi video-camera (model HV-620k), fitted with a vidicon tube sensitive to infra-red frequencies and a zoom lens (f 1.8), was positioned in front of the screen and provided a face-on view of the infant. The experimenter crouched between the infant and the camera for presentation of the stimulus object and controlled the room lighting by means of a remote switch.

Procedure

Infants were brought to the testing room, and spent 5-10min playing with toys with the mother and the experimenter. The mother then placed the infant in the chair, fastened a safety harness to prevent the infant from slipping out, and sat in a chair behind the infant. The experimenter crouched in front of the infant and commenced a block of three trials. At the start of each trial the object was presented at the infant's midline for a short period of manipulation to arouse interest. The object was then removed from the infant's sight, and the mother restrained the infant's hands by holding them. Three trials were given, either with the original object presented to the infant's left or right, or with no object. On object trials it was positioned at one side of the infant within reaching distance and level with the infant's waist. When the infant was attending to the object, the room lights were switched off and the object was removed. After a brief delay the mother released the infant's hands. The experimenter and mother remained silent for a period of 25 s after which the room lights were switched on again. The object was then presented at the midline for manipulation, and after an inter-trial interval of about 15 s the next trial was started. On control trials with no object the experimenter removed the object from the midline, the mother restrained the infant's hands and after a delay of 10 s the room lights were switched off. The trial then proceeded as outlined above. Within each block of three trials infants received a random sequence of two trials with the object at the left and right, and one no-object control trial. Further blocks of trials were given until testing had to stop because the infant became too distressed. The infant's behaviour on all trials was recorded on videotape.

All of the infants who took part eventually became distressed during the periods of darkness, and when this occurred no further trials were run. Their behaviour was scored from the videotapes only for each block of three trials that was successfully completed. Infants who became distressed before the end of the first block of trials were dropped from the study, and this explains the high proportion of subject loss. Of the remaining 13 infants, six completed only one block of trials, six completed two blocks, and only one infant managed three blocks. All the trials were scored independently by both authors, the first author being the experimenter. A rectangular region around the object was marked on the screen of the TV monitor by drawing vertical and horizontal lines. These lines were positioned 1cm beyond the upper and innermost edges of the object (i.e. approximately one infant hand width beyond the object's edges. A corresponding region of equal size was drawn on the opposite side of the screen where no object was located. On the no-object control trials, these regions were drawn by taking the position of the object from the preceding object trial unless the control trial was first, in which case the position from the following object trial was used. These regions were used to identify reaches to the target and non-target locations. This method of constructing the regions took account of slight variations in the position of the object. The infant was scored as reaching if the whole of the hand crossed one of the boundaries and entered a region. The termination of a reach was scored when the whole hand crossed a boundary and left the region. For each trial, the number of reaches was scored for regions to the left and right of the infant. Scoring was continued until 25 s had elapsed from the start of the trial (the point at which the infant's hands were released). It was possible for infants to reach to both regions at the same time, although this behaviour was infrequent. When it occurred, two reaches were scored, one to each region.

Scoring could not be done blind with regard to the type of trial or the location of the object because it was necessary for the scorer to see the position of the object in order to mark the regions on the TV monitor. Agreement between scorers was 0.89 for reaches to the left, and 0.88 for reaches to the right. Disagreements were resolved by reviewing the tapes jointly, and trials on which agreement could not be reached were discarded from any further analysis.

Results

Within each block there were two trials on which an object had been presented, and one control trial on which no object had been presented. The total number of reaches to both regions was greater on the object trials (mean = 3.04) than on the no-object trials (mean = 2.65), but the difference was not significant on a two-tailed Wilcoxon test ($T = 35$, $n = 12$, n.s.). The number of reaches on any trial was moderate (mean = 2.89), and may have been reduced on later trials because there was no object to contact and therefore all reaches were unsuccessful. However, a Page's L test on the scores for all subjects across the first three trials showed no evidence for such a decline in reaching ($L = 159.5$, $z = 0.69$, n.s.), and there was no indication of any decline in reaching across the six trials completed by seven infants ($L = 510$, $z = -0.22$, n.s.).

On object trials, the region where the object had been presented was the target, and the region on the opposite side was the non-target. On no-object control trials, both regions were non-targets. The mean number of reaches to these regions on object and no-object control trials was calculated in different ways. For object trials, the mean number of reaches to the target and non-target regions was obtained by averaging across trials for each infant. For the no-object control trials, a mean score for each trial was first obtained by summing the scores for left and right non-target regions and dividing by two. These means were then averaged across the total number of control trials for each infant. The mean number of reaches to the target, control non-target and non-target regions for individual infants are given in Table 1.

A Friedman's test showed that the number of reaches to these regions differed significantly ($\chi^2 = 7.03$, d.f. = 2, $P < 0.05$). Individual comparisons with two-tailed Wilcoxon tests revealed that there were significantly more reaches to the target region than to the non-target region on object trials ($T = 5.5$, $n = 12$, $P < 0.02$), but that the number of reaches to the control non-target regions did not differ from the number of reaches to the other two regions on object trials. The results in Table 1 suggested an ordering in the number of reaches across regions, and this was confirmed as a significant trend with a two-tailed Page's L test ($L = 169.0$, $z = 2.55$, $P < 0.02$).

Infants produced significantly more reaches to the target region than to the non-target region on the object trials. One simple strategy that might account for this finding would be that the infant maintained fixation of the place where the object had been seen, and then reached towards that place when his or her hands were released. To check on

Table 1 **Mean number of reaches per trial for individual infants to target, control non-target and non-target regions**

Subject	Object trial target	No-object trial control non-target	Object trial non-target
1	0.50	1.00	0.00
2	2.00	0.00	2.50
3	2.75	3.25	1.50
4	6.25	2.50	2.25
5	0.75	1.00	0.50
6	2.50	2.00	2.00
7	0.50	0.00	0.00
8	3.00	2.50	3.50
9	1.25	0.50	0.00
10	1.00	1.00	1.00
11	0.50	0.75	0.25
12	2.50	2.25	1.50
13	1.00	0.00	0.50
Mean	1.88	1.33	1.15

whether such a strategy was used, the recording of each object trial was examined to see if infants did maintain fixation of the target region or looked away prior to making the first reach or before the end of the trial if no reaching occurred. In addition, the direction of the first reach (target or non-target region) was identified. There was a total of 42 object trials, but data from two were discarded because of lack of agreement between scorers. Of the remaining 40 trials, infants looked away from the target region on 36 trials, and maintained fixation on only four trials. There were 17 first reaches into the target region, 15 reaches into the non-target region, and eight trials on which no reaches occurred to either region. On the majority of trials infants looked away from the target region before reaching, and the first reach was as likely to be directed towards the target region as to the non-target region. There were only two trials on which an infant did not look away and reached first to the target region.

One reason for the apparent random direction of the first reach could be that infants reached accurately to the target region on the first object trial but persisted in reaching to the same region on later trials. However, examination of the direction of first reaches on the first and second object trials did not confirm such a pattern. On the first object trial, six infants reached first to the target and six to the non-target, while on the second object trial, six reached to the target and five to the non-target. Five infants changed the direction of their first reach across the first two object trials, and five infants reached in the same direction. The direction of first reaches on the first two object trials was therefore random.

Finally, the data were examined for evidence of position preferences. There were more reaches to the right (mean = 3.46) than to the left (mean = 2.1), but the difference was not significant ($T = 22.5$, $n = 12$, n.s.).

Discussion

Five-month-old infants reached more to the place where they had seen an object than to a control place where no object had been shown, even though the room was in darkness and nothing at all was visible. The location of the object was changed on each presentation, but infants adjusted their reaching to take account of its last seen position. Thus 5-month-old infants showed the same capacity to adjust their reaching for an object's remembered position as they did when the object was visible (Willatts, 1979).

The fact that the number of reaches on object and control trials did not differ significantly suggested there was a general level of activity in darkness that infants were prepared to sustain. The significant trend in the number of reaches directed to particular regions, showed that infants altered the distribution of reaches according to the experimental condition. On no-object control trials reaches were directed to both non-target regions, while on object trials the same level was maintained by increased reaching to the target region and decreased reaching to the non-target region. The finding that infants reached out in darkness on trials when no object had been presented justifies our criticism of the Bower & Wishart study which did not control for such behaviour.

The Haith & Campos (1977) criticisms of Bower & Wishart's procedure do not apply to our study. Although infants were allowed to manipulate the object between trials in order to maintain their interest, this was only at the midline and never at the two target locations. It would be difficult to argue that infants engaged in tactile groping when they reached more to the object's last seen (but not felt) position. It is possible that infants who are able to reach to the place where they remember seeing an object will also use a more primitive method of tactile groping when they have handled the object as well. We did not examine the videotapes for evidence of reaching to the midline because this behaviour would have been ambiguous. Any reach to the midline might have been accidental or an attempt at tactile groping. As far as we know, there are no published reports of tactile groping other than the few observations reported by Piaget, and this behaviour remains to be investigated.

The infants in our study were restrained and could not have been in the act of reaching when the lights were switched off. However, it could be argued that restraining infants does not prevent them from preparing to reach, so that when the mother let go, the infant followed through with a movement that had already been primed. This argument is not supported by the findings for direction of first reach and gaze prior to reaching. Sustained fixation and reaching towards the target region occurred on only two out of 40 trials, and on the majority the infants looked away. When the first reach did occur, it was as likely to be to the non-target region as to the target. Similar behaviour was also reported by Wishart et al. (1978) who noted that all but one infant 'looked around in some astonishment when the lights went out', and that the probability of an accurate first reach in the dark was 0.5 for 5-month-olds. The fact that infants in our study eventually reached more towards the target location despite such interruptions suggests that they had an enduring representation of the object and its previous location.

It is possible that our infants had already developed Stage 4 search skills and that reaching in the dark was an example of such an ability. Wishart & Bower (1984) claimed that over half of their sample of 5-month-olds showed a Stage 4 level of search, but a criticism of their study is that they did not examine infants' behaviour in sufficient detail to identify whether Stage 3 or Stage 4 strategies were used. In a similar study, Willatts (1984) found that 6-month-olds searched with a transitional Stage 3 strategy, and intentional Stage 4 search generally appeared one or two months later. It is unlikely that 5-month-olds would be superior in their search skills to 6-month-olds, and although the search ability of infants in the present study was not tested it is reasonable to conclude that they would not have produced Stage 4 search and that this may be rejected as an explanation for reaching in the dark.

One difficulty was the distress produced by darkness which resulted in a high level of subject loss. Both Bower & Wishart and Wishart *et al.* (1978) reported similar distress, and some infants who failed to complete a session had to be tested again (Wishart, personal communication). For some infants it appeared to be the sudden onset of darkness that was upsetting and they began to fuss and cry during the first trials. For the remainder it seemed to be frustration brought about by being allowed only short periods for play with the object that were interrupted by longer periods in which nothing could be seen. The experience of darkness is not always distressing for infants if they feel secure (e.g. are sitting on the mother's lap), and are engaged in some activity such as manipulating objects (Soroka *et al.*, 1979; Gottfried & Rose, 1980). One way of reducing this distress in future studies might be to place the infant on a mat or in a cot because they would be more accustomed to lying on their backs in darkness. Another method might be to avoid the sudden change to darkness by gradually dimming the room lights.

Our findings support the claim of Bower & Wishart that 5-month-old infants show a form of object permanence by reaching for objects in the dark. Young infants remembered the location of an object despite its perceptual disappearance, and we conclude from our observations that 5-month-olds are able to represent objects that can no longer be perceived. This finding does not support the Piagetian view that young infants lack a concept of object permanence, although such a concept may continue to develop during infancy (Wishart & Bower, 1984).

However, we are left with a confusing picture of infants' behaviour at this age. A 5-month-old will carry an unseen object into view for visual inspection (*Piaget*, 1955: White *et al.*, 1964), yet will drop an object when the hand holding it is covered with a cloth (Bruner, 1969; Gratch, 1972), or even when the hand closes over the object (*Bower*, 1982, p. 126). In some of our own pilot work we also noticed that infants who were holding an object dropped it after the room lights were turned off. The infant apparently has the same tactual information in these different situations, but the object is retained in some circumstances and released in others. Harris (1975) has suggested that the 'loss of visibility rather than invisibility appears to disrupt the infant', but the findings of Bower & Wishart (1972) and the present study show that this is not always the case. Further studies will be necessary to resolve these apparent contradictions.

Acknowledgements

The authors thank Aileen Sandilands, Anna Shewan and Margaret Grubb for all their assistance.

References

Bower, T.G.R. (1974) *Development in Infancy*, 1st ed. San Francisco: Freeman.

Bower, T.G.R. (1982) *Development in Infancy*, 2nd ed. San Francisco: Freeman.

Bower, T.G.R. & Wishart, J.G. (1972) 'The effects of motor skill on object permanence.' *Cognition*, 1, 28-35.

Bruner, J.S. (1969) 'Eye, hand and mind.' In D. Elkind & J.H. Flavell (eds). *Studies in Cognitive Development*, London: Oxford University Press.

Corman, H. & Escalona, S. (1969) 'Studies of sensorimotor development: A replication study.' *Merrill-Palmer Quarterly*, 15, 351-361.

Gottfried, A.W. & Rose, S.A. (1980) 'Tactile recognition memory in infants.' *Child Development*, 51, 69-74.

Gratch, G. (1972) 'A study of the relative dominance of vision and touch in six-month-old infants.' *Child Development*, 43, 615-623.

Gratch, G. & Landers, W.F. (1971) 'Stage IV of Piaget's theory of infants' object concepts: A replication study.' *Child Development*, 42, 359-372.

Haith, M.M. & Campos, J.J. (1977) 'Human infancy'. *Annual Review of Psychology*, 28, 251-294.

Harris, P.L. (1975) 'Development of search and object permanence during infancy.' *Psychological Bulletin*, 82, 332-344.

Harris, P.L. (1983) 'Infant cognition.' In P.H. Mussen, M.M. Haith & J.J. Campos (eds), *Handbook of Child Psychology*, 4th ed., vol. 2, *Infancy and Developmental Psychology*, London: Wiley.

Miller, D.G., Cohen L.B. & Hill, K.T. (1970) 'A methodological investigation of Piaget's theory of object concept development in the sensory-motor period.' *Journal of Experimental Child Psychology*, 9, 59-85.

Piaget, J. (1955) *The Construction of Reality in the Child. London: Routledge & Kegan Paul.*

Rader, N., Spiro, D.J. & Firestone, P.B. (1979) 'Performance on a Stage IV object permanence task with standard and non-standard covers.' *Child Development*, 50, 908-910.

Scofield, L. & Uzgiris, I.C. (1969) 'Examining behavior and the development of the object concept.' Paper presented at the meeting of the Society of Research in Child Development, Santa Monica, CA.

Soroka, S.M., Corter, C.M. & Abramovitch, R. (1979) 'Infants' tactual discrimination of novel and familiar stimuli.' *Child Development*, 50, 1251-1253.

Uzgiris, I.C. (1973) 'Patterns of cognitive development in infancy.' *Merrill-Palmer Quarterly*, 19, 181-204.

White, B.L., Castle, P. & Held, R. (1964) 'Observations on the development of visually directed reaching.' *Child Development*, 35, 349-364.

Willatts, P. (1979) 'Adjustment of reaching to change in object position by young infants. *Child Development*, 50, 911-913.

Willatts, P. (1984) 'Stages in the development of intentional search by young infants.' *Developmental Psychology,* 20, 389-396.

Wishart, J.G. (1979) 'The development of the object concept in infancy.' Unpublished PhD thesis University of Edinburgh.

Wishart, J.G. & Bower, T.G.R. (1984) 'Spatial relations and the object concept: A normative study.' In. L.P. Lipsitt & C.K. Rovee-Collier (eds), *Advances in Infancy Research*, vol. 3, Norwood, NJ: Ablex.

Wishart, J.G., Bower, T.G.R. & Dunkeld, J. (1978) 'Reaching in the dark', *Perception*, 7, 506-512.

8. Object Permanence in 3½- and 4½-Month-Old Infants

Renée Baillargeon

These experiments tested object permanence in 3½- and 4½-month-old infants. The method used in the experiments was similar to that used by Baillargeon, Spelke, and Wasserman (1985). The infants were habituated to a solid screen that rotated back and forth through a 180° arc, in the manner of a drawbridge. Following habituation, a box was placed behind the screen and the infants were shown two test events. In one (possible event), the screen rotated until it reached the occluded box; in the other (impossible event), the screen rotated through a full 180° arc, as though the box were no longer behind it. The 4½-month-olds, and the 3½-month-olds who were fast habituators, looked reliably longer at the impossible than at the possible event, suggesting that they understood that (a) the box continued to exist after it was occluded by the screen and (b) the screen could not rotate through the space occupied by the occluded box. Control experiments conducted without the box supported this interpretation. The results of these experiments call into serious question Piaget's (1954) claims about the age at which object permanence emerges and about the processes responsible for its emergence.

Adults believe that an object cannot exist at two separate points in time without having existed during the interval between them. Piaget (1954) held that infants do not begin to share this belief until they reach about 9 months of age. The main evidence for this conclusion came from observations of young infants' reactions to hidden objects. Piaget noticed that prior to 9 months, infants do not search for objects they have observed being hidden. If a toy is covered with a cloth, for example, they make no attempt to lift the cloth and grasp the toy, even though they are capable of performing each of these actions. Piaget speculated that for young infants objects are not permanent entities that exist continuously in time but transient entities that cease to exist when they are no longer visible and begin to exist anew when they come back into view.

Although Piaget's (1954) observations have been confirmed by numerous researchers (see Gratch, 1975, 1977, Harris, in press, and Schuberth, 1983, for reviews), his interpretation of these observations has been questioned. A number of researchers (e.g., Baillargeon, Spelke, & Wasserman, 1985; Bower, 1974) have suggested that young infants might fail Piaget's search task, not because they lack object permanence, but because they are generally unable to perform coordinated actions. Studies of the development of action (e.g., Piaget, 1952; Uzgiris & Hunt, 1970) have shown that it is not until infants reach about 9 months of age that they begin to coordinate actions directed at separate objects into means-end sequences. In these sequences, infants

Renée Baillargeon: 'Object Permanence in 3½- and 4½-Month-Old Infants.' *DEVELOPMENTAL PSYCHOLOGY* (1987), Vol. 23, No. 5. pp. 655-664. Copyright © 1987 by the American Psychological Association, Inc. Reprinted by permission.

apply one action to one object so as to create conditions under which they can apply another action to another object (e.g., pulling a cushion to get a toy placed on it or deliberately releasing a toy so as to grasp another toy). Thus, young infants could fail Piaget's task simply because it requires them to coordinate separate actions on separate objects.

This interpretation suggests that young infants might show evidence of object permanence if given tests that did *not* require coordinated actions. Bower (1967, 1974; Bower, Broughton, & Moore, 1971; Bower & Wishart, 1972) devised several such tests and obtained results that he took to indicate that by 2 months of age, if not sooner, infants already possess a notion of object permanence. Bower's tests, however, have been faulted on methodological and theoretical grounds (e.g., Baillargeon, 1986, in press; Baillargeon *et al.*, 1985; Gratch, 1975, 1977; Harris, in press; Muller & Aslin, 1978).

Because of the problems associated with Bower's tests, Baillargeon *et al.* (1985) sought a new means of testing object permanence in young infants. The test they devised was indirect: It focused on infants' understanding of the principle that a solid object cannot move through the space occupied by another solid object. The authors reasoned that if infants were surprised when a visible object appeared to move through the space occupied by a hidden object, it would suggest that they took account of the existence of the hidden object. In their study, 5½-month-old infants were habituated to a screen that rotated back and forth through a 180° arc, in the manner of a drawbridge. Following habituation, a box was placed behind the screen and the infants were shown two test events. In one (possible event), the screen rotated until it reached the occluded box and then returned to its initial position. In the other (impossible event), the screen rotated until it reached the occluded box and then continued as though the box were no longer behind it! The screen rotated through a full 180° arc before it reversed direction and returned to its initial position, revealing the box standing intact in the same location as before. The infants looked reliably longer at the impossible than at the possible event, suggesting that they understood that (a) the box continued to exist after it was occluded by the screen and (b) the screen could not rotate through the space occupied by the occluded box.

The results of Baillargeon et al. indicate that, contrary to Piaget's claims, 5½-month-old infants understand that an object continues to exist when occluded. The first experiment reported here attempted to extend these results by examining whether younger infants, 4½-month-olds, expect the continued existence of occluded objects.

There are two reasons to ask whether younger infants have object permanence. The first is purely descriptive: Before we can propose a theory of the development of infants' beliefs about objects, we must establish *what* beliefs they hold at different ages. The second is more theoretical: The age at which infants are granted a notion of object permanence will undoubtedly constrain the nature of the mechanism we invoke to explain the attainment of this notion. Piaget (1952, 1954) attributed the emergence of object permanence to the coordination of sensorimotor schemes, which, as was mentioned earlier, begins at about 9 months of age. The discovery by Baillargeon et al. that 5½-month-olds already possess a notion of object permanence is clearly inconsistent with Piaget's account. What mechanism could explain the presence of this notion in infants aged 5½ months or less? This question will be addressed in the General Discussion section.

Experiment 1

The method used in Experiment I was similar to that used by Baillargeon et al. (1985); it is depicted in Figure 1.

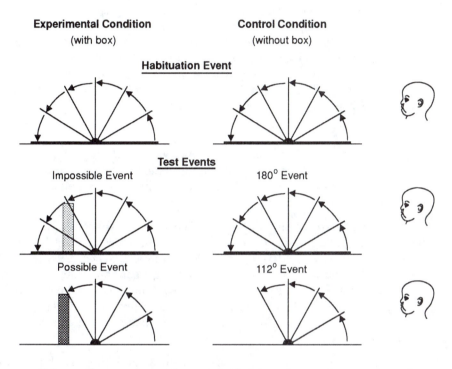

Figure 1 **Schematic representation of the habituation and test events shown to the infants in the experimental and control conditions in Experiment 1**

There was one foreseeable difficulty with the design of Experiment 1. The infants might look longer at the impossible than at the possible event, not because they were surprised to see the screen rotate through the space occupied by the occluded box, but because they found the 180° screen rotation more interesting than the shorter, 112° rotation shown in the possible event. In order to check this possibility, a second group of $4\frac{1}{2}$-month-olds was tested in a control condition identical to the experimental condition except that there was *no box* behind the screen during the test events (see Figure 1). If the infants in the experimental condition looked longer at the impossible event because they preferred the 180° to the 112° rotation, then the infants in the control condition should also look longer at the 180° event. On the other hand, if the infants in the experimental condition looked longer at the impossible event because they were surprised when the screen failed to stop against the occluded box, then the infants in the control condition should look equally at the 180° and the 112° events because no box was present behind the screen.[1]

Method

Subjects

Subjects were 24 full-term infants ranging in age from 4 months, 2 days to 5 months, 2 days (M = 4 months, 14 days). Half of the infants are assigned to the experimental condition and half to the control condition. Another 5 infants were excluded from the experiment, 3 because of fussiness, 1 because of drowsiness, and 1 because of equipment failure. The infants' names in this experiment and in the succeeding experiments were obtained from birth announcements in a local newspaper. Parents were contacted by letters and follow-up phone calls; they were offered reimbursement for their travel expenses but were not compensated for their participation.

Apparatus

The apparatus consisted of a large wooden box that was 120 cm high, 95 cm wide, and 74 cm deep. The infant faced an opening, 49 cm high and 95 cm wide, in the front wall of the apparatus. The interior of the apparatus was painted black and was decorated with narrow pink and green stripes.

At the center of the apparatus was a silver cardboard screen that was 31 cm high, 28 cm wide, and 0.5 cm thick. The lower edge of the screen, which was set 0.5 cm above the floor of the apparatus, was affixed to a thick metal rod that was 28.5 cm long and 1 cm in diameter. This rod was connected to a right-angle gear box that was 2 cm high, 3.5 cm wide, and 4 cm deep. A drive rod, which was 0.5 cm in diameter, was also connected to the gear box. This rod was 54 cm long and protruded through the back wall of the apparatus. By rotating this rod, an experimenter could rotate the screen back and forth through a 180° arc.[2]

A wooden box, 25 cm high, 15 cm wide, and 5 cm thick, could be introduced into the apparatus through a hidden door in its back wall. This box was painted yellow and was decorated with a two-dimensional clown face. The box was placed on a platform, which was 21 cm wide and 28 cm long, in the floor of the apparatus, behind the screen. This platform was mounted on a vertical slide located underneath the apparatus. By lowering the platform, after the screen occluded the box from the infants view, an experimenter could surreptitiously remove the box from the path of the screen.

The infant was tested in a brightly lit room. Four clip-on lights (each with a 40-W lightbulb) were attached to the back and side walls of the apparatus to provide additional light. Two frames, each 183 cm high and 71 cm wide and covered with black cloth, stood at an angle on either side of the apparatus. These frames isolated the infant from the experimental room. At the end of each trial, a muslin-covered curtain 65 cm high and 95 cm wide, was lowered in front of the opening in the front wall of the apparatus.

Experimental-condition events

Two experimenters worked in concert to produce the events in the experimental condition. The first operated the screen, and the second operated the platform.

Impossible test event. To start, the screen lay flat against the floor of the apparatus toward the infant. The yellow box stood clearly visible, centered 12.5 cm behind the screen. The first experimenter rotated the screen at the approximate rate of 45°/s until it had completed a 90° arc at which point she paused for 1 s. This pause allowed the second experimenter to lower the platform supporting the box. The first experimenter then continued to rotate the screen toward the back wall at the same rate of about 45°/s until it lay flat against the floor of the apparatus, covering the space previously occupied by the box. The entire process was then repeated in reverse: The first experimenter rotated the screen 90° and paused for 1 s, allowing the second experimenter to raise the platform; the first experimenter then lowered the screen to its original position against the floor of the apparatus, revealing the box standing intact in the same position as before.

Each full cycle of movement thus lasted approximately 10 s. The box remained occluded for about 8 of these 10 s: It was in view only during the first and last seconds, when the screen was raised less than 45°. There was a 1-s pause between successive cycles. Cycles were repeated until the computer signaled that the trial had ended (see below). At that point, the second experimenter lowered the curtain in front of the apparatus.

Possible test event. As before, the first experimenter rotated the screen 90° at the rate of about 45°/s and then paused for 1 s, allowing the second experimenter to lower the platform. The first experimenter then continued to rotate the screen 22.5^o toward the back wall (where the screen would have contacted the box had the latter not been lowered), taking about 0.5 s to complete this movement. The first experimenter held the screen in this position for 2 s, and then the entire process was repeated in reverse: The first experimenter returned the screen to the 90° position, paused for 1 s (to allow the second experimenter to raise the platform), and then lowered the screen to its initial position against the floor of the apparatus. Each full cycle of movement thus lasted about 9 s, with the box remaining totally occluded for about 7 of these 9 s.[3]

Habituation event. The habituation event was exactly the same as the impossible test event, except that the box was absent.

Control-condition events

180° and 112° test events. The 180° and the 112° test events shown to the infants in the control condition were identical to the impossible and possible test events (respectively) shown to the infants in the experimental condition, except that the box was absent.

Habituation event. The habituation event shown to the infants in the control condition was identical to that shown to the infants in the experimental condition.

The platform was moved in the same manner in all of the events to ensure that the sounds that accompanied the lowering and raising of the platform could not contribute to differences in the infants' looking times between and within conditions.

Procedure

Prior to the beginning of the experiment, each infant was allowed to manipulate the yellow box for a few seconds while the parent filled out consent forms. During the experiment, the infant sat on the parent's lap in front of the apparatus. The infant's head was approximately 65 cm from the screen and 100 cm from the back wall. The parent was asked not to interact with the infant while the experiment was in progress. At the start of the test trials, the parent was instructed to close his or her eyes.

The infant's looking behavior was monitored by two observers who viewed the infant through peepholes in the cloth-covered frames on either side of the apparatus. The observers could not see the experimental events and did not know the order in which the test events were presented. Each observer held a button box linked to a MICRO/PDP-11 computer and depressed the button when the infant attended to the experimental events. Interobserver agreement was calculated for each trial on the basis of the number of seconds for which the observers agreed on the direction of the infant's gaze out of the total number of seconds the trial lasted. Disagreements of less than 0.1 s were ignored. Agreement in this experiment as well as in the subsequent experiments averaged 88% (or more) per trial per infant. The looking times recorded by the primary observer were used to determine when a trial had ended and when the habituation criterion had been met (see below).

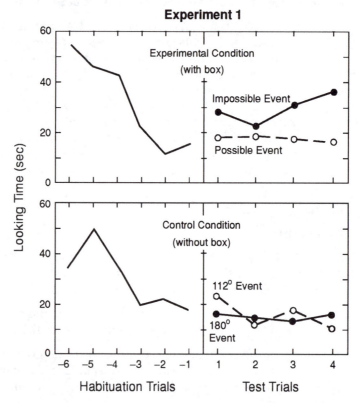

Figure 2   **Looking times of the infants in the experimental and control conditions in Experiment 1 during the habituation and test trials. (Note that the habituation trials are numbered backward from the trial in which habituation was reached.)**

At the start of the experiment, each infant received a familiarization trial to acquaint him or her with the position of the box behind the screen. During this trial, the screen lay flat against the floor of the apparatus, with the box standing clearly visible behind it. The trial ended when the infant (a) looked away from the display for 2 consecutive seconds after having looked at it for at least 10 cumulative seconds, or (b) looked at the display for 30 cumulative seconds without looking away for 2 consecutive seconds.

Following the familiarization trial, each infant was habituated to the habituation event described above, using an infant-control procedure (after Horowitz, 1975). The main purpose of this habituation phase was to familiarize the infant with the (relatively unusual) motion of the screen.[4] Each habituation trial ended when the infant (a) looked away from the event for 2 consecutive seconds after having looked at it for at least 5 cumulative seconds (the duration of a half-cycle), or (b) looked at the event for 60 cumulative seconds without looking away for 2 consecutive seconds. The intertrial interval was 2-3 s. Habituation trials continued until the infant reached a criterion of habituation of a 50% or greater decrease in looking time on three consecutive trials, relative to the infant's looking time on the first three trials. If the criterion was not met within nine trials, the habituation phase was ended at that point. Therefore, the minimum number of habituation trials an infant could receive was six, and the maximum number was nine. Only 3 of the infants failed to reach the habituation criterion within nine trials; the other 21 infants took an average of 6.62 trials to satisfy the criterion. It should be noted that, in this experiment as in the subsequent experiments, infants who failed to reach the habituation criterion within nine trials were not terminated: At the completion of the ninth habituation trial, the experimenters simply proceeded to the test phase.

After the habituation phase, the infants in the experimental condition saw the impossible and the possible test events on alternate trials until they had completed four pairs of test trials. Similarly, the infants in the control condition saw the $180°$ and the $112°$ test events on alternate trials until they had completed four pairs of test trials. Within each condition, half of the infants saw one test event first and the other half saw the other test event first. At the beginning of each test trial, the first experimenter waited to move the screen until the computer signaled that the infant had looked inside the apparatus for 2 cumulative seconds. This ensured that the infants in the experimental condition had noted the presence of the box behind the screen. The criteria used to determine the end of each test trial were the same as for the habituation trials.

Six of the 24 infants in the experiment completed fewer than four pairs of test trials. Five infants completed only three pairs, 3 because of fussiness, 1 because of procedural error, and 1 because the primary observer could not follow the direction of the infant's gaze. The other infant completed only two pairs, because of fussiness. All subjects (in this experiment as well as in the subsequent experiments) were included in the data analyses, whether or not they had completed the full complement of four pairs of test trials.

Results

Figure 2 presents the mean looking times of the infants in the experimental and control conditions during the habituation and test phases of the experiment. It can be seen that the infants in the experimental condition looked longer at the impossible than at the possible event, whereas the infants in the control condition looked equally at the $180°$ and the $112°$ events.

The infants' looking times to the test events were analyzed by means of a 2 x 2 x 4 x 2 mixed-model analysis of variance (ANOVA), with Condition (experimental or control) and Order (impossible/$180°$ or possible/$112°$ event first) as the between-subjects factors, and with Event (impossible/ $180°$ or possible/$112°$) and Test Pair (first, second, third, or fourth pair of test trials) as the within-subjects factors. Because the design was unbalanced, the SAS GLM procedure was used to calculate the ANOVA (SAS Institute, 1985). There was a significant main effect of condition, $F(1, 20) = 8.53, p < .01$, and of event, $F(1, 126) = 6.16, p < .05$, and a significant Condition x Event interaction, $F(1, 126) = 8.50, p < .005$. Planned comparisons indicated that the infants in the experimental condition looked reliably longer at the impossible ($M = 29.2, SD = 20.6$) than at the possible ($M = 17.7, SD = 13.1$) event, $F(1, 126) = 14.48, p < .0005$, whereas the infants in the control condition looked equally at the $180°$ ($M = 15.1, SD = 9.3$) and the $112°$ ($M = 16.2, SD = 12.3$) events, $F(1, 126) = 0.12$.

The analysis also revealed a significant Order x Event interaction, $F(1, 126) = 4.64, p < .05$. Post hoc comparisons indicated that the infants who saw the impossible/$180°$ event first looked reliably longer at this event ($M = 24.17, SD = 16.88$) than at the possible/$112°$ event ($M = 14.45, SD = 9.51$), $F(1, 126) = 10.56, p < .005$, whereas the infants who saw the possible/$112°$ event first tended to look equally at the impossible/$180°$ ($M = 20.24, SD = 18.01$) and the possible/$112°$ ($M = 19.67, SD = 14.99$) events, $F(1, 126) = 0.03$. Such order effects are not uncommon in infancy research and are of little theoretical interest.

Discussion

The infants in the experimental condition looked reliably longer at the impossible than at the possible event, suggesting that they understood that (a) the box continued to exist after it was occluded by the screen, and (b) the screen could not move through the space occupied by the occluded box. In contrast to the infants in the experimental condition, the infants in the control condition tended to look equally at the $180°$ and the $112°$ events. This finding provides evidence that the infants in the experimental condition looked longer at the impossible event, not because they found the $180°$ screen rotation intrinsically more interesting than the $112°$ rotation, but because they expected the screen to stop when it reached the occluded box and were surprised that it failed to do so.

The results of Experiment 1 suggest that, contrary to Piaget's (1954) claims, infants as young as $4\frac{1}{2}$ months of age understand that an object continues to exist when occluded. Experiment 2 investigated whether infants aged $3\frac{1}{2}$-4 months also possess a notion of object permanence. The design of this experiment was identical to that of Experiment 1.

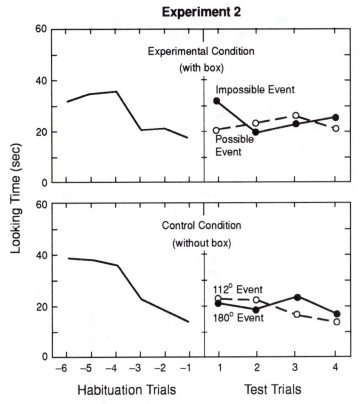

Figure 3   **Looking times of the infants in the experimental and control conditions in Experiment 2 during the habituation and test trials**

Experiment 2

Method

Subjects

Subjects were 40 full-term infants ranging in age from 3 months, 15 days to 4 months, 3 days (M = 3 months, 24 days). More infants were tested in Experiment 2 than in Experiment 1 because pilot data indicated that the responses of these younger infants tended to be more variable; some infants produced consistently short looks, and other infants produced consistently long looks. Half of the infants were assigned to the experimental condition and half to the control condition. Six other infants were excluded from the experiment, 5 because of fussiness and 1 because of drowsiness.

Apparatus, events, and procedure

The apparatus, events, and procedure used in this experiment were the same as in Experiment 1. Of the 40 infants in the experiment, 12 failed to reach the habituation criterion within 9 trials; the others took an average of 7.14 trials to reach the criterion.

111

Ten infants contributed only three pairs of test trials to the data analyses, 7 because of fussiness, 1 because he would not look at the events, 1 because of procedural error, and 1 because of equipment failure.

Results

Figure 3 presents the mean looking times of the infants in the experimental and control conditions during the habituation and test phases of the experiment. The infants' looking times during the test phase were analyzed as in the preceding experiment. The analysis revealed no significant main effects or interactions, all Fs < 2.69, ps > .05.

Fast and slow habituators

Examination of the infants' looking times during the habituation and test phases of the experiment suggested that the pattern revealed by the initial analysis (statistically equal looking times to the impossible/180° and the possible/112° events) represented the average of two distinct looking patterns. Specifically, it appeared that, in the experimental condition, the infants who reached the habituation criterion within six or seven trials tended to look longer at the impossible than at the possible event, whereas the infants who required eight or nine trials to reach the criterion or who did not reach the criterion tended to look equally at the two test events. In the control condition, in contrast, both groups of infants tended to look equally at the 180° and the 112° events. These patterns were not unexpected, because rate of habituation is known to relate to posthabituation performance (Bornstein & Benasich, 1986; DeLoache, 1976; McCall, 1979).

The infants were therefore classified as *fast* habituators (the infants who took six or seven trials to reach the habituation criterion) and *slow* habituators (the infants who required eight or nine trials to reach the criterion or who failed to reach the criterion within nine trials). In the experimental condition, 9 infants were classified as fast habituators and 11 as slow habituators. In the control condition, 7 infants were classified as fast habituators and 12 as slow habituators (the remaining infant could not satisfy the habituation criterion because he produced very short looks on each trial[5]; because it was unclear how this infant should be classified, he was excluded from the next analyses).

The looking times of the fast and slow habituators in the experimental and control conditions to the test events were analyzed by means of a 2 x 2 x 2 x 4 x 2 mixed-model ANOVA with Habituation (fast or slow habituators), Condition (experimental or control), and Order (impossible/180° or possible/112°) as the between-subjects factors, and with Test Pair (first, second, third, and fourth pair of test trials) and Event (impossible/180° or possible/112°) as the within-subject factors. As anticipated, this analysis yielded a significant Habituation x Condition x Event interaction, $F(1, 189) = 6.54, p < .05$. In order to study this interaction, four comparisons were carried out. These indicated that in the experimental condition, the fast habituators looked reliably longer at the impossible ($M = 23.78, SD = 18.28$) than at the possible ($M = 14.68, SD = 11.79$) event, $F(1, 189) = 7.38, p < .01$, whereas the slow habituators looked about equally at the two events (impossible, $M = 23.45, SD = 19.05$; possible, $M = 27.68, SD = 20.97$), $F(1, 189) = 1.75, p > .05$ (see Figure 4).[6] In the control condition, the fast habituators looked about equally at the $180°$ ($M = 17.06$, $SD = 15.45$) and $112°$ ($M = 19.80$, $SD = 18.09$) events, $F(1, 189) = 0.48$, as did the slow habituators ($180°$ event, $M = 20.34$, $SD = 16.87$; $112°$ event, $M = 18.30$, $SD = 15.10$), $F(1, 189) = 0.41$. There were no other significant main effects or interactions (all Fs < 3.53, $ps > .05$).

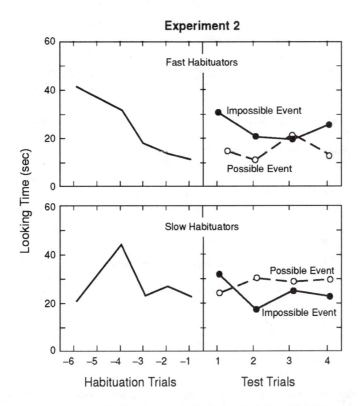

Figure 4   Looking times of the fast and slow habituators in Experiment 2 (experimental condition) during the habituation and test trials

At the end of each habituation and test trial, the observers rated the state of the infant. Examination of these ratings revealed that during the habituation trials, the slow and fast habituators did not differ in amount of fussiness: Only four (17%) slow and three (19%) fast habituators were judged by the observers to have been slightly or moderately fussy on two or more trials. During the test trials, however, the slow habituators tended to be slightly fussier than the fast habituators. Seven (30%) slow habituators, but only one (6%) fast habituator, completed fewer than four pairs of test trials because of fussiness. Furthermore, nine (39%) slow habituators, but only four (25%) fast habituators, were rated as slightly or moderately fussy on two or more test trials.

Why were the slow habituators fussier than the fast habituators during the test trials? One reason might be that, having looked longer during the habituation phase, the slow habituators were more likely to become tired or bored during the test phase. A one-way ANOVA indicated that the slow habituators ($M = 254.59$, $SD = 99.90$) looked reliably longer overall during the habituation trials than did the fast habituators (M = 180.94, SD = 62.87), $F(1, 35)$ = 6.39, $p < .05$. Hence, the slow habituators might have been somewhat fussier during the test trials because they were more tired, bored, or restless.

Discussion

The fast habituators in the experimental condition showed a pronounced preference for the impossible over the possible event, a preference akin to that observed in the $4\frac{1}{2}$-month-olds in Experiment 1. In contrast, the fast habituators in the control condition tended to look equally at the 180° and the 112° events. Together, these results indicate that the fast habituators in the experimental condition looked longer at the impossible event, not because they found the 180° rotation of the screen more interesting than the 112° rotation, but because they were surprised or puzzled to see the screen rotate through the space occupied by the occluded box. Such results suggest that at least some infants between the ages of $3\frac{1}{2}$ and 4 months realize that an object continues to exist when occluded.

The slow habituators in the experimental condition, in contrast to the fast habituators, tended to look equally at the impossible and the possible events. The marked discrepancy in the responses of these two groups of infants will be discussed in the General Discussion.

Experiment 3: Replication

Given the unexpected nature and potential significance of the results obtained in the experimental condition of Experiment 2, it seemed important that they be confirmed. Experiment 3 attempted to do so with $3\frac{1}{2}$-month-old infants.

Method

Subjects

Subjects were 24 full-term infants ranging in age from 3 months, 6 days to 3 months, 25 days (M = 3 months, 15 days). Five additional infants were eliminated from the experiment, 4 because of fussiness, and 1 because the primary observer could not follow the direction of the infants gaze.

Apparatus and events

The apparatus was the same as that used in the preceding experiments, with one exception. Instead of the yellow box, a brightly colored, three-dimensional *Mr. Potato Head* was used. Casual observations indicated that most infants found this toy more attractive than the box.

Because Mr. Potato Head was shorter than the box (15.5 cm as opposed to 25 cm), the screen was rotated 135°, instead of 112°, in the possible event. That is, after rotating the screen 90° at the usual rate of $45^{\circ}/s$ and then pausing for 1 s, as before, the primary experimenter rotated the screen 45° toward the back wall of the apparatus, taking 1 s to complete the movement. The first experimenter paused for 2 s and then repeated the same actions in reverse. Each full cycle of movement thus lasted approximately 10 s, as in the impossible event. Mr. Potato Head was totally occluded for about 8 of the 10s.

Procedure

The procedure was the same as that of the experimental condition in Experiment 2, with one exception. In an attempt to abbreviate the test phase of the experiment, no pretrials were given at the beginning of the test trials.

Of the 24 infants in the experiment, 8 failed to reach the habituation criterion within 9 trials; the other infants took an average of 6.94 trials to reach the criterion. Five infants completed only three pairs of test trials, 4 because of fussiness, and 1 because the primary observer could not follow the direction of the infant's gaze. Another 2 infants completed only two test pairs because of fussiness.

Results

The looking times of the infants to the impossible and possible test events were first analyzed by means of a 2 x 4 x 2 mixed-model ANOVA, with Order (impossible or possible event first) as the between-subjects factor, and with Test Pair (first, second, third, or fourth pair of test trials) and Event (impossible or possible event) as the within-subjects factors. The analysis yielded no significant main effects or interactions, all Fs < 2.05, ps > .11.

Fast and slow habituators

Of the 24 infants who participated in the experiment, 12 were classified as fast habituators, and 12 were classified as slow habituators, using the same criteria as in Experiment 2.

Figure 5 shows the mean looking times of each group of infants during the habituation and test trials. The looking times of the two groups to the test events were analyzed by means of a 2 x 2 x 4 x 2 mixed-model ANOVA, with Habituation (fast or slow habituators) and Order (impossible or possible event first) as the between-subjects factors, and with Test Pair (first, second, third, or fourth test pair) and Event (impossible or possible event) as the within-subjects factors. As expected, the analysis yielded a significant Habituation x Event interaction, $F(1, 122) = 5.13, p < .05$. Planned comparisons showed that the fast habituators looked reliably longer at the impossible ($M = 21.97, SD = 16.33$) than at the possible ($M = 14.24, SD = 10.56$) event, $F(1, 122) = 6.35, p < .02$, whereas the slow habituators looked at the impossible ($M = 23.24, SD = 20.00$) and the possible ($M = 26.42, SD = 21.15$) events about equally, $F(1, 122) = .91$.

Comparison of the fast and slow habituators indicated that they did not differ in fussiness during the habituation trials: Only one infant, a slow habituator, was judged to have been fussy on two or more habituation trials. However, as in Experiment 2, the slow habituators tended to be fussier than the fast habituators during the test trials. Five of the slow habituators, but only one of the fast habituators, completed fewer than four test pairs due to fussiness. In addition, seven slow habituators, but only three fast habituators, were fussy on two or more trials. A one-way ANOVA showed that, as in Experiment 2, the slow habituators ($M = 218.59, SD = 139.75$) tended to look longer overall during the habituation trials than did the fast habituators ($M = 140.25, SD = 37.80$), $F(1,21) = 3.50, p = .075$.

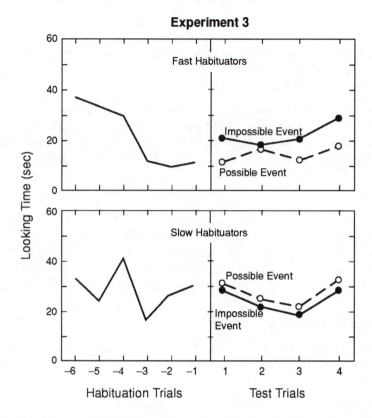

Figure 5 **Looking times of the fast and slow habituators in Experiment 3 during the habituation and test trials**

Discussion

The results of Experiment 3 replicated those of the experimental condition in Experiment 2. The fast habituators looked reliably longer at the impossible than at the possible event, suggesting that they were surprised or puzzled to see the screen move through the space occupied by Mr. Potato Head.

Could the fast habituators' preference for the impossible event be due to their having found the 180° screen rotation intrinsically more interesting than the shorter rotation shown in the possible event? This interpretation seems highly unlikely for two reasons. First, the fast habituators in the control conditions of Experiments 1 and 2 did not show an overall preference for the 180° rotation. Second, the slow habituators in Experiment 3 looked about equally at the impossible and the possible events. It is difficult to imagine why the fast, but not the slow, habituators would have found the 180° rotation intrinsically more interesting than the shorter, 135° rotation shown in the possible event.

General Discussion

The $4^{1}/_{2}$-month-olds in Experiment 1 and the $3^{1}/_{2}$-month-olds in Experiments 2 and 3 who were fast habituators all looked reliably longer at the impossible than at the possible event, suggesting that they understood that (a) the object behind the screen (i.e., box or Mr. Potato Head) continued to exist after the screen rotated upward and occluded it and (b) the screen could not move through the space occupied by the object. The results of the control conditions in Experiments 1 and 2 provide support for this interpretation. These results indicated that when no object was present behind the screen, the infants did not look longer at the 180° screen rotation.

These results call into question Piaget's (1954) claims about the *age* at which object permanence is attained, about the *processes* responsible for its emergence, and about the *behaviors* by which it is manifested. These are discussed in turn.

Piaget maintained that it is not until infants reach about 9 months of age that they begin to view objects as permanent. However, the results of the experiments reported here indicate that infants as young as $3^{1}/_{2}$ months of age already realize that objects continue to exist when occluded. This finding does not mean that by $3^{1}/_{2}$ months, infants' conception of occluded objects is as sophisticated as that of older infants. Further research is necessary to determine whether young infants are able to represent not only the existence but also the physical and spatial characteristics of occluded objects (e.g., Baillargeon, 1986, in press; Baillargeon & Graber, in press).

Piaget also held that the emergence of object permanence depends on the coordination of sensorimotor schemes, which begins at about 9 months of age. The present findings, like those of Baillargeon *et al.* (1985), are inconsistent with this explanation, because they suggest that infants possess a notion of object permanence long before they begin to perform coordinated actions.

How can we account for the presence of a notion of object permanence in $3^{1}/_{2}$-month-old infants? One possibility is that this notion is innate (e.g., Bower, 1971; Spelke, 1985). Spelke (1985), for example, hypothesized that infants are born with a conception of objects as spatially bounded entities that exist continuously in time and move continuously in space, maintaining their internal unity and external boundaries. This conception, according to Spelke, provides infants with a basis for recognizing that objects continue to exist when occluded. A second possibility is that infants are born, not with a substantive belief in the permanence of objects, but with a learning mechanism that is capable of arriving at this notion given a limited set of pertinent observations.[7] These observations could arise from infants' examination of the displacements and interactions of objects (Mandler, 1986) as well as from infants' actions upon objects. Although infants do not show mature reaching for objects until about 4 months of age (e.g., Granrud, 1986: von Hofsten, 1980), infants less than 4 months often perform arm extensions in the presence of objects (e.g., Bruner & Koslowski, l972; Field, 1976; Provine & Westerman, 1979). Infants might notice, when performing these arm extensions, that their hands sometimes occlude and sometimes are occluded by objects (Harris,1983). The same point can be made about infants' manipulations of objects. White (1969) reported that beginning at about 3 months of age, objects that are placed in one hand are often brought to the midline to be simultaneously viewed and explored tactually by the other hand. Infants might notice in the course of these manipulations that their hands occlude (parts of) the objects.

The results of the present experiments are not sufficient to determine which (if either) of the two hypotheses mentioned above better explains the presence of object permanence in 3½-month-old infants. What these results do indicate, however, is that whatever explanation is proposed cannot depend on perceptual or motor abilities more sophisticated than those available after the third month of life.

Piaget viewed the search for hidden objects as the hallmark of object permanence. Yet the present results indicate that infants possess object permanence long before they begin to engage in search activities. How can we explain this discrepancy? Why do infants' actions lag so far behind their understanding? One possibility, alluded to in the introduction, is that young infants may fail to search because they are generally unable to perform sequences of actions in which one action is applied to one object in order to create conditions under which another action can be applied to another object (e.g., pulling a cushion to get an object placed on it). Why infants should have difficulty with these types of action sequences remains somewhat of a mystery. Piaget's (1952) remarkable observations of the development of action in infancy make it clear that 3- and 4-month-old infants can perform means-end sequences in which one action is applied to one object (e.g., pulling a chain) in order to produce a result involving another object (e.g., shaking a toy attached to the other end of the chain). Further research is needed to compare the cognitive and motor requirements of the means-end sequences observed at 3-4 and at 7-8 months to identify the source of the latter's difficulty.

A final issue raised by the results of the present experiments concerns the differences between the performances of the fast and slow habituators in Experiments 2 (experimental condition) and 3. Recall that the fast habituators looked longer at the impossible than at the possible event, whereas the slow habituators looked about equally at the two events. At least two explanations could be offered for the discrepancy between these two groups, one appealing to transient and the other to more stable differences between the fast and slow habituators.

The first possibility is that the slow habituators were less engaged by the experimental events than the fast habituators. Perhaps the slow habituators were less alert, or more distressed by their novel surroundings. In any case, they were less involved with the events: (a) they required more trials to reach the habituation criterion, if they reached it at all, and (b) they were more likely to become fussy during the test trials. In other words, because the task of interpreting the impossible and possible events was a difficult one for the young infants in Experiments 2 and 3, only the infants whose attention was fully engaged were able to grasp the underlying structure of the events (i.e., realized that the screen rotated through the space occupied by the occluded box). The infants whose attention wandered — because they were fussy, bored, hungry, or ill at ease in their unfamiliar surroundings — were apparently unable to do so.

Two predictions follow from this first interpretation. One is that whether a given 3½-month-old looks longer at the impossible event in any one test session should depend on his or her attentional state at the time of the session. The other is that, as infants grow older and the task of understanding the impossible and possible events becomes less difficult, attentional states should have less impact on their performances. Partial support for this prediction comes from the experimental condition of Experiment 1. Of the 12 infants in this condition, 8 were fast habituators (6-7 trials to criterion), and 4 were slow habituators (8-9 trials to criterion). Six of the 8 fast habituators (75%) and 3 of the 4 slow habituators (75%) looked at the impossible event for at least 9 s longer than at the possible event. For the younger infants in Experiments 2 (experimental condition) and 3 combined, the comparable figures were 17 of 21 (81%) fast habituators and 7 of 23 (31%) slow habituators.

The second interpretation for the discrepancy in the responses of the fast and slow habituators is that it reflects, not transient fluctuations in alertness and mental involvement, but stable, meaningful differences between the two groups of infants. Suppose that the fast habituators were generally more efficient than the slow habituators at processing information about the physical world — at detecting, discriminating, representing, and categorizing regularities about objects and events. One consequence might be that at the time of testing, the fast habituators had already formed strong expectations about the permanence and the solidity of objects, whereas the slow habituators had just begun developing these expectations. This would explain why the fast habituators showed marked and consistent attention to the impossible event and why the slow habituators did not.

Note that the hypothesized difference between fast and slow habituators need not be cognitive in origin: It could also be motivational (e.g., fast habituators might be more motivated or more persistence in their examination of the physical world), social (e.g., fast habituators might have caretakers who consistently direct their attention toward objects), or physiological (e.g., fast habituators might have better state control) (cf. Bornstein & Benasich, 1986; Bornstein & Sigman, 1986).

Longitudinal data will be needed to decide which (if either) of the two interpretations put forth is accurate. If one finds that the same infants show a preference for the impossible event when they habituate quickly and fail to show this preference when they habituate more slowly, one might be warranted to conclude that the infants possess a notion of object permanence but only manifest this notion when they are sufficiently alert and calm to attend to the events. A simpler test of object permanence, one necessitating less sustained attention, might be less subject to the vagaries of infants' attentional states.

The results of the experiments reported in this article indicate that by $3\frac{1}{2}$ months of age, infants already possess expectations about the behavior of objects in time and space. Specifically, infants assume that objects continue to exist when occluded and that objects cannot move through the space occupied by other objects. It is likely that further investigations of young infants' physical knowledge will bring to light further competence. As the picture of infants' physical world becomes more complex, the task of describing how they attain, represent, and use their physical knowledge will undoubtedly open new avenues into the central issue of the origins of human cognition.

Acknowledgements

This research was supported by a grant from the National Institute of Child Health and Human Development (HD-21104).

I thank Jerry DeJong, Judy Deloache, Julia DeVos, Marcia Graber, Stephanie Hanko-Summers, and Jerry Parrott for their careful reading of the manuscript. I also thank Earle Heffley, Tom Kessler, and Oskar Richter for their technical assistance; Dawn Iacobucci and Stanley Wasserman for their help with the statistical analyses; and Marcia Graber, Stephanie Hanko-Summers, Julie Toombs, Anna Szado, and the undergraduates working in the Infant Cognition Laboratory at the University of Illinois for the help with the data collection. I also thank the parents who kindly agreed to have their infants participate in the studies.

Notes

1. The control condition was conducted without the box, rather than with the box to the side of the screen as in Baillargeon *et al.* (1985), to avoid a possible ambiguity. If the infants looked equally at the 180° and the 112° events, with the box to the side, one could not be sure whether (a) they had an equal preference for the two rotations or (b) they fixated the box and ignored the screen. Baillargeon *et al.* found, in their control experiment, that the order in which the infants saw the two screen events had a reliable effect on their looking behavior; such a finding rules out the possibility that the infants were merely staring at the box. Nevertheless, because of this potential confound, it seemed best to conduct the control experiment without the box.

2. In order to help the experimenter move the screen at a constant, steady pace, a protractor was attached to the drive rod. In addition, the experimenter listened through headphones to a metronome clicking once per second.

3. The 2-s pause in the possible event was introduced to make the rate of disappearance and reappearance of the box more similar in the two events. With the pause, the occlusion time of the box was 8 out of 10 s in the impossible event and 7 out of 9 s in the possible event. Making these two figures highly similar helped ensure that (a) the infants could not discriminate between the two events on the basis of rate differences and (b) the observers could not identify the events by the rate at which the platform was lowered and raised. Pilot data collected with the two observers indicated that they were unable to guess which event was being shown on the basis of the sounds associated with the movement of the platform.

4. It is interesting to speculate about the role of the habituation trials in the experiment. As stated in the text, the main rationale for including these trials was to familiarize the infants with the (presumably unfamiliar) movement of the screen. However, it could be that such familiarization was not necessary and that the infants would have responded in the same way had they received no habituation trials. Another possibility is that the habituation trials served to acquaint the infants with the fact that the screen rotated freely through empty space but stopped rotating when it encountered a hard surface. This hypothesis predicts that the infants would look less at the possible event (in which the screen rotated freely until it reached the occluded box) than at the impossible event (in which the screen continued to rotate after encountering the box). Further research is needed to evaluate these and related alternatives.

5. Because the minimal looking time for any test trial was 5 s, an infant had to cumulate at least 30 s of looking across three consecutive trials in order to show a 50% decline in looking time.

6. It may seem puzzling that, although the fast and slow habituators differed in how long they looked at the possible event (fast, $M = 14.68$: slow, $M = 27.68$), both groups of infants looked about equally at the impossible event (fast, $M = 23.78$; slow, $M = 23.45$). One might want to suggest, on the basis of these data, that although both groups of infants dishabituated to the impossible event (because it was impossible), only the slow habituators dishabituated to the possible event (perhaps because of the novel screen rotation). However, examination of the habituation data in Figure 4 argues against this interpretation. The fast habituators' mean looking time on their last three habituation trials ($M = 14.13$) was similar to their mean looking time to the possible ($M = 14.68$) but not to the impossible ($M = 23.78$) event. In contrast, the slow habituators' mean looking time on their last three habituation trials ($M = 22.46$) was similar to their mean looking time to the impossible ($M = 23.45$) and, to a lesser extent, to the possible ($M = 27.68$) event. The fast and slow habituators' equal looking times to the impossible event would thus reflect differences in their absolute levels of looking at the events, rather than similarities in their processing of the events.

7. I have left open the question of whether the learning mechanism is constrained in terms of the types of observations it can detect or the nature of the generalizations it can derive.

References

Baillargeon, R. (1986) 'Representing the existence and the location of hidden objects: Object permanence in six- and eight-month-old infants.' *Cognition*, 23, 21-41.

Baillargeon, R. (in press) 'Young infants' reasoning about the physical and spatial properties of a hidden object.' *Cognitive Development*.

Baillargeon, R., & Graber, M. (in press) 'Where is the rabbit?: 5.5-month-old infants' representation of the height of a hidden object.' *Cognitive Development*.

Baillargeon, R., Spelke, E. S., & Wasserman, S. (1985) 'Object permanence in five-month-old infants.' Cognition, 20, 191-208.

Bornstein, M.H., & Benasich, A.A. (1986) 'Infant habituation: Assessments of individual differences and short-term reliability at five months.' Child Development, 57, 87-99.

Bornstein, M.H., & Sigman, M.D. (1986) 'Continuity in mental development from infancy.' *Child Development*, 57, 251-274.

Bower, T.G.R. (1967) 'The development of object permanence: Some studies of existence constancy.' *Perception and Psychophysics*, 2, 411-418.

Bower, T.G.R. (1971) 'The object in the world of the infant.' *Scientific American*, 225, 30-38.

Bower, T.G.R. (1974) *Development in infancy.* San Francisco: Freeman.

Bower, T.G.R., Broughton, J., & Moore, M.K (1971) 'Development of the object concept as manifested in changes in the tracking behavior of infants between 7 and 20 weeks of age.' *Journal of Experimental Child Psychology*, 11, 182-193.

Bower, T.G.R., & Wishart, J.G. (1972) 'The effects of motor skill on object permanence.' *Cognition*, 1, 165-171.

Brune:, J.S., & Koslowski, B. (1972) 'Visually preadapted constituents of manipulatory action.' *Perception,* 1, 3- 14.

DeLoache, J.S. (1976) 'Rate of habituation and visual memory in infants.' *Child Development*, 47, 145-154.

Field, J. (1976) 'Relation of young, infants' reaching to stimulus distance and solidity.' *Developmental Psychology*, 12, 444-448.

Granrud, C.E. (1986) 'Binocular vision and spatial perception in 4- and 5-month-old infants.' *Journal of Experimental Psychology: Human Perception and Performance*, 12, 36-49.

Gratch, G. (1975) 'Recent studies based on Piaget's view of object concept development.' In L.B. Cohen & P. Salapatek (Eds.), *Infant Perception: From sensation to cognition* (Vol. 2, pp. 51-99). New York: Academic Press.

Gratch, G. (1977) 'Review of Piagetian infancy research: Object concept development.' In W.F. Overton & J.M. Gallagher (Eds.), *Knowledge and development: Advances in research and theory* (*1*) (pp. 59-91). New York: Plenum.

Harris, P.L. (1983) 'Infant cognition.' In P.H. Mussen (Series Ed.) & M.M. Haith & J.J. Campos (Vol. Eds.), *Handbook of child psychology*: Vol. 2. *Infancy and developmental psychobiology* (4th ed.) New York: Wiley.

Harris, P.L. (in press) 'The development of search.' In P. Salapatek & L.B. Cohen (Eds.), *Handbook of infant perception.* New York: Academic Press.

Hofsten, C. von (1980) 'Predictive reaching for moving objects by human infants.' *Journal of Experimental Child Psychology*, 30, 369-382

Horowitz, F.D. (Ed.). (1975) 'Visual attention, auditory stimulation and language discrimination in young infants.' *Monographs of the Society for Research in Child Development*. 39 (Whole Nos.5-6).

Mandler, J.M. (1986) *How to build a baby: On the development of an accessible representational system.* Manuscript submitted for publication.

McCall, R.B. (1979) 'Individual differences in the pattern of habituation at 5 and 10 months of age.' *Developmental Psychology*, 15, 559-569.

Muller, A.A., & Aslin, R.N. (1978) 'Visual tracking as an index of the object concept.' *Infant Behavior and Development*, 1, 309-319.

Piaget, J. (1952) *The origins of intelligence in children.* New York: International University Press.

Piaget, J. (1954) *The construction of reality in the child.* New York: Basic.

Provine, R.B., & Westerman, J.A. (1979) 'Crossing the midline: Limits of early eye-hand behavior.' *Child Development*, 50, 437-441.

SAS User's Guide: Statistics, 1985 Edition. (1985) Gary, NC: SAS Institute Inc.

Schuberth, R.E. (1983) 'The infant's search for objects: Alternatives to Piaget's theory of concept development.' In L.P. Lipsitt & C.K. Rovee-Collier (Eds.), *Advances in Infancy Research* (Vol. 2). Norwood, NJ: Ablex.

Spelke, E.S. (1985) 'Perception of unity, persistence, and identity: Thoughts on infants' conceptions of objects.' In J. Mehler & R. Fox (Eds.), *Neonate cognition: Beyond the blooming buzzing confusion.* Hillsdale, NJ: Erlbaum.

Uzgiris, I. C., & Hunt, J. McV. (1970) *Assessment in infancy: Ordinal scales of psychological development.* Urbana, IL: University of Illinois Press.

White, B.L. (1969) 'The initial coordination of sensorimotor schemas in human infants: Piaget's ideas and the role of experience.' In D. Elkind & J.H. Flavell (Eds.), *Studies in cognitive development* (pp. 237-256). New York: Oxford University Press.

Social Attachment in Infancy

Since John Bowlby's influential work on the contribution of security of infant attachment to later life, researchers have attempted to investigate more objectively the range and sequelae of social attachments in infancy. Much of the impetus for this work came from Mary Ainsworth's studies in the 1960s and 1970s which provided a technique for assessing and classifying attachment behaviours shown by infants to their caregivers. Ainsworth's 'Strange Situation' comprises a series of episodes in which the infant's reactions to the leave-taking and reappearance of the parent in conjunction with the appearance of a stranger in a strange environment are recorded. The 'Strange Situation' is very much an analogue of the stressful situations created in Harry Harlow's studies of attachment in rhesus monkeys. According to the argument from evolution put forward by Bowlby, attachment behaviour (seeking close proximity to the primary caregiver) fulfils an adaptive function when the infant is stressed by an unfamiliar (and thus potentially harmful) event.

On this basis it is argued that the absence of the caregiver and the presence of a stranger will create fear or wariness in the infant. If the infant views the caregiver as a source of security, the infant will seek comfort from the caregiver upon his/her return. If, on the other hand, the infant does not view the caregiver as a source of security, then proximity seeking behaviour will either be absent or reduced/altered in some way.

Ainsworth identified three main types of attachment which have since been used by other researchers. 'Secure infants' (Type B) are those who seek proximity with the caregiver at reunion; 'Anxious-Avoidant' (Type A) infants are those who effectively ignore the caregiver upon reunion; 'Anxious-Resistant' (Type C) infants are those who initially approach the caregiver, but then show 'ambivalence' through refusing to be picked up or in other ways comforted. Ainsworth also identified a number of subgroups, but most of the published research does not make use of these. Indeed, many studies break down the categories into 'Secure' (Type B) versus 'Insecure' (Type A and Type C) infants.

The three articles appearing in this section deal with various issues relating to Bowlby's theory of attachment. For Bowlby, security of attachment was related to the quality of parenting received in the first two or three years of life. The paper by Alan Sroufe reviews the evidence from this perspective (the 'relationship model') and juxtaposes this with evidence relating to the view that security of attachment reflects the infant's character, rather than the relationship between caregiver and infant (the 'temperament model').

A related theme concerns 'sensitive periods' (see section on *Early Experience*) and developmental continuity. Bowlby argued that once established, the quality of the child's relations with adults was relatively stable and unchanging. In the *Early Experience* section, we encountered suggestive evidence relating to adopted children that indicated this view is likely to be erroneous. The article by Thompson *et al.* provides more direct evidence concerning how changing circumstances have an impact on the quality of attachments shown by infants. However, it is also the case that in some families' parenting styles and personal difficulties can be handed down to further generations. The article by Dowdney *et al.* explores how mothers who themselves received inadequate parenting as children relate in their turn to their own children. While this study does not relate directly to Bowlby's views of attachment, the evidence nonetheless resonates with his ideas. The reader is invited to conceive various explanations for this apparent cross-generational transmission of parent-child relationships.

9. Attachment Classification from the Perspective of Infant-Caregiver Relationships and Infant Temperament

L. Alan Sroufe

Recently a number of investigators have suggested that classification differences in the Ainsworth Strange Situation (anxious and secure patterns of attachment) may be due largely or in part to endogenous temperamental variation. In doing so, these investigators have suggested a dimensional-trait approach in place of a qualitatively different taxonomic approach. Moreover, much evidence is directly contrary to a strong temperament interpretation of attachment patterns (changing attachments, differing attachments with different caregivers, prospective data on the early characteristics of infants later classified as securely or anxiously attached). Other interactionist temperament models currently have not been tested sufficiently. At the same time, a host of research findings support the interpretation that Ainsworth assessments capture aspects of the relationship between infant and caregiver, as derived from the history of their interaction. This includes direct evidence from observations of infants and mothers over time, the influence of varying patterns of care within and between cultures, the impact of factors presumed to influence quality of care (e.g., social support, life stress, caregiver family history), and predictions of later parent behavior from strange situation assessments of infant behavior. The importance of understanding attachment as a relational concept is twofold: (1) it represents a theoretical and paradigmatic shift of importance for many aspects of developmental psychology, and (2) it opens the way for more productive research on temperament, the interaction between temperament and experience, and important process studies of the unfolding of the infant-caregiver relationship.

The Strange Situation procedure introduced by Ainsworth and Wittig (1969) has spurred extensive predictive research over the last decade. The research has been diverse, suggesting on the one hand that patterns of behavioral organization with respect to the caregiver (relationships) may be stable even when specific behaviors change and, on the other hand, that numerous aspects of later functioning may be predicted.

Attachment relationships in infancy are stable in usual circumstances, and even changes in attachment are predictable. When trained coders assess randomly selected, middle-class infant-caregiver pairs, following the methods of Ainsworth, the quality of attachment is highly concordant between two assessments across a 6-month period (Connell, 1976; Main & Weston, 1981; Waters, 1978). Even when the infant shows a different pattern of attachment with two caregivers, the assessment of each dyad is

L.Alan Sroufe: 'Attachment Classification from the Perspective of Infant-Caregiver Relationships and Infant Temperament'. *CHILD DEVELOPMENT* (1985), 56, pp. 1-14. © 1985 by the Society for Research in Child Development, Inc.

stable over time (Main & Weston, 1981). In poverty samples, there is still significant stability, though here there is also substantial change (Vaughn, Egeland, Sroufe, & Waters, 1979). Such change, however, is related meaningfully to changes in life stress, that is, changes from anxious to secure attachment are associated with reductions in life stress.

Beyond this evidence for stability, Strange Situation classifications have been shown to have a number of external correlates. In dozens of reports based on numerous samples, secure attachment (in contrast to anxious attachment) has been related to peer competence, self-esteem, curiosity, coping with novelty, coping with failure, enthusiasm and persistence in problem solving, independence and infrequency of behavior problems, among other things (e.g., Arend, Gove, & Sroufe, 1979; Bates, Maslin, & Frankel, in press; Erickson, Sroufe, & Egeland, in press; Grossman & Grossman, in press; Lewis, Feiring, McGuffog, & Jaskir, 1984; Londerville & Main, 1981; Matas, Arend, & Sroufe, 1978; Sroufe, 1983; Sroufe, Fox, & Pancake, 1983; Waters, Wippman, & Sroufe, 1979). These studies all have used coders blind to attachment history and to other data on the children. In some cases persons totally unfamiliar with attachment theory collected outcome data prior to attachment classifications, which were then done by blind coders from previously recorded videotapes (Waters et al., 1979). Sometimes the data were derived from persons who could not be biased with respect to attachment theory (e.g., sociometric choices of children). And sometimes outcome data have been highly objective, for example, frequency of sitting on the preschool teacher's lap (Sroufe et al., 1983).

All in all, this body of research makes it clear that something reliable and meaningful is being assessed with the Ainsworth procedure. Differences often are substantial and always in the predicted direction, commonly with controls for moderator variables such as IQ. But how are these differences to be interpreted?

In the Bowlby/Ainsworth tradition, attachment (in contrast to attachment behavior) is viewed as a relational construct (Sroufe & Fleeson, in press). While researchers within this framework may not always have been clear on this point, the Strange Situation, as used by Ainsworth, was devised to capture the quality of functioning of the infant-caregiver *dyad*. As stated in our first empirical paper (Matas et al., 1978), attachment classifications, while based solely on infant behavior, are presumed to reflect the history of caregiver sensitivity. "The effectiveness of the pair is being captured even in assessing infant behavior" (p. 555). In fact, the Strange Situation was introduced and widely adopted only because it was related to contemporaneous patterns of infant-caregiver behavioral organization (the attachment/exploration balance in the home) and because it was shown in Ainsworth's original work to be related to earlier patterns of interaction (caregiver responsivity to infant behavior). Distinct patterns of attachment with each caregiver, predictions to later caregiver behavior (including behavior with siblings), predictions from caregiver developmental history, or predictions of change in attachment in the face of changing caregiver circumstances would have made little sense outside of the relational perspective (all discussed later).

In sharp contrast to this relational position, a number of writers recently have suggested that Ainsworth classifications may to some extent be a reflection of individual differences in infant temperament (Campos, Barrett, Lamb, Goldsmith, & Sternberg, 1983; Chess & Thomas, 1982; Kagan, 1982). In particular, Kagan has argued that attachment group status (A, B, or C) may be due to endogenous individual differences in the disposition to become distressed at separation.

While bodies of data generally are open to multiple interpretations, the differences between these two positions are pronounced and the consequences of accepting one position or the other are substantial. The whole Ainsworth scheme is trivialized if differences in attachment classification may be reduced to endogenous infant variation. In fact, if these assessed differences are due largely to temperament, then they cannot be measures of attachment at all in the Bowlby/Ainsworth sense, because within their framework, attachment (the affective/organizational bond between infant and caregiver) is inherently a relationship concept.

Establishing that the Ainsworth approach yields assessments of qualitative aspects of the relationship between infant and caregiver, rather than inborn dispositions for separation distress or some other endogenous characteristic, is important for several reasons: First, the full implications and potential of the Ainsworth approach are only beginning to be realized. As developmental psychology moves beyond the study of individuals to the study of relationships, it is important to have demonstrations that *relationships* can be assessed. Second, the assessment of qualitative aspects of behavior and behavioral organization, as represented by the Ainsworth procedure, currently provides a model for research on other periods of development and other domains of functioning. Third, if in the Ainsworth procedure the infant-caregiver relationship is assessed (and not simply the infant), and yet these assessments predict later individual functioning outside of the caregiving context (peer competence, curiosity, etc.), this has important theoretical consequences. The most obvious implication is that qualities that arise in relationships ultimately lead to qualities of individuals — an old idea, but one that has proved difficult to demonstrate empirically. Very important process questions automatically follow. With attachment assessments trivialized as temperamental variation, all of this is lost.

Relationship and temperament models

Both the relationship and temperament interpretations of Strange Situation classifications can take many forms. Moreover, viewing attachment classifications as reflections of the infant-caregiver relationship would not exclude viewing temperament as an important concept in explaining many aspects of infant or caregiver behavior. Similarly, those ascribing a key role for temperament may still allow a substantial role for experience. Most researchers adopt some kind of interactional model.

For example, within a relationship perspective one can assume that: (1) attachment classifications (secure/insecure) and temperamental dimensions may be orthogonal, that is, (a) temperamental variation influences various aspects of behavior but not behavior *organization* (attachment classification), or (b) temperament influences subcategory classification (B1, B4, etc.) but not major category placement, or (c) quality of care determines security of attachment (B, non-B), while the *particular* pattern of anxious attachment (A, C) may result from an interaction of infant robustness with

127

insensitive care; (2) relationship history so totally transforms constitutional temperamental variation that its contribution to Strange Situation assessments or attachment behavior more generally is negligible or unknown. Each of these positions acknowledges the reality of temperamental variation.

Those suggesting a more prominent role for temperament can believe that such influences are partial or interact with experience in variously complex ways. For example, Goldsmith and Campos (1982) summarize three possible relations: (1) temperament might influence the caregiver's (degree of) social responsiveness, which then influences attachment and strange situation classification; (2) caregivers' social responsiveness might influence both attachment and temperament *expression*; (3) temperament differences may directly influence Strange Situation assessments, which then are not measures of attachment. The first two of these may be compatible with a relationship perspective; the third is not.

We will examine this range of potential models in light of cumulated research evidence. But first it will be useful to examine certain sources of confusion concerning the meaning and validity of Strange Situation assessments.

Attachment and Strange Situation behavior

In part, the confusion of attachment and temperament concepts (as also was the case with attachment and dependency; Sroufe *et al.*, 1983) arises because attachment researchers and temperament researchers attend to many of the same behaviors, for example clinging, crying, and soothability. Thus, infants classified by Ainsworth as having "avoidant" relationships generally cry little and seek little contact, while "resistant" cases show much crying and contact seeking. Such consistent individual differences in attachment could be readily assimilated to a temperament position. Thus, Kagan (1982) has written: ". . . a child who becomes distressed following maternal departure is more likely to rush to and to greet the mother than one who fails to cry or one who is minimally distressed by the departure. As a result the former child is more likely to be classified as securely attached. Infants who ignore or do not greet the mother on return, *because they were not upset*, are more likely to be classified as less securely attached" (p. 24, italics added).

Such an interpretation, in addition to being factually incorrect (see below), overlooks central aspects of the classification approach. Behaviors such as crying or clinging may or may not be influenced by temperamental variation. But individual differences in such behavioral manifestations are at a different level of analysis than attachment classification. The point has been made previously (e.g., Sroufe & Waters, 1977) that the *organization* among behaviors and across contexts lies at the root of the Ainsworth procedure, not presence or frequency of particular behaviors. No single behavior can index quality of attachment independent of context and organization with other behaviors. Crying at separation and contact upon reunion are not exceptions. "Even separation protest and proximity seeking, hallmarks of attachment, are indicative of the quality of attachment *only* as they are organized with respect to context and to other behaviors . . ." (Sroufe & Waters, 1977, p. 1189, italics added).

Whether an infant cries none, a little, some, or a lot is of little relevance to the determination of the *security* of attachment (i.e., B or non-B). Rather, it is how the infant responds to the caregiver when distressed (contact seeking, absence of anger, returning to play when settled) or not distressed (greeting, seeking interaction upon reunion) that allows the classification of secure attachment.

The main point is that children in secure attachment relationships are behaviorally quite heterogeneous. There is as much variation in separation distress (and contact seeking) *within* the secure group as between the secure and anxious groups. Infants in subgroup B_1 (judged to be secure because of active greeting and interaction upon reunion) cry as little as infants in the A group, as do many B_2's. Infants in subgroup B_4 (judged to be secure because contact is effective in terminating distress) cry as much during separation as children in the C group, as do many B_3's (see Table 1A). The split on crying clearly falls within the secure (B) group, not between the secure and anxious groups. Thus, one baby shows a great deal of separation distress, followed by much contact seeking and clinging, while another cries little or not at all and at no point seeks physical contact. Despite such differences in manifest behavior (temperament?), both may well be classed as securely attached on the basis of behavioral patterns. Other infants cry a lot and seek much contact, and the relationship still is classified as anxious. Separation distress alone does not discriminate secure from anxious patterns. Since the beginning, Ainsworth (1967) has been clear that distress at separation is not an adequate index of quality of attachment. Kagan, a proponent of the temperament position, reached this same conclusion some years later (e.g., Kagan, Kearsley, & Zelazo, 1978).

The relation between separation distress and avoidance or contact maintenance within the Strange Situation

Some researchers have suggested (1) that there is a strong relation between separation distress and behavior during reunion in the Strange Situation, and (2) that such a relationship shows that classifications are therefore second order and of limited validity (Campos *et al.*, 1983; Connell & Goldsmith, 1982; Gaensbauer, Shultz, & Connell, 1983). Several points need to be made here.

First, certainly there are relations between behaviors across episodes of the Strange Situation. This is the whole point behind the organizational conception (Sroufe & Waters, 1977). It is the same dyad across contexts. In fact, in 1979 we showed that we could predict classifications from positive affective exchanges during *preseparation* (Waters *et al.*, 1979). We, of course, did not argue that the affective sharing caused the later separation or reunion behavior, but rather that the organization of behavior is coherent across context, that secure attachment is manifest in positive affective exchanges as well as comforting when distressed.

Second, in fact, the negative correlation between separation protest and avoidance is quite modest (−.10 to −.35, the highest correlations being between crying in Episode 4 and Avoidance in Episode 5) when this variable is assessed by trained coders (Sroufe & Waters, 1977; Waters, 1978, and personal communication). While many avoidant infants do not cry during separation, some children who do cry show marked avoidance, and some who do not cry at all show no avoidance. Thus, crying and later avoidance are inversely correlated, but they are not redundant. There is a somewhat stronger correlation between separation distress and contact maintenance, of course. Children who are engaged in play and not upset are unlikely to seek prolonged physical contact. But contact maintenance does not distinguish secure (B's) from anxious (C's) dyads (see Table 1B). The correlation between separation distress and contact resistance is modest (−.02 to +.34), and it is *contact resistance* (anger, struggling, difficulty settling) that distinguishes B and C dyads. Some children cry a lot and show no or little contact resistance (B3's or B4's). Some cry a lot *and* show much resistance (C's).

Table 1   Crying and contact maintaining during separation in the Strange Situation

	A. Crying						B. Contact maintaining			
	Episode 4		Episode 6		Episode 7		Episode 5		Episode 8	
	M	SD	*M*	SD	*M*	SD	*M*	SD	*M*	SD
Group A	.17	1.16	3.41	4.20	.61	1.44	1.04	.15	2.11	1.09
Group B$_1$	.37	.90	2.67	3.57	1.35	2.33	1.20	.63	2.20	1.14
Group B$_2$	1.25	3.60	3.85	4.10	2.98	2.64	1.36	.81	4.50	1.53
Group B$_3$	4.17	4.11	8.62	4.69	7.24	4.98	3.23	2.32	5.73	1.44
Group B$_4$	6.63	3.04	12.00	0	9.80	4.40	2.75	2.06	4.50	.58
Group C	7.33	4.26	9.77	4.37	9.18	3.09	4.07	1.88	4.43	1.80

Source: — Ainsworth *et al.*, 1978, p. 372.

The issue of external validity

Even if these correlations between reunion behavior and separation protest were substantial, they would be irrelevant to the validity of the classifications or of avoidance scores or amount of separation protest as measures of meaningful individual differences in attachment. Strange Situation classifications are established as valid measures of individual differences because of their range of external correlates. They may be claimed to be valid assessments of individual differences in attachment because of the particular nature of many of these correlates, including relations with crying and exploration in the home (as well as independent laboratory assessments) and earlier measures of infant-caregiver interaction (discussed below). Separation distress, or other temperamental variables assessed in the Strange Situation, have not been shown to have any external correlates. The fact that they may show some correlation with reunion behavior is not relevant. Two variables may be correlated and not share criterial correlates.

As a concrete example, crying in the laboratory was not found to relate to any attachment-related behavior in the home, not even crying (Ainsworth, Blehar, Waters, & Wall, 1978). Crying in the home *was* predicted by Strange Situation classification, and specifically by contact resistance, which had a range of other home correlates. Avoidance also had a range of home correlates, including responding negatively to being put down, tentative contact, and anger. Thus, avoidance and resistance, while correlated with laboratory separation distress, have home correlates that laboratory crying does not share.

The fact that crying in the laboratory does not predict even crying at home, while resistance and avoidance do predict home behavior, is not paradoxical. Discrete behaviors such as crying are influenced by a host of situational factors and generally require extensive sampling for adequate stability. Thus, crying in the novel lab situation not only does not predict to the very different home situation, brief assessments of crying may not even predict to other unfamiliar situations. Avoidance and resistance during reunions with the caregiver in the Strange Situation are not conceived of as reflections of general dispositions. Rather, they are viewed as signs of anomalous organization of the attachment behavioral system (revealed in the context of a modest threat to the attachment bond). Therefore, as reflections of attachment relationship difficulty, they are expected to predict attachment problems in the home context, though not in an isomorphic way. As "signs" of atypical attachment and as behavioral categories, avoidance and resistance are not so dependent on extensive sampling as discrete behavioral referents of general dispositions.

Empirically, crying during separation shows a stability over 6 months of .41, while avoidance shows a stability correlation of .62. Classifications in the same sample showed 96% stability (Waters, 1978). It would seem obvious that classifications based on the overall organization of behavior would yield stronger predictions of future behavior than separation distress (Kagan, 1982) or other specific affective variables (Gaensbauer *et al.*, 1983). To argue that such specific measures should be adopted as measures of attachment, or meaningful individual differences at all, investigators must provide data on stability and external correlates.

Recent data suggested to implicate temperament

Neonatal neurological status and attachment

The finding from the Egeland and Sroufe longitudinal project of a relationship between nonoptimal status on the Brazelton exam at age 7 days and C-group classification at 12 months (Waters, Vaughn, & Egeland, 1980) has been cited as evidence that Strange Situation classifications may be due to temperament (Campos *et al.*, 1983). Such a suggestion, of course, links Brazelton status with temperament; yet, "the NBAS is not exclusively, or even primarily a temperament scale" (Goldsmith & Campos, 1982, p. 171). Moreover, in this study, the 7-day Brazelton was not even stable over the 3 days to our second Brazelton assessment, one obvious criterion of temperament (Plomin, 1982). Our interpretation was, and remains, that given a poorly organized newborn and an overly taxed, economically disadvantaged mother, a difficult interaction (and ultimately anxious attachment) would be expected. It was predicted from the relationship perspective that this set of circumstances would predict resistant (Group C) but not avoidant attachment. We did this study to test these predictions, and both were borne out.

Fortunately, other data are available that allow further clarification concerning a direct causal link between neonatal status and Strange Situation classification. Crockenberg (1981) also examined the relation between newborn Brazelton and 12-month Ainsworth assessments, but with a middle-class sample. As was predictable from a relationship perspective, there was no overall relation between Brazelton and attachment classification. Her further analyses confirmed that when caregivers have the resources they can cope with the challenges of a difficult infant; irritability in infants predicted anxious attachments only for mothers without adequate social support. Strange Situation assessments capture the history of the interaction over the first year, however complexly determined, not endogenous infant factors.

As an additional note here, there have been several efforts to examine directly links between attachment and temperament (as usually conceived), using the Carey Temperament Questionnaire or a similar instrument (e.g., Bates *et al.*, in press, Meyer, 1984; Vaughn, Taraldson, Crichton, & Egeland, 1981). None of these prospective studies found a relation, although one may, of course, question the validity of these temperament assessments. We will return to this issue later.

Cultural group differences in Strange Situation classifications

Recent reports of elevated avoidance in a West German sample (Grossman, Grossman Huber, & Wartner, 1981) and elevated Group C proportions in a Japanese sample also have been interpreted as supporting the temperament position (Campos *et al.*, 1983, Kagan 1982). What is striking about this interpretation is that (1) the data obviously are open to multiple interpretations, including cultural caregiving differences or the inappropriateness of the assessment for the particular sample, and (2) the various interpretations easily are sorted out with further data collection. The relevant data are now available.

First, in the case of Germany, a subsequent study done with a non-working-class sample in south Germany, and with mothers born some time after the War (in contrast to the original Bielefeld sample), revealed proportions of attachment classifications comparable to U.S. samples, with no increase in the proportion of avoidance. Child-rearing attitudes and caregiving practices are implicated, not the German character. As will be discussed below, the high avoidance in the Bielefeld sample itself was, in fact, associated with earlier patterns of care.

The Japanese case is more striking. In the first sample to be reported there were 37% C's (compared to 10%-20% in U.S. samples) and no A's, a notable finding (Miyake, Chen, & Campos, in press). This was interpreted by Kagan and others as evidence that Strange Situation classifications reflect temperament. But Freedman (1974), among others, has described the Oriental newborn as "less changeable, less perturbable, tend[ing] to habituate themselves more readily, and tending to *clam themselves or to be consoled more readily when upset*" (p. 154, italics added). Given this description, the temperament interpretation of the Strange Situation classifications seems on the surface to be paradoxical. These Japanese infants were called C's because they cried without settling. How is this the result of their placid temperament? Moreover, the temperament interpretation glosses over an obvious cultural explanation of these reactions. The "traditional" Japanese mother never leaves her infant alone — even briefly — over the entire course of the first year. It is understandable then that they would be thoroughly distressed when left alone in a strange setting. The Strange Situation was designed to be a mild "everyday" stressor. Clearly, in the context of traditional Japanese culture, it is a stress situation of great magnitude, qualitatively different from all but the most unusual American cases. Moreover, in their effort to duplicate Ainsworth's procedure, the investigators allowed the separations to go on for

3 min regardless of amount of distress, rather than cutting the separations short, as is done here. Many infants will cry without readily settling if stressed enough. Given these distortions in the intent of the Ainsworth procedure, these assessments cannot be valid predictors of home attachment behavior (valid assessments of attachment), and for this reason Takahashi (who carried out the assessments) referred to the so-called anxiously attached infants as "pseudo-C's". In contrast to Group C infants in U.S. studies, these infants showed good quality play in preseparation, casting further doubt on their classification as anxious.

Miyake *et al.* (in press) report that neonatal frustration to nipple withdrawal was related to crying without settling in this Japanese sample. Such a finding tentatively suggests that degree of upset when severely stressed may be related to endogenous variation. However, this finding is not relevant to the relation between temperament and attachment. Crying and exploratory behavior of these subjects in the home would have to be assessed to assert such a tie.

Furthermore, the validity of a strong temperament interpretation of the cultural group differences is easily checked: one needs only to examine Japanese subjects not reared according to traditional patterns. The cultural/experiential interpretation is confirmed by a recent study involving "modern" Japanese families (i.e., mothers oriented toward careers who at times leave their infants in the care of others and otherwise behave like Western mothers). In this study, the proportion of A's (13%), B's, and C's (18%) was comparable to U.S. samples (Durrett, Otaki, & Richards in press). A related study with Chinese Americans is also revealing (Li-Repac, 1982). An overall increase in C's was found. However, C status was linked to degree of acculturation; more fully acculturated Chinese families had the same proportion of C's as Caucasian samples.

Findings suggested to support a relationship perspective

The neonatal predictors of C status in a poverty sample but not a middle-class sample, and the cultural differences just discussed, are quite congruent with the view that Strange Situation classifications reflect differences in the dyadic relationship between infant and caregiver. A host of other empirical studies converge to support this interpretation. Some of these involve direct observations of caregiver responsiveness to infants earlier in the first year; others involve factors that would be expected to influence the quality of care and thereby the infant-caregiver relationship, such as social support or changing life stress.

Attachment and quality of earlier care

Bowlby's (1969) major hypothesis was that quality of attachment was dependent upon the quality of care. Therefore, central in Ainsworth's original research (summarized in Ainsworth *et al.*, 1978) was the finding that sensitive responding to the infant's communications in the first year was related to secure attachment in the Strange Situation at 12 months (while early infant behavior *per se* was not; see also Blehar, Lieberman, & Ainsworth, 1977). Without this finding, further research with the Strange Situation would not have been inspired.

Given the centrality of this finding, it is important that it has been replicated widely with diverse samples and in several laboratories (Bates, Maslin, & Frankel, in press; Bell, in press; Egeland & Farber, 1984, Grossman & Grossman, in press; Smith & Pederson, 1983). These five studies are exact replications. In each, Ainsworth's sensitivity scales at 6 months (and sometimes other ages as well) were related to attachment classifications at 12 months, always done by coders blind to earlier sensitivity scores. In each study, responsive care was associated significantly with secure attachment.

Since two of these studies (Egeland and Grossman) sometimes have been interpreted as failing to support Ainsworth (e.g., Campos *et al.*, 1983; Lamb, Thompson, Gardner, Charnov, & Estes, 1984), a further word is required. In the Egeland and Sroufe project, we assessed discrete infant and mother behaviors in feeding and play situations, in addition to obtaining sensitivity ratings. Few relationships came out of the discrete behavioral analyses. This reflects negatively on the power of discrete behaviors for prediction, but it is not a reflection on Ainsworth's hypothesis. Our only *a priori* prediction was that sensitivity as assessed by Ainsworth's scales would be related to security of attachment. Her findings were replicated (beyond the .001 level of confidence).

Grossman reported that sensitivity ratings at 2 and 6 months predicted attachment classification at 12 months, but ratings at 10 months did not (*Grossman & Grossman*, in press). This was because in the Bielefeld sample caregivers in general begin to push for independence and "proper" deportment late in the first year. The variance in sensitivity disappears and mean sensitivity moves down. Rather than disconfirming Ainsworth, these findings support the predictive power of quality of care. Despite changes in sensitivity late in the first year, earlier assessment still predicted attachment classification, that is, individual differences in attachment still were predicted despite the general cultural press.

The relation between responsive care and later quality of attachment has proven to be extremely robust. It should be noted that sensitivity, as assessed by Ainsworth, entails responsivity to the particular moods, needs, and signals of the individual baby (i.e., temperamental differences already are encompassed) and therefore cannot likely be reduced to endogenous infant factors (see below).

Factors influencing quality of care

An array of studies have been carried out on factors that reasonably would be expected to relate to quality of care and therefore the attachment relationship. In many cases predictions have been quite specific (e.g., avoidant attachment and maternal "unavailability") and few would follow from a strict temperament perspective.

Caregiver social support and life stress. — These factors, which would be expected to affect the quality of caregiver infant interaction, have been found to be related predictably to attachment (Crockenberg, 1981; Durrett *et al.*, in press; Vaughn *et al.*, 1979). They are likely to be independent of endogenous infant characteristics.

Personal resources of caregivers. — For a number of years we have been following a sample of poverty families in Minneapolis. The stress, living situation instability, and often disorganized patterns of care led us to expect an elevation in the Group C (resistant) attachment pattern (see also Ainsworth, in press; Bretherton, in press). We found 22% Group C at 12 months, a significant elevation from middle-class samples.

Abuse and neglect. — Extreme forms of maltreatment are predictably associated with marked elevations in anxious attachment. In the case of physical neglect (with the infant's basic needs for food, hygiene, and safety not attended) there is an elevation in Group C attachments; in the case of physical abuse and "emotional unavailability" there is a marked increase in avoidant attachment (Crittenden, 1983; Egeland & Sroufe, 1981; George & Main, 1979; Schneider-Rosen & Cicchetti, 1984). While one could argue that mothers neglect irritable infants and physically abuse (or fail to respond to) unresponsive infants, such interpretations would be post hoc, and are contradicted by evidence to be presented below. The findings here were predicted from the relationship perspective.

Maternal history. — From a relationship perspective, the caregiver's responsiveness to her infant should be predictable from her own early care. The ideal prospective study had not yet been completed. However, three interview studies have obtained a relation between maternal reports of childhood experiences and an anxious attachment between her and her infant (Main & Goldwyn, 1983; Morris, 1980; Ricks, in press). In the Morris study, for example, mothers who reported that their own mothers were available to them and were viewed as competent in the caregiving role, and whose early lives were characterized by stability, regularity and parental warmth, were dramatically more likely to have securely attached infants. The history data and attachment classifications were as usual obtained independently. Blind judges were able to classify correctly (as secure or anxious) an average of 79% of these cases. More objective criteria from the interviews also yielded significant relations between quality of early care experienced by mother and attachment relationships between this new mother and her infant.

Ill infants. — From a relational view there is, of course, a role for the infant. Some infants are more challenging and more likely to be a source of caregiver anxiety. Such is the case with infants having a severe respiratory disorder. In a recent study, Meisels, Plunkett, Stiefel, Pasick, and Roloff (1984) found that 42% of these infants formed anxious/resistant attachment relationships. This is in direct accord with predictions from the relationship theory, as one would expect chronic illness to create anxiety in caregivers but not necessarily make them unavailable (the avoidance precursor). Note also that these are serious illnesses, not minor temperamental variations. Premature infants are no more likely to be anxiously attached than full terms, given normal health (Rode, Chang, Fisch, & Sroufe, 1981).

Some clearly differentiating data

All of the findings reported above are in accord with, and were predicted from, a relationship perspective. Many of the findings are, of course, open to post hoc temperament interpretations (e.g., unresponsive mothers are genetically atypical or exert prenatal influences on infant temperament; mother's own early care was due to her temperament, etc.). Some of the findings, such as differences among the Japanese samples, stretch a temperament interpretation rather severely. Still other data are strongly differentiating between temperament and relationship interpretations.

First, infants may have secure attachments with one caregiver and anxious attachments with another (Grossman *et al.*, 1981; Main & Weston, 1981). This is not paradoxical from the point of view that attachment classification is the product of interaction; it is paradoxical from a strict temperament interpretation. Temperamental characteristics (e.g., disposition to fearful reactions to novelty) should show some stability across partners (Plomin, 1982).

Second, the quality of attachment, even with the same caregiver, is subject to change if the life stress experienced by the caregiver changes (Vaughn *et al,* 1979). Again, if the quality of interaction changes, attachment pattern, as a reflection of this relationship, changes. Temperamental differences, as usually conceived, should not be so readily modifiable (Plomin, 1982).

Third, Strange Situation assessments, though focused on infant behavior, predict maternal behavior at later ages and in other contexts (Matas *et al.*, 1978). They even predict maternal behavior with a sibling (Meyer, 1984; Ward, 1983). In the Ward study, attachment classification of the firstborn predicted both the mothers' emotional support and quality of assistance with second-borns in an assessment at age 2 years (i.e., up to 3 years later). This follows directly from the notion that the infant-caregiver relationship is being assessed (and therefore both members of the dyad), rather than endogenous infant variation (Mata *et al.*, 1978; Sroufe & Fleeson, in press). If attachment assessments are products of dyadic interaction (orchestrated by caregiver responsiveness), then it is not surprising that security of attachment with a mother-firstborn pair predicts mother's responsiveness to a second-born years later.

Finally, prospective data show that nonoptimal patterns of care precede infant maladaptation and anxious patterns of attachment (Egeland & Sroufe, 1981). Results are most clear in the case of what we have defined as "emotionally unavailable" caregivers ($N = 19$). These mothers were observed as early as age 3 months to be uninvolved, detached, and affectless in interacting with the infant. Even in the hospital they were rated by nurses as showing less interest in their infants than the sample as a whole. By contrast, these infants showed normal Apgars, normal Brazelton exams at 7 and 10 days (not significantly different from any other subgroups in our sample), and were still quite robust at age 3 months (being, in fact, significantly higher than their control group on a summary factor score). Their means on all individual infant variables assessed in our 3-month feeding and play observations were comparable to those of infants who later were securely attached. The infants showed a notable decline between 3 and 6 months, however, and maladaptation became more notable at each assessment thereafter. By 12 months, 42% of these infants showed the avoidant pattern of attachment, and by 18 months 86% were avoidant (despite the fact that the sample as a whole showed less anxious attachment at this age). By age 2 they were virtually without exception unenthusiastic in engaging challenges, easily frustrated, and excessively angry and negativistic in interacting with their mothers in a problem-solving task (Egeland & Sroufe, 1981). Such prospective data are the final arbiter of explanations of attachment differences.

Evaluation of models

Temperament positions

From this review of available evidence concerning Strange Situation classifications, it is clear that the strong temperament interpretation is without basis. It is supported only by post hoc assertions, which cannot be given the same status as a network of specifically predicted relations. Moreover, it is countered by overwhelming evidence. Differences in attachment classification cannot be accounted for by endogenous disposition to distress or other inherent temperament characteristics. As discussed below, other interactionist temperament positions remain intuitively more appealing, but at present are without support by evidence.

1. It may be argued that, while temperament clearly is not the sole determinant of attachment classification, perhaps it is a partial determinant (Campos *et al.*, 1983); that is, experience and temperament add together to determine attachment status. This seems difficult to square with the absence of a relation between attachment assessments with two caregivers, and it is not supported by evidence (except in extreme cases; see model 3 below). In fact, behavior of infants in early infancy is not stable, nor does it predict later attachment (though caregiver behavior in the same assessments does, Blehar *et al.*, 1977). It sometimes is argued that important temperamental variations emerge later in the first year (Goldsmith & Campos, 1982), when stable differences can be detected, and that these late-emerging variations exert influence on attachment assessments. This certainly is possible, but such a position is untested and, at the present time, perhaps untestable, since such late-appearing endogenous variation cannot easily be separated out from experience. Given the predictability of attachment status from caregiver behavior, such an assumption seems gratuitous at present.

2. Related to position 1, caregiver responsiveness may influence both the development of attachment and the expression of temperament (Goldsmith & Campos, 1982). Strange Situation assessments then would represent some unknown combination of attachment variation and temperamental expression (e.g., learned thresholds of expressed fearfulness; high for avoidant infants, moderate for secure infants, and low for resistant infants). There is no evidence that specifically supports this position, and there is evidence that is challenging for it. The home observation of negative responses of avoidant infants to being put down already has been mentioned. It also is the case that outcome assessments in preschool (Sroufe *et al.*, 1983) show that children with histories of avoidant attachment are high on emotional dependency with preschool teachers (equal to resistant infants and significantly higher than secure infants). They also are high on negative affect (Sroufe 1983). This directly followed from the view that avoidance reflects anxious attachment but would not seem to be a likely prediction from the view that avoidance reflects a low fearfulness threshold.

3. Another alternative is that certain infant temperament characteristics may lead to caregiver nonresponsiveness (the caregiver-infant mismatch hypothesis). This position has been popular and, in fact, was a major hypothesis in early stages of the Egeland and Sroufe project. However, we have found little evidence to support such a view (i.e., neither caregiver behavior nor attachment were predicted by infant behavior early in the first year), nor is there evidence in the literature that, within the broad normal range, variation in infant behavior causes nonresponsiveness in caregivers. In extreme circumstances (such as poverty) or with extreme infant conditions (severe respiratory disorder, Down's syndrome), caregiver responsiveness is at times negatively influenced. In more usual circumstances, however, caregivers seem to respond to the particular nature of the particular infant. In fact, there is evidence that in usual circumstances caregivers are *more* responsive to premature infants than to full-term infants (Cohen & Beckwith, 1979). Thus, the usual caregiver response to mild anomalies or minor variations in infant reactivity is to adjust behavior appropriately. This fails to occur only in unusual circumstances. That is, based on current data, it is plausible to argue that nonresponsiveness occurs when infant temperament is *not* having an effect. The reason Ainsworth sensitivity scores are so powerful in predicting attachment is that they take into account responsivity to particular infants. It seems to be that *the caregiving context determines responsiveness; infant temperament perhaps determines what responsiveness entails*. While a role for temperament may be seen in this revised model, it is not viewed as causal, even partially, of attachment quality.

Some infants would challenge many parents. Therefore, 44% C's were found in infants with respiratory distress syndrome; but note that the majority still were securely attached. *Some infants would tax some parents* (nonoptimal Brazelton status and type C attachment with a poverty, but not a middle-class, sample). But for most infants, most parents provide good enough care, and the general quality of that care seems unrelated to normal range variations in temperament.

Relationship positions

The evidence clearly supports the general interpretation that attachment classifications reflect the relationship history of the infant-caregiver dyad. But how might temperament concepts be considered in such a developmental account ?

1. Attachment and temperament may be orthogonal. Temperamental variation may underlie differences in activity level, cuddliness, reactivity thresholds, and so forth, but such dimensions may play little role in determining attachment behavioral organization (e.g., attachment/exploration balance or whether comfort is sought when the distress threshold is exceeded, etc.). That is, attachment assessments and temperament assessments may be directed at different levels of analysis. An alternative here is that subgroups *within* the major classification categories (B_1, B_4, etc.) are influenced by temperamental variation, but major category placement is not. There is nothing in the literature counter to the proposition that subgroupings reflect temperament; neither is there any evidence for it. From this position it would be expected that there would be some congruence in attachment

with two caregivers, if subcategories were considered (e.g., if A_1 with mother, then A *or* B_1 with father, etc.).

2. Alternatively, security of attachment (B–non-B) may be determined by caregiver responsiveness, whereas temperamental variation (broadly conceived) may be implicated in distinguishing between the avoidant (A) and resistant (C) patterns of anxious attachment. As one possibility here, Gordon Bronson (personal communication) has suggested that avoidant attachment results when a robust infant encounters insensitive care, and resistant attachment when a nonoptimally functioning infant encounters insensitive care. In contrast to the infant-caregiver mismatch position discussed above, this interactional position is congruent with the data from our poverty sample. However, more data would be required to confirm this hypothesis. Almost all of the infants in our "psychologically unavailable" group were avoidant, and not all of these were robust as infants. Any such interactional viewpoint still suggests that attachment classifications are capturing the quality of the relationship and not simply endogenous infant characteristics.

3. Finally, it may be that endogenous temperamental differences, however extensive, are thoroughly transformed within the caregiving relationship system; that is, they become part of a totality. Such endogenous variation may continue to unfold after the early months, but it unfolds within the relationship and cannot be factored out. By 12 months all one has is the relationship history, not relationship and temperament in two separate suitcases (Sroufe & Fleeson, in press).

Thus, in usual circumstances if a caregiver has an infant that is easily overaroused, the caregiver will be prompted to provide modulated stimulation, smooth transitions, and so forth. In time the infant develops sufficient arousal tolerance and selfmodulating capacity. A placid, hard to arouse infant elicits more vigorous stimulation and articulated expressiveness. In time the infant becomes more actively engaged. Within this perspective, which truly respects infant plasticity, such change is viewed in terms of real transformation. The original temperament no longer is "there." What has been challenged here is not the concept of temperament but views of temperament as a causal concept (as in the child's temperament causes attachment pattern or causes behavior in the Strange Situation or causes poor parenting). The "child effects" idea is turned around to imply prompting of required parental care, rather than as causing poor parenting.

Admittedly, this is a radical position. Something short of the total transformation of endogenous behavioral dispositions seems intuitively likely. And infants would seem to vary in terms of the demands they make on the skill and responsiveness of the caregivers. But the position deserves more attention than it has yet been given. It is no more presumptive than any of the temperament positions outlined above. Moreover, it is congruent with all of the data yet published on attachment.

Implications for research

Further research on temperament influences on attachment or a new emphasis on process research both would be possible. Some issues for temperament researchers will first be indicated, followed by a discussion of outcome and process studies.

Temperament research

Those who advocate that differences in individual physiology play a large role in attachment classifications must (1) provide evidence for reliable and stable behavioral differences in the early weeks of life that are related to later attachment classifications, or (2) show that twins reared apart are largely concordant for attachment class. Observing differences in attachment and simply asserting that they are due to temperament is not enough.

Those who, in the face of instability in early behavior, argue that stable temperamental differences emerge later in the first year (a plausible idea) must find some way of assessing such variation independent of caregiver influence, if any causal role is to be implied. If one believes that temperament is inextricably interwoven with caregiving experience (the relationship position), then the assumption of a causal role for temperament is gratuitous.

Those who argue that the role of temperament in attachment is not directly causal but rather is indirect, via influences on the caregiver, again must find some way of assessing infant behavior independent of caregiving and also must assess caregiver reactions. The mere existence of behavioral variation in infants and caregivers is not enough. Commonalities in negative caregiving of twins reared apart from birth would again be one approach. The match-mismatch hypothesis and other models of negative influence on caregiver behavior certainly merit further study. While not supported by evidence at the present time, such positions nonetheless remain logically plausible and probably testable.

Many of the same points apply when considering positions based on the idea that temperamental variation may be orthogonal to security of attachment and yet influence attachment behaviors (amount of crying, clinging, etc.). Researchers would need to show that such behavior may be predicted from earlier assessments of infant behavior shown to be at least partially independent of caregiving experience. The existence of differences in crying, clinging, fear of novelty, etc., assessed at the end of the first year, even if then stable, cannot be used by themselves as evidence for physiologically based variation. These too may be the result of caregiving experience. To date there is no discriminating evidence.

There is some support for Bronson's idea that B–non-B (security of attachment) is the result of experience, while pattern of anxious attachment (A or C) results from an interaction of infant robustness with insensitive care. It would be quite worthwhile to do further work on this position.

Outcome and process research

Each of the relationship models of attachment has implications for research. The view that attachment and temperament are strictly orthogonal has clear implications for predictive studies. If cognitive ability, temperamental variation, and social/personality organization were to be defined independently, our ability to understand and predict behavior (based on all three sources of variation) should be enhanced greatly. Moreover, as Plomin (1982) has suggested, research on temperament itself is hampered when researchers ascribe any and all individual differences to temperament. Were we more discriminating in our interpretations, it might become possible to establish firmly certain temperamental characteristics. We then could study the interaction of temperament and experience, opening up new frontiers of knowledge.

When researchers embrace the view that much of temperamental variation is encompassed within the relationship system, important process questions arise. How are these transformations accomplished? How do they vary across various temperamental patterns and caregiving circumstances? Which aspects of temperament are more readily modified, which less so? These are questions that have been raised before, but generally within a view of temperamental dimensions as trait concepts (modifiable but nonetheless remaining intact). Here the idea would be that the same set of temperamental characteristics could be transformed into totally (qualitatively) different end products in given caregiving systems. Thus, twins reared apart no doubt show similarity in terms of certain characteristics of behavioral expression (Freedman, 1974), but in terms of many socioemotional aspects of behavior (especially quality of relationships with parents, peers, intimate partners, and offspring) they may be no more similar than any other separately reared individuals.

It is time once again to put aside the nature-nurture debate. Given the general agreement that experience transforms endogenous characteristics and that even newborn behavioral variation (including Brazelton status) may be predicted by prenatal assessments of maternal anxiety and other factors (Davids, Holden, & Gray, 1963; Molitor, Joffe, Barglow, Benveniste, & Vaughn, 1984), it generally will not be possible to prove that child factors cause developmental outcomes independent of caregiver influences. A more productive use of research energy would be study of the unfolding of infant-caregiver relationships themselves.

Conclusion

It should not be surprising that temperament concepts seem to have little power in explaining security of attachment. Attachment and temperament concepts operate at different levels of analysis. Temperament and attachment, as defined by Bowlby and his followers, are fundamentally different constructs, and research guided by the attachment perspective cannot meaningfully be assimilated to the temperament construct (Cronbach & Meehl, 1955). Qualitative aspects of relationships (dyadic behavioral organization) simply cannot be reduced to individual behavioral dimensions. Expectations of comforting, security in the presence of the other, and shared affect are not well conceived as temperamental variations. In a fundamental way, relationships are the result of experience, that is, the history of the interaction of the dyad.

In accepting a relationship interpretation of Strange Situation classifications, one does not have to abandon an interest in physiological factors. Attachment and temperament constructs refer to different domains, and there is no inherent incompatibility between relationship and temperamental concepts in moving toward a wholistic understanding of the child. The most urgent need is for process studies of how caregivers typically adjust their behavior to accommodate to the particular needs and nature of a given child.

Moreover, the relationship view, with its stress on parental history, social support, and life stress, carries no implication of blame for parents (Sroufe & Waters, 1982). However, there are implications of the position that parent-child relationships profoundly influence personality development. As a member of society one shares a responsibility with respect to the quality of care available to all children. If responsibility for the child's well-being does not reside in his or her inborn variation, then it is ours.

References

Ainsworth, M.D.S. (1967) *Infancy in Uganda*. Baltimore: Johns Hopkins University Press.

Ainsworth, M. D. S. (in press) 'Patterns of infant-mother attachment as related to maternal care.' In D. Magnusson & V. Allen (Eds), *Human development: An international perspective*. New York: Academic Press.

Ainsworth, M., Blehar, M. , Waters, E., & Wall, S. (1978) *Patterns of attachment*. Hillsdale, NJ: Erlbaum.

Ainsworth, M., & Wittig, B. (1969) 'Attachment and exploratory behavior of one-year-olds in a strange situation.' In B. Foss (Ed.), *Determinants of infant behavior* (Vol. 4) London: Methuen.

Arend, R., Gove, F., & Sroufe, L.A. (1979) 'Continuity of individual adaptation from infancy to kindergarten: A predictive study of egoresilience and curiosity in preschoolers.' *Child Development,* 50, 950-959.

Bates. J., Maslin, C., & Frankel, K. (in press) 'Attachment security, mother-child interaction, and temperament as predictors of behavior problem ratings at age three years.' *Monographs of the Society for Research in Child Development*.

Bell, S.M. (in press) *Cognitive development and mother-child interaction in the first three years of life*. Monograph in preparation.

Blehar, M., Lieberman, A., & Ainsworth, M. (1977) 'Early face-to-face interaction and its relation to later infant-mother attachment.' *Child Development*, 48, 182-194.

Bowlby, J. (1969) *Attachment and loss: Vol. 1. Attachment*. New York: Basic.

Bretherton, I. (in press) 'Attachment theory: Retrospect and prospect.' *Monographs of the Society for Research in Child Development*.

Campos, J., Barrett, K., Lamb, M., Goldsmith, H., & Sternberg, C. (1983) 'Socioemotional development.' In M. Haith & J. Campos (Eds.), P. H. Mussen (Series Ed.), *Handbook of child psychology: Vol. 2. Infancy and deuelopmental psychobiology* (pp. 783-916) New York: Wiley.

Chess, S., & Thomas, A. (1982) 'Infant bonding: Mystique and reality.' *American Journal of Orthopsychiatry,* 52, 213-222.

Cohen, S., & Beckwith, L. (1979) 'Preterm infant interaction with the caregiver in the first year of life and competence of age two.' *Child Development*, 50, 767-776.

Connell, D.B. (1976) *Individual differences in attachment: An investigation into stability, implications, and relationships to structure of early language development*. Unpublished doctoral dissertation, University of Syracuse.

Connell, J., & Goldsmith, H.A. (1982) 'A structural modeling approach to the study of attachment and strange situation behaviors.' In R. Emde & R. Harmon (Eds.), *The development of attachment and affiliative systems* (pp. 213-244) New York: Plenum.

Crittenden, P. (1983) *Mother and infant patterns of interaction: Developmental relationships.* Unpublished doctoral dissertation, University of Virginia.

Crockenberg, S. (1981) 'Infant irritability, mother responsiveness, and social support influences on the security of infant-mother attachment.' *Child Development*, 52, 857-865.

Cronbach. L.J., & Meehl, P.E. (1955) 'Construct validity in psychological tests.' *Psychological Bulletin*, 52, 281-302.

Davids, A., Holden, R., & Gray, G. (1963) 'Maternal anxiety during pregnancy and adequacy of mother and child adjustment eight months following childbirth.' *Child Development*, 34, 993-1002.

Durrett, M.E., Otaki, M., & Richards, P. (in press) 'Attachment and mother's perception of support from the father.' *Journal of the International Society for Studies in Behavioral Development.*

Egeland, B., & Farber, E. (1984) 'Infant-mother attachment: Factors related to its development and changes over time.' *Child Development*, 55, 753-771.

Egeland, B., & Sroufe, L.A. (1981) 'Developmental sequelae of maltreatment in infancy.' In R. Rizley & D. Cicchetti (Eds.), *Developmental perspectives in child maltreatment* (pp. 77-92) San Francisco: Jossey-Bass.

Erickson, M., Sroufe, A., & Egeland, B. (in press) 'The relationship of quality of attachment and behavior problems in preschool children from a high risk sample.' *Monographs of the Society for Research in Child Development.*

Freedman, D. (1974) *Human infancy: An evolutionary perspective.* Hillsdale, NJ: Erlbaum.

Gaensbauer, T., Shultz, L., & Connell, J. (1983) 'Emotion and attachment: Interrelationships in a structured laboratory paradigm.' *Developmental Psychology*, 19, 815-831.

George, C., & Main, M. (1979) 'Social interactions of young abused children: Approach, avoidance and aggression.' *Child Development*, 50, 306-318.

Goldsmith, H., & Campos, J. (1982) 'Toward a theory of infant temperament', In R. Emde & R. Harmon (Eds.), *The development of attachment and affiliative systems* (pp. 161-194) New York: Plenum.

Grossman, K., & Grossman, K.E. (in press) 'Maternal sensitivity and newborns' orienting responses as related to quality of attachment in Northern Germany.' *Monographs of the Society for Research in Child Development.*

Grossman, K.E., Grossman, K., Huber, F., & Wartner, U. (1981) 'German children's behavior toward their mothers at 12 months and their fathers at 18 months in Ainsworth's strange situation.' *International Journal of Behavioral Development*, 4, 157-181.

Kagan, J. (1982) *Psychological research on the human infant: An evaluative summary.* New York: W. T. Grant Foundation.

Kagan, J., Kearsley, R., & Zelazo P. (1978) *Infancy: Its places in human development.* Cambridge, MA: Harvard University Press.

Lamb, M., Thompson, R., Gardner, W., Charnov, E., & Estes, D. (1984) 'Security of infantile attachment as assessed in the strange situation: Its study and biological interpretation.' *Behavioral and Brain Sciences*, 7, 127-147.

Lewis, M., Feiring, C., McGuffog, C., & Jaskir, J. (1984) 'Predicting psychopathology in six-year-olds from early social relations.' *Child Development*, 55, 123-136.

Li-Repac, D. (1982) *The impact of acculturation on the child-rearing attitudes and practices of Chinese-American families*. Unpublished doctoral dissertation, University of California at Berkeley.

Londerville, S., & Main, M. (1981) 'Security of attachment, compliance, and maternal training methods in the second year of life.' *Developmental Psychology*, 17, 289-299.

Main, M., & Goldwyn, R. (1983) *Predicting rejection of her infant from mother's representation of her own experience: A preliminary report*. Unpublished manuscript.

Main, M., & Weston, D. (1981) 'The quality of the toddler's relationship to mother and father.' *Child Development*, 52, 932-940.

Matas, L., Arend, R., & Sroufe, L. A. (1978) 'Continuity of adaptation in the second year: The relationship between quality of attachment and later competence.' *Child Development*, 49, 547-556.

Meisels, S., Plunkett, J., Stiefel, G., Pasick, P., & Roloff, D. (1984) *Patterns of attachment among preterm infants of differing biological risk*. Paper presented at the biennial conference of the International Conference on Infant Studies, New York.

Meyer, H. (1984) *Similarity in the quality of attachment between first- and second-born siblings and their mothers*. Paper submitted to the International Conference on Infant Studies, New York.

Miyake, K., Chen, S., & Campos, J. (in press) 'Infant temperament, mother's mode of interaction, and attachment in Japan.' *Monographs of the Society for Research in Child Development*.

Molitor, N., Joffe, L., Barglow, P., Benveniste, R., & Vaughn, B. (1984) *Biochemical and psychological antecedents of newborn performance on the Neonatal Behavioral Assessment Scale*. Paper presented at the International Conference on Infant Studies, New York, April.

Morris, D. (1980) *Infant attachment and problem solving in the toddler: Relations to mother's family history*. Unpublished doctoral dissertation, University of Minnesota.

Plomin, R. (1982) 'Childhood temperament.' In B. Lahey & A. Kazdin (Eds.), *Advances in clinical child psychology* (Vol. 6) New York: Plenum.

Ricks, M. (in press) 'The social inheritance of parenting.' *Monographs of the Society for Research in Child Development*.

Rode, S., Chang, P., Fisch, R., & Sroufe, L.A. (1981) 'Attachment patterns of infants separated at birth.' *Developmental Psychology*, 17, 188-191.

Schneider-Rosen, K., & Cicchetti, D. (1984) 'The relationship between affect and cognition in maltreated infants: Quality of attachment and the development of visual self-recognition.' *Child Development*, 55, 648-658.

Smith, P., & Pederson, D. (1983) *Maternal sensitivity and patterns of infant-mother attachment*. Paper presented at the biennial meeting of the Society for Research in Child Development, Detroit.

Sroufe, L.A. (1983) 'Infant-caregiver attachment and patterns of adaptation in preschool: The roots of maladaptation and competence.' In M. Perlmutter (Ed.), *Minnesota symposia in child psychology* (Vol. 16, pp. 41-83) Hillsdale, NJ: Erlbaum.

Sroufe, L.A., & Fleeson, J. (in press) 'Attachment and the construction of relationships.' In W. Hartup & Z. Rubin (Eds.), *Relationships and development*. Hillsdale, NJ: Erlbaum.

Sroufe, L. A., Fox, N., & Pancake, V. (1983) 'Attachment and dependency in developmental perspective.' *Child Development*, 54, 1335-1354.

Sroufe, L.A., & Waters, E. (1977) 'Attachment as an organizational construct.' *Child Development*, 48, 1184-1199.

Sroufe, L.A., & Waters, E. (1982) 'Issues of temperament and attachment.' *American Journal of Orthopsychiatry*, 52, 743-746.

Vaughn, B., Egeland, B., Waters, E., & Sroufe, L.A. (1979) 'Individual differences in infant-mother attachment at 12 and 18 months: Stability and change in families under stress.' *Child Development*, 50, 971-975.

Vaughn, B., Taraldson, B., Crichton, L., & Egeland, B. (1981) 'The assessment of infant temperament: A critique of the Carey infant temperament questionnaire.' *Infant Behavior and Development*, 4, 1-17.

Ward, M.J. (1983) *Maternal behavior with firstborns and secondborns: Evidence for consistency in family relations*. Unpublished doctoral dissertation, University of Minnesota.

Waters, E. (1978) 'The stability of individual differences in infant-mother attachment.' *Child Development*, 49, 483-494.

Waters, E., Vaughn, B., & Egeland, B. (1980) 'Individual differences in infant-mother attachment relationships at age one: Antecedents in neonatal behavior in an urban, economically disadvantaged sample.' *Child Development*, 51, 203-216.

Waters, E., Wippman, J., & Sroufe, L.A. (1979) 'Attachment, positive affect, and competence in the peer group: Two studies in construct validation.' *Child Development*, 50, 821-829.

10. Stability of Infant-Mother Attachment and Its Relationship to Changing Life Circumstances in an Unselected Middle-Class Sample

Ross A. Thompson, Michael E. Lamb and David Estes

43 infants and mothers were observed in the Strange Situation procedure when the infants were 12.5 and 19.5 months old. Following each assessment, mothers completed a questionnaire concerning changes in family and caregiving circumstances over the assessment period. Although the proportions of securely attached and insecurely attached infants were similar at both ages and conformed to previous findings, temporal stability was only 53% for overall classifications and 26% for subgroups. Changes in family circumstances which seemed likely to influence the ongoing quality of infant-mother interaction (such as maternal employment or regular nonmaternal care) were associated with changes in attachment status. However, these influences were associated with bidirectional changes in attachment status. Family and caregiving circumstances were less strongly associated with attachment security or insecurity at either assessment. These results indicate that the security of attachment reflects the current status of infant-mother interaction, and that this is affected by changing family and caregiving circumstances.

Recently, students of socioemotional development in infancy have devoted a great deal of attention to the security of the infant-mother attachment relationship. Much of this interest has been evoked by a set of research findings concerning the conditions which foster stability or change in the security of attachment over time. Waters (1978), for example, tested 50 mothers and infants in the Strange Situation procedure (Ainsworth, Blehar, Waters & Wall 1978) at 12 and 18 months, and reported that 96% of his sample obtained the same overall attachment classification at both assessments. In contrast, Vaughn, Egeland, Sroufe, and Waters (1979) observed a sample of 100 socioeconomically disadvantaged families in the Strange Situation at 12 and 18 months and reported much lower stability (62%) over the two assessments. They accounted for this difference by noting that a greater proportion of their lower-income families were likely to experience instability and stress in family circumstances, and data were presented linking the frequency of stressful events to changes in attachment status over time. Vaughn and colleagues (1979, p. 971) noted that Waters's middle-class sample had been specially selected to minimize the likely incidence of family stress and change in order to maximize the possibility of finding consistent individual differences in infant-mother relationships.

Ross A. Thompson, Michael E. Lamb and David Estes: 'Stability of Infant-Mother Attachment and Its Relationship to Changing Life Circumstances in an Unselected Middle-Class Sample'. *CHILD DEVELOPMENT* (1982), 53. pp. 144-148. © 1982 by the Society for Research in Child Development, Inc. All rights reserved.

These findings leave unanswered the question of the temporal stability of attachment classifications in an unselected middle-class sample, and how the family changes and stresses commonly encountered in middle-class homes influence the stability of attachment classifications over time. We sought to address this question by means of a short-term longitudinal study.

Method

A sample of 43 infants (21 males, 22 females) and their mothers were observed in the Strange Situation procedure at 12.5 and 19.5 months of age. We succeeded in recruiting a relatively heterogeneous middle-class sample: Scores on Hollingshead's[1] Index of Social Status revealed that 14 families were in class I (major professional and business), 12 in class II (minor professional and technical), 13 in class III (skilled craftsmen, clerical, sales workers), and four in class IV (machine operators and semiskilled workers). Following each Strange Situation assessment, mothers completed questionnaires concerning changes in family circumstances and caregiving arrangements for the child over the assessment period. With these data, we were able to examine both the stability of attachment status during the second year, as well as the factors associated with changes in attachment classification over time.

The Strange Situation is a semistandardized assessment paradigm designed to appraise the security of the infant-mother attachment relationship. The procedure consists of a series of seven 3-min episodes which are designed to create a situation of gradually escalating stress for the baby (e.g., unfamiliar room, interaction with a strange adult, separation from mother in the company of that adult, and finally being left alone), so that the organization of the infant's behavior in relation to the parent can be observed. Particular attention is devoted to the quality of the baby's reunion responses following brief separations from the mother.

From videotaped records, episode-by-episode assessments of the infant's social interactive behaviors were conducted using Ainsworth's seven-point scales (Ainsworth et al. 1978). These entailed assessments of the baby's (a) proximity- and contact-seeking activities, (b) contact-maintaining behaviors, (c) resistance to interaction or contact, (d) avoidance of social interaction, (e) distance interaction, and (f) search behaviors during separation episodes. In addition, an overall classification of the security of attachment was assigned, which focused on the infant's ability to use the adult as a secure base to explore in an unfamiliar setting, and the ability to reunite positively with the parent after brief separations. Infants who are securely attached (group B) are able to play comfortably in the parent's presence during preseparation episodes and greet and/ or seek contact with the parent upon reunion. Insecure-avoidant (group A) babies exhibit noninteractive exploration during preseparation, and avoid or ignore the parent during reunion episodes. Insecure-resistant (group C) babies seek proximity and contact even during preseparation episodes, and contact-seeking behaviors during reunions are accompanied by angry, resistant behaviors. Subgroups within each of the three classifications focus largely on variations in these reunion behaviors (see Ainsworth *et al.* [1978] for further details concerning procedure and scoring).

Scoring of the 19.5-month tapes was conducted without knowledge of the 12.5-month classifications and was performed by highly trained research assistants who used consistent scoring criteria at each age. Correlation coefficients between independent ratings of the interactive behaviors were high for both assessments (12.5 months: mean $r = .95$, range = .90–.98; 19.5 months: mean $r = .93$, range = .89–.95). Exact agreement on overall attachment classifications was 90% for the 12.5-month assessment, and 98% at 19.5 months; agreement for subgroups was 86% and 93%, respectively.

Following the Strange Situation at each age, mothers were given a brief (15–17-item) questionnaire to complete at home and return by mail. Questionnaires were designed to yield descriptive demographic data and information concerning changes in family circumstances and caregiving arrangements over the assessment period. Some questions focused on enduring aspects of caregiving for the baby, such as mother's return to work and the identities of the baby's regular caregivers. Other questions concerned general family circumstances, such as moving to a new home. We also inquired into specific experiences, such as the occurrence of major separations of 24 hours or longer from the mother. Response measures were scored on an occurrence/nonoccurrence basis for the purposes of analysis.

Results

At each age, the distribution of infants across attachment classifications was very similar, and accorded with the normative findings reported by Ainsworth (Ainsworth et al. 1978) and others. However, only 53% of the infants were assigned the same overall attachment classification at both ages (see table 1). Temporal stability of classification subgroups was 26%.

Table 1   Temporal stability of attachment classifications

	19.5-Month Classification			
	Avoidant	Secure	Resistant	Total
12.5-Month Classification:				
Avoidant .	1	5	1	7
Secure	5	20	5	30
Resistant .	0	4	2	6
Total	6	29	8	43

Temporal consistency and change in overall attachment status was mirrored in the correlations of scores on the interactive variables at 12.5 and 19.5 months (see table 2). Although mother-directed behaviors during preseparation episodes were nonsignificantly correlated, four out of five interactive variables during reunions correlated significantly when overall attachment classification was temporally consistent. In contrast, when attachment status changed over time, correlations between interactive behaviors during reunions were all small and nonsignificant. These findings on the interactive variables thus provide corroborative evidence for temporal stability and change in overall attachment classifications.

149

Table 2   **Correlations of 12.5-month and 19.5-month scores of mother-directed interactive behaviors in the Strange Situation**

	Temporal stability of attachment classification			
	Unstable		Stable	
	Pre-separation	Reunion	Pre-separation	Reunion
Proximity seeking	— .09	— .09	— .09	— .18
Contact maintaining	— .05	— .15	.26	.54**
Resistance	.39	— .15	— .04	.77**
Avoidance	.15	— .19	— .03	.42*
Distance interaction	.15	.04	.17	.45*

Note — Preseparation episodes (episodes 1 and 2) and reunion episodes (episodes 4 and 7) were combined to increase the reliability of episode-by-episode scores.
  $* p < .05$
$** p < .01$

Table 1 shows that changes in attachment status occurred more often for infants who were insecurely attached (i.e., groups A and C) at 12.5 months than for those initially deemed securely attached. Furthermore, while infants who were classified secure at 12.5 months tended to remain so, insecurely attached infants were more likely to become securely attached by the follow-up assessment than to remain insecure. This pattern of findings suggests that insecurity of attachment may be a developmentally less robust phenomenon, so to speak, than attachment security. In this middle-class sample, there was also a tendency toward the development of secure mother-infant attachment relationships over time, even though the relative proportions of securely attached and insecurely attached infants remained the same.

We examined the questionnaire responses in order to understand the kinds of circumstances which were associated with temporal changes in attachment classifications (see table 3) Between the two assessments, five of the mothers in our sample returned to work; in four cases, the baby's attachment status changed. More than half (12 of 20) of those infants whose classification changed over time had mothers who had returned to work by the time of the 19.5-month assessment, while this was true of less than 15% (3 of 23) of those whose classification remained the same ($\chi^2 = 10.28$, $df = 1$, $p < .005$). Similarly, changes in attachment status were also more likely to occur when the infant regularly (i.e., ≥ 15 hours weekly) experienced caregiving from father, a relative, babysitter, child-care agency, or other nonmaternal caregivers (11 of 20) than when attachment status was consistent (2 of 23) ($\chi^2 = 11.09$, $df = 1$, $p < .001$). All infants who entered into a nonmaternal caregiving arrangement between the two assessments changed in attachment status. Obviously, maternal employment and nonmaternal care co-occurred in many families. Importantly, in both cases, changes in attachment status associated with such events were bidirectional: Some infants changed from securely to insecurely attached, but others shifted from insecurely attached to secure over time. In contrast, critical events, such as a major (≥ 24 hours) separation from the mother, were not associated with changes in attachment status (the impact of much longer separations could not be assessed, since they were experienced by very few infants in our sample). Nor were changes in more general family conditions, such as moving to a new home. In short, the circumstances most directly associated with changes in attachment classification were those which were most likely to directly affect the ongoing quality or quantity of mother-infant interaction. The bidirectional effects of these circumstances on attachment status suggest that in middle-class homes they do introduce change in mother-infant interaction, but do not necessarily bias toward attachment insecurity (see Thompson & Lamb, in press).

Table 3 **Maternal employment and regular nonmaternal care: temporal relationships to stability of attachment classifications**

	Before 12.5 months	Between 12.5 and 19.5 months
	Maternal employment	
Initially insecure — change ($N = 10$)	5 (50)	2 (20)
Initially secure — change ($N = 10$)	3 (30)	2 (20)
Initially insecure — stable ($N = 3$)	0	0
Initially secure — stable ($N = 20$)	2 (10)	1 (5)
	Regular nonmaternal care	
Initially insecure — change ($N = 10$)	3 (30)	2 (20)
Initially secure — change ($N = 10$)	4 (40)	2 (20)
Initially insecure — stable ($N = 3$)	2 (67)	0
Initially secure — stable ($N = 20$)	0	0

Note: Figures shown in parentheses are percentages.

Few of the family or caregiving factors were related to attachment security or insecurity at either age. The only significant relationship indicated that infants who were insecurely attached at 19.5 months were more likely to experience regular nonmaternal care (9 of 14) than were securely attached babies (4 of 29) ($\chi^2 = 9.30$, $df = 1$, $p < .005$, with Yates's correction). In general, however, the family circumstances and stresses we assessed were more likely to influence the temporal stability of attachment relationships than to be associated with A-, B-, or C-group classifications at either age.

Discussion

These results indicate that in nearly half the infants in an unselected, middle-class sample, the security of attachment changed between 12.5 and 19.5 months of age. We also found that these changes were associated with changes in caregiving arrangements which were likely to affect infant-mother interaction. In middle-class homes, however, these events which occurred during the baby's lifetime did not result in a bias toward attachment insecurity, but rather forced a renegotiation, so to speak, of the mother-infant relationship — sometimes resulting in changes from secure to insecure attachment relationships, sometimes in the opposite direction. Even events occurring during the baby's first year were associated with changes in attachment status, perhaps by introducing short-term changes in mother-infant interaction which influenced the 12.5-month Strange Situation assessment, but not the follow-up one. Clearly, temporal changes in attachment classifications are more typical of normal populations than we had earlier thought. In light of this, we suggest that attachment classifications be viewed as an index of the current status of the infant-mother relationship, the quality of which is likely to change in response to changing family and caregiving circumstances.

This research is based on a dissertation project conducted by the first author in partial fulfillment of the requirements for the degree Doctor of Philosophy in the Rackham School of Graduate Studies at the University of Michigan. It was supported by a grant from the Riksbankens Jubileumsfond of Sweden to author Lamb, and by a dissertation grant from Rackham to author Thompson. While the research was conducted, Thompson was a predoctoral fellow in the Bush Program in Child Development and Social Policy at the University of Michigan and a National Science Foundation predoctoral fellow, while Estes was a United States Public Health Service predoctoral trainee. We are very grateful for the assistance provided by Lisa Colvin, Susan Dickstein, Michael Iskowitz, Margaret Madden, Susan Piconke, Jane Stein, Jamie Steinberg, Susan Strzelecki, and Michele Tukel. Catherine Malkin provided special help in both testing and scoring. We are also appreciative of technical assistance provided by Lee Davis. Finally, we wish to express a special debt to the families who participated in this study. An earlier version of this paper was presented at the annual meetings of the Midwestern Psychological Association, Detroit, April 30-May 2, 1981.

Reference Note

1.   Hollingshead, A.B. (1975), Four-factor index of social status. Unpublished manuscript, Yale University.

References

Ainsworth, M.D.S.; Blehar, M.C.; Waters, E.; & Wall, S. (1978) *Patterns of attachment*. Hillsdale, N.J.: Erlbaum.

Thompson, R.A., & Lamb, M.E. 'Infants, mothers, families, and strangers.' In N. Lewis & L. Rosenblum (Eds.), *Beyond the dyad*. New York: Plenum, in press.

Vaugn, B.; Egeland, B.; Sroufe, L.A.; & Waters, E. (1979) 'Individual differences in infant-mother attachment at twelve and eighteen months: stability and change in families under stress.' *Child Development*, 50, 971-975.

Waters, E. (1978) 'The reliability and stability of individual differences in infant-mother attachment.' *Child Development*, 49, 483-494.

11. The Nature and Qualities of Parenting Provided by Women Raised in Institutions

Linda Dowdney, David Skuse, Michael Rutter,
David Quinton and David Mrazek

Abstract — *A repeated pattern of difficulties in parenting is often found in successive generations of the same families. That finding, together with a concern to identify potential adverse influences upon child behaviour and development, was the focus of this study into the parenting provided by women who were raised within institutions. Relationships with their 2- to 3-year-old infants were assessed using complementary interview and naturalistic observational techniques. Differences in parenting styles between the case and comparison groups were on the whole subtle. Ex-care women were relatively less sensitive to their children's cues and, in response to their demands and opposition, exercised control by confrontation rather than by circumvention.*

Keywords: *Mother-child interaction, institutional rearing, parenting skills, observation / interview study.*

Introduction

The social, emotional and cognitive development of young children takes place within the context of the family. The relationships that children have with their parents are crucial, for it is the parents who assume the primary caretaking, nurturing and teaching roles. The recognition of the importance of these relationships has led to decades of research into parenting (for reviews see Clarke-Stewart & Apfel, 1978; Maccoby & Martin, 1983). While there have been major changes in the particular features of parenting that preoccupy theoreticians and empirical researchers, a concern to delineate those parental attributes and qualities that foster *optimal* child development has been the main emphasis of this research, whatever its theoretical orientation.

A separate but related issue concerns the observation that a repeated pattern of difficulties in parenting is often found in successive generations of the same families. This is shown, for instance, in the data concerning child abuse (Oliver & Taylor, 1971; Spinetta & Rigler, 1972) and that relating to the parents of 'problem families' (Ferguson, 1966; Philp, 1963; Wright & Lunn, 1971). Given that serious parenting problems show some intergenerational continuity it is important to determine which features of parenting are involved in such continuities.

A study of mothers with children recently admitted into care showed their patterns of child-rearing to be substantially different from those of a general population comparison group (Quinton & Rutter, 1984a, b). Specifically, they were more insensitive and

Linda Dowdney, David Skuse, Michael Rutter, David Quinton and David Mrazek: 'The Nature and Qualities of Parenting Provided by Women Raised in Institutions.' *THE JOURNAL OF CHILD PSYCHOLOGY AND PSYCHIATRY* (1985), Vol. 26, No. 4, pp. 599-625. © 1985 Association for Child Psychology and Psychiatry.

negative, demonstrating less warmth towards their children. Their discipline attempts were frequently both ineffective and inconsistent. The mothers of children admitted into care had often experienced seriously adverse family conditions in their own childhoods, and significantly more of them had at some time been taken into care themselves.

The sample in that study had been defined in terms of a breakdown in parental care, so that it was not surprising to find many areas of difficulty in parenting. The finding that many of the mothers had experienced serious difficulties in their own upbringing suggested that there was likely to be some intergenerational continuity in factors associated with parenting. A prospective study was designed to test that possibility; it comprised a follow-up into adult life of girls who spent a substantial portion of their childhood years in an institution. Some of the general outcome findings of the study are reported elsewhere (Quinton, Rutter & Liddle, 1984; Rutter, Quinton & Liddle, 1983). This paper provides a more detailed account of the parenting qualities of the women.

Method

Selection of total sample

The study consisted of a follow-up into early life of individuals who, in 1964, were then in one or other of two children's homes run on group cottage lines. The children had been admitted to institutional care because their parents could not cope with child-rearing rather than because of any type of disturbed behaviour shown by the children themselves. The regimes in the cottages had been studied systematically by King and his colleagues (King, Raynes & Tizard, 1971) and the children's behaviour at school bad been assessed by means of a standardized questionnaire (the Rutter 'B' scale — Rutter, 1967). Both sets of data were made available to us. This 'ex-care' sample was restricted to all children defined as 'white' in the original study and who were aged between 21 and 27 years on 1 January 1978. This age criterion was applied in the hope of obtaining a high proportion of subjects with young children.

The contrast group comprised a quasi-random general population sample[1] of individuals of the same age, never admitted 'into care', who had lived as children with their families in the same general area in inner London and whose behaviour at school had been assessed at approximately the same age by means of the same questionnaire. The contrast sample was similarly followed into early adult life using methods of assessment identical to those employed for the 'ex-care' sample. This report considers only the women in both groups who had become parents.

Parenting sample

In total, 94 ex-care women fulfilled the criterion for selection into the study (Quinton *et al.*, 1984). Of the 89 still alive at the time of follow-up, 81 were traced and interviewed. In the comparison group, 41 women out of a potential 51 subjects were traced and interviewed.

Of the ex-care women, 49 had given birth to live children, of whom 42 had at least one child living with them at home. Only 16 comparison women had become mothers, 13 of whom were successfully interviewed. In order to provide a sample large enough for a comparative assessment of parenting, this group was expanded by the inclusion of 14 women who were the wives of male controls (these comprised the wives with children in the age group used for observations of parent-child interactions). The findings for the comparison women and the female spouses were generally similar (Quinton *et al.*, 1984).

The observation sample consisted of 23 ex-care and 21 comparison mothers with children between the ages of two and three and a half years. This age range was chosen as the period of development during which children become more oppositional and negative, and place demands upon parental strategies of management. Two years was chosen as the lower limit because most children have acquired some language by that age, allowing relatively greater reliance on verbal communication as a basis for observational recording. Choosing an upper limit of 3½ years meant that it would be unusual for the children to have entered playschool. Thus they would have had relatively little experience outside the nuclear family, and would probably still have such dependence on their mother that interaction between them would be frequent during a restricted period of observation.

The assessment of parenting

Concepts. The conceptualization of parenting in terms of relevant skills and crucial functions is relatively well researched, findings having been consistent in their demonstration of aspects that are maladaptive for the child. For example, it is well established that the family characteristics most strongly associated with delinquency include ineffective supervision and disciplines; family discord and disharmony; weak parent-child relationships; and large family size (Rutter & Giller, 1983).

Furthermore, there is a reasonable consensus on the specific dimensions of parenting that are most important for children's optimal development (Harman & Brim, 1980; Pringle, 1974; Rutter, 1975). Thus parenting 'skills' are thought to include sensitivity to children's cues and a responsiveness to the differing needs at different developmental stages; in social problem solving and coping skills; in knowing how to play and talk with children; and in the use of disciplinary techniques that are effective in the triple sense of bringing about the desired child behaviour, doing so in a way that results in harmony and increasing the child's self-control.

It was with these considerations in mind that we chose to study the following characteristics of the mother-child relationship: (1) control with respect to difficult or disruptive child behaviours; (2) affective tone as demonstrated by the expression of positive or negative emotion by the mother; and (3) maternal responsivity, or sensitivity to the child's cues. Finally, an assessment was made of the type and quality of social communications when the mother and child were engaged together in mutual activities such as play. Recognition of the different strengths of both interview and observational techniques in the study of parenting has led to their combined use (see, for example, Dunn & Kendrick, 1982; Lytton, 1973), as it was in this study.

Assessment of parenting by interview. Interviews conducted with subjects lasted 2½- 4 hours and used a non-schedule standardized approach based on methods established in earlier investigations (Brown & Rutter, 1966; Graham & Rutter, 1968; Quinton, Rutter & Rowlands, 1976: Rutter & Brown, 1966). Mothers were encouraged to talk freely about the child's daily routine, including the regularity and timing of waking, mealtimes and bedtimes, as well as the parental handling of any problems associated with daily routines. Detailed accounts were obtained of disruptive and oppositional behaviour, peer and sib disputes, fears and anxieties, together with the mother's response and handling of these issues. For each type of issue the mother was asked for a detailed account of the most recent incident. The frequency and typicality of such interactions were established as well as the frequency of less often occurring parenting issues or parenting techniques.

In this way a detailed day-to-day picture of parenting style was built up from a wide range of individual ratings. In addition to these handling characteristics, information was systematically obtained on the kind and range of toys available and the frequency with which the mother and child played together. Individual ratings were made on a number of categories such as reading, imaginative (role) play, rough and tumble play, involvement in household tasks or watching television. Finally the mother was asked to describe the previous day's activities in detail so that scores of the amount of concentrated, continuously available separate activity could be rated.

Overall ratings of parenting style and consistency were made taking all the information into account. This included the level of expressed warmth; the sensitivity shown in the handling of the child; the style, effectiveness and consistency of control and the management of anxieties and fears. These overall ratings allowed the interviewer to take into account a number of features of parenting and parenting contexts which could not be derived directly from the individual ratings.

Observational assessment of parenting. The observational methodology was designed to provide information that would be complementary to that obtained by interview. A detailed description of the methodology, its reliability and validity can be found in Dowdney, Mrazek, Quinton & Rutter (1984) and Mrazek, Dowdney, Rutter & Quinton (1982).

Observations took place in the home on two occasions, each session being 2 hours in length. The mothers were asked to follow their usual routine as closely as possible, although we requested that the television should not be turned on. We emphasized that we would not interact with either mother or child during the period of observation. This was important in order to avoid children speaking and doing things with us rather than with their mother.

Three different systems of measurement of mother-child interaction were employed. First, 10-sec *time-interval sampling* was used to provide a basic frequency count of specified behaviours (any particular behaviour could be recorded once only in each time interval). This gave rise to measures of the duration and form of mother-child interaction. There was also recording of positive or negative expressions of affect by the mother (such as affectionate contact or smacks); maternal initiations of interaction; the proximity of mother and child in terms of whether or not they were in the same room; and frequency and duration of independent activities on the part of the mother or child.

Secondly, *sequential* measures were used to assess how mothers responded to each of three different sets of circumstances: (a) episodes involving discipline or control; (b) situations in which their child showed distress; and (c) their child's attempts to gain attention or initiate an interaction. For each of these there was specification of the 'key' events that served to initiate sequential recording (see Dowdney *et al.*, 1984). For example, in the area of control, sequential recording began if a child showed opposition to or non-compliance with a maternal instruction. Pre-specified 'outcomes' determined the termination of sequential recording. For instance, in the case of control episodes, the sequence continued until either the child complied or the mother ceased attempting to assert control. Time intervals were abandoned while sequences were being noted; rather, single or multi-element maternal and child behaviours were recorded in turn-taking fashion without concern for the precise duration of each behavioural event. However, as an audiotape recording was made of the entire observation, the duration of sequences could be obtained later.

The third system of measurement concerned the mother's *verbal interactions* with her child. The measures were obtained from a detailed analysis of the audiotape recording of the observation period; the mode of coding was primarily oriented to the social functions of maternal communications. The mother's contribution to the dialogue was coded according to a scheme consisting of eight categories of social communication.

Sample. Table 1 summarizes the characteristics of the observed children in the ex-care and comparison samples. The children in the two groups did not differ in ordinal position and were closely comparable in age. However, although the sex distributions did not differ significantly, it was notable that girls outnumbered boys in the comparison group. In an older age-group this might have constituted a possible bias but sex differences in behaviour among 2-year-olds are few compared with those generally found among 4- to 5-year-olds (Maccoby & Jacklin, 1974), and none were found in our sample. As the dimensions of parenting we studied were found not to differ by sex, the sexes have been pooled hereafter.

Table 1   Characteristics of the observed sample

	Ex-care ($n = 23$)	Comparison group ($n = 21$)
Sex of child		
Boys	13	7
Girls	10	14
Exact probability 0.21 (two-tailed)		
Age of child		
24-30 months	12	11
31-37 months	5	3
38-42 months	6*	7
No statistically significant differences		
Ordinal position		
Only child	5	7
First born	6	6
A middle child	5	2
Youngest	7	6
No statistically significant differences		

* One child was 44 months old by the time of observation.

Results

Parenting history

A substantial contrast existed between the social histories of women who had been raised in children's homes and those who comprised the comparison group. The findings are discussed more fully in Quinton et al. (1984) and Rutter et al. (1983), but they were nowhere more striking than in the realm of parenting experiences and actions, Nearly twice as many of the ex-care women had become pregnant and given birth to a surviving child by the time of the follow-up interview. While two-fifths of the ex-care sample had become pregnant before their nineteenth birthday, this was true for only two of the 42 comparison women. Serious breakdowns in parenting were evident only in the institutional sample; nearly one-fifth had had children taken into care for fostering or placement in a children's home and there had been one case of infanticide. Altogether, for one reason or another, 18% of the 'ex-care' mothers had children who were no longer being looked after by them and with no apparent likelihood of being returned, compared with none of the control group. Moreover, just over one-third (35%) had experienced some form of transient or permanent parenting breakdown with at least one of their children; this occurred with *none* of the comparison group mothers (Table 2). In most cases the women had left their children to the care of others because they could not cope with the demands of life as they faced them at the time, rather than because the children had been compulsorily removed as a result of gross neglect or physical abuse. Among the nine women who had permanently given up a child, five subsequently gave birth to a second child who was not taken into care.

Table 2   Pregnancy and parenting histories

	Ex-care women ($n = 81$)	Comparison group ($n = 42$)	Statistical significance		
	%	%	χ^2	d.f.	P
Ever pregnant	72	43	8.50	1	< 0.01
Pregnant by 19	42	5	16.75	1	< 0.001
Had surviving child	60	36	5.85	1	< 0.02
Of those with children	($n = 49$)	($n = 15$)			
	%	%			
Without male partner	22	0	Exact test, $P = 0.039$		
Any children ever in care/fostered	18	0	Exact test, $P = 0.075$		
Any temporary or permanent parenting breakdown	35	0	Exact test, $P = 0.02$		
Living with father of all children	61	100	6.52	1	< 0.02

Current parenting: overall interview measures

Taking all information into account it was possible to derive overall 'good', 'medium' and 'poor' categories of current parenting style at the time of follow-up, based upon a mother's level of expressed warmth, her effectiveness and consistency of control, maternal sensitivity and handling of the child's anxieties and fears. 'Poor' parenting was rated if there was a marked lack of warmth to the child (score of 0-2 on a 6-point scale) or low sensitivity to a child's needs (score of 1-2 on a 5-point scale) *and* difficulties in at least two out of three areas of disciplinary control (consistency, effectiveness or style). Conversely, 'good' parenting was rated if there were no difficulties on any scales of current parenting. An intermediate ranking indicated some current problems.

Over two-fifths of the ex-care mothers had a current rating of poor parenting compared with one in ten of the comparison group — a four-fold difference (Table 3). On the other hand, nearly one-third (31%) of the women reared in institutions showed good parenting, a rating made on just less than half of the comparison group. It is clear that in spite of the fact that *all* of the ex-care group had experienced an institutional rearing for part of their childhoods and that most had experienced poor parenting when with their own families, there was great heterogeneity of outcome in the ex-care sample, with a substantial minority showing *good* parenting. It is evident also that a surprisingly high proportion (just over half) of the comparison group mothers showed some problems in parenting, although far fewer showed severe difficulties.

Table 3   Current parenting outcome

	Ex-care (n = 42) %	Comparison group* (n = 27) %	Residuals
Good	31	48	1.44
Intermediate	29	41	1.05
Poor	40	11	− 2.62

$$\chi^2 = 6.91, \text{ 2 d.f., } P < 0.05$$

Observation findings: overall measures

In the first stage of analysis, observational measures were combined to provide, for each mother, an overall assessment of the quality of her parenting. For this purpose the two groups of women were pooled. Seven aspects of parenting quality were chosen on the basis of concepts regarding the dimensions of parenting that are most important for children's socio-emotional development. These comprised control and distress issues, maternal affective tone, play interaction, and aspects of maternal sensitivity and responsivity. Preliminary analysis enabled individual mothers to be rated on each one of the seven dimensions, and for the scores to be ranked. The rankings on each measure were then divided into quartiles. Difficulties in parenting were defined in terms of being in the *extreme* quartiles for low positive affect, high negative affect, high frequency of child distress, high frequency of control episodes, high number of child initiations, high proportion of child initiations ignored and low frequency of joint play. An overall assessment of problems in parenting was obtained by summing, for each mother, the number of dimensions on which she was ranked in the quartile that reflected the greatest 'difficulty'.

Table 4   Overall observation measure of parenting (No. of areas of difficulty)

No. of areas of difficulty	Ex-care women ($n = 23$)	Comparison women ($n = 21$)
None	3	10
1 to 2	12	11
At least 4	8	0

$$\chi^2 = 11.746; \text{d.f.} = 2; P < 0.01$$

A comparison of the two groups on these dimensions indicated that a higher proportion of the ex-care women were experiencing *more* difficulties (Table 4). A third (35%) fell into the lowest quartile on at least four out of these seven areas of parenting. This was not the case for any mother in the comparison group. Conversely, over two-thirds (71%) of the comparison group mothers had parenting qualities that placed them in the top quartile on at least *one* of these measures; this was true for only one in nine of the ex-care sample. The difference between the groups was significant ($\chi^2 = 11.75$, 2 d.f., *P < 0.01*).

These overall findings raise two major issues. The first question concerns the extent to which the parenting difficulties experienced by the ex-care women are set in a context of broader psychosocial adversities. The second issue relates to the particular characteristics of those parenting problems that were detected by interview and by observation, and whether the groups could be distinguished by such molecular measures.

Current psychosocial functioning

Individual measures of psychosocial functioning showed marked differences between the two samples (Table 5). Over one-quarter (26%) of the ex-care group had currently handicapping psychiatric disorders, the great majority of which consisted of long-standing personality problems. Only 7% of the comparison group had a psychiatric condition and none of them was rated as having a handicapping personality disorder [both measures being based on well tested interview methods; see Quinton *et al.* (1984) and Rutter *et al.* (1983) for criteria]. In addition, criminality, broken cohabitation, marital discord and substantial difficulties in love/sex relationships were substantially more frequent in the ex-care group.

Overlap between parenting and overall psychosocial functioning. An overall psychosocial assessment was obtained by combining these measures (see Quinton *et al.*, 1984). Table 6 shows the extent of overlap between this overall measure of social functioning and the overall interview assessment of quality of parenting. Four main conclusions may be drawn. First, there was no association between the two measures in the comparison group. The implication is that parenting difficulties need not be a consequence of overall psychosocial impairment. Secondly, the two measures overlapped to a very considerable extent in the ex-care. As a consequence, there are very few ex-care women with poor parenting but a good psychosocial outcome on non-parenting measures (3/42), and scarcely any with good parenting but a poor psychosocial outcome (2/24). Thirdly, the main differences between the two groups applied to the proportions with both or neither set of difficulties. There was little evidence of parenting links across the two generations if parenting difficulties *occurring in isolation* are considered. Indeed, intermediate level parenting difficulties shown by women with generally good psychosocial functioning were largely a feature of the comparison group (8/28 vs 5/42 in the ex-care group). That observation suggests the inference for the fourth conclusions — namely, that the explanation for isolated parenting difficulties of mild-to-moderate degree may well be different from that for severe and generalised psychosocial problems which include parenting difficulties as one of the many areas of concern.

Table 5   Current psychosocial functioning (women)

	Ex-care ($n = 42$)	Comparison ($n = 27$)d	Statistical significance		
	%	%	χ^2	d.f.	P
Current psychiatric disorder	26	7	2.66	1	N.S.
Personality disorder	17	0	3.35	1	N.S.
Criminality (self-report)	26	0	6.57	1	$P < 0.02$
Criminality (official records)	33	8*	2.12	1	N.S.
One or more broken cohabitations	40	11	5.33	1	$P < 0.01$
Marked marital problems (of those cohabiting)	31	7	4.06	1	$P < 0.01$
Substantial difficulties in love/sex relationships	19	0	4.11	1	$P < 0.01$

* Data available only on subjects $n = 13$ (i.e. not spouses).

Table 6   Overlap between parenting and overall psychosocial functioning

	Psychosocial outcome	
	Good	Intermediate/poor
'Ex-care' group parenting:		
Good	11	2
Intermediate	6	6
Poor	2	15
Comparison group parenting:		
Good	8	4
Intermediate	8	4
Poor	2	1

Current parenting and social circumstances. The ex-care women were living in worse social circumstances than the comparison group women at the time of follow-up. Nearly twice as many (44 vs 24%) were living in intermediate/poor circumstances, operationally defined in terms of a score based on lack of facilities such as a washing machine, telephone or evidence of overcrowding such as the children having to share a bed. However, poor parenting was more likely to occur in the ex-care group, whatever their social situation (see Quinton *et al.*, 1984).

Changes in parenting with subsequent children. Substantial overlap has been shown to exist between serious parenting difficulties and generally poor psychosocial functioning in the ex-care group (e.g. Table 6). This might seem to suggest that parenting problems could be an intrinsic and persistent aspect of maladaptive personality functioning. There is, however, the contrary evidence that these women's parenting is significantly improved when they have the support of a non-deviant spouse (see Quinton et al., 1984). The modifiability of parenting skills could be more stringently tested by measuring changes over time, but that could not be examined directly in the present study as only one follow-up assessment was made. However, an indirect measure of change is provided by the comparison of first-born and subsequent-born children. Two lines of approach may be taken with this question. The first concerns parenting breakdown and separation. The second examines the direct assessments of parenting functioning by interview and by observation.

If parenting skills were indeed modifiable this hypothesis could be tested by examining families with at least two children, where the mother's relationship with her first-born had suffered breakdown. The experience of the second- and subsequent-born children could then be contrasted with that of the first-born. Altogether there were 15 (out of 42) women in the ex-care group who had had parenting breakdowns with their first-born children. 'Breakdown' means, in this context, that the children were either taken into care or that they went to live apart from their mother — with friends or relatives — for a period of at least 6 months. The figure excludes one woman who had given birth twice during her adolescence but who did not parent at that time because her infants were put up for adoption straight away; she had no separations from her subsequent children. One other woman had a breakdown in parenting with her second-born only. It was considered premature to judge the parenting of five of the remaining group on the basis of lack of breakdown, because at the time of assessment their second child was less than 2 years of age.[2] Four women had had no further children, including one whose first-born had been the victim of infanticide. Of the remaining six women with subsequent-born children who were not infants, two were not parenting any children at the time of interview — one because of a long-term fostering arrangement and the other because her offspring had all gone together to live with their father. Thus a currently parenting group of only four was left on which to test the hypothesis that breakdowns might be more frequent with first-born children. In one of these four cases all the children experienced parenting breakdown at the same time as a result of the parents' separation. Of the remaining three mothers one had had no separations from her second child and was rated as parenting well at interview and by observation. Another had been separated from each of her three children at various times and was considered to be functioning poorly when interviewed. When this woman was observed some months later in more favourable social circumstances she was rated intermediate in parenting. The third was not observed. She had had all her children in care at various times, and at interview her parenting was considered to be poor. In total there were 27 of the 42 ex-care women who had had *at least two* children. Seven of those 27 (25.9%) had experienced parenting breakdowns with their first-born child. This compared with 6 (28.6%) of the 21 subsequent-born children over the age of 2 years who had been the subjects of breakdown.

The second line of approach to the question of whether the parenting of women raised in care improves with experience is to compare the current parenting of first- and subsequent-born children for women who have had at least two children. Interview and observational assessments were, of course, only possible on those children who were currently living with their mothers; this group comprised 22 mothers with first-born and 20 with subsequent-born children. Interview and observational findings on *current* parenting provide evidence on which to test the hypothesis that mothers who have been raised in care parent second- or subsequent-born children better than their first-borns. Of course, this evidence is indirect because it is not the same women whose parenting on first- and subsequent-born children is being compared. Nevertheless, no support for the hypothesis is obtained from interview data, poor parenting being rated in 36% of the group with first-borns, 45% in those with subsequent-born children.

Table 7   Ex-care families with temporary or permanent parenting breakdown

Family	Age	Sex	Nature of breakdown	Currently with	Current parenting rating
1	10 years	boy	in-care	long-term fostering	not parenting
	8 years	boy	in-care	long-term fostering	
2	4 years	girl	in-care	long-term fostering	
	6 weeks	girl	none	with mother	not rateable
3	7 years	girl	in-care	adopted	poor
	$2^1/_2$ years	girl	fostered	with mother	
	2 weeks	girl	none	with mother	
4	$2^1/_2$ years	boy	fostered	long-term/adoption	poor
	5 years	boy	in-care	with mother	
	3 years	girl	in-care	with mother	
5	11 years	girl	in-care	adopted	
	10 years	boy	in-care	adopted	
	8 years	girl	none	with mother	intermediate
	$3^1/_2$ years	girl	none	with mother	
	14 months	girl	none	with mother	
	2 months	boy	none	with mother	
6	—	girl	infanticide	—	

163

Table 7 **Ex-care families with temporary or permanent parenting breakdown (cont.)**

Family	Age	Sex	Nature of breakdown	Currently with	Current parenting rating
7	8 years	boy	foster-care	short-term foster care	poor
	5 years	boy	foster-care	with mother	
	15 months	boy	foster-care	with mother	
8	4 years	boy	none	with mother	poor
	$2\,^1/_2$ years	girl	foster-care	with mother	
	$1^1/_2$ years	girl	none	with mother	
9	5 years	boy	short-term care	with mother	poor
	17 months	boy	none	with mother	
10	$4^1/_2$ years	girl	marital breakdown	with father	not parenting
11	9 years	boy	marital breakdown	with father	
	8 years	girl	marital breakdown	with father	not parenting
	5 years	boy	marital breakdown	with father	
	4 years	girl	marital breakdown	with father	
12	7 years	boy	marital breakdown	with father	not rateable
	10 months	girl	none	with mother	
13	10 years	girl	marital breakdown	with mother	
	9 years	girl	marital breakdown	with mother	good
	4 years	girl	marital breakdown	with mother	
	1 year	girl	none	with mother	
14	2 years	girl	failure to cope	with mother	poor
	7 months	girl	failure to cope	with mother	
15	9 years	girl	failure to cope	with mother	poor
16	$7^1/_2$ years	girl	failure to cope	with mother	good
	$3^1/_2$ years	boy	none	with mother	
17	2 years	boy	marital breakdown	with mother	poor

All separations due to marital breakdown lasted 6 months or longer. Breakdowns categorised as 'failure to cope' involve the child being looked after by other adults but not being in-care or fostered. The majority of those thus admitted were for failure to cope as well.

The observational findings are in sharp contrast, in that a marked difference was found in the extent of parenting difficulties according to ordinal position. Of the eight women with difficulties in at least four out of seven areas of parenting, seven were parenting first-born or only children. In order to examine whether women in the comparison group experienced a similar ordinal position effect it was necessary to redefine parenting problems as difficulties in two or more areas, as none of the comparison group women had four or more.

As Table 8 shows, the ex-care mothers parenting first-borns were more likely to have wide-ranging problems than were comparison group mothers assessed on their eldest children. Women from the ex-care group with first-borns also had significantly greater difficulties than those assessed on the parenting of subsequent children. Examining the seven specific areas of parenting difficulty defined by observational analysis, a similar distinct ordinal position effect is seen — both within the ex-care group and between groups. Interestingly, comparison group women did not show any significant differences in such problem areas with subsequent-born children.

It is not entirely clear why the observational measures should show an ordinal position effect whereas interview data did not. Historical findings on first and subsequent breakdowns seem too limited to shed light on the issue. Possible explanations include differences in the nature of the data. First, it is apparent that some of the most socially impaired women who had experienced breakdowns in parenting were no longer caring for children aged 2 years or more, hence their parenting was not subject to examination. (This applied to five of the 16 mothers with an overall rating of 'poor' social functioning but only one of the 31 remaining mothers) Secondly, the interview rating applied to parenting as it ordinarily took place. This contrasts with the one-to-one situation usually used for home observation, and may be of relevance because obviously the mothers of subsequent-born children were having to deal with several children whereas those of first-born children were not. It may be, therefore, that the mothers of subsequent-born children were having to parent in more difficult family circumstances. If that is so, the observational data would suggest that their parenting skills may have improved but that they remained vulnerable to the effects of social stressors and pressures. We must conclude that the evidence is ambiguous on whether or not parenting improves with experience in these circumstances but, probably, it does so in some women (although clearly not in all cases). Perhaps it is least likely to do so in those with the greatest initial social impairment.

Table 8   Two or more areas of parenting difficulty and ordinal position of child

| | Ex-care women | | Comparison women | |
	%	n	%	n
First-born or only child	82	(11)	23	(13)
Other	25	(12)	36	(8)

Exact probability (two-tailed): within groups: ex-care = 0.018, comparison = 0.82; between groups: first-born = 0.012; other = 0.91.

Specific dimensions of current parenting: interview measures

In order to consider in greater detail just what form those difficulties might take, it is necessary to turn to the findings for the various specific measures of individual aspects of parenting. Those derived from the interviews will be considered first.

Degree of involvement. There were few sizeable differences of note between the two groups with respect to the overall patterns of affection and playful interaction between the mothers and their children (Table 9). Most of the women in both groups showed a high level of expressed warmth to their children. Only one-quarter (24%) of the ex-care women were low in warmth and although this rate was above that (7%) in the comparison group, the difference fell short of statistical significance (Exact test, *P* = 0.15). Similarly, most mothers played with their children on a regular basis and the groups did not differ in the amount of joint play. Attention was paid to the type of play activities between the mothers and their children, with a differentiation between those (such as make-believe games and drawing) that required creative involvement from the child and those (such as watching T.V. or helping about the house) in which such individual initiative was less important. There was a tendency, that fell short of statistical significance, for more ex-care mothers (40 vs 19%) to engage in interactions that included no creative involvement but, otherwise, the types of play were broadly comparable in the two groups.

Table 9   Interview measures of affection and play

Expressed warmth	Ex-care (n = 42) %	Comparison group (n = 27) %	χ^2	d.f.	P
Low	24	7			
Moderate	21	37	4.00	2	N.S.
High	55	56			

(low vs rest, Exact test, *P* = 0.146)

Daily play with child	Ex-care (n = 24)* %	Comparison group (n = 21)* %			
Type (i)					
Let's pretend games	24	38			N.S.
Constructional games	28	43			N.S.
Drawing, writing, reading	56	67			N.S.
None of the above	40	19	1.48	1	N.S.
Type (ii)					
Watching T.V.	28	33			N.S.
Rough and tumble	36	19			N.S.
Help with housework	56	48			N.S.

*Comparison based on 2- to 3$\frac{1}{2}$-year-old children only.

Disciplinary style. In both groups there was a good deal of inconsistency in disciplinary control, and this was as frequent in the comparison group as in the ex-care sample (Table 10). There was, however, a significant tendency for the ex-care women to include a higher proportion in which disciplinary episodes involved unreconciled disputes (meaning that the episode failed to result in harmony or any attempt to 'make-up' or restore the relationship). An aggressive style of discipline (with frequent recourse to smacking, irritable shouting and the like) was relatively frequent in both groups. The ex-care mothers were somewhat more likely to use a definitely aggressive style than the preponderant disciplinary method, but the difference was statistically non-significant. This contrast between the groups was reflected also in the frequency of smacking (Table 10), where twice as many of the ex-care mothers resorted to daily smacking (40 vs 19%), although the difference fell short of statistical significance. Most of the mothers in both groups showed at least moderately effective disciplinary control (effective, that is to say, in that the disciplinary act resulted in the intended change in the child's behaviour). However, definitely ineffective control was substantially more frequent in the ex-care group (26 vs 4%), a difference that was statistically significant.

Table 10   Interview measures of sensitivity and of control

	Ex-care (n = 42)	Comparison group (n = 27)	Statistical significance		
	%	%	χ^2	d.f.	P
(a) Consistency of control					
Somewhat/very inconsistent	50	44	0.04	1	N.S.
(b) Reconciliation of disputes					
0-4/10 reconciled	26	8			
5-7/10 reconciled	21	8	6.62	2	< 0.05
8+/10 reconciled	54	85			
(c) Control style					
Indulgent	12	7			
Firm – not aggressive	26	41	3.95	3	N.S.
Mildly aggressive	29	37			
Definitely aggressive	33	15			
Definitely aggressive vs rest, Exact test, $P = 0.148$					
(d) Frequency of smacking					
Once a fortnight or less	24	33			
1-6 times per week	36	48	3.65	2	N.S.
Daily or more often	40	19			
Daily vs rest, Exact test, $P = 0.096$					

Table 10 Interview measures of sensitivity and of control (cont.)

	Ex-care (n = 42)	Comparison group (n = 27)	Statistical significance		
	%	%	χ^2	d.f.	P
(e) Effectiveness of control					
Ineffective	26	4			
Some control	21	22	4.29	1	N.S.
Moderate control	29	41	(χ^2 for trends)		
Firm control	24	37			
Ineffective vs rest, χ^2 = 4.33, 1 d.f., $P < 0.05$					
(f) Sensitivity					
Low	42	7			
Moderate	19	22	10.58	2	< 0.01
High	38	70			

Maternal sensitivity. Much the biggest difference between the groups concerned the mother's 'sensitivity' in her handling of distress or disputes — a rating based on the interviewers' judgement of the mothers' overall handling of their children (Table 10). Insensitivity was rated when mothers seemed unable to perceive reasons for their children's distress ("he's always crying for no reason"), or when they moved excessively rapidly into control without first trying to evaluate or sort out what was happening, or when they described the child's fears or anxieties as 'naughty' behaviour. 'Sensitivity', on the other hand, meant that the mothers showed some appreciation (in overt behavioural terms) of why their children behaved in the way they did, that they made differential responses according to the specifics of the child's behaviour, and that in general they showed a flexible and adaptive approach to child-rearing with an appropriate variation according to what was going on and according to the child's response and whether the parental action 'worked' in doing whatever it intended to do. Forty-two per cent of currently parenting ex-care mothers were rated as low on sensitivity compared with only 7% of the comparison group — a highly significant difference.

Specific dimensions of current parenting: observational measures

Demanding child behaviours. Control episodes (i.e. sequences of interaction initiated by the child's aggressive, destructive, oppositional or non-compliant behaviour) occurred at a rate more than 50% higher than that in the comparison group (Table 11). The relatively high frequency of disciplinary issues in the ex-care group mirrors the interview finding that the ex-care mothers were more likely to be inefficient in their discipline. Distress episodes were also somewhat more common in the ex-care group but the frequency varied greatly within both the groups (especially within the ex-care group as shown by the particularly high standard deviation), and the overall between-group difference fell well short of statistical significance. However, perhaps the most striking difference lay in the substantially higher rate of child initiations in the ex-care group. Both verbal and physical initiations were included in this category, but to be counted as a new overture from the child the initiation had to have been preceded by at least 20 sec of non-interaction. The most common single type of initiation concerned the children's attempts to share with their mothers their interest and excitement in some play activity (34% in the ex-care group and 38% in the comparison group) but they also included non-specific verbalizations (25 and 27% respectively), requests (16% in each group), questions (15 and 9% respectively) and other forms of approach.

Table 11   Child behaviours during observation

	Ex-care women (n = 23)		Comparison women (n = 21)		Statistical significance		
	Mean	(S.D.)	Mean	(S.D.)	t	d.f.	P
Control episodes per 4 hours	19.34	(11.48)	12.63	(7.79)	2.236	42	< 0.05
Distress episodes per 4 hours	7.87	(7.85)	5.67	(4.87)	1.105	42	N.S.
Child initiations per 4 hours	37.96	(15.48)	25.05	(11.68)	3.099	42	< 0.01

Maternal affect. In both groups there was immense variation in the frequency with which positive affect was expressed (as reflected in a warm tone of voice, encouraging remarks, words of approval or physical actions such as affectionate touches or cuddles), and the difference between the groups was non-significant. However, there was a tendency for positive affect to be marginally less common in the ex-care group (Table 12). Although negative affect (comprising a critical or hostile tone of voice, disapproving or threatening comments and physically aggressive behaviour such as smacking or shaking) also showed great individual variation, the rate was over 70% higher in the ex-care group — a difference significant at the 5% level.[3]

Table 12   Maternal affect

	Ex-care women (n – 23)		Comparison women (n = 21)		Statistical significance		
	Mean	(S.D.)	Mean	(S.D.)	t	d.f.	P
Negative affect;							
overall rate per 4 hours*	35.52	(26.72)	20.56	(16.99)	2.12	40†	< 0.05
within confrontation only	16.83	(14.09)	10.37	(9.36)	1.71	40†	N.S.
with other social interactions	18.70	(14.12)	10.21	(8.28)	2.31	40†	< 0.05
Positive affect;							
overall rate per 4 hours	221.26	(111.94)	271.76	(138.80)			N.S.

*Rate = No. of 10-sec intervals per hour of observation during which the specified effect occurred.
† These date exclude two women in the comparison group with rates of negative affect several standard deviations outside the range of both groups. In both cases this was due to prolonged episodes of an atypical type, not represented in the other observations. The exclusion was based, therefore, on the fact that both statistically and qualitatively they could not be pooled with the rest of either sample.

Examination of the social contexts within which maternal affect was expressed showed that the negative feelings were *not* mainly a feature of disciplinary episodes. In both groups just over half the negative affect was expressed in the context of social interactions (such as playing or talking together) rather than in the context of some form of confrontation (i.e. a control or distress episode). The between-groups differences for the separate affect-within-context measures showed that the higher rate of negative maternal affect in the ex-care group applied across all contexts, although the difference was most marked *outside* confrontations.

Mother-child social interactions. The interview data showed no difference between the groups in the overall extent to which the mothers played and talked with their children. The observational findings (Table 13) showed the same. There was a very wide variation between mother-child pairs on the amount of social interaction during the 4 hours of observation — ranging from just over 1½ hours (38% of the total time) to nearly the full 4 hours (93% of the total time). Broadly speaking, four main types of interaction were seen: (1) joint play; (2) talking together; (3) some joint action such as polishing the furniture; and (4) caretaking activities, such as dressing or washing the child. The activity that accounted for the bulk of social interactions was joint play but, again, the amount showed huge individual variation (over a range extending from 23 min to over 3 hours). However, on none of these activities did the groups differ to any substantial or significant extent.

Table 13   Mother-child social interactions

	Ex-care women (n = 23)		Comparison group (n = 21)	
	Mean	(S.D.)	Mean	(S.D.)
Play: No. of 10-sec units	502	(257)	604	(261)
Talking: No. of 10-sec units	228	(100)	225	(152)
Joint activity: No. of 10-sec units	41	(48)	30	(46)
Caretaking: No. of 10-sec units	38	(35)	27	(25)

There were no statistically significant differences between the groups on these measures.

Interactions were considered separately according to whether or not the mother or child initiated them. As already noted, child initiations of social interactions were more frequent in the ex-care group. However, the rate of maternal initiations did not differ significantly between the groups — the rate per 4 hours in the ex-care group was 39 and that in the comparison group was 31. Moreover, neither the topic of the maternal initiations (i.e. whether to express interest in the children's play or to exercise control, or to engage in caretaking activities, etc.) nor the form of the initiation (i.e. whether a question, instruction or an explanation) differentiated the groups. In both groups some two-fifths of the maternal initiations failed to lead to any established form of interaction, the exchange terminating within three verbal elements (Table 14). The most likely outcome for interactions persisting beyond three elements was a conversation (28% of outcomes) but one in six (15%) resulted in joint play. The children in the ex-care group were slightly less likely to be engaged in play through their mother's initiations (12 vs 19%). The ex-care group mothers were also somewhat more likely to precipitate children's distress or confrontation following their approaches (12 vs 8%).

Table 14   Outcome of maternal initiations (% of all initiations)

	Ex-care women (n = 23) %	Comparison group (n = 21) %
No continuing interaction beyond 3 elements	41.54	38.19
Precipitation of child distress or control episode	11.83	8.28
Resulting joint play	11.71	18.71
Resulting joint conversation	28.52	27.60
Resulting joint activity	2.96	3.06
Caretaking	3.55	3.68
Other	0	0.01

No differences were statistically significant.

We may conclude that the explanation for the higher rate of child initiations in the ex-care group does *not* lie in any lack of social interaction nor in any lack of initiation of activities by the mothers. There was some suggestion, perhaps, that the ex-care mothers may have attempted to engage their children's involvement less skilfully, in that they were *less* likely to succeed in initiating joint play and *more* likely to provoke distress or confrontation. However, these differences were small and fell short of statistical significance.

Maternal communications. The middle hour of each 2-hour observation period was transcribed from the audio-taped record, with the aid of narrative notes made during the original observations. Non-verbal behaviour and happenings or circumstances that imparted meaning to verbal statements were noted down at the time for use later in enabling an accurate production of the verbal transcription. Thus 2 hours of potential dialogue were coded according to a scheme that comprised eight categories of social communication (Table 15).

In both groups there was a high rate of usage of minimal acknowledgements (one word responses such as "oh", "mmm" or "right"), with no between-group differences for that category. However, the ex-care mothers were nearly twice as likely (8.5 vs 4.4 per hour) to give no response at all to their children's communications. The finding raises the possibility that the higher rate of child initiations in the ex-care group may have been the result of a relative lack of maternal responsiveness — the children 'needed' to make more overtures in order to obtain their mothers' attention This issue is considered further in relation to the analysis of sequences of interaction (see later).

Table 15 Maternal communications

	Ex-care women (n = 20)		Comparison group (n = 20) Hourly rate of communication		Statistical significance		
	Mean	(S.D.)	Mean	(S.D.)	t	d.f.	P
Minimal acknowledge	47.38	(25.06)	46.06	(26.99)	0.16	39	N.S.
Ignore	17.16	(12.20)	8.86	(9.14)	2.51	39	< 0.01
Praise	8.14	(7.84)	8.25	(7.52)	0.05	39	N.S.
Facilitating comments	123.85	(49.21)	142.08	(41.69)	1.28	39	N.S.
Non-facilitating comments	25.75	(15.52)	21.42	(17.85)	0.83	39	N.S.
Description/naming	41.59	(29.65)	43.73	(29.17)	0.23	39	N.S.
Elaborating comments	39.13	(19.23)	62.66	(27.09)	3.22	39	< 0.01
Other	258.44	(70.38)	283.16	(94.02)	0.96	39	N.S.

Praise (i.e. comments such as "well done" or "that's a good girl") was little used by either group of mothers, the rate being about 4 per hour. Facilitating comments constituted much the largest category (apart from 'other'; see below) in both groups. This included structuring activities to help participation (e.g. bringing a stool to the sink so that the child could help wash up); suggesting new activities; giving verbal help or practical assistance (e.g. showing the child where to put a piece in a jigsaw puzzle); open, rather than closed, questions or comments; maternal compliance to children's suggestions or requests; and relevant maternal responses to children's make-believe play. The ex-care mothers were slightly less likely to facilitate (a rate of 62 vs 72 per hour) but the difference fell short of statistical significance.

Non-facilitating comments (e.g. simple negations without explanation, "that's not a dog", or postponement of compliance, "I'll help you later") were much less common and occurred at about the same rate in both groups. Descriptions or naming were much more frequent, with similar rates in both groups. This category included labelling or description of objects *without* elaboration.

The large 'other' category comprised a heterogeneous collection of remarks with a less clearly defined social communication purpose. Thus closed questions, requests for clarification, repetition of the child's utterances, "don't know" responses and confirmations all fell into this non-specific category. The rates of 'other' remarks were closely similar in the two groups.

The largest difference between the groups concerned maternal comments that provided elaboration by widening the scope of conversation, by introducing new ideas or information (e.g. "Look at those horses going up the road; they're going to have new shoes at the blacksmith's"), by the teaching of abstractions or relative relationships (e.g. "that's hotter than that, isn't it?"), by the introduction of pretend activities, by the extension of a pre-existing make-believe game or by linking a current activity to some other aspect of the child's experience outside the immediate situation. Such elaborating comments occurred at a rate of just over 30 per hour in the comparison group but just under 20 in the ex-care group. Of course, elaborating statements of this type may play an important role in the provision of information that aids children's cognitive performance; equally, their reciprocal quality may facilitate the development of children's conversational skills. However, it is also likely that they are important emotionally and socially because they serve as a way of the mother showing an active interest in her child's activities and because they constitute the pabulum for a developing relationship that has a content and context outside that of dealing with distress and disruptive behaviour.

Maternal responses to child overtures. As already discussed, the children of ex-care mothers had a substantially higher rate of approaches, overtures or initiations of interactions—about 10 per hour compared with 6 per hour in the comparison group. Table 16 summarizes the findings on the nature of the mother's responses to their children's overtures. The most striking feature is that the ex-care mothers were more likely to *ignore* their children's attempts to gain their attention; the difference was statistically significant both for the mothers' first response to the children's approaches and for subsequent responses in the same sequence initiated by the children's attempts to gain attention. However, when the ex-care women *did* respond to their children's approaches they did so in a broadly comparable fashion to that shown by the women in the comparison group.

Table 16   Maternal responses to child overtures

	Ex-care women (n = 23)		Comparison group (n = 21)		Statistical significance*	
	Mean	(S.D.)	Mean	(S.D.)	z	P
% ignore as first response†	15.30	(8.28)	10.81	(3.49)	1.98	< 0.05
% ignore as any response†	9.09	(4.19)	4.95	(3.49)	3.11	< 0.01
% acknowledge	18.91	(7.76)	19.43	(9.38)		N.S.
% question	19.34	(5.79)	20.05	(8.19)		N.S.
% instruct	15.26	(5.77)	13.62	(8.03)		N.S.
% explain	9.43	(4.25)	11.14	(5.21)		N.S.
% maternal compliance	4.22	(2.26)	4.14	(4.29)		N.S.
% maternal non-compliance	4.91	(3.12)	4.69	(4.43)		N.S.
% approve	3.39	(3.75)	3.48	(2.48)		N.S.
% other	15.69	(4.08)	18.43	(5.14)		N.S.

* Mann-Whitney *U* test. This non-parametric statistic is used because the data comprise proportions of responses. The distribution of variables thus tends to be binomial rather than normal.
†The % 'ignore' as first response is based on the total No. of first responses, whereas % 'ignore' as any response, like the rest of the table, is based on the total No. of all responses within child approach sequences. The difference between these two proportions for 'ignore' indicates that 'ignores' were less likely to occur later in the sequences; Mann-Whitney *U* test.

Maternal responses to child opposition. The ex-care mothers experienced more incidents per hour in which the children's aggressive or oppositional behaviour initiated an episode that required some form of maternal response or control. Each of these episodes was recorded in the form of a continuous sequence of mother and child behaviours in order to make possible an analysis of the process of mother-child interaction throughout the course of disciplinary episodes. Although the ex-care group had more episodes of control per hour of observation, the overall period of time spent in such episodes was only marginally (and non-significantly) higher (See Table 17). The explanation lay in the high rate of very short control episodes in the ex-care group. The ex-care women showed a slight excess of control episodes of all lengths but the main excess (and the only one to reach statistical significance) lay in control episodes lasting two 10-sec units or less.

Table 17   Duration of control sequences

	Ex-care women (n = 23)		Comparison group (n = 20)*		Statistical significance		
	Mean	(S.D.)	Mean	(S.D.)	*t*	d.f.	*P*
No. of control episodes per 4 hours	19.35	(11.48)	13.30	(7.42)	2.02	41	< 0.05
Duration of control time per 4 hours†	66.26	(43.88)	55.25	(50.24)			N.S.
No. of 10-sec units per control episode	3.32	(0.91)	3.82	(2.42)			N.S.
No. of control episodes ≥ 3 10-sec units	8.04	(5.24)	6.55	(5.17)	0.94	41	N.S.
No. of control episodes < 2 10-sec units	11.30	(7.24)	6.75	(4.48)	2.43	41	< 0.05

* The *n* refers to the number of women in each group who experienced episodes of control, i.e. it omits the one women in the comparison group whose observation sessions included no control episodes.
† No. of 10-sec units.

Table 18   Characteristics of control episodes

	Ex-care women (n = 23)		Comparison women (n = 20)		Statistical significance
	Mean	(S.D.)	Mean	(S.D.)	*P*
% control episodes associated with distress	14.50	(14.75)	18.05	(23.24)	N.S.
% child compliance with maternal control	75.74	(15.12)	72.30	(21.31)	N.S.
% repeated confrontations	23.61	(18.27)	27.20	(22.45)	N.S.

Table 18 provides a summary of some of the main findings on the characteristics of control episodes. It examines 'success' in terms of several different criteria — first, whether the control episode was associated with the child showing distress; secondly, whether the episode ended with the child's compliance with the mother's control attempt; and thirdly, whether the episode involved a confrontation over a behaviour identical to that dealt with in an earlier episode (i.e. the child was once again doing something that the mother had previously made clear was forbidden). On none of these three criteria were there major differences between the groups.

Table 19   Maternal responses within control episodes

	Ex-care women (n = 23)		Comparison women (n = 21)		Statistical significance*	
	Mean	(S.D.)	Mean	(S.D.)	z	P
% managerial as any response (e.g. suggest/distract)	14.56	7.60	10.45	8.40	2.32	< 0.02
% instructions	33.09	12.72	36.60	11.37		N.S.
% imperative (e.g. prohibition/restrain)	7.26	6.22	7.00	5.93		N.S.
% passive (e.g. ignore/leave room)	15.35	13.42	16.20	16.74		N.S.
% aggressive† (e.g. smack/threat)	11.74	7.93	10.75	8.54		N.S.
% other	19.22	8.19	19.95	15.05		N.S.

* Mann-Whitney U test.
† This category comprises a range of aggressive responses, including threats, smacks, rough handling and sarcastic remarks, but excluding negative intonation as such.

Table 19 shows the various ways in which the mothers responded to their children's oppositional or non-compliant behaviour. The data refer to the proportion of episodes in which the specified maternal behaviour occurred at any point in the sequence. Within both groups there was a wide variety of styles with which the mothers handled control issues (as shown by the high standard deviations for all categories). Some women displayed patience and good humour, whereas others adopted a more confronting approach, threatening or shouting at their children. However, the majority employed a mixture of styles — on some occasions being forceful and overtly disapproving but yet at other times using persuasion and reasoning in an attempt to achieve compliance. It may be that the explanation for the significantly higher proportion of 'managerial' responses by the ex-care women (responses which comprise distractions, explanations, persuasion and suggestions) arises from the fact that this group had more brief episodes of control (Table 17). But Patterson's (1982) model of coercive interchanges and relatively low-key maternal managerial response would in some circumstances act as a negative reinforcer for the child's coercive (i.e. oppositional or non-compliant) behaviour. Thus the short-term goal of control resolution would be achieved only at the expense of an increased likelihood of further child coercion. There was also a tendency for the ex-care women to employ a mixture of styles in control episodes: 87% using all modes of responding compared with 65% of the comparison group.

Maternal responses to child distress. Distress episodes, in which the children whined or cried, occurred at some point during the observation sessions in all but seven of the families. As already noted, such episodes were somewhat more frequent in the ex-care group, but not significantly so. Table 20 provides a more detailed breakdown of the distress episodes according to their type. Five varieties were categorized: (a) that which accompanied a control episode; (b) that associated with the child hurting itself or getting into some sort of difficulty; (c) that in which the child started to whine for no discernible reason; (d) that precipitated by the mothers smacking or threatening their children during the preceding 10-sec time interval; and (e) 'coercive' distress in which the child whined or cried to protest against some prohibition. In the vast majority of instances (93%) this last variety arose after the mother had refused to comply with some request from their children or had ignored their demands. In a small proportion of incidents the mothers had taken objects away from the child or had curtailed activities in which they were engaged. All forms of distress were slightly more frequent in the ex-care group but only in the case of coercive distress was the difference a large one. Because of the large within-group variation the difference fell short of statistical significance. However, it is clear from a consideration of mother-child pairs (rather than overall rates in the group as a whole) that more mothers in the ex-care group experienced coercive distress. Such distress occurred in 17 of the 23 (73.9%) ex-care families as against ten of the 21 (47.6%) comparison group — a significant difference. In other words, the main feature of the distress in the ex-care group was that it arose out of some aspect of the mothers' handling of prohibited behaviour.

Table 20   Types of distress

Rates of distress per 4 hours	Ex-care women (n = 23)		Comparison women (n = 21)		Statistical significance		
	Mean	(S.D.)	Mean	(S.D.)	t	d.f.	P
Distress associated with control	2.478	(3.06)	2.190	(2.66)			N.S.
Non-control distress	5.390	(6.34)	3.476	(3.50)	1.22	42	N.S.
Associated hurt/difficulty	1.739	(2.72)	1.380	(2.19)			N.S.
Non-specific	1.217	(2.36)	0.619	(1.02)			N.S.
Precipitated by mother	0.304	(0.93)	0.238	(0.89)			N.S.
Coercive	2.130	(2.01)	1.238	(1.45)	1.677	42	N.S.

Maternal responses to distress arising outside of control sequences were grouped into four main categories (Table 21): negative, positive passive and minimal (plus 'other'). A response was considered 'positive' if it involved maternal compliance or helping, explaining, suggesting or distraction. 'Positive' responses also included those with an approving or encouraging tone of voice, and verbal or physical expressions of warmth (such as making comforting statements or cuddling the child). The category of 'negative' responses comprised those with an angry or hostile tone of voice, the verbal or physical expression of negative emotion such as threatening the child or smacking him, high-level imperatives and non-compliance to his demands. A 'passive' response was scored if a mother ignored or left her child in a distressed condition. The category of 'minimal' response was used for instances in which the mother responded with just an acknowledgement or non-specific comment.

Table 21   Maternal responses to non-control distress

Proportion of responses	Ex-care women (n = 17)		Comparison group (n = 11)	
	Mean %	(S.D.) %	Mean %	(S.D.) %
Positive (e.g. help/comfort, comply)	24.12	(13.06)	27.76	(33.71)
Negative (e.g. threat/disapprove)	20.76	(15.33)	12.18	(15.50)
Passive (ignore/leave)	8.82	(9.95)	13.06	(18.71)
Minimal (acknowledge/non-specific verbalisation)	14.88	(23.58)	8.94	(10.40)
Other	31.65	(15.12)	38.18	(32.23)

There were no statistically significant differences between the groups on these measures.

As evident from Table 21 the two groups of mother tended to respond to their children's distress in a broadly comparable fashion — with positive responses being by far the most frequent reaction. However, although falling short of statistical significance, it is apparent that responses involving negative affect were substantially more frequent in the ex-care group. This parallels the general finding that in all contexts the ex-care women showed a tendency to exhibit more negative affect. When considered in terms of mothers (rather than group means) it was apparent that half (50%) of the ex-care women displayed negative affect in response to their children's emotional upset, in contrast to one in six (15.8%) of the comparison group women — a difference that approached statistical significance (two-tailed exact test, $P = 0.06$).

Discussion

The implications of the results presented in this paper may be considered first in the context of the broad sweep of parenting histories, and secondly with respect to the detailed and specific observations on the quality of mothering.

A central question of this study was whether particular types of parenting inadequacies would be found in women who were raised in children's homes. As has been mentioned, for a minority the parent–child relationship itself could not be sustained. Of those with a surviving child, over one-third (35%) had experienced temporary or permanent separation from that child or, in a few cases, from all their children. This result might suggest that an institutional upbringing is significantly likely to result in extreme parenting deficits of a serious and lasting kind. However, an examination of the case histories showed that this was likely to be true of only a small handful of cases. The majority of parenting breakdowns occurred several years ago, with first-born children, and at times of great psychosocial stress and adversity. The findings discussed in this paper refer to *current* parenting, usually in more favourable social circumstances. The observational data, for instance, usually referred to parenting in circumstances which were, by arrangement, relatively non-stressful in terms of a period of interaction with just one child at a time when the mother did not have other competing demands. To that extent, the measures concerned the mothers' parenting skills under good circumstances. On the other hand, the interview and observational data agreed well and gave rise to a closely similar picture; such agreement would not have been likely had the behaviours seen at observation been unrepresentative of average domestic interaction.

Taken as a whole, these assessments of parenting suggest both negative and positive conclusions. On the one hand, the findings did *not* suggest that the institutional rearing had commonly resulted in any general emotional deficit. A few of the ex-care women were low in expressed warmth but the great majority were both affectionate to their children and actively involved with them. Moreover, the evidence did not suggest any gross defect in parenting skills nor did it indicate that cruelty or punitiveness were other than infrequent occurrences. It would thus be quite wrong to regard the ex-care women as generally rejecting or neglectful. On the other hand, there *were* important differences between the groups. The ex-care women were much more likely to show insensitivity to their children, they were more prone to exhibit irritability and to use frequent smacking, discipline was more likely to be ineffective and there was a trend for there to be less play with their children in activities that relied on the children's creativity, initiative and independence. The overall picture from the data suggests that ex-care women were concerned and trying to parent well but that they were not particularly skilful or adept in picking up their children's cues or in responding to their children's needs in ways that circumvented difficulties through an appropriate recognition of the best way to sort out problems, rather than just to provide immediate control.

This aspect of relative lack of competence is perhaps best illustrated by a consideration of their handling of control issues. Altogether, the data indicate that the greater inefficiency of discipline in the ex-care group did not stem from any particular management style in response to major episodes of disruptive behaviour. Rather, the difference between the groups lay in the ex-care women's greater tendency to use brief negative interventions for minor oppositional behaviours. Moreover, the between–groups differences for the separate affect-within-context measures showed that a higher rate of negative maternal affect occurred in the ex-care group across all contexts. Interestingly, this difference was most marked *outside* confrontations (the difference within confrontations falling just short of statistical significance). This means that the observation that the ex-care women tended to be more negative towards their children was not just a function of the fact that they experienced relatively more episodes of confrontation (involving both control and distress). In other words, the finding seems to reflect a general affective style rather than a form of discipline.

Nevertheless, they engaged in a statistically significant excess of brief control episodes, lasting 20 sec or less. It seemed that, to some extent, these very brief episodes tended to be of a somewhat different character from the longer episodes. Rather than a determined disciplinary attempt on the mother's part to change some particular aspect of the child's behaviour, they seemed to represent a less-differentiated and less-focused negative response of general irritation or disapproval. Although, of course, his sample and age-group was quite different, Patterson (1982) has commented on the tendency for mothers of aggressive children to 'natter' and 'nag' their children frequently over nothing in particular rather than concentrate discipline on child behaviours that they really wished to alter. Whether or not the pattern of very brief control episodes we observed in the ex-care group shared this quality shown by mothers of aggressive children requires further exploration, but it is important to recognize that the brevity of the episodes does not necessarily reflect efficiency and, indeed, it may represent inefficiency of disciplinary style.

The point emphasizes the complexity of the issue of disciplinary efficiency. The ex-care mothers' descriptions of child discipline showed that a higher proportion of them (than comparison group mothers) were markedly inefficient in discipline. The observational data confirmed this picture in their demonstration of a higher rate of control episodes in the ex-care group. The most important mark of successful discipline, of course, is the lack of disruptive behaviour — that is, the crucial aim is to prevent unacceptable behaviour rather than to bring it to a halt once it has occurred. Whether or not such success is mainly a consequence of maternal actions following oppositional behaviour or, rather, actions outside disciplinary episodes is an empirical question that requires systematic study.

There is certainly more to discipline than how misbehaviour is managed, and in understanding the process that leads to efficient discipline one needs to consider broader aspects of parent-child interaction. Discipline involves anticipatory as well as reactive elements (see Radke-Yarrow & Kuczynski, 1983). Occasions for discipline may be averted by the prior statements of rules, prompts, cautions and lessons. Also, the emotional context of interactions has implications for disciplinary efficiency (Patterson, 1982). Additionally, the frequency with which parent-child confrontations arise is likely to be influenced by the parents' skills in responding to children's needs and in helping them acquire effective approaches to problem-solving. The ex-care mothers' style of interaction may have been less than optimal in this connection — in terms of the relative lack of elaborating comments, the greater exhibition of negative effect both within and outside confrontation, and the tendency to make frequent brief unfocused disciplinary interventions. However, their tendency to ignore or not to respond to their children's overtures and their relative lack of sensitivity to their children's needs may have had important disciplinary implications. Perhaps parents need to acquire a disciplinary 'currency'. That is to say, if children are to be expected to comply with parental demands, it may be necessary that parents first show that they are willing to comply with children's demands. In that respect, the ex-care mothers' greater tendency to ignore or rebuff their children's approaches may have been influential. It was not that the mothers did not play or talk with their children — they did that as much as the comparison group mothers. Nor was it that the mothers did not initiate interactions — again, they did so as often. Rather, the difference lay in the fact that the interactions were less likely to have arisen as a response to the *child's* demands.

This finding should be considered in relation to the fact that the children of ex-care women were seen throughout observations to exhibit a much higher rate of spontaneous approaches to their mothers. That distinction between the groups may reflect the need of these children to take overt action in order to engage their mothers' attention, and would link to the interview finding that these women lacked sensitivity. However, the observational finding that parenting problems in the ex-care group were more frequent with first-born than subsequent-born children suggests that the parenting of their first children may have provided the women with a learning experience from which they were able to profit (although the interview data did not show this effect).

The implications from both the interview and observational data are that the skills of successful parenting may lie more in the patterns of parent-child interaction that *prevent* conflict and distress arising than in how such conflict and distress are dealt with once they have occurred. The data suggest that the important dimensions may include sensitivity to children's needs, awareness of their cues and responsiveness to their calls for attention. The sheer amount of parent-child play and conversation seemed less crucial than that such interaction should allow initiation and creativity by the child as well as by the parent. The affective quality seemed influential in terms of its overall effect on the tone of the interaction and on the quality of the parent-child relationship, rather than in terms of its reflection of a strict or punitive disciplinary approach. The inter-group differences concerned the extent to which negative affect (irritability, critical tone, derogatory remarks and the like) characterized non-disciplinary interchanges, at least as much as the extent to which they constituted a feature of discipline. Of course, it should be clear that these represent hypotheses rather than facts (we have no direct measures of the outcome of parenting), but the general pattern is in keeping with the findings that have emerged from studies of other, quite different, groups (Maccoby & Martin, 1984; Patterson, 1982). Obviously, cases of gross neglect, physical abuse and hopelessly inept discipline can and do occur. However, these features applied to only a tiny minority of the parents whom we studied. It may be, too, that parental *responses* to disruptive behaviour are more important with older children.

The possible association of current handicapping psychiatric disorder with other indices of current psychosocial adversity and with particular styles of parenting, by individual mothers, is a potentially interesting subject for future examination. Evidently, there is a need to develop ways of recognizing potential difficulties in parenting at an earlier stage, and there is a need for knowledge on the features that characterize successful parenting if aspirations in the field of parent education are to be matched by accomplishments. Whereas our findings do not as yet provide answers that can be used as an unambiguous guide to policy and practice, they do provide pointers to aspects of parenting that would warrant further study. Moreover, even at this point, they indicate aspects of parenting that require attention by those involved in the care of children.

Portions of this work were conducted independently by Linda Dowdney as part of the requirements for a Ph.D Thesis (University of London).

Notes

1   The sample departed from truly random only insofar as it was restricted to children in the same school classes as the children of mentally ill parents. The available data show that this introduced no relevant distortions or biases. (Further details on both samples are given in Quinton & Rutter, 1984c).

2   Of the total 29 children who had experienced separation, in 16 cases (55%) this had occurred before their second birthday.

3   These date exclude two women in the comparison group with rates of negative affect several standard deviations outside the range of both groups. In both cases this was due to prolonged episodes of an atypical type, not represented in the other observations. The exclusion was based, therefore, on the fact that both statistically and qualitatively they could not be pooled with the rest of either sample.

References

Brown, G.W. & Rutter, M.L. (1966) 'The measurement of family activities and relationships: a methodological study.' *Human Relations*, 19, 241-263.

Clarke-Stewart, K.A. & Apfel, N. (1978) 'Evaluating parental effects on child development.' In L. Shulman (Ed.), *Review of research in education*, Vol. 6 (pp. 47-119) Ithaca, IL: F.E. Peacock.

Dowdney, L., Mrazek, D.A., Quinton, D. & Rutter, M. (1984) 'Observations of parent-child interaction with two- to three-year olds.' *Journal of Child Psychology and Psychiatry*, 25, 379-407.

Dunn, J. & Kendrick, C. (1982) *Siblings: love, envy and understanding*. London: Grant McIntyre.

Ferguson, T. (1966) *Children in care — and after*. Oxford: Oxford University Press.

Graham, P. & Rutter, M.L. (1968) 'The reliability and validity of the psychiatric assessment: II. Interview with the parent.' *British Journal of Psychiatry*, 114, 581-492.

Harman, D. & Brim, O. (1980) *Learning to be parents: principles, programs and methods*. London: Sage Publications.

King, R.D., Raynes, N.V. & Tizard, J. (1971) *Patterns of residential care: sociological studies in institutions for handicapped children*. London: Routledge & Kegan Paul.

Lytton, H. (1973) 'Three approaches to the study of parent-child interaction: ethological, interview and experimental.' *Journal of Child Psychology and Psychiatry*, 14, 1-17.

Maccoby, E. & Jacklin, C.N. (1974) *The psychology of sex differences*. Stanford, CA: Stanford University Press.

Maccoby, E. & Martin, J. (1983) 'Parent-child interaction.' In E.M. Hetherington (Ed.), *Socialization, personality and social development, Vol. 4. Handbook of child psychology* (4th ed.) (pp. 1-101) New York: Wiley.

Mrazek, D., Dowdney, L., Rutter, M. & Quinton, D. (1982) 'Mother and pre-school child interaction: a sequential approach.' *Journal of the American Academy of Child Psychiatry*, 21, 453-464.

Oliver, J.E. & Taylor, A. (1971) 'Five generations of ill treated children in one family pedigree.' *British Journal of Psychiatry*, 119, 473-480.

Patterson, G. (1982) *Coercive family process*. Eugene, OR: Castalia Press.

Philp, A.F. (1963) *Family failure: a study of 129 families with multiple problems*. London: Faber & Faber.

Pringle, M.K. (1974) *The needs of children*. London: Hutchinson.

Quinton, D. & Rutter, M. (1984a) 'Parents with children in care — I. Current circumstances and parenting skills.' *Journal of Child Psychology and Psychiatry*, 25, 211-229.

Quinton, D. & Rutter, M. (1984b) 'Parents with children in care — II. Intergenerational continuities.' *Journal of Child Psychology and Psychiatry*, 25, 231-250.

Quinton, D. & Rutter, M. (1984c) 'Parenting behaviour of mothers raised 'in care'.' In A.R. Nicol (Ed.), *Longitudinal studies in child care and child psychiatry: practical lessons from research experience*. Chichester: Wiley (in press)

Quinton, D. & Rutter, M. & Liddle, C. (1948) 'Institutional rearing, parenting difficulties, and marital support.' *Psychological Medicine*, 14, 107-124.

Quinton, D., Rutter, M. & Rowlands, O. (1976) 'An evaluation of an interview assessment of marriage.' *Psychological Medicine*, 6, 577-586.

Radke-Yarrow, M. & Kuczynski, L. (1983) 'Perspectives and strategies in child-rearing. Studies of rearing in normal and depressed mothers.' In D. Magnusson & V. Allen (Eds), *Human development: an interactional perspective* (pp. 57-74) New York: Academic Press.

Rutter, M. (1967) 'A children's behaviour questionnaire for completion by teachers: preliminary findings.' *Journal of Child Psychology and Psychiatry*, 8, 1-11.

Rutter, M. (1975) *Helping troubled children*. Harmondsworth: Penguin Books.

Rutter, M. & Brown, G.W. (1966) 'The reliability and validity of measures of family life and relationships in families containing a psychiatric patient.' *Social Psychiatry*, 1, 38-53.

Rutter, M. & Giller, H. (1983) *Juvenile delinquency: trends and perspectives*. Harmondsworth: Penguin Books.

Rutter, M., Quinton, D. & Liddle, C. (1983) 'Parenting in two generations: looking backwards and looking forwards.' In N. Madge (Ed.), *Families at risk* (pp. 60-98) London: Heinemann Educational.

Spinetta, J.J. & Rigler, D. (1972) 'The child-abusing parent: a psychological review.' *Psychological Bulletin*, 77, 296-304.

Wright, C. H. & Lunn, J. E. (1971) 'Sheffield problem families: follow-up study of their sons and daughters (Parts I-III)' *Community Medicine*, 126, 301-307, 315-321.

Acquiring Language

Much of the interest in children's language acquisition arose from Noam Chomsky's work in the 1950s and 1960s on generative grammars. Chomsky's main thesis is that the rules governing the deployment of word order (syntax) in the generation of various types of sentence are both implicit and complex: how then do young children master many of these rules so quickly? Both common observation and systematic studies revealed that parents did not explicitly teach children these rules – so how were they acquired? Chomsky proposed a hypothetical (L)anguage (A)cquisition (D)evice as part of the solution to this problem. Essentially, he argued that the human brain is genetically endowed with the capacity to extract the underlying principles of sentence structure in a given language from mere exposure to a language. A relatively simple account of his view is reproduced in the first article in this section.

Later investigators, while conceding that adults did not teach syntax directly to children, focused on various aspects of adult-child interchanges that may facilitate language acquisition. Catherine Snow was one of the foremost investigators of adults' adaptations of speech style (referred to as 'speech registers' by linguists) when addressing young children. From her evidence, Snow argued that parents often simplified their speech to young children, thereby facilitating the extraction of rules. The article by Snow is a good example of this line of enquiry. However, some anthropological work suggests that these adaptations in speech are not universal, which begs the question as to the necessity of such adapted input for language acquisition to proceed 'normally'. The article by Schieffelin and Ochs provides observations somewhat at odds with Snow's thesis. The article by Nelson explores the theme of modified input in the presentation of an experimental intervention study.

One other issue that has received considerable attention relates to 'critical periods' in language acquisition. In the 1960s Eric Lenneberg argued that language acquisition would not proceed normally if a child were deprived of natural language exposure beyond the early teenage years. Various case studies, such as the case of Genie (cited by Skuse in the section on *Early Experience*), have been culled in this debate. The article by Johnson and Newport represents a more direct analysis of the issue of 'critical' or 'sensitive' periods in language acquisition.

12.   Language Acquisition

Noam Chomsky

1. Introductory

There would seem to be at least three reasons why research into children's acquisition of language is important.

(i)   It is interesting in its own right.

(ii) The results of studies in language acquisition may throw light on a variety of educational and medical problems, e.g. aphasia, speech-retardation and cognitive development.

(iii) Since the study of language acquisition may confirm or disconfirm the universal categories postulated by linguistic theories with an explicitly mentalist basis, it is clear that the phenomena of language acquisition are relevant to the development of linguistic theory.

Many linguists and non-linguists have studied language acquisition without making any real effort to define how the results of their studies might be applied, and without wishing to prove anything about the nature of language. The result of this rather casual approach has been a mass of observations which inevitably tend to be of an anecdotal and therefore unsystematic nature. Moreover, the lack of any coherent theory of language acquisition means that the link between the data and what we assume to be the 'facts' of language acquisition are necessarily extremely tenuous. For example, it is difficult to describe, let alone explain, the facts of slow speech development without knowing precisely what constitutes normal speech development. Unfortunately we know very little at the present time about what constitutes normal speech development. This is due partly to the immense practical difficulties involved in studying child speech but also to the fact that there is no linguistic theory yet available which provides a sufficiently detailed apparatus to enable us either to describe the facts or to catalogue them comprehensively.

It may be useful, before turning to Chomsky's views on the subject, to give some indication of the practical and theoretical difficulties involved in studying language acquisition. Firstly, it is difficult for obvious practical reasons to study input-data, that is the amount and nature of speech to which the child is exposed over a period of two to three years (what Chomsky calls 'primary linguistic data'). It is clear that such studies are necessary if we wish, for example, to test Skinner's theory that language is learned by 'reinforcement', or to find out precisely what is learned by the child and what we must assume to be part of his innate capacity for acquiring language.

Secondly, it is difficult to study output-data, that is, to describe in precise grammatical terms the utterances that the child produces. Child speech is by its very nature structurally impoverished. Usually, and certainly in the earliest stages, we need a lot of situational (and phonological) information to determine the meaning of a child's utterances. For example, 'mummy chair' might mean 'that's mummy's chair' or 'mummy has a chair'. Should we be content simply to describe this utterance as a sequence of Noun + Noun or should we try to determine the nature of the underlying sentences, in order to describe the utterance as ambiguous?

Thirdly, it is difficult to study input-output relations. This is mainly due to the fact that there may be a considerable time-lag between what the child hears and what he produces.

Fourthly, it is extremely difficult to test the child's competence and to sort out performance variables. How do we know, for example, when a young child 'makes a mistake' in terms of his own system of competence? Children are notoriously difficult subjects to test.

Lastly, although it seems clear that the deep-surface distinction is valid for child-language it is not so clear what the exact relationship is between the deep component of an adult grammar and the deep component of a child grammar given, say, a base component the type that Chomsky describes in *Aspects*. To illustrate this difficulty let us compare on the one hand the following synonymous set of child utterances: *juice, me juice, want juice, my juice* (all meaning: 'give me some juice' or 'I want some juice') and on the other hand the adult utterances *give me some juice. I want some juice*. Given this data, the researcher faces the following dilemma. If he assumes that an adult grammar and a child grammar share the same deep component, then the data is not describable in terms of a base component such as Chomsky provides in *Aspects*. In order to describe the data, a far more abstract universal deep component would be required. On the other hand, if the researcher assumes that an adult grammar and a child grammar do not share the same deep component, then the notion of substantive linguistic universals is in danger of becoming incoherent.

It is probably true to say that for descriptive purposes most researchers in the field of language acquisition would favour the assumption that an adult grammar and a child grammar share the same deep component (most changes in 'transitional competence' could be conveniently stated in the transformational component of a standard grammar) — if only we had a well-developed linguistic theory based on this assumption, not to mention a theory based on *evidence* for such an assumption! [Eds.]

2. Experimental approaches

The attempt to write a grammar for a child raises all of the unsolved problems of constructing a grammar for adult speech, multiplied by some rather large factor. To mention just the most obvious difficulty, since the language is constantly changing rather dramatically, it is impossible to use the one 'method' available to linguists who attempt to go beyond surface description, namely learning the language oneself. Clearly the general problem is at least as difficult, and, in fact, much more difficult than the problem of discovering the grammar of the language of a mature speaker, and this, I think, is a problem of much greater difficulty than is often realized. In fact, the only remarks I would like to make reflect an impression that underlying these descriptions of children's speech[*], laudable and interesting as they are, there is a somewhat oversimplified conception of the character of grammatical description, not unrelated, perhaps, to a similarly oversimplified view that is typical of much recent work on language in psychology and linguistics.

For one thing, it should be clearly recognized that a grammar is not a description of the performance of the speaker, but rather of his linguistic competence, and that a description of competence and a description of performance are different things. To illustrate, consider a trivial example where one would want to distinguish between a description of competence and a description of performance. Suppose that we were to attempt to give an account of how a child learns to multiply (rather than how he acquires his language). A child who has succeeded in learning this has acquired a certain competence, and he will perform in certain ways that are clearly at variance with this competence. Once he has learned to multiply, the correct description of his competence is a statement, in one or another form of some of the rules of arithmetic — i.e. a specification of the set of triples (x, y, z) such that z is the product of x and y. On the other hand, a description of the performance of either an adult or a child (or a real computer) would be something quite different. It might, for example, be a specification of a set of quadruples (x, y, z, w) such that w is the probability that, given x and y, the person will compute the product as z. This set of quadruples would incorporate information about memory span, characteristic errors, lapses of attention, etc., information which is relevant to a performance table but not, clearly, to an account of what the person has learned — what is the basic competence that he has acquired. A person might memorize the performance table and perform on various simple-minded tests exactly as the person who knows the rules of arithmetic but this would not, of course, show that he knows these rules. It seems clear that the description which is of greatest psychological relevance is the account of competence, not that of performance, both in the case of arithmetic and the case of language. The deeper question concerns the kinds of structures the person has succeeded in mastering and internalizing, whether or not he utilizes them, in practice, without interference from the many other factors that play a role in actual behaviour. For anyone concerned with intellectual processes, or any question that goes beyond mere data arranging, it is the question of competence that is fundamental. Obviously one can find out about competence only by studying performance, but this study must be carried out in devious and clever ways, if any serious result is to be obtained.

These rather obvious comments apply directly to study of language, child or adult. Thus it is absurd to attempt to construct a grammar that describes observed linguistic behaviour directly. The tape-recordings of this conference give a totally false picture of the conceptions of linguistic structure of the various speakers. Nor is this in the least

---

[*] This paper was originally read at a Conference on First-Language Acquisition held at Endicott House, Dedham, Massachusetts, 27-29 October 1961, and contains comments on a paper by Wick Miller and Susan Ervin entitled 'The Development of Grammar in Child Language'. In this paper Miller and Ervin suggest that grammatical systems arise in the child's exposure to differing probabilities in adult speech and that the 'correct' patterns are reinforced, thus enabling the child to approximate adult patterns more closely. [Eds.]

bit surprising. The speaker has represented in his brain a grammar that gives an ideal account of the structure of the sentences of his language, but, when actually faced with the task of speaking or 'understanding', many other factors act upon his underlying linguistic competence to produce actual performance. He may be confused or have several things in mind, change his plans in midstream, etc. Since this is obviously the condition of most actual linguistic performance, a direct record — an actual corpus — is almost useless as it stands, for linguistic analysis of any but the most superficial kind.

Similarly, it seems to me that, if anything far-reaching and real is to be discovered about the actual grammar of the child, then rather devious kinds of observations of his performance, his abilities, and his comprehension in many different kinds of circumstance will have to be obtained, so that a variety of evidence may be brought to bear on the attempt to determine what is in fact his underlying linguistic competence at each stage of development. Direct description of the child's actual verbal output is no more likely to provide an account of the real underlying competence in the case of child language than in the case of adult language, ability to multiply, or any other nontrivial rule-governed behaviour. Not that one shouldn't start here, perhaps, but surely one shouldn't end here, or take too seriously the results obtained by one or another sort of manipulation of data of texts produced under normal conditions.

It is suggested in this paper — and this is a view shared by many psychologists and linguists — that the relation between competence and performance is somehow a probabilistic one. That is, somehow the higher probabilities in actual output converge towards the actual underlying grammar, or something of the sort. I have never seen a coherent presentation of this position, but, even as a vague idea, it seems to me entirely implausible. In particular, it surely cannot be maintained that the child forms his conceptions of grammatical structure by just assuming that high probabilities correspond to 'rules' and that low probabilities can be disregarded, in some manner. Most of what the child actually produces and hears (and this is true for the adult as well) is of extremely low probability. In fact, in the case of sentence structure, the notion of probability loses all meaning. Except for a ridiculously small number (e.g. conventionalized greetings, etc., which, in fact, often do not even observe grammatical rules), all actual sentences are of a probability so low as to be effectively zero, and the same is true of structures (if, by the 'structure' of a sentence, we mean the sequence of categories to which its successive words or morphemes belong). In actual speech, the highest probability must be assigned to broken and interrupted fragments of sentences or to sentences which begin in one way and end in a different, totally incompatible way (surely the tapes of this meeting would be sufficient to demonstrate this). From such evidence it would be absurd to conclude that this represents in any sense the linguistic consciousness of the speakers, as has been noted above. In general, it is a mistake to assume that — past the very earliest stages — much of what the child acquires is acquired by imitation. This could not be true on the level of sentence formation, since most of what the child hears is new and most of what be produces, past the very earliest stages, is new.

In the papers that have been presented here — and again, this is not unrepresentative of psychology and linguistics — there has been talk about grammars for the decoder and grammars for the encoder. Again, there are several undemonstrated (and, to me, quite implausible) assumptions underlying the view that the speaker's behaviour should be modelled by one sort of system, and the hearer's by another. I have never seen a precise characterization of a 'grammar for the encoder' or a 'grammar for the decoder' that was not convertible, by a notational change, into the other. Furthermore, this is not surprising. The grammars that linguists construct are, in fact, quite neutral as between speaker and hearer. The problems of constructing models of performance, for the speaker and hearer, incorporating these grammars, are rather similar. This, of course, bears again on the question of relation between competence and performance. That is, the grammar that represents the speaker's competence is, or course, involved in both his speaking and interpreting of speech, and there seems no reason to assume that there are two different underlying systems, one involved in speaking, one in 'understanding'. To gain some insight into this underlying system, studies of the speaker's actual output, as well as of his ability to understand and interpret, are essential. But again, it cannot be too strongly emphasized that the data obtained in such studies can only serve as the grounds for inference about what constitutes the linguistic consciousness that provides the basis for language use.

A few other minor remarks of this sort might be made to indicate areas in which experimental methods that go far beyond mere observation of speech in normal situations will be needed to shed some light on underlying competence. To take just one example, it is often remarked, and, in particular, it is remarked in this paper, that in the case of lexical items (as distinct from 'function words', so-called) it is generally possible to assign referential meaning rather easily. Of course, as clearly stated in the paper, this is in part a matter of degree. However, I think that the notion that it is generally a straightforward matter in the case of lexical items is a faulty conclusion derived from concentration on atypical examples. Perhaps in the ease of 'green', 'table', etc., it is not difficult to determine what is the 'referential meaning'. But consider, on the other hand, such words as 'useful', where the meaning is clearly 'relational' — the things in the world cannot be divided into those that are useful and those that are not. In fact, the meaning of 'useful', like that of a function word, in some respects, must be described in partly relational terms. Or, to take a more complicated example, consider a word like 'expect'. A brief attempt to prescribe the behaviours or situations that make application of this word appropriate will quickly convince one that this is entirely the wrong approach and that 'referential meaning' is simply the wrong concept in this case. I don't think that such examples are at all exotic. It may be that such atypical examples as 'table' and 'green' are relatively more frequent in the early stages of language learning (though this remains to be shown, just as it remains to be shown that determination of referential meaning in such cases is in some sense 'primitive'), and, if true, this may be important. However, this is clearly not going to carry one very far.

Consider now a rather comparable phonetic example. One of the problems to be faced is that of characterizing the child's phonemic system. Phonemes are often defined by linguists as constituting a family of mutually exclusive classes of phones, and this is the definition adopted in this paper. If this were true, there would be, in this case, a fairly simple relation between performance (i.e. a sequence of phones) and the underlying abstract system (i.e. the phonemic representation of this sequence). One might hope that by some simple classification technique one might determine the phonemic system from the phonetic record or the phonemic constitution of an utterance from the sequence of its phones. There is, however, extremely strong evidence (so it seems to me, at least) that phonemes cannot be defined as classes of sounds at all (and certainly not as mutually exclusive classes) and that the relation between a phonemic system and the phonetic record (just as the relation between a phonemic representation of an utterance and its actual sound) is much more remote and complex.

These two examples are randomly chosen illustrations of a general tendency to oversimplify drastically the facts of linguistic structure and to assume that the determination of competence can be derived from description of a corpus by some sort of sufficiently developed data-processing techniques. My feeling is that this is hopeless and that only experimentation of a fairly indirect and ingenious sort can provide evidence that is at all critical for formulating a true account of the child's grammar (as in the case of investigation of any other real system). Consequently, I would hope that some of the research in this area would be diverted from recording of texts towards attempting to tap the child's underlying abilities to use and comprehend sentences, to detect deviance and compensate for it, to apply rules in new situations, to form highly specific concepts from scattered bits of evidence, and so on. There are, after all, many ways in which such study can be approached. Thus, for example, the child's ability to repeat sentences and nonsentences, phonologically possible sequences and phonologically impossible ones, etc., might provide some evidence as to the underlying system that he is using. There is surely no doubt that the child's achievements in systematizing linguistic data, at every stage, go well beyond what he actually produces in normal speech. Thus it is striking that advances are generally 'across the board'. A child who does not produce initial s + consonant clusters may begin to produce them all, at approximately the same time, thus distinguishing for the first time between 'cool' and 'school', etc. — but characteristically will do this in just the right words, indicating that the correct phonemic representation of these words was present to the mind even at the stage where it did not appear in speech. Similarly, some of the data of Brown and Fraser seem to suggest that interrogatives, negatives, and other syntactically related forms appear and are distinguished from declaratives at approximately the same time, for some children. If so, this suggests that what has actually happened is that the hitherto latent system of verbal auxiliaries is now no longer suppressed in actual speech, as previously. Again, this can be investigated directly. Thus a child producing speech in a 'telegraphic style' can be shown to have an underlying, fuller conception of sentence structure (unrealized in his speech, but actively involved in comprehension) if misplacement of the elements he does not produce leads to difficulties of comprehension, inability to repeat, etc., while correct placement gives utterances intelligible to him, and so on.

'Formal discussion' in *The Acquisition of Language*,
Bellugi and Brown (1964)

3. Rationalist and empiricist views

Applying a rationalist view to the special case of language learning, Humboldt (1836) concludes that one cannot really teach language but can only present the conditions under which it will develop spontaneously in the mind in its own way. Thus the *form of a language*, the schema for its grammar, is to a large extent given, though it will not be available for use without appropriate experience to set the language-forming processes into operation. Like Leibniz, he reiterates the Platonistic view that, for the individual, learning is largely a matter of *Wiedererzeugung*, that is, of drawing out what is innate in the mind.

This view contrasts sharply with the empiricist notion (the prevailing modern view) that language is essentially an adventitious construct, taught by 'conditioning' (as would be maintained, for example, by Skinner or Quine) or by drill and explicit explanation (as was claimed by Wittgenstein), or built up by elementary 'data-processing' procedures (as modern linguistics typically maintains), but, in any event, relatively independent in its structure of any innate mental faculties.

In short, empiricist speculation has characteristically assumed that only the procedures and mechanisms for the acquisition of knowledge constitute an innate property of the mind. Thus for Hume, the method of 'experimental reasoning' is a basic instinct in animals and humans, on a par with the instinct 'which teaches a bird, with such exactness, the art of incubation, and the whole economy and order of its nursery' — it is derived 'from the original hand of nature' (Hume, 1748, § IX). The form of knowledge, however, is otherwise quite free. On the other hand, rationalist speculation has assumed that the general form of a system of knowledge is fixed in advance as a disposition of the mind, and the function of experience is to cause this general schematic structure to be realized and more fully differentiated. To follow Leibniz's enlightening analogy, we may make

> '. . . the comparison of a block of marble which has veins, rather than a block of marble wholly even, or of blank tablets, i.e. of what is called among philosophers a *tabula rasa*. For if the soul resembled these blank tablets, truths would be in us as the figure of Hercules is in the marble, when the marble is wholly indifferent to the reception of this figure or some other. But if there were veins in the block which would indicate the figure of Hercules rather than other figures, this block would be more determined thereto, and Hercules would be in it as in some sense innate, although it would be needful to labour to discover these veins, to clear them by polishing, and by cutting away what prevents them from appearing. Thus it is that ideas and truths are for us innate, as inclinations, dispositions, habits, or natural potentialities, and not as actions; although these potentialities are always accompanied by some actions, often insensible, which correspond to them' [Leibniz, *New Essays*, pp. 45-6].

It is not, of course, necessary to assume that empiricist and rationalist views can always be sharply distinguished and that these currents cannot cross. Nevertheless, it is historically accurate as well as heuristically valuable to distinguish these two very different approaches to the problem of acquisition of knowledge. Particular empiricist and rationalist views can be made quite precise and can then be presented as explicit hypotheses about acquisition of knowledge, in particular, about the innate structure of a language-acquisition device. In fact, it would not be inaccurate to describe the taxonomic, data-processing approach of modern linguistics as an empiricist view that contrasts with the essentially rationalist alternative proposed in recent theories of transformational grammar. Taxonomic linguistics is empiricist in its assumption that general linguistic theory consists only of a body of procedures for determining the grammar of a language from a corpus of data, the form of language being unspecified except in so far as restrictions on possible grammars are determined by this set of procedures. If we interpret taxonomic linguistics as making an empirical claim, this claim must be that the grammars that result from application of the postulated procedures to a sufficiently rich selection of data will be descriptively adequate — in other words, that the set of procedures can be regarded as constituting a hypothesis about the innate language-acquisition system. In contrast, the discussion of language acquisition in preceding sections was rationalistic in its assumption that various formal and substantive universals are intrinsic properties of the language-acquisition system, these providing a schema that is applied to data and that determines in a highly restricted way the general form and, in part, even the substantive features of the grammar that may emerge upon presentation of appropriate data. A general linguistic theory of the sort roughly described earlier, and elaborated in more detail in the following chapters and in other studies of transformational grammar, must therefore be regarded as a specific hypothesis, of an essentially rationalist cast, as to the nature of mental structures and processes.

Aspects of the Theory of Syntax, 51-3

4. Criticism of reinforcement theory

It is a common observation that a young child of immigrant parents may learn a second language in the streets, from other children, with amazing rapidity, and that his speech may be completely fluent and correct to the last allophone, while the subtleties that become second nature to the child may elude his parents despite high motivation and continued practice. A child may pick up a large part of his vocabulary and 'feel' for sentence structure from television, from reading, from listening to adults, etc. Even a very young child who has not yet acquired a minimal repertoire from which to form new utterances may imitate a word quite well on an early try, with no attempt on the part of his parents to teach it to him. It is also perfectly obvious that, at a later stage, a child will be able to construct and understand utterances which are quite new, and are, at the same time, acceptable sentences in his language. Every time an adult reads a newspaper, he undoubtedly comes upon countless new sentences which are not at all similar, in a simple, physical sense, to any that he has heard before, and which he will recognize as sentences and understand; he will also be able to detect slight distortions or misprints. Talk of 'stimulus generalization' in such a case simply perpetuates the mystery under a new title. These abilities indicate that there must be fundamental processes at work quite independently of 'feedback' from the environment. I have been able to find no support whatsoever for the doctrine of Skinner and others that slow and careful shaping of verbal behaviour through differential reinforcement is an absolute necessity. If reinforcement theory really requires the assumption that there be such meticulous care, it seems best to regard this simply as a *reductio ad absurdum* argument against this approach. It is also not easy to find any basis (or, for that matter, to attach very much content) to the claim that reinforcing contingencies set up by the verbal community are the single factor responsible for maintaining the strength of verbal behaviour. The sources of the 'strength' of this behaviour are almost a total mystery at present. Reinforcement undoubtedly plays a significant role, but so do a variety of motivational factors about which nothing serious is known in the case of human beings.

As far as acquisition of language is concerned, it seems clear that reinforcement, casual observation, and natural inquisitiveness (coupled with a strong tendency to imitate) are important factors, as is the remarkable capacity of the child to generalize, hypothesize, and 'process information' in a variety of very special and apparently highly complex ways which we cannot yet describe or begin to understand, and which may be largely innate, or may develop through some sort of learning or through maturation of the nervous system. The manner in which such factors operate and interact in language acquisition is completely unknown. It is clear that what is necessary in such a case is research, not dogmatic and perfectly arbitrary claims based on analogies to that small part of the experimental literature in which one happens to be interested.

The pointlessness of these claims becomes clear when we consider the well-known difficulties in determining to what extent inborn structure, maturation, and learning are responsible for the particular form of a skilled or complex performance. To take just one example, the gaping response of a nestling thrush is at first released by jarring of the nest, and, at a later stage, by a moving object of specific size, shape, and position relative to the nestling. At this later stage the response is directed towards the part of the stimulus object corresponding to the parent's head, and characterized by a complex configuration of stimuli that can be precisely described. Knowing just this, it would be possible to construct a speculative, learning-theoretic account of how this sequence of behaviour patterns might have developed through a process of differential reinforcement, and it would no doubt be possible to train rats to do something similar. However, there appears to be good evidence that these responses to fairly complex 'sign stimuli' are genetically determined and mature without learning. Clearly, the possibility cannot be discounted. Consider now the comparable case of a child imitating new words. At an early stage we may find rather gross correspondences. At a later stage, we find that repetition is, of course, far from exact (i.e. it is not mimicry, a fact which itself is interesting), but that it reproduces the highly complex configuration of sound features that constitute the phonological structure of the language in question. Again, we can propose a speculative account of how this result might have been obtained through elaborate arrangement of reinforcing contingencies. Here too, however, it is possible that ability to select out of the complex auditory input those features that are phonologically relevant may develop largely independently of reinforcement, through genetically determined maturation. To the extent that this is true, an account of the development and causation of behaviour that fails to consider the structure of the organism will provide no understanding of the real processes involved.

It is often argued that experience, rather than innate capacity to handle information in certain specific ways, must be the factor of overwhelming dominance in determining the specific character of language acquisition since a child speaks the language of the group in which he lives. But this is a superficial argument. As long as we are speculating, we may consider the possibility that the brain has evolved to the point where, given an input of observed Chinese sentences, it produces (by an 'induction' of apparently fantastic complexity and suddenness) the 'rules' of Chinese grammar, and given an input of observed English sentences, it produces (by, perhaps, exactly the same process of induction) the rules of English grammar; or that given an observed application of a term to certain instances it automatically predicts the extension to a class of complexly related instances. If clearly recognized as such, this speculation is neither unreasonable nor fantastic; nor, for that matter, is it beyond the bounds of possible study. There is, of course, no known neural structure capable of performing this task in the specific ways that observation of the resulting behaviour might lead us to postulate; but for that matter, the structures capable of accounting for even the simplest kinds of learning have similarly defied detection.

Summarizing this brief discussion, it seems that there is neither empirical evidence nor any known argument to support any specific claim about the relative importance of 'feedback' from the environment and the 'independent contribution of the organism' in the process of language acquisition.

A Review of B.F. Skinner's Verbal Behavior (1959), 42-4

5. Formal and substantive universals

A theory of linguistic structure that aims for explanatory adequacy incorporates an account of linguistic universals, and it attributes tacit knowledge of these universals to the child. It proposes, then, that the child approaches the data with the presumption that they are drawn from a language of a certain antecedently well-defined type, his problem being to determine which of the (humanly) possible languages is that of the community in which he is placed. Language learning would be impossible unless this were the case. The important question is: What are the initial assumptions concerning the nature of language that the child brings to language learning, and how detailed and specific is the innate schema (the general definition of 'grammar') that gradually becomes more explicit and differentiated as the child learns the language? For the present we cannot come at all close to making a hypothesis about innate schemata that is rich, detailed, and specific enough to account for the fact of language acquisition. Consequently, the main task of linguistic theory must be to develop an account of linguistic universals that, on the one hand, will not be falsified by the actual diversity of languages and, on the other will be sufficiently rich and explicit to account for the rapidity and uniformity of language learning, and the remarkable complexity and range of the generative grammars that are the product of language learning.

The study of linguistic universals is the study of the properties of any generative grammar for a natural language. Particular assumptions about linguistic universals may pertain to either the syntactic, semantic, or phonological component, or to interrelations among the three components.

It is useful to classify linguistic universals as *formal* or *substantive*. A theory of substantive universals claims that items of a particular kind in any language must be drawn from a fixed class of items. For example, Jakobson's theory of distinctive features can be interpreted as making an assertion about substantive universals with respect to the phonological component of a generative grammar. It asserts that each output of this component consists of elements that are characterized in terms of some small number of fixed universal, phonetic features, each of which has a substantive acoustic-articulatory characterization independent of any particular language. Traditional universal grammar was also a theory of substantive universals, in this sense. It not only put forth interesting views as to the nature of universal phonetics, but also advanced the position that certain fixed syntactic categories (Noun, Verb, etc.) can be found in the syntactic representations of the sentences of any language and that these provide the general underlying syntactic structure of each language. A theory of substantive semantic universals might hold for example, that certain designative functions must be carried out in a specified way in each language. Thus it might assert that each language will contain terms that designate persons or lexical items referring to certain specific kinds of objects, feelings, behaviour, and so on.

It is also possible, however, to search for universal properties of a more abstract sort. Consider a claim that the grammar of every language meets certain specified formal conditions. The truth of this hypothesis would not in itself imply that any particular rule must appear in all or even in any two grammars. The property of having a grammar meeting a certain abstract condition might be called *a formal* linguistic universal, if shown to be a general property of natural languages. Recent attempts to specify the abstract conditions that a generative grammar must meet have produced a variety of proposals concerning formal universals, in this sense. For example, consider the proposal that the syntactic component of a grammar must contain transformational rules (these being operations of a highly special kind) mapping semantically interpreted deep structures into phonetically interpreted surface structures, or the proposal that the phonological component of a grammar consists of a sequence of rules, a subset of which may apply cyclically to successively more dominant constituents of the surface structure (a transformational cycle, in the sense of much recent work on phonology). Such proposals make claims of a quite different sort from the claim that certain substantive phonetic elements are available for phonetic representation in all languages, or that certain specific categories must be central to the syntax of all languages, or that certain semantic features or categories provide a universal framework for semantic description. Substantive universals such as these concern the vocabulary for the description of language; formal universals involve rather the character of the rules that appear in grammars and the ways in which they can be interconnected.

On the semantic level, too, it is possible to search for what might be called formal universals, in essentially the sense just described. Consider, for example, the assumption that proper names, in any language, must designate objects meeting a condition of spatiotemporal contiguity, and that the same is true of other terms designating objects; or the condition that the colour words of any language must subdivide the colour spectrum into continuous segments; or the condition that artifacts are defined in terms of certain human goals, needs, and functions instead of solely in terms of physical qualities. Formal constraints of this sort on a system of concepts may severely limit the choice (by the child, or the linguist) of a descriptive grammar, given primary linguistic data.

The existence of deep-seated formal universals, in the sense suggested by such examples as these, implies that all languages are cut to the same pattern, but does not imply that there is any point by point correspondence between particular languages. It does not, for example, imply that there must be some reasonable procedure for translating between languages*.

In general, there is no doubt that a theory of language, regarded as a hypothesis about the innate 'language-forming capacity' of humans, should concern itself with both substantive and formal universals. But whereas substantive universals have been the traditional concern of general linguistic theory, investigations of the abstract conditions that must be satisfied by any generative grammar have been undertaken only quite recently. They seem to offer extremely rich and varied possibilities for study in all aspects of grammar.

6. Descriptive and explanatory theories

Let us consider with somewhat greater care just what is involved in the construction of an 'acquisition model' for language. A child who is capable of language learning must have

(1)   (i)   a technique for representing input signals

      (ii) a way of representing structural information about these signals

      (iii) some initial delimitation of a class of possible hypotheses about language structure

      (iv) a method for determining what each such hypothesis implies with respect to each sentence

      (v) a method for selecting one of the (presumably, infinitely many) hypotheses that are allowed by (iii) and are compatible with the given primary linguistic data.

Correspondingly, a theory of linguistic structure that aims for explanatory adequacy must contain

(2)   (i)   a universal phonetic theory that defines the notion 'possible sentence'

      (ii) a definition of 'structural description'

      (iii) a definition of 'generative grammar'

      (iv) a method for determining the structural description of a sentence, given a grammar

      (v) a way of evaluating alternative proposed grammars

---

* By a 'reasonable procedure' I mean one that does not involve extralinguistic information — that is, one that does not incorporate an 'encyclopedia'. The possibility of a reasonable procedure for translation between arbitrary languages depends on the sufficiency of substantive universals. In fact, although there is much reason to believe that languages are to a significant extent cast in the same mould, there is little reason to suppose that reasonable procedures of translation are in general possible. [Chomsky]

196

A theory meeting these conditions would attempt to account for language learning in the following way. Consider first the nature of primary linguistic data. This consists of a finite amount of information about sentences, which, furthermore, must be rather restricted in scope, considering the time limitations that are in effect, and fairly degenerate in quality. For example, certain signals might be accepted as properly formed sentences, while others are classed as nonsentences, as a result of correction of the learners' attempts on the part of linguistic community. Furthermore, the conditions of use might be such as to require that structural descriptions be assigned to these objects in certain ways. That the latter is a prerequisite for language acquisition seems to follow from the widely accepted (but, for the moment, quite unsupported) view that there must be a partially semantic basis for the acquisition of syntax or for the justification of hypotheses about the syntactic component of a grammar. Incidentally, it is often not realized how strong a claim this is about the innate concept-forming abilities of the child and the system of linguistic universals that these abilities imply. Thus what is maintained, presumably, is that the child has an innate theory of potential structural descriptions that is sufficiently rich and fully developed so that he is able to determine, from a real situation in which a signal occurs, which structural descriptions may be appropriate to this signal, and also that he is able to do this in part in advance of any assumption as to the linguistic structure of this signal. To say that the assumption about innate capacity is extremely strong is, of course, not to say that it is incorrect. Let us, in any event, assume tentatively that the primary linguistic data consists of signals classified as sentences and nonsentences, and a partial and tentative pairing of signals with structural descriptions.

A language-acquisition device that meets conditions (i)-(iv) is capable of utilizing such primary linguistic data as the empirical basis for language learning. This device must search through the set of possible hypotheses $G_1, G_2, \ldots$, which are available to it by virtue of condition (iii), and must select grammars that are compatible with the primary linguistic data, represented in terms of (i) and (ii). It is possible to test compatibility by virtue of the fact that the device meets condition (iv). The device would then select one of these potential grammars by the evaluation measure guaranteed by (v). The selected grammar now provides the device with a method for interpreting an arbitrary sentence, by virtue of (ii) and (iv). That is to say, the device has now constructed a theory of the language of which the primary linguistic data are a sample. The theory that the device has now selected and internally represented specifies its tacit competence, its knowledge of the language. The child who acquires a language in this way, of course, knows a great deal more than he has 'learned'. His knowledge of the language, as this is determined by his internalized grammar, goes far beyond the presented primary linguistic data and is in no sense an 'inductive generalization' from these data.

This account of language learning can, obviously, be paraphrased directly as a description of how the linguist whose work is guided by a linguistic theory meeting conditions (i)-(v) would justify a grammar that he constructs for a language on the basis of given primary linguistic data.

Notice, incidentally, that care must be taken to distinguish several different ways in which primary linguistic data may be necessary for language learning. In part, such data determine to which of the possible languages (that is, the languages provided with grammars in accordance with the *a priori* constraint (iii)) the language learner is being exposed, and it is this function of the primary linguistic data that we are considering here. But such data may play an entirely different role as well; namely, certain kinds of data and experience may be required in order to set the language-acquisition device into operation, although they may not effect the manner of its functioning in the least. Thus it has been found that semantic reference may greatly facilitate performance in a syntax-learning experiment, even though it does not, apparently, effect the *manner* in which acquisition of syntax proceeds; that is, it plays no role in determining which hypotheses are selected by the learner (Miller and Norman, 1964). Similarly, it would not be at all surprising to find that normal language learning requires use of language in real-life situations, in some way. But this, if true, would not be sufficient to show that information regarding situational context (in particular, a pairing of signals with structural descriptions that is at least in part prior to assumptions about syntactic structure) plays any role in determining how language is acquired, once the mechanism is put to work and the task of language learning is undertaken by the child. This distinction is quite familiar outside of the domain of language acquisition. For example, Richard Held has shown in numerous experiments that under certain circumstances reafferent stimulation (that is stimulation resulting from voluntary activity) is a prerequisite to the development of a concept of visual space, although it may not determine the character of this concept (cf. Held and Hein, 1963; Held and Freedman, 1963, and references cited there). Or, to take one of innumerable examples from studies of animal learning, it has been observed (Lemmon and Patterson, 1964) that depth perception in lambs is considerably facilitated by mother-neonate contact, although again there is no reason to suppose that the nature of the lamb's 'theory of visual space' depends on this contact.

In studying the actual character of learning, linguistic or otherwise, it is, of course, necessary to distinguish carefully between these two functions of external data — the function of initiating or facilitating the operation of innate mechanisms and the function of determining in part the direction that learning will take.

Returning now to the main theme, we call a theory of linguistic structure that meets conditions (i)-(v) an *explanatory theory,* and a theory that meets conditions (i)-(iv) a *descriptive theory*. In fact, a linguistic theory that is concerned only with descriptive adequacy will limit its attention to topics (i)-(iv). Such a theory must, in other words, make available a class of generative grammars containing, for each language, a descriptively adequate grammar of this language — a grammar that (by means of (iv)) assigns structural descriptions to sentences in accordance with the linguistic competence of the native speaker. A theory of language is empirically significant only to the extent that it meets conditions (i)-(iv). The further question of explanatory adequacy arises in connection with a theory that also meets condition (v). In other words, it arises only to the extent that the theory provides a principled basis for selecting a descriptively adequate grammar on the basis of primary linguistic data by the use of a well-defined evaluation measure.

This account is misleading in one important respect. It suggests that to raise a descriptively adequate theory to the level of explanatory adequacy one needs only to define an appropriate evaluation measure. This is incorrect, however. A theory may be descriptively adequate, in the sense just defined, and yet provide such a wide range of potential grammars that there is no possibility of discovering a formal property distinguishing the descriptively adequate grammars, in general, from among the mass of grammars compatible with whatever data are available. In fact, the real problem is almost always to restrict the range of possible hypotheses by adding additional structure to the notion 'generative grammar'. For the construction of a reasonable acquisition model, it is necessary to reduce the class of attainable grammars compatible with given primary linguistic data to the point where selection among them can be made by a formal evaluation measure. This requires a precise and narrow delimitation of the notion 'generative grammar' — a restrictive and rich hypothesis concerning the universal properties that determine the form of language, in the traditional sense of this term.

The same point can be put in a somewhat different way. Given a variety of descriptively adequate grammars for natural languages, we are interested in determining to what extent they are unique and to what extent there are deep underlying similarities among them that are attributable to the form of language as such. Real progress in linguistics consists in the discovery that certain features of given languages can be reduced to universal properties of language, and explained in terms of these deeper aspects of linguistic form. Thus the major endeavour of the linguist must be to enrich the theory of linguistic form by formulating more specific constraints and conditions on the notion 'generative grammar'. Where this can be done, particular grammars can be simplified by eliminating from them descriptive statements that are attributable to the general theory of grammar. For example, if we conclude that the transformational cycle is a universal feature of the phonological component, it is unnecessary, in the grammar of English, to describe the manner of functioning of those phonological rules that involve syntactic structure. This description will now have been abstracted from the grammar of English and stated as a formal linguistic universal, as part of the theory of generative grammar. Obviously, this conclusion, if justified, would represent an important advance in the theory of language, since it would then have been shown that what appears to be a peculiarity of English is actually explicable in terms of a general and deep empirical assumption about the nature of language, an assumption that can be refuted, if false, by study of descriptively adequate grammars of other languages.

In short, the most serious problem that arises in the attempt to achieve explanatory adequacy is that of characterizing the notion 'generative grammar' in a sufficiently rich, detailed, and highly structured way. A theory of grammar may be descriptively adequate and yet leave unexpressed major features that are defining properties of natural language and that distinguish natural languages from arbitrary symbolic systems. It is for just this reason that the attempt to achieve explanatory adequacy — the attempt to discover linguistic universals — is so crucial at every stage of understanding of linguistic structure, despite the fact that even descriptive adequacy on a broad scale may be an unrealized goal. It is not necessary to achieve descriptive adequacy before raising questions of explanatory adequacy. On the contrary, the crucial questions, the questions that have the greatest bearing on our concept of language and on descriptive practice as well, are almost always those involving explanatory adequacy with respect to particular aspects of language structure.

To acquire language, a child must devise a hypothesis compatible with presented data — he must select from the store of potential grammars a specific one that is appropriate to the data available to him. It is logically possible that the data might be sufficiently rich and the class of potential grammars sufficiently limited so that no more than a single permitted grammar will be compatible with the available data at the moment of successful language acquisition, in our idealized 'instantaneous' model. In this case, no evaluation procedure will be necessary as a part of linguistic theory — that is, as an innate property of an organism or a device capable of language acquisition. It is rather difficult to imagine how in detail this logical possibility might be realized, and all concrete attempts to formulate an empirically adequate linguistic theory certainly leave ample room for mutually inconsistent grammars, all compatible with primary data of any conceivable sort. All such theories therefore require supplementation by an evaluation measure if language acquisition is to be accounted for and selection of specific grammars is to be justified; and I shall continue to assume tentatively, as heretofore, that this is an empirical fact about the innate human *faculté de langage* and consequently about general linguistic theory as well.

Aspects of the Theory of Syntax, 27-37

7. Conclusion

The child who learns a language has in some sense constructed the grammar for himself on the basis of his observation of sentences and nonsentences (i.e. corrections by the verbal community). Study of the actual observed ability of a speaker to distinguish sentences from nonsentences, detect ambiguities, etc., apparently forces us to the conclusion that this grammar is of an extremely complex and abstract character, and that the young child has succeeded in carrying out what from the formal point of view, at least, seems to be a remarkable type of theory construction. Furthermore, this task is accomplished in an astonishingly short time, to a large extent independently of intelligence, and in a comparable way by all children. Any theory of learning must cope with these facts.

It is not easy to accept the view that a child is capable of constructing an extremely complex mechanism for generating a set of sentences, some of which he has heard, or that an adult can instantaneously determine whether (and if so, how) a particular item is generated by this mechanism, which has many of the properties of an abstract deductive theory. Yet this appears to be a fair description of the performance of the speaker, listener, and learner. If this is correct, we can predict that a direct attempt to account for the actual behaviour of speaker, listener, and learner, not based on a prior understanding of the structure of grammars, will achieve very limited success. The grammar must be regarded as a component in the behaviour of the speaker and listener which can only be inferred, as Lashley has put it, from the resulting physical acts. The fact that all normal children acquire essentially comparable grammars of great complexity with remarkable rapidity suggests that human beings are somehow specially designed to do this, with data-handling or 'hypothesis-formulating' ability of unknown character and complexity. The study of linguistic structure may ultimately lead to some significant insights into this matter. At the moment the question cannot be seriously posed, but in principle it may be possible to study the problem of determining what the built-in structure of an information-processing (hypothesis-forming) system must be to enable it to arrive at the grammar of a language from the available data in the available time. At any rate, just as the attempt to eliminate the contribution of the speaker leads to a 'mentalistic' descriptive system that succeeds only in blurring important traditional distinctions, a refusal to study the contribution of the child to language learning permits only a superficial account of language acquisition, with a vast and unanalysed contribution attributed to a step called 'generalization' which in fact includes just about everything of interest in this process. If the study of language is limited in these ways, it seems inevitable that major aspects of verbal behaviour will remain a mystery.

A Review of B.F. Skinner's Verbal Behavior (1959), 57-8

13.   Mothers' Speech to Children Learning Language

Catherine E. Snow

The assumption that language acquisition is relatively independent of the amount and kind of language input must be assessed in light of information about the speech actually heard by young children. The speech of middle-class mothers to 2-year-old children was found to be simpler and more redundant than their speech to 10-year-old children. The mothers modified their speech less when talking to children whose responses they could not observe, indicating that the children played some role in eliciting the speech modifications. Task difficulty did not contribute to the mothers' production of simplified, redundant speech. Experienced mothers were only slightly better than nonmothers in predicting the speech-style modifications required by young children. These findings indicate that children who are learning languages have available a sample of speech which is simpler, more redundant, and less confusing than normal adult speech.

The speech young children hear is their only source of information about the language they are to learn. As such, it must be taken into account in any attempt to explain the process of language acquisition. Despite its unquestioned importance for language learning, very little is actually known about the kind of language which is addressed to children. Developmental psycholinguists have assumed that children hear a random sample of adult utterances, characterized by all the stutters, mistakes, garbles, inconsistencies, and complexities which are common in adults' speech to other adults (Chomsky 1965, 1968; Lenneberg 1969; McNeill 1970). This assumption about the primary linguistic data has been offered as a key bit of evidence in support of the view that infants must be largely preprogrammed for the task of language learning.

Considering the theoretical importance of the child's early linguistic environment, not only to students of language acquisition, but also to those trying to explain social class differences in linguistic ability (Bernstein 1970; Hess & Shipman 1965; Olim 1970), it seemed valuable to study the language actually heard by young children. Accordingly, the present experiments were performed in order to investigate: (a) whether the speech of mothers to children just learning to talk differed from the speech of those same mothers to older children, (b) whether speech-style modifications for young children depended on the presence of the child with the mother, as opposed to the mother's mere intention to address a 2-year-old, (c) whether the difficulty of the tasks for the child affected the mother's production of speech-style modifications, and (d) whether nonmothers differed from mothers in their ability to modify their speech for young children.

Catherine E. Snow: 'Mothers' Speech to Children Learning Language'. *CHILD DEVELOPMENT* (1972), 43, pp. 549-565. © 1972 by the Society for Research in Child Development, Inc. All rights reserved.

Experimental investigations

Subjects

The women who served as subjects were all college graduates who volunteered after being contacted through their alumni association. The women were told that the experiments dealt with "how children learn to talk." Apparently none of them suspected that her own speech and not the child's behavior was of primary interest. Twelve of the women tested had children in the age range 9-5 to 12-4. These children participated with their mothers in experiment 1, serving as the stimulus children for the 10-year-old condition. Twenty-four of the subjects had children ranging in age from 2-0 to 3-4. Twelve of these mothers and their children participated in experiment 1; and 12, in experiment 2. Six women who had no children and who were not frequently in the company of children participated in experiment 3.

Scoring procedure

Tape recordings of all experimental sessions were transcribed, and scoring of the following nine measures was done on the typewritten transcriptions.

1. Quantity of speech: total number of words spoken.

2. Mean length of utterance: ratio of the total number of words spoken to the total number of utterances. Utterances were scored by listening to the tapes and marking the transcriptions as indicated by the phonetic cues and pauses in the mothers' speech. Run-on sentences were scored as two or more utterances. Phrases and sentence fragments were accepted as utterances if they were characterized by a complete intonation pattern. Thus, what was scored as a complete utterance often was not a complete sentence as defined by traditional grammar.

3. Sentence complexity: ratio of the number of compound verbs plus subordinate clauses to the total number of utterances.

4. Mean preverb length: ratio of the total number of words before the main verb in all clauses to the total number of clauses. Imperatives were excluded from both these counts.

5. Incidence of utterances without verbs: ratio of the number of utterances that did not contain verbs to the total number of utterances.

6. Incidence of third-person pronouns: ratio of the total number of occurrences of the pronouns he, she, it, they, him, her, them, his, her, hers, its, their, and theirs to the total number of words.

7. Incidence of complete repetitions: ratio of the number of complete repetitions of sentences (i.e. utterances which contain both subject and verb) to the total number of utterances. Repetitions were scored only if they occurred within three utterances of the original.

8. Incidence of partial repetitions: ratio of the number of repetitions of one or more major units within an utterance (e.g. repetition of the subject phrase or a subordinate clause) or of an entire utterance without a verb to the total number of utterances. If all major units were repeated, a complete repetition was scored. If

only some of the units were repeated, a partial repetition was scored. Again, the repetition was scored only if it occurred within three utterances of the original.

9. Incidence of semantic repetitions: ratio of the number of repetitions of the meaning of a previous utterance which did not include repetition of any of its grammatical units to the number of utterances. An utterance was scored as a semantic repetition only if it was a true paraphrase and did not qualify as a complete or partial repetition. The repetition was scored only if it occurred within three utterances of the original.

Measures 1-6 were simple counting procedures and were scored in all cases by the experimenter. Since measures 7, 8, and 9 involved some subjective judgment, an independent observer also scored these. The reliability coefficients for the experimenter and the independent judge ranged from .7 to .9 and were in all cases highly significant, so a mean of the two scores was assigned as the subject's score.

Experiment 1

The primary purpose of experiment 1 was to investigate whether mothers modified their speech styles when addressing young children. Second, the absence or presence of the child in the room with the mother was varied in an attempt to separate the effects of the mothers' expectations about the linguistic capabilities of young children from the effects of any implicit demands the children might make on the adult speakers.

Method. — Appointments were scheduled so that a mother of a 2-year-old came to the laboratory with her child at the same time as a mother of a 10-year-old came with her child. Each of the two mothers then performed three verbal tasks with both children. In addition to performing the tasks with the child of either age group actually present in the room, the mother was asked to perform the tasks while speaking into a tape recorder in the absence of the child, but as if she were speaking to a child of the appropriate age group. Thus, each mother performed the tasks four times, with an absent 2-year-old, a present 2-year-old, an absent 10-year-old, and a present 10-year-old. The three tasks consisted of (a) making up and telling a story to the child, based on a picture provided by the experimenter, (b) telling the child how to sort a number of small plastic toys in several ways, and (c) explaining a physical phenomenon to the child. The speech during the three tasks was pooled for scoring. Half the mothers performed the tasks first with their own children, and half performed the tasks first with a 2-year-old. All the mothers performed the absent condition for each age before the present condition for that age. The experimenter was not present during any of the testing.

Results. — Each measure was analyzed separately with a three-way analysis of variance. A small number of missing scores which resulted from mechanical failure of the tape recorder or from recalcitrance among the 2-year-olds were estimated using the procedure described in Winer (1962), so that an analysis for repeated measures could be applied. Degrees of freedom were subtracted from the error terms to compensate for the effects of estimation. The groups factor (mothers of 2-year-olds versus mothers of 10-year-olds) yielded no significant differences, so the two groups will be considered together in discussion of the results. Whenever the analysis of variance showed overall significance, cell means within the presence and age factors were compared using Scheffé (1953) tests.

The analysis of variance for quantity of speech indicates that mothers talked longer when a child was present in the room and that mothers talked longer to 2-year-olds than to 10-year-olds (see table 1). The age x presence interaction was significant, reflecting a much greater effect of the presence of the child in the 2-year-old than in the 10-year-old condition. Results of the Scheffé tests (indicated by lines between the cell means in table 1) show that the 2-year-old present condition was significantly different from all the others, and that the 10-year-old present condition was significantly different from the 10-year-old absent condition. The primary reason for quantity-of-speech differences was probably the greater difficulty of the tasks for the younger children and the greater interest of the tasks for the mothers in the present condition.

Mean length of utterance, sentence complexity, and mean preverb length are all measures of the grammatical complexity of speech. In each case, a higher score indicates more complex speech. For every measure, the absent condition elicited more complex speech than the present condition, and the 10-year-olds elicited more complex speech than the 2-year-olds. All the differences were significant except the difference between the 2-year-old and the 10-year-old conditions for mean preverb length, which approached significance. Mean preverb length and sentence complexity showed significant age x presence interactions; both these interactions reflect a much greater difference between present and absent scores in the 2-year-old than in the 10-year-old condition. Scheffé tests for all three measures show an identical pattern; there were no significant differences among the 2-year-old absent, 10-year-old absent, and 10-year-old present conditions, but all of these differed significantly from the 2-year-old present condition. On every measure of complexity, the speech produced in the 2-year-old present condition was significantly simpler than that produced in any other condition.

All three repetition measures showed significant age and presence effects. In all cases, mothers made more repetitions to 2-year-olds than to 10-year-olds. Also, complete repetitions and semantic repetitions occurred more frequently in the present than in the absent condition. Scheffé tests for these two repetition measures show the same pattern as for the complexity measures; more repetitions occurred in the 2-year-old present condition than in any other condition, and the other conditions did not differ from one another. This pattern is confirmed by the significant age x presence interaction for semantic repetitions. However, the results for the presence factor were reversed for incidence of partial repetitions; there were more partial repetitions in the absent condition than in the present condition. Scheffé tests indicate that there were more partial repetitions in the 2-year-old absent condition than in any other condition. The 2-year-old present condition also elicited more partial repetitions than the 10-year-old present condition. The production of more partial repetitions in the absent condition indicates that mothers predicted the need for this kind of repetition, though they were unable to predict the need for complete repetitions, paraphrases, or grammatical simplification. Why this should be the case is unclear.

Table 1 Results of three-way analyses of variance and Scheffé tests, Experiment 1

Measures	Means		ANOVA Significant Effects		
	2-Year-Olds	10-Year-Olds	Age	Presence	Age x Presence
Quantity of speech:					
Absent	426.7	390.0	.01	.01	.05
Present	1448.2	861.2			
Mean length of utterance:					
Absent	9.839	11.245	.01	.01	. . .
Present	6.596	9.633			
Sentence complexity:					
Absent	0.473	0.543	.01	.01	.05
Present	0.189	0.464			
Mean preverb length:					
Absent	2.685	2.594	. . .	.01	.01
Present	2.044	2.448			
Utterances without verbs:					
Absent	0.074	0.043	.05	.01	. . .
Present	0.165	0.121			
Third-person pronouns:					
Absent	0.049	0.062	.01	.01	. . .
Present	0.039	0.051			
Complete repetitions:					
Absent	0.008	0.003	.01	.01	. . .
Present	0.029	0.007			
Partial repetitions:					
Absent	0.284	0.138	.01	.01	. . .
Present	0.157	0.105			
Semantic repetitions:					
Absent	0.059	0.032	.01	.01	.05
Present	0.136	0.049			

Note - Scheffé test results are indicated by lines between cell means: ———— , $p < .01$, ········ , $p < .05$.

Significantly fewer third-person pronouns were used in the present and in the 2-year-old conditions. Scheffé tests indicate that fewer third-person pronouns were used in the 2-year-old present condition than in either 10-year-old condition, and fewer were used in the 2-year-old absent than in the 10-year-old absent condition. Mothers tended to repeat nouns, especially subject and direct object nouns, when speaking to 2-year-olds rather than substituting pronouns for them.

Incidence of utterances without verbs was higher in the 2-year-old condition and in the present condition. Scheffé tests show that the 2-year-old present condition elicited more utterances without verbs than either absent condition, and the 10-year-old present condition elicited more utterances without verbs than the 10-year-old absent condition. This suggests that mothers did not maintain formal correctness in their speech to 2-year-olds. Rather, they produced sentence fragments, many of which were repetitions of phrases from preceding sentences.

Cell means for measures which showed significant groups x age interactions are given in table 2. These interactions can perhaps best be understood as differences between mothers talking to their own children and strangers' children. The interaction for quantity of speech occurred because mothers of 2-year-olds talked more to their own children than to the older children, while mothers of 10-year-olds talked about the same amount to both groups of children. The two complexity measures, mean length of utterance and sentence complexity, reveal that mothers of 2-year-olds used less complex language when speaking to the younger children and more complex language when speaking to the older children than did the mothers of 10-year-olds. The mothers of 10-year-olds simplified their speech somewhat for 2-year-olds but also spoke more simply to the 10-year-olds than did the other group of mothers. In general, it seems that the mothers of 2-year-olds were more sensitive than the mothers of 10-year-olds to the demands for simplified speech made by 2-year-old children.

Table 2   Cell means for the measures which showed groups x age interactions in Experiment 1

Measures and Condition	Means		Significance Level
	Mothers of 2-Year-Olds	Mothers of 10-Year-Olds	
Quantity of speech:			
2-year-old	1084.7	790.2	.05
10-year-old	567.7	680.8	
Mean length of utterance:			
2-year-old	7.833	8.603	.01
10-year-old	11.399	9.479	
Sentence complexity:			
2-year-old	0.284	0.379	.01
10-year-old	0.578	0.429	

Experiment 2

Experiment 2 was performed with two purposes in mind. The first was to confirm the results found for the presence factor in experiment 1. The procedure for the absent condition was changed somewhat in an attempt to motivate the mothers maximally to produce the speech modifications. The second purpose was systematically to vary task difficulty to ensure that the differences between the 2-year-old and 10-year-old conditions found in experiment 1 were not simply a result of greater difficulty of the tasks for the 2-year-olds.

Method. — Each of 12 mothers performed a number of tasks with her own 2-year-old child. In the first task, called block selection, the mother described a specific block (chosen by the experimenter) in terms of its size, its color, and the animal(s) pictured on it. The child had to pick out the block described from among a group of several similar blocks. The easy level of the task consisted of finding a small block with only one animal pictured on it from among 12 alternatives; the difficult level consisted of finding a large block with two animals pictured on it from among 24 alternatives. In the pattern-construction task, the mother described a pattern composed of light and dark wooden blocks of different sizes and shapes so that the child could reproduce the pattern with the blocks. In the easy task, the pattern consisted of five or six easily described blocks; in the difficult task the pattern consisted of 14–16 blocks, including shapes for which the children had no names. Each mother performed an easy and a difficult version of each task with her child in both the absent and the present condition. To ensure maximum similarity of the absent and present conditions, the mothers were warned that the tapes made in the absent condition would actually be played to the children, and this was done. Half the mothers performed the absent condition first and half performed the present condition first. The mothers scored the children's responses in all the tasks; the experimenter was not present during the testing.

Results. — Each measure was analyzed separately with a two-way analysis of variance. The two tasks were analyzed separately because of the problem of ranking difficulty within the two disparate tasks. The cell means and levels of significance for the analyses of variance are given in table 3.

In general, the findings for the presence factor were the same as those of experiment 1, except that some of the measures which showed an absent-present difference in experiment 1 no longer showed this difference under the more rigorous conditions of experiment 2. As predicted from experiment 1, quantity of speech was greater in the present condition. Significantly less complex speech occurred in the present condition in the pattern-construction task, as reflected in mean length of utterance and mean preverb length. For the block-selection task, however, only mean length of utterance decreased significantly in the present condition. Results for repetition measures were similar to those obtained in experiment 1. Complete repetitions increased in the present condition, and partial repetitions decreased. There were no significant differences for semantic repetitions. Whereas incidence of third-person pronouns, incidence of utterances without verbs, and incidence of semantic repetitions showed presence effects in experiment 1, these were not affected by the absence of the child in experiment 2. Thus, it seems that experienced mothers under properly motivating conditions can predict to some extent what kinds of speech modifications their children will require. They can produce speech in the absent condition which is in some ways similar to their normal speech to children, but the presence of the child remains a potent factor in eliciting still more extensive modifications.

Table 3   Results of two-way analyses of variance in Experiment 2

Measures and Task[a]	Means				ANOVA Significant Effects		
	Absent		Present				Presence x
	Easy	Difficult	Easy	Difficult	Presence	Difficulty	Difficulty
Quantity of speech:							
A	147.2	148.9	321.0	269.0	.05	. . .	. . .
B	181.6	631.3	398.8	889.2	.05	.01	. . .
Mean length of utterance:							
A	8.555	8.497	6.314	6.037	.01	. . .	. . .
B	9.851	10.180	6.497	6.749	.01	. . .	. . .
Sentence complexity:							
A	0.214	0.163	0.118	0.104	. . .	. . .	. . .
B	0.195	0.246	0.126	0.171	. . .	.05	. . .
Mean preverb length:							
A	2.111	2.353	2.003	2.101	. . .	.01	. . .
B	2.260	2.598	2.204	2.242	.01	. . .	. . .
Utterances without verbs:							
A	0.163	0.247	0.212	0.213	. . .	. . .	. . .
B	0.159	0.122	0.191	0.176	. . .	. . .	. . .
Third-person pronouns:							
A	0.052	0.029	0.044	0.025	. . .	.01	. . .
B	0.039	0.034	0.034	0.046	. . .	. . .	. . .
Complete repetitions:							
A	0.030	0.022	0.055	0.087	.05	. . .	. . .
B	0.042	0.031	0.057	0.085	.05	. . .	. . .
Partial repetitions:							
A	0.259	0.325	0.164	0.134	.01	. . .	.05
B	0.273	0.208	0.182	0.143	.05	. . .	. . .
Semantic repetitions:							
A	0.016	0.027	0.015	0.022	. . .	. . .	. . .
B	0.047	0.030	0.026	0.013	. . .	. . .	. . .

[a] Task A denotes the block-selection task; task B denotes the pattern-construction task.

The difficulty factor had only scattered effects, as indicated by the fact that for any given measure the difficulty factor was never significant for both tasks. As might be expected, quantity of speech increased with more difficult problems. This was only true for the pattern-construction task, however, where greater difficulty was partly a function of the need for more steps to solve the problem. Of the speech-complexity measures, sentence complexity increased in the difficult condition in the pattern-construction task, and mean preverb length increased in the difficult condition in the block-selection task. Mean length of utterance tended to increase in the difficult condition in the pattern-construction task, but this difference did not reach statistical significance. If the mothers in experiment 1 were responding to the children's difficulty with the tasks, they would be expected to have simplified their speech in the difficult condition; instead they produced more complex speech in this condition, suggesting that it was in fact the children's linguistic immaturity that was crucial in stimulating the mothers' speech modifications.

No repetition measures showed any difficulty effects in either of the tasks. Incidence of third-person pronouns decreased in the difficult condition only in the block-selection task. Incidence of utterances without verbs was not affected by difficulty.

The only presence x difficulty interaction effect occurred for incidence of partial repetitions in the block-selection task. Mothers produced more partial repetitions in the difficult condition if the child was absent, but not if the child was present to offer some feedback about the kind of information needed.

Experiment 3

In experiment 3, the speech of highly motivated mothers in the absent condition was compared to the speech of nonmothers who had had very little experience with children. This was done in order to determine whether their past experience in talking to children had taught the mothers who served as subjects in experiments 1 and 2 anything about the speech modifications that young children require.

Method. — Nonmothers were asked to make stimulus tapes for 2-year-old children, for use in "an experiment in cognitive development." They recorded instructions, only in the absent-condition, for the same tasks as used in experiment 2. These tapes were compared to absent-condition data collected from mothers in experiment 2.

Results. — The most striking finding was the general absence of differences between the speech of mothers and nonmothers (see table 4). Only quantity of speech, mean length of utterance, and incidence of utterances without verbs showed significant differences; in the first two cases nonmothers' scores were higher; in the last case, lower. Inspection of the protocols reveals that nonmothers' speech was more detailed, precise, and formal-sounding than mothers' speech. Nonmothers' speech was also more complex and less repetitive, but not significantly so.

The difficulty factor produced three differences. Quantity of speech increased in the difficult condition, as it had in experiment 2. Mean length of utterance was significantly greater in the difficult condition in both tasks. Comparison of easy and difficult conditions for the other complexity measures indicates that, although the differences were not significant, almost all of them were in the direction of greater complexity in the difficult condition. There were significantly more partial repetitions in the difficult condition in the block-selection task. However, in the pattern-construction task, there were fewer partial repetitions in the difficult condition, although this was not a significant difference. No other repetition measures showed any difficulty effects.

There were two significant groups x difficulty interaction effects. The increase in quantity of speech in the difficult condition in the pattern-construction task was much greater for nonmothers than for mothers. Mothers' mean length of utterance decreased slightly in the difficult condition in the block-selection task, while nonmothers' mean length of utterance increased substantially. In both cases, the difference between the conditions affected the nonmothers more than it affected the mothers.

Table 4   Results of two-way analyses of variance in Experiment 3

| Measures and Task[a] | Means | | | | ANOVA Significant Effects | | |
| | Mothers | | Nonmothers | | | | |
	Easy	Difficult	Easy	Difficult	Groups	Difficulty	Groups x Difficulty
Quantity of speech:							
A	147.2	148.9	192.2	157.3	...	...	...
B	181.6	631.4	472.2	1328.0	.01	.01	.05
Mean length of utterance:							
A	8.555	8.497	9.747	12.640	.05	.05	.05
B	9.851	10.180	10.008	11.242	...	.05	...
Sentence complexity:							
A	0.214	0.163	0.218	0.267	...	...	...
B	0.195	0.246	0.327	0.341	...	...	...
Mean preverb length:							
A	2.111	2.353	2.582	2.587	...	...	...
B	2.260	2.598	2.733	2.947	...	...	...
Utterances without verbs:							
A	0.163	0.247	0.019	0.022	.01	...	...
B	0.159	0.122	0.051	0.065	.05	...	...
Third-person pronouns:							
A	0.052	0.029	0.040	0.031	...	...	...
B	0.039	0.034	0.035	0.041	...	...	...
Complete repetitions:							
A	0.030	0.022	0.014	0.014	...	...	...
B	0.042	0.031	0.011	0.016	...	...	...
Partial repetitions:							
A	0.259	0.325	0.177	0.227	...	.01	...
B	0.273	0.208	0.227	0.178	...	...	...
Semantic repetitions:							
A	0.016	0.027	0.036	0.011	...	...	...
B	0.047	0.030	0.014	0.010	...	...	...

[a] Task A denotes the block-selection task; task B denotes the pattern-construction task.

Discussion

To recapitulate the findings of the present experiments: (a) mothers' speech to young children was simpler and more redundant than their normal speech, (b) these modifications in mothers' speech styles depended to some extent on the reactions of the child being addressed, (c) task difficulty did not contribute to the mothers' production of simplified, redundant speech, and (d) experienced mothers were only slightly better than nonmothers in predicting the speech-style modifications required by young children.

The present findings strongly suggest that middle-class children such as those included in this study do not learn language on the basis of a confusing corpus full of mistakes, garbles, and complexities. They hear, in fact, a relatively consistent, organized, simplified, and redundant set of utterances which in many ways seems quite well designed as a set of "language lessons." It might be useful to explore in some detail how these speech-style modifications function as tutorial devices.

Potential value of grammatical simplification

One striking feature of mothers' speech in the presence of young children was the reduction in the length of their utterances. Since run-on sentences were scored as two or more utterances, the shorter utterances which were produced in the presence of 2-year-olds were, on the average, less elaborated than normal utterances. Elaboration can occur in many ways. Sentence complexity scores were lower in the 2-year-old present condition, indicating less use of subordinate clauses and compound verbs. Incidence of utterances without verbs was greater, indicating increased use of constructions so simple they did not even qualify as sentences. Mean preverb-length scores were lower, indicating less left-branching and self-embedding. It is clear that the number of words before the verb is very high in a left-branching sentence such as, "Bill who is the son of the woman who lives next door cuts my lawn." Such sentences occurred very rarely in speech to 2-year-olds. Similarly, self-embedded sentences such as, "The rat that the cat that the dog worried killed ate the malt," never occurred in speech to 2-year-olds. Whatever the specific changes leading to shorter utterances, it seems clear that, in general, these changes are correlated with grammatical (and semantic) simplicity. This means that the surface structure, which the child hears, is related by a smaller number of steps to the base structure, which must be reached if the sentence is to be interpreted correctly. Further, the child's work in searching for the major units in a sentence is considerably lightened if there are fewer minor units to process. Finally, there are fewer inflections in a shorter sentence; this may improve the chances that the child will notice, remember, and induce the rules governing the inflections that do occur.

Mothers used fewer subordinate clauses and compound verbs when speaking to young children; for example: "That's a lion. And the lion's name is Leo. Leo lives in a big house. Leo goes for a walk every morning. And he always takes his cane along." If there are fewer clauses in a sentence, then the child is faced with fewer subject-verb and subject-verb-object relations to puzzle out, and related subjects and verbs are more likely to follow one another directly. Thus, the child might discover the subject-verb-object rule for sentence production with greater ease than if he were faced with sentences composed of many interembedded clauses. Evidence presented by Slobin and Welsh (1968) suggests that children do process sentences by searching out the subject and verb. If the subject or verb were somehow obscured in the sentences offered to their subject for imitation, she would treat the sentence as a word list. But she could extract a subject, verb, and object from a scrambled sentence if she could identify two nouns and a verb which had some semantically acceptable relationship.

Mean preverb length was shorter in speech addressed to 2-year-olds. Greater mean preverb length can result from center-embedding or leftbranching; such sentences are known to be more difficult to process for children (Gaer 1969) and for adults (Miller 1962). Since the subject is normally the first element in an English sentence, greater mean preverb length would often involve separation between the subject and the verb. This kind of sentence is probably both difficult and confusing to a child who is just mastering a subject-verb rule for forming sentences. Furthermore, considering the evidence that a meaningful verb is important in making it possible for children to process sentences (Herriot 1968), sentences in which the verb is placed toward the end may be more difficult to understand.

About 16% of the utterances spoken to 2-year-olds were simple phrases, which were not produced on the basis of a subject-verb rule. This is quite a high percentage for a child who will have to deduce subject-verb rules for producing sentences. Inspection of the protocols indicates that much of the increase of utterances without verbs in the 2-year-old condition can be attributed to repetition of important phrases from preceding sentences; for example: "Put the red truck in the box now. The red truck. No, the red truck. In the box. The red truck in the box." The value of this kind of repetition for guiding the child's behavior is obvious. Grammatically, it may have yet another value. It gives information about the boundaries of units within utterances, since only complete units — noun phrases and prepositional phrases, primarily — are repeated in this way. A major step in decoding a sentence is assigning a phrase structure to it. Information about the limits of subunits within the sentence is extremely valuable in this task.

Fewer third-person pronouns were used in speech to young children. Mothers repeated the subjects and objects of their sentences rather than substituting pronouns for them. Thus, the children were not required, in the early stages of rule formation, to deal with the difficulties of pronoun reference. Furthermore it is possible that the existence of subject-verb relations in sentences is somewhat obscured when a pronoun is substituted for the subject noun phrase, which has a more obvious semantic reference to an actor or a topic. The difficulties would be especially great for a child who is not yet sure which pronouns refer to which classes of nouns.

Potential value of repetition

Repetition of complete sentences was about four times as frequent for 2-year-olds as for 10-year-olds. Depending on the task, 3%-8% of the utterances that 2-year-olds heard were repeated shortly afterwards. Short-term memory limits the time available for processing input. Repetition of a sentence would give added processing time, thus increasing the child's chances of successfully processing the sentence. For example, if a child had decoded the major components of a sentence at first hearing, repetition would give him an opportunity to pay attention to the more minor constructions, such as modifiers and subordinate clauses. Perhaps the function of these unstressed constructions in long sentences first becomes obvious to the child only following repetition of the sentence.

Repetition of phrases was much more common in speech addressed to 2-year-olds. As discussed above, the repetition of noun and prepositional phrases is clearly of value, assuming that one of the child's tasks is to assign a phrase structure to what he hears. Often, when mothers repeated phrases, they used a new frame for the repeated phrase; for example: "Pick up the red one. Find the red one. Not the green one. I want the red one. Can you find the red one?" This is a valuable object lesson in the basic linguistic skill of rearranging units to form new utterances. Interestingly, it is quite similar to language games that children themselves play with their newly learned words (Weir 1962).

In experiment 1, 14% of mothers' utterances to 2-year-olds in the present condition were paraphrases of preceding utterances; for example: "Give mummy all the red toys. I would like all the things that look like this. Can you give me all the red things?" This is more than twice as many paraphrases as in the absent condition and three times as many as provided for 10-year olds. Some of this was undoubtedly due to the child's failure to comprehend the mother's first statement. Thus, the mother was required to find a new way to say what she meant. Interestingly, the mothers did not predict this need as readily as they predicted the need for partial repetition. The ability to paraphrase represents another basic feature of language. The relationship between sound and meaning is arbitrary, and therefore several different sound signals can have the same meaning. Thus, it makes no sense to memorize sentences; new ones meaning the same thing can always be created without waste of memory stores. Hearing adults paraphrase their own utterances could be a valuable demonstration of this basic feature of language to a child whose vocabulary and grammar are still so small that he has only one way to say most things. Furthermore, if the child has figured out the meaning of the sentence, he needs less time to interpret its paraphrase and thus can spend more time decoding grammatically less important units of the paraphrase.

Conclusions

The modifications which mothers produce for young children may be valuable in at least two ways. The first value, no doubt intended by the speaker, is to keep his speech simple, interesting, and comprehensible to young children. The second value, unintended by the adult but potentially as important as the first, is that simplified speech is admirably designed to aid children in learning language. This makes it somewhat easier to understand how a child can accomplish the formidable task of learning his native language with such relative ease. The willingness of the child's parents to produce simplified and redundant speech, combined with the child's own ability to attend selectively to simple, meaningful, and comprehensible utterances (Shipley, Gleitman, & Smith 1969; Snow 1971; also see Friedlander 1968, 1970; Turnure 1971), provide the child with tractable, relatively consistent, and relevant linguistic information from which to formulate the rules of grammar.

This paper is based on a doctoral dissertation submitted to McGill University. The author wishes to thank Dr. M. Sam Rabinovitch, thesis advisor, for his help, and Dr. Ellis Olim for making available the Language Styles Scoring Manual, from which several of the measures used in the present experiments were borrowed or adapted. The author was supported by a National Science Foundation graduate fellowship during the time the research was completed.

References

Bernstein, B. (1970) 'A sociolinguistic approach to socialization: with some reference to educability'. In F. Williams (Ed.), *Language and poverty: perspectives on a theme.* Chicago: Markham.

Chomsky, N. (1965) *Aspects of the theory of syntax.* Cambridge: M.I.T. Press.

Chomsky, N. (1968) *Language and mind.* New York: Harcourt, Brace & World.

Friedlander, B.Z. (1968) 'The effect of speaker identity, voice inflection, vocabulary, and message redundancy on infants' selection of vocal reinforcement'. *Journal of Experimental Child Psychology*, 6, 443-459.

Friedlander, B.Z. (1970) 'Receptive language development in infancy: issues and problems'. *Merrill-Palmer Quarterly*, 16, 7-51.

Gaer, E.P. (1969) 'Children's understanding and production of sentences'. *Journal of Verbal Learning and Verbal Behavior*, 8, 289-294.

Herriot, P. (1968) 'The comprehension of syntax'. *Child Development*, 39, 273-282.

Hess, R.D., & Shipman, V.C. (1965) 'Early experience and the socialization of cognitive modes in children'. *Child Development*, 36, 869-886.

Lenneberg, E.H. (1969) 'On explaining language'. *Science*, 164, 635-643.

McNeill, D.A. (1970) *The acquisition of language: the study of developmental psycho-linguistics.* New York: Harper & Row.

Miller, G.A. (1962) 'Some psychological studies of grammar'. *American Psychologist*, 748-762.

Olim, E. (1970) 'Maternal language styles and the cognitive development of children'. In F. Williams (Ed.), *Language and poverty: perspectives on a theme.* Chicago: Markham.

Scheffé, H. (1953) 'A method for judging all contrasts in the analysis of variance'. *Biometrika*, 40, 87-104.

Shipley, E.F.; Gleitman, C.S.; & Smith, L.R. (1969) 'A study of the acquisition of language: free responses to commands'. *Language*, 45, 322-342.

Slobin, D.I., & Welsh, C.A. (1968) 'Elicited imitations as a research tool in developmental psycholinguistics'. Working Paper No. 10, Language-Behavior Research Laboratory, University of California at Berkeley.

Snow, C.E. (1971) 'Language acquisition and mothers' speech to children'. Unpublished doctoral dissertation, McGill University.

Turnure, C. (1971) 'Response to voice of mother and stranger by babies in the first year'. *Developmental Psychology*, 4, 182-190.

Weir, R. (1962) *Language in the crib.* The Hague: Mouton.

Winer, B. J. (1962) *Statistical principles in experimental design.* New York: McGraw-Hill.

14. A Cultural Perspective on the Transition from Prelinguistic to Linguistic Communication

Bambi B. Schieffelin and Elinor Ochs

Ethnographic orientation

To most middle-class Western readers, the descriptions of verbal and non-verbal behaviors of middle-class caregivers with their children seem very familiar, desirable, and even natural. These descriptions capture in rich detail what does go on in many middle-class households, to a greater or lesser extent. The characteristics of caregiver speech (baby-talk register) and comportment that have been specified are highly valued by members of white middle-class society, including researchers, readers, and subjects of study. They are associated with good mothering and can be spontaneously produced with little effort or reflections. As demonstrated by Shatz and Gelman (1973), Sachs and Devin (1976), and Andersen and Johnson (1973), children as young as 4 years of age can speak and act in these ways when addressing small children.

From our research experience in other societies as well as our acquaintance with some of the cross-cultural studies of language socialization (Blount 1972; Bowerman 1981; Fischer 1970; Hamilton 1981; Harkness 1975; Harness and Super 1977; Heath 1983; Miller 1982; Philips 1982; Schieffelin and Eisenberg 1984; Scollon and Scollon 1981; Stross 1972; Ward 1971; Wills 1977), the general patterns of caregiving that have been described in the psychological literature on white middle class are neither characteristic of all societies nor of all social groups (e.g., all social classes within one society). We would like the reader, therefore, to reconsider the descriptions of caregiving in the psychological literature as *ethnographic descriptions*.

By ethnographic we mean *descriptions that take into account the perspective of members of a social group, including beliefs and values that underlie and organise their activities and utterances*. Ethnographers gather their evidence, and draw their conclusions through elicitation of members' reflections and interpretations as a basis for analysis (Geertz 1973). Typically the ethnographer is not a member of the group under study. Further, in presenting an ethnographic account the researcher faces the problem of communicating world views or sets of values that may be unfamiliar and strange to the reader. Ideally such statements provide a set of organising principles that give coherence and an analytic focus to the behaviors described.

Psychologists who have carried out research on verbal and nonverbal behavior of caregivers and their children draw on both of the methods articulated above. However, unlike most ethnographers, typically the psychological researcher *is* a member of the social group under observation. (In some cases, the researcher's own children are the

Bambi B. Schieffelin and Elinor Ochs: 'A Cultural Perspective on the Transition from Prelinguistic to Linguistic Communication' in *THE TRANSITION FROM PRELINGUISTIC TO LINGUISTIC COMMUNICATION*, edited by R.M. Golinkoff (Lawrence Erlbaum Associates, Inc., 1983), pp. 211-229.

subjects of study). Further, unlike the ethnographer, the psychologist addresses a readership familiar with the social scenes portrayed.

That researcher, reader, and subjects of study tend to have in common a white middle-class literate background has had several consequences. For example, by and large, the psychologist has not been faced with the problem of cultural translation, as has the anthropologist — there has been a tacit assumption that readers can provide the larger cultural framework for making sense out of the behaviors documented. A consequence of this in turn is that the cultural nature of the behaviors and principles presented is not explicit. From our perspective, *language and culture as bodies of knowledge, structures of understanding, conceptions of the world, collective representations, are both extrinsic to and far more extensive than any individual could know or learn. Culture encompasses variation in knowledge between individuals, but such variation, while crucial to what an individual may know and to the social dynamic between individuals, does not have its locus within the individuals.* Our position is that culture is not something that can be considered separately from the accounts of caregiver-child interactions; it is what organizes and gives meaning to that interaction. This is an important point, as it affects the definition and interpretation of the behaviors of caregivers and children. How caregivers and children speak and act towards one another is linked to cultural patterns that extend and have consequences beyond the specific interactions observed. For example, how caregivers speak to their children may be linked to other institutional adaptations to young children. These adaptations in turn may be linked to how members of a given society view children more generally (their 'nature', their social status and expected comportment) and to how members think children develop.

We are suggesting here that sharing of assumptions between researcher, reader, and subjects of study is a mixed blessing In fact, this sharing presents a *paradox of familiarity*. We are able to apply without effort the cultural framework for interpreting the behavior of caregivers and young children in our own social group; indeed as members of a white middle-class society, we are socialized to do this very work, that is interpreting behaviors, attributing motives, and so on. The paradox is that in spite of this ease of effort, we can not easily isolate and make explicit these cultural principles. As Goffman's work on American society has illustrated, articulation of norms, beliefs, and values is often possible only when faced with violations, that is with gaffes, breaches, misfirings, and the like (Goffman 1963, 1967; Much and Shweder 1979).

Another way to see the cultural principles at work in our own society is to examine the ways in which *other* societies are organized in terms of social interaction and in terms of the society at large. In carrying out such research, the ethnographer offers a point of contrast and comparison with our own everyday activities. Such comparative material can lead us to reinterpret behaviors as cultural that we have assumed to be natural. From the anthropological perspective, every society will have its own cultural constructs of what is natural and what is not. For example, every society has its own theory of procreation. Certain Australian Aboriginal societies believe that a number of different factors contribute to conception. Von Sturmer (1980) writes that among the Kugu-Nganychara (West Cape York Peninsula, Australia) the spirit of the child may first enter the man through an animal that he has killed and consumed. The spirit passes from the man to the woman through sexual intercourse, but several sexual acts are necessary to build the child. (See also Montagu 1937; Hamilton 1981.) Even within a single society, there may be different beliefs concerning when life begins and ends, as the recent debates in the United States and Europe concerning abortion and mercy killing indicate. The issue of what is nature and what is nurture (cultural) extends to patterns of caregiving and child development. Every society will have (implicitly or explicitly) given notions concerning the capacities and temperament of children at different points in their development (see, for example, Ninio 1979; Snow, de Blauw and van Roosmalen 1979; Dentan 1978). The expectations and responses of caregivers will be directly related to these notions.

Two developmental stories

At this point, using an ethnographic perspective, we will recast selected behaviors of white middle-class caregivers and young children as pieces of one 'developmental story'. The white middle-class 'developmental story' that we are constructing is based on various descriptions available, and focuses on those patterns of interaction (both verbal and non-verbal) that have been emphasized in the literature. This story will be compared with another developmental story: the Kaluli (Papua New Guinea), a society that is strikingly different.

One of the major goals in presenting and comparing these developmental stories is to demonstrate that communicative interactions between caregivers and young children are culturally constructed. In our comparisons, we will focus on three facts of communicative interaction: (1) the social organisation of the verbal environment of very young children; (2) the extent to which children are expected to adapt to situations or that situations are adapted to the child; and (3) the negotiation of meaning by caregiver and child. We first present a general sketch for each social group and then discuss in more detail the consequences of the differences and similarities in communicative patterns in these two groups.

These developmental stories are not timeless, but rather are linked in complex ways to particular historical contexts. Both the ways in which caregivers behave towards young children and the popular and scientific accounts of these ways may differ at different moments in time. The stories that we present represent ideas currently held in the two social groups.

The two stories show that there is more than one way of becoming social and using language in early childhood. All normal children will become members of their own social group. But the process of becoming social including becoming a language user is culturally constructed. In relation to this process of construction, every society has its own developmental stories that are rooted in social organisation, beliefs, and values. These stories may be explicitly codified and/ or tacitly assumed by members.

Anglo-American white middle-class developmental story

Middle class in Britain and the United States covers a broad range of white-collar and professional workers and their families, including lower-middle-, middle-middle-, and upper-middle-class strata. The literature on communicative development has been largely based on middle-middle- and upper-middle-class households. These households tend to consist of a single nuclear family with one, two, or three children. The primary caregiver almost without exception is a child's natural or adopted mother. Researchers have focused on communicative situations in which one child interacts with his or her mother. The generalizations proposed by these researchers concerning mother child communication could be an artifact of this methodological focus. However, it could be argued that the attention to two-party encounters between a mother and her child reflects the most frequent types of communicative interaction to which most young middle-class children are exposed. Participation in two-party as opposed to multi-party interactions is a product of many considerations, including the physical setting of households, where interior and exterior walls bound and limit access to social interactions.

Soon after an infant is born, many mothers will hold their infants in such a way that they are face to face and will gaze at them. Mothers have been observed to address their infants, vocalize to them, ask questions, and greet them. In other words, from birth on, the infant is treated as a *social being* and as an *addressee* in social interaction. The infant's vocalizations, physical movements, and states are often interpreted as meaningful and will be responded to verbally by the mother or other caregiver. In this way, proto-conversations are established and sustained, along a *dyadic, turn-taking* model. Throughout this period and the subsequent language-acquiring years, caregivers treat very young children as communicative partners. One very important procedure in facilitating these social exchanges is the mother's (or other caregiver's) act of *taking the perspective of the child*. This perspective is evidenced in her own speech through the many simplifying and affective features of baby-talk register that have been described and through the various strategies employed to identify what the young child may be expressing.

Such perspective-taking is part of a much wider set of accommodations by adults to young children. These accommodations are manifested in several domains. For example, there are widespread material accommodations to infancy and childhood in the form of cultural artifacts designed for this stage of life, that is baby clothes, baby food, miniaturization of furniture, and toys. Special behavioral accommodations are coordinated with the infant's perceived needs and capacities, for example, putting the baby in a quiet place to facilitate and insure proper sleep; 'babyproofing' a house as a child becomes increasingly mobile, yet not aware of or able to control the consequences of his own behavior. In general, *situations and the language used in them are adapted or modified to the child* rather than the reverse. Further, the child is a *focus of attention*, in that the child's actions and verbalizations are often the *starting point* of social interaction with more mature persons.

While developmental achievements such as crawling, walking, and first words are awaited by caregivers, the accommodations noted above have the effect of keeping the child dependent on and separate from the adult community for a considerable period of time. The child is protected from certain experiences which are considered harmful (e.g.

playing with knives, climbing stairs), but such protection delays his knowledge and developing competence in such contexts.

The accommodations of white middle-class caregivers to young children can be examined for other values and tendencies. Particularly among the American middle class, these accommodations reflect a *discomfort with the competence differential* between adult and child. The competence gap is reduced by two strategies. One is for the adult to simplify her or his speech to match more closely what the adult considers to be the verbal competence of the young child. Let us call this strategy the *self-lowering* strategy, following Irvine's (1974) analysis of intercaste demeanor. A second strategy is for the caregiver to interpret (Brown 1973) richly what the young child is expressing. Here the adult acts as if the child were more competent than his behavior more strictly would indicate. Let us call this strategy the *child-raising* strategy. Other behaviors conform to this strategy, such as when an adult cooperates in a task with a child but treats that task as an accomplishment of the child.

For example, in eliciting a story from a child, a caregiver will often cooperate with the child in the telling of the story. This cooperation typically takes the form of posing questions to the child, such as 'Where did you go?', 'What did you see?', and so on, to which the adult knows the answer. The child is seen as telling the story even though she or he is simply supplying the information the adult has preselected and organised (Ochs, Schieffelin and Platt 1979; Schieffelin and Eisenberg 1984; Greenfield and Smith 1976). Bruner's (1978) descriptions of scaffolding, in which a caregiver constructs a tower or other play object, allowing the young child to place the last block, are also good examples of this tendency. Here the tower may be seen by the caregiver and others as the child's own work. Similarly, in later life, caregivers playing games with their children may let them win, acting as if the child can match or more than match the competence of the adult.

A final aspect of this white middle-class developmental story concerns the willingness of many caregivers to interpret unintelligible or partially intelligible utterances of young children (cf. Ochs 1982). One of the recurrent ways in which interpretation is carried out is for the caregiver to offer a paraphrase (or 'expansion' (Brown and Bellugi 1964; Cazden 1965)), using a question intonation. This behavior of caregivers has continuity with their earlier attributions of intentionality directed towards ambiguous utterances (from the point of view of the infant). For both the prelinguistic and language-using child, the caregiver provides an explicitly verbal interpretation. This interpretation or paraphrase is potentially available to the young child to affirm, disconfirm, or modify.

Through exposure to and participation in these clarification exchanges, the young child is being socialized into several cultural patterns. The first of these is a way of recognizing and defining what constitutes unintelligibility, that an utterance or vocalization may in fact not be immediately understood. Second, the child is presented with the procedures for dealing with ambiguity. Through the successive offerings of possible interpretations, the child learns that more than one understanding of a given utterance or vocalization may be possible. The child is also learning who can make these interpretations, and the extent to which they may be open to modification. Finally the child is learning how to settle upon a possible interpretation and how to show disagreement or agreement. *This entire process socializes the child into culturally specific models of organizing knowledge, thought, and language.*

A kaluli developmental story

The Kaluli people (population approximately 1200) are an example of a small-scale, nonliterate egalitarian society (Schieffelin 1976). Kaluli, most of whom are monolingual, speak the Kaluli language, a non-Austronesian verb-final ergative language. They live in the tropical rain forest on the Great Papuan Plateau in the Southern Highlands of Papua New Guinea. Kaluli maintain large gardens and hunt and fish in order to obtain protein. Villages are composed of 60-90 individuals who traditionally lived in one large longhouse that had no internal walls. Currently, while the longhouse is maintained, many families are living in smaller dwellings so that two or more extended families may live together. It is not unusual then for at least a dozen individuals of different ages to be living together in one house which consists essentially of one semi-partitioned room.

Men and women utilize extensive networks of obligation and reciprocity in the organisation of work and sociable interaction. Everyday life is overtly focused around verbal interaction. Kaluli think of and use talk as a means of control, manipulation, expression, assertion, and appeal. It gets you what you want, need, or feel owed. Talk is a primary indicator of social competence and a primary way to be social. Learning how to talk and become independent is a major goal of socialization.

For the purpose of comparison and for understanding something of the cultural basis for the ways in which Kaluli act and speak to their children, it is important to first describe selected aspects of a Kaluli developmental story which I have constructed from various kinds of ethnographic data. Kaluli describe their babies as helpless, 'soft' (*taiyo*), and 'having no understanding' (*asugo andoma*). They take care of them, they say, because they 'feel sorry for them'. Mothers, who are primary caregivers, are attentive to their infants and physically responsive to them. Whenever an infant cries it is offered the breast. However, while nursing her infant, a mother may also be involved in other activities, such as food preparation, or she may be engaged in conversation with individuals in the household. Mothers never leave their infants alone and only rarely with other caregivers. When not holding their infants, mothers carry them in netted bags which are suspended from their heads. When the mother is gardening, gathering wood, or just sitting with others, the baby will sleep in the netted bag next to the mother's body.

Kaluli mothers, given their belief that infants 'have no understanding' never treat their infants as partners (speaker/addressee) in dyadic communicative interactions. While they greet their infants by name and use expressive vocalizations they rarely address other utterances to them. Furthermore, mothers and infants do not gaze into each other's eyes, an interactional pattern that is consistent with adult patterns of not gazing when vocalizing in interaction with one another. Rather than facing their babies and speaking to them, Kaluli mothers tend to face their babies outwards so that they can be seen by, and see others that are part of the social group. Older children greet and address the infant and in response to this, the mother while moving the baby, speaks in a high-pitched nasalized voice 'for' the baby. Triadic exchanges such as the one shown in Figure 1 is typical of these situations.

Figure 1   Example of a triadic exchange

Mother	Abi
(Abi to baby)	[1]Bage!/do you see my box here?/do you see it?/do you see it?/
(high nasal voice talking as if she is the baby, moving the baby who is facing Abi):	
[2]My brother, I'll take half, my brother.	
(holding stick out)	[3]Mother, give him half/give him half/mother, my brother here, here take half/X/
(in a high nasal voice as baby):	
[4]My brother, what half do I take? What about it, my brother, put it on the shoulder!	
[5](to Abi in her usual voice): 'Put it on the shoulder'.	
(Abi rests stick on baby's shoulder)	
[6]There, carefully put it on, (stick accidentally pokes baby) Feel sorry, stop.	

Notes: Mother is holding her infant son Bage (3 months). Abi (35 months) is holding a stick on his shoulder in a manner similar to that in which one would carry a heavy patrol box (the box would be hung on a pale placed across the shoulders of the two men). (Transcription conventions follow Bloom and Lahey (1978).)

When a mother takes the speaking role of an infant she uses language that is well-formed and appropriate for an older child. Only the nasalization and high pitch mark it as 'the infant's'. When speaking as the infant to older children, mothers speak assertively, that is, they never whine or beg on behalf of the infant. Thus, in taking this role the mother does for the infant what the infant cannot do for itself, appear to act in a controlled and competent manner, using language. These kinds of interactions continue until a baby is between 4-6 months of age.

Several points are important here. First, these triadic exchanges are carried out primarily for the benefit of the older child and help create a relationship between the two children. Second, the mother's goals in these exchanges are not based on, nor do they originate with anything that the infant has initiated — either vocally or gesturally. Recall the Kaluli claim that infants have no understanding. How could someone with 'no understanding' initiate appropriate interactional sequences?

However, there is an even more important and enduring cultural construct that helps make sense out of the mother's behaviors in this situation and in many others as well. Kaluli say that 'one cannot know what another thinks or feels'. Now, while Kaluli obviously interpret and assess one another's available behaviors and internal states, these interpretations are not culturally acceptable as topics of talk. Individuals often talk about their own feelings (I'm afraid, I'm happy, etc.). However, there is a cultural dispreference for talking about or making claims about what another might think, what another might feel, or what another is about to do, especially if there is no external evidence. As we shall see, these culturally constructed behaviors have several important consequences for the ways in which Kaluli caregivers verbally interact with their children, and are related to other pervasive patterns of language use which shall be discussed below.

As infants become older (6-12 months) they are usually held in the arms or carried on the shoulders of the mother or an older sibling. They are present in all on-going household activities, as well as subsistence activities that take place outside the village in the bush. During this time period babies are addressed by adults to a limited extent. They are greeted by a variety of names (proper names, kinterms, affective and relationship terms) and receive a limited set of both negative and positive imperatives. In addition, when they do something they are not to do, such as reach for something that is not theirs to take, they will often receive such rhetorical questions such as 'Who are you?!' (meaning 'not someone to do that') or 'It is yours?!' (meaning 'it is not yours') to control their actions by shaming them (*sasidiab*). What is important to stress here is that the language addressed to the preverbal child consists largely of 'one-liners' which call for no verbal response. Either an action or termination of an action is appropriate. Other than these utterances, very little talk is directed to the young child by the adult caregiver.

This pattern of adults not treating infants as communicative partners continues even when babies begin babbling. Kaluli recognize babbling (*debedan*) but say that this verbal activity is not communicative and has no relationship to speech that will eventually emerge. Adults and older children occasionally repeat vocalizations back to the young child (ages 12-16 months) reshaping them into the names of persons in the household or into kinterms, but they do not say that the baby is saying the name nor do they wait for or expect the child to repeat those vocalizations in an altered form. In addition, vocalizations are not generally treated as communicative and given verbal expression. Nor are they interpreted by adults, except in one situation, an example of which follows.

When a toddler shrieks in protest at the assaults of an older child, mothers will say 'I'm unwilling' (using a quotative particle) referring to the toddler's shriek. These were the only circumstances in which mothers treated vocalizations as communicative and provided verbal expression for them. In no other circumstances in the four families in the study did adults provide a verbally expressed interpretation of a vocalization of a preverbal child. Thus, throughout the preverbal period very little language is directed to the child, except for imperatives, rhetorical questions, and greetings. A child who by Kaluli terms has not yet begun to speak is not expected to respond either verbally or vocally. What all of this means is that in the first 18 months or so very little sustained dyadic verbal exchange takes place between adult and infant. The infant is only minimally treated as an addressee, and is not treated as a communicative partner in dyadic exchanges. One immediate conclusion is: the conversational model that has been described for many white middle-class caregivers and their preverbal children has no application in this case. Furthermore, if one defines language input as language directed to the child then it is reasonable to say that for Kaluli children who have not yet begun to speak, there is very little. However, this does not mean that Kaluli children grow up in an impoverished verbal environment and do not learn how to speak. Quite the opposite is true. The verbal environment of the infant is rich and varied, and from the very beginning the infant is surrounded by adults and older children who spend a great deal of time talking to one another. Furthermore, as the infant develops and begins to crawl, engage in play activities, and other independent actions, these actions are frequently referred to, described, and commented upon by members of the household speaking to one another especially by older children. Thus, the ongoing activities of the preverbal child are an important topic of talk between members of the household, and this talk about the here-and-now of the infant is available to the infant, though only a limited amount of talk is addressed to the infant. For example, in referring to the infant's actions, siblings and adults use the infant's name or kinterm. They will say, 'Look at Seligiwo! He's walking'. Thus the child may learn from these contexts to attend to the verbal environment in which he or she lives.

Every society has its own ideology about language, including when it begins and how children acquire it. The Kaluli are no exception. Kaluli claim that language begins at the time when the child uses two critical words, 'mother' (*no*) and 'breast' (*bo*). The child may be using other single words, but until these two words are used, the beginning of language is not recognised. Once a child had used these words, a whole set of inter-related behaviors is set into motion. Kaluli claim once a child has begun to use language he or she then must be 'shown how to speak' (Schieffelin 1979). Kaluli show their children language in the form of a teaching strategy which involves providing a model for what the child is to say followed by the word ɛlɛma, an imperative meaning 'say like that'. Mothers use this method of direct instruction to teach the social uses of assertive language (teasing, shaming, requesting, challenging, reporting). However, object labeling is never part of an ɛlɛma sequence, nor does the mother ever use ɛlɛma to instruct the child to beg or appeal for food or objects. Begging, the Kaluli say, is natural for children. They know how to do it. In contrast, a child must be taught to be assertive through the use of particular linguistic expressions and verbal sequences.

A typical sequence using ɛlɛma is triadic, involving the mother, child (between 20-36 months), and other participant(s). Figure 2 gives an example. *In this situation, as in many others, the mother does not modify her language to fit the linguistic ability of the young child. Instead her language is shaped so as to be appropriate (in terms of form and content) for the child's intended addressee.* Consistent with the ways she interacts with her infant, what a mother instructs her young child to say usually does not have its origins in any verbal or nonverbal behaviors of the child, but in what the mother thinks should be said. The mother pushes the child into ongoing interactions that the child may or may not be interested in, and will at times spend a good deal of energy in trying to get the child verbally involved. This is part of the Kaluli pattern of fitting (or pushing) the child into the situation rather than changing the situation to meet the interests or abilities of the child. Thus, mothers take a directive role with their young children, teaching them what to say so that they may become participants in the social group.

Figure 2   Example of a triadic exchange using ɛlɛma

---

[1]Mother → Wanu → > Binalia:[a]
Whose is it? say like that.

         [2]whose is it?!/

[3]Is it yours?! say like that.

         [4]is it yours?!/

[5]Who are you?! say like that.

         [6]who are you?!/

[7]Mama → Wanu → > Binalia:
Did you pick (it)?! say like that.

         [8]did you pick (it)?!/

[9]Mother → Wanu → > Binalia:
My G'ma picked (it)! say like that.

         [10]my G'ma picked (it)!/

[11]Mama → Wanu → > Binalia:
This my G'ma picked! say like that.

         [12]this my G'ma picked!/

Notes: Mother, daughter Binalia (5 years), cousin Mama ($3^1/_2$ years), and son Wanu (27 months) are at home, dividing up some cooked vegetables. Binalia has been begging for some but her mother thinks that she has had her share. (Transcription conventions follow Bloom and Lahey (1978).)
[a] → = speaker → addressee.
→ > = addressee → > intended addressee.

In addition to instructing their children by telling them what to say in often extensive interactional sequences, Kaluli mothers pay attention to the form of their children's utterances. Kaluli will correct the phonological, morphological, or lexical form of an utterance or its pragmatic or semantic meaning. Since the goals of language acquisition include a child becoming competent, independent, and mature-sounding in his language, Kaluli use no baby-talk lexicon, for they said (when I asked about it) that to do so would result in a child sounding babyish, which was clearly undesirable and counter-productive. The entire process of a child's development, of which language acquisition plays a very important role, is thought of as hardening process and culminates in the child's use of 'hard words' (Feld and Schieffelin 1982).

The cultural dispreference for saying what another might be thinking of feeling has important consequences for the organization of dyadic exchanges between caregiver and child. For one, it affects the ways in which meaning is negotiated during an exchange. For the Kaluli the responsibility for clear expression is with the speaker, and child speakers are not exempt from this. Rather than offering possible interpretations or guessing what a child is saying or meaning, caregivers make extensive use of clarification requests such as 'huh?' and 'what?' in an attempt to elicit clearer expression from the child. Children are held to what they say and mothers will remind them that they in fact have asked for food or an object if when given it they don't act appropriately.

Since responsibility of expression does lie with the speaker, children are also instructed with ɛlɛma to request clarification (using similar forms) from others when they do not understand what someone is saying to them.

Another important consequence of not saying what another thinks is the absence of adult expansions of child utterances. Kaluli caregivers will put words into the mouths of their children but these words originate from the caregiver. However, caregivers do not elaborate or expand utterances initiated by the child. Nor do they jointly build propositions across utterances and speakers except in the context of sequences with ɛlɛma in which they are constructing the talk for the child.

All of these patterns of early language use, such as the lack of expansions or verbally attributing an internal state to an individual, are consistent with important cultural conventions of adult language usage. The Kaluli very carefully avoid gossip and often indicate the source of information they report. They make extensive use of direct quoted speech in a language that does not allow indirect quotation. They utilize a range of evidential markers in their speech to indicate the source of speakers' information — for example, whether something was said, seen, heard, or gathered from other kinds of evidence. These patterns are also found in early child speech and, as such, affect the organization and acquisition of conversational exchanges in this small-scale egalitarian society.

A discussion of the developmental stories

We propose that infants and caregivers do not interact with one another according to one particular 'biologically designed choreography' (Stern 1977). There are many choreographies within and across societies. Cultural systems as well as biological ones contribute to their design, frequency, and significance. The biological predisposi-caregivers must be broader than thus far conceived in that the use of eye gaze, vocalization and body alignment are orchestrated differently in the social groups we have observed. As noted earlier, for example, Kaluli mothers do not engage in sustained gazing at, or elicit and maintain direct eye contact with, their infants as such behavior is dispreferred, associated with witchcraft.

Another argument in support of a broader notion of biological predisposition to be social, concerns the variation observed in the participant structure of social interactions. The literature on white middle-class child development has been orientated, quite legitimately, towards the two-party relationship between infant and caregiver, typically infant and mother. The legitimacy of this focus rests on the fact that this relationship is primary for infants within this social group. Further, most communicative interactions are dyadic in the adult community. While the mother is an important figure in the Kaluli developmental story, the interactions in which infants are participants are typically triadic or multi-party. As noted, Kaluli mothers will organise triadic interactions in which infants and young children will be oriented away from their mothers towards a third party.

This is not to say that Kaluli caregivers and children do not engage in dyadic exchanges. Rather, the point is that *such exchanges are not accorded the same significance as in white middle-class society*. In white middle-class households that have been studied the process of becoming social takes place predominantly through dyadic interactions, and social competence itself is measured in terms of the young child's capacity to participate in such interactions. In Kaluli [. . .] households, the process of becoming social takes place through participation in dyadic, triadic, and multi-party social interactions, with the latter two more common than the dyad.

From an early age, Kaluli children must learn how to participate in interactions involving a number of individuals. To do this minimally requires attending to more than one individual's works and actions, and knowing the norms for when and how to enter interactions, taking into account the social identities of at least three participants. Further, the sequencing of turns in triadic and multi-party interactions has a far wider range of possibilities vis-à-vis dyadic exchanges and thus requires considerable knowledge and skill. While dyadic exchanges can only be ABABA . . ., triadic or multi-party exchanges can be sequenced in a variety of ways, subject to social constraints such as speech act content and status of speaker. For Kaluli children, triadic and reflect the ways in which members of these societies routinely communicate with one another.

Conclusions

This chapter contains a number of points but only one message — that the process of acquiring language and the process of acquiring sociocultural knowledge are intimately linked. In pursuing this generalization, we have formulated the following proposals:

The specific features of caregiver speech behavior that have been described as simplified register are neither universal nor necessary for language to be acquired. White middle-class and Kaluli children, become speakers of their languages within the normal range of development and yet their caregivers use language quite differently in their presence.

The use of simplified registers by caregivers in certain societies may be part of a more general orientation in which situations are adapted to young children's perceived needs. In other societies, the orientation may be the reverse — that is, children at a very early age are expected to adapt to requirements of situations. In such societies, caregivers direct children to notice and respond to others' actions. They tend not to simplify their speech and frequently model appropriate utterances for the child to repeat to a third party in a situation.

The cross-cultural research raises many questions. The extent to which we are developing culturally specific theories of development needs to be considered. To add to what we know we must examine the prelinguistic and linguistic behaviors of the child of the ways in which they are continually and selectively affected by the values and beliefs held by those members of society who interact with the child.

It is tempting to speculate about what differences these differences make. Cross-cultural research invites that. However, at this point in our research it seems premature to focus on answers. Instead we prefer to use these data to generate questions — questions that will suggest new ways to think about language acquisition and socialization. And when we identify a new phenomenon or find old favorites missing

— such as the absence of expansions and lack of extensive modified speech to the child in diverse societies — we must identify the sociocultural factors that organize and make sense of communicative behaviors. Because these behaviors are grounded in culturally specific norms we can expect that the reason for the 'same' phenomenon will be different.

While biological factors play a role in language acquisition, sociocultural factors have a hand in this process as well. It is not a trivial fact that small children develop in the context of organized societies. Cultural conditions for communication organise even the earliest interactions between infants and others. Through participation as audience, addressee, and/or 'speaker', the infant develops a range of skills, intuitions, and knowledge enabling him or her to communicate in culturally preferred ways. The development of these competencies is an integral part of becoming a competent speaker.

References

Anderson, E.S. and Johnson, C.E. (1973) 'Modifications in the speech of an eight-year-old to younger children', *Stanford Occasional Papers in Linguistics* 3: 149-60.

Bloom, L. and Lahey, M. (1978) *Language Development and Language Disorders*, New York: Wiley.

Blount, B. (1972) 'Aspects of socialization among the Luo of Kenya', *Language in Society* 235-48.

Bowerman, M. (1981) 'Language development', in H.C. Triandis and A, Heron (eds) *Handbook of Cross-Cultural Psychology*, vol. 4. *Developmental Psychology*, Boston, Mass: Allyn & Bacon.

Brown, R. (1973) *A First Language: The Early Stages*, Cambridge, Mass.: Harvard University Press.

Brown, R. and Bellugi, U. (1964) 'Three processes in the child's acquisition of syntax', *Harvard Educational Review* 34: 133-51.

Bruner, J.S. (1978) 'The role of dialogue in language acquisition', in A. Sinclair, R.J. Jarvella and W.J.M. Levelt (eds) *The Child's Conception of Language*, New York: Springer-Verlag.

Cazden, C. (1965) 'Environmental assistance to the child's acquisition of grammar', unpublished Ph.D. dissertation, Harvard University.

Dentan, R.K. (1965) 'Notes of childhood in a nonviolent context: the Semai case', in A. Montagu (ed.) *Learning Non-Aggression: The Experience of Nonliterate Societies*, Oxford: Oxford University Press.

Feld, S.and Schieffelin, B.B. (1982) 'Hard talk: a functional basis for Kaluli discourse', in D. Tannen (ed.) *Analyzing Discourse: Talk and Text*, Washington, D.C. Georgetown University Press.

Fischer, J. (1970) 'Linguistic socialization: Japan and the United States', in R. Hill and R. Konig (eds) *Families in East and West*, The Hague: Mouton.

Geertz, C. (1973) *The Interpetation of Cultures*, New York: Basic Books.

Goffman, E. (1963) *Behavior in Public Places*, New York: Free Press,

Goffman, E. (1967) *Interaction Ritual: Essays on Face-to-Face Behavior*, Garden City, New York: Anchor Books.

Greenfield, P.M. and Smith, J.H. (1976) *The Structure of Communication in Early Language Development*, New York: Academic Press.

Hamilton, A. (1981) 'Nature and nurture: Aboriginal childrearing in north-central Arnhem land', Institute of Aboriginal Studies, Canberra.

Harkness, S. (1975) 'Cultural variation in mother's language', in W. von Raffler-Engel (ed.) *Child Language, Word* 27: 495-8.

Harkness, S. and Super, C. (1977) 'Why African children are so hard to test', in L.L. Adler (ed.) *Issues in Cross-Cultural Research. Annals of the New York Academy of Sciences* 285: 326-31.

Heath, S.B. (1983) *Ways with Words: Language, Life and Work*. London: Cambridge University Press.

Irvine, J. (1974) 'Strategies of status manipulation in the Wolof greeting', in R. Bauman and J. Sherzer (eds) *Explorations in the Ethnography of Speaking*, New York: Cambridge University Press.

Miller, P. (1982) *Amy, Wendy and Beth: Learning Language in South Baltimore*, Austin, Tex: University of Texas Press.

Montagu A. (1937) *Coming into Being among the Australian Aborigines: a Study of the Procreative Beliefs of the Native Tribes of Australia*, London: Routledge.

Much, N. and Shweder R. (1979) 'Speaking of rules: The analysis of culture in breach', in W. Damon (ed.) *New Directions for Child Development: Moral Development* 2, San Francisco, California: Jossey-Bass.

Ninio, A. (1979) 'The naive theory of the infant and other maternal attitudes in two subgroups in Israel', *Child Development* 50: 976-80.

Ochs, E. (1982) 'Talking to children in Western Samoa', *Language in Society* 11: 77-104.

Ochs, E., Schieffelin, B.B. and Platt, M. (1979) 'Propositions across utterances and speakers', in E. Ochs and B.B. Schieffelin (eds) *Developmental Pragmatics*, New York: Academic Press.

Philips, S. (1982) *The Invisible Culture*, New York: Longman, Inc.

Sachs, J. and Devin, J. (1976) 'Young children's use of age-appropriate speech styles', *Journal of Child Language* 3: 81-98.

Schieffelin, B.B. (1979) 'Getting it together: an ethnographic approach to the study of the development of communicative competence', in E. Ochs and B.B. Schieffelin (eds) *Developmental Pragmatics*, New York: Academic Press.

Schieffelin, B.B. (1981) 'A developmental study of pragmatic appropriateness in word order and case marking in Kaluli', in W. Deutsch (ed.) *The Child's Construction of Language*, London: Academic Press.

Schieffelin, B.B. and Eisenberg, A. (1984) 'Cultural variation in children's conversations', in R.L. Schiefelbusch and J. Pickar (eds) *Communicative Competence: Acquisition and Intervention*, Baltimore, Md.: University Park Press.

Schieffelin, E.L. (1976) *The Sorrow of the Lonely and the Burning of the Dancers*, New York: St Martins Press.

Scollon, R. and Scollon, S. (1981) 'The literate two-year old: the fictionalization of self. Abstracting themes: a Chipewyan two-year-old', in R.O. Freedle (ed.) *Narrative, Literacy and Face in Interethnic Communication*, vol. VII: *Advances in Discourse Processes*, Norwood, N.J.: Ablex.

Shatz, M. and Gelman, R. (1973) 'The development of communication skills: modifications in the speech of young children as a function of listener' *Monographs of the Society for Research in Child Development* 152, 38 (5).

Snow, C., de Blauw, A. and van Roosmalen, G. (1979) 'Talking and playing with babies: the role of ideologies of childrearing', in M. Bullowa (ed.) *Before Speech: The Beginnings of Interpersonal Communication*, Cambridge: Cambridge University Press.

Stern, D. (1977) *The First Relationship: Infant and Mother, Cambridge,* Mass.: Harvard University Press.

Stross, B. (1972) 'Verbal processes in Tzeltal speech socialization', *Anthropological Linguistics* 14(1).

von Sturmer, D.E. (1980) 'Rights in nurturing', unpublished M.A. thesis, Australian National University, Canberra.

Ward, M. (1971) *Them Children: A Study in Language Learning,* New York: Holt, Rinehart & Winston.

Wills, D. (1977) Culture's cradle: social, structural and interactional aspects of Senegalese socialization, unpublished Ph.D. dissertation, University of Texas, Austin.

15. Facilitating Children's Syntax Acquisition

Keith E. Nelson

How adults can assist children's acquisition of new syntactic forms is unclear from prior research. In this 2-month study, when 2½-year-olds produced sentences, adults gave replies designed to speed acquisition of particular kinds of sentence structures that were lacking before intervention. Children received intervention that was selectively directed toward acquisition either of question forms or of verb forms. The impact of intervention also was selective. Children who encountered verb intervention sessions acquired new verb structures, and children who received question intervention sessions acquired new forms of questions. This evidence appears to provide the first demonstration that adults' verbal intervention with children who are learning a first language can lead the children to acquire particular syntactic forms that they lacked before intervention.

Young children receive much speech from adults, and gradually young children master the language they hear. Currently much is known about the characteristics of adult speech directed to young children (Berko Gleason, 1973; Moerk, 1972; Snow, 1972; Newport, in press); even more is known about the child's successively refined levels of using words (Clark, 1973; Maratsos, 1974; Nelson & Bonvillian, 1973) and sentences (Bloom, 1970; Brown, 1973; McNeill, 1970; Menyuk, 1971). But to understand how the child learns language, it is also essential to know how the child's progress is facilitated or hindered by available adult examples of language use.

Some general characteristics of the relations between adult speech and children's speech have been reported again and again. One characteristic is that the young child does *not* imitate adult sentences with great frequency. Even when the child does imitate the adult, the child's imitations do not serve to introduce new grammatical constructions into the child's system of syntax. In typical dialogues, the child is not imitating the immediately preceding adult sentence structures and adults are not giving the child direct feedback indicating whether the child's sentence is well formed or poorly formed (Brown, Cazden, & Bellugi-Klima, 1969; Brown & Hanlon, 1970).

This brief summation leaves a puzzle. The young child obviously does extract information about syntax, somehow, from sentences spoken by adults. But immediate imitation by the child and immediate feedback about syntax from adults do not appear to play much of a role. Furthermore, when correlations have been examined between the general characteristics of mothers' speech and their children's progress in syntax acquisition, few strong clues emerged concerning what characteristics of adult speech or of adult-child dialogues could facilitate syntax acquisition. A final problem is that

Keith E. Nelson: 'Facilitating Children's Syntax Acquisition'. *DEVELOPMENTAL PSYCHOLOGY* (1977), Vol. 13, No. 2, pp. 101-107. Copyright © 1977 by the American Psychological Association. Reprinted by permission.

when concurrent dialogues between mothers and children are recorded, there is no way of determining direction of influence. That is, it is not possible to specify to what extent the mother's language is influencing the child's language and to what extent the reverse holds true.

All of these considerations point to one conclusion: that experimental studies are needed to help discover how children's syntax acquisition is facilitated or hindered by adult language-users. The present study was designed to test the notion that experimental intervention can lead children to acquire particular, new, syntactic forms that they had never used before. Among prior intervention studies (Amnon & Amnon, 1971; Cazden, 1965; Feldman,[1]), only one study (Nelson, Carskaddon, & Bonvillian, 1973) has shown clearly that intervention can promote children's progress toward mastering syntax. And we did not know of any studies which had demonstrated that particular syntactic structures were lacking before intervention but then were acquired as a result of intervention. So at the outset we considered this present study to be open in terms of what syntactic structures would be studied. A group of children were needed, all of whom clearly lacked some set of syntactic forms. Then we could see if selective intervention would lead children to begin using the forms. From an available sample of 25 normal 2½-year-olds we selected 12, all of whom initially lacked two categories of syntactic structures — complex questions and complex verbs. There were three kinds of complex questions that were absent. One kind is represented by the following sentence: "I changed them around, didn't I?" This is a tag question, with the "didn't I" tagged on the end to form a question. The other generally absent questions were such *Wh*-negative questions as "Why can't I go?" and negative questions like "Doesn't it hurt?" or "It won't fit?" For verbs, the complex forms the children lacked were of two general types: (a) single verbs in future tense or in conditional tense, such as "He could help me" ; and (b) sentences with two verbs in which past tense, conditional tense, or future tense were involved — that is, the children were not saying things like "He will run and jump," or "The bear ate the girl who visited."

After making certain that these 12 children lacked many or all of the forms just mentioned, five 1-hour intervention sessions were scheduled. If all the childen had received the same intervention, any changes in syntax might have been partly attributable to other factors besides intervention. Therefore, two intervention groups were formed, each serving as a control for the other. One group of 6 children received treatment directed only at facilitating the acquisition of complex verbs, whereas the other group of 6 received intervention directed only at facilitating the acquisition of complex questions. Except for the particular content of experimenter-child interactions, however, the nature of the intervention was the same. The idea was to use many complex verbs or many complex questions in such a way that the child would relate them to his or her own sentences. To this end, there were no set topics for the sessions, the attempt instead being to follow the child's topics and meanings. Within these general guidelines, it was also an aim of the experimenter to present many sentences that were "reworkings" or "recastings" of the child's preceding sentence (cf. Brown *et al.*, 1969; Nelson *et al.*, 1973). Such recastings kept the basic meaning of the child's sentence but expressed this meaning in a revised sentence structure. Thus the child might say, "The donkey ran," and the experimenter might say, "The donkey did run, didn't he?" or perhaps, "The donkey ran and jumped." Particularly in examples like these recast sentences, the child's attention could be drawn to the ways in which very similar meanings can be expressed in different syntactic structures. In short, the child might see relations between his or her own sentence structures and those of the adults. And on the basis of such comparison, the child might begin to use new aspects of syntax.

To determine if children did pick up new forms, recordings of the last two sessions of intervention were transcribed and analyzed. For each child, two points were at issue: Were any complex question forms used that weren't used prior to intervention, and were any complex verb forms used that weren't used prior to intervention?

Method

Subjects

Subjects were six boys and six girls. At the beginning of intervention sessions each child was either 28 or 29 months of age and was learning English as a first language.

All sessions were conducted and taped in the child's home. Regardless of whether the conversation sessions were intervention sessions or sessions for establishing the child's initial language levels, the child and an experimenter conversed while the child played and the child established the topics for most of the conversation.

Initial language levels for the two intervention groups

Two 1-hour sessions of conversation were taped for each child across a 3-week period. These tapes were transcribed and analyzed. Children's utterances that were direct imitations of other speakers were excluded from all analyses, as were one-word utterances. For each child the mean (average) length of utterance was calculated.

Assignment of subjects to groups was based in part on mean length of utterance in words. Three boys and three girls were scheduled to receive intervention focused on complex verbs. The remaining three boys and three girls comprised the second intervention group, scheduled to receive intervention designed to facilitate acquisition of complex questions. Each group averaged 3.69 words per utterance in the two initial sessions (range = 3.09–4.29).

The question intervention group and the verb intervention group were closely comparable initially in terms of their use of complex verb forms. Each child's initial transcripts were scored for presence or absence of any sentences containing verbs in the following five categories (a) single verb in future tense, (b) single verb in conditional tense, (c) two verbs with one or both verbs in future tense, (d) two verbs with one or both verbs in conditional tense, (e) two verbs with one or both verbs in past tense. No child showed initial use of sentences with verbs in all five categories. In each intervention group, two was the median number of the five verb categories that were initially present. The average number of categories included in the child's initial speech samples was 1.83 for the verb intervention group and 2.17 for the question intervention group ($t < 1$). Sentences with a single verb in the past tense were present for all children prior to intervention.

As a check on the children's initial levels of development in terms of complex questions, each child's transcripts were scored in terms of presence or absence of any examples of the following kinds of sentence structures (a) tag questions, in which the tag is formed by adding an auxiliary and appropriate pronoun at the end of a statement — for example, "They eat flowers, don't they?" or "The boy is not afraid, is he?" ; (b) *Wh*-negative questions beginning with *why, who, what, where, which, how,* or *when (Wh* words), followed immediately by an auxiliary, as in "Who isn't ready?" or "Why doesn't it work?" ; (c) other negative questions (exclusive of the previous two categories) such as "It won't shut?" or "Can't we go now?" The question intervention and verb intervention groups were precisely equal in terms of presence or absence of these forms of questions — three children in each group lacked all of the forms, and three children in each group lacked tag questions and negative questions beginning with *Wh* words.

Additional information was also available to support the above analyses of sentence forms that were absent in the children's speech prior to intervention. For each child, the particular complex question forms and complex verb forms absent in this study's initial tapes also were absent in 3 hours of taped conversation (from a separate project) collected across the 3 months preceding this study.

Finally, the two intervention groups were compared before and after intervention on two measures expected to be largely unaffected by either form of selective intervention — mean length of utterance, as specified above, and average complexity of noun phrases. Complexity of noun phrases was measured in terms of mean number of elements per noun phrase. In general, an element was counted for each English morpheme (see Nelson *et al.*, 1973). The initial levels were 2.15 elements per noun phrase and 2.02 elements per noun phrase for the verb intervention and question intervention groups ($t < 1$), respectively. Reliability (*rs*) between pairs of scorers was .94 both for average complexity of noun phrases and for mean length of utterance. There was 100% agreement between two scorers concerning presence or absence of the complex question and verb forms specified above.

Intervention procedures

Five 1-hour sessions of intervention were scheduled across a 2-month period for each child. Regardless of which intervention was used with a child, one experimenter met individually with the child for all sessions and on each occasion tried to elicit many sentences from the child. Three women served as experimenters, with each one working individually with four different children — two assigned to verb intervention and two assigned to question intervention.

In question intervention sessions the experimenter frequently responded to the child's sentence with a recasting or reworking of the sentence to illustrate negative questions or tag questions. For example, when one child said "You can't get in!" the experimenter gave the reply "No, I can't get in, can I?" Recasting into new, grammatically complete sentences that maintained the basic meaning of the child's sentence was done both when the child's sentence was grammatically complete and when the child's sentence was grammatically incomplete. If suitable recastings of the child's sentences did not come to mind, the experimenter constructed new examples of negative questions and tag questions as often as possible. Thus, when a child said "And you're a girl," the response given by an experimenter was "Right. And aren't you a little girl?" As part of this question intervention treatment, negative questions beginning with *Wh* words (e.g., *why, what)* were also included.

Similarly, in the verb intervention sessions, experimenters used both recastings and new constructions to illustrate use of the complex verbs that children lacked initially. Thus, experimenters employed many sentences with a single verb in the future or conditional tense and many sentences with two verbs in which one or both verbs were in future, conditional, or past tense . Two examples of exchanges that occurred are (a) child: "Where it go?" ; adult: "It will go there" ; (b) child: "I got it, I reached it" ; adult: "You got under the bed and reached it."

In verb intervention sessions experimenters minimized use of the forms concentrated on in question intervention, whereas verb forms that were stressed in verb intervention were used infrequently by experimenters during question intervention sessions.

Checks on intervention procedures were made by transcribing and analyzing the children's and experimenters' sentences in the final two treatment sessions. First, these analyses show that experimenters were engaged in similar ($t < 1$) numbers of overall verbal exchanges (or "turns") with the children who received verb intervention ($M = 273$) and question intervention ($M = 227$). In addition, the experimenters were about equally successful with the two intervention groups in eliciting sentences, as indicated by means of 338 and 291 utterances produced respectively by verb and question intervention subjects ($t < 1$). However, the selected forms that were the focus of intervention showed sharply contrasting patterns of use. Experimenters averaged a total of 291.8 complex questions (tag and negative questions) for each child in the last two question intervention sessions but only 6.2 such questions in the last two verb intervention sessions, $t(10) = 2.78, p < .02$. On the other hand, the five kinds of sentences with complex verbs that were the focus of verb intervention (as specified above) were used by experimenters much more frequently in the final verb intervention sessions (232.2 sentences per child) than in the final question intervention sessions (23.5 sentences per child), $t(10) = 3.13, p < .02$. In each of the latter two comparisons, there was no overlap between the frequency distributions for the question intervention and verb intervention children.

Language levels in the last two intervention sessions

Transcripts of each child's fourth and fifth intervention sessions were scored in terms of all measures used in assessing initial language levels. Excluded from analysis were all one-word utterances and all direct imitations of other speakers. As in the case of initial language assessment, each child's transcripts were scored for presence or absence of any sentences that represented the complex verbs or the complex questions at issue in this investigation. Direct imitations by a child of those complex verbs or complex questions he or she initially lacked occurred very rarely, and in no instance did a child show imitation of a form prior to use of the form in spontaneous (nonimitative) speech.

Results

Clear and selective effects of the interventions were obtained. Complex question forms lacking before intervention were picked up by all six children who received intervention directed at these forms. In contrast, use of new complex questions was shown by just one of the six children whose intervention was focused on complex verb forms. The reverse pattern held for the acquisition of new verb forms. All six of the verb intervention children acquired new verb constructions that were not used before intervention, such as two-verb sentences involving past, future, or conditional tense, but only one child in the question intervention group made such progress on verbs. Sign tests show this outcome for verbs and the outcome for questions to be significant ($p < .01$ in each case). Table 1 specifies the particular verb and question structures used by each child.

Table 1   **Sentence structure used (+) by each subject after intervention but not prior to intervention**

Sentence type	Question intervention subject						Verb intervention subject					
	1	2	3	4	5	6	1	2	3	4	5	6
Tag question	+		+	+	+							+
Wh + negative question			+									
Other negative question		+			+							
Future, 1 verb						+				+		
Conditional, 1 verb						+	+	+				+
Future, 2 verbs							+	+			+	
Conditional, 2 verbs							+					
Past, 2 verbs						+		+	+			+

Note. Wh = questions beginning with *why, who, what, how, when,* or *which.*

Examples of sentences with negative questions or complex verb structures that were acquired after intervention began are given in Tables 2 and 3.

As expected, the two treatments did not differentially affect the children's progress in terms of mean utterance length or mean elements per noun phrase. Difference scores on each of these measures were computed between the final two treatment sessions and the two sessions preceding treatment for each child. Mean changes in mean length of utterance[2] were small and did not differ appreciably ($t < 1$) for the question intervention group (mean change of +.03) and the verb intervention group (mean change of − .17). Average difference scores in number of elements per noun phrase were +.08 and +.11, respectively, for the verb intervention and question intervention groups ($t < 1$). These findings provide further support for the selective nature of the treatment effects.

Table 2   Question intervention subjects: examples of newly acquired question forms

Question

Tag
   He's shaking, isn't he?
   You're not leaving, are you?
   It does fit, doesn't it?
   Look I changed them around, didn't I?
   Wow it does fit, doesn't it?
Other negative
   You don't see it?
   Isn't it bigger?
   Why don't got a giraffe?
   No more, okay?
   Can't go through?

Table 3   Verb intervention subjects: examples of newly acquired verb forms

Sentence

One-verb
   I could take mine!
   He'll bite my finger.
   Will you draw a baby?
   I could make a ball.
   Could this fit right there?
Two-verb
   He fell and he broke.
   And mommy didn't do it, I did it.
   Member [remember] that ugly dinosaur, he would just bite.
   I will get up, hide it.
   You do this and I will do this.

Discussion

The interventions of the present study were selective attempts by adults to accelerate the young child's acquisition either of new complex verb forms or new complex question forms. The verb intervention treatment did selectively facilitate syntactic progress in terms of verbs, and the question intervention did selectively facilitate syntactic progress in terms of questions. This new finding takes us one step closer to understanding how the child derives necessary information about syntax from examples adults provide.

In interpreting the findings, it is important to note both the similarity and differences between what the experimenters did in intervention and what parents say in interaction with their children. Tapes of these same children with their mothers show that mothers do use negative questions and tag questions and they do use complex verbs. But these forms are not used frequently by the mothers. So the experimenters were using intervention techniques that did not introduce completely new forms to the child but that did tend to draw the child's attention to the forms. In part, an increase in frequency of complex questions or of complex verbs served this purpose. But it should also be recalled that the experimenters often reworked or recast the child's own sentence to produce a new sentence — as when "Donkey ran" or "The donkey ran" becomes "The donkey did run, didn't he?" This recasting technique, in which the meaning of the child's sentence is substantially unchanged but is recast in a new sentence structure, may be a central part of the facilitation of syntax. One reason for thinking so is that a previous study with 3-year-olds showed that intervention sessions involving recasting led to children's increased progress in syntax as measured by general indexes of syntactic level (Nelson *et al.*, 1973). In addition, that study indicated that a bias toward introducing predicate rather than subject information in the adults' recast replies was matched by a selective effect on syntactic progress: The children's clearest advances were seen in terms of measures of verb complexity.

Stated most broadly, the present study establishes some sufficient conditions for facilitating the young child's acquisition of new syntactic forms. Beyond this we would like to know the necessary conditions for the child's mastery of new elements of syntax. In trying to extend the present line of inquiry, a central factor to keep in mind is that to master syntax the child must in some way make comparisons between his or her own sentence structures and those of others. Recasting could aid these comparisons, as the child could compare the ways in which the contrasting sentence structures of the adult's reply and the child's preceding utterance serve to express very similar meanings. Such opportunities for comparison do arise outside experimental intervention, in that some use of recasts occurred for mothers of the present study's 28- to 29-month-olds as well as for mothers of young children in other observations in which no syntax intervention techniques were used (Nelson & Bonvillian, in press; Newport, in press). However, whether recasting the child's sentence is essential to the child's acquisition of new forms remains to be determined. Moreover, further evidence is needed to establish whether the child can make the needed comparisons with adult linguistic structures even if the child does not converse directly with the particular adults who provide examples useful to the child. An adequate theoretical model of language acquisition would specify what comparisons the child makes between his own sentence structures and those of adults, and it would further specify when such comparisons are made and how they influence particular revisions the child makes in his own system of sentence generation.

In this study, children's acquisition of new syntactic forms was selectively speeded during the course of intervention by adult verbal intervention. Because it was not possible to follow up this sample of children systematically after intervention ceased, it remains to be determined whether such intervention has lasting consequences for the child's syntactic development and whether newly acquired elements are used broadly with many listeners and across varying situations. In future research another question of interest will concern the optimal degree of difference between a child's initial syntactic forms and the forms to be targeted for acquisition through intervention. As for the present experiment, we can observe only that the targeted verb forms and negative question forms were just moderately more advanced (in developmental terms) than the children's initial syntax; for example, all children initially were using regular past tense verbs as well as affirmative questions of some complexity. An additional variable that may influence the effectiveness of intervention is whether the adult who intervenes with a child speaks the same dialect as the adults who routinely interact with the child, as was the case in the present study and the study by Nelson *et al.* (1973) but not in the studies by Cazden (1965) and Feldman[1]. A final element bearing on the outcome and interpretation of this study was our analysis of extensive samples of the children's speech prior to intervention, which reduced any probability that a child would possess an undetected form before treatment and then begin using the form more frequently when the experimenter modeled the form during intervention.

It is suggested above that the present intervention techniques were successful in furthering syntax acquisition because they furthered a comparison process in which the young child examines the relation between his or her own sentences and sentences spoken by adults. If so, the present and similar techniques should be effective with a broad range of syntactic forms, not just with complex verbs and questions. Furthermore, since emerging evidence on sign language acquisition demonstrates many parallels to speech acquisition (Bonvillian, Nelson, & Charrow, in press), it is conceivable that an adequate model of language acquisition will explain speech and sign acquisition in a highly similar fashion and that the same kinds of adult techniques (e.g., recasting) will facilitate syntax acquisition in both modes.

This research was supported in part by Grant 1-R03-MH19826-01 from the National Institute of Health. A previous version of this paper ("Facilitating Syntax Acquisition") was presented at the Eastern Psychological Association meeting held in New York, April 1975.

Special thanks for assistance go to Judi Chun, Kris Olson, Cheryl Quinn, Ellen Ogo Tanouye, Barbara Kaplan, Arthur Lehman, Nathaniel Floyd, Michele Silverman, Barbara Gombach, and the mothers of the children in this June 1973 study.

Reference notes

1. Feldman, C. (1971) *The effects of various types of adult responses in the syntactic acquisition of two- to three-year olds*. Unpublished manuscript, Department of Psychology, University of Chicago.

2. The measure of mean length of utterance (MLU) used here and also in the initial composition of groups was the mean number of words per utterance. One-word utterances were excluded because frequency of one-word utterances (e.g., *yes* answers to adults) often reflects more on the adult's use of language within a recorded observation than on the child's language level. When one-word utterances are included, the result pattern, however, is unchanged. An MLU measure in words has the advantage for broad use in many studies of straightforward calculation for either large or small samples of a child's utterances at any point in development. The MLU measures in morphemes, in contrast, are far from straightforward (cf. Brown, 1973; Cazden, 1965), with the appropriateness of decisions about morphemes (e.g., whether *got* is a past tense verb or a synonym of *have*) very much dependent on the sample size and on the language level of the child. Nevertheless, to further between-study

comparisons, MLU in morphemes (see Brown, 1973), including one-word utterances, was calculated also. The MLU in these terms paralleled the results reported above, with an average MLU in the final two treatment sessions of 2.88 for question intervention subjects and 3.03 for verb intervention subjects.

References

Amnon, P.R., & Amnon, M.S. (1971) 'Effects of training black preschool children in vocabulary vs. sentence construction'. *Journal of Educational Psychology*, 33, 421-426.

Berko Gleason, J. (1973) 'Code-switching in children's language'. In T.E. Moore (Ed.). *Cognitive development and the acquisition of language*, New York: Academic Press.

Bloom, L. (1970) *Language development: Form and function in emerging grammars*, Cambridge, Mass.: MIT Press.

Bonvillian, J.D., Nelson, K.E., & Charrow, V.R. 'Languages and language-related skills in deaf and hearing children'. *Sign Language Studies*, in press.

Brown, R. (1973) *A first language*. Cambridge, Mass.: Harvard University Press.

Brown, R., Cazden, C., & Bellugi-Klima, U. (1969) 'The child's grammar from I to III'. In J.P. Hill (Ed.), *Minnesota symposia on child psychology*, Minneapolis: University of Minnesota Press.

Brown, R., & Hanlon, C. (1970) 'Derivational complexity and order of acquisition in child speech'. In J.R. Hayes (Ed.), *Cognition and the development of language,* New York: Wiley.

Cazden, C. (1965) *Environmental assistance to the child's acquisition of grammar*. Unpublished doctoral dissertation, Harvard University.

Clark, E. (1973) 'What's in a word?' In T.E. Moore (Ed.), *Cognitive development and the acquisition of language*. New York: Academic Press.

Maratsos, M.P. (1974) 'When is a high thing the big one?' *Developmental Psychology*, 10, 367-375.

McNeill, D.(1970) *The acquisition of language: The study of developmental psycholinguistics*. New York: Harper & Row.

Menyuk, P. (1971) *The acquisition and development of language,* Englewood Cliffs, N.J.: Prentice-Hall.

Moerk, E. (1972) 'Principles of interaction in language learning'. *Merrill-Palmer Quarterly*, 18, 229-257.

Nelson, K.E., & Bonvillian, J. D. (1973) 'Concepts and words in the two-year-old: Acquisition of concept names under controlled conditions'. *Cognition*, 2, 435-450.

Nelson, K.E., & Bonvillian, J. D. 'Early semantic development: Conceptual growth and related semantic and syntactic processes'. In K.E. Nelson (Ed.), *Children's language, Vol 1*. New York: Gardner Press, in press.

Nelson, K.E., Carskaddon, G., & Bonvillian, J.D. (1973) 'Syntax acquisition: Impact of experimental variation in adult verbal interaction with the child'. *Child Development, 44,* 497-504.

Newport, E.L. 'Motherese: The speech of mothers to young children'. In N.J. Castellan, D.B. Pisoni, & G.R. Potts (Eds.). *Cognitive theory: Vol. II,* Hillsdale, N.J.: Erlbaum, in press.

Snow, C.E. (1972) 'Mothers' speech to children learning language'. *Child Development*, 43, 549-565.

16.   Critical Period Effects in Second Language Learning: the Influence of Maturational State on the Acquisition of English as a Second Language

Jacqueline S. Johnson and Elissa L. Newport

In most behavioral domains, competence is expected to increase over development, whether gradually or in stages. However, in some domains, it has been suggested that competence does not monotonically increase with development, but rather reaches its peak during a "critical period,"[1] which may be relatively early in life, and then declines when this period is over. For example, in the development of early visual abilities, the development of attachment, or — in the case considered here — the acquisition of language, it has been suggested that learners are best able to achieve the skill in question during a maturationally limited period, early in life. Elsewhere we have presented evidence that first language learning is indeed limited in this way (Newport and Supalla, 1987). The present paper focuses on the acquisition of a *second* language, asking whether this type of learning, undertaken only after a native language is already acquired, is nevertheless still maturationally constrained.

We will begin by reviewing prior evidence on this hypothesis, for both first and second language learning, and will then present a new empirical study which we believe shows evidence for a maturational function in second language learning. Such evidence leaves open, however, whether the underlying maturational change occurs in a specific language faculty, or rather in more general cognitive abilities involved in language learning. We will conclude by considering the types of mechanisms which are consistent with our findings.

Evidence for a critical period effect in first language acquisition

The critical period hypothesis, as advanced by Lenneberg (1967), holds that language acquisition must occur before the onset of puberty in order for language to develop fully. As will be detailed in the subsequent section, Lenneberg's hypothesis concerned only first language acquisition; he left open the question of whether this critical period extended to second language acquisition, which would occur after a first language was already in place.

Lenneberg's argument contained two parts. First, he reviewed available behavioral evidence suggesting that normal language learning occurred primarily or exclusively within childhood. At the time his book was written, no direct evidence for the hypothesis (from normal individuals who had been deprived of exposure to a first language for varying lengths of time in early life) was available. His review therefore included

Jacqueline S. Johnson and Elissa L. Newport: 'Critical Period Effects in Second Language Learning: the Influence of Maturational State on the Acquisition of English as a Second Language' in *COGNITIVE PSYCHOLOGY* (1989), 21, pp. 60-99. Copyright © 1989 by Academic Press, Inc.

various types of indirect evidence; for example, differences in recovery from aphasia for children *vs* adults, and differences in progress in language acquisition, before *vs* after puberty, in the mentally retarded.

Second, he proposed a mechanism which might be responsible for a maturational change in learning abilities. The proposed mechanism was fundamentally neurological in nature. He suggested that the brain, having reached its adult values by puberty, has lost the plasticity and reorganizational capacities necessary for acquiring language. Subsequent research has questioned whether all of the neurological events he cited occur at an appropriate time for them to serve as the basis for a critical period (Krashen, 1975). Nevertheless, the hypothesis that there *is* such a critical period for language learning has remained viable.

Since Lenneberg's writing, behavioral studies approximating a direct test of the critical period hypothesis for first language acquisition have become available. One such study is a well-known case of Genie, a girl who was deprived of language and social interaction until her discovery at the age of 13 (Curtiss, 1977). Her lack of linguistic competence, particularly in syntax, after seven years of rehabilitation supports the critical period hypothesis. However, the abnormal conditions under which Genie was reared, including nutritional, cognitive, and social deprivation, have led some investigators to question whether her language difficulties have resulted only from lack of linguistic exposure during early life.

More recently, Newport and Supalla (Newport, 1984: Newport and Supalla, 1987) have studied language acquisition in the congenitally deaf, a population in which exposure to a first language may occur at varying ages while other aspects of social and cognitive development remain normal. Their data come from congenitally deaf subjects for whom American Sign Language (ASL) is the first language. However, since 90 percent of the congenitally deaf have hearing (speaking) parents, only a few deaf individuals are exposed to this language from birth. The majority of deaf people are exposed to ASL only when they enter residential school for the deaf and first associate with other deaf individuals; this can be as early as age four or as late as early adulthood.

Newport and Supalla separated subjects by their age of exposure into three groups: *native learners*, who were exposed to ASL from birth by their deaf parents; *early learners*, who were first exposed to ASL between the ages of four and six; and *late learners*, who were first exposed to ASL at age 12 or later. Wishing to test asymptotic performance (i.e. ultimate command of the language), they chose subjects who had at least 40 years of experience with the language as their primary, everyday communication system. The subjects were tested on their production and comprehension of ASL verb morphology. The results show a linear decline in performance with increasing age of exposure, on virtually every morpheme tested. That is, native learners scored better than early learners, who scored better than late learners, on both production and comprehension.

This study thus provides direct evidence that there is a decline over age in the ability to acquire a first language. It also tells us, however, that Lenneberg's portrayal is at least partially incorrect in two regards. First, the results show a continuous linear decline in ability, instead of a sudden drop-off at puberty as his hypothesis implies. (This study does not tell us whether the linear function asymptotes or continues to decline after puberty, since separate groups of later learners, before *vs* after puberty, were not tested.) Second, it should be noted that, while the postpubescent learners did not reach as high a level of proficiency as the native or early learners, language had not become totally unlearnable for them. This rules out any extreme interpretation of the critical period hypothesis.

In sum, current evidence supports the notion of a maturationally delimited critical period for first language acquisition, with some modifications from Lenneberg's original formulation. However, this evidence is compatible with a number of quite different accounts of the nature of the underlying maturational change. Evidence concerning age effects on *second* language learning can contribute to a further delineation of critical period accounts.

Second language acquisition

What it can and cannot tell us about the critical period

Given the early difficulties of performing a direct test of the critical period hypothesis on first language acquisition, many researchers undertook studies of second language acquisition over age as a test of the hypothesis. Some investigators have suggested that a critical period theory must predict that children are better than adults at learning second languages, as well as first languages. Consequently, they have viewed any evidence to the contrary as evidence against the critical period hypothesis (see Snow, 1983, for discussion).

In our opinion, data on this issue do have an important consequence for a critical period theory of language acquisition. However, it is not that the critical period hypothesis could be rejected on such evidence but rather that it can be refined or clarified by such evidence. A critical period theory for language acquisition would have quite a different character depending upon whether second language acquisition were included in its effects.

To capture this distinction there are two different ways we can state the critical period hypothesis, one that does not include second language acquisition in its effects and one that does:

Version one: the exercise hypothesis. Early in life, humans have a superior capacity for acquiring languages. If the capacity is not exercised during this time, it will disappear or decline with maturation. If the capacity is exercised, however, further language learning abilities will remain intact throughout life.

Version two: the maturational state hypothesis. Early in life, humans have a superior capacity for acquiring languages. This capacity disappears or declines with maturation.

Notice that, although very different in character, the two versions make the same predictions with regard to first language acquisition. They differ, however, in their predictions for second language acquisition.

The exercise hypothesis predicts that children will be superior to adults in acquiring a first language. By this account, if learners are not exposed to a first language during childhood, they will be unable to acquire any language fully at a later date. However, as long as they have acquired a first language during childhood, the ability to acquire language will remain intact and can be utilized at any age. On such a hypothesis, second language learning should be equivalent in children and adults, or perhaps even superior in adults owing to their greater skills in their first language as well as in many related domains.

This hypothesis is not unlike the conception of the visual critical period described for cats (Hubel and Wiesel, 1963), where early visual experience is required to maintain and refine the structure of the visual cortex, or the conception of the critical period described for attachment in dogs (Scott, 1980), where early attachment to one dog is required for subsequently normal socialization and permits unlimited later attachments to other members of the same species. Indeed, as will be discussed below, some of the current evidence on second language learning could be interpreted to support an exercise hypothesis.

In contrast, the maturational state hypothesis claims that there is something special about the maturational state of the child's brain which makes children particularly adept at acquiring *any* language, first as well as second. This hypothesis predicts that language learning abilities decline with maturation, regardless of early linguistic experience: acquiring a first language early in life will not guarantee the ability to acquire a second language later in life. In this version, then, children will be better in second language learning as well as first.

With certain qualifications, the critical period hypothesis that Lenneberg put forth can be subsumed under either version. In fact, it is not absolutely clear which version he would have favored. Some comments he made suggest that he thinks the young learner has a superior capacity for acquiring second languages, and therefore that he would favor the maturational state hypothesis:

> the incidence of "language learning blocks" rapidly increases after puberty. Also automatic acquisition from mere exposure to a given language seems to disappear after this age and foreign languages have to be taught and learned through a conscious and labored effort. Foreign accents cannot be overcome easily after puberty.

> (Lenneberg, 1967, p. 176)

However, other comments within the same paragraph sound as if he would have favored the exercise hypothesis:

> our ability to learn foreign languages tends to confuse the picture. Most individuals of average intelligence are able to learn a second language after the beginning of their second decade . . . a person can learn to communicate in a foreign language at the age of forty. This does not trouble our basic hypothesis on age limitation because we may assume that the cerebral organization for language learning as such has taken place during

childhood, and since natural languages tend to resemble one another in many fundamental aspects the matrix for language skills is present.

(Lenneberg, 1967, p. 176)

Since Lenneberg's was one of the first proposals in this area, it is not surprising that he did not take a definitive stand on this issue, particularly since there were at that time few data to support either view. Nevertheless, it is a crucial distinction that should be made in any subsequent account of a critical period.

Research on age effects on second language acquisition

Is there an age-related limitation on the learning of a second language? A number of studies have investigated this question since the time of Lenneberg's book, focusing particularly on the acquisition of phonology and grammar. Superficially, these studies appear to contradict one another; some have been said to demonstrate an adult advantage, some a child advantage.

This apparent contradiction is resolved when one separates performance in the early stages of learning from eventual attainment in the language (for a review of these studies, with a conclusion similar to the one presented here, see Krashen *et al.*, 1982). Most of the studies of second language learning have examined just the early stages of learning; these studies tend to show an adult advantage in both phonology (Asher and Price, 1967; Olson and Samuels, 1973; Snow and Hoefnagel-Hohle, 1977) and syntax (Snow and Hoefnagel-Hohle, 1978). Adults thus seem to begin moving toward second language proficiency more quickly. However, this advantage appears to be short-lived.

In contrast, studies of eventual attainment in the language shows a superiority for subjects who began learning in childhood, both in phonology (Asher and Garcia, 1969; Seliger *et al.*, 1975; Oyama, 1976) and in syntax (Oyama, 1978; Patkowski, 1980). However, most of the studies of child-adult differences in ultimate attainment have focused on pronunciation. With anecdotal evidence that late learners do carry an accent and experimental findings that support it, most investigators will concede a child advantage for acquiring phonology (though not necessarily a maturational one; see, for example, Snow and Hoefnagel-Hohle, 1977; Olson and Samuels, 1973).

There is much less available evidence on child-adult differences in the ultimate attainment of grammar. To our knowledge, only two studies have been done. In both, the subjects were US immigrants who were exposed to English upon moving to the United States and who had lived in the United States for at least five years at time of the test.

In one study, subjects' syntactic ability was assessed by trained judges who assigned syntactic ratings to written transcripts of the subjects' speech from tape recorded interviews (Patkowski, 1980). For purposes of analysis, subjects' scores were divided along two variables; age of arrival in the United States (before *vs* after age 15), and years in the United States (under *vs* over 18 years). Additionally, measures of the subjects' exposure to English in both natural and classroom settings were taken. Using either the results from the analysis of variance test or correlations, age of arrival was the only significant predictor of syntactic proficiency, with the prepubescent learners outperforming the postpubescent learners. The correlation of age of arrival with score was -0.74, which indicates a linear trend; however, the exact shape of the relationship cannot be determined from the reported results.

In the second study mentioned, subjects were measured on their ability to repeat spoken English sentences which had been masked with white noise (Oyama, 1978). This task was meant to tap the ability to integrate different sources of linguistic knowledge including phonology, syntax, intonation, and redundancy patterns. Admittedly this is not a pure measure of syntactic ability; however, it presumably involves syntactic knowledge (along with other factors). This study found the same pattern of results just reported: age of arrival was the only significant predictor of test performance.

In addition, the Oyama study addressed important claims regarding whether children's superiority over adults in final attainment is due to factors other than maturation which happen to be correlated with age. For example, it has been argued that the adult is less *motivated* than the child to learn the language fully, is more *self-conscious* about speaking (i.e. practicing and making errors), does not have the cultural *identification* with the host country necessary to become fluent, and in general is less able to achieve the open attitudinal and affective state required for language acquisition to take place (for reviews of this view, see Schumann, 1975; Krashen, 1982). To test these claims, Oyama measured each of these variables, plus other candidate predictors, using interview and questionnaire material. Simple correlations showed a good association between these variables and test score; however, partial correlations removing the effects of age of arrival became essentially zero. In contrast, when the reverse procedure was performed, removing each of these variables from the relationship between age of arrival and test score, the partial correlation remained large and significant. In short, age of arrival rather than the attitudinal variables, predicted language performance.

These are important findings, for they support the view that age effects are not simply an artifact of child-adult differences in affective conditions of learning. However, a more rigorous test of this question could be performed. Nonmaturational hypothesis do not typically propose that one attitudinal variable, for example, self-consciousness, will alone predict performance; rather, they propose that the combination of all of these variables favors children over adults. Thus a more stringent test would involve partialling out all of the attitudinal variables together from age of arrival, and then determining whether there is any predictive power left.

The study we present in the present paper is an attempt to supplement the findings of these earlier studies. It is similar to the two studies discussed above, in that the focus is on ultimate command of the grammar of the second language as a function of age of exposure to that language. It differs from previous studies, however, in the way subjects' proficiency in the language is assessed and in the types of analyses performed. First, a detailed evaluation of subjects' knowledge of numerous aspects of English morphology and syntax is performed. This allows us to examine the relationship between age of exposure and an overall measure of English proficiency, as well as the possible differential effects of age of exposure on various aspects of grammatical structure. Second, a wide range of ages of exposure is examined, so that the precise shape of the function relating age to proficiency can be determined. Third, multivariate analyses are used to evaluate the relative contributions to proficiency of age as well as a number of affective, sociological, and environmental conditions of learning.

In detail, the primary questions that we address are as follows:

1. Is there an age-related effect on learning the grammar of a second language?
2. If so, what is the nature of this relationship? What is the shape of the function relating age to learning and ultimate performance, and where (if anywhere) does the relationship plateau or decline?
3. Can experimental or attitudinal variables, separately or together, explain the effects obtained for age of learning?
4. What areas of the grammar are the most and least problematic for learners of different age groups?

In answering these questions we hope to gain a better understanding of the nature of the critical period and, most particularly, to be able to decide between the two versions of the critical period outlined above.

Method

Subjects

Subjects were 46 native Chinese or Korean speakers who learned English as a second language. Chinese and Korean were chosen as the native languages because of their typological dissimilarity to English. (For consideration of the effects of the first language on the second, see Discussion.) No differences were found in the results for the two language groups, so they will be presented together throughout the paper.

The primary criterion for selecting subjects was that they varied in the age at which they moved to the United States and thereby first became immersed in English. All subjects were exposed to English by native speakers in the United States. In addition, to be sure that subjects had sufficient experience with English to be considered at their ultimate attainment in the language, every attempt was made to obtain subjects who had lived in the United States for many years. Minimum criteria were as follows: all subjects had to have at least five years of exposure to English and had to have lived in the United States for an unbroken stay of at least three years prior to the time of test. Finally, to ensure ample exposure to English and to ensure some homogeneity of social background, all subjects were selected from the student and faculty population at an American university (University of Illinois). Subjects were recruited through posted sign-up sheets, letters, and by word of mouth.

The resulting 46 subjects varied in age of arrival in the United States from ages 3 to 39; throughout that range there was a fairly even distribution of ages of arrival. Age of arrival was considered the age of first exposure to English. Three additional subjects were tested but eliminated from data analysis when our posttest interview revealed that they did not meet the above criteria: one did not have an unbroken stay in the United States for three years prior to test; the second did not arrive in the United States until adulthood but was immersed in English through attending an all-English-speaking school in a foreign country. For both of these subjects, then, age of immersion could not be determined unambiguously. The third subject was eliminated because her early exposure to English was from her Chinese parents, who had no prior experience with English but nevertheless decided to speak only English in the home upon their arrival in the United States. Most of her early exposure to English was therefore not to standard English.

Additional experiential characteristics of the subjects varied for subjects arriving in the United States early *vs* late in life, and will be discussed separately for these two groups. In all cases, these experiential characteristics, as well as age of arrival, will be evaluated for their relationship to performance in English.

Early arrivals. There were 23 subjects, 12 males and 11 females, who had arrived in the United States before age 15. These early arrivals were, at the time of test, for the most part freshman or sophomore undergraduates who received money or class credit for their participation. All of these subjects, from the time of arrival until college, lived in an environment where their native language was spoken in the home and English spoken outside of the home. Once they entered college, all lived predominantly in an English-speaking environment.

Late arrivals. The remaining 23 subjects were 17 males and six females who had arrived in the United States after age 17. Prior to coming to the United States, all of these subjects had had between 2 and 12 years of mandatory formal English instruction in their native country. This raised two possible concerns. One, the classroom experience might reduce the effect of age of arrival on learning, since age of first exposure to English for these subjects is earlier than age of arrival. Two, "age of learning" may turn out to be better defined by age of starting classes rather than age of arrival, which would result in a narrower range of ages than desired. Whether point two is true is an interesting question itself and will be examined empirically in the results section.

At the time of test, these subjects were primarily professors, research associates, and graduate students. All subjects, in both the early and late arrivals groups, had at least some years of schooling while in the United States. Within the late arrivals, the smallest number of years of school in the United States was three years, the largest ten, with an average of six years for the group.

For some of the subjects, the language environment was analogous to that of the early arrivals, in which the native language was spoken in the home and English spoken at school and work: for others, particularly those that were unmarried, the language environment was almost all English. Thus in terms of exposure on a day to day basis, it does not appear that the early arrivals have any advantage over the late arrivals.

In terms of years of exposure in the United States the late and early arrivals also are fairly even (see table 1). The average number of years in the United States for early and late arrivals is 9.8 and 9.9, respectively. The main difference between the two groups is that the late arrivals have a larger range of years in the United States.

Table 1   **The distribution of early and late arrival in terms of the number of years they lived in the USA**

	Age of arrival	
Years in the USA	3-15	17-39
3-6	4	7
7-10	10	11
11-15	9	3
23-26	0	2

To provide a baseline performance on tests of English, 23 native speakers of English were run. Two additional native subjects participated but were not included in the analysis, one because the posttest interview revealed that he acquired English outside of the United States, and one because she spoke a nonstandard dialect of English.

Procedure

The subjects were tested on their knowledge of English syntax and morphology by being asked to judge the grammaticality of spoken English sentences of varying types (see Materials). While such a task, of course, in principle requires metalinguistic skills in addition to knowledge of the language, virtually perfect performance is shown on the same task by six and seven year old native speakers in subsequent studies (Johnson, Newport, & Strauss, in press). This suggests that the metalinguistic skills necessary for our task can only be minimally demanding for an adult and that any variation obtained in performance on the task among adults must be due to variation in knowledge of the language.

The test sentences were recorded on tape by a native American female voice (E.N.). Each sentence was read twice, with a 1-2 second pause separating the repetitions. They were said clearly, with normal intonation at a slow to moderate speed. The ungrammatical sentences were spoken with the intonation pattern of the grammatical counterpart. There was a 3-4 second delay between the different sentences.

Subjects were tested individually in the laboratory. They were instructed to make a grammaticality judgement for each sentence, guessing if they were not sure. It was made clear to the subject that if the sentence was incomplete or otherwise wrong for any reason, they should regard it as ungrammatical. The subject recorded yes/no responses on an answer sheet by circling Y or N. To avoid giving cues to the subject, the experimenter did not face the subject during the testing session while the tape was going. Subjects were given a break halfway through the test, but were told prior to starting that they should tell the experimenter to stop the tape at any time if they need to break sooner, either if the tape was too fast for them or if they were simply getting tired.

Following the grammaticality judgement test, subjects were interviewed for approximately half an hour about their language background. Information was gathered about the type and amount of exposure to English they had, from when they were first learning the language until the time of test. Motivational and additudinal measures were also taken, by having the subjects rate themselves on a scale of 1 to 5 with regard to those measures.

None of the subjects were blind as to the nature of the experiment. They were told prior to participating that we were interested in determining whether children or adults are better at learning second languages; they were not told, however, what type of results were expected.

Materials

The judgements of grammaticality test was modeled loosely after one used by Linebarger *et al.* (1983) in a study unrelated to the present one. Our test, however, has a different set of English constructions and corresponding test sentences than those of Linebarger *et al.*, with the exception of two rule types which are noted.[2]

Our test was composed of 276 sentences.[3] Of these, 140 were ungrammatical. The other 136 formed the grammatical counterparts of these sentences.[4] The pairs that were formed, between the ungrammatical and grammatical counterparts, were sentences that were exactly the same except for one rule violation contained in the ungrammatical sentence. The pairs of sentences were constructed to test 12 types of rules of English, listed in table 2. The test contained between six and 16 pairs of sentences testing each rule type. The members of a pair were, however, not adjacent to each other, but rather were placed in opposite halves of the test. Within each half, sentences were presented in random order (see Design for further details).

To ensure as much as possible that the sentences tested the rules under study and not extraneous factors, sentences were constructed to contain only relatively high frequency words, most of which were only one or two syllables in length. The location of the grammatical error (at the beginning, middle, or end of the sentence), the basic phrase structure of the sentence, and the sentence length (ranging from five to eleven words per sentence) were balanced across pairs of sentences testing each rule type, so that each rule type was tested by a set of sentences comparable in all of these regards.

The 12 rule types we tested were chosen to represent a wide variety of the most basic aspects of English sentence structure. (Indeed, according to our expectations, native speakers of English found the test very easy, with ungrammatical sentences producing strong feelings of ungrammaticality.) Within the 12 rules types, there were four rule types which dealt specifically with English morphology: past tense, plural, third person singular, and present progressive. They will be discussed together since many of the violations were constructed along similar lines. The other eight types involved various rules of English syntax. Within each rule type, the violations were formed on the basis of a few basic formats, with several pairs of sentences (typically four) using each format. These are discussed in more detail, with examples of the structure of the pairs, overleaf.

Table 2   Twelve rule types tested in grammaticality judgement task

1	Past tense	7	Particle movement
2	Plural	8	Subcategorization
3	Third person singular	9	Auxiliaries
4	Present progressive	10	Yes/no questions
5	Determiners	11	Wh-questions
6	Pronominalization	12	Word order

Morphology: Past tense, plural, third person singular, and present progressive. For morphology, the grammatical sentence always contained the target morpheme in a required context, while the grammatical violation was created using one of four formats:

1. by omitting the required morpheme;
2. by replacing the required morpheme with an inappropriate morpheme from a different class;
3. by making an irregular item regular;
4. by attaching a regular marking to an already irregularly marked item.

The first format was used to make ungrammatical sentences for all four types of morphology. The sentence pairs were constructed so that the grammatical context required the target morpheme, making it a grammatical violation when the morpheme was omitted in one of the sentences of the pair. For example, in sentences (1a) and (1b), a plural marker is required on the noun "pig", and is present in (1a) but is omitted in (1b). In sentences (2a) and (2b), the present progressive ending is required on the verb "speak"; it is present in (2a) but omitted in (2b).

(1a) The farmer bought two pigs at the market.
*(1b) The farmer bought two pig at the market.
(2a) The little boy is speaking to a policeman.
*(2b) The little boy is speak to a policeman.

Sentences were structured similarly for the other classes of morphemes.

The second format applied only to the verb morphology. One sentence of the pair was correct; the other had an inappropriate tense marking for the context. Consider, for example, sentences (3a) and (3b).

(3a) Yesterday the hunter shot a deer.
*(3b) Yesterday the hunter shoots a deer.

In (3a), the verb is in the past tense form as required, while in (3b) the verb "shoot" occurs in present tense form in a past tense context.

The last two formats for creating the ill-formed sentences could be used only for past tense and plural forms. An ill-formed sentence created by making an irregular item regular is exemplified in sentence (4b), with its grammatical counterpart in (4a).

Similarly, the ungrammatical sentence (5b) has a regular marking added on an already marked irregular.

    (4a) A shoe salesman sees many feet throughout the day.
  *(4b) A shoe salesman sees many foots throughout the day.
    (5a) A bat flew into our attic last night.
  *(5b) A bat flewed into our attic last night.

The test was constructed so that there was an equal number of sentence pairs (4) in each format used for each type of morphology. However, due to the nature of the morphemes, it was impossible for all of the formats to be applied to all of the four rule types. Therefore the past tense and plural are tested by more sentence pairs than are the third person or the present progressive.

Determiners. To test subjects' knowledge of determiners, the grammatical member of the sentence pairs was constructed so that a determiner in a particular position was either necessary or not allowed. The ungrammatical counterparts were then formed by one of three methods: (a) by omitting them in required contexts, as in sentence (6b); (b) by substituting the indefinite for the definite, as in (7b); and (c) by inserting them where neither article is allowed, see (8b). These examples can be contrasted with their grammatical counterparts (6a), (7a), and (8a), respectively:

    (6a) Tom is reading a book in the bathtub.
  *(6b) Tom is reading book in the bathtub.
    (7a) The boys are going to the zoo this Saturday.
  *(7b) A boys are going to the zoo this Saturday.
    (8a) Larry went home after the party.
  *(8b) Larry went the home after the party.

In many cases, there are other ways of construing the errors; for example, (6b) may be construed as a plural error, instead of a determiner error, for not having the plural marking on the noun "book." In cases like these, where the error classification was ambiguous, the semantic contexts were created to try to bias the listener into the preferred reading. For example, in (6) the reason Tom is in the bathtub is to sway the subject into expecting that he is reading only one book rather than many.

Pronominalization. The sentence pairs for this rule type contain some type of pronominal. The ungrammatical sentences were formed to include one of the following violations: (a) the wrong case marking on the pronoun; (b) an error in gender or number agreement for the pronoun; or (c) an erroneous form of the possessive adjective.

The violations of case involved using nominative pronouns in objective positions (see (9a) and (9b) and objective pronouns in nominative positions:

    (9a) Susan is making some cookies for us.
  *(9b) Susan is making some cookies for we.

Gender and number were tested by capitalizing on the fact that reflexive pronouns have to agree with the noun they are coindexed with. Sentence (10a) is an example of correct gender agreement, while (10b) shows a gender agreement violation:

(10a) The girl cut herself on a piece of glass.
*(10b) The girl cut himself on piece of glass.

For possessive adjectives, the error is in the form the word takes. So, for example, some ungrammatical items have a possessive adjective with the possessive marker added, as in (11b). Compare this to the correct form in (11a):

(11a) Carol is cooking dinner for her family.
*(11b) Carol is cooking dinner for hers family.

Particle movement. With some minor changes, all of the items in this rule type are from Linebarger *et al.* (1983). Here the sentences take advantage of the differences between particles and prepositions. The ill-formed sentences were created by treating prepositions as particles, that is, by moving the preposition to the right of the object NP as in (12b), as compared to the correct form in (12a). These were contrasted with grammatical sentences with particles in their moved and unmoved positions, as in (13a) and (13b). Additionally, other sentences were ill-formed by moving the particle outside its own clause, as in (13c). Notice that, for this rule type, the sets of counterpart sentences are not pairs but triples:

(12a) The man climbed up the ladder carefully.
*(12b) The man climbed the ladder up carefully.
(13a) Kevin called up Nancy for a date.
(13b) Kevin called Nancy up for a date.
*(13c) Kevin called Nancy for a date up.

Subcategorization. The items in this rule type are also from Linebarger *et al.* (1983). These items test subjects' knowledge of the subcategorization frames of various verbs. In English, individual verbs determine the type of syntactic frames that may follow them. For example, some verbs require a direct object, while others require propositional phrases. Because the details of these frames are lexically determined, ill-formed sentences could be created by changing the structure of the required frame for a particular verb while keeping the meaning intact. Thus, the change in these sentences involved using the subcategorization frame of a semantically similar verb. See, for example, the contrasts below.

(14a) The man allows his son to watch TV.
*(14b) The man allows his son watch TV.
(15a) The man lets his son watch TV.
*(15b) The man lets his son to watch TV.

The ungrammatical sentences were formed by exchanging the different subcategorization frames of the two semantically similar verbs "allow" and "let."

Auxilliaries. In this rule type, the affix requirements for different auxiliary verbs were tested. In particular, the ungrammatical sentences were formed by violating three rules of auxiliaries. Each rule, with an example of the correct and incorrect forms, is given overleaf:

"Have" requires a past participle.

(16a) The baby bird has fallen from the oak tree.

*(16b) The baby bird has fall from the oak tree.

Following any form of "be," the main verb must take the progressive.

(17a) Fred will be getting a raise next month.

*(17b) Fred will be get a raise next month.

Only the first element of Aux is tensed.

(18a) Leonard should have written a letter to his mother.

*(18b) Leonard should has written a letter to his mother.

Yes/no questions. For this rule type, the ungrammatical sentences contain primarily errors in subject–aux inversion. The errors are of three types. In one, two auxiliaries are moved in front of the subject, as in (19b). In another, both the auxiliary and the verb are fronted (20b); and in the third, the verb is fronted in a sentence where do-insertion would normally occur, as in (21b). The grammatical counterparts are (19a), (20a), and (21a), respectively.

(19a) Has the king been served his dinner?

*(19b) Has been the king served his dinner?

(20a) Can the little girl ride a bicycle?

*(20b) Can ride the little girl a bicycle?

(21a) Did Bill dance at the party last night?

*(21b) Danced Bill at the party last night?

Additionally, there were some ungrammatical sentences formed by copying, instead of moving, the auxiliary verb, the difference being shown in (22a) and (22b):

(22a) Can the boy drive a tractor?

*(22b) Can the boy can drive a tractor?

Wh-questions. The ungrammatical wh-questions have three forms, two of them also dealing with aux. In one form, no subject–aux inversion occurs, as in (23b) as compared with (23a); in the other, do-insertion is omitted, as in (24b) compared to (24a):

(23a) When will Sam fix his car?

*(23b) When Sam will fix his car?

(24a) What do they sell at the corner store?

*(24b) What they sell at the corner store?

The third form of the ungrammatical wh-questions was lexical. A question was ill-formed by substituting an incorrect wh-word for a correct one. In sentence (25b), for example, "why" cannot be used unless the subcategorization frame of the verb "put" is satisfied by supplying a locative. Sentence (25a) satisfies this restriction by replacing the locative with a locative wh-word.

(25a) Where did she put the book?

*(25b) Why did she put the book?

Word Order. In this last rule type, basic word order rules are tested. Sentences of three types were used: intransitive (NP–V), transitive (NP–V–NP), and dative (NP–V–NP–NP). Within each type, the ungrammatical sentences were formed by systematically rearranging the verbs and noun phrases so that all of the possible orders of constituents occurred. Thus the simplest ill-formed sentence involves the reversal of an NP and intransitive verb, as in (26a) versus (26b); the most complex involves the rearrangement of NPs and V in double-object structures, as in (27a) versus (27b).

> (26a) The woman paints.
> *(26b) Paints the woman.
> (27a) Martha asked the policeman a question.
> *(27b) Martha a question asked the policeman.

Design

The test was divided into two halves. An equal number of exemplars of each rule type and subrule type were represented in each half. The grammatical and ungrammatical members of a pair were in opposite halves of the test. Within each half, sentences were randomized in such a way that no rule type was concentrated in one section of the test, and no run of grammatical or ungrammatical sentences was longer than four.

Results

Age of acquisition

Age of acquisition and ultimate performance. The primary questions of this study involved examining the relationship between age of learning English as a second language and performance on the test of English grammar. The results show a clear and strong relationship between age of arrival in the United States and performance. Subjects who began acquiring English in the United States at an earlier age obtained higher scores on the test than those that began later, $r = -0.77$, $P < 0.01$.

A more detailed understanding of this relationship can be gained from table 3 and figure 1. Subjects were grouped by age of arrival into categories similar to those used in past research (e.g. Snow and Hoefnagel-Hohle, 1978). Table 3 presents the mean score, standard deviation, and the ranges of the number of correct responses and the number of errors for each group and for the native English comparison group. The means are also presented graphically figure 1. The adjacent age groups were compared, two at a time, by a set of two-sample t tests using separate variance estimates.[5]

The first comparison involved determining whether there was any difference between the age 3-7 group and the native group in their performance in English. The two groups were not significantly different from each other, $t(10.4) = 1.28$, $P > 0.05$; indeed, the two groups were entirely overlapping in performance. In contrast, all of the other age groups performed significantly below the natives (for natives *vs* the next closest group (8–10), $t(8.1) = 6.67$, $P < 0.01$). This suggests that, if one is immersed in a second language before the age of seven, one is able to achieve native fluency in the language;[6] however, immersion even soon after that age results in a decrement in ultimate performance.

Table 3   Mean scores of nonnative and native speakers of English

		Age of arrival			
	Natives (n = 23)	*3–7* (n = 7)	*8–10* (n = 8)	*11–15* (n = 8)	*17–39* (n = 23)
Means	268.8	269.3	256.0	235.9	210.3
SD	2.9	2.8	6.0	13.6	22.8
Range	275–265	272–264	263–247	251–212	254–163
(Errors)	(1–11)	(4–12)	(13–29)	(25–64)	(22–113)

Note: Maximum score = 276

Given that the 3–7 group is the only group that reached native performance, it is perhaps not surprising that the different between the means of the 3–7 and 8–10 age groups is significant, $t(10) = 5.59$, $P > 0.01$. As can be seen in table 3, while the absolute difference between the means of these two groups is small, both groups have very small SDs, and the range of scores for the 3–7 group is entirely nonoverlapping with the 8–10 group. All of the later adjacent age groups are also significantly different from each other. The age 8–10 group obtained higher scores than the 11–15 group, $t(9.7) = 3.83$, $P < 0.01$, with almost nonoverlapping distributions between the two groups, and the age 11-15 group obtained higher scores than the 17–39 (adult) group, $t(21) = 3.78$, $P < 0.01$.

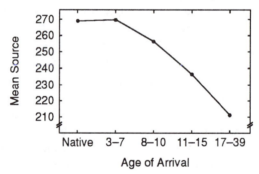

Figure 1   The relationship between age of arrival in the United States and total score correct on a test of English grammar.

In sum, there appears to be a strong linear relationship between age of exposure to the language and ultimate performance in the language, up to adulthood. In the next section we examine the shape of this function in more detail.

The effects of age of acquisition before versus after puberty. An important question to answer is whether, throughout adulthood, performance continues to decline as a function of age of exposure or whether it plateaus at some point (H. Gleitman, personal communication). If the explanation for late learners' poorer performance relates to maturation, performance should not continue to decline over age, for presumably there are not many important maturational differences between, for example, the brain of a 17 year old and the brain of a 27 year old. Instead, there should be a consistent decline in performance over age for those exposed to the language before puberty, but no systematic relationship to age of exposure, and a leveling off of ultimate performance, among those exposed to the language after puberty. This is precisely what was found.

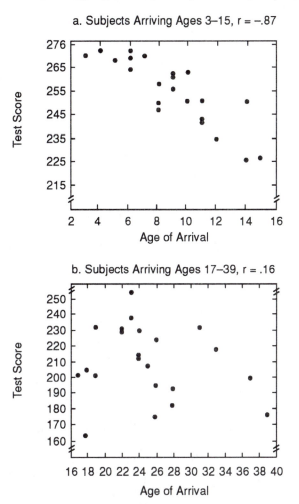

a. Subjects Arriving Ages 3–15, r = −.87

b. Subjects Arriving Ages 17–39, r = .16

* Note: The Y-axes are on different scales.

Figure 2   Scatterplots of test score in relation to age of arrival for subjects arriving in the USA before versus after puberty.

Subjects were divided into two groups in terms of age of exposure, from age 3–15, versus 17–39, with an equal number of subjects ($N = 23$) in each group. The correlations between age of exposure and performance for these two groups were strikingly different. For the group first exposed to English between the ages of 3 and 15, the correlation was − 0.87, $P < 0.01$. Note that this correlation is even more substantial than that for the subjects as a whole. In contrast, for the group first exposed to English between the ages of 17 and 39, there is no significant correlation, $r = -0.16$, $P > 0.05$. Scatterplots demonstrating this effect are presented in figure 2a and b.

Age of acquisition and variance in ultimate performance. Another age-related result, which is obvious from inspecting the scatterplots of figure 2 and the SDs in table 3, is the heterogeneous variance. For groups who acquired English at early ages, the variance is very small; with increasing age of exposure, variance gets larger, creating a megaphone shape, so that for subjects exposed to English after 15 the variance is very large. Note that it would have been quite possible to find that the means of these groups increased but the variance stayed constant over the age groups. The heterogeneity of variance obtained, and the relation between age of acquisition and variance, is an independent result.

This heterogeneity of variance underscores two simple but important points:

1. Before age 15, and most particularly before age 10, there are very few individual differences in ultimate ability to learn language within any particular age group; success in learning is almost entirely predicted by the age at which it begins.

2. For adults, later age of acquisition determines that one will not become native or near-native in a language; however, there are large individual variations in ultimate ability in the language, within the lowered range of performance.

Age of exposure to format instruction. It has been assumed thus far that age of arrival in the United States is the best measure of age of exposure to the language. For early arrivals it is the only measure available, since these subjects had no prior experience with English at all. However, for the late arrivals there are two measures possible: age of arrival in the United States, or age of beginning English instruction in school within the native country. There is already a high correlation between age of arrival and test score for the subjects as a whole, $r = -0.77$; if age of classes is a better measure of first exposure for the late arrivals, then the correlation should be even higher when using that as a measure of time of exposure. This is not what was found. The correlation for the subjects as a whole between age of exposure, defined as classes or immersion (whichever came first), and test score is -0.67. These correlations, however, are not statistically different from each other, $t(43) = 1.26$, $P > 0.05$. This is not surprising since, due to the early arrivals, half of the measurements are exactly the same; moreover, most of the late arrivals are defined as later learners (pubescent or postpubescent) either way they are measured. Because of this overlap in measurement, the best way to evaluate the effect of age of classes is to do so using only the subjects who had classroom instruction. For these subjects alone ($N = 23$), the correlation between age of classes and test score is -0.33, which is not significant, $P > 0.05$.

This result has two implications. First, it means that we are using the right measure for "age of exposure"; age of arrival in the United States, with its resulting immersion in English, is more strongly related to ultimate performance in English than is age of beginning formal English instruction. More profoundly, it means that the learning which occurs in the formal language classroom may be unlike the learning which occurs during immersion, such that early instruction does not necessarily have the advantage for ultimate performance that is held by early immersion. It should be noted, however, that this last conclusion may be limited by the relatively narrow age range for formal instruction found in our subjects: our subjects all began their English classes between the ages of 7 and 16, with most subjects beginning at ages 12–15. This conclusion may also be restricted to the type of formal instruction received in Chinese and Korean schools (and, of course, any other schools in which the instruction is similarly formal), and should be less true the more formal instruction approximates immersion in the United States. In any event, age of arrival in the United States appears to be the better measure of age of acquisition for the population we studied.

Experiential and attitudinal variables

Experiential variables. Years of exposure in the United States was also a variable of interest in this study. First, careful attention was paid to balance the years of exposure between early and late learners. This was done in order to avoid the possibility that obtained age effects would be due to differences in years of exposure, rather than to true differences in age of exposure. That we were successful in controlling for years of exposure between the early and late learners is apparent from the lack of correlation between age of arrival and years in the US, $r = -0.09$, $P > 0.05$.

Beyond controlling for this potential confound, it is also important to ask what effect years of exposure has on learning, independent of the age effects. It is known that number of years has some effect on subjects' competence during the initial stages of learning a second language (see, for example, Snow and Hoefnagel-Hohle, 1978). At an extreme, people who have been in a host country for one and a half years must perform better than those who have only been there half a year. The question here is, however, do people continue to improve over time through continued exposure to the language, or do they reach an asymptote after a certain number of years? To answer this question, a correlation coefficient was computed between years of exposure in the United States and test performance. The resulting correlation, $r = 0.16$, is not significant, $P > 0.05$ (see also table 4). This is in agreement with other studies (Oyama, 1978; Patkowski, 1980), also showing no significant effect of the number of years of exposure on language performance for learners beyond the first few years of exposure.

In addition to years of exposure, table 4 also presents other variables which we considered possible experiential correlates with ultimate performance, such as amount of initial exposure to English, classroom experience, and attitude. Most of these variables were computed from information provided by the subjects; amount of initial exposure (measured as the percentage of time English was used during the first year or two in the United States) and motivation to learn in English classes (rated 1 to 5) were estimates provided by the subjects. None of the correlations are significant.

Regarding amount of initial exposure, the mean percentage for the group is 51.4 percent, with a standard deviation of 20.2 percent. Unless subjects' estimates are inaccurate, it appears that ultimate performance is not sensitive to fairly large differences in amount of initial exposure to the language, at least not after the subjects have been immersed in the language for a number of years.

Table 4   Correlation coefficients of experimental variables with score

Interview variable	Correlation w/score
Length of exposure (years in the USA)	0.16
Amount of initial exposure (first year or two in USA)	0.03
Age of English classes[a]	−0.33
Years of English classes[a]	0.25
Motivation to learn in classes[a]	0.05

[a] Correlation for late learners only; measure not applicable to other subjects.

The classroom variables include the age at which the subjects began English classes in their native country (already discussed in the previous section), the number of years they took English classes, and their ratings of how motivated they were to learn English in the classroom. Again, none of these variables correlates significantly with performance. It may be of interest for future research, however, that age of starting English classes is the highest of the (nonsignificant) experiential correlations. This may suggest some benefit of early classroom exposure, if classroom exposure occurred earlier than in the population we studied, and particularly if the classroom were more like immersion.

Attitudinal variables. Some investigators (see Schumann, 1975, and Krashen, 1982, for reviews) have suggested that age effects are secondary by-products of changes in people's level of self-consciousness, in their cultural identification, and in their motivation to learn a second language well, rather than maturational changes in learning. To address this claim, correlation and regression analyses were performed. Table 5 presents correlations of such attitudinal variables with test score as well as with age of arrival. These variables were measured by asking subjects to rate themselves according to the questions presented at the bottom of table 5.

The correlations show a strong relationship between these attitudinal variables and both test score and age of arrival. Higher ratings of American identification and increased measures of motivation were associated with better performance in English and with younger age of arrival, while higher ratings of self-consciousness were associated with poorer performance and with later age of arrival. Both of these sets of results would be predicted by a theory which attempted to explain age differences in language learning as a function of attitudinal variables correlated with age, rather than a function of maturation. The other possibility is, of course, the reverse; the attitudinal variables may have obtained their correlations with test score as a result of the correlation with age of arrival. Thus it becomes a question as to which is the better measure: age of arrival or attitudinal variables?

Table 5 Correlation coefficients of attitudinal variables with test score and age of arrival

Attitudinal variables	Test score	Age of arrival
Identification	0.63**	−0.55**
Self-consciousness	−0.36*	0.19
Motivation	0.39**	−0.48**

* P < 0.05.

** P < 0.01.

Questions:

1 How strongly would you say you identify with American culture? (subject's reply). If 5 means you identify with the American culture, that is, you feel like a complete American, and 1 means not at all, how would you rate your identification?

2 Did you feel self-conscious while learning English in the United States? (most often an explanation was needed here). How would you rate that on a scale from 1 to 5, where 5 is very self-conscious and 1 is not at all?

3 Motivation is a composite of two questions. (a) Is it important to you to be able to speak English well? (subject's reply). On a scale of 1 to 5, where 5 means very important and 1 means not at all, how would you rate it? (b) Do you plan on staying in the United States? The composite was formed by adding one point to their importance rating if they planned on staying in the United States, and by subtracting one point if they did not.

It is clear that age of arrival is the better measure over any of the attitudinal variables considered alone. The correlation between age of arrival and test score ($r = -0.77$) surpasses the correlation between any of the attitudinal variables and test score. Furthermore, the attitudinal variables are more adversely affected when age of arrival is partialled out than is age of arrival when each of the attitudinal variables is partialled out, as shown in table 6. This is in complete agreement with Oyama's (1978) results.

As stated earlier, however, the most powerful evidence against this alternative hypothesis is to show that age of arrival can account for variance not accounted for by the attitudinal variables combined. To test this, a regression analysis was performed using the three attitudinal variables together, which resulted in a regression coefficient of 0.47. This was compared to the 0.69 regression coefficient obtained with the three attitudinal variables plus age of arrival. The contribution made by age of arrival is statistically significant $F(1,41) = 28.1$, $P < 0.01$. This shows that, independent of any possible attitudinal effects, age of arrival has an effect on learning a second language.

Table 6 Partial correlation of age of arrival and attitudinal variables with test score

	Attitudinal variables w/age of arrival removed	Age of arrival w/attitudinal variables removed
Identification	0.39*	−0.65**
Self-consciousness	−0.34*	−0.76**
Motivation	−0.04	−0.72**

* P < 0.05.

** P < 0.01.

Of independent interest is whether the attitudinal variables can account for any of the variance not accounted for by age of arrival. Even though it is clear that age of exposure to a language is an important variable for predicting ultimate performance, other variables may contribute to this as well. Unlike previous studies (e.g. Oyama, 1978), we did find added predictive value with two attitudinal variables: self-consciousness and American identification. Each of the two makes a significant contribution to a regression model including only age of arrival ($F(1,43) = 5.6$, $P < 0.05$, for self-consciousness, and $F(1,43) = 7.5$, $P < 0.05$, for identification), as well as a significant contribution to a regression model including age of arrival and the other attitudinal variable ($F(1,42) = 5.0$, $P < 0.05$, for the addition of self-consciousness to age plus identification, and $F(1,42) = 6.9$, $P < 0.05$, for the addition of identification to age plus self-consciousness). Motivation, whether analyzed separately or in conjunction with the other two variables, failed to add significantly to the regression coefficient. Thus it appears at first glance that a model of second language learning would have to include both age effects and the effects of self-consciousness and identification, though not the effects of motivation. Such a model might argue, for example, that while age of arrival affects language learning, so does the self-consciousness and the cultural identification of the learner.

At this time one might, however, be cautious about inferring a direct causal link between self-consciousness and cultural identification to language learning, until this result is corroborated in future studies. Not only are the effects of self-consciousness and cultural identification not supported in other studies, but also possible mediating variables have not been ruled out. For example, language performance may be correlated with subjects' evaluation of their performance, which may in turn affect how self-conscious they are and how much they identify with the host country. Thus poorer learners may, as a result of their performance problems, become more self-conscious and identify less with the United States. In this account, greater self-conscious and less identification would be the result rather than the cause of the performance problems. In any case, apart from whether attitudinal variables do or do not play a role, there is a clear independent effect of age of arrival on ultimate performance.

Age of acquisition and rule type

The results show a striking effect of age of acquisition on performance in our test of English syntax and morphology. It is of interest to know what particular areas of the grammar create the most and least problems for second language learners. Are the errors random, with an even dispersal across rule type, or do late learners err more frequently on a particular type of rule? To answer this question, an analysis was performed on age of learning in relation to the differing types of rules evaluated on the test. This analysis used only the ungrammatical items, since it is only the ungrammatical items which can be said to be testing any particular rule type. That is, when a subject marks a grammatical sentence as ungrammatical, it is unclear what part of the sentence, or grammar, (s)he is having problems with. In contrast, when a subject marks an ungrammatical sentence as grammatical, (s)he must have failed to represent just that structure under test as a native speaker would. For purposes of this analysis, the age groups were the same as those used previously, except that the late learner group was further divided into two groups, (17–24) and (25–39), with an approximately equal number of subjects in each. This was done to reach a more nearly equal number of subjects in each of the age of learning groups. A two-way analysis of variance was performed, using the 12 rule types (outlined in the Methods section above) and six ages of acquisition.

The results of the anova showed a significant effect of rule type F (11,693) = 53.2, $P < 0.01$, a significant effect of age of acquisition. $F(5,63) = 32.3$, $P < 0.01$, and an interaction between rule type and age of acquisition, $F(55,693) = 8.3$, $P < 0.01$. The age effect here is simply a reproduction of the finding that early learners perform better than the late learners; apparently there is no reduction of this effect when scoring only the ungrammatical test items. The effect of rule type shows that subjects made more errors on certain rule types than on others. Finally, the interaction appears mainly to be the result of late learners making proportionately more errors on some rule types, and proportionately fewer on others. Thus, many of the late learners' errors do not appear to be random; rather, there are particular parts of the grammar that seem more difficult.

The pattern of errors for each age group across the 12 rule types can be seen in figure 3. In figure 3, rule types are ordered along the x-axis in decreasing order of difficulty for later learners.[7] As can be seen, determiners and plural morphology appear to be the most difficult for the two latest groups of learners, with scores significantly worse than chance for determiners ($t = 3.35$, $P < 0.01$), and no different from chance for plurals ($t = 0.16$, $P > 0.05$). While all of the remaining rule types receive scores significantly better than chance (t ranges from 3.46 to 26.1, $P < 0.01$), they vary widely in level of performance. Most notably, basic word order rules and the present progressive are giving very few problems, with most subjects getting virtually all of the items of these types correct.[8]

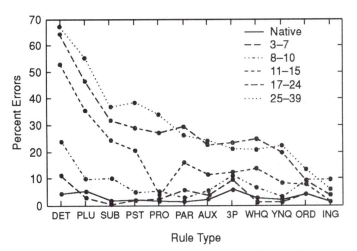

Figure 3   **Mean percentage of errors in 12 types of English rules.**

Why are subjects performing better on some rule types and worse on others? One uninteresting possibility is that the items testing some rule types are inherently easier than those testing other rule types, since in some cases different rules are tested by quite different sentential variations. On the other hand, it is clear that this is not the whole account of our effects. Rule types tested in very similar ways on our test (e.g. the various rule types involving morphology) did not show similar degrees of difficulty for late learners, suggesting that these rule type effects are not due to the difficulty of the format by which we tested the rules.

A second possibility is that the subjects suffered from phonological difficulties which made the items for that rule type difficult to process. Again, although we cannot definitely eliminate this possibility, we do not believe it is the whole account of the rule type effects. Rule types with exactly the same phonological form (e.g. plural and third person singular, both -s) did not show similar degrees of difficulty for late learners. Also, rule types testing forms which were phonologically more substantial and therefore easier to hear (e.g. rule types with whole words reversed or eliminated) were not necessarily easier for late learners than those that involved smaller phonological units.

A third possibility is that subjects suffered from interference from the nature of their first language (Chinese or Korean), and so should show special difficulty with rule types most different from the first language. Once again this did not appear to be the full account of our effects. Rule types equally absent from Chinese and Korean (e.g. past tense and present progressive) did not show similar degrees of difficulty for late learners.

Most important, our rule type ordering corresponds in certain striking ways to the order of difficulty obtained in studies of second language learners from other first language backgrounds, as well as in studies of the isolated girl Genie. In particular, the relative ease of word order and the present progressive show up in all of these studies. We believe, then, that the rule type effects we obtained are at least in part reflections of what is generally difficult or easy for a late learner. We will return to this issue in the Discussion section below.

One final question involved the relationship between age of arrival and each of the individual rule types. Given that late learners' competence varies over rule types, it is of interest to know whether age of arrival predicts performance on only certain selected rules of the second language. The data show, however, that this is not the case. Table 7 presents the correlations between age of arrival and the scores on each of the 12 rule types. Despite late learners' proficiency on some rule types, all of the rule types showed significant correlations with age of arrival. This result shows that age of exposure to the language affects all of the structures we examined, despite variations across rule types in the absolute level of performance late learners achieved.

Table 7   Correlation coefficients between age of arrival and rule type[a]

Rule type	Correlations
Determiners	0.64**
Plural	0.75**
Subcategorization	0.53**
Past tense	0.79**
Pronouns	0.73**
Particles	0.44**
Auxiliaries	0.45**
Third person singular	0.29*
Wh-questions	0.39**
Yes/no questions	0.50**
Word order	0.48**
Present progressive	0.32*

[a] These correlations, unlike others with age of arrival, are positive correlations, since they relate age of arrival to number of errors.

* $P < 0.05$.

** $P < 0.01$.

Discussion

This study was designed to answer certain empirical questions about critical period effects in second language learning, and thereby to clarify and refine theoretical proposals regarding a critical period for language acquisition more generally. We will begin our discussion by reviewing the empirical findings and then turn to the general theoretical issues.

The basic empirical findings

Age of acquisition and ultimate performance. The first question we asked was whether there was a relation between age of acquisition and ultimate performance in the grammar of a second language. The results of this study clearly show such a relation, and therefore support the notion that children have an advantage over adults in acquiring a second language. The overall correlation between age of arrival in the United States and performance on our test of English grammar was − 0.77; and, for those subjects arriving in the United States before puberty, this correlation was − 0.87. Indeed, there was a significant correlation between age of arrival and performance on every type of syntactic and morphological rule we tested.

These findings are in accord with the results of the previous studies which have tested asymptotic performance, despite the fact that these studies used very different measures of English proficiency. (Oyama, (1978) measured number of words detected through white noise; Patkowski (1980) measured syntactic ratings of production.) The 'present study enhances the previous studies' findings by providing a much more detailed examination of English syntax and morphology. The three studies, however, complement each other well, for each emphasizes a different aspect of language use. Oyama's study, for example, taps some aspect of on-line processing in comprehension. Patkowski's measures free production, and in our study we presume to be measuring underlying grammatical competence via sentence judgements. Because these studies complement each other, the compatibility of the results is all the more impressive. Together they provide a strong case for the conclusion that children are indeed better than adults in their ultimate attainment in a second language.

The effects of age of acquisition before versus after puberty. The second question we asked concerned the shape of the relationship between age of acquisition and ultimate performance. Due to the large range of ages in the learners we tested, and our division of the early learners into small age groups, we are able to make a fairly good generalization about the shape of this relationship. Subjects who arrived in the United States before the age of seven reached native performance on the test. For arrivals after that age, there was a linear decline in performance up through puberty. Subjects who arrived in the United States after puberty performed on the average much more poorly than those who arrived earlier. After puberty, however, performance did not continue to decline with increasing age. Instead, the late arrival groups while performing on the whole more poorly than the younger arrivals, distinguished itself by having marked individual differences in performance, something which was not found in the earlier arrivals.

The pattern of this relationship supports a maturational account of the age effects found. It does this by the fact that the age effect is present during a time of ongoing biological and cognitive maturation and absent after maturation is complete (i.e. at puberty). Thus it appears as if language learning ability slowly declines as the human matures and plateaus at a low level after puberty. The precise level of this plateau differs between individuals.

Again, these findings are in line with previous studies, although no previous study has asked this question in detail. Both Oyama (1978) and Patkowski (1980) reported only overall correlations and grouped means, with groupings which were larger and slightly different from our own and with a more limited range of ages of acquisition than our own. Both studies found the general linear decline of performance with age of acquisition that we found, but the groupings of their subjects make it difficult to tell whether the precise ages at which we found changes in the function are supported by their results as well. In addition, in a study of age of acquisition in relation to first (rather than second) language acquisition, Newport and Supalla (1987) and Newport (1984) found a linear decline in ultimate performance over three age groups: subjects exposed to American Sign Language from birth *vs* at age 4-6 *vs* after age 12.[9] In short, the surrounding literature on both first and second language acquisition appears to be generally consistent with the more detailed results obtained in the present study.

Experiential and attitudinal variables. The third question we asked was whether the effects of age of acquisition could be due to experiential or attitudinal variables coincidentally related to age, rather than to maturational changes in language learning. Our results suggest that entirely nonmaturational explanations for the age effects would be difficult to support. Certainly the attitudinal variables (motivation, American identification, and self-consciousness) were unable to explain away the age effects, in accord with Oyama's (1978) study. This held true in the present data even when all three variables together were pitted against age.

It is also doubtful that the age effects are the result of differences in the amount of English exposure between the younger and older arrivals. This is true for several reasons. First, the younger arrivals did not differ significantly, if at all, from the adult arrivals in the amount of English they were exposed to during learning (see the Method section for description of the subjects' experiential characteristics). Second, the nonsignificant correlation between amount of initial exposure and performance suggests that second language learning is not particularly sensitive to differences in the amount of exposure, at least when that exposure has occurred over a number of years and is fairly high in the first place.

Some researchers have claimed that there are differences in the quality of the exposure that adults and children receive, rather than in the mere quantity, and that this difference may account for the age differences found in language learning success. According to this view, children receive the ideal type of input for successful language learning, while adults do not. Many have said, for example, that children receive "simple," reduced input which refers to concrete objects, existing in the here and now. Adults, on the other hand, are exposed to syntactically more complex input which most often refers to abstract concepts and events that are displaced in space and time. The simple concrete input of the child is thought to be helpful for language acquisition, while the complex input of the adult is thought to interfere with language acquisition (Dulay *et al.*, 1982).

Both the empirical and theoretical assumptions underlying this approach have been disputed. First, the assumption that language is easier to learn from limited simple input has been questioned (Wexler and Culicover, 1980; Gleitman *et al.*, 1984). Second, the empirical evidence for this claim has also been brought into question. Freed (1980) performed a study which compared the type of input given to adult and child second language learners and found that adults and children actually receive comparable input in terms of syntactic complexity (as measured by the number of clause boundaries). Interestingly, however, the adult-directed input contained a more limited range of constructions than the child-directed input. Adults received input which tended to maintain the canonical shape of a sentence, while children received sentences with more deformations. Thus in terms of transformational complexity, adults received the simpler input. From this it would be just as reasonable to argue that adults learn less well because their input is not as complex and varied as the child's. In any case, the role of input in second language learning needs to be better formulated before we can decide whether children have any advantage in learning a language due to the type of input they receive.

Age of acquisition and rule type. The fourth question we asked concerned the nature of the effects of age on the attained grammar of the second language. Our results suggested that, although there was an effect of age of acquisition on every rule type we examined, some rules of English grammar were more profoundly affected by age of acquisition than others. In particular, knowledge of the basic word order of the language was acquired by all of our subjects, regardless of their age of learning. Similarly, knowledge of the present progressive (-ing) was acquired by all of our subjects. These areas of competence likewise appear in other studies of second language learning (see Krashen (1982) for a review of the order of morpheme difficulty in second language learning). Perhaps even more striking, they are the only two aspects of English which were successfully acquired by Genie, who was exposed to English as a first language only after puberty (Curtiss, 1977; Goldin-Meadow, 1978). In contrast, other aspects of English syntax and morphology gave late learners much more difficulty.

We believe that these rule type results are at least in part reflections of universal factors in learnability, and not merely the result of item difficulty or transfer from the first language. Newport *et al.* (1977), Gleitman *et al.* (1984), and Goldin-Meadow (1978) have suggested that basic word order is a highly resilient property of languages, appearing in the acquisition of a first language under widely varying conditions of both input and age of exposure. The present results on the acquisition of a second language under varying conditions of age of exposure are in accord with these claims. However, accounting for why word order and -ing are particularly easy for learners remains for future research.

Before turning to a more general discussion of critical period hypotheses in language learning, we must consider whether the set of results we have obtained will be replicable on other second language learning groups or whether they are confined in any way to the particular second language learners (Chinese and Koreans) we have studied.

Possible effects of the first language on second language learning. We have thus far presented our results as though the findings were generalizable to second language learning, regardless of the nature of the first language or the relationship between the grammar of the first language and that of the second language. Indeed we believe this is the case, although we also recognize that certain aspects of the structure of one's first language are likely to have some effects on the learning of the second language (see, for example, Zehler (1987) and Hakuta and Cancino (1977) for a review of transfer effects in second language learning). Here we wish to raise two points of relevance to the question of whether our results are limited in any way to the Chinese and Korean speakers we studied.

First, we do not believe that the relationship found here between age of exposure and ultimate performance in the second language is unique to the circumstances where Chinese or Korean is the first language and English is the second. We did purposely choose to concentrate on first and second languages where the grammars were sufficiently different that a significant second language learning problem would arise. Chinese and Korean are relatively more isolating languages than English and have syntaxes which are different in many ways from that of English. However, studies currently underway, as well as certain details of our present results, suggest that the basic findings do not depend on these particular language combinations.

Several studies in progress (Johnson and Newport, in press) examine performance on our test by subjects with a wide variety of first languages. It is too early to say from these data whether there is any effect of the nature of the first language (we expect that there might be); however, it is already clear that the strong correlation between age of arrival and test performance replicates with subjects from these other first-language backgrounds.

In addition, the detailed results of the present study suggest that the nature of the first language cannot fully explain the difficulties of the second language learner. The examination of performance on the 12 rule types reveals relationships to age of arrival on every structure we examined, regardless of how similar or different these structures were to ones in the first language. For example, determiners and plural inflection, which gave late learners their most serious difficulties on our test, are notably lacking in Chinese and Korean; but so are inflections for the present progressive, on which late learners performed exceptionally well. A more detailed understanding of which of our effects, if any, may arise from first language characteristics should emerge from our studies in progress.

Second, we do not believe that our results derive in any important way from the input or cultural circumstances which characterize Chinese and Korean speakers. The Chinese and Korean speakers we tested were perhaps unusual, compared with many second language learners of English, in that they often continued close associations with other speakers of their first language. One might wonder, therefore, whether their exposure to English or their maintenance of their first language somehow influenced their second language learning. Again, this is an empirical question which is best resolved by the results of our studies in progress, which include many speakers isolated from their first language group as well as speakers of first languages with large communities. Within the present study, all of our subjects (both early and late learners) continued speaking their first language with their families and others into adulthood, and all were exposed to English from native English speakers. In addition, all had a significant amount of exposure to English, since they were all active members of an English-speaking community (that is, American schools and universities). These factors therefore could not be responsible for the differences we found between early and late learners of English. Whether these factors have an additional effect on learning, beyond the effect of age of exposure, was not the focus of our study, although some of our results do bear on this question.

In sum, we believe that in other language groups the strong effects of age of acquisition may be accompanied by effects of input, first language typology, or other variables that do not appear in our data on Chinese and Korean learners. Most importantly, however, we have reason to expect, on the basis of our data, that these effects of age of acquisition will persist.

Theoretical conclusions for a crtical period hypothesis in language acquisition

The present study was performed primarily for the purpose of understanding the nature of the critical period for language acquisition. In particular, we wanted first to discover whether the critical period occurs at all in second language acquisition or whether it is exclusively a first-language phenomenon. To delineate this distinction we began by presenting two possible versions of a critical period hypothesis. They are repeated here for convenience.

Version one: the exercise hypothesis. Early in life, humans have a superior capacity for acquiring languages. If the capacity is not exercised during this time, it will disappear or decline with maturation. If the capacity is exercised, however, further language learning abilities will remain intact throughout life.

Version two: the maturational state hypothesis. Early in life, humans have a superior capacity for acquiring languages. This capacity disappears or declines with maturation.

To reiterate the differences between these two versions, the exercise hypothesis only requires that a first language be acquired during childhood; as long as this occurs the capacity for successful language learning will remain intact. Thus it predicts no differences between child and adult learners, due to maturation itself, in the ability to acquire a second language to native proficiency. In contrast, the maturational state hypothesis says that any language, be it first or second, must be acquired during childhood in order for that language to develop fully. Our results support the maturational state hypothesis, and not the exercise hypothesis. Human beings appear to have a special capacity for acquiring language in childhood, regardless of whether the language is their first or second.

The maturational state hypothesis is, however, not itself an explanation of critical period phenomena in language; rather, it merely outlines a class of explanations which would be compatible with our results (namely, those which posit maturational changes in general language learning abilities). In order to approach a more precise theoretical account of the phenomena, our study has also provided additional information which should aid in understanding the nature of the critical period: namely, information about the shape of the function relating age of acquisition and ultimate performance. Our results provide three sets of facts which any theory regarding critical periods would have to account for: the gradual decline of performance, the age at which a decline in performance is first detected, and the nature of adult performance.

The gradual decline of performance. Lenneberg's original proposal of a critical period in language acquisition seemed to predict a rectangular function in the relationship between age of acquisition and ultimate performance. That is, Lenneberg hypothesized that "normal" language learning was possible during the period from infancy to puberty, with a loss of abilities after puberty. However, the data on second language learning in the present study did not have this shape. We did not find a flat relationship between performance and age of learning throughout childhood, with a sudden drop in performance marking the end of the critical period; instead, performance gradually declined from about age seven on, until adulthood. Insofar as such data are available from other studies of first and second language acquisition, the same linear trend seems to appear (Oyama, 1978; Patkowski, 1980; Newport, 1984; Newport and Supalla, 1987).

Although this gradual decline is not in accord with Lenneberg's implied function, it is in accord with results from other behavioral domains in which critical periods have been hypothesized. As research accumulates on critical periods, whether it be in imprinting in ducks (Hess, 1973), socialization in dogs (Scott, 1978), or song learning in birds

(Kroodsma, 1981), it is becoming apparent that most, if not all, critical periods conform to the more gradual function. This point has recently been noted by several investigators (Tanner, 1970; Immelman and Suomi, 1981).

> usually these periods consist of . . . beginning and end parts . . . [during] which the organism is slightly sensitive to the specific influence, with a period of maximum sensitivity in the middle. It is not as a rule an all-or none phenomenon. (Tanner, 1970, p. 131)

Whatever mechanisms underlie a critical period effect in language learning, then, must be compatible with this gradual decline of performance over age.

The age at which a decline in performance is first detected. Lenneberg's proposal also seemed to imply that a decline in performance should first appear at puberty. Instead of puberty, we found a small but significant decline in performance in subjects who had arrived in the United States as early as age 8–10. Indeed, the only discrepancy we know of between our results and other data is that, in first language acquisition, this decline may occur even earlier (Newport, 1984; Newport and Supalla, 1987); in the Newport and Supalla data, a 4–6 age group scored consistently, although not always significantly, below native performance. It is possible that a similar early decline may occur in second language acquisition as well on a test that included more complex aspects of syntax than our own; on our present test, the age 3–7 group scored at ceiling.

Further research is therefore necessary to determine with certainty the exact point at which a decline in learning begins for second language acquisition. It is clear from the present data, however, that this decline begins well before puberty. It also appears that this early decline is small, and that another more major change occurs around puberty. Proposed mechanisms underlying a critical period effect in language learning must therefore account for the details of timing of these changes and, particularly, for the fact that the decline in learning ability begins earlier than initially thought by most researchers.

The nature of adult performance. There are two aspects of adult performance with which any theoretical account of the critical period must be compatible. The first is that language does not become totally unlearnable during adulthood. This has held true in all of the studies which have tested age differences in asymptotic performance, including both first and second language learning. In the present study, late learners scored significantly above chance on all of the rule types tested except for determiners and plurals. It appears to be the case, then, that quite a few aspects of language are learnable to a fair degree at any age, even though deficiencies in this learning occur.

The second aspect of adult performance with which any theory must be compatible is the great variability found among individuals. For adult learners, age does not continue to be a predictor of performance; thus any proposed mechanism accounting for adult performance likewise cannot be correlated with age. Moreover, while early learners are uniformly successful in acquiring their language to a high degree of proficiency, later learners show much greater individual variation (see also Patkowski, 1980, for related comments). A theoretical account of critical period effects in language learning must therefore consider whether the skills underlying children's uniformly superior performance are similar to those used by adult learners, or rather whether adult language learning skill is controlled by a different set of variables.

Final remarks on a critical period theory of language acquisition. In sum, we now have a number of findings which should be accounted for in any explanation of a critical period. There is the nature of the relationship between age of arrival and performance: a linear decline in performance up through puberty and a subsequent lack of linearity and great variability after puberty. There is also the pattern of errors found for the wide range of aspects of syntax and morphology of English studied: age effects were found for every rule type, with low levels of performance on every rule type except word order and present progressive. The primary and most general finding to accommodate for any critical period theory, of course, is that the critical period is not just a first language phenomenon, but extends to a second language as well.

These findings rule out certain types of accounts of critical period for language acquisition and make other types of accounts more plausible. We have suggested that our results are most naturally accommodated by some type of maturational account, in which there is a gradual decline in language learning skills over the period of on-going maturational growth and a stabilization of language learning skills at a low but variable level of performance at the final mature state. This leaves open, however, the precise explanation of such a phenomenon. The traditional view of critical period effects in language learning has been that there is maturational change in a specific language acquisition device (Lenneberg, 1967; Chomsky, 1981). Such a view, with some modifications to incorporate the detailed points of maturational change, is consistent with our results. Also consistent with our results are views which hypothesize more general cognitive changes over maturation (see, for example, Newport, 1984). From this view, an increase in certain cognitive abilities may, paradoxically, make language learning more difficult. We are hopeful that future research will provide more detailed results which may differentiate these views from one another. In any event, the present study makes clear that some type of critical period account for language acquisition is necessary and that the proper account of a critical period will include both first and second language in its effects.

Acknowledgements

This research was supported in part by NIH Grant NS16878 to E. Newport and T. Supalla, and by NIH Training Grant HD07205 to the University of Illinois. We are grateful to Geoff Coulter, Henry Gleitman, and all of the members of our research group for discussion of the issues raised here, to Lloyd Humphreys for advice on statistical matters, to Marcia Linebarger for the loan of test materials, and to Carol Dweck, John Flavell, Dedre Gentner, Doug Medin, and two anonymous reviewers for helpful comments on earlier drafts of this paper.

Notes

1. In this paper we use the term *critical period* broadly, for the general phenomenon of changes over maturation in the ability to learn (in the case under consideration in this paper, to learn language). We therefore include within this term maturational phenomena which other investigators have called sensitive, rather than critical, periods. By using the term in this broad fashion, we mean to avoid prejudging what the degree or quality of such maturational change may be (e.g. is it a sharp qualitative change *vs* a gradual quantitative one?) and what

the nature of the underlying maturational mechanism may be (e.g. is it a change in a special language faculty *vs* a more general change in cognitive abilities?). These further questions will be addressed in part by the nature of our findings, and in part by future research.

2. We thank Marcia Linebarger for making these and other tests available to us.

3. An additional six sentences, three ungrammatical and three the grammatical counterparts of these, were included in the test but were eliminated from scoring because native speakers of English made large numbers of errors in judging their grammaticality, due to either auditory problems or dialect variations.

4. The numbers of ungrammatical and grammatical sentences are unequal because some rule types have more than one grammatical sentence, or more than one ungrammatical sentence, within each set of counterparts (see, for example, the section on particle movement). For the most part, however, the grammatical and ungrammatical sentences form pairs, and for ease of presentation they will be referred to as "pairs" throughout the paper.

5. Using a two-sample t statistic where the variance of each group is estimated separately is appropriate whenever the population variances are not assumed to be equal, as is the case here.

6. It is always possible, however, that the equivalence in performance between natives and the 3–7 group is due to a ceiling effect on our test, and that tests of more complex aspects of English syntax would show differences even between these groups.

7. This ranking of rule type difficult remains the same when using other criteria; for example, ordering rule type according to the number of subjects who score almost perfectly on that rule (that is, 0 or 1 item wrong, out of 6 to 16 possible, depending on the rule type).

8. Some other rule type scores also benefited from subjects' apparent ease with basic word order rules. For example, those items testing yes/no question formation by presenting questions in a V-N-N order (e.g. "Learns Jane math from Mr Thompson?") were particularly easy for subjects. This pattern fits in with a general tendency for V-first items to be easily judged ungrammatical.

9. One discrepancy between the Newport and Supalla results for first language acquisition and the present results for second language acquisition is in the level of performance attained by subjects who began learning the language between the ages of 3 and 7. In the Newport and Supalla data, the 4–6 age group performed consistently, although not always significantly, below natives. In the present study, the 3–7 age group was entirely within native performance. This difference will be discussed below, in the section entitled "The age at which a decline in performance is first detected."

References

Asher, J., & Garcia, R. (1969) 'The optimal age to learn a foreign language'. *Modern Language Journal*, 53, 334-341.

Asher, J., & Price, B. (1967) 'The learning strategy of total physical response: Some age differences'. *Child Development*, 38, 1219-1227.

Chomsky, N. (1981) *Lectures on government and binding*. Dordrecht, Netherlands: Foris.

Curtiss, S. (1977) *Genie: A psycholinguistic study of a modern day "wild child."* New York: Academic Press.

Dulay, H., Burt, M., & Krashen, S. (1982) *Language two*. New York: Oxford University Press.

Freed, B. (1980) 'Talking to foreigners versus talking to children: Similarities and differences'. In R. Scarcella and S. Krashen (eds), *Research in second language acquisition*. Rowley, MA: Newbury House.

Goldin-Meadow, S. (1978) 'A study in human capacities'. *Science*, 200, 649-651.

Gleitman, L.R., Newport, E.L., & Gleitman, H. (1984) 'The current status of the motherese hypothesis'. *Journal of Child Language*, 11, 43-79.

Hakuta, K., & Cancino, H. (1977) 'Trends in second language acquisition research'. *Harvard Educational Review*, 47, 294-316.

Hess, E.H. (1973) *Imprinting*, New York: Van Nostrand.

Hubel, D., & Weisel, T. (1963) 'Receptive fields of cells in striate cortex of very young, visually inexperienced kittens'. *Journal of Neurophysiology*, 26, 994-1002.

Immelmann, K., & Suomi, S.J. (1981) 'Sensitive phases in development'. In K. Immelmann, G.W. Barlow, L. Petrinovich, & M. Main (eds), *Behavioral development: The Bielefeld Interdisciplinary Project*. Cambridge: Cambridge University Press.

Krashen, S. (1975) 'The development of cerebral dominance and language learning: More new evidence'. In D, Dato (ed.), *Developmental psycholinguistics: Theory and applications: Georgetown Round Table on Language and Linguistics*. Washington, DC: Georgetown University.

Krashen, S. (1982) 'Accounting for child-adult differences in second language rate and attainment'. In S. Krashen R. Scarcella, & M. Long (eds). *Child-adult differences in second language acquisition*. Rowley, MA: Newbury House.

Krashen, S., Long, M., & Scarcella, R. (1982) 'Age, rate, and eventual attainment in second language acquisition'. In S. Krashen, R. Scarcella, & M. Long (eds), *Child-adult differences in second language acquisition*. Rowley, MA: Newbury House.

Kroodsma, D.E. (1981) 'Ontogeny of bird song'. In K. Immelmann, G.W. Barlow, L. Petrinovich, & M. Main (eds), *Behavioral development: The Bielefeld Interdisciplinary Project*. Cambridge: Cambridge University Press.

Lenneberg, E. (1967) *Biological foundations of language*. New York: Wiley.

Linebarger, M.C., Schwartz, M.F., & Saffran, E.M. (1983) 'Sensitivity to grammatical structure in so-called grammatic aphasics'. *Cognition*, 13, 361-392.

Newport, E.L. (1984) 'Constraints on learning: Studies in the acquisition of American Sign Language'. *Papers and Reports on Child Language Development*, 23, 1-22.

Newport, E.L., Gleitman, H., & Gleitman, L.R. (1977) 'Mother, I'd rather do it myself: Some effects and non-effects of maternal speech style'. In C.E. Snow & C.A. Ferguson (eds.), *Talking to children: Language input and acquisition*. Cambridge: Cambridge University Press.

Newport, E.L. & Supalla, T. (1987) *A critical period effect in the acquisition of a primary language*. University of Illinois, manuscript under review.

Olson, L., & Samuels, S. (1973) 'The relationship between age and accuracy of foreign language pronunciation'. *Journal of Educational Research*, 66, 263-267.

Oyama, S. (1976) 'A sensitive period for the acquisition of a nonnative phonological system'. *Journal of Psycholinguistic Research*, 5, 261-285.

Oyama, S. (1978) 'The sensitive period and comprehension of speech'. *Working Papers on Bilingualism*, 16, 1-17.

Patkowski, M. (1980) 'The sensitive period for the acquisition of syntax in a second language'. *Language Learning*, 30, 339-472.

Schumann, J. (1975) 'Affective factors and the problem of age in second language acquisition'. *Language Learning*, 2, 209-235.

Scott, J.P. (1978) 'Critical periods for the development of social behavior in dogs'. In J.P. Scott (ed.), *Critical periods*. Stroudsburg, PA: Dowden, Hutchinson, & Ross.

Scott, J.P. (1980) 'The domestic dog: A case of multiple identities'. In. M.A. Roy (ed.), *Species identity and attachment: A phylogentic evaluation*. New York: Garland STPM Press.

Seliger, H., Krashen, S., & Ladefoged, P. (1975) 'Maturational constraints in the acquisition of a native-like accent in second language learning'. *Language Sciences*, 36, 20-22.

Snow, C. (1983) 'Age differences in second language acquisition: Research findings and folk psychology'. In. K. Bailey, M. Long, and S. Peck (eds), *Second language acquisition studies*. Rowley MA: Newbury House.

Snow, C., & Hoefnagel-Hohle, M. (1977) 'Age differences in pronuciation of foreign sounds'. *Language and Speech*, 20, 357-365.

Snow, C., & Hoefnagel-Hohle, M. (1978) 'The critical period for language acquisition: Evidence from second language learning'. *Child Development*, 49, 1114-1128.

Tanner, J.M. (1970) 'Physical growth'. In P.H. Mussen (Ed.), *Carmichael's manual of child psychology*. New York: Wiley.

Wexler, K., & Culicover, P. (1980) *Formal principles of language acquisition*. Cambridge, MA: The MIT Press.

Zehler, A.M. (1982) *The reflection of first language-derived experience in second language acquisition*. Unpublished doctoral dissertation, University of Illinois.

Cognitive Development in Childhood

Piaget's work on the middle-childhood, or primary school years, has received a lot of attention from psychologists and educationists: he coined the term 'concrete operations' to refer to the mental abilities that develop during these years prior to the 'emergence' of formal logical abilities in adolescence.

Concrete operations comprise mental activities (operations) that deal with physically present attributes. For example, a child in this stage of development may be able to understand that the time of arrival of an approaching car will be jointly determined by its speed and by its distance from its destination. However, the child will not understand the formal abstract properties of this relationship: i.e., that travel time = distance/velocity. Piaget was concerned with a number of evolving competences during this stage. Apart from the 'concrete' character of such intellectual competences, all concrete operations require the co-ordination of two or more sources of information. In the example of the approaching car, the child needs to co-ordinate distance and speed. According to Piaget, this ability does not begin to surface until the child is around seven years of age.

A number of researchers have claimed that the tasks used by Piaget to assess concrete operations contain confounding effects which artificially depress young children's performance. The articles by Hughes and Donaldson and by McGarrigle and Donaldson report their much-cited studies of concrete operations using modified tasks. In addition to focusing on the arguments and findings reported in these two papers, the reader is invited to examine how visual perspective-taking ability and conservation require integration of two sources of information, as argued by Piaget. The article by Demetre and Gaffin explores the implications of the Hughes and Donaldson work for our understanding of children's pedestrian accidents.

A second major approach to cognitive development is represented in the work of the Russian psychologist, Lev Vygotsky. Vygotsky argued that cognitive development is to be understood essentially as the internalisation of social intercourse, including language and various didactic routines. In this model of development, the child is viewed as an 'apprentice' to more experienced and more skilful members of the community, as opposed to the 'explorer' found in Piaget's model. Vygotsky's work has begun to have a major impact in developmental psychology in recent years, and a number of European and American researchers are currently elaborating on the theory and investigating the process by which social interaction facilitates cognitive changes. The two articles by Vygotsky provide a summary of some of his major views. The chapter by Rogoff provides a review of recent studies of 'guided participation', which is assumed to play a central role in Vygotsky's theory.

17. The Use of Hiding Games for Studying the Coordination of Viewpoints

Martin Hughes and Margaret Donaldson

One of Piaget's best known claims is that children below the age of six or seven years are highly egocentric, and cannot take account of another person's point of view (e.g. Piaget, 1926; Piaget & Inhelder, 1969). Piaget has devised several tasks for demonstrating the egocentrism of young children, one of which is the classic mountain task (Piaget & Inhelder, 1956, chapter 8).

The mountain task was designed to test whether young children could take another person's point of view in the literal sense of being able to calculate what that person could *see*. In a typical version of the task the child is seated before a model of three mountains, each of which is a different colour, and a doll is placed so that it is looking at the mountains from a different point of view. The child is shown a set of pictures of the mountains taken from different angles and is asked to choose the picture which shows what the doll sees. Piaget & Inhelder found that children below about eight years were unable to do this; indeed there was a powerful tendency among children below the age of six or seven to choose the picture showing their *own* point of view. This finding is extremely reliable, and has been replicated several times (e.g. Aebli, 1967; Dodwell, 1963; Garner & Plant, 1972).

Piaget & Inhelder concluded from their findings that the children's egocentrism was preventing them from working out what the doll could see: "the children . . . all really imagine that the doll's perspective is the same as their own, they all think the little man sees the mountains in the way they appear from where they themselves sit" (Piaget & Inhelder, 1956, p. 220). According to Piaget and Inhelder, the young child is unable to *decentre*: that is, he is unable to see his own viewpoint as one of a set of possible viewpoints, and to coordinate these different points of view into a single coherent system.

The child's performance on the mountain task would indeed seem to justify the conclusions of Piaget & Inhelder. However the mountain task is not the only way to test children's ability to recognise and coordinate different points of view. In the present paper we outline a different way of investigating these abilities.

In the studies described below the task is presented to the child as a hiding game. The child is asked to hide a small boy doll from one or more toy policemen who are 'looking for the boy'. In the first study the child has to do this by placing a small model wall between one of the policemen and the boy; in the other studies he has to hide the boy within various configurations of walls. Thus the child is not asked directly to calculate

Martin Hughes and Margaret Donaldson: 'The Use of Hiding Games for Studying the Coordination of Viewpoints'. *EDUCATIONAL REVIEW* (1979) Vol. 31. No. 2, pp. 133-140. Reprinted with permission of Carfax Publishing Company, PO Box 25, Abingdon, Oxfordshire OX14 3UE.

what the policemen can see. Nevertheless, this demand is implicit in the task: he cannot succeed without taking account of what the various policemen can see.

In choosing a task that in many ways resembles a game we were implicitly following the example of Peel (1967), who devised a game to investigate children's understanding of logical terms such as 'if . . . then . . .'. In Peel's game the experimenter and child took turns to put coloured beads or counters into a box, according to rules such as: 'If and whenever I draw a red bead you are not to draw a red counter'. Peel argued that games such as this are particularly useful for studying children's thinking skills, in that a formally complex task can be presented to children in a way that retains their interest and enjoyment. This belief also underlies the studies presented here.

Study One

The task used in our first study was the most straightforward of the three. The child was seated at a low table, in the middle of which were placed a policeman, the boy and a wall. The policeman and boy were about 6 cm high, and the wall was 7 cm high by 4 cm wide. The experimenter told the child that the policeman was looking for the boy, and that the boy wanted to hide from the policeman. The policemen and boy were then placed facing each other near the edge of the table, at P and B respectively (see Fig. 1(a)), and the child was asked to *put the wall so that the policeman cannot see the boy*. The child had thus to place the wall so that it blocked the line PB.

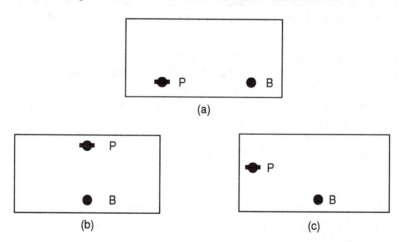

Figure 1   Positions of policeman (P) and boy (B) in Study One

The task was repeated for two more positions of the policeman and boy: first, with the line PB perpendicular to the edge of the table (Fig. 1(b)), and secondly, with the line PB across the corner of the table (Fig. 1(c)). We included this last position because of the claim by Piaget & Inhelder that young children find it particularly difficult to imagine a straight line across the corner of a table (Piaget & Inhelder, 1956, chapter 6). In each case the policeman and boy always faced each other and the child could always see the policeman's face.

These three versions of the task were given to a group of 10 three-year-olds (range 3 : 3 to 3 : 11, mean 3 : 8) and 10 four-year-olds (range 4 : 2 to 4 : 9, mean 4 : 6). Somewhat surprisingly, the children's performance was virtually errorless, with nine out of ten children in each age group placing the wall correctly in all versions of the task. There were no differences between the various versions of the task: all children, three- and four-year-olds alike, succeeded on the 'across the corner' version.

These results already make it clear that three- and four-year-old children can perform in a non-egocentric fashion in certain situations. None of the children showed any signs of confusing their own view of the boy with the policeman's view (for example, by placing the wall between *themselves* and the boy). All the children were clearly aware that placing the wall on the line PB prevented the policeman from seeing the boy, and the fact that the boy was still clearly visible to them did not seem to influence their judgements. Accordingly, we decided to use the same basic idea to see if young children could coordinate two different points of view at once.

Study Two

In the second study we used three small dolls — two policeman and a boy — and a cross-shaped configuration of walls (see Fig. 2). The children were asked to hide the boy from *both* the policeman, and thus had to keep in mind two different points of view at once.

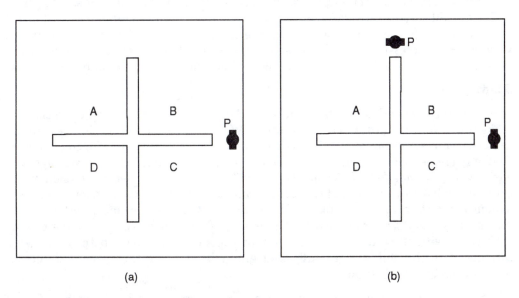

(a)   (b)

Figure 2   Positions of policemen (P) in Study Two

Each child was introduced to the task very carefully to give him every chance of fully understanding the situation. The experimenter placed the boy, the walls and a single policeman on the table and told the child, as in the first study, that the policeman was looking for the boy and that the boy wanted to hide from the policeman. The experimenter then arranged the walls and the policeman as shown in Fig. 2(a), so that the policeman could see into the sections marked B and C, but not into sections A and D. The boy doll was then placed in section A, and the child was asked 'can the policeman see the boy?' This was repeated for sections B, C and D in turn. The experimenter then moved the policeman to the opposite side, so that he could see into sections A and D, but not sections B and C. This time the child was asked to 'hide the boy so that the policeman can't see him'. If the child made any mistakes at these preliminary stages, his error was pointed out to him and the question repeated until the correct answer was given. But in fact very few mistakes were made (only 8% overall).

When it was clear that the child fully understood the situation, the experimenter brought out the other policeman, saying 'Here's another policeman. He is also looking for the boy. The boy must hide from BOTH policemen'. The two policemen were then positioned as shown in Fig. 2(b), leaving only section D unobserved. The child was asked to 'hide the boy so that BOTH the policemen can't see him'. This was repeated three times, each time leaving a different section as the only hiding place.

The task was given to 30 children aged between 3 : 6 and 4 : 11, with a mean age of 4 : 3. The overall success rate was again surprisingly high, with 22 children correct on all four trials, and five children correct on three out of four trials. The younger children were no less successful than the older ones, and it was clear that virtually all the children tested were able to take account of and coordinate two different points of view.

Study Three

In view of the ease with which the children had performed in Study Two, we decided to make the task even harder in the next study. We used two versions of the task. In the first, the wall arrangement had five sections, and the two policemen were positioned so that only one section was left unobserved (see Fig. 3(a)). The child's task was again to 'hide the boy so that BOTH the policemen can't see him'. In the second version of the task, the wall arrangement had six sections, and this time there were three policemen looking for the boy (see Fig. 3(b)). The child was asked to 'hide the boy so that NONE of the policemen can see him'. Each task consisted of four trials, corresponding to four different positions of the policeman. As in the previous study, both tasks were introduced to the children carefully and gradually, to give them every chance of understanding the situation.

The subjects in this study were 20 three-year-olds (range 3 : 1 to 3 : 11, mean 3 : 6) and 20 four-year-olds (range 4 : 0 to 4 : 9, mean 4 : 5). None of these children had been subjects in either of the two previous studies. The children were divided into two groups, matched as far as possible for age and sex. One group performed the first version of the task, while the other group performed the second version.

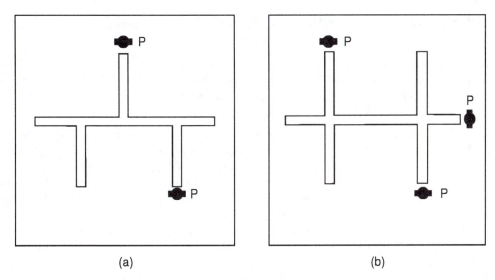

(a) (b)

Figure 3   Typical positions of policemen (P) in Study Three

Despite the increased complexity of the task, the four-year-olds still had little trouble with either version. Nine out of 10 four-year-olds made no errors at all on the five-section, two-policeman task, and eight out of 10 made no errors in the six-section, three-policemen task. The three-year olds had more difficulty with the tasks, although their performance was still fairly high: six out of 10 made one or no errors in the first task and seven out of 10 made one or no errors on the second task. The difference between three- and four-year-olds was significant at the 0.05 level for the first task only (U = 23, Mann-Whitney U test, two-tailed). As can be seen, there were no major differences between the two versions of the task. This finding was somewhat surprising as we had predicted that the three-policemen task would be harder than the two policemen task.

Very few of the errors produced by the three-year-olds could in any sense be termed egocentric. No child confused his own view with the policemen's by consistently hiding the boy so that the boy was out of sight from the child. Indeed, two of the children who failed on the task consistently placed the boy doll in the sections *nearest* to them, so that the doll was fully visible to them as well as to the policemen. Two children chose to play a different game from the one which the experimenter had in mind; one consistently hid the boy under the table, and the other hid him in her hand! These responses — which were perfectly adequate in their own way — were somewhat reluctantly scored as incorrect. The remaining errors were mainly the occasional mistakes made in calculation by children who otherwise performed well on the task.

Discussion

The level of performance found in these three studies is remarkably high. Very few of the children — three-year-olds or four-year-olds — had any difficulty either with the one-policeman task used in Study One, or with the simpler two-policemen task used in Study Two. It was only when the task was made more complex still, in Study Three, that the three-year-olds started to make an appreciable number of errors, and even then the majority of children still performed extremely well.

These findings clearly have important implications for the notion of early childhood egocentrism, and we will return to these implications shortly. First, however, it is worth pausing to look at the children's performance on the tasks in more detail, and to consider the kinds of thinking skills they might be using.

When one watches the children perform these tasks, it often seems as though they are playing an enjoyable little game with the experimenter, somewhat like a simple form of chess. The experimenter places the policemen in position, and asks the child to hide the boy: the child responds by putting the boy within one of the sections of the walls. The experimenter then moves one of the policemen to another position, so that the boy is now visible: the child in turn replies by moving the boy to a new safe position. The experimenter moves the policemen again, the child replies again and so it goes on: move and counter-move, threat and reply. These games are obviously very enjoyable to the children and they seem to have no difficulty in understanding what to do. Indeed, the child will often respond before any instructions are given, as if he understands the rules of the game well enough and does not need reminding of what he has to do. This, as we shall see later, is an important point.

The analogy with chess is reinforced by the habit of some children who pick up the boy, move him to a section of the walls and, *without letting go of him*, look around to see if he is visible to any of the policemen. If he is, they move him to another section and try again. This is very similar to what often happens when a beginner starts to play chess: he will pick up a piece, move it to a square on the board, and without letting go, will look around to see if the piece can be captured, or if the move is otherwise unsafe. This practice soon disappears as the beginner learns to internalise the whole process instead. By analogy, it is tempting to suppose that the children who succeed on the policemen task without moving the boy from one section to another have likewise managed to internalise the process of trying each section to see which is safe.

If this is so, then it raises interesting questions about the thought processes which might be involved. Do they involve imagery — in that the child imagines the boy in a particular section and then works out if he is visible or not — or is it rather a primitive case of inference, with the child thinking along the lines:

> 'If I move him to section A, then he will be visible. I don't want this, so I won't move him to Section A.
>
> 'If I move him to section B, . . . etc'?

The process could, of course, involve both imagery and inference. Indeed, it is likely that for advanced chess players, who can 'see' many moves ahead, both imagery and inferences are involved. This kind of thinking has been little studied, however, either in adults or in children, and at present we can only speculate on what might be involved.

While it remains unclear precisely what thought processes are required to succeed on our tasks, there can be little doubt that they reveal the presence of well-coordinated, 'decentred' thinking in three- and four-year-old children. In successfully coordinating the viewpoints of three different policemen at once, the children show themselves to be virtually unhampered by the constraints of egocentrism. These findings thus add further support to a growing body of evidence which shows that young children can — in certain circumstances — calculate what another person can see (see review by Flavell, 1974; also Borke, 1975). In addition, there are findings from two further studies which support those presented here. In one study, Light (1974) gave two tasks involving hide and seek situations to a group of children around their fourth birthdays, and one of the tasks was similar to that used in Study Two. Light found that performance was high on both tasks, with well over half the children giving predominantly correct responses. In the other study, Flavell, Shipstead & Croft (1978) gave various versions of a hiding task, similar to that used in Study One, to children aged between 2½ and 3½ years. They found that almost all the children could hide an object from a toy dog by moving the object behind a screen, but that it was significantly harder to hide the object by moving the screen. All the same, most of the 3 and 3½ year-olds were able to do this latter version of the task.

There is thus substantial evidence to show that three- and four-year-olds are by no means as egocentric as Piaget has claimed. But why, in that case, do they fail on the mountain task? Why do so many children pick their own view of the mountains when asked to select the doll's view? One factor which undoubtedly influences the children's performance is the complexity of the array. The mountain task is particularly difficult in that it requires the child to perform both front/back and left/right reversals in order to work out the doll's view, and there is indeed evidence that performance improves as the array is simplified (Fishbein, Lewis & Keffer, 1972; Flavell *et al.*, 1968). However it seems that another factor may also be involved. It could well be that in the mountain task the child has considerable difficulty in *understanding what he is supposed to do.*

Support for this idea comes from a study one of us carried out with a simplified version of the mountain task (Hughes, 1978). Instead of mountains, Hughes used three dolls of different colours each facing outwards from the corner of a triangular base. The array was positioned between the child and the experimenter, so that the child saw the face of the doll nearest him (say, a red doll) and the experimenter saw the face of a different doll, the one nearest him (say, a blue doll). Hughes found that when three- and four-year-olds were asked, in the standard manner, to select a picture showing the experimenter's view, very few could do this. However, the great majority of them could succeed when this question was preceded by questions referring to particular features of the array ('which doll's face do I see?/do you see?', etc.) and to the same features of the pictures ('which doll's face do you see in this picture?', etc.). By drawing the child's attention to these features, the preliminary questions helped him understand what was involved in the task.

In contrast, the tasks used in the present studies were extremely clear to the children, and they immediately grasped what they were supposed to do. We were careful to introduce the tasks in ways which would help the child understand the situation, but in fact these precautions were largely unnecessary. The children understood the rules of the game at once and, as we have already seen, they often responded to each trial without any reminders from the experimenter as to what the game was about.

Why do children find these tasks so easy to grasp, compared with problems like the mountain task? We believe it is because the policemen tasks make *human sense* in a way that the mountain task does not. The motives and intentions of the characters (hiding and seeking) are entirely comprehensible, even to a child of three, and he is being asked to identify with — and indeed do something about — the plight of a boy in an entirely comprehensible situation. This ability to understand and identify with another's feelings and intentions is in many ways the exact opposite of egocentrism, and yet it now appears to be well developed in three-year-olds. Indeed, as one of us has argued at greater length (Donaldson, 1978), it seems likely that it constitutes a very fundamental human skill, the origins of which may be present even in the first few months of life.

References

Aebli, H. (1967) 'Egocentrism (Piaget) not a phase of mental development but a substitute solution for an insoluble task'. *Pedagogica Europaea*, 3, pp. 97-103.

Borke, H. (1975) 'Piaget's mountains revisited: changes in the egocentric landscape.' *Developmental Psychology*, 11, pp. 240-243.

Dodwell, P.C. (1963) 'Children's understanding of spatial concepts'. *Canadian Journal of Psychology*, 17, pp. 141-161.

Donaldson, M. (1978) *Children's Minds* (London, Fontana/Croom Helm).

Fishbein, H.D., Lewis, S. & Keiffer, K. (1972) 'Children's understanding of spatial relations: co-ordination of perspectives'. *Developmental Psychology*, 7, pp. 21-33.

Flavell, J.H. (1974) 'The developmental of inferences about others'. In: Mischel, T. (Ed.) *Understanding Other Persons* (Oxford, Blackwell).

Flavell, J.H., Botkin, P.T., Fry, C.L., Wright, J.W. & Jarvis, P.E. (1968) *The Development of Role-taking and Communication Skills in Children* (New York, J. Wiley).

Flavell, J.H., Shipstead, S.G. & Croft, K. (1978) 'Young children's knowledge about visual perception: hiding objects from others' (unpublished manuscript).

Garner, J. & Plant, E. (1972) 'On the measurement of egocentrism: a replication and extension of Aebli's findings'. *British Journal of Educational Psychology*, 42, pp. 79-83.

Hughes, M. (1978) 'Selecting pictures of another person's view'. *British Journal of Educational Psychology*, 48, pp. 210-219.

Light, P. (1974) 'The role-taking skills of four-year-old children', unpublished *Ph.D. thesis*, University of Cambridge.

Peel, E.A. (1967) 'A method for investigating children's understanding of certain logical connectives used in binary propositional thinking'. *British Journal of Mathematical and Statistical Psychology*, 20, pp. 81-92.

Piaget, J. (1926) *The Language and Thought of the Child* (London, Routledge & Kegan Paul).

Piaget, J. & Inhelder, B. (1956) *The Child's Conception of Space* (London, Routledge & Kegan Paul).

Piaget J. & Inhelder, B. (1969) *The Psychology of the Child* (London, Routledge & Kegan Paul).

18.   The Salience of Occluding Vehicles to Child Pedestrians

James D. Demetre and Susan Gaffin

Young children have a disproportionate number of pedestrian accidents whilst trying to cross roads near parked vehicles. Three competing hypotheses as to the basis of this problem were tested under controlled conditions. Children aged 6 (N=32), 8 (N=30) and 10 years (N=36) were presented with a two-choice road crossing task, comprising a crossing point bounded by occluding vehicles and a crossing point providing a clear view of oncoming traffic. At 6 years, choices were random, whereas at 8 years, and especially at 10 years, the clear view crossing choice predominated. There was also a strong association between preference for the clear view crossing point and experience as an independent road user.

Pedestrian accidents are among the most common causes of death and serious injury to children growing up in the developed world (Ampofo-Boateng & Thomson, 1989; Haight & Olsen, 1981; Thomson, 1991). Accident statistics have for a long time shown that children in the age range 5 to 9 years are particularly over-represented in pedestrian accident statistics, despite their relatively low exposure to traffic (Hillman, Adams & Whitelegg, 1990; Routledge, Repetto-Wright & Howarth, 1974; Thomson, 1991).

One source of young children's vulnerability is suggested by accident statistics showing that a disproportionate number of young children have accidents whilst attempting to cross a road near parked vehicles, which frequently hamper visibility (Downing & Spendlove, 1981; Lawson, 1990; van der Molen, 1981). While figures vary, it is reported that between 40 and 70 per cent of 5- to 6-year-old children's accidents involve attempts to cross near a parked vehicle, compared with about 20 per cent of 13- to 14-year-olds' accidents (van der Molen, 1981). The current state of the evidence permits three different accounts of this distribution of accidents. The aim of the present study is to provide evidence for adjudicating among the following three alternatives.

First, it is possible that young children fail to take account of the occluding properties of parked vehicles, which will place them at greater risk as pedestrians, and would account for their disproportionate involvement in accidents near parked vehicles. A second possibility is that parked vehicles are indeed highly salient to the young child, but not as a sign of danger but rather are viewed as protective barriers from oncoming traffic. Thus, young children may unwittingly increase the likelihood of accident involvement through a selective preference for crossing roads in the vicinity of parked vehicles. Another possibility is that younger children's difficulty with parked vehicles reflects ecological, rather than psychological constraints. A greater proportion of young

James D. Demetre and Susan Gaffin: 'The Salience of Occluding Vehicles to Child Pedestrians'. *BRITISH JOURNAL OF EDUCATIONAL PSYCHOLOGY* (1994), 64. pp. 243-251. © 1994 The British Psychological Society.

children's accidents occur on minor roads in residential areas where parked cars are commonplace (Lawson, 1990; van der Molen, 1981). Thus, the association between age and accidents involving parked vehicles may simply reflect differential exposure to various traffic environments.

To date, studies have addressed several issues relating to children's problems with occluding vehicles, but none has directly addressed the question of salience in children's road crossing decisions. Several studies using a wide range of methodologies, including unobtrusive observation of children, reveal that children below the age of 9 or 10 years generally fail to compensate for the constraints imposed by occluding vehicles. Only a small proportion of young children crossing near a parked car position themselves near the outer edge of the car in order to gain visibility for oncoming traffic (Downing & Spendlove, 1981; van der Molen, 1983; Sandels, 1975).

Other studies have shown that children below the age of 10 or 11 years tend to opt for a seemingly efficient, direct route across a road, frequently failing to take account of various occluding features, such as blind bends in the road and parked vehicles (Ampofo-Boateng & Thomson, 1991; Ampofo-Boateng, Thomson, Crieve, Pitcairn, Lee & Demetre, 1993; Thomson, Ampofo-Boateng, Pitcairn, Grieve, Lee & Demetre, 1992). However, it is possible that these children may have opted for an unsafe road crossing point simply because it was more expeditious, rather than out of any inherent disregard for the problems posed by occlusion.

Studies of perspective-taking using scaled models and real-world contexts have found that most children aged 5 years and older were able to predict correctly when they would be occluded by a parked vehicle and when their view of oncoming traffic would be occluded by a parked vehicle (Gunther & Limbourg, 1976; Vinje & Groeneveld, 1981). However, approximately 30 per cent of 5-year-olds and 20 per cent of 6- to 7-year-olds in these studies failed to make correct predictions. This contrasts with studies of 3- to 4-year-old children's understanding of occlusion in other contexts, where far fewer children make errors (Cox, 1980, 1986; Flavell, 1988; Flavell, Shipstead & Croft, 1978; Hughes & Donaldson, 1979).

The available evidence does not provide a firm basis for assessing the salience of occluding vehicles to young children's road crossing decisions. The paucity of direct evidence leaves the three hypotheses of children's accident involvement with parked vehicles in equal contention. The present study seeks to provide a firmer basis for evaluating these hypotheses by investigating children's road crossing choices under controlled conditions. The present study employed a two-choice task which permitted a controlled assessment of children's road crossing choices. The two choices comprised a crossing point bounded by two cars, which occluded the child's view of oncoming traffic, and a crossing point that provided a clear view of oncoming traffic. The two crossing points were equally accessible, being equidistant from both the starting point and the destination target. Other potentially confounding aspects surrounding choices were also controlled. Three groups of children aged 6 years, 8 years and 10 years were tested. The distribution of road crossing choices would permit arbitration among the three alternative interpretations of children's vulnerability with parked vehicles posed above.

If occluding vehicles are not salient signs of danger for the youngest children, it would be expected that their distribution of choices would be random, and that preferences for the clear view crossing point would increase with age. In contrast, if occluding vehicles are perceived as protective barriers by the youngest children, it would be expected that they would show a preference for the occluding cars crossing point, this preference weakening, and possibly reversing, with age. If age-related differences in children's accident involvement with parked cars is due to base rate differences in exposure to environments containing parked cars, then no age-related differences in road crossing choices would be expected to emerge under controlled conditions.

A secondary aim of the present study was to ascertain whether there is an association between children's unsupervised use of roads and the road crossing choices made on the two-choice task. Unobtrusive observations of children's road user behaviour suggest that children accompanied by adults tend to allow themselves to be passively led across the road, and engage little in orienting behaviour relative to solitary pedestrians (van der Molen, 1983). Thus, it seems reasonable to expect that children who take responsibility for navigating through the environment are more likely to be receptive to experience, and hence show a greater awareness of the problems posed by parked vehicles.

Method

Sample

A total of 98 children participated in the present study. Children were divided into three age groups: 32 in the 6-year group (mean = 6 years 1 month; range = 5 years 9 months – 6 years 6 months); 30 in the 8-year group (mean = 8 years 1 month; range = 7 years 9 months – 8 years 8 months); and 36 in the 10-year group (mean = 10 years 1 month; range = 9 years 7 months – 10 years 8 months). Each group contained an equal number of boys and girls. All the children attended a state school in a predominantly working class district on the outskirts of London. Prior consent was obtained from the parents of all participating children.

Procedure

The two-choice road crossing task comprised two adjacent road crossing points situated on the kerb of a minor road near the school. One crossing point was free of parked cars and provided a fairly clear view of oncoming traffic. The other crossing point was bounded by two parked cars which occluded oncoming traffic. The two crossing points were separated by a distance of approximately 15 metres. The occluding crossing point was contrived by the experimenter who parked her car behind another parked car prior to meeting the child. A plastic cone, serving as the pedestrian's hypothetical destination point, was placed across the road on the opposite sidewalk. A schematic representation of the task is provided in Figure 1.

Children were tested individually. Once escorted to the test site, children were asked questions to ascertain whether they ever crossed roads alone, or whether they were always supervised by an adult or older sibling. Children were then introduced to the two-choice road crossing task. Children were escorted to a point on the pavement midway between the two crossing points (position Z in Figure 1), where they were told they would be shown two different places from which to cross the road to reach the target cone (position W in Figure 1). Children were explicitly told that they were not actually going to cross the road but they would have to indicate which place they would choose as a crossing point. Children's comprehension of the task was assessed through questioning, and queries answered. Children were then escorted successively to each crossing point (positions X and Y in Figure 1). On approaching each crossing point, children were asked to stop and look both ways for oncoming traffic. Children were then escorted back to the midpoint (position Z in Figure 1), where they were asked to indicate their choice of crossing point.

Once their road crossing choice had been established, children were asked to provide an explanation of their choice. Where necessary, corrective feedback was provided at the end of the session, and children were enjoined to keep the 'game' a secret from their classmates.

Design

Order of exposure to the two crossing points was counterbalanced, with half the children being shown the occluding cars crossing point first, and half being shown the clear view crossing point first. Position of crossing point was also counterbalanced, with half the children having the occluding cars crossing point on their right, and half having the occluding cars crossing point on their left. A fully counterbalanced design was used, with four unique combinations of order of crossing point exposure and position of crossing point (see Figure 1).

Results

Association of age and road crossing choice

Sex of child, order of crossing point exposure and position of crossing point did not influence children's road crossing choices, hence the data were combined across these variables.

The numbers of children in each age group who made each road crossing choice are presented in Table 1. Approximately half of the 6-year-olds chose the occluding cars crossing point, this choice becoming progressively less frequent at the two older ages.

An overall chi square test of association revealed a highly significant relationship between age and road crossing choice, $\chi^2(2) = 16.32, p < .001$. Chi square goodness-of-fit tests revealed that 8-year-olds, $\chi^2(1) = 4.8, p < .05$, and particularly 10-year-olds, $\chi^2(1) = 25, p < .001$, had a selective preference for the clear view crossing point. In contrast, 6-year-olds' choices did not deviate from a random distribution, $\chi^2(1) = .13, p > .50$.

The apparently random basis of 6-year-olds' choices was further reflected in the explanations they provided for their choices. Only three of the 15 children who chose the clear view crossing point made any mention of visibility or the need to avoid the problem of occlusion. By contrast, children in the two older groups who made the clear view choice almost invariably mentioned visibility and occlusion in defending their choice. The latter almost always mentioned two aspects of the occlusion problem: that the parked cars would occlude traffic from the pedestrian, and that the parked cars would occlude the pedestrian from drivers.

Figure 1   Schematic illustrations of the two-choice road crossing task

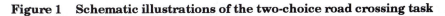

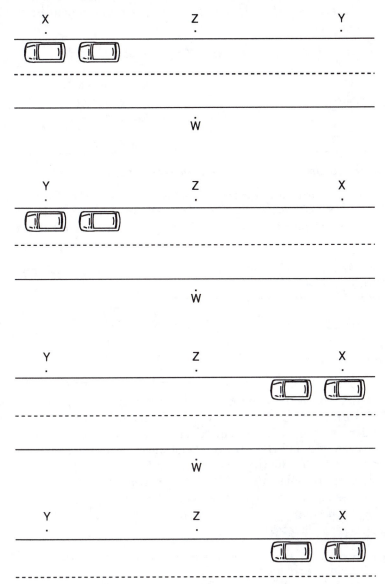

The four illustrations correspond to each of the two orders of crossing point exposure (2) x (2) positions of crossing point. Z was the initial point and decision point, X was the first crossing point shown to a subject, Y was the second crossing point shown to a subject, W was the plastic cone representing the destination point.

The obtained pattern of age-related changes in children's road crossing choices is consistent with the notion that occluding vehicles are not salient at the outset but become increasingly salient with age.

Table 1   Frequency of road crossing as a function of age

Road crossing choice	Age group (years)		
	6	8	10
Occluding cars	17	9	3
Clear view	15	21	33

Association of pedestrian experience and road crossing choice

Table 2 shows that very few 6-year-olds crossed roads alone. By contrast, all the 10-year-olds crossed roads alone. The 8-year-olds showed the most variability, and were thus the most appropriate group to use in testing the association between pedestrian experience and road crossing choice.

Table 2   Frequency of children crossing roads alone or only with supervision as a function of age

Pedestrian experience	Age group (years)		
	6	8	10
Cross alone	2	21	36
Cross only with supervision	30	9	0

Table 3 shows that the overwhelming majority of 8-year-olds who crossed roads alone chose the clear view crossing point. Conversely, the majority of 8-year-olds who crossed roads only under supervision chose the occluding cars crossing point. A chi square test of association revealed a highly significant relationship between pedestrian experience and road crossing choice in this age group, $\chi^2(1) = 13.98$, $p < .001$. Chi square goodness-of-fit tests revealed that children who crossed roads alone had a highly significant preference for the clear view crossing point, $\chi^2(1) = 13.76$, $p < .001$. In contrast, supervised children's choices did not deviate significantly from a random distribution, $\chi^2(1) = 2.78$, $p > .10$.

Table 3   Frequency of road crossing choices in 8-year-olds as a function of pedestrian experience

Road crossing choice	Pedestrian experience	
	Cross alone	With supervision
Occluding cars	2	7
Clear view	19	22

The findings indicate that children with independent experience as pedestrians are highly likely to select a crossing point that provides a clear view of traffic. However, the direction of any cause-effect relationship between these two variables is impossible to establish with the existing data.

Discussion

The findings indicate that occluding vehicles are not salient to 6-year-olds' road crossing selections. Six-year-olds' selections on the two-choice road crossing task were essentially random, and their justifications for these choices largely reflected guesswork. By 8 years of age, the majority of children did show a preference for crossing the road from the clear view point. However, almost 30 per cent of children in this age group chose to cross between occluding cars; the majority of these were children who did not have experience of crossing roads alone. By 10 years of age, almost 92 per cent of children chose the clear view crossing point.

These findings support the hypothesis that occluding vehicles are not salient in early middle childhood, despite this being a period in development when understanding of perspective-taking in relation to occlusion is believed to be well consolidated (Cox, 1980, 1986; Flavell, 1988). The salience of occluding vehicles increases with age, and is strongly associated with experience of crossing roads alone. The data are inconsistent with the notion that the youngest children's difficulties with occluding vehicles arise from their perceiving these as protective barriers. It is possible that even younger children show such a preference for occluding vehicles, but very young children do not feature very strongly in accident statistics.

Why are occluding vehicles so low in salience below the age of 8 years? It was noted previously that children's perspective-taking abilities in pedestrian contexts seem to lag behind similar abilities for other contexts of occlusion (Gunther & Limbourg, 1976; Vinje & Groeneveld, 1981). This lag may reflect the relative complexities surrounding visibility and occlusion in relation to vehicles. However, on the face of it, it would seem unlikely that this putative lag is sufficient to account for the lack of salience accorded to occluding cars among as many as 30 per cent of 8-year-olds and 9 per cent of 10-year-olds. It is likely that other factors over and above problems in perspective-taking contribute to these children's difficulties with occluding vehicles.

In characterising the other factors involved in children's decision-making in complex, potentially dangerous environments, one is tempted to invoke the notion of 'self-regulative' functions proposed by Vygotsky (1978). It seems likely that in middle childhood, competences are not automatically brought 'on line' until a child has first had meaningful, purposive experience in a given domain of activity. It is also possible that more general cognitive changes underlying the so-called 5-to-7 shift, which coincides with assignment by adults of various roles of responsibility in a number of cultures, ordinarily plays a role in bringing such competences to the fore (Rogoff, Sellers, Pirrotta, Fox & White, 1975).

Another aspect of the findings merits discussion. The majority of children who claimed to have used roads independently made appropriate road crossing choices. Among the 8-year-olds, only two out of 21 children who used roads alone made an inappropriate road crossing choice. Future research needs to address two issues relating to this finding. First, the contribution of road-user experience to children's road-crossing decisions needs to be more directly assessed, in order to establish the causal linkage underpinning the association found in the present study. This can best be tackled through outcome evaluations of intervention procedures aimed at providing children with analogues of road-user experience (see Ampofo-Boateng et al., 1993, for possibilities). A second issue concerns the bases upon which parents decide to grant their children license to use roads independently. At present, very little is known about how systematic such parental choices are, and whether parents assess their child's road-user competence (at least informally) before granting road-user privileges.

In conclusion, the present study shows that children below the age of 8 years are largely random in their selection of road crossing points, failing to take account of occluding vehicles. Even at 8 years of age, a large minority of children fail to take account of occluding vehicles in their road crossing choices. The association found between independent use of roads and road crossing choices may suggest that experience as a road user contributes to the salience of occluding vehicles in decision making. Future research needs to address the issue of how such experience can best be provided before children attain the status of independent road users.

References

Ampofo-Boateng, K., & Thomson, J.A. (1989) 'Child pedestrian accidents: a case for preventive medicine.' *Health Education Research*, 5, 265-274.

Ampofo-Boateng, K. & Thomson, J.A. (1991) 'Children's perception of safety and danger on the road.' *British Journal of Psychology*, 82, 487-505.

Ampofo-Boateng, K. Thomson, J.A., Grieve, R., Pitcairn, T., Lee, D.N. & Demetre, J.D. (1993) 'A developmental and training study of children's ability to find safe routes to cross the road.' *British Journal of Developmental Psychology*, 11, 31-45.

Cox, M.V. (1980) 'Visual perspective-taking in children.' In M.V. Cox (Ed), *Are Young Children Egocentric?*, pp. 61-79. London: Batsford Academic.

Cox, M.V. (1986) *The Child's Point of View*. Brighton: Harvester Press.

Downing, C.S. & Spendlove, J. (1981) 'Effectiveness of a campaign to reduce accidents involving children crossing roads near parked cars.' *Transport and Road Research Laboratory Report, No. 986*. Crowthorne, Berks.

Flavell, J.H. (1988) 'The development of children's knowledge about the mind: from cognitive connections to mental representations.' In J.W. Astington, P.L. Harris & D.R. Olson (Eds), *Developing Theories of Mind*, pp. 244-267. New York: Cambridge University Press.

Flavell, J.H., Shipstead, S.G. & Croft, K. (1978) 'Young children's knowledge about visual perception: hiding objects from others.' *Child Development*, 49, 1208-1211.

Gunther, R. & Limbourg, M. (1976) 'Bedingungen für das Erleben und Verhalten von Kindern im Strassenverkehr.' *Unfallund Sicherheitsforschung Strassenverkehr, Heft 4*. Koln, Germany: Bundesanstalt fur Strassenwesen (cited in Vinje & Groeneveld, 1981).

Haight, F. & Olsen, R.A. (1981) 'Pedestrian safety in the United States: some recent trends.' *Accident Analysis and Prevention*, 13, 43-55.

Hillman, M., Adams, J. & Whitelegg, J. (1990) *One False Move . . . A Study of Children's Independent Mobility*. London: Institute for Policy Studies.

Hughes, M. & Donaldson, M. (1979) 'The use of hiding games for studying co-ordination of viewpoints.' *Educational Review,* 31, 133-140.

Lawson, S.D. (1990) *Accidents to Young Pedestrians: Distributions, Circumstances, Consequences and Scope for Countermeasures*. Basingstoke: Automobile Association Foundation for Road Safety Research.

Molen, H.H. van der (1981) 'Child pedestrian exposure, accidents and behavior.' *Accident Analysis and Prevention,* 13, 193-224.

Molen, H.H. van der (1983) 'Pedestrian ethology.' Doctoral dissertation, University of Groningen, Netherlands.

Rogoff, B., Sellers, M.J., Pirrotta, S., Fox, N. & White, S.H., (1975) 'Age of assignment of roles and responsibilities to children: a cross-cultural survey.' *Human Development,* 18, 353-369.

Routledge, D.A., Repetto-Wright, R. & Howarth, C.I. (1974) 'The exposure of young children to accident risk as pedestrians.' *Ergonomics,* 17, 457-480.

Sandels, S. (1975) *Children in Traffic*. London: Elek.

Thomson, J.A. (1991) *The Facts about Child Pedestrian Accidents*. London: Cassell.

Thomson, J.A., Ampofo-Boateng, K., Pitcairn, T., Grieve, R., Lee, D.N. & Demetre, J.D. (1992) 'Behavioural group training of children to find safe routes to cross the road.' *British Journal of Educational Psychology,* 62, 173-183.

Vinje, M.P. & Groeneveld, J. (1981) 'Understanding visibility in traffic: an experiment with preschool children.' *University of Groningen Traffic Research Center Reports No. 78-05,* Netherlands.

Vygotsky, L.S. (1978) *Mind in Society*. Cambridge, MA: Harvard University Press.

19.   Conservation Accidents

James McGarrigle and Margaret Donaldson

Abstract

Eighty children aged between 4 years 2 months and 6 years 3 months were tested on length and number conservation, both when the transformation occurred because of a direct action by the experimenter and when it happened 'accidentally' as the by-product of an activity directed towards a different goal. Fifty children conserved when the transformation was 'accidental', whereas only 13 were successful when it was intentional. These results are interpreted as evidence that characteristics of the experimenter's behaviour, in particular his actions towards the task materials, can influence children's interpretation of utterances by suggesting the experimenter is thinking about a different attribute from that specified linguistically. It is suggested that traditional procedures may underestimate children's cognitive abilities.

Introduction

A substantial body of research has grown up around Piaget's conservation tasks (Piaget, 1952; Piaget and Inhelder, 1969). Piaget's findings have been replicated by many investigators using standardized procedures based on Piaget's original method (Elkind, 1961; Dodwell, 1960; Hood, 1962; Smedslund, 1964). However a considerable amount of evidence has accumulated suggesting that children may have the knowledge necessary for conservation long before they succeed in the traditional conservation task (e.g., Frank, 1964; Gelman, 1972; Rose and Blank, 1974). These studies have usually involved ingenious methods for circumventing those features of the conservation task which the authors thought were particularly problematic for the child. For example, those suggesting attentional/perceptual difficulties have used screening procedures (Frank, 1964) or trained children to attend to the relevant attributes (Gelman, 1969). Those postulating linguistic difficulties have used pretraining in the use of the relational terms of the task (Gruen 1965) or developed conservation games not involving the relational terms (Gelman, 1972). Each of these diverse procedures gave indications that children can conserve at an earlier age than is suggested by traditional methods.

This paper is addressed to the paradox presented by these conflicting results — results which show that the child can, in some contexts, demonstrate his knowledge about the invariance of certain attributes of objects while at the same time he fails to exhibit such knowledge in the typical Piagetian situation. The traditional method of assessing conservation is scrutinized and one potentially important feature of the situation is identified. It is suggested that this feature, which is irrelevant to the logical requirements of the conservation task, contributes substantially to the child's difficulty in the classic situation.

James McGarrigle and Margaret Donaldson: 'Conservation accidents'. *COGNITION* (1974), Vol. 3, No. 4. pp. 341-350. Reprinted by permission of Elsevier Science B.V.

Consider the usual procedure for assessing conservation of number. Two lines of counters, equal in number, are arranged in one-to-one correspondence in front of the child, and a question about their relative numerosity is presented (Q1, e.g., are there more counters here or more counter here or are they both the same number?) The child makes the judgement (J1) that they are the same and the experimenter then rearranges one of the rows and repeats the original question (Q2). The nonconserving child typically changes his judgement in favour of the longer row (J2). It is customary to associate the child's changing choice from J1 to J2 with what appears to be the only other feature of the situation that has changed — the perceptual configuration of the row of counters — so that the explanation of the child's behaviour focusses on his susceptibility to perceptual influences.

Suppose however that, despite their formal or surface identity, Q1 and Q2 are given differing interpretations by the child. This is not as unlikely as it seems on first reflection, and it is not difficult to imagine how two identical questions might be used to interrogate different aspects of a static array. For example, some of the counters might be covered in spots. In this situation the original conservation question (Q1 and Q2) could be used to enquire about the relative numerosity of just the counters with spots, provided that preceding contextual information, either linguistic or non-linguistic, made it clear that the questioner was now interested in this aspect of the array. The point of this unlikely sounding example is that we do not know the sources of 'contextual information' which could lead the child to vary his interpretation of an unchanging question.

One conspicuous event that intervenes between J1 and the presentation of Q2 is the experimenter's simple action of changing the length of one of the rows of counters. Could this provide the contextual information which leads the child to misinterpret Q2? Recent theoretical proposals in the area of language acquisition indicate the paramount importance, for the development of language, of the actions of the participants in early interactions. These suggestions draw upon the communication of intent model proposed by philosophers of language in which an important distinction is made between speaker's meaning and utterance meaning (Grice, 1968). Macnamara (1972) has suggested that children learn language on the basis of their independent hypotheses about speaker's meaning, derived from their intercourse with the world. Ryan (1973) and Bruner (1975) have argued that mother-child interactions provide contexts of mutual action in which intentions, initially communicated non-linguistically, come to be mapped on to their linguistic means of expression. They suggest a central role for non-linguistic means of collaboratively directing attention as a basis for the referential function of language. Although the detail of these processes remains to be specified, this approach clearly indicates the importance of the intentional structure of the speaker's non-linguistic behaviour for the child's interpretation of utterances. Since language acquisition continues at least until the period of concrete operations (Palermo and Molfese, 1973) then it is important to consider the possible effect of the intentional activity of the experimenter on the child's interpretation of the language of the conservation task.

The structure of the conservation task seems to involve a significant deviation from normal adult-child interactions. In the conservation task the adult's non-linguistic behaviour is uncoupled from the linguistic element, in that the non-linguistic component is irrelevant to the interpretation of the utterance. Moreover the non-linguistic behaviour is highly relevant for an utterance of a different type — one concerned with the length of the row rather than number. It could be that the experimenter's simple direct action of changing the length of the row leads the child to infer an intention on the experimenter's part to talk about what he has just been doing. It is as if the experimenter refers behaviourally to length although he continues to talk about number. If the young child's procedures for interpreting language initially depend heavily on the non-linguistic component of the interaction, it would not be surprising if he ignored normal word-referent relationships and interpreted the question on the basis of the experimenter's intentions as evidenced in his behaviour.

If this proposal is correct, it follows that it should be possible to vary the incidence of conservation success by manipulating the intentional structure of the circumstances leading to the transformation. One way to do this is to make the transformation appear accidental. It cannot of course be genuinely accidental. The notion of 'deliberate accident' is self-contradictory, so one cannot build true accident into an experimental design. However one can attempt to ensure that an event will not appear to the subject to have been produced with calculated intent by the experimenter. One can make it seem to be a by-product of some other activity and to that extent fortuitous. The method employed here exploits the child's willingness to attribute agency to inanimate objects. A small teddy bear with malicious intentions towards the task materials is operated by the experimenter to effect the transformation. The child makes his judgements before and after the transformation. In one condition, the transformation results from a direct intentional action of the experimenter like that used in the classic method. In the other condition the same transformation happens 'accidentally' in the course of the teddy bear's activity which is directed towards the goal of 'spoiling the game'. Since in both conditions the child is faced with the usual misleading perceptual array then, if orthodox accounts of conservation performance are correct, both methods of assessment should yield similar results. If, on the other hand, the intentional character of the experimenter's actions can govern the child's interpretation of the question, then better performance is predicted where the transformation occurs without this intentional background.

Method

Subjects: Eighty children, of mean age 5 years and 4 months (range 4 years 2 months to 6 years 3 months) took part in the study. Forty of these were attending Edinburgh nursery schools and their mean age was 4 years 10 months (range 4 years 2 months to 5 years 4 months). The other 40 were attending a local State primary school and their mean age was 5 years 10 months (range 5 years 3 months to 6 years 3 months). There was an equal number of boys and girls in each of the samples.

Design: Each child received number and length conservation problems under conditions in which the transformation was effected intentionally (Intentional Transformation, IT), and under conditions in which it occurred accidentally (Accidental

Transformation, AT). There were two situations involving the conservation of number (equal and unequal) and two involving length conservation (equal and unequal). Children were assigned to one of two groups, with care taken to balance the sex and age composition of the groups. Group I completed all the judgements involving AT before encountering any in the IT condition; Group II received the IT condition first. Within these groups, one half of the children received the number situations first and the other half received the length situations first. The equal and unequal situations appeared first equally often. The order of presentation of situations was held constant across the IT and AT conditions.

Materials and Situations: The task materials were counters of 1½" diameter, some lengths of string, and a small teddy bear (height 3") with a box large enough to conceal him.

In the *number equal* situation, four red and four white counters were arranged in one to-one correspondence into two rows of equal length. The transformation, for both IT and AT conditions, involved moving the counters of one row until they were touching each other, thereby shortening that row. Before and after the transformation the child was asked:

"Is there more here or more here or are they both the same number?"

while the experimenter pointed along each of the rows at the appropriate points in the utterance. For the *number unequal* situation, rows of four and five counters were used and the question was:

"Which is the one with more — this one or this one?"

For the *length equal* situation, two 10" lengths of red and black string were used. These were placed beside each other, with their end-points coinciding, and the child was asked:

"Is this one longer than this one or are they both the same length?"

while the experimenter touched each of the pieces of string in turn.* One piece of string was then transformed by bending it into a crescent shape, and the question was repeated. For the *length unequal* situation one of the 10" strings and an 8" length of white string were used and the question was:

"Which is the long one — this one or this one?"

Procedure

At the beginning of the session only the cardboard box containing teddy was present on the table. E lifted teddy out of the box, and showed him to the child, explaining that teddy was very naughty and that he was liable to escape from his box from time to time and try to 'mess up the toys' and 'spoil the game'.

E then arranged the materials for the child's first situation. During the IT condition, the teddy bear did not appear. The IT procedure was modelled on the traditional method

---

* It has been objected, perhaps with some reason, that it was unwise to touch the string, since the children might regard even this act as somehow transforming the material. It seems unlikely that they did so, however, in view of the large differences between the IT and AT conditions which were nonetheless obtained.

used in conservation studies. After the child's first judgement, E said "Now watch..." and rearranged the materials with a single direct action, and then repeated the question.

In the AT condition, following the initial judgement, E pretended to experience surprise and alarm as he moved teddy towards the materials making such remarks as: "It's naughty teddy!" "Oh! look out, he's going to spoil the game." At this point E quickly moved teddy over the string or the row of counters making sure that they were appropriately disarranged in apparently haphazard fashion.

Then he allowed the child to return teddy to his box.

On four occasions during the AT procedure the child, having removed teddy, restored the string or counters to their original state before E could elicit the conservation judgement. When this happened that situation was begun again using a modified procedure.* Instead of chasing teddy back to his box, the child was asked to keep teddy prisoner — that is, to hold him in his hands. This ensured that the transformation remained unaltered until the judgement was elicited.

The transformation, for both AT and IT conditions, was always carried out on the material furthest from the child. This procedure was adopted to allow teddy more opportunity for carrying out his mischief before the child could intervene. Each child saw both red and white counters undergo transformation within any condition (i.e., in one situation the red row was transformed, in the other the white), and similarly for the red and black string. When each situation was encountered again under the second condition (IT or AT), the child witnessed the same material being transformed as on the first occasion. The order in which E pointed to the materials in conjunction with the question was varied systematically. E gave no feedback concerning the child's performance.

The method employed here for assessing conservation does not involve the eliciting of justifications. This strategy was adopted for two reasons. In the first place, Brainerd (1973) has argued that, even from the point of view of Piagetian theory, the justification criterion is too strict. More important for present purposes, the attempt to elicit justifications would have involved the child and E in further complex interaction, the characteristics of which could have influenced the child's subsequent behaviour in a number of ways.

Results

Tables 1 and 2 show that correct responses were far more frequent when the transformation occurred accidentally than when it was affected in the traditional manner. Nearly three-quarters of responses were correct in the AT condition, whereas only one-third were correct in the IT condition. If the criterion for successful conservation is set at four out of four judgements correct, then 50 of the 80 children are diagnosed as conservers under the AT method. In contrast, when these same 80 children

---

* It might have been better simply to stop testing in these cases. But since they were so few in number, the pattern of the results is not substantially affected.

made their judgements in the IT condition, only 13 achieved the criterion of successful conservation. This conclusion remains essentially unaltered if a laxer criterion is employed.

Table 1 **Total of correct responses given by Groups I and II for each situation under AT and IT conditions**

Situations	Group I ($n = 40$)		Group II ($n = 40$)	
	AT ⟶ IT		IT ⟶ AT	
A Number Equal	32	19	14	22
B Number Unequal	36	18	13	22
C Length Equal	34	15	8	24
D Length Unequal	37	12	9	23
Totals	139	64	44	91

Table 2 **Percentages of correct responses for Groups I and II under AT and IT conditions**

Situations	Group I			Group II	
	AT ⟶ IT			IT ⟶ AT	
Nursery School Children	80.0	31.25		22.5	46.25
Primary School Children	93.7	48.8		32.5	67.5
Overall	86.9	40.0		27.5	56.9
Mean AT Performance			71.9		
Mean IT Performance			33.7		

The performance in the AT condition of Group II, which had received the IT condition first, was significantly poorer than that of Group I ($\chi^2 = 4.85$, $p < 0.05$). Hence it may be more appropriate to compare only the initial four judgements of each group. On this analysis 30 of the 40 children of Group I successfully conserved (AT condition) whereas only 5 of Group II did so (IT condition) ($\chi^2 = 29.2$, $p < 0.001$).

Discussion

These results give clear indications that traditional procedures for assessing conservation seriously underestimate the child's knowledge. Most of these four- and five-year olds achieved the criterion for successful conservation of length and number when the transformation was accidental, and yet most of the same children failed when the transformation was effected in the traditional manner. Indeed the results suggest that the performance in the AT condition of Group II subjects was depressed because of their prior experience with IT, so that even the AT procedure may have underestimated their knowledge of conservation. The verbalisations of those Group II subjects who were unsuccessful in the AT condition suggest they ignored the teddy's stated intentions and interpreted his activity as being directed towards changing the length of the row of counters, presumably because they had just witnessed the experimenter exhibit such activity. For example one child in the *length equal* situation chose the untransformed string as being longer after the teddy's activity "because you bent that one doing it and it's the shortest one".

The present approach differs from earlier ones which have emphasized language comprehension difficulties in that it considers the possibility that extralinguistic features of the testing situation, in particular the non-verbal behaviour of the experimenter, can influence the child's interpretation of the language. Several investigators have suggested there is a failure to understand key words in the question, and Griffiths, Shantz and Sigel (1967) have argued for the use of pretests which assess the comprehension of the relational terms in non-conservation contexts. However it is possible to understand a word in one context while failing to do so in others. The framework adopted here has allowed the identification of one feature of the testing situation which has precisely this effect — the intentional character of the experimenter's behaviour. It appears that this feature of interactions is implicated in the young child's normal procedures for interpreting language.

In the early stages of language acquisition, the child interprets the meaning of behavioural events to arrive at a notion of speaker's meaning and this knowledge is utilized to make sense of the language around him. Eventually the child acquires a semblance of linguistic meaning, in that he can respect certain properties of the language where the non-linguistic components of the speaker's activities do not conflict with the utterance. During this phase the intentional nature of the speaker's activities, where this is at variance with the utterance, can govern what the child thinks is being talked about, so that his understanding of such concepts as number and length can be obscured.

Hence when the experimenter has effected an intentional action which changes the *length* of a row of counters, the child behaves as if the experimenter is asking a question about length rather than number. When the length of the row changes, but without the experimenter appearing to have intended it, the child has no conflicting behavioural evidence relevant to his interpretation of the question, and so can correctly answer the experimenter's question on the basis of number. Similarly, when the experimenter carefully arranges one of the pieces of string into a crescent shape, the child compares the length of the untransformed string with one of the properties of the new figure — usually the distance between the sides of the crescent. In contrast, when the crescent shape appears as a result of the teddy's activity, the child is able to base his comparisons on the appropriate attribute.

Issues closely related to these have recently been discussed by Donaldson and McGarrigle (1974). They presented evidence that children, in judging which of two sets of toy cars had 'more', were systematically influenced by the presence of garages around the cars. The irrelevant attribute, fullness of the garage, was used as a criterion for response by about one-third of the children when the garages were present; when they were absent a different criterion was employed. Donaldson and McGarrigle suggested that these and related findings were evidence of the operation of non-linguistic rules which function in particular contexts to provide a specific interpretation of utterances when the child's linguistic knowledge by itself cannot do so. These rules, known as local rules, specify a hierarchy of attributes of the referent which are used in interpreting utterances. The results of the present experiment indicate that characteristics of the speaker's actions can also influence the child's interpretation of utterances, suggesting the existence of a different kind of local rule, one which is sensitive to the intentions of the speaker.

It is difficult to find alternative explanations for the present findings.* It is clear that accounts which emphasize perceptual effects are inadequate by themselves, since in both IT and AT conditions the child faced the usual misleading configuration of materials. Gelman (1969) has argued that attentional deficiencies could explain conservation failure. She proposed that young children define quantity multi-dimensionally so that a variety of irrelevant attributes are attended to, and suggested that the change in value of an irrelevant attribute brought about by the transformation increased the likelihood of attention to that attribute. Gelman used discrimination learning set training to overcome this tendency, and showed that five-year olds could, after extensive training, succeed in conservation tasks. However it is not easy to reconcile the results reported here with the attentional analysis since in the AT procedure the children were able, without any training whatsoever, to continue responding on the basis of the criterial attribute even though an irrelevant attribute had changed. Nonetheless the framework adopted in the present paper does have implications for attentional processes. Rather than postulating an attentional deficit, we are suggesting that the child's normal procedures for interpreting language encourage special sensitivity to certain characteristics of the speaker's behaviour.

If the explanation of the findings reported here is correct then there are important implications for those procedures which combine questions with intentional manipulative activity by an adult as a means of examining cognitive abilities. Far greater attention must be given to the features of the interactional setting in which the child's knowledge is assessed before any conclusions about the child's competence can be drawn. Further evidence is needed concerning the precise characteristics of speaker's intentional actions and how these influence the child's interpretation of utterances. It is possible that the achievements of the concrete operational stage are as much a reflection of the child's increasing independence from features of the interactional setting as they are evidence of the development of a logical competence.

* The interval between the first and second judgements for each situation was approximately 30 seconds in the AT condition, whereas it was only 3 - 5 seconds in the IT condition. A separate study on a small number of children found no evidence that the longer time interval between J1 and J2 could account for the improved performance in the AT procedure.

References

Brainerd, C.J. (1973) 'Judgements and explanations as criteria for the presence of cognitive structures.' *Psychol. Bull.,* 79, 172-179.

Bruner, J.S. (1973) 'The ontogenesis of speech acts.' *J. Child Language,* 2, 1-19.

Dodwell, P.C. (1961) 'Children's understanding of number concepts: Characteristics of an individual and of a group test.' *Can. J. Psychol.,* 15, 191-205.

Elkind, D. (1961) 'The development of quantitative thinking: A systematic replication of Piaget's studies.' *J. gen. Psychol.,* 98, 37-46.

Frank, cited in Bruner, J.S., Olver, R.O., and Greenfield, P.M. (1966) *Studies in Cognitive Growth,* Wiley, New York, p. 193.

Donaldson, M., & McGarrigle, J. (1974) 'Some clues to the nature of semantic development.' *J. Child Language, 1,* 185-194.

Gelman, R. (1969) 'Conservation acquisition: A problem of learning to attend to relevant attributes.' *J. Exper. child Psychol., 7,* 67-87.

Gelman, R. (1972) 'Logical capacity of very young children: Number invariance rules.' *Child Devel., 43,* 75-90.

Grice, H.P. (1968) 'Utterer's meaning, sentence-meaning, and word-meaning.' *Foundations of Language, 4,* 225-242.

Griffiths, J.A., Shantz, C.A., & Sigel, I.E. 'A methodological problem in conservation studies: The use of relational terms.' *Child Devel., 38,* 841-848.

Gruen, G.E. (1965) 'Experiences affecting the development of number conservation in children.' *Child Devel., 36,* 963-979.

Hood, H.B. (1962) 'An experimental study of Piaget's theory of the development of number in children.' *Brit. J. Psychol., 53,* 273-286.

Macnamara, J. (1972) 'Cognitive basis of language learning in infants.' *Psychol. Rev., 79,* 1-13.

Palermo, D.S., & Molfese, D.L. (1972) 'Language acquisition from age five onward.' *Psychol. Bull., 78,* 409-428.

Piaget, J. (1952) *The child's conception of number.* London: Routledge and Kegan Paul.

Piaget, J., & Inhelder, B. (1969) *The psychology of the child.* New York: Basic Books.

Rose, S.A., & Blank, M. (1974) 'The potency of context in children's cognition: An illustration through conservation.' *Child Devel., 45,* 499-502.

Ryan, J. (1973) 'Interpretation and imitation in early language development.' In R. Hinde & J.S. Hinde (Eds) *Constraints on learning — Limitations and predispositions.* London: Academic Press.

Smedslund, J. (1964) 'Concrete reasoning: A study of intellectual development.' *Mono. Soc. Res. Child. Devel., 29.*

20.

Tool and Symbol in Child Development*

L.S. Vygotsky

The primary purpose of this book is to characterize the uniquely human aspects of behavior, and to offer hypotheses about the way these traits have been formed in the course of human history and the way they develop over an individual's lifetime.

This analysis will be concerned with three fundamental issues: (1) What is the relation between human beings and their environment, both physical and social? (2) What new forms of activity were responsible for establishing labor as the fundamental means of relating humans to nature and what are the psychological consequences of these forms of activity? (3) What is the nature of the relationship between the use of tools and the development of speech? None of these questions has been fully treated by scholars concerned with understanding animal and human psychology.

Karl Stumpf, a prominent German psychologist in the early years of the twentieth century, based his studies on a set of premises completely different from those I will employ here.[1] He compared the study of children to the study of botany, and stressed the botanical character of development, which he associated with maturation of the whole organism.

The fact is that maturation *per se* is a secondary factor in the development of the most complex, unique forms of human behavior. The development of these behaviors is characterized by complicated, qualitative transformations of one form of behavior into another (or, as Hegel would phrase it, a transformation of quantity into quality). The conception of maturation as a passive process cannot adequately describe these complex phenomena. Nevertheless, as A. Gesell has aptly pointed out, in our approaches to development we continue to use the botanical analogy in our description of child development (for example, we say that the early education of children takes place in a "kindergarten").[2] Recently several psychologists have suggested that this botanical model must be abandoned.

In response to this kind of criticism, modern psychology has ascended the ladder of science by adopting zoological models as the basis for a new general approach to understanding the development of children. Once the captive of botany, child psychology is now mesmerized by zoology. The observations on which these newer models draw come almost entirely from the animal kingdom, and answers to questions about children are sought in experiments carried out on animals. Both the results of experiments with animals and the procedures used to obtain these results are finding their way from the animal laboratory into the nursery.

This convergence of child and animal psychology has contributed significantly to the study of the biological basis of human behavior. Many links between child and animal behavior, particularly in the study of elementary psychological processes, have been established. But a paradox has now emerged. When the botanical model was fashionable, psychologists emphasized the unique character of higher psychological functions and the difficulty of studying them by experimental means. But this zoological approach to the higher intellectual processes — those processes that are uniquely human — has led psychologists to interpret the higher intellectual functions as a direct continuation of corresponding processes in animals. This style of theorizing is particularly apparent in the analysis of practical intelligence in children, the most important aspect of which concerns the child's use of tools.

Practical intelligence in animals and children

The work of Wolfgang Köhler is particularly significant in the study of practical intelligence.[3] He conducted many experiments with apes during World War I, and occasionally compared some of his observations of chimpanzees' behavior with particular kinds of responses in children. This direct analogy between practical intelligence in the child and similar response by apes became the guiding principle of experimental work in the field.

K. Buhler's research also sought to establish similarities between child and ape.[4] He studied the way in which young children grasp objects, their ability to make detours while pursuing a goal, and the manner in which they use primitive tools. These observations, as well as his experiment in which a young child is asked to remove a ring from a stick, illustrate an approach akin to Köhler's. Buhler interpreted the manifestations of practical intelligence in children as being of exactly the same type as those we are familiar with in chimpanzees. Indeed, there is a phase in the life of the child that Buhler designated the "chimpanzee age" (p. 48). One ten-month-old infant whom he studied was able to pull a string to obtain a cookie that was attached to it. The ability to remove a ring from a post by lifting it rather than trying to pull it sideways did not appear until the middle of the second year.[5] Although these experiments were interpreted as support for the analogy between the child and apes, they also led Buhler to the important discovery, which will be explicated in later sections, that the beginnings of practical intelligence in the child (he termed it "technical thinking"), as well as the actions of the chimpanzee, are independent of speech.

Charlotte Buhler's detailed observations of infants during their first year of life gave further support to this conclusion.[6] She found the first manifestations of practical intelligence took place at the very young age of six months. However, it is not only tool use that develops at this point in a child's history but also systematic movement and perception, the brain and hands — in fact, the child's entire organism. Consequently, the child's system of activity is determined at each specific stage *both by the child's degree of organic development and by his or her degree of mastery in the use of tools.*

K. Buhler established the developmentally important principle that the beginnings of intelligent speech are preceded by technical thinking, and technical thinking comprises the initial phase of cognitive development. His lead in emphasizing the chimpanzee-like features of children's behavior has been followed by many others. It is in extrapolating this idea that the dangers of zoological models and analogies between human and animal behaviors find their clearest expression. The pitfalls are slight in research that focuses on the preverbal period in the child's development, as Buhler's did. However, he drew a questionable conclusion from his work with very young children when he stated, "The achievements of the chimpanzee are quite independent of language and in the case of man, even in later life, technical thinking, or thinking in terms of tools, is far less closely bound up with language and concepts than other forms of thinking."[7]

Buhler proceeded from the assumption that the relationship between practical intelligence and speech that characterizes the ten-month-old child remains intact throughout her lifetime. This analysis postulating the independence of intelligent action from speech runs contrary to our own findings, which reveal the integration of speech and practical thinking in the course of development.

Shapiro and Gerke offer an important analysis of the development of practical thinking in children based upon experiments modeled after Köhler's problem-solving studies with chimpanzees.[8] They theorize that children's practical thinking is similar to adult thought in certain respects and different in others, and emphasize the dominant role of social experience in human development. In their view, social experience exerts its effect through imitation: when the child imitates the way adults use tools and objects, she masters the very principle involved in a particular activity. They suggest that repeated actions pile up, one upon another, as in a multi-exposure photograph; the common traits become clear and the differences become blurred. The result is a crystalized scheme, a definite principle of activity. The child, as she becomes more experienced, acquires a greater number of models that she understands. These models represent, as it were, a refined cumulative design of all similar actions: at the same time, they are also a rough blueprint for possible types of action in the future.

However, Shapiro and Gerke's notion of adaptation is too firmly linked to a mechanical conception of repetition. For them, social experience serves only to furnish the child with motor schemas; they do not take into account the changes occurring in the internal structure of the child's intellectual operations. In their descriptions of children's problem solving, the authors are forced to note the "specific role fulfilled by speech" in the practical and adaptive efforts of the growing child. But their description of this role is a strange one. "Speech," they say, "replaces and compensates for real adaptation; it does not serve as a bridge leading to past experience but to a purely social adaptation which is achieved via the experimenter." This analysis does not allow for the contribution speech makes to the development of a new structural organization of practical activity.

Guillaume and Meyerson offer a different conclusion regarding the role of speech in the inception of uniquely human forms of behavior.[9] From their extremely interesting experiments on tool use among apes, they concluded that the methods used by apes to accomplish a given task are similar in principle and coincide on certain essential points to those used by people suffering from aphasia (that is, individuals who are deprived of speech). Their findings support my assumption that speech plays an essential role in the organization of higher psychological functions.[10]

311

These experimental examples bring us full circle to the beginning of our review of psychological theories regarding child development. Buhler's experiments indicate that the practical activity of the young child prior to speech development is identical to that of the ape, and Guillaume and Meyerson suggest that the ape's behavior is akin to that observed in people who are deprived of speech. Both of these lines of work focus our attention on the importance of understanding the practical activity of children at the age when they are just beginning to speak. My own work as well as that of my collaborators is directed at these same problems. But our premises differ from those of previous investigators. Our primary concern is to describe and specify the development of those forms of practical intelligence that are specifically human.

Relation between speech and tool use

In his classic experiments with apes Köhler demonstrated the futility of attempting to develop even the most elementary sign and symbolic operations in animals. He concluded that tool use among apes is independent of symbolic activity. Further attempts to cultivate productive speech in the ape have also produced negative results. These experiments showed once more that the purposive behavior of the animal is independent of any speech or sign-using activity.

The study of tool use in isolation from sign use is common in research work on the natural history of practical intellect, and psychologists who studied the development of symbolic processes in the child have followed the same procedure. Consequently, the origin and development of speech, as well as all other sign-using activity, were treated as independent of the organization of the child's practical activity. Psychologists preferred to study the development of sign use as an example of pure intellect and not as the product of the child's developmental history. They often attributed sign use to the child's spontaneous discovery of the relation between signs and their meanings. As W. Stern stated, recognition of the fact that verbal signs have meaning constitutes "the greatest discovery in the child's life."[11] A number of authors fix this happy "moment" at the juncture of the child's first and second year, regarding it as the product of the child's mental activity. Detailed examination of the *development of* speech and other forms of sign use was assumed to be unnecessary. Instead, it has routinely been assumed that the child's mind contains all stages of future intellectual development; they exist in complete form, awaiting the proper moment to emerge.

Not only were speech and practical intelligence assumed to have different origins, but their joint participation in common operations was considered to be of no basic psychological importance (as in the work of Shapiro and Gerke). Even when speech and the use of tools were closely linked in one operation, they were still studied as separate processes belonging to two completely different classes of phenomena. At best, their simultaneous occurrence was considered a consequence of accidental, external factors.

The students of practical intelligence as well as those who study speech development often fail to recognize the interweaving of these two functions. Consequently, the children's adaptive behavior and sign-using activity are treated as parallel phenomena — a view that leads to Piaget's concept of "egocentric" speech.[12] He did not attribute an important role to speech in the organization of the child's activities, nor did he stress its communicative functions, although he was obliged to admit its practical importance.

Although practical intelligence and sign use can operate independently of each other in young children, the dialectical unity of these systems in the human adult is the very essence of complex human behavior. Our analysis accords symbolic activity a specific *organizing* function that penetrates the process of tool use and produces fundamentally new forms of behavior.

Social interaction and the transformation of practical activity

Based on the discussion in the previous section, and illustrated by experimental work to be described later, the following conclusion may be made: *the most significant moment in the course of intellectual development, which gives birth to purely human forms of practical and abstract intelligence, occurs when speech and practical activity, two previously completely independent lines of development, converge.* Although children's use of tools during their preverbal period is comparable to that of apes, as soon as speech and the use of signs are incorporated into any action, the action becomes transformed and organized along entirely new lines. The specifically human use of tools is thus realized, going beyond the more limited use of tools possible among the higher animals.

Prior to mastering his own behavior, the child begins to master his surroundings with the help of speech. This produces new relations with the environment in addition to the new organization of behavior itself. The creation of these uniquely human forms of behavior later produce the intellect and become the basis of productive work: the specifically human form of the use of tools.

Observations of children in an experimental situation similar to that of Köhler's apes show that the children not only *act* in attempting to achieve a goal but also *speak*. As a rule this speech arises spontaneously and continues almost without interruption throughout the experiment. It increases and is more persistent every time the situation becomes more complicated and the goal more difficult to attain. Attempts to block it (as the experiments of my collaborator R. E. Levina have shown) are either futile or lead the child to "freeze up."

Levina posed practical problems for four- and five-year-old children such as obtaining a piece of candy from a cupboard. The candy was placed out of reach so the child could not obtain it directly. As the child got more and more involved in trying to obtain the candy, "egocentric" speech began to manifest itself as part of her active striving. At first this speech consisted of a description and analysis of the situation, but it gradually took on a "planful" character, reflecting possible paths to solution of the problem. Finally, it was included as part of the solution.

For example, a four-and-a-half-year-old girl was asked to get candy from a cupboard with a stool and a stick as possible tools. Levina's description reads as follows: (Stands on a stool, quietly looking, feeling along a shelf with stick.) "On the stool." (Glances at experimenter. Puts stick in other hand.) "Is that really the candy?" (Hesitates.) "I can get it from that other stool, stand and get it." (Gets second stool.) "No, that, doesn't get it. I could use the stick." (Takes stick, knocks at the candy.) "It will move now." (Knocks candy.) "It moved, I couldn't get it with the stool, but the, but the stick worked."[13]

In such circumstances it seems both natural and necessary for children to speak while they act: in our research we have found that speech not only accompanies practical activity but also plays a specific role in carrying it out. Our experiments demonstrate two important facts:

(1) A child's speech is as important as the role of action in attaining the goal. Children not only speak about what they are doing; their speech and action are part of *one and the same complex psychological function*, directed toward the solution of the problem at hand.

(2) The more complex the action demanded by the situation and the less direct its solution, the greater the importance played by speech in the operation as a whole. Sometimes speech becomes of such vital importance that, if not permitted to use it, young children cannot accomplish the given task.

These observations lead me to the conclusion that *children solve practical tasks with the help of their speech, as well as their eyes and hands*. This unity of perception, speech, and action, which ultimately produces internalization of the visual field, constitutes the central subject matter for any analysis of the origin of uniquely human forms of behavior.

To develop the first of these two points, we must ask: What is it that really distinguishes the actions of the speaking child from the actions of an ape when solving practical problems?

The first thing that strikes the experimenter is the incomparably greater *freedom* of children's operations, their greater independence from the structure of the concrete, visual situation. Children, with the aid of speech, create greater possibilities than apes can accomplish through action. One important manifestation of this greater flexibility is that the child is able to ignore the direct line between actor and goal. Instead, he engages in a number of preliminary acts, using what we speak of as instrumental, or mediated (indirect), methods. In the process of solving a task the child is able to include stimuli that do not lie within the immediate visual field. Using words (one class of such stimuli) to create a specific plan, the child achieves a much broader range of activity, applying as *tools* not only those objects that lie near at hand, *but searching for and preparing such stimuli as can be useful in the solution of the task, and planning future actions*.

Second, the practical operations of a child who can speak become much less impulsive and spontaneous than those of the ape. The ape typically makes a series of uncontrolled attempts to solve the given problem. In contrast, the child who uses speech divides the activity into two consecutive parts. She plans how to solve the problem through speech and then carries out the prepared solution through overt activity. Direct manipulation is replaced by a complex psychological process through which inner motivation and intentions, postponed in time, stimulate their own development and realization. This new kind of psychological structure is absent in apes, even in rudimentary forms.

314

Finally, it is decisively important that speech not only facilitates the child's effective manipulation of objects but also controls the *child's own behavior*. Thus, with the help of speech children, unlike apes, acquire the capacity to be both the subjects and objects of their own behavior.

Experimental investigation of the egocentric speech of children engaged in various activities such as that illustrated by Levina produced the second fact of great importance demonstrated by our experiments: *the relative amount of egocentric speech*, as measured by Piaget's methods, increases in relation to the difficulty of the child's task.[14] On the basis of these experiments my collaborators and I developed the hypothesis that children's egocentric speech should be regarded as the transitional form between external and internal speech. Functionally, egocentric speech is the basis for inner speech, while in its external form it is embedded in communicative speech.

One way to increase the production of egocentric speech is to complicate a task in such a way that the child cannot make direct use of tools for its solution. When faced with such a challenge, the children's emotional use of language increases as well as their efforts to achieve a less automatic, more intelligent solution. They search verbally for a new plan, and their utterances reveal the close connection between egocentric and socialized speech. This is best seen when the experimenter leaves the room or fails to answer the children's appeals for help. Upon being deprived of the opportunity to engage in social speech, children immediately switch over to egocentric speech.

While the interrelationship of these two functions of language is apparent in this setting, it is important to remember that egocentric speech is linked to children's social speech by many transitional forms. The first significant illustration of the link between these two language functions occurs when children find that they are unable to solve a problem by themselves. They then turn to an adult, and verbally describe the method that they cannot carry out by themselves. The greatest change in children's capacity to use language as a problem-solving tool takes place somewhat later in their development, when socialized speech (which has previously been used to address an adult) *is turned inward*. Instead of appealing to the adult, children appeal to themselves: language thus takes on an *intrapersonal function* in addition to its *interpersonal use*. When children develop a method of behavior for guiding themselves that had previously been used in relation to another person, when they organize their own activities according to a social form of behavior, they succeed in applying a social attitude to themselves. The history of the process of *the internalization of social speech* is also the history of the socialization of children's practical intellect.

The relation between speech and action is a dynamic one in the course of children's development. The structural relation can shift even during an experiment. The crucial change occurs as follows: At an early stage speech *accompanies* the child's actions and reflects the vicissitudes of problem solving in a disrupted and chaotic form. At a later stage speech moves more and more toward the starting point of the process, so that it comes to *precede* action. It functions then as an aid to a plan that has been conceived but not yet realized in behavior. An interesting analogy can be found in children's speech while drawing. Young children name their drawings only after they have completed them; they need to see them before they can decide what they are. As children get older they can decide in advance what they are going to draw. This displacement of the naming process signifies a change in the function of speech. Initially speech follows actions, is provoked by and dominated by activity. At a later stage, however, when speech is moved to the starting point of an activity, a new relation between word and action emerges. Now speech guides, determines, and dominates the course of action; *the planning function of speech* comes into being in addition to the already existing function of language to reflect the external world.[15]

Just as a mold gives shape to a substance, words can shape an activity into a structure. However, that structure may be changed or reshaped when children learn to use language in ways that allow them to go beyond previous experiences when planning future action. In contrast to the notion of sudden discovery popularized by Stern, we envisage verbal, intellectual activity as a series of stages in which the emotional and communicative functions of speech are expanded by the addition of the planning function. As a result the child acquires the ability to engage in complex operations extending over time.

Unlike the ape, which Köhler tells us is "the slave of its own visual field," children acquire an independence with respect to their concrete surroundings; they cease to act in the immediately given and evident *space*. Once children learn how to use the planning function of their language effectively, their psychological field changes radically. A view of the future is now an integral part of their approaches to their surroundings. In subsequent chapters, I will describe the developmental course of some of these central psychological functions in greater detail.

To summarize what has been said thus far in this section: The specifically human capacity for language enables children to provide for auxiliary tools in the solution of difficult tasks, to overcome impulsive action, to plan a solution to a problem prior to its execution, and to master their own behavior. Signs and words serve children first and foremost as a means of social contact with other people. The cognitive and communicative functions of language then become the basis of a new and superior form of activity in children, distinguishing them from animals.

The changes I have described do not occur in a one-dimensional, even fashion. Our research has shown that very small children solve problems using unique mixtures of processes. In contrast with adults, who react differently to objects and to people, young children are likely to fuse action and speech when responding to both objects and social beings. This fusion of activity is analagous to syncretism in perception, which has been described by many developmental psychologists.

The unevenness I am speaking of is seen quite clearly in a situation where small children, when unable to solve the task before them easily, combine direct attempts to obtain the desired end with a reliance upon emotional speech. At times speech expresses the children's desires, while at other times it serves as a substitute for actually achieving the goal. The child may attempt to solve the task through verbal formulations *and* by appeals to the experimenter for help. This mixture of diverse forms of activity was at first bewildering; but further observations drew our attention to a sequence of actions that clarify the meaning of the children's behavior in such circumstances. For example, after completing a number of intelligent and interrelated actions that should help him solve a particular problem successfully, the child suddenly, upon meeting a difficulty, ceases all attempts and turns for help to the experimenter. Any obstacle to the child's efforts at solving the problem may interrupt his activity. The child's verbal appeal to another person is an effort to fill the hiatus his activity has revealed. By asking a question, the child indicates that he has, in fact, formulated a plan to solve the task before him, but is unable to perform all the necessary operations.

Through repeated experiences of this type, children learn covertly (mentally) to plan their activities. At the same time they enlist the assistance of another person in accordance with the requirements of the problem posed for them. The child's ability to control another person's behavior becomes a necessary part of the child's practical activity.

Initially this problem solving in conjunction with another person is not differentiated with respect to the roles played by the child and his helper; it is a general, syncretic whole. We have more than once observed that in the course of solving a task, children get confused because they begin to merge the logic of what they are doing with the logic of the same problem as it has to be solved with the cooperation of another person. Sometimes syncretic action manifests itself when children realize the hopelessness of their direct efforts to solve a problem. As in the example from Levina's work, children address the objects of their attention equally with words and sticks, demonstrating the fundamental and inseparable tie between speech and action in the child's activity; this unity becomes particularly clear when compared with the separation of these processes in adults.

In summary, children confronted with a problem that is slightly too complicated for them exhibit a complex variety of responses including direct attempts at attaining the goal, the use of tools, speech directed toward the person conducting the experiment or speech that simply accompanies the action, and direct, verbal appeals to the object of attention itself.

If analyzed dynamically, this alloy of speech and action has a very specific function in the history of the child's development; it also demonstrates the logic of its own genesis. From the very first days of the child's development his activities acquire a meaning of their own in a system of social behavior and, being directed towards a definite purpose, are refracted through the prism of the child's environment. The path from object to child and from child to object passes through another person. This complex human structure is the product of a developmental process deeply rooted in the links between individual and social history.

References

1. K. Stumpf, "Zur Methodik der Kinderpsychologie," *Zeitsch. f. pädag. Psychol.*, 2 (1900).

2. A. Gesell, *The Mental Growth of the Preschool Child* (New York: Macmillan, 1925; Russian ed., Moscow-Leningrad: Gosizdat., 1930).

3. W. Köhler, *The Mentality of Apes* (New York: Harcourt Brace, 1925).

4. K. Buhler, *The Mental Development of the Child* (New York: Harcourt, Brace, 1930; Russian ed., 1924).

5. This particular experiment was described by D. E. Berlyne, "Children's Reasoning and Thinking," in *Carmichael's Manual of Child Psychology*, 3rd ed., Paul H. Mussen, ed. (New York: John Wiley, 1970), pp. 939-981.

6. C. Buhler, *The First Year of Life* (New York: Day, 1930).

7. K. Buhler, *Mental Development*, pp. 49-51. See also C. Buhler, *First Year*. The linguistic capabilities of chimpanzees are currently the subject of controversy among psychologists and linguists. It seems clear that chimpanzees are capable of more complex signing than expected at the time Buhler and Vygotsky wrote these passages. However, the inferences about cognitive and linguistic competence warranted by these observations are still hotly debated.

8. S. A. Shapiro and E. D. Gerke, described in M. Ya. Basov, *Fundamentals of General Pedology* (Moscow-Leningrad: Gosizdat., 1928).

9. P. Guillaume and I. Meyerson, "Recherches sur l'usage de l'instrument chez les singes," *Journal de Psychologie*, 27 (1930): 177-236.

10. Research on aphasia was barely begun by Vygotsky during his own lifetime. The error of this conclusion and subsequent changes in his theory regarding aphasia may be found in the work of A. R. Luria; see *Traumatic Aphasia* (The Hague: Mouton, 1970).

11. W. Stern, *Psychology of Early Childhood up to the Sixth Year of Age* (New York: Holt, Rinehart and Winston, 1924; Russian ed., Petrograd, 1915).

12. J. Piaget, *The Language and Thought of the Child* (New York: Meridian Books, 1955; also International Library of Psychology, 1925). The differences between Vygotsky's and Piaget's views of early language development and the role of egoecentric speech is treated extensively in chapter 3 of Vygotsky's *Thought and Language* (Cambridge: MIT Press, 1962) and in Piaget's volume of essays, *Six Psychological Studies* (New York: Random House, 1967).

13. See R. E. Levina, for L. S. Vygotsky's ideas on the planning role of speech in children, *Voprosi Psikhologii*, 14 (1938): 105-115. Although Levina made these observations in the late 1920s, they remain unpublished except for this brief explication.

14. Piaget, *Language and Thought*, p. 110.

15. A fuller description of these experiments is presented in chapter 7 of *Thought and Language*.

21. Interaction between Learning and Development*

L.S. Vygotsky

The problems encountered in the psychological analysis of teaching cannot be correctly resolved or even formulated without addressing the relation between learning and development in school-age children. Yet it is the most unclear of all the basic issues on which the application of child development theories to educational processes depends. Needless to say, the lack of theoretical clarity does not mean that the issue is removed altogether from current research efforts into learning; not one study can avoid this central theoretical issue. But the relation between learning and development remains methodologically unclear because concrete research studies have embodied theoretically vague, critically unevaluated, and sometimes internally contradictory postulates, premises, and peculiar solutions to the problem of this fundamental relationship; and these, of course, result in a variety of errors.

Essentially, all current conceptions of the relation between development and learning in children can be reduced to three major theoretical positions.

The first centers on the assumption that processes of child development are independent of learning. Learning is considered a purely external process that is not actively involved in development. It merely utilizes the achievements of development rather than providing an impetus for modifying its course.

In experimental investigations of the development of thinking in school children, it has been assumed that processes such as deduction and understanding, evolution of notions about the world, interpretation of physical causality, and mastery of logical forms of thought and abstract logic all occur by themselves, without any influence from school learning. An example of such a theory is Piaget's extremely complex and interesting theoretical principles, which also shape the experimental methodology he employs. The questions Piaget uses in the course of his "clinical conversations" with children clearly illustrate his approach. When a five-year-old is asked "why doesn't the sun fall?" it is assumed that the child has neither a ready answer for such a question nor the general capabilities for generating one. The point of asking questions that are so far beyond the reach of the child's intellectual skills is to eliminate the influence of previous experience and knowledge. The experimenter seeks to obtain the tendencies of children's thinking in "pure" form, entirely independent of learning.[1]

Similarly, the classics of psychological literature, such as the works by Binet and others, assume that development is always a prerequisite for learning and that if a child's mental functions (intellectual operations) have not matured to the extent that he is capable of learning a particular subject, then no instruction will prove useful. They especially feared premature instruction, the teaching of a subject before the child was ready for it. All effort was concentrated on finding the lower threshold of learning ability, the age at which a particular kind of learning first becomes possible.

Because this approach is based on the premise that learning trails behind development, that development always outruns learning, it precludes the notion that learning may play a role in the course of the development or maturation of those functions activated in the course of learning. Development or maturation is viewed as a precondition of learning but never the result of it. To summarize this position: Learning forms a superstructure over development, leaving the latter essentially unaltered.

The second major theoretical position is that learning *is* development. This identity is the essence of a group of theories that are quite diverse in origin.

One such theory is based on the concept of reflex, an essentially old notion that has been extensively revived recently. Whether reading, writing, or arithmetic is being considered, development is viewed as the mastery of conditioned reflexes; that is, the process of learning is completely and inseparably blended with the process of development. This notion was elaborated by James, who reduced the learning process to habit formation and identified the learning process with development.

Reflex theories have at least one thing in common with theories such as Piaget's: in both, development is conceived of as the elaboration and substitution of innate responses. As James expressed it, "Education, in short, cannot be better described than by calling it the organization of acquired habits of conduct and tendencies to behavior."[2] Development itself is reduced primarily to the accumulation of all possible responses. Any acquired response is considered either a more complex form of or a substitute for the innate response.

But despite the similarity between the first and second theoretical positions, there is a major difference in their assumptions about the temporal relationship between learning and developmental processes. Theorists who hold the first view assert that developmental cycles precede learning cycles; maturation precedes learning and instruction must lag behind mental growth. For the second group of theorists, both processes occur simultaneously; learning and development coincide at all points in the same way that two identical geometrical figures coincide when superimposed.

The third theoretical position on the relation between learning and development attempts to overcome the extremes of the other two by simply combining them. A clear example of this approach is Koffka's theory, in which development is based on two inherently different but related processes, each of which influences the other.[3] On the one hand is maturation, which depends directly on the development of the nervous system; on the other hand is learning, which itself is also a developmental process.

Three aspects of this theory are new. First, as we already noted, is the combination of two seemingly opposite viewpoints, each of which has been encountered separately in the history of science. The very fact that these two viewpoints can be combined into one theory indicates that they are not opposing and mutually exclusive but have something essential in common. Also new is the idea that the two processes that make up development are mutually dependent and interactive. Of course, the nature of the interaction is left virtually unexplored in Koffka's work, which is limited solely to very general remarks regarding the relation between these two processes. It is clear that for Koffka the process of maturation prepares and makes possible a specific process of learning. The learning process then stimulates and pushes forward the maturation process. The third and most important new aspect of this theory is the expanded role it ascribes to learning in child development. This emphasis leads us directly to an old pedagogical problem, that of formal discipline and the problem of transfer.

Pedagogical movements that have emphasized formal discipline and urged the teaching of classical languages, ancient civilizations, and mathematics have assumed that regardless of the irrelevance of these particular subjects for daily living, they were of the greatest value for the pupil's mental development. A variety of studies have called into question the soundness of this idea. It has been shown that learning in one area has very little influence on overall development. For example, reflex theorists Woodworth and Thorndike found that adults who, after special exercises, had achieved considerable success in determining the length of short lines, had made virtually no progress in their ability to determine the length of long lines. These same adults were successfully trained to estimate the size of a given two-dimensional figure, but this training did not make them successful in estimating the size of a series of other two-dimensional figures of various sizes and shapes.

According to Thorndike, theoreticians in psychology and education believe that every particular response acquisition directly enhances overall ability in equal measure.[4] Teachers believed and acted on the basis of the theory that the mind is a complex of abilities — powers of observation, attention, memory, thinking, and so forth — and that any improvement in any specific ability results in a general improvement in all abilities. According to this theory, if the student increased the attention he paid to Latin grammar, he would increase his abilities to focus attention on any task. The words "accuracy," "quick-wittedness," "ability to reason," "memory," "power of observation," "attention," "concentration," and so forth are said to denote actual fundamental capabilities that vary in accordance with the material with which they operate; these basic abilities are substantially modified by studying particular subjects, and they retain these modifications when they turn to other areas. Therefore, if someone learns to do any single thing well, he will also be able to do other entirely unrelated things well as a result of some secret connection. It is assumed that mental capabilities function independently of the material with which they operate, and that the development of one ability entails the development of others.

Thorndike himself opposed this point of view. Through a variety of studies he showed that particular forms of activity, such as spelling, are dependent on the mastery of specific skills and material necessary for the performance of that particular task. The development of one particular capability seldom means the development of others. Thorndike argued that specialization of abilities is even greater than superficial observation may indicate. For example, if, out of a hundred individuals we choose ten who display the ability to detect spelling errors or to measure lengths, it is unlikely that these ten will display better abilities regarding, for example, the estimation of the weight of objects. In the same way, speed and accuracy in adding numbers are entirely unrelated to speed and accuracy in being able to think up antonyms.

This research shows that the mind is not a complex network of *general* capabilities such as observation, attention, memory, judgment, and so forth, but a set of specific capabilities, each of which is, to some extent, independent of the others and is developed independently. Learning is more than the acquisition of the ability to think; it is the acquisition of many specialized abilities for thinking about a variety of things. Learning does not alter our overall ability to focus attention but rather develops various abilities to focus attention on a variety of things. According to this view, special training affects overall development only when its elements, material, and processes are similar across specific domains; habit governs us. This leads to the conclusion that because each activity depends on the material with which it operates, the development of consciousness is the development of a set of particular, independent capabilities or of a set of particular habits. Improvement of one function of consciousness or one aspect of its activity can affect the development of another only to the extent that there are elements common to both functions or activities.

Developmental theorists such as Koffka and the Gestalt School — who hold to the third theoretical position outlined earlier — oppose Thorndike's point of view. They assert that the influence of learning is never specific. From their study of structural principles, they argue that the learning process can never be reduced simply to the formation of skills but embodies an intellectual order that makes it possible to transfer general principles discovered in solving one task to a variety of other tasks. From this point of view, the child, while learning a particular operation, acquires the ability to create structures of a certain type, regardless of the diverse materials with which she is working and regardless of the particular elements involved. Thus, Koffka does not conceive of learning as limited to a process of habit and skill acquisition. The relationship he posits between learning and development is not that of an identity but of a more complex relationship. According to Thorndike, learning and development coincide at all points, but for Koffka, development is always a larger set than learning. Schematically, the relationship between the two processes could be depicted by two concentric circles, the smaller symbolizing the learning process and the larger the developmental process evoked by learning.

Once a child has learned to perform an operation, he thus assimilates some structural principle whose sphere of application is other than just the operations of the type on whose basis the principle was assimilated. Consequently, in making one step in learning, a child makes two steps in development, that is, learning and development do not coincide. This concept is the essential aspect of the third group of theories we have discussed.

Zone of proximal development: a new approach

Although we reject all three theoretical positions discussed above, analyzing them leads us to a more adequate view of the relation between learning and development. The question to be framed in arriving at a solution to this problem is complex. It consists of two separate issues: first, the general relation between learning and development; and second, the specific features of this relationship when children reach school age.

That children's learning begins long before they attend school is the starting point of this discussion. Any learning a child encounters in school always has a previous history. For example, children begin to study arithmetic in school, but long beforehand they have had some experience with quantity — they have had to deal with operations of division, addition, subtraction, and determination of size. Consequently, children have their own preschool arithmetic, which only myopic psychologists could ignore.

It goes without saying that learning as it occurs in the preschool years differs markedly from school learning, which is concerned with the assimilation of the fundamentals of scientific knowledge. But even when, in the period of her first questions, a child assimilates the names of objects in her environment, she is learning. Indeed, can it be doubted that children learn speech from adults; or that, through asking questions and giving answers, children acquire a variety of information; or that, through imitating adults and through being instructed about how to act, children develop an entire repository of skills? Learning and development are interrelated from the child's very first day of life.

Koffka, attempting to clarify the laws of child learning and their relation to mental development, concentrates his attention on the simplest learning processes, those that occur in the preschool years. His error is that, while seeing a similarity between preschool and school learning, he fails to discern the difference — he does not see the specifically new elements that school learning introduces. He and others assume that the difference between preschool and school learning consists of non-systematic learning in one case and systematic learning in the other. But "systematicness" is not the only issue; there is also the fact that school learning introduces something fundamentally new into the child's development. In order to elaborate the dimensions of school learning, we will describe a new and exceptionally important concept without which the issue cannot be resolved: the zone of proximal development.

A well known and empirically established fact is that learning should be matched in some manner with the child's developmental level. For example, it has been established that the teaching of reading, writing, and arithmetic should be initiated at a specific age level. Only recently, however, has attention been directed to the fact that we cannot limit ourselves merely to determining developmental levels if we wish to discover the actual relations of the developmental process to learning capabilities. We must determine at least two developmental levels.

The first level can be called the *actual developmental level*, that is, the level of development of a child's mental functions that has been established as a result of certain already *completed* developmental cycles. When we determine a child's mental age by using tests, we are almost always dealing with the actual developmental level. In studies of children's mental development it is generally assumed that only those things that children can do on their own are indicative of mental abilities. We give children a battery of tests or a variety of tasks of varying degrees of difficulty, and we judge the extent of their mental development on the basis of how they solve them and at what level of difficulty. On the other hand, if we offer leading questions or show how the problem is to be solved and the child then solves it, or if the teacher initiates the solution and the child completes it or solves it in collaboration with other children — in short, if the child barely misses an independent solution of the problem — the solution is not regarded as indicative of his mental development. This "truth" was familiar and reinforced by common sense. Over a decade even the profoundest thinkers never questioned the assumption; they never entertained the notion that what children can do with the assistance of others might be in some sense even more indicative of their mental development than what they can do alone.

Let us take a simple example. Suppose I investigate two children upon entrance into school, both of whom are ten years old chronologically and eight years old in terms of mental development. Can I say that they are the same age mentally? Of course. What does this mean? It means that they can independently deal with tasks up to the degree of difficulty that has been standardized for the eight-year-old level. If I stop at this point, people would imagine that the subsequent course of mental development and of school learning for these children will be the same, because it depends on their intellect. Of course, there may be other factors, for example, if one child was sick for half a year while the other was never absent from school; but generally speaking, the fate of these children should be the same. Now imagine that I do not terminate my study at this point, but only begin it. These children seem to be capable of handling problems up to an eight-year-old's level, but not beyond that. Suppose that I show them various ways of dealing with the problem. Different experimenters might employ different modes of demonstration in different cases: some might run through an entire demonstration and ask the children to repeat it, others might initiate the solution and ask the child to finish it, or offer leading questions. In short, in some way or another I propose that the children solve the problem with my assistance. Under these circumstances it turns out that the first child can deal with problems up to a twelve-year-old's level, the second up to a nine-year-old's. Now, are these children mentally the same?

When it was first shown that the capability of children with equal levels of mental development to learn under a teacher's guidance varied to a high degree, it became apparent that those children were not mentally the same age and that the subsequent course of their learning would obviously be different. This difference between twelve and eight, or between nine and eight, is what we call *the zone of proximal development. It is the distance between the actual developmental level as determined by independent problem solving and the level of potential development as determined through problem solving under adult guidance or in collaboration with more capable peers.*

If we naively ask what the actual developmental level is, or, to put it more simply, what more independent problem solving reveals, the most common answer would be that a child's actual developmental level defines functions that have already matured, that is, the end products of development. If a child can do such-and-such independently, it means that the functions for such-and-such have matured in her. What, then, is defined by the zone of proximal development, as determined through problems that children cannot solve independently but only with assistance? The zone of proximal development defines those functions that have not yet matured but are in the process of maturation, functions that will mature tomorrow but are currently in an embryonic state. These functions could be termed the "buds" or "flowers" of development rather than the "fruits" of development. The actual developmental level characterizes mental development retrospectively, while the zone of proximal development characterizes mental development prospectively.

The zone of proximal development furnishes psychologists and educators with a tool through which the internal course of development can be understood. By using this method we can take account of not only the cycles and maturation processes that have already been completed but also those processes that are currently in a state of formation, that are just beginning to mature and develop. Thus, the zone of proximal development permits us to delineate the child's immediate future and his dynamic developmental state, allowing not only for what already has been achieved developmentally but also for what is in the course of maturing. The two children in our example displayed the same mental age from the viewpoint of developmental cycles already completed, but the developmental dynamics of the two were entirely different. The state of a child's mental development can be determined only by clarifying its two levels: the actual developmental level and the zone of proximal development.

I will discuss one study of preschool children to demonstrate that what is in the zone of proximal development today will be the actual developmental level tomorrow — that is, what a child can do with assistance today she will be able to do by herself tomorrow.

The American researcher Dorothea McCarthy showed that among children between the ages of three and five there are two groups of functions: those the children possess, and those they can perform under guidance, in groups, and in collaboration with one another but which they have not mastered independently. McCarthy's study demonstrated that this second group of functions is at the actual developmental level of five-to-seven-year-olds. What her subjects could do only under guidance, in collaboration, and in groups at the age of three-to-five years they could do independently when they reached the age of five-to-seven years.[5] Thus, if we were to determine only mental age — that is, only functions that have matured — we would have but a summary of completed development, while if we determine the maturing functions, we can predict what will happen to these children between five and seven, provided the same developmental conditions are maintained. The zone of proximal development can become a powerful concept in developmental research, one that can markedly enhance the effectiveness and utility of the application of diagnostics of mental development to educational problems.

A full understanding of the concept of the zone of proximal development must result in reevaluation of the role of imitation in learning. An unshakable tenet of classical psychology is that only the independent activity of children, not their imitative activity, indicates their level of mental development. This view is expressed in all current testing systems. In evaluating mental development, consideration is given to only those solutions to test problems which the child reaches without the assistance of others, without demonstrations, and without leading questions. Imitation and learning are thought of as purely mechanical processes. But recently psychologists have shown that a person can imitate only that which is within her developmental level. For example, if a child is having difficulty with a problem in arithmetic and the teacher solves it on the blackboard, the child may grasp the solution in an instant. But if the teacher were to solve a problem in higher mathematics, the child would not be able to understand the solution no matter how many times she imitated it.

Animal psychologists, and in particular Köhler, have dealt with this question of imitation quite well.[6] Köhler's experiments sought to determine whether primates are capable of graphic thought. The principal question was whether primates solved problems independently or whether they merely imitated solutions they had seen performed earlier, for example, watching other animals or humans use sticks and other tools and then imitating them. Köhler's special experiments, designed to determine what primates could imitate, reveal that primates can use imitation to solve only those problems that are of the same degree of difficulty as those they can solve alone. However, Köhler failed to take account of an important fact, namely, that primates cannot be taught (in the human sense of the word) through imitation, nor can their intellect be developed, because they have no zone of proximal development. A primate can learn a great deal through training by using its mechanical and mental skills, but it cannot be made more intelligent, that is, it cannot be taught to solve a variety of more advanced problems independently. For this reason animals are incapable of learning in the human sense of the term: *human learning presupposes a specific social nature and a process by which children grow into the intellectual life of those around them.*

Children can imitate a variety of actions that go well beyond the limits of their own capabilities. Using imitation, children are capable of doing much more in collective activity or under the guidance of adults. This fact, which seems to be of little significance in itself, is of fundamental importance in that it demands a radical alteration of the entire doctrine concerning the relation between learning and development in children. One direct consequence is a change in conclusions that may be drawn from diagnostic tests of development.

Formerly, it was believed that by using tests, we determine the mental development level with which education should reckon and whose limits it should not exceed. This procedure oriented learning toward yesterday's development, toward developmental stages already completed. The error of this view was discovered earlier in practice than in theory. It is demonstrated most clearly in the teaching of mentally retarded children. Studies have established that mentally retarded children are not very capable of abstract thinking. From this the pedagogy of the special school drew the seemingly correct conclusion that all teaching of such children should be based on the use of concrete, look-and-do methods. And yet a considerable amount of experience with this method resulted in profound disillusionment. It turned out that a teaching system based solely on concreteness — one that eliminated from teaching everything associated with abstract thinking — not only failed to help retarded children overcome their innate handicaps but also reinforced their handicaps by accustoming children exclusively to concrete thinking and thus suppressing the rudiments of any abstract thought that such children still have. Precisely because retarded children, when left to themselves, will never achieve well-elaborated forms of abstract thought, the school should make every effort to push them in that direction and to develop in them what is intrinsically lacking in their own development. In the current practices of special schools for retarded children, we can observe a beneficial shift away from this concept of concreteness, one that restores look-and-do methods to their proper role. Concreteness is now seen as necessary and unavoidable only as a stepping stone for developing abstract thinking — as a means, not as an end in itself.

Similarly, in normal children, learning which is orientated toward developmental levels that have already been reached is ineffective from the viewpoint of a child's overall development. It does not aim for a new stage of the developmental process but rather lags behind this process. Thus, the notion of a zone of proximal development enables us to propound a new formula, namely that the only "good learning" is that which is in advance of development.

The acquisition of language can provide a paradigm for the entire problem of the relation between learning and development. Language arises initially as a means of communication between the child and the people in his environment. Only subsequently, upon conversion to internal speech, does it come to organize the child's thought, that is, become an internal mental function. Piaget and others have shown that reasoning occurs in a children's group as an argument intended to prove one's own point of view before it occurs as an internal activity whose distinctive feature is that the child begins to perceive and check the basis of his thoughts. Such observations prompted Piaget to conclude that communication produces the need for checking and confirming thoughts, a process that is characteristic of adult thought.[7] In the same way that internal speech and reflective thought arise from the interactions between the child and persons in her environment, these interactions provide the source of development of a child's voluntary behavior. Piaget has shown that cooperation provides the basis for the development of a child's moral judgment. Earlier research established that a child first becomes able to subordinate her behavior to rules in group play and only later does voluntary self-regulation of behavior arise as an internal function.

These individual examples illustrate a general developmental law for the higher mental functions that we feel can be applied in its entirety to children's learning processes. We propose that an essential feature of learning is that it creates the zone of proximal development; that is, learning awakens a variety of internal developmental processes that are able to operate only when the child is interacting with people in his environment and in cooperation with his peers. Once these processes are internalized, they become part of the child's independent developmental achievement.

From this point of view, learning is not development; however, properly organized learning results in mental development and sets in motion a variety of developmental processes that would be impossible apart from learning. Thus, learning is a necessary and universal aspect of the process of developing culturally organized, specifically human, psychological functions.

To summarize, the most essential feature of our hypothesis is the notion that developmental processes do not coincide with learning processes. Rather, the developmental process lags behind the learning process; this sequence then results in zones of proximal development. Our analysis alters the traditional view that at the moment a child assimilates the meaning of a word, or masters an operation such as addition or written language, her developmental processes are basically completed. In fact, they have only just begun at that moment. The major consequence of analyzing the educational process in this manner is to show that the initial mastery of, for example, the four arithmetic operations provides the basis for the subsequent development of a variety of highly complex internal processes in children's thinking.

Our hypothesis establishes the unity but not the identity of learning processes and internal developmental processes. It presupposes that the one is converted into the other. Therefore, it becomes an important concern of psychological research to show how external knowledge and abilities in children become internalized.

Any investigation explores some sphere of reality. An aim of the psychological analysis of development is to describe the internal relations of the intellectual processes awakened by school learning. In this respect, such analysis will be directed inward and is analogous to the use of x-rays. If successful, it should reveal to the teacher how developmental processes stimulated by the course of school learning are carried through inside the head of each individual child. The revelation of this internal, subterranean developmental network of school subjects is a task of primary importance for psychological and educational analysis.

A second essential feature of our hypothesis is the notion that, although learning is directly related to the course of child development, the two are never accomplished in equal measure or in parallel. Development in children never follows school learning the way a shadow follows the object that casts it. In actuality, there are highly complex dynamic relations between developmental and learning processes that cannot be encompassed by an unchanging hypothetical formulation.

Each school subject has its own specific relation to the course of child development, a relation that varies as the child goes from one stage to another. This leads us directly to a reexamination of the problem of formal discipline, that is, to the significance of each particular subject from the viewpoint of overall mental development. Clearly, the problem cannot be solved by using any one formula; extensive and highly diverse concrete research based on the concept of the zone of proximal development is necessary to resolve the issue.

Notes

1. J. Piaget, *The Language and Thought of the Child* (New York: Meridian Books, 1955).

2. William James, *Talks to Teachers* (New York: Norton, 1958), pp. 36-37

3. Koffka, *Growth of the Mind.*

4. E. L. Thorndike, *The Psychology of Learning* (New York: Teachers College Press, 1914).

5. Dorothea McCarthy, *The Language Development of the Pre-school Child* (Minneapolis: University of Minnesota Press, 1930).

6. W. Köhler, *The Mentality of Apes* (New York: Harcourt Brace Press, 1925).

7. J. Piaget, *The Language and Thought of the Child* (New York: Meridian Books, 1955).

22. Evidence of Learning from Guided Participation with Adults

Barbara Rogoff

David, age 7½ months, was at a restaurant with his parents and seemed to be getting bored. His mother handed him a dinner roll, although until then he had eaten only strained foods, zwieback toast, and Cheerios. David happily took the roll, examined it, looked up at his mother, and said, "Da?" as he held the roll up near his mouth. His mother replied automatically. "Yes, you can eat it."

The child acts (or is made to act) as if he or she had a plan or strategy before it is possible to devise and carry out that strategy independently. The child does not first master a strategy that guides action and then begin to act, but first acts and then begins to master the strategy that guides the action.... The child begins to regulate his or her own activity by becoming aware of what has already been going on for some time under the direction of others. (Wertsch, "Adult-Child Interaction and the Roots of Metacognition")

The fluency with which Mozart composed seems to be the outcome of his particular, intensive apprenticeship, of his opportunities to internalize, while still very young, the musical possibilities developed before his time.

(John-Steiner, *Notebooks of the Mind*)

This chapter examines research on the consequences of children's interactions with adults for their cognitive development. In the routine and recurrent interactions between adults and children are many thousands of opportunities for guided participation in solving everyday problems. We tend to overlook the numerous, implicit everyday opportunities for children to gain understanding and skills of the world around them. As Rheingold (1985) argues, development is largely a process of becoming familiar. It may be through repeated and varied experience in supported routine and challenging situations that children become skilled in specific cognitive processes. For example, Ferrier (1978) and Newson and Newson (1975) argue that the opportunity for language development occurs in routine participation in shared experiences and efforts to communicate as caregivers and infants carry out the thousands of diaperings, feedings, baths, and other recurring activities of daily life.

The advances that appear with development may build on these many opportunities to stretch knowledge and skills. In this perspective, development is built on learning, and, at the same time, learning is based on development. Children contribute to their own development through their eagerness and management of learning experiences as well as through their building on the knowledge and skill they have already developed. At the earliest ages, this "knowledge" includes their reflexes and aspects of behavior necessary for eating and protection, as well as primordial schemas for social interaction and learning systems such as language (Slobin, 1973). Soon, however, children's inborn behavioral and motivational repertoire is modified by experience, with their history reflected in the knowledge they bring to each new situation.

The research evidence on the influence of children's interaction with adults on their cognitive development provides clues about the means by which specific features of guided participation facilitate individual development. This literature goes beyond asking whether there is a relation between social interaction and children's individual skills to begin to address questions of how and under what circumstances social interaction may guide cognitive development.

There are important limitations, however, in this body of research:

1. It extracts for observation one session or a few sessions in children's lives to examine its (their) impact on individual development; it does not do justice to the repeated and adjusted nature of routine interaction in children's lives.

2. It focuses on dyadic situations, overlooking the richness of routine social situations. An apprenticeship model would involve not only a novice and an expert, but also other novices and experts jointly engaged in the same activity over time.

3. It involves situations in which adults are in charge and are focused on interaction with children. Thus it does not represent the many occasions in which children and adults are in each other's presence without interaction as their agenda, and the many times that the interaction is initiated and controlled by children seeking assistance, entertainment, or companionship. In keeping with the adult-initiated nature of the observed situations, there is little research on how children initiate and direct interaction or guide the assistance of others.

4. It concentrates on social interaction without considering the larger social context of arrangements for children and the societal context of the interactions and the cognitive skills. Skills in language, object manipulation, memory, and planning are, of course, closely tied to their application in cultural practices. The research on social interaction ignores the nature of the cultural tools used in the skills studied, overlooking the tools of language for categorization and analysis of events, technologies for constructing and analyzing objects, taxonomies for organizing lists of information to be remembered, and conventions such as maps for planning efficient routes in advance of actual navigation. In its emphasis on one cultural setting, the research examines the types of interactions (dyadic, often face-to-face) and specific cognitive skills that are of importance in that setting — Euroamerican middle class. It does not address the relations between interaction and cognitive skills in other settings.

5. In its frequent reliance on speed of development as a measure of the impact and excellence of social interaction, it reflects an assumption that the earlier that children develop a particular competence, the more skilled they will become in the

long run and the better they will compete in life. This assumption is not universal; in many cultures, the pace of development is not a matter of concern except for the very extreme cases in which children lag substantially behind what is expected. It is reasonable to question the assumption that faster is better, held by professionals as well as by the public. Piaget criticized it in identifying it as "The American Question." Children who are hurried to attain a recognizable competence in, say, number skills or reading may attain superficial evidence of skill (e.g., counting, knowing the alphabet, decoding written words) that does not help or, indeed, even hinders the development of deeper understandings in those domains, such as concepts of numerical properties or reading for comprehension.

6. The research situations are managed by an investigator who sets the problem, the goals, and the rules for the participants, removing these activities from analysis and limiting the roles of the participants, who might otherwise define their own problem or goals or rules.

With recognition of these limitations in the research — some an inevitable consequence of finite resources and time for programs of research, some a reflection of biases in approach — let us examine the relation between children's keeping with the adult-initiated nature of the observed situations, there is lit-social interaction with adults and their language development, skills in object exploration and construction, memory, and planning. These topics cover most of the available literature examining the role of social guidance and cognitive development. I do not review much of the research on the relation between social context and IQ, and between teaching and classroom learning, because it often does not closely examine either social interaction or cognitive processes. My preference is for research that investigates the processes of social interaction and cognition, rather than that which deals with summary scores that are often attributed to individuals as general characteristics.

Language and conceptual development

Language development

The relation between social interaction (or adult "input") and children's language development has received a great deal of attention. Many early studies correlated some features of maternal language with children's language skill, often including variables without predicting on a conceptual basis which ones should correlate. It is not surprising that shotgun correlational studies yield inconsistent results.

Researchers in this area disagree about what to make of the pattern of negative and positive correlations between linguistic input and children's language development. (See Hoff-Ginsberg & Shatz, 1982, and Snow, 1984, for reviews.) Some scholars conclude from research that fails to document relationships between linguistic input and child language acquisition that social interaction has little impact on language development (e.g., Bates, Bretherton, Beeghly-Smith, & McNew, 1982). However, this conclusion assumes that the methods used have been adequate to answer the question.

Camaioni, de Castro Campos, and DeLemos (1984) argue that the reason many studies have not found a relationship between social interaction and language is that they have reified both the social and the linguistic as separate, given categories rather than as processes in formation. They suggest that an adequate examination of the question requires scholars to

1. Look at social interaction and language as constitutive processes rather than as rules operating on already given categories

2. Consider language as a means to structure reality through social or communicative functions (stressing that linguistic activities are, right from the start, intersubjective processes)

3. Adopt linguistic models whose basic unit of analysis is not the single utterance but the *dialogue*

Similarly, John-Steiner and Tatter (1983) point out that approaches that assume that the social and individual aspects of development are separable rend apart the inherent unity of social and individual contributions. They argue that the limited findings of studies that test influences of separated social and cognitive processes on language development show the futility of separating these aspects of development, rather than diminishing the credibility of the mutual roles of individual and social features of development.

John-Steiner and Tatter (1983) stress that language development occurs within a system in which the primary goal is a functional one — achieving understanding between child and caregiver. With communication as the goal, child and caregiver together structure their interaction and advance their understanding of each other, with adjustments in adult speech and progress in language development as by-products.

These views, which stress that language development occurs in the process of functional communication, recast the question of social impact on language development. Instead of separating input (i.e., characteristics of maternal speech) from output (e.g., tests of children's vocabulary or grammatical skill), they focus on features of the communication of social partners with the child and on the child's skill in communication. Early language use involves conversations and propositions that are built in dialogue between people. Even infants in the one-word period build discussions with adults through taking successive turns that layer comments on topics of joint attention, as in "Shoe" . . . "Is that your shoe?" . . . "On" . . . "Oh, shall I put on your shoe?" (Greenfield & Smith, 1976; Scollon, 1976).

Consistent with the perspective that language development occurs in the context of functional communication, research shows a relationship between the extent and responsivity of adult–child interaction and the language development of children (Hoff-Ginsberg & Shatz, 1982; Snow, 1984). For example, mothers' frequency of and responsivity in interaction are related to infants' and toddlers' greater communicative competence (Hardy-Brown, Plomin, & DeFries, 1981; Olson, Bates, & Bayles, 1984). The extent to which mothers encourage attention to objects and events, and label the objects at which infants point, is associated with vocabulary size (Adamson, Bakeman, & Smith, in press; Masur, 1982; Papousek, Papousek, & Bornstein, 1985). Snow (1984) and Moerk (1985) argue that a great deal of speech addressed to children is sensitive to their linguistic skills and is contingent (both temporally and topically) with their previous utterances, and that the more children experience such contingency, the greater the facilitation of language acquisition.

Several studies demonstrate the importance of joint attention that focuses on children's interests rather than requiring children to refocus their attention. Tomasello and Farrar (1986) found that the extent of mothers' references to objects that were already the focus of their toddlers' attention correlated with the children's vocabulary 6 months later, while the extent of object references that redirected the children's attention was not related to vocabulary development. In addition, in an experimental study, toddlers learned words better if their attention was already focused on the objects of reference than if the words were presented when the children were not attending to the objects (Tomasello & Farrar, 1986).

Similarly, preschool children who heard new vocabulary items (Spanish labels for toys) contingent on their own expression of interest in the toys were better able to produce the newly learned words than were children who heard the labels at the same time as the experimental children, with timing unrelated to their own attention and interest in the toys being named (Valdez-Menchaca, 1987). Three-month-old infants interacting with adults who responded contingently to their vocalizations produced utterances that seemed more speech-like (syllabic) to adults than the utterances of infants whose partners interacted with them equally often but not contingently (Bloom, Russell, & Wassenberg, 1985). Recasts of children's comments enhance language development if they occur in smoothly continuing discourse (Nelson, Denninger, Bonvillian, Kaplan, & Baker, 1984). Snow (1982a) summarizes:

> A major facilitator of language acquisition is *semantic contingency* in adult speech. Adult utterances are semantically contingent if they continue topics introduced by the preceding child utterances. Semantically contingent utterances thus include a) expansions, which are limited to the content of the previous child utterance, b) semantic extensions, which add new information to the topic, c) clarifying questions, which demand clarification of the child utterance, and d) answers to child questions. (pp. 3-4)

It is noteworthy that the adult's semantically contingent speech builds from the child's comments, hence stressing the involvement of the child's interests and skills in the shared process. In addition, middle-class parents tailor their feedback in conversation to their children's contributions, responding differently to 2- to 3-year-olds' well-formed or ill-formed utterances: they expand, correct, or ask clarifying questions in response to children's ill-formed utterances, and extend the topic or move the conversation on more frequently in response to well-formed utterances (Demetras, Post, & Snow, 1986; Moerk, 1985; Penner, 1987).

Hoff-Ginsberg (1986) argues that maternal speech contributes to language acquisition by providing the child with data that illustrate regularities in the language: "These data feed into the child's proclivity to look for regularities in the system, to extract those patterns, and to use them as a basis for generalizations" (p. 160). In the process of communication, adults provide data and structure, of which children make active use.

Research on the communication environment of twins, who generally have to divide parental resources, supports the idea that the extent of parents' conversation and attention focusing may relate to children's language development. Papousek *et al.* (1985) report research by Bornstein and Ruddy suggesting that the lag in vocabulary learning of 12-month-old twins (compared with singletons) may result from the fact that each twin receives half as much maternal verbal input and encouragement of attention to objects, properties, or events in the environment during the first year as would a singleton. Since twins did not differ from singletons at age 4 months in manipulation, vocalization, and looking, their lag at age 12 months may reveal the effect of having to share the interactional energy of their mother. Tomasello, Mannle, and Kruger (1986), reporting similar findings, suggest that the economics of interacting with two babies at once reduces the opportunities for interaction for each baby and may account for the slower language development of twins compared with singletons.

The tailored responses of middle-class adults communicating with young children, focusing their attention, and expanding and improving the children's contributions appear to support children's advancing linguistic and communication skills in ways valued by their community.

Conceptual development

Research on conceptual development similarly illustrates the role of communication in advancing knowledge and gives evidence that children's level of understanding provides an important starting point for adult-child discussion of concepts.

Children's conceptual development was enhanced in a study that encouraged mothers to provide more advanced concepts in conversation as they read picture books to their 3-year-olds over a period of 2 weeks (Adams, 1987). To encourage the mothers to discuss concepts and use taxonomic labels, some of the books were designed with the pictures of animals arranged with taxonomic families together. The mothers hedged and modified their children's labels and made statements of class inclusion, providing taxonomic information, when using the books that were organized by family. The children whose mothers read those books showed advances in their categorization of animals to a level approaching adult usage, compared with children whose mothers read books with the same pictures arranged randomly. Thus social interaction that encouraged discussion of category hierarchies induced children to progress toward appropriately handling a body of culture- and domain-specific knowledge.

In a study of understanding of the concept of seriation, Heber (1981) found improvement in 5- to 6-year-olds' seriation skills in a condition in which an adult engaged each child in dialogue about the child's seriation decisions, especially when the dialogue encouraged the child to specify the rationale for decisions (to an "ignorant" puppet) or guided the child in discussing relations of "more" and "less." In contrast, there was no improvement in the seriation skills of children who received a didactic explanation of the rationale, worked with peers of equal skill, or worked independently, compared with children who received no opportunity to work on the problem. The fact that the conditions that encouraged development involved dialogue is consistent with the idea that benefits of social interaction derive from shared thinking in intersubjective communication.

Object exploration and construction

Adult support appears to encourage children's attention to objects and exploration, and infants' and older children's skills in handling objects, especially if the adults' support is contingent on the children's efforts.

Children's attention and skill with objects can be channeled by adults' highlighting of events during social interaction. The active and supportive involvement of an adult in children's exploration of novel objects led to more exploration by 3- to 7-year-olds than did the simple presence of the adults (Henderson, 1984a, 1984b). Adult object demonstration, focusing of the infant's attention, and collaborative engagement with objects relates to infant attentiveness, skill, and learning of new uses of objects (Bornstein, 1988; Hay, Murray, Cecire, & Nash, 1985; Hodapp, Goldfield, & Boyatzis, 1984; Parrinello & Ruff, 1988; Rogoff, Malkin, & Gilbride, 1984). An intervention to increase the level of maternal focusing on her infant's attention (by having an encouraging observer comment on the effectiveness of the mother's natural efforts to stimulate her infant) produced greater exploratory competence by the infants as much as 2 months later (Belsky, Goode, & Most, 1980).

Kaye (1977a) found that mothers' attempts to teach 7-month-olds to reach around a barrier to grasp a toy were tailored to the infants' motivation, attention, and competence. The mothers modeled detouring or simplified the task when the infants looked back at the toy after having just looked away but not when the infants were reaching for it. They simplified the task when the infants were not succeeding at it or were not interested in it. When infants had been close to success but were becoming fretful, the mothers moved the infants' hands around the screen toward the toy. Simplification of the task enhanced the infants' success in the training phase, although not in a posttest.

Puzzle construction

In a series of studies with preschool children on the task of constructing complex block pyramids, Wood and his colleagues have found that adults sensitively tailor their support of children's efforts according to the children's skill and that such contingency may help children to advance their skills.

The level of assistance by a tutor who was instructed to help the children only when they had run into difficulty was adjusted to the children's ages (Wood, Bruner, & Ross, 1976). With 3-year-olds, the tutor's efforts focused on maintaining the children's attention to the task. With 4-year-olds, the tutor could concentrate on pointing out the nature of mistakes. With 5-year-olds, the tutor was needed only to check the construction or to help with critical difficulties.

When mothers helped their 3- to 4-year-olds in the same task, most of them tailored their instruction to their children's needs, guiding at a level that was near the limits of the children's performance, taking into account the children's responses to the most recent instruction, and adjusting the specificity of instruction according to whether the children had been successful on that step (Wood & Middleton, 1975). Whereas the *number* of interventions by mothers did not relate to the children's performance, children performed best on the posttest of independent construction if their mothers had intervened in their region of sensitivity to instruction and had adjusted appropriately to their success.

The type of sensitivity shown by the mothers in tailoring their scaffolding (Wood & Middleton, 1975) was effective in improving 3- to 4-year-old children's performance when a tutor followed the mothers' patterns in systematically accommodating the contingency of her instruction to children's needs (Wood, Wood, & Middleton, 1978). Children who were taught contingently, with the tutor moving to less intervention after success and to more intervention after failure, were more capable of carrying out the task in the posttest than were children who were taught according to scripts that focused on modeling the whole task, describing the task, or arbitrarily switching between these levels of intervention. In these studies, children's skills in particular situations can be seen to advance as a result of supportive guidance provided in social interaction.

Children's remembering and planning

Planning and memory activities have been suggested as tasks in which collaboration and guidance may be especially fruitful (Brown & Reeve, 1987; Hartup, 1985; Lomov, 1978). Adults may be able to carry out metacognitive or metamnemonic roles that are beyond children, while demonstrating to the children how such processing can be accomplished. Wertsch (1978) argues that the regulation supplied by adults while assisting young children is a form of metacognition, with shifts across development moving from executive control by the adult (with step-by-step commands for carrying out a task); to questions and suggestions aimed at revealing to the child the overall strategy or the next step; and, finally, to general executive assistance by the adult, with children handling the details of carrying out strategies.

DeLoache (1983) notes that mothers' memory questions (regarding names or attributes of objects) during picture-book reading with toddlers are structured to elicit the best the children can do, but with some requests for information that are too difficult for the child. When the child fails to respond, the mother quickly answers her own question, providing a model that may be especially effective in its timing and filling a slot that allows the child to compare a well-formed response with whatever "inchoate thought" the child has formulated in answer to the question.

Correlational data suggest a link between parental memory demands and children's memory skills. Two- and 3-year-old children whose mothers made frequent memory demands on them evidenced better performance on memory tests up to a year following the observation of maternal memory demands (Ratner, 1984). Children whose mothers managed conversations about past events by rephrasing and elaborating their previous questions when the children were 2½ years old recounted more information in a more coherent narrative when they were 4 years old (Fivush, 1988).

Although these suggestions of connections between joint mnemonic activity and children's memory skills are intriguing, it is important to remember that correlational links allow multiple explanations. Children who remember skillfully are likely to act differently in joint mnemonic activities from children who are less skilled in memory tasks.

Experimental data examining the relation between collaborative memory or planning activities and children's subsequent independent performance do not yield entirely consistent results that would support the assumption that social interaction automatically fosters development. The inconsistencies across studies suggest that it is not the presence of a partner that matters, but the *nature of interaction* between the partners. The child's partner's skill in the task and the achievement of joint problem solving seem to be critical. The variation in results may have to do with young children's difficulties in participating in joint decision making in planning, although they can benefit from social guidance in more concrete tasks, such as remembering categories or lists of items.

The rest of this chapter is divided into a discussion of research with young children (ages 4 and 5) and older children, since the inconsistencies appear in studies with the younger children. The research with both age groups underlines the importance of considering shared decision making, with intersubjectivity between the partners, rather than just comparing groups that vary in the presence or expertise of partners.

Guided participation and young children

Studies with young children have occasionally found no benefits from having an adult partner present when compared to the success of children working alone (Kontos, 1983). In our research, we have found that 4- and 5-year-olds benefited from working with adult partners in memory tasks but were no more effective in learning to plan routes than were those who worked alone.

Memory tasks

Several memory studies with young children have shown that the children benefit from working with supportive adults. A pilot study compared the free recall of 4-year-olds whose parents were either encouraged to assist them in learning a list of items or instructed to simply present the list without elaboration, as in standard laboratory procedures (Mistry & Rogoff, 1987). In both conditions, the parents were constrained as to number and order of item presentations. The children whose parents were instructed to provide strategic assistance performed slightly better than those whose parents were instructed to simply present the list. Children who recalled more items were somewhat more likely to have had the memory goal emphasized by their parents, to have labeled the items, and to have received more parental suggestions about strategies to use to organize the items.

In two studies that varied the support of an adult experimenter, 5-year olds benefited from guidance in learning and remembering the organization of common items (Göncü & Rogoff, 1987). The experimenter followed scripts designed to adjust the extent of guidance in determining category labels and the extent of children's participation in decision making. The children remembered the classification scheme better in the individual posttest if the adult had offered any type of guidance on category rationales (whether suggesting that the child find categories or explaining, demonstrating, or collaborating with the child in determining the categories) rather than having children work alone or simply providing feedback on the placement of individual items.

Planning tasks

Maze Routes. Two studies found that 4-year-olds who solved practice mazes with their mothers' assistance were no more skilled in planning maze solutions as matched children who worked alone in the practice session (Radziszewska, Germond, & Rogoff). During the practice session, children either worked by themselves, with their mothers seated nearby, or solved mazes with their mothers' assistance. In the practice phase, children in the two groups were yoked in pairs to ensure that they practiced on an equal number of mazes.

In both the original study and a replication (designed to decrease instructions from the experimenter that we thought might have made the mothers' help unnecessary), children who had worked alone and those who had had their mothers' assistance in the practice phase solved an equal number of mazes in the posttest, with an equal degree of planfulness. We are currently doing a third version of this study, with mazes differing in the degree to which planfulness is appropriate, to learn whether task variation in the need for advance planning makes the assistance of mothers more useful to the children in distinguishing when to plan in advance and when to plan opportunistically, a skill that is difficult for 4-year-olds (Gardner & Rogoff, 1988).

Grocery-Store Routes. Another study involving young children in spatial planning revealed a similar absence of differences between children who had worked alone and those who had worked with a partner. Five-year-olds were asked to devise routes to pick up grocery items (presented in a pictorial list) without backtracking through the aisles of a three-dimensional model store (Gauvain & Rogoff, 1989). Children who had worked alone on planning efficient routes through the store performed as well on a later test as children who had worked with peers or with their mothers. Simply having a partner did not make children more likely to plan routes efficiently.

The children who actually shared decision making in their interactions with partners (rather than working independently or dividing the task into independent turns), however, did perform better than both the children who had worked alone and the children who had had a partner but had not worked jointly. These results, although correlational, support the idea that intersubjectivity between partners is an important aspect of interaction. The presence of a partner may be irrelevant unless the partners truly work together in problem solving.

An explanation: difficulty of sharing thinking in some tasks

Piaget's suggestion that young children have difficulty coordinating problem solving with another person (Azmitia & Perlmutter, in press; *Piaget*, 1977) appears to be a plausible explanation for the lack of benefits of social interaction for young children in the planning tasks — unless decision making is shared. But an explanation based solely on egocentricity at a young age would not explain the fact that adult guidance benefits young children's memory performance (as well as their language and conceptual development and object exploration and construction).

The nature of the tasks is crucial to consider. In some situations, the presence of a partner may serve as a distraction, requiring attention to be focused on the division of labor and on social issues rather than providing support. Some tasks may be difficult to coordinate with another person, and this may be especially true for young children.

The spatial planning tasks that we have used may be particularly difficult for young children to work on collaboratively. Some cognitive processes, such as planning, may be less accessible both to reflection by the individual and to discussion or joint attention in action. Planning tasks involve limitations in the concrete contexts for description and instances to "point to" in conversation or demonstration, since they deal with future events. It may be more difficult to share decision making or understanding of a problem that deals with abstract concepts or future events than to achieve intersubjectivity in dealing with concrete, present referents. Perhaps it is easier for young children to work with others on memory tasks, learning information that is physically presented without the need for complicated interpersonal understanding, than it is on planning tasks, which require discussion of future possibilities and strategies for dealing with the efficient coordination of several possible actions.

There do not seem to be general difficulties for young children in profiting from social interaction, as they benefit from guided participation in remembering as well as in language and conceptual development and object exploration and construction. I attribute the findings on difficulties in guided participation in planning to task-specific challenges for young children in sharing problem solving in the development of efficient plans and dealing with coordination for the future, which contrast with greater ease of establishing intersubjectivity in concrete tasks involving objects to be remembered, referred to, and handled appropriately. This is supported by the evidence that young children who actually shared decision making in planning routes through the grocery store performed better in subsequent independent planning. Simply being with a skilled adult may have no direct link to children's learning. Interaction in which the adult and the child manage to achieve intersubjectivity in decision making, with adult guidance, may relate to better subsequent performance by young children.

Further evidence for the importance of intersubjectivity for cognitive benefits of social interaction is provided by the observation that a joint focus of attention during conversations in a museum between mothers and young children — with joint discussion — led to greater memory for the information discussed, no matter which member of the pair initially focused attention on it (Tessler, cited by Fivush, 1988). Details that the children pointed out but that did not become a focus of joint discussion were not as well remembered by the children.

If we investigate the extent to which children actually participate in specific, sophisticated thinking in social interaction, we may be able to delineate features of social interaction that are influential in cognitive development. Just as research on language development points to the importance of joint attention and of expansions of young middle-class children's attempts to communicate, building on children's interest and level of skill, research on the development of memory and planning skills suggests that a crucial aspect of social interaction is the extent to which children participate in a shared thinking process with the support of a more skilled partner. This notion is supported by research on remembering and planning with older children.

Guided participation and older children

The studies of remembering and planning undertaken with older children compare interaction with middle-class adults (as skilled partners) with that with peers (as less skilled partners). Such a comparison provides a control for having a social partner and facilitates the examination of memory and planning processes that are made public when they are performed socially. Partners in problem solving provide information to each other on decision making that can be used by researchers to infer decision-making processes.

The research with older children is consistent in showing advantages of working with a skilled partner in memory and planning tasks. Adult partners consistently evidence greater sensitivity, demonstration, and modeling of sophisticated strategies than peer partners. Since peers have been purposefully used as less skilled partners in these tasks, the results are unlikely to apply to situations in which peers are skilled or in control.

Memory tasks

In tasks involving learning a classification system to organize sets of common objects, 6-year-old children performed better after having had the assistance of adults than of 8-year-old children (Ellis & Rogoff, 1982, 1986). The adult teachers almost always explained the tasks before beginning to place items, referred to the need to categorize, and provided category rationales for the groups of items; less than half of the child teachers did so. Most of the adult teachers prepared their learners for the memory test through rehearsal and mnemonics for the classification system, while very few of the child teachers provided explicit preparation for the test beyond admonishing their partners to study. The children whose mothers offered guidance and who participated in working out the organization of items and in preparing for the test remembered the items and the conceptual organization better in the individual posttest (Rogoff & Gauvain, 1986).

The example given in [Chapter 5] involving joint development of a mnemonic strategy for remembering the locations of the categories (Rogoff & Gardner, 1984, using the same data as Ellis & Rogoff, 1982, 1986) illustrates the mnemonic support that mothers provided. The mother created a temporal mnemonic for the locations of the first groups of objects, thinking aloud as she suggested making up a little story organized according to daily routine. Then she reviewed the categories and enlisted the child's help in creating the story for the remaining groups. She provided guidance and invention in suggesting the mnemonic and getting the child started on it, and she and the child collaborated on the level of the child's participation in producing the mnemonic. Once the child showed some grasp of the mnemonic, the mother turned it over to the child to manage for further review.

Most of the child teachers appeared insensitive to their partners' need to learn, providing little guidance and almost no preparation for the test (Ellis & Rogoff, 1986). More than half of them did not include the learners in the task, placing the items themselves without explanation and often without even looking to see if the learner were watching. Others required the learners to perform the task with minimal guidance, having them guess the location of items without explanation. The peer dyads did not evidence the intersubjectivity and shared decision making observed with the adult-child dyads; they appeared to focus on the immediate task of sorting items.

When the child teachers did try to guide the learners, their hints were not effective for placing later items in the group or for the long-term goal of communicating the category structure in preparation for the test. For example, one child who wanted the learner to put an item in a white box pointed to the background of the photograph of the item. This hint was effective in getting the item placed, but would have been of little help for other items in the group or for the test. The child teachers had difficulty formulating hints that were useful but still allowed the learner some independence in solving the problem, failing to interject helpful information at the level the learner needed. (On occasion, it appeared that this was the child teachers' idea of the role of a teacher, as they used schoolteacher intonations to praise the learners' correct guesses.)

Similar contrasts between the teaching interactions of adults and children teaching younger children have been found by McLane (1987) and Koester and Bueche (1980): the child teachers seemed to focus on accomplishing the concrete task rather than ensuring that their partners understood the rationale, and they usually did too much (taking over the performance of the task) or too little (insisting that their young partners "figure it out" without giving them guidance in doing so). Child teachers may have difficulty coordinating communication when the cognitive task is unfamiliar or especially challenging.

The learners' interaction with the adults in Ellis and Rogoff's (1982, 1986) study appeared to involve more effective guided participation: the adults attempted to orient the children to the task, to provide links between current knowledge and the new situation, and to structure the task, and the children participated in guided decision making with their roles collaboratively adjusted so that they were involved at a level that was challenging but within reach. The interactions involving child teachers did not show these features of guidance, and the learners who were paired with child teachers made more attempts to direct the teaching, especially by trying to become involved in the task when the child teachers took over all the responsibility and excluded the learners. These results support the idea that interaction with skilled partners is useful for children's learning in the memory task through guided participation in skilled problem solving.

Planning studies

In the first study in this series, Radziszewska and Rogoff (1988) found that 9-year-old children gained more skill in errand planning from collaborating with parents than with 9-year-old partners. Partners were given a map of an imaginary downtown (Figure 4) and two lists of errands and were asked to plan a trip to get materials for a school play. Each partner had a list with five items to be picked up, such as uniforms from the Theatrical Supplies store and paintbrushes from the Paint Shop or the Shopping Center. The dyad had to coordinate their planning of the route so the driver could make one trip efficiently (to save gasoline). To produce an optimal route, subjects needed to devise a plan incorporating the stores that had to be visited (i.e., to get items that were available from only one store), and to decide which of two alternatives would be more efficient to include for items that could be bought at a choice of stores. The map was the same for all trials, and the optimal route was similar, but the lists of items were different for each trial. Partners planned two trips together; then each planned a trip independently.

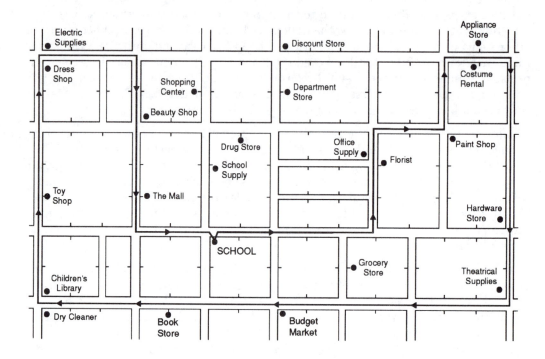

Figure 4   **Map of imaginary downtown for errand-planning task, showing an optimal route. (Reprinted by permission of the publisher, from Radziszewska & Rogoff, 1988, copyright 1988 by the American Psychological Association**

The collaborative planning of adult-child dyads was much more sophisticated than that of peer dyads. The peer dyads planned by making decisions on a step-by-step basis, as is common in children's individual planning (Magkaev, 1977). They usually proceeded by identifying the store closest to the current location and checking to see if it was on either of the lists; much less efficient routes were the result. Adult-child dyads planned longer sequences of moves, averaging 4.9 stores per move decision compared with the peer dyads' average sequences of 1.3. Almost half of the adult-child dyads planned the whole route at once, whereas none of the peer dyads did so. Adult-child dyads were also twice as likely to explore the layout before making moves, often marking the choice and no-choice stores with different colors and symbols to facilitate planning an optimal route. Furthermore, adult-child dyads were 11 times as likely to verbalize planning strategies.

During collaboration with adults, children usually participated in the more sophisticated planning strategies organized by the adults. Statements of strategy came primarily from the adults, but the sophisticated planning decisions were made jointly by the adults and children. Differences in the performance of the children who performed well and those who performed poorly after collaborating with adults appeared to relate to the extent of shared and guided decision making with the adults during collaboration.

The interaction between peers resembled that between adults and children in dyads in which the children subsequently performed poorly. They were also similar to the peer teachers in the study by Ellis and Rogoff (1986) who focused on immediate actions with a step-by-step approach and poorly communicated their problem-solving strategies. The more skilled peer partners often dominated decision making, ignored their partners, and communicated little.

It appears that planning with a skilled partner provides an opportunity for children to practice skills that are in advance of those that they can manage independently, and that such collaboration enhances children's later independent planning. Children who had worked with adults produced routes that were about 20% shorter than those of children who had worked with peers, and they applied specific aspects of the sophisticated planning strategy they had practiced with adults. For example, 14 of the 16 children from adult-child pairs started the individual trial by searching for and marking the choice and the no-choice stores on the map, as was common in their collaborative trials, whereas only 1 of the 16 children from peer dyads marked the stores in advance of making moves.

Although the differences in performance that resulted from having had a peer or adult partner were striking, both during collaboration and in independent performance, the advantage of working with adults could be attributed either to adults' greater skill in the planning task or to guidance and children's participation in the collaborative planning decisions. The next study examined the roles of the child's partner's expertise in the planning task and of guided participation in planning.

Radziszewska and Rogoff (manuscript) replicated their earlier study (Radziszewska & Rogoff, 1988) and added a condition in which peer partners were individually trained to employ the optimal strategy in the errand-planning task, prior to their collaboration with target children. A pretest determined that the errand-planning efficiency of the trained peers approached that of the adults. During collaboration, dyads with a trained peer partner and dyads with an adult partner evidenced equally sophisticated planning (i.e., planning sequences of moves rather than single steps), and both groups showed more sophisticated planning than dyads with an untrained peer partner.

The results suggested that expertise in errand planning as well as availability of guidance and participation in skilled decision making contributed to the effectiveness of working with adults. Target children who had collaborated with adults performed best, and those who had worked with trained peers performed no better than those who had worked with untrained peers.

Despite the adults' and the trained peers' similar planning strategies and efficiency during collaborative errand planning, the adults more frequently communicated the optimal strategy to target children. In addition, more than half of the adult-child dyads evidenced strategic thinking aloud during collaboration, whereas none of the peer dyads (with trained or untrained partners) showed strategic thinking aloud. Almost all the children working with adults were active participants, observing or participating in decisions, whereas fewer than half of the children working with trained peers were active participants. Children who worked with untrained peers often collaborated, but without a partner skilled in errand planning, such involvement was least effective for the target children's learning. The children who performed best in subsequent independent errand planning had the benefit of participating in skilled planning decisions, with guidance: posttest performance by target children was related to the production of efficient routes on collaborative trials, active involvement of children in planning decisions, and discussion of decisions and of the optimal strategy in joint planning.

Together, the results with younger and older children suggest that intersubjectivity in remembering and planning is a central feature of social interaction that allows children to take advantage of the bridging, structuring, and transfering of responsibility that were suggested as processes involved in guided participation. Children appear to benefit from participation in problem solving with the guidance of partners who are skilled in accomplishing the task at hand.

Caveats in the comparison of peers with adults

The initial purpose of using peers in the studies just discussed was as a less skilled comparison group for the skilled adult partners. The results may not represent the positive aspects of peer interaction in activities in which children are more skilled or in situations they regard as being in the domain of peer (rather than adult-child) activities, such as play and exploration. Hence the findings reported in the sections on older children's remembering and planning — that interaction with adults is more sensitive and instructive and that children learn more from their interactions with adults than from those with peers — must be qualified as limited to adult-world tasks in which adults are more skilled.

The generality of the results with regard to peer interaction is also limited to middle-class groups, not only because the adults' strategies and the tasks used are tied to such groups, but also because the role of peers varies greatly across cultures. In many cultures, children play a more central role in the socialization of other children than they do in the American middle class. In such cultures, children who have served as caregivers of younger siblings from the age of 4 or 5 and who work and play in mixed-age groups responsible for their own functioning may have the opportunity to develop skills in guiding other children: such skills are less available to middle-class U.S. children, who have little responsibility for other children and more limited contact with children of ages different from their own.

The value of cooperative classroom learning, in which peers work together on academic tasks and provide one another with motivation, guidance, and feedback (Damon, 1984; Slavin, 1987), also suggests that in circumstances in which children have practice in interaction, they may be very helpful to one another. Peers can serve as guides in academic activities in the classroom, especially if such interaction is encouraged in the classroom social structure, giving children experience as onlookers and in coordinated parallel activity, guidance, and collaboration (Aronson, Blaney, Stephan, Sikes, & Snapp, 1978; Cooper, Marquis, & Edward, 1986). When teachers encourage and support peer interaction, children may develop skill in academically useful forms of interaction.

Researchers will have to address the naturalistic interaction between peers in tasks they do well or choose for themselves — tasks that peers might teach each other or collaborate on when away from adult influence. As an approximation of this situation. Tudge and Rogoff (in progress) are investigating peer and adult-child collaboration on learning two spatial-planning computer games. The 9-year-old children were more comfortable handling the computer games than were the adults, although all participants began the study as novices. We are analyzing the progress in skill and in collaborative processes as peer and adult-child pairs gain expertise in the games over repeated sessions and examining the way, once the participants have become somewhat proficient, each teaches other novice children to play the games. Both games involve complex spatial planning, but one was presented as educational and the other as recreational, to see whether children take more control of the recreational game and rely more on adults in the educational game.

We expect that the collaboration and teaching processes, and perhaps the children's subsequent individual performance, may differ from those observed in the studies in which children were under the direction of adults, participating in tasks in which adults are more skilled. For, rather than being merely unskilled foils for comparison with skilled adults, children play special roles in one another's cognitive development.

References

Adams, A. K. (1987, January) 'A penguin belongs to the bird family': Language games and the social transfer of categorical knowledge. Paper presented at the Third International Conference on Thinking, Honolulu.

Adamson, L. B., Bakeman, R., & Smith, C. B. (in press) 'Gestures, words, and early object sharing'. In V. Volterra & C. Erting (Eds.), From gesture to symbol in hearing and deaf children. New York: Springer-Verlag.

Aronson, E., Blaney, N., Stephan, C., Sikes, J., & Snapp, M. (1978) The jigsaw classroom. Beverly Hills, CA: Sage.

Azmitia, M., & Perlmutter, M. (in press) 'Social influences on children's cognition: State of the art and future directions'. In H. Reese (Ed), Advances in child development and behavior. San Diego, CA: Academic Press.

Bates, E., Bretherton, I., Beeghly-Smith, M., & McNew, S. (1982) 'Social base of language development'. In H. W. Reese & L. P. Lipsitt (Eds.), *Advances in child development and behavior* (Vol. 16). New York: Academic Press.

Belsky, J., Goode, M. K., & Most, R. K. (1980) 'Maternal stimulation and infant exploratory competence: Cross-sectional, correlational, and experimental analyses'. *Child Development,* 51, 1163-1178.

Bloom, K., Russell, A., & Wassenberg, K. (1985, April) *Turn taking affects the quality of infant vocalizations.* Paper presented at the meetings of the Society for Research in Child Development, Toronto.

Bornstein, M. H. (1988) 'Mothers, infants, and the development of cognitive competence'. In H. E. Fitzgerald, B. M. Lester, & M. W. Yogman (Eds.), *Theory and research in behavioral pediatrics* (Vol. 4). New York: Plenum Press.

Brown, A. L., & Reeve, R. A. (1987) 'Bandwidths of competence: The role of supportive contexts in learning and development'. In L. S. Liben (Ed.), *Development and learning: Conflict or congruence?* Hillsdale, NJ: Erlbaum.

Camaioni, L., de Castro Campos, M. F. P., & DeLemos, C. (1984). 'On the failure of the interactionist paradigm in language acquisition: A re-evaluation'. In W. Doise & A. Palmonari (Eds.) *Social interaction in individual development.* Cambridge: Cambridge University Press.

Cooper, C. R., Marquis, A., & Edward, D. (1986) 'Four perspectives on peer learning among elementary school children'. In E. C. Mueller & C. R. Cooper (Eds.), *Process and outcome in peer relationships.* San Diego, CA: Academic Press.

Damon, W. (1984). 'Peer education: The untapped potential'. *Journal of Applied Developmental Psychology,* 5, 331-343.

DeLoache, J. S. (1983, April) *Joint picture book readings as memory training for toddlers.* Paper presented at the meetings of the Society for Research in Child Development, Detroit.

Demetras, M. J., Post, K. N., & Snow, C. E. (1986) 'Feedback to first language learners: The role of repetitions and clarification questions'. *Journal of Child Language,* 13, 275-292.

Ellis, S., & Rogoff, B. (1982) 'The strategies and efficacy of child versus adult teachers'. *Child Development,* 53, 730-735.

Ellis, S., & Rogoff, B. (1986) 'Problem solving in children's management of instruction'. In E. Mueller & C. Cooper (Eds.), *Process and outcome in peer relationships.* Orlando, FL: Academic Press.

Ferrier, L. (1978) 'Word, context and imitation'. In A. Lock (Ed.), *Action, gesture and symbol: The emergence of language.* New York: Academic Press.

Fivush, R. (1988) *Form and function in early autobiographical memory.* Unpublished manuscript, Emory University, Atlanta.

Gardner, W. P., & Rogoff, B. (1988) *Children's adjustment of deliberateness of planning to task circumstances.* Unpublished manuscript, University of Virginia, Charlottesville.

Gauvain, M., & Rogoff, B. (1989) 'Collaborative problem solving and children's planning skills'. *Developmental Psyschology,* 25, 139-151.

Göncü, A. & Rogoff, B. (1987, April) *Adult guidance and children's participation in learning.* Paper presented at the meetings of the Society for Research in Child Development, Baltimore.

Greenfield, P. M., & Smith, J. (1982) *The structure of communication in early language development*. New York: Academic Press.

Hardy-Brown, K.., Plomin, R., & DeFries, J. C. (1981) 'Genetic and environmental influences on the rate of communicative development in the first year of life'. *Developmental Psychology,* 17, 704-717.

Hartup, W. (1985) 'Relationships and their significance in cognitive development'. In R. Hinde & A. Perret-Clermont (Eds.), *Relationships and cognitive development*. Oxford: Oxford University Press.

Hay, D. F., Murray, P., Cecire, S., & Nash, A. (1985) 'Social learning of social behavior in early life'. *Child Development*, 56, 43-57.

Heber, M. (1981) 'Instruction *versus* conversation as opportunities for learning'. In W. P. Robinson (Ed.), *Communications in development*. London: Academic Press.

Henderson, B. B. (1984a) 'Parents and exploration: The effect of context on individual differences in exploratory behavior'. *Child Development,* 55, 1237-1245.

Henderson, B. B. (1984b) 'Social support and exploration'. *Child Development,* 55, 1246-1251.

Hoff-Ginsberg, E. (1986) 'Function and structure in maternal speech: Their relation to the child's development of syntax'. *Developmental Psychology,* 22, 155-163.

Hoff-Ginsberg, E., & Shatz, M. (1982) 'Linguistic input and the child's acquisition of language'. *Psychological Bulletin,* 92, 3-26.

John-Steiner, V. (1985) *Notebooks of the mind: Explorations of thinking*. Albuquerque: University of New Mexico Press.

John-Steiner, V., & Tatter, P. (1983) 'An interactionist model of language development'. In B. Bain (Ed.), *The sociogenesis of language and human conduct*. New York: Plenum Press.

Kaye, K. (1977a) 'Infants' effects upon their mothers' teaching strategies'. In J. D. Glidewell (Ed.), *The social context of learning and development*. New York: Gardner Press.

Koester, L. S., & Bueche, N. A. (1980) 'Preschoolers are teachers: When children are seen but not heard'. *Child Study Journal,* 10, 107-118.

Kontos, S. (1983) 'Adult-child interaction and the origins of metacognition'. *Journal of Educational Research,* 77, 43-54.

Lomov, B. F. (1978) 'Psychological processes and communication'. *Soviet Psychology,* 17, 3-22.

Magkaev, V. K. (1977) 'An experimental study of the planning function of thinking in young school children'. In M. Cole (Ed.), *Soviet developmental psychology: An anthology*. White Plains, NY: Sharpe.

Masur, E. F. (1982). 'Mothers' responses to infants' object-related gestures: Influences on lexical development'. *Journal of Child Language,* 9, 23-30.

McLane, J. B. (1987) 'Interaction, context, and the zone of proximal development'. In M. Hickmann (Ed.), *Social and functional approaches to language and thought*. San Diego, CA: Academic Press.

Mistry, J., & Rogoff, B. (1987, April) *Influence of purpose and strategic assistance on preschool children's remembering*. Paper presented at the meetings of the Society for Research in Child Development, Baltimore.

Moerk, E. L. (1985) 'A differential interactive analysis of language teaching and learning'. *Discourse Processes*, 8, 113-142.

Nelson, K. E., Denninger, M. S., Bonvillian, J. D., Kaplan, B. J., & Baker, N. D. (1984) 'Maternal input adjustments and non-adjustment as related to children's linguistic advances and to language acquisition theories'. In A. D. Pellegrini & T. D. Yawkey (Eds.), *The development of oral and written language in social contexts*. Norwood, NJ: Ablex.

Newson, J., & Newson, E. (1975) 'Intersubjectivity and the transmission of culture: On the social origins of symbolic functioning'. *Bulletin of the British Psychological Society, 28*, 437-446.

Olson, S. L., Bates, J. E., & Bayles, K. (1984) 'Mother-infant interaction and the development of individual differences in children's cognitive competence'. *Developmental Psychology, 20*, 166-179.

Papousek, M., Papousek, H., & Bornstein, M. H. (1985) 'The naturalistic vocal environment of young infants'. In T. M. Field & N. Fox (Eds.), *Social perception in infants*. Norwood, NJ: Ablex.

Parrinello, R. M., & Ruff, H. A. (1988) 'The influence of adult intervention on infants' level of attention'. *Child Development, 59*, 1125-1135.

Penner, S. G. (1987) 'Parental responses to grammatical and ungrammatical child utterances'. *Child Development, 58*, 376-384.

Piaget, J. (1977) 'Logique génétique et sociologie'. In *Etudes sociologiques*. Geneva: Librairie Droz. (Reprinted from *Revue Philosophique de la France et de l'Etranger*, 1928, *53*, 161-205).

Piaget, J. (1977) 'Les operations logiques et la vie sociale'. In *Etudes sociologiques*. Geneva: Librairie Droz.

Piaget, J. (1977) 'Problèmes de la psycho-sociologie de l'enfance'. In *Etudes sociologiques*. Geneva: Librairie Droz. (Reprinted from *Traité de sociologie*, G. Gurvitch, Paris: Presses Universitaires de France, 1963, pp. 229-254).

Radziszewska, B., & Rogoff, B. (1988) 'Influence of adult and peer collaborators on children's planning skills'. *Developmental Psychology, 24*, 840-848.

Ratner, H. H. (1984) 'Memory demands and the development of young children's memory'. *Child Development, 55*, 2173-2191.

Rheingold, H. L. (1985) 'Development as the acquisition of familiarity'. *Annual Review of Psychology*, 36, 1-17.

Rogoff, B., & Gardner, W. P. (1984) 'Guidance in cognitive development: An examination of mother-child instructional interaction'. In B. Rogoff & J. Lave (Eds.), *Everyday cognition: Its development in social context*. Cambridge, MA: Harvard University Press.

Rogoff, B., & Gauvain, M. (1986) 'A method for the analysis of patterns illustrated with data on mother-child instructional interaction'. In J. Valsiner (Ed.), *The role of the individual subject in scientific psychology*. New York: Plenum Press.

Rogoff, B., & Malkin, C., & Gilbride, K. (1984) 'Interaction with babies as guidance in development'. In B. Rogoff & J. V. Wertsch (Eds.), *Children's learning in the 'zone of proximal development.'* San Francisco: Jossey-Bass.

Scollon, R. (1976) *Conversations with a one-year-old*. Honolulu: University Press of Hawaii.

Slavin, R. E. (1987) 'Developmental and motivational perspectives on cooperative learning: A reconciliation'. *Child Development, 58*, 1161-1167.

Slobin, D. I. (1973) 'Cognitive prerequisites for the development of grammar'. In C. A. Ferguson & D. I. Slobin (Eds.), *Studies of child language development*. New York: Holt, Rinehart and Winston.

Snow, C. E. (1982a) 'Are parents language teachers?' In K. Borman (Ed.), *Social life of children in a changing society*. Hillsdale, NJ: Erlbaum.

Snow, C. E. (1984) 'Parent-child interaction and the development of communicative ability'. In R. Schiefelbusch & J. Pickar (Eds.), *The acquisition of communicative competence*. Baltimore: University Park Press.

Tomasello, M., & Farrar, M. J. (1986) 'Joint attention and early language'. *Child Development, 57*, 1454-1463.

Tomasello, M., Mannle, S., & Kruger, A. C. (1986) 'Linguisitc environment of 1- to 2-year-old twins'. *Developmental Psychology, 22*, 169-176.

Tudge, J. R. H., & Rogoff, B. (1989) 'Peer influences on cognitive development: Piagetian and Vygotskian perspectives'. In M. Bornstein & J. Bruner (Eds.), *Interaction in human development*. Hillsdale, NJ: Erlbaum.

Valdez-Menchaca, M. C. (1987, April) *The effects of incidental teaching on vocabulary acquisition by young children*. Paper presented at the meeting of the Society for Research in Child Development, Baltimore.

Wertsch, J. V. (1978) 'Adult-child interaction and the roots of metacognition'. *Quarterly Newsletter of the Institute for Comparative Human Development, 2*, 15-18.

Wood, D., Bruner, J. S., & Ross, G. (1976) 'The role of tutoring in problem-solving'. *Journal of Child Psychology and Psychiatry, 17*, 89-100.

Wood D. J., & Middleton, D. (1975) 'A study of assisted problem-solving'. *British Journal of Psychology, 66*, 181-191.

Wood, D., Wood, H., & Middleton, D. (1978) 'An experimental evaluation of four face-to-face teaching strategies'. *International Journal of Behavioral Development, 2*, 131-147.

Social Relationships in Childhood

A number of investigators have recently begun to explore the impact of friendships and their absence on the development of school-aged children. A number of arguments have been proposed *vis-à-vis* the likely contributions of friendship and peer relationships to social, intellectual and emotional development (see Hartup's chapter for an overview).

One of the most ambitious reviews undertaken of the field is presented in the article by Parker and Asher, which attempts to collate evidence from a number of studies to establish whether problems in friendship formation are a cause of later social and psychiatric difficulties, or whether they are a mere symptom of earlier disturbances.

The articles by Ladd and by Bierman *et al.* explore themes generated by the Parker and Asher review. The article by Ladd represents a detailed report of one attempt to establish whether success in making and keeping friends is predictive of later social and academic adjustment in school. The article by Bierman *et al.* provides a detailed account of an experimental evaluation of intervention procedures aimed at enhancing the peer status of rejected boys.

23. Friendships and their Developmental Significance

Willard W. Hartup

Introduction

Most children and adolescents have a "best friend" and several "good friends". Infants and toddlers have friends, too, although these relationships are not as extensively differentiated as among older children and adolescents. Mothers sometimes argue that their young children have best friends when, in fact, the children are merely regular playmates and their interaction harmonious. Nevertheless, mutually-regulated "friendships" can be observed among many young children (Howes, 1983). By 4 and 5 years of age, approximately three out of four children are involved in a close relationship with some other child, and about three out of ten have more than one (Hinde, Titmus, Easton & Tamplin, 1985; Howes, 1989).

Friendship networks remain relatively small during the preschool years, with the number of mutual friends averaging 0.88 for boys and 0.63 for girls. Unilateral relationships (i.e., unreciprocated friendship choices) supplement these mutual ones, averaging 1.68 and 0.86 for boys and girls, respectively (Hartup, Laursen, Stewart, & Eastenson, 1988). School-aged children, in contrast, average five best friends, a number that declines only slightly among adolescents (Hallinan, 1980). About 80% of today's teenagers have at least one best friend and several good friends, and fewer than 10% have no contact with friends outside school (Crockett, Lossoff, & Petersen, 1984).

Conversations with school-aged children and adolescents confirm that these relationships are exceedingly important to the youngsters themselves (Goodnow & Burns, 1988; Youniss & Smollar, 1986) and that, when "on their own", more time is spent by children and adolescents with friends than with family members or any other associate (Medrich, Rosen, Rubin, & Buckley, 1982; Laursen, 1989). Becoming friends and maintaining these relationships are regarded by children themselves as among the most significant achievements of childhood and adolescence.

Our interest in children's friendships, however, extends beyond their ubiquity. We need to know whether having friends, as contrasted with not having friends, predicts good developmental outcome and, if so, why. We need to know whether friendships between socially competent children differ from friendships between less competent children. We need to know whether friendship relations are as necessary to good developmental outcome as parent-child relations. Friendships furnish children with socialisation opportunities not easily obtained elsewhere, including experience in conflict management as well as experience in cooperation and sharing. But how important is it

Willard W. Hartup: 'Friendships and their Developmental Significance' from *CHILDHOOD SOCIAL DEVELOPMENT: CONTEMPORARY PERSPECTIVES*, edited by Harry McGurk (1992), pp. 175-205. Reprinted by permission of Lawrence Erlbaum Associates Ltd., Hove, UK.

that these experiences occur with friends? At the moment, we know more about the ubiquity of children's friendships than about their developmental significance.

Children's friendships are discussed in this essay in four sections: First, conceptual and significance issues will be considered, including the "markers" of friendship (i.e., how friendships may be defined), the "conditions" of friendship (i.e., what circumstances are responsible for the formation and maintenance of friendships), the "stages" of friendship (i.e., the temporal dimensions of these relationships), and the "functions" of friendship (i.e., the contributions these relationships may make to social development). "Beginnings" will then be discussed, including the processes that appear to be implicated in becoming friends, the friendships of infants and toddlers, and behavioural manifestations in early childhood. Childhood and adolescent friendships will be examined next, with emphasis on friendship selection and "being friends". Age and sex differences will also be considered. Finally, friendship experience and its contribution to developmental outcome will be discussed, considering both what contemporary studies show us and what they don't. The theme running through the essay is essentially that friendships are developmental advantages for children and adolescents rather than developmental necessities.

Conceptual issues and significance

The conditions of friendship

The essentials of friendship are reciprocity[1] and commitment between individuals who see themselves more or less as equals. Children's attachments to their friends are not as exclusive or as robust as their attachments to their mothers and fathers. In addition, interaction between friends rests on a more equal power base than the interaction between children and their parents. Recognising this egalitarian structure, some writers regard friendships as "affiliative" relations rather than "attachments" (Weiss, 1986). Children make a considerable emotional investment in their friends, however, and these relationships are relatively enduring. Separation from friends sometimes elicits anxiety and a sense of loss similar to the manner in which separation from an attachment figure elicits these emotions (Park & Waters, 1988; Howes, 1989). Similarities as well as differences thus exist between the relationships that children construct with friends and the attachments they construct with their elders.

The main themes in friendship relations — affiliation and common interests — are understood by children beginning in early childhood. Among preschool and younger school-aged children, friendship expectations centre on common pursuits and concrete reciprocities ("When you have got something wrong, they help. And I give them food, so they give me food back" [Grade 2][2]). Later on, children's views about their friends centre on mutual understanding, loyalty, and trust; children also expect to spend time with their friends, share interests, and engage in self-disclosure with them. ("A good friend is someone who likes you and spends time with you and forgives you and doesn't actually bash you up" [Grade 6]). Friends have fun with one another; they enjoy doing things with one another and care about one another. Although school-aged children and adolescents never use words like empathy or intimacy to describe their friends, these constructs also distinguish friends from other children in the child's thinking. Friends:

"tell you their secrets and you tell them yours", "will listen to you and understand you", "don't drop you as soon as something goes wrong". Children recognise that conflicts may occur with their friends, but they believe that friends have a special commitment to one another in the management of conflict ("A good friend is someone you fight with, but not forever") and that conflicts may also strengthen these relationships. Overall, then, friendships are understood by children and adolescents as delicate balances of social exchange occurring within egalitarian contexts: within these relationships, self-interest is weighed against consideration for the other and conflicts are weighed against cooperation. Ordinarily, children believe that the social exchanges occurring between friends are mutually beneficial.

Children's friendship expectations have been studied extensively (Peevers & Secord, 1973; Bigelow & LaGaipa, 1975; Selman, 1980; Furman & Bierman, 1984; Goodnow & Burns, 1988). Considerable agreement exists in these accounts: with age, increases occur in the number of psychological constructs used, the flexibility and precision with which they are used in children's talk about their friends, the complexity and organisation of children's information and ideas about friends, the level of analysis used in interpreting the behaviour of other children, and recognition that certain attributes (e.g., intimacy and loyalty) are characteristic of these relationships.

Most writers assume that these age differences in children's notions about their friends derive from more general changes in cognitive and language development. Some investigators, however, argue that these changes are elaborations of the child's understanding of a single construct — social reciprocity (Youniss, 1980). Others believe that they reflect structural transformations in the child's understanding of social relations (Selman, 1980). And still others argue that these age differences represent cumulative representations of basically unrelated "themes" or expectations, e.g., common interests, commitment, and intimacy (Berndt, 1981). These theoretical differences have not been resolved, although the evidence shows clearly that children's notions about friendship relations become more and more differentiated as they grow older (Berndt & Perry, 1986).

The markers of friendship

Children's friendships can be identified in four ways: (1) by asking someone to identify the child's friends; (2) by asking someone to assess the degree of "liking" or attraction that exists between two children; (3) by assessing the extent to which two children seek and maintain proximity with one another over time; and (4) by measuring the reciprocities and coordinated actions existing in the social interaction between two children.

Best Friends. Asking someone to identify the child's friends is the most common method used to single out these relationships. One may simply ask children to nominate their best friends from among their classmates or their acquaintances, assuming that children understand and use the word "friend" consistently and in the same way that other people do. Although systematic studies do not exist, the available evidence indicates that children use the word more or less consistently by the fourth year — earlier in many cases. One may also ask teachers or parents to identify children's friends, thus assuming that these respondents know enough about children's feelings towards one another to be able to make valid assessments.

Mutual Liking. Children's friendships can also be identified by asking children to name other children who are "especially liked". This strategy assumes that close relationships between children rest on strong, affectively toned attraction as well as a sense that children feel supported and cared for by one another. The validity of this method depends on children's knowing what it means to "like" someone. According to the evidence, usage is reliable by the time children are 6 or 7 years of age, although questions can be raised about the consistency with which younger children nominate one another as "liked" (Hymel, 1983). One other difficulty with mutual liking as a means of identifying children's friendships is that this method does not make it easy to distinguish "best friends" from "friends", a distinction that children themselves regard as significant (Goodnow & Burns, 1988). Once again, teachers or other individuals who know the children can also be used as respondents in assessing mutual liking (McCandless & Marshall, 1957).

Proximity. "Moving sociometrics", through which close relationships are singled out by observing proximity-maintenance, were invented long ago (Hyde & York, 1948). Used originally to identify interpersonal relationships in a mental hospital, these techniques were later adapted for use with children (McCandless & Marshall, 1957) and have proved useful for identifying strong associations existing among very young children (Hinde, *et al.*, 1985; Hartup, *et al.*, 1988; Howes, 1989; Ladd, Price, & Hart, 1990) as well as adolescents (Wong & Csikzentmihalyi, 1991). In this instance, measurement assumes that friends are more motivated to spend time together than nonfriends and, conversely, that children who spend time together usually like one another.

Behavioural Reciprocities. Coordinations and reciprocities in social interaction are sometimes employed as methods for identifying children's friendships (Howes, 1983). Actually, more attention has been given to these complementarities as relationship concomitants than as relationship indicators. Behavioural reciprocities clearly differentiate friends from nonfriends but self-reports, mutual liking, and proximity-seeking are easier ways to identify these relationships.

Concordances among these Markers. Concordances among these methods are substantial: First, among preschool-aged children, significant agreement exists between best friends identified by means of sociometric nominations and best friends identified through observational measurement of proximity-seeking. In one investigation (Howes, 1989), agreement between these indicators was 72% among the 4154 dyads studied, and most of the disagreements occurred because a behaviourally-identified friend received a unilateral rather than a mutual sociometric nomination. Other studies show somewhat lower concordances between these two identification methods but, always, the average amount of social interaction is considerably higher with preferred companions than with disliked ones (Chapman, Smith, Foot, & Pritchard, 1979; Hymel, Hayvren, & Lollis, 1982).

Children who are considered to be best friends by outside observers also stand out in terms of proximity-seeking: among preschool children, teacher nominations and observational methods were in agreement for 85% of the available dyads, with nearly all of the disagreements involving unilateral nominations (Howes, 1989). In an earlier study (Howes, 1983), 97% of the friends identified by behavioural criteria were also identified by teachers, and 100% of the friendships identified by the teachers were also identified by the behavioural criteria. Mother-nominations (when the children were both enrolled in the same nursery school) agreed 53% for 42-month olds with proximity-based methods for identifying friends and 69% for 50-month olds (Hinde, *et al.*, 1985).

Numerous studies show that friendships identified by asking children whom they "like" or "like to play with" are also concordant with observed proximity-seeking. Biehler (1954) reported that 80% of preschool-aged children's most preferred companions, as determined by observations, were named as either first or second choices on a picture sociometric test requiring the children to name the classmates whom they liked best. Other investigators have also shown that children spend more time with their best liked companions than with other classmates (Hartup, *et al.*, 1988). Finally, self-reports and teacher-reports are in good agreement concerning which children have friends and who they are. Teacher and child nominations agreed for 78% of the dyads studied in one instance (Howes, 1989).

Contextual variations must be taken into account in examining the concordances among these friendship markers for school-aged children. Sociometric choices are not strongly related to proximity-seeking in the classroom or playground (Chapman, *et al.*, 1979), for example, since social interaction in these settings is externally constrained. Seating arrangements and classroom activities are teacher-determined, thereby attenuating these concordances; games and sports activities reduce the extent to which social attraction accounts for proximity between children in the playground. In contrast, time-use studies show that, when outside school and on their own, school-aged children spend most of their time with their friends rather than nonfriends (Medrich, *et al.*, 1982).

The stages of friendship

Close relationships have beginnings, middles, and ends. Relationship dynamics vary accordingly. Children's friendships differ from one another in their temporal course, and this needs to be taken into consideration in studying them. Some relationships progress more-or-less directly from acquaintanceship to termination without much consolidation in between. Others undergo extensive "build-up" and last for long periods of time. And age differences are evident: preschool-aged children's friendships, for example, are not as stable as older children's (Hartup, 1983).

These variations are well-recognised but seldom studied. We know that children whose friendships are destined to end within a short time tend to talk more frequently about disloyalty and lack of intimacy than children whose friendships are stable (Berndt, Hawkins, & Hoyle, 1986). We also know that children with emotional difficulties are more likely to have unstable friendships than children without difficulties (Rutter & Garmezy, 1983). But, otherwise, relatively little can be said about temporal variations in children's friendships and their significance.

Research attention is currently centred on five relationship "stages": acquaintance, build-up, continuation and consolidation, deterioration, and termination (Levinger, 1983; Levinger & Levinger, 1986). Although some relationships do not move through every one of these stages, those relationships that we call friendships encompass most of them.

Propinquity. Close relationships begin with propinquity (i.e., physical proximity). For this reason, every demographic force that brings two children together is relevant to their becoming friends. That is, the conditions that bring two families to the same neighbourhood or two children to the same school or classroom have as much to do with the beginnings of friendship as who the children are (Sancilio, 1989).

Propinquity alone is not a sufficient condition for the establishment of friendship relations. Whether two children become friends depends on the benefits each child perceives as deriving from interaction with the other, especially in relation to what the relationship is believed to "cost". Most individuals (children not excepted) assume that these benefits will be greater in exchanges with someone who is similar to themselves than with someone who is not (Byrne, 1971). Direct experience with one another also contributes to expectations that continued social interaction will be mutually rewarding.

First Encounters. Although a considerable amount is known about the attributes that attract children to one another (see Hartup, 1983), relatively little is known about their first encounters. The available evidence suggests that these encounters are largely devoted to establishing common ground (or the lack thereof). Social interaction during first encounters is mostly driven by the activities or tasks in which the children are engaged. Social interdependencies are likely to be confined to these tasks, and the empirical evidence confirms this (Furman & Childs, 1981). On first meeting, children are more likely to be concerned with who gets the first turn with an attractive toy than with "being friends". At this stage, relationships are relatively superficial, emotionally-speaking.

Build-up. In time, some relationships achieve a momentum of their own, i.e., their existence does not depend so much on environmental monitoring or the activities in which the individuals engage. Among adults, this transition is marked by a shift from an "I-centred" to a "we-centred" orientation (Kelley, 1979); other increases in mutuality also occur. Among children who are "hitting it off", communication becomes increasingly connected, conflicts are confronted and managed successfully, similarities between themselves are stressed, and self-disclosure is initiated (Gottman, 1983). Relationships are not especially stable during this stage; seeking common ground remains a necessity. Should children not maintain their common interests, it is necessary to re-engage in information exchange much like the information exchanges that take place during first encounters.

Continuation. The transition from "build-up" to "continuation" is marked by increasing stability in the interactions between individuals. Stability, itself, emerges mainly on the basis of commitment — a condition that rests, in turn, on each individual's investment in the relationship (Levinger, 1983).

Virtually nothing is known about the conditions that strengthen children's commitments to one another, but several studies demonstrate that commitment becomes significant in children's thinking about friendship relations by 10 to 11 years of age (Bigelow & LaGaipa, 1975; Bigelow, 1977). One should not rule out the possibility that commitment is important to younger children, but information is too sketchy to say much about these dynamics in early childhood.

One interesting convergence suggests that a causal connection does indeed exist between commitment and stability in children's friendships. Between 10 and 11 years, two transitions are evident:

1. For the first time, significant numbers of children mention commitment in interviews about their friendship expectations ("A friend is a person that sticks by you when all the troubles come" [Goodnow & Burns, 1988]).

2. An increase (to two-thirds) occurs in the number of these relationships that last for at least a year (Berndt *et al.*, 1986).

Friendships would surely be more stable among younger children were commitments more salient among them. But, as intriguing as these notions are, more needs to be learned about commitment and friendship relations, especially the conditions that foster commitment and weaken it, and its relation to the stability of these relationships.

Deterioration. Children may cease to "hit it off" at any time and the circumstances are not always clear-cut. Breakdown is sometimes marked by disagreements, similar to the manner in which disagreements sometimes accompany marital distress (Gottman, 1979). At other times, breakdown is marked only by alienation; overt contention and disagreement are notably absent. Sometimes one child will be dissatisfied while the other remains happy with the relationship. Clearly, no single dynamic signals deterioration in children's friendships.

Since commitment emerges for the first time in children's thinking about these relationships in middle childhood, one would not expect commitment violations to be important in friendship breakdown among younger children; contemporary studies bear this out (Bigelow, 1977; Rizzo, 1989). Conflicts themselves can be distress signals among both younger and older children but, as mentioned, alienation between children often occurs in the absence of argument; children simply drift apart (and sometimes regret it) but are not able to explain exactly why. Observations conducted in one first-grade classroom confirmed that friendships frequently terminate simply because children cease to interact; neither emotional outbursts nor arguments forecast their demise, nor were overt declarations made (Rizzo, 1989). Similar ethnographic work, however, has not been conducted with older children.

Endings. Friendships terminate when common ground dissolves and children cease to be behaviourally interdependent. Deterioration does not lead inevitably to termination. Relationships can be renewed, providing the children can discover a basis for restoring their commitment to one another. Nevertheless, friendships (unlike parent-child relationships) cannot withstand betrayal and disloyalty for very long nor can they weather incessant disagreement.

Ordinarily, termination means that children reduce the time they spend together; conflicts seldom occur following breakup simply because the children avoid one another rather than interact. Actually, friendship endings have not been studied, so relatively little can be said about the transition from deterioration to endings or about the relation between endings with old friends and beginnings with new ones.

Friendship functions

Mutual attraction ensures continuing interaction between the children involved. Four other functions can be identified that friendships serve:

1. these relationships are contexts in which basic social skills are acquired or elaborated (e.g., social communication, cooperation, and group entry skills);

2. they are information sources for acquiring self-knowledge, knowledge about others, and knowledge about the world;

3. they are emotional and cognitive resources (both for "having fun" and adapting to stress); and

4. they are forerunners of subsequent relationships (modelling the mutual regulation and intimacy that most close relationships require).

One must remember that these contributions to the child's development derive from an egalitarian context: friendships are symmetrically or horizontally structured in contrast to adult-child relationships, which are asymmetrically or vertically structured (Youniss, 1980). Friends are similar to one another in developmental status; friends engage one another mostly in play and "socialising". Friendship residuals among individual children undoubtedly reflect these egalitarian dimensions.

One must remember, too, that friendship functions may vary with age. Or, rather, some functions may vary with age while others remain constant (Price & Ladd, 1986). Mutual attraction, for example, supports proximity-seeking and continued social interaction between companions among both children and adolescents (Hartup et al., 1988; Laursen, 1989). Social interaction, however, consists mostly of play among young children and "socialising" among older ones (Whiting & Whiting, 1975; Medrich et al., 1982). Play and socialising have certain similarities (e.g., both are fun), but these activities are also different. Socialising involves camaraderie, intimacy, caring, and other support manifestations that play does not. Developmental considerations, then, need to be taken into account in speculating about the functions of friendship.

Friendships and social competence. Considerable evidence shows that friendships are cooperative socialisation contexts (Hartup, 1989). Preschool-aged friends engage in more frequent positive exchanges (as well as neutral ones) than unselected partners or children who don't like one another (Masters & Furman, 1981). Mutual attraction also goes along with sustained social exchanges, complementarities in social interaction, and mutually-directed affect (Howes, 1983; 1989). Conflicts between friends are less intense and resolved more frequently by mutual disengagement than conflicts between nonfriends (Hartup, et al., 1988); competition is less intense (Charlesworth & LaFreniere, 1983). Older children, too, cooperate more readily with friends than nonfriends, are more interactive, smile and laugh more, play closer attention to equity rules in their conversations, and direct their conversations toward mutual rather than egocentric ends (Newcomb & Brady, 1982). Conflict and competition are experienced differently, too, by school-aged friends and nonfriends, although these differences vary greatly according to context (Hartup, in press a).

Longitudinal evidence corroborates the notion that children's relationships with their friends support cooperation and reciprocity between individuals. One investigator (Howes, 1983) assessed infants (5-14 months), (toddlers 16-23 months), and preschool-aged children (35-49 months) on six occasions during the course of a school year. "Maintained friends" (consistent mutual attraction verified by observations as well as teacher nominations) were contrasted with "sporadic" friends (who were friends only once during the year or inconsistently) and "nonfriends" (children who were never friends at any time). Social overtures (successful ones), elaborated exchanges, reciprocal play, positive emotional exchanges, and vocalising increased significantly over time among maintained friends; only vocalising increased among sporadic friends and none of the observed behaviours increased among the nonfriends. Socialising between mutual friends thus became more complex during the year but remained constant among the other dyads. Other longitudinal evidence shows that, among preschool-aged children, social behaviour with a stable friend is generally more competent than with an unstable one: children are more successful in group entry, more complementary and reciprocal in their social play, more cooperative, and more likely to engage in pretend play. After losing friends, competence is diminished (Howes, 1989).

Among school-aged children, talk about intimacy also differentiates stable and unstable friends. Across the transition to adolescence, intimacy considerations differentiate friendship relations more sharply than anything else. Comments about sharing thoughts and feelings increase, along with comments about self-disclosure (Berndt & Perry, 1986). Both self-disclosure and intimate knowledge are endorsed as friendship expectations more and more commonly between the ages of 11 and 17 (Sharabany, Gershoni, & Hofman, 1981). Frankness and spontaneity, knowing and sensitivity, attachment, exclusiveness, and giving and sharing are the specific dimensions of intimacy that increase most with age.

Overall, then, friendships support cooperation, reciprocity, and effective conflict management, beginning in early childhood and extending through adolescence. Intimacy considerations become increasingly salient during middle childhood and, along with commitment, are the social skills most extensively utilised by adolescents in these contexts.

Friendships as information sources. Children teach one another in many situations and are generally effective in this capacity.[3] Peer teaching occurs in three main varieties (Damon & Phelps, 1989): peer tutoring, cooperative learning, and peer collaboration. Peer tutoring refers to the didactic transmission of information from one child to another, ordinarily from an "expert" to a "novice". Peer tutoring is sometimes employed in schools, but also occurs when children are on their own. Cooperative learning refers to schemes in which children are asked to combine their contributions in problem-solving and to share rewards. Peer collaboration, in contrast, refers to situations in which novices work together on tasks that neither is able to do separately. Empirical studies indicate that each of these methods works, although some are content specific. Collaboration, for example, works best in mastering abstract, basic concepts (e.g., proportionality) whereas tutoring works best with mechanics and specific skills (Damon & Phelps, 1989).

Quite possibly, friends interact differently in these situations from nonfriends. Mutual friends know one another better than nonfriends; they are more accurate than "unilateral associates" in assessing the characteristics they have in common as well as more knowledgeable about their differences (Ladd & Emerson, 1984). Close relationships require that the individual ". . . know the other's needs and goals and how the individual impinges on those, know the responses the other is likely to exhibit in reaction to the individual's own behavior, and, then, possess the capability of performing the responses necessary to bring about the desired effect" (Berscheid, 1985, p. 71). Given these considerations, friends should be uncommonly good teachers and collaborators, better than nonfriends in most circumstances.

Empirical studies relating to these hypotheses are scant. Tutoring effects have never been studied in relation to the attraction existing between tutor and tutee. Earlier studies suggest that on-task behaviour actually declines when a young child is observed by a friend; in contrast, on-task behaviour is sustained when the observer is a nonfriend (Hartup, 1964). But whether friends are better tutors (and whether children like to be tutored better by friends than by nonfriends) is not known. Similarly, we know almost nothing about friendship relations and cooperative learning. Cooperative experiences promote solidarity and social attraction within classrooms (Johnson, Johnson, Johnson, & Anderson, 1976) but no one knows whether cooperative outcomes are better among groups of friends than among groups of nonfriends.

Peer collaboration, however, has been examined among both friends and nonfriends. Newcomb and Brady (1982) observed children who were asked to explore a many-faceted "creativity box" with either a friend or a nonfriend. More extensive exploration occurred among children with their friends; conversation was also more vigorous and connected. Most important, the children who explored the box with a friend remembered more about it afterwards. Other evidence shows that when children were observed while attempting to resolve conflicts about social ethics, friends gave more explanations to one another than nonfriends, as well as criticised their companions more freely (Nelson & Aboud, 1985). Once again, outcomes also differed: friends changed to more mature solutions through these discussions to a greater extent than did nonfriends, although the total number of changes did not differ.

Friends and nonfriends also differ in group collaboration. Social interaction is more democratic and cooperative as well as more efficient in some tasks, e.g., making up stories (Scofield, 1960). This efficiency may not last long, though, since friends feel freer to stop working with one another than nonfriends (Shaw & Shaw, 1962).

While the empirical documentation is relatively weak, existing studies thus suggest that friendships are unique contexts for transmitting information from one child to another. Since friends may be more effective as teachers or collaborators in some situations than others, these functions need to be explored more extensively.

Friends as resources. Friendships are cognitive and emotional resources furnishing the child with maximum capacity for problem-solving as well as security for striking out into new territory, meeting new people, and tackling new problems. According to these hypotheses, friendships extend children's problem-solving capabilities as well as provide buffering from stress.

Logically, friendships should facilitate reaching goals and meeting challenges simply because two children working as a well-meshed "team" work more efficiently than two children who are strangers. Friends share motives; children and their friends also work out verbal and motor "scripts" that enable them to combine their talents and achieve their goals more extensively than nonfriends. New studies show clearly that child-child collaboration is effective in mastering certain tasks (Azmitia, 1988) but the evidence is scanty concerning the hypothesis that friends cooperate better than nonfriends in obtaining desired resources. One investigation (Charlesworth & LaFreniere, 1983), though, demonstrates that small groups of friends actually gained access to a scarce resource (movie cartoons) more readily and with fewer conflicts than small groups of nonfriends.

As emotional resources, friendships support both "having fun" and stress-reduction. Once again, the evidence is not extensive. Foot, Chapman and Smith (1977) observed children while they watched a comedy film. The duration and frequency of laughing, smiling, looking and talking were greater between friends than between strangers, as well as response matching (a measure of behavioural concordance between the children). Strangers may not be the best dyads to compare to friends (the comparison confounds familiarity with liking) but these results nevertheless suggest that friendships support "having fun".

Friends furnish one another, too, with a sense of security in strange situations. In one investigation (Ipsa, 1981), preschool-aged children were observed, together with either a classmate or another child enrolled in a different classroom, in the presence of a strange adult. With familiar companions, the children displayed little distress at the departure of the adult, whereas children with unfamiliar companions were upset. Schwartz (1972) also observed more positive affect, greater mobility, and more frequent talk in a strange situation between preschool children who were considered by their teachers to be friends than between children who were unacquainted. Once again, the studies confound friendship and familiarity, but the results are suggestive.

The most important issue to be explored in this area has not been touched: whether stable friendships buffer children and adolescents from the adverse effects of negative events occurring in everyday life, e.g., family conflict, terminal illness, unemployment, or school failure. One investigation (Wallerstein & Kelly, 1981) suggests that friendships may indeed ameliorate the stress associated with divorce. School-aged boys turned readily to friends, seemingly to distance themselves from the troubled household. Girls, however, entered into friendships only when their mothers were especially supportive. Similar results were obtained by Elder (1974), who studied the records of children reared in the United States during the Great Depression. When their fathers lost their jobs, boys continued with their friends more-or-less as before; girls, on the other hand, stayed home, experienced strain in their relations with age-mates, and evidenced greater concern about having friends than before the family economic situation deteriorated. Considering the centrality of stress management in child health and social relations, additional work in this area is badly needed.

Friendships and subsequent relationships. Sullivan (1953, pp. 245-246) has stated that:

> . . . when he finally finds a chum — somewhere between eight-and-a-half and ten — you will discover something very different in the relationship — namely, that your child begins to develop a real sensitivity to what matters to another person . . . preadolescence is marked by the coming of the integrating tendencies which, when they are completely developed, we call love, or, to say it another way, by the manifestation of the need for interpersonal intimacy.

These words express one of the best-known notions about friendships, namely, that children acquire dispositions within them that generalise to other relationships with their contemporaries. In this sense, children's friendships are thought to be templates used in constructing subsequent relationships. To be sure, new relationships are never exact copies of old ones; relationships always reflect the idiosyncracies of one's partners (Hinde, 1979). This theory suggests, however, that the organisation of behaviour within relationships generalises from old ones to new ones. Only the most indirect evidence supports this claim. Friendship experience is correlated with an altruistic outlook and other manifestations of interpersonal sensitivity (Mannarino, 1976). Children with many friends are generally effective in child-child relations and are well-liked (Ladd, Price, & Hart, 1990). On the other side of the coin, children who are involved in bully/victim relationships (as either bullies or victims) are likely to be involved in other bully/victim relationships subsequently (Olweus, 1980). Clearly, continuities exist from relationship to relationship, but continuities from one friendship to another have not been studied.

Beginnings

Becoming friends[4]

"Exchange theories" (and their variants) are based on the argument that close relationships emerge only to the extent that interaction between individuals is mutually satisfying (Kelley, 1979). We don't know exactly how children evaluate what is "received" from the many social exchanges in which they are involved, why they are so strongly motivated to make comparisons between themselves and others, and why they are so concerned with "fairness" (see Hinde, 1979). Nevertheless, exchange theory is a viable explanation for the emergence and maintenance of the relationships that children construct with their friends.

Most of the basic information needed by children about exchange outcomes can be divided into two classes: affirmations and conflicts. Affirmations (or agreements) provide children with a sense of what is correct and workable in an exchange, and provide them with a basis for estimating the likelihood that a continuing relationship will "work" or "pay off". Especially when their occurrence coincides with anxiety-reduction, affirmations establish other children as emotional and cognitive resources. Affirmations are also the events suggesting to the child that exchanges with similar individuals are likely to be more gratifying than exchanges with dissimilar ones.

Conflicts (or disagreements) create doubts about what might be correct and workable, thereby motivating change in thinking and acting. Conflicts are instrumental in establishing friendships since they illuminate the "fit" between individuals, i.e., by demonstrating when the skills, interests, and goals of two children are not concordant, as well as by marking relationship boundaries, i.e., those behavioural "limits" that can be exceeded only by risking separation. Stated another way: conflicts assist children, in reverse, in recognising the common ground that exists between them.

A continuous dialectic between affirmation and disaffirmation is needed in order to construct and maintain relationships. Affirmations, alone, carry little information about exchange possibilities except in contrast with disaffirmations. Similarly, disaffirmations establish common ground only through contrasts with affirmations. Disagreements and agreements are therefore "tandem essentials" in friendship formation and maintenance. Beyond suggesting that agreement/disagreement ratios must be favourable, exchange theory does not specify the "climate of agreement" needed for friendships to emerge and endure. Available studies suggest that these ratios must exceed unity: Gottman (1983), for example, observed children interacting with their friends with agreement/disagreement ratios that averaged somewhat less than 2:1.

Overall, exchange theory furnishes a good general account of the manner in which agreements and disagreements are involved in "becoming friends". Disagreement/agreement ratios need to be better specified, equilibration in social exchanges better understood, and contextual variations need to be taken into account. Agreements and disagreements need clarification, especially, as "tandem essentials" in mutual attraction.

The friendships of infants and toddlers

Observations in child care centres show considerable differentiation in the social interaction occurring among infants and toddlers. Sociometric "stars" are evident: certain infants are approached more consistently than others, and some are more consistently avoided. Sought-after babies are likely to be more active in initiating contacts with other babies as well as to react contingently to their overtures. Least sought-after babies are likely to be asocial; both the number and complexity of their social interactions are likely to depend on whether they themselves initiated them (Lee, 1973). Social responsiveness, in this sense, is closely akin to generalised reciprocity, and sociometric stars make overtures to which other children readily respond, as well as responding to other children contingently and more-or-less equivalently.

When reciprocity and complementarity are mutual, social attraction will be too: a "climate of agreement" is established and children become friends. One investigator (Howes, 1983) empirically established this occurrence. Observing infants, toddlers, and preschool children, the investigator distinguished dyads from one another according to three criteria:

1. their social overtures needed to result in interaction at least half the time;

2. complementarities needed to occur in their play; and

3. positively-toned affective exchanges needed to be evident (e.g., smiling and laughing).

Sheer amount of social interaction was not used as a criterion, although dyads meeting the other criteria turned out to be more interactive than those that didn't. The most interesting results, though, were these: most of the dyads displaying successful social overtures, complementary play, and shared affect were considered by the children's teachers to be "friends". Other investigators have also reported that special relationships are mirrored in the social interaction occurring among infants and toddlers, and that their actions vary according to the identity of their companions (Ross & Lollis, 1989).

The commodities exchanged between infant friends differ from those exchanged by older ones. Babies who are stable friends exchange objects more frequently than toddlers or preschool-aged friends. Concomitantly, preschool children and their friends spend more time in reciprocal and complementary play than infants and toddlers, and vocalise more to them (Howes, 1983). Seemingly, then, the child's development does not change the basis for mutual attraction (i.e., reciprocity in social relations), merely the commodities exchanged (i.e., from objects to complementarities in play).

Conflict and aggression are not closely connected to friendship relations among very young children. Relationships based mainly on enmity are difficult to find, mainly because children who don't like one another don't interact. Generally, toddlers fight most with classmates who are also their friends, although not all toddlers fight with their friends. Consequently, one sees "fighting friends" from time to time, although many toddlers are friends without the accompanying conflict (Ross, Conant, & Cheyne, 1987).

Children and adolescents

Similarities between friends

Age. Children and their friends are concordant in age, reflecting the egalitarian nature of these relationships. Age concordances between friends are not great within single classrooms but are considerable within entire schools. This situation extends from early childhood through adolescence (Kandel, 1978b).

Sex. Children and their friends are same-sex. Opposite-sex friendships are relatively rare, even among preschoolers. Among school-aged children, opposite-sex relationships are ordinarily seen as romantic or sexual, and frequently invite teasing and joking (Thorne, 1986; Goodnow & Burns, 1988). Romantic relationships become increasingly evident during adolescence, but most teenagers continue to choose members of their own sex as best friends. Only one in twenty friendships among adolescents is opposite-sex (Duck, 1975). Gender concordances decline slightly among older adolescents from high school through adulthood (Epstein, 1983).

Race. Racial concordances between friends are also evident, increasing from early childhood through adolescence. Among American children, own-race choices increase during middle childhood; choices of own-race play or work companions then stabilise but own-race friendship choices continue to increase through adolescence (Asher, Singleton, & Taylor, 1988). Similar concordances (including the age differences) exist among British children: friendship choices are own-race more often than chance among primary grade children, increasingly progressively among older children, and especially among adolescents (Jelinek & Brittan, 1975).

Behavioural similarities. Behavioural concordances among friends and nonfriends are not especially well-studied in early and middle childhood. Existing evidence suggests that these similarities are not as great as the similarities between friends in age, sex, and race (Hartup, in press b). Better studies exist for young adolescents, although behavioural similarities between friends are not especially great at this time, either. The most striking concordances occur in three areas: school attitudes, including educational aspirations and attitudes about achievement; attitudes about certain normative behaviours in contemporary teen culture, e.g., drinking and drug-taking (Kandel, 1978b); and sexual experience — among girls only (Billy, Rodgers, & Udry, 1984).

Determinants. Similarities between friends occur for two main reasons:

1. similar children and adolescents choose one another as friends, and

2. friends socialise one another in similar directions.

Unfortunately, selection and socialisation effects are not easy to disentangle empirically. One investigator (Kandel, 1978a) succeeded, however, by studying continuity and change among adolescents in drug use, educational attitudes, and delinquent involvement across one school year. Both selection and socialisation effects were evident, in equal amounts. Gender and race concordances, of course, represent selection effects only.

Behaviour with friends

Friendship formation in early and middle childhood is more elaborate than among infants and toddlers, although first indications of social attraction continue to include sustained social exchanges, complementarities in these exchanges, and mutually-regulated affect. Gottman (1983) examined conversations between children (strangers) on three successive occasions and also obtained estimates from mothers of how well the children were "hitting it off" after two months. Results revealed that the clarity and connectedness of communication during the children's first encounters was the best predictor of hitting it off; information exchange, conflict resolution, and common play activities were also correlated with this outcome. Communication clarity in subsequent sessions was also closely related to hitting it off, and self-disclosure assumed significance. Regression analyses showed that these variables accounted for more than 80% of the variance in the children's becoming friends, an unusually large amount.

Once friendships are established, cooperation and reciprocity become markers of these relationships. Competition and conflict are related to friendship functioning according to context, i.e., friends differ from nonfriends in conflict management according to the setting in which social interaction occurs. On playgrounds and in other "open" situations, friends disagree less often per unit time than nonfriends, but have more total disagreements because friends spend more time with one another than nonfriends. Conflicts are less heated between friends than between nonfriends, mutual disengagements are used more commonly as resolution strategies, and outcomes are more equal. Friends remain together more frequently than nonfriends in open situations, too, once the conflict is over (Hartup, et al., 1988). In "closed" situations, however, (i.e., when the children must interact with one another, not changing partners or activities) friends actually disagree more often per unit time (Hartup, in press a). Conflicts in closed situations are also more intense between friends than between nonfriends (Gottman, 1983; Nelson & Aboud, 1985). Friends thus seem to make more vigorous efforts than nonfriends to reduce the damage resulting from their disagreements in open situations and to ensure continued interaction. In closed situations, they apparently feel "freer" to disagree.

This interaction between friendship and context in conflict management can only be inferred currently by comparing the results of different studies. Setting and friendship variations have not been examined simultaneously within a single investigation, and this omission needs to be corrected. Age differences must also be looked at: certain studies, for example, suggest that adolescents generate more conflicts with friends than with nonfriends in open situations (Laursen, 1989) but fewer conflicts in open ones (Berndt et al., 1986), exactly the opposite of the case with children.

With increasing age, children's friendships become suffused with expectations of loyalty, trust, self-disclosure, and intimacy. Children themselves confirm these generalisations, primarily in interviews and questionnaires. Observational methods are difficult to use for capturing intimate nuances among older children and adolescents.

Sex differences

Sex differences are evident in the interaction that occurs between children and their friends, reflecting general differences between boys and girls in social orientation and behaviour (Huston, 1983). Few investigators have examined sex differences in social interaction among friends and nonfriends separately. Since most observational studies centre on events occurring between children who spend time together, one can assume that the resulting sex differences characterise friends, but this may not always be the case. Friendships themselves differ between boys and girls. Among school-aged children, for example, girls' relationships are usually more "intensive" and less "extensive" than boys'. Using factor analytic methods, Waldrop and Halverson (1975) found that intensiveness (i.e., the extent to which the child's mother discusses best friends and their importance) loaded highly on a peer-orientation factor among girls but not boys. At the same time, extensiveness (i.e., emphasis on group activities and games) loaded on peer-orientation only among boys.

Friendship networks vary in exclusiveness, too. Eder and Hallinan (1978) obtained sociometric choices from five classrooms, determined the number of triads in each classroom that included an exclusive, reciprocated friendship, and divided this number by the total number of same-sex triads existing in the class. Exclusive friendship dyads were more common among girls' triads than boys', while non-reciprocated choices were more common among boys'. Girls' choices also grew more exclusive during the school year whereas boys' choices either became non-exclusive or didn't change. What are the origins of these sex differences? We are uncertain. Play interests may be partly responsible: boys' activities commonly involve numerous individuals whereas girls' activities are likely to be dyadic. One can also argue, however, that the extensiveness in boys' friendship networks supports strivings for autonomy and mastery, while the intensiveness in girls' networks supports needs for closeness and intimacy in social relations.

Whatever their determinants, these sex differences are widely recognised among adolescents. Girls spend more time with their friends, on average, than boys do (Wong & Csikzentmihalyi, 1991). Both boys and girls characterise girls' friendships as more intimate than boys' (Bukowski & Kramer, 1986). Intimacy is more commonly mentioned in girls' talk about their friendships than in boys' talk, and ratings of their same-sex friendships are, in general, more intimate (Sharabany et al., 1981). Girls also report the occurrence of self-disclosure between themselves and their friends more frequently than boys do (Rivenbark, 1971). Finally, male adolescents are more likely than females, on average, to believe that their conflicts don't affect their close relationships. Conversely, females talk more often about the long-term implications of disagreements with their friends (Laursen, 1989).

Mean differences, however, may not tell the entire story with respect to sex differences. Boys' friendships, for example, are more variable than girls' with respect to intimacy. Youniss and Smollar (1986) found that most adolescent girls describe their friendships in terms of shared activities, intimacy, and mutual understanding, and 40% of the adolescent boys in this investigation also described their friendships in this way. Only 30% of the boys characterised their friendships as communicatively guarded and lacking in mutual understanding.

Friendship experience and developmental outcome

Children who are disliked by other children are at risk generally, mostly of mental health difficulties in adolescence and early adulthood and of early school leaving. Being disliked is a common experience among aggressive children, but early aggressiveness is more closely related to later criminality than is social rejection. Shyness is sometimes accompanied by peer rejection, but only among older children (Hartup, in press b).

Being disliked and being without friends, however, are not the same. Indeed, some children who are disliked by other children have best friends, most commonly children who are socially rejected themselves (Cairns, Cairns, Neckerman, Gest, & Garieppy, 1988). Since friendship experience may have its own social functions, one cannot assume that it will be related to the same developmental outcomes as peer rejection. Relatively few investigators have sought to verify the developmental significance of friendship experience. A small number of correlational studies establish the relation between having friends, on the one hand, and social competence, on the other. These investigations show that:

1. Preschool-aged children with emotional difficulties are friendless more frequently than better-adapted children, and are less likely to maintain the friendships they have. Even so, many young children with emotional difficulties also have friends (Howes, 1983).

2. Among school-aged children referred to child guidance clinics, 30% to 75% (depending on age) are reported by parents as having peer difficulties (Achenbach & Edelbrock, 1981). Referred children have fewer friends as well as less contact with them than nonreferred children, and their friendships are less stable over time (Ruttel & Garmezy, 1983).

3. Referred children understand the reciprocities and intimacies in friendships less maturely than non-referred children (Selman, 1980).

Other studies show that, among unselected children and adolescents, friendship experience is correlated with various indicators of social skill:

1. Among preschoolers, children with mutual friends evidence more mature affective perspective taking than children who only have unilateral (i.e., unreciprocated) relationships (Jones & Bowling, 1988).

2. Preschoolers with mutual friends enter groups more easily than children with no mutual friends, engage in more cooperative pretend play, have fewer difficulties with other children, and are more sociable (Howes, 1989).

3. Among preadolescents, those with stable chums are more altruistic than those without them, as measured by concern for others and defaults in a prisoner's dilemma game (Mannarino, 1976).

4. Children with friends display greater altruism than children without friends, as assessed by both teacher ratings and observations (McGuire & Weisz, 1982).

5. Finally, the transition to adolescence is marked by increasing positive correlations between social competence, sociability, and self-esteem, on the one hand, and the intimacy, satisfaction, and companionability of the individual's friendships, on the other. Negative correlations between hostility and anxiety/depression, respectively, and friendship intimacy also increase (Buhrmester, 1990).

Although this evidence is impressive, the results cannot be used to specify causal direction: close relationships may support good adjustment and its development but, alternatively, well-adjusted children may simply be better at establishing friendships than poorly-adjusted ones. Causality can be better argued from regression models used with longitudinal data. Thus far, two short-term studies have been conducted, both yielding results supporting the thesis that friendship experience contributes to socialisation outcome.

In one investigation (Ladd, *et al.*, 1990), the playground behaviour of preschool children was observed on three occasions during the school year in order to assess friendship relations. Friendship variables included number of frequent play companions (i.e., playmates present in more than 30% of a child's observations) and network affinity (i.e., the proportion of frequent companions who also indicated they liked the subject). Social adjustment was measured in terms of sociometric status and teacher ratings. Results indicated, first, that the number of frequent companions was significantly correlated with the adjustment measures in each measurement interval separately but, also, that the correlations between network affinity and these measures increased over time. Most interestingly, the results indicated that the number of frequent companions at the beginning of the year predicted social ratings at the end of the year, but social ratings at the beginning did not predict companion scores at the end.

In a second investigation, Ladd (1990) obtained repeated measures of friendship relations, sociometric status, and school adjustment (perceptions, anxiety/avoidance, and performance) among kindergarten children. Personal attributes (e.g., mental age and prior school experience) predicted early school performance to some extent, but regression analyses also showed that children with many friends at school entrance developed more favourable school perceptions in the early months than children with fewer friends. Those who maintained these relationships also liked school better as the year went by. Making new friends in the classroom also predicted gains in school performance over the year whereas being disliked by other children forecast unfavourable school perceptions, school avoidance, and progressively poorer school performance. Contrasting analyses, estimating the regression of friendship status on school adjustment, showed relatively weak results: e.g., favourable school perceptions predicted friendship maintenance over the year but, otherwise, school adjustment did not forecast friendship experience. Friendship relations thus predicted school adjustment in these data better than the reverse.

Taken together, the results suggest that early adaptation to school derives partly from personal attributes (e.g., mental age) but also from friendship experience (Ladd, 1990, p. 1097):

> ... children's classroom peer relationships tended to add to the prediction of school adjustment, above and beyond that which could be accounted for by their personal attributes and experiences. Furthermore, features of children's classroom peer relationships forecasted both their adjustment during the early weeks of kindergarten and changes in their adjustment during the school year. The fact that changes in children's school adjustment were predicted by these variables lends support to the hypothesis that children's personal attributes, their prior experiences, and their relationships with classmates affect their adaptational progress ...

While the processes through which friendship relations contribute to social competence are not illuminated by these results, the contention that these relationships contribute importantly and directly to socialisation is supported. Most important, several different dimensions in friendship relations turn out to be significant: i.e., having friends in one's classroom to begin with, keeping them, and making new ones.

Prospective studies are time-consuming and laborious, but without them the developmental significance of children's friendships cannot be established. Currently, one wishes for longer-term studies and studies that extend beyond the school milieu. One also wishes for studies in which family relations are included in the regression model as well as child-child relations, since qualitative differences in early relationships between mothers and children are related to making friends later and, possibly, to what those friendships are like (Elicker, Englund, & Sroufe, in press). Even so, the weight of the current evidence suggests that friendship relations have considerable developmental significance.

Whether friends are "necessities" in child and adolescent development remains uncertain. Should friends not be available, other relationships may be elastic enough to serve the friendship functions enumerated earlier. Children with friends may be better off than children without friends but, if necessary, other relationships may be substituted for friendships. Stated another way: friendships may be optimal settings for learning about egalitarian relationships and the social exchanges necessary to them, but children may be able to exploit other relationships to learn these same things. Nature seldom leaves us with only one means to an adaptational end; numerous means are usually available. These redundancies, of course, assure successful adaptation when primary adaptational mechanisms cannot be used. Consequently, we argue that friendships are best viewed as developmental advantages rather than developmental necessities, and we read the current evidence concerning friendships and their developmental significance in this light (Hartup & Sancilio, 1986).

Conclusion

Children understand that reciprocity and equality are the basic conditions of friendship. These conditions are understood by young children in relatively concrete terms and by older children in more psychological ones. Emotional investment in these relationships is taken for granted, especially among older children and adolescents: caring and social support are expected to be exchanged with one's friends. Commitment and trust eventually become important conditions undergirding these relationships, and intimacy becomes a major issue during adolescence. Whether these expectations are manifestations of a single, over-riding concern with equity or separate social considerations remains to be established.

Beginning in early childhood, children reliably identify certain children as best friends, whether they are asked to classify their associates as friends or as individuals who are liked. Parents and teachers identify these same children as friends, and children spend more time with those classmates whom they designate as friends than with other children. Liking one another and spending time together are the most obvious markers of these relationships.

Friendship relations can be divided into a series of "stages" ranging from first encounters through deterioration and endings . Wide variation exists from friendship to friendship in these time-related elements. Common ground is especially significant in establishing relationships; commitment is especially important to their continuation and maintenance. Children's relationships with one another deteriorate for many different reasons, although commitment violations are salient beginning in preadolescence. Conflicts sometimes signal friendship endings, but not always. Endings are as likely to be accompanied by alienation as argument.

Children's friendships serve proximally as mechanisms for ensuring interaction with agemates. More distally, friendships serve as contexts for acquiring social skill, sources of information about both the social and nonsocial world, cognitive and emotional resources, and precursors of other relationships. Empirical evidence concerning these functions is scattered, diverse, and mostly circumstantial (as evidence about distal function inevitably is). Better understanding of friendship functions is among the greatest needs in this area.

A "climate of agreement" seems to be required for friendships to begin. Close relationships, however, are always constructed on the basis of a dialectic between agreements and disagreements, as these are involved in establishing common ground between individuals and reciprocity in their social interaction. Infants and toddlers display both reciprocities and complementarities with one another, and these characteristics (along with shared affect) distinguish friends from nonfriends. Reciprocity continues to be the basis for mutual attraction through the preschool years, although the commodities exchanged between friends undergo considerable change.

Friends are concordant in age, sex, and race. Behavioural concordances are not as strong, although school-aged children and their friends evidence moderate similarity in educational and normative attitudes. Based on current evidence, behavioural similarities both contribute to friendship selection and result from these relationships. Conflict as well as cooperation differentiates the social interaction of friends and nonfriends from early childhood through adolescence. Contextual variations are evident, however, especially in manifestations of conflict and competition. Children's own accounts of their friendship expectations increasingly emphasise commitment, but behavioural manifestations of these developments are not well documented.

Boys interact differently with their friends from girls, although sex differences have rarely been examined among friends and nonfriends separately. Girls' relationships appear to be more intensive and less extensive than boys', and to encompass greater concerns with intimacy. Boys may be more variable with their friends than girls, however, suggesting caution in making simple statements about sex differences in friendship relations.

Correlational studies show that children with friends are more socially competent than children who do not have friends, and that troubled children have difficulty in friendship relations. Causal models, tested with longitudinal data, suggest that friendship experience forecasts developmental outcome in conjunction with personal attributes and other experiences. Making friends, keeping them, and making new ones are all relevant. The current evidence suggests, however, that we can better argue that friendships are developmental advantages than argue that these relationships are developmental necessities.

Support in the completion of this manuscript was provided by the Rodney S. Wallace Endowment, College of Education, University of Minnesota.

Notes

1. The term reciprocity is not used consistently in the literature. Reciprocity sometimes refers to the contingent occurrence of the same actions during social interaction (e.g., talk followed by talk). At other times, the term refers to behavioural "complements" (e.g., chase/being chased; give/take). The construct also refers to equivalencies in the "benefits" deriving from a social exchange. Contingency and equivalence seem to be the core elements in this word's meaning.

2. The quotations from children's interviews given in the text were obtained by Goodnow and Burns (1988) and are used with permission.

3. The instructional methods they use are remarkably similar to those employed by adults in teaching children (Ludeke & Hartup, 1983).

4. This section derives from a manuscript appearing elsewhere (Hartup, in press a) and is used with permission.

References

Achenbach, T. M., & Edelbrock, C.S. (1981) 'Behavioral problems and competence reported by parents of normal and disturbed children aged 4 through 16'. *Monographs of the Society for Research in Child Development*, 46 (1, No. 188).

Asher, S.R., Singleton, L.C., & Taylor, A.R. (1988) *Acceptance versus friendship: A longitudinal study of racial integration*. Manuscript submitted for publication.

Azmitia, M. (1988) 'Peer interaction and problem-solving: When are two heads better than one?' *Child Development*, 59, 87-96.

Berndt, T. J. (1981) 'Relations between social cognition, nonsocial cognition, and social behavior: The case of friendship'. In J.H. Flavell, & L. Ross (Eds.), *Social cognitive development* (pp. 176-199). Cambridge, U.K.: Cambridge University Press.

Berndt, T.J., Hawkins, J.A., & Hoyle, S.G. (1986) 'Changes in friendship during a school year: Effects on children's and adolescents' impressions of friendship and sharing with friends'. *Child Development*, 57, 1284-1297.

Berndt, T.J., & Perry, T.B. (1986) 'Children's perceptions of friendships as supportive relationships'. *Developmental Psychology*, 22, 640-648.

Berscheid, E. (1985) 'Interpersonal modes of knowing. In E.W. Eisner (Ed.), Learning the ways of knowing'. *The 85th yearbook of the national society for the study of education* (pp. 60-76). Chicago: University of Chicago Press.

Biehler, R.F. (1954) 'Companion choice behavior in the kindergarten'. *Child Development*, 25, 45-50.

Bigelow, B.J. (1977) 'Children's friendship expectations: A cognitive developmental study'. *Child Development*, 48, 246-253.

Bigelow, B.J., & LaGaipa, J.J. (1975) 'Children's written descriptions of friendship: A multidimensional analysis'. *Developmental Psychology*, 11, 857-858.

Billy, J.O.G., Rodgers, J.L., & Udry, J.R. (1984) 'Adolescent sexual behavior and friendship choice'. *Social Forces*, 62, 653-678.

Buhrmester, D. (1990) 'Intimacy of friendship, interpersonal competence, and adjustment during preadolescence and adolescence'. *Child Development*, 61, 1101-1111.

Bukowski, W.M., & Kramer, T.L. (1986) 'Judgments of the features of friendship among early adolescent boys and girls'. *Journal of Early Adolescence*, 6, 331-338.

Byrne, D. (1971) *The attraction paradigm*. New York: Academic Press.

Cairns, R.B., Cairns, B.D., Neckerman, H.J., Gest, S., & Garieppy, J.-L. (1988) 'Peer networks and aggressive behavior: Peer support or peer rejection?' *Developmental Psychology*, 24, 815-823.

Chapman, A.J., Smith, J.R., Foot, H.C., & Pritchard, E. (1979) 'Behavioural and sociometric indices of friendship in children'. In M. Cook, & G.D. Wilson (Eds.), *Love and attraction* (pp. 127-130). Oxford, U.K.: Pergamon.

Charlesworth, W.R., & LaFreniere, P. (1983) 'Dominance, friendship, and resource utilization in preschool children's groups. *Ethology and Sociobiology*, 4, 175-186.

Crockett, L., Losoff, M., & Petersen, A.C. (1984) Perceptions of the peer group and friendship in early adolescence'. *Journal of Early Adolescence*, 4, 155-181.

Damon, W., & Phelps, E. (1989) 'Strategic uses of peer learning in children's education'. In T. J. Berndt, & G.W. Ladd (Eds.) *Peer relationships in child development* (pp. 135-157). New York: Wiley.

Duck, S.W. (1975) 'Personality similarity and friendship choices by adolescents'. *European Journal of Social Psychology*, 5, 351-365.

Eder, D., & Hallinan, M.T. (1978) 'Sex differences in children's friendships'. *American Sociological Review*, 43, 237-250.

Elder, G. (1974) *Children of the Great Depression*. Chicago: University of Chicago Press.

Elicker, J., Englund, M., & Sroufe, L.A. (in press) 'Predicting peer competence and peer relationships in childhood from early parent-child relationships'. In R.D. Parke, & G.W. Ladd (Eds.), *Family-peer relationships: Modes of linkage*. Hillsdale, N.J.: Lawrence Erlbaum Associates Inc.

Epstein, J. L. (1983) 'Selection of friends in differently organized schools and classrooms'. In J. L. Epstein, & N. Karweit (Eds.), *Friends in school: Patterns of selection and influence in secondary schools* (pp. 73-92). New York: Wiley.

Foot, H.C., Chapman, A.J., & Smith, J.R. (1977) 'Friendship and social responsiveness in boys and girls'. *Journal of Personality and Social Psychology*, 35, 401-411.

Furman, W., & Bierman, K.L. (1984) 'Children's conceptions of friendship: A multi-dimensional study of developmental changes'. *Developmental Psychology*, 20, 925-931.

Furman, W., & Childs, M.K. (1981, April) *A temporal perspective on children's friendships*. Paper presented at the biennial meetings of the Society for Research in Child Development, Boston.

Goodnow, J.J., & Burns, A. (1988) *Home and school: Child's eye view*. Sydney: Allen & Unwin.

Gottman, J.M. (1979) *Marital interaction: Experimental investigations*. New York: Academic Press.

Gottman, J.M. (1983) 'How children become friends'. *Monographs of the Society for Research in Child Development*, 48, (No. 201).

Hallinan, M.T. (1980) 'Patterns of cliquing among youth'. In H.C. Foot, A.J. Chapman, & J.R. Smith (Eds.), *Friendship and peer relations in children* (pp. 321-342). New York: Wiley.

Hartup, W.W. (1964) 'Friendship status and the effectiveness of peers as reinforcing agents'. *Journal of Experimental Child Psychology*, 1, 154-162.

Hartup, W.W. (1983) 'Peer relations'. In E. M. Hetherington (Ed.), & P. H. Mussen (Series Ed.), *Handbook of child psychology, Vol. 4, Socialization, social development, and personality* (pp. 103-196). New York: Wiley.

Hartup, W.W. (1989) 'Behavioral manifestations of children's friendships'. In T.J. Berndt, & G.W. Ladd (Eds.), *Peer relationships in child development* (pp. 46-70). New York: Wiley.

Hartup, W.W. (in press, a) 'Conflict and friendship relations'. In C.U. Shantz, & W.W. Hartup (Eds.), *Conflict in child and adolescent development*. Cambridge, U.K.: Cambridge University Press.

Hartup, W.W. (in press, b) 'Peer relations in early and middle childhood'. In V.B. van Hasselt, & M. Hersen (Eds.), *Handbook of social development: A lifespan perspective*. New York: Plenum.

Hartup, W.W., Laursen, B., Stewart, M.A., & Eastenson, A. (1988) 'Conflict and the friendship relations of young children'. *Child Development*, 59, 1590-1600.

Hartup, W.W., & Sancilio, M.F. (1986) 'Children's friendships'. In E. Schopler, & G. Mesibov (Eds.), *Social behavior in autism* (pp. 61-79). New York: Plenum.

Hinde, R.A. (1979) *Towards understanding relationships*. New York: Academic Press.

Hinde, R.A., Titmus, G., Easton, D., & Tamplin, A. (1985) 'Incidence of "friendship" and behavior with strong associates versus non-associates in preschoolers'. *Child Development*, 56, 234-245.

Howes, C. (1983) 'Patterns of friendship'. *Child Development*, 54, 1041-1053.

Howes, C. (1989) 'Peer interaction of young children'. (1989). *Monographs of the Society for Research in Child Development*, 53 (Serial No. 217).

Huston, A.C. (1983) 'Sex-typing'. In E. M. Hetherington (Ed.), & P.H. Mussen (Series Ed.), *Handbook of child psychology, Vol. 4, Socialization, personality, and social development* (pp. 387-467). New York: Wiley.

Hyde, R.W., & York, R.H. (1948) 'A technique for investigating interpersonal relationships in a mental hospital'. *Journal of Abnormal and Social Psychology*, 43, 287-299.

Hymel, S. (1983) 'Preschool children's peer relations: Issues in sociometric assessment'. *Merrill-Palmer Quarterly*, 29, 237-260.

Hymel, S., Hayvren, M., & Lollis, S. (1982, May) *Social behavior and sociometric preferences: Do children really play with peers they like?* Paper presented at the annual meeting of the Canadian Psychological Association, Montreal.

Ipsa, J. (1981) 'Peer support among Soviet day care toddlers'. *International Journal of Behavioral Development*, 4, 255-269.

Jelinek, M.M., & Brittan, E.M. (1975) 'Multiracial education: I. Inter-ethnic friendship patterns'. *Educational Research*, 18, 44-53.

Johnson, D.W., Johnson, R.T., Johnson, J., & Anderson, D. (1976) 'Effects of cooperative versus individualized instruction on student prosocial behavior, attitudes toward learning, and achievement'. *Journal of Educational Psychology*, 68, 446-452.

Jones, D.C., & Bowling, B. (1988, March) *Preschool friends and affective knowledge: A comparison of mutual and unilateral friends*. Paper presented at the Conference on Human Development, Charleston, S.C.

Kandel, D.B. (1978a) 'Homophily, selection, and socialization in adolescent friendships'. *American Journal of Sociology*, 84, 427-436.

Kandel, D.B. (1978b) 'Similarity in real-life adolescent friendship pairs'. *Journal of Personality and Social Psychology*, 36, 306-312.

Kelley, H.H. (1979) 'Personal relationships: Their structures and processes'. Hillsdale , N.J.: Lawrence Erlbaum Associates Inc.

Ladd, G.W. (1990) 'Having friends, keeping friends, making friends, and being liked by peers in the classroom: Predictors of children's early school adjustment?' *Child Development*, 61, 1081-1100.

Ladd, G.W., & Emerson, E.S. (1984) 'Shared knowledge in children's friendships'. *Developmental Psychology*, 20, 932-940.

Ladd, G.W., Price, J.M., & Hart, C.H. (1990) 'Preschoolers' behavioral orientations and patterns of peer contact: Predictive of peer status?' In S.R. Asher, & J.D. Coie (Eds.), *Peer rejection in childhood* (pp. 90-115). Cambridge, U.K.: Cambridge University Press.

Laursen, B. (1989) *Interpersonal conflict during adolescence*. Unpublished doctoral dissertation, University of Minnesota.

Lee, L.C. (1973, July) *Social encounters of infants: The beginnings of popularity*. Paper presented at the biennial meeting of the International Society for the Study of Behavioural Development, Ann Arbor, Mich.

Levinger, G. (1983) 'Development and change'. In H.H. Kelley, E. Berscheid, A. Christensen , J.H. Harvey, T.L. Huston, G. Levinger, E. McClintock, L.A. Peplau, & D.R. Peterson (Eds.), *Close relationships* (pp. 315-359). New York: W.H. Freeman.

Levinger, G., & Levinger, A.C. (1986) 'The temporal course of close relationships: Some thoughts about the development of children's ties'. In W.W. Hartup, & Z. Rubin (Eds.), *Relationships and development* (pp. 111-133). Hillsdale, N.J.: Lawrence Erlbaum Associates Inc.

Ludeke, R.J., & Hartup, W.W. (1983) 'Teaching behaviors of nine- and eleven-year-old girls in mixed-age and same-age dyads'. *Journal of Educational Psychology*, 75, 908-914.

Mannarino, A.P. (1976) 'Friendship patterns and altruistic behavior in preadolescent males'. *Developmental Psychology*, 12, 555-556.

Marshall, H.R., & McCandless B. R. (1957) 'A study in prediction of social behavior of preschool children'. *Child Development*, 28, 149-159.

Masters, J.C., & Furman, W. (1981) 'Popularity, individual friendship selections, and specific peer interaction among children'. *Developmental Psychology*, 17, 344-350.

McCandless, B.R., & Marshall, H.R. (1957) 'A picture sociometric technique for preschool children and its relation to teacher judgments of friendship'. *Child Development*, 28, 139-148.

McGuire, K.D., & Weisz, J.R. (1982) 'Social cognition and behavior correlates of preadolescent chumship'. *Child Development*, 53, 1478-1484.

Medrich, E.A., Rosen, J., Rubin,V., & Buckley, S. (1982) *The serious business of growing up*. Berkeley, Cal.: University of California Press.

Nelson, J., & Aboud, F.E. (1985) 'The resolution of social conflict between friends'. *Child Development*, 56, 1009-1017.

Newcomb, A.F., & Brady, J.E. (1982) 'Mutuality in boys' friendship selections'. *Child Development*, 53, 392-395.

Olweus, D. (1980) 'Bullying among school boys'. In R. Barnen (Ed.), *Children and violence.* Stockholm: Akademic Litteratur.

Park, K.A., & Waters, E. (1988) *Security of attachment and preschool friendships.* Unpublished manuscript, State University of New York, Stony Brook.

Peevers, B.H., & Secord, P.F. (1973) 'Developmental changes in attribution of descriptive concepts to persons'. *Journal of Personality and Social Psychology*, 27, 120-128.

Price, J.M., & Ladd, G.W. (1986) 'Assessment of children's friendships: Implications for social competence and social adjustment'. In R.J. Prinz (Ed.), *Advances in behavioral assessment of children and families*, Vol 2 (pp. 121-149). Greenwich, C.T.: J.A.I. Press.

Rivenbark, W.H. (1971) 'Self-disclosure patterns among adolescents'. *Psychological Reports*, 28, 35-42.

Rizzo, T.A. (1989) *Friendship development among children in school.* Norwood, N.J.: Ablex.

Ross, H.S., Conant, C., & Cheyne, J.A. (1987) *Reciprocity in the relationships of kibbutz toddlers.* Poster presented at the biennial meetings of the Society for Research in Child Development, Baltimore.

Ross, H.S., & Lollis, S.P. (1989) 'A social relations analysis of toddler peer relationships'. *Child Development*, 60, 1082-1091.

Rutter, M., & Garmezy, N. (1983) 'Developmental psychopathology'. In E.M. Hetherington (Ed.), P.H. Mussen (Series Ed.), *Handbook of child psychology, Vol 4, Socialization, social development, and personality* (pp. 775-911). New York: Wiley.

Sancilio, M.F. (1989) *Making friends: The development of dyadic social relationships among previously unacquainted adolescent boys.* Unpublished doctoral dissertation, University of Minnesota.

Schwartz, J.C. (1972) 'Effects of peer familiarity on the behavior of preschoolers in a novel situation'. *Journal of Personality and Social Psychology*, 24, 276-284.

Scofield, R.W. (1960) 'Task productivity of groups of friends and nonfriends'. *Psychological Reports*, 6, 459-460.

Selman, R.L. (1980) 'The growth of interpersonal understanding'. New York: Academic Press.

Sharabany, R., Gershoni, R., & Hofman, J.E. (1981) 'Girlfriend, boyfriend: Age and sex differences in intimate friendship'. *Developmental Psychology*, 17, 800-808.

Shaw, M.E., & Shaw, L.M. (1962) 'Some effects of sociometric grouping upon learning in a second grade classroom'. *Journal of Social Psychology,* 57, 453-458.

Thorne, B. (1986) 'Girls and boys together . . . but mostly apart: Gender arrangements in elementary schools'. In W.W. Hartup, & Z. Rubin (Eds.), *Relationships and development* (pp. 167-184). Hillsdale, N.J.: Lawrence Erlbaum Associates Inc.

Waldrop, M.F., & Halverson, C.F. (1975) 'Intensive and extensive peer behavior: Longitudinal and cross-sectional analyses'. *Child Development*, 46, 19-26.

Wallerstein, J.S., & Kelly, J.B. (1981) *Surviving the breakup: How children and parents cope with divorce*. New York: Basic Books.

Weiss, R.S. (1986) 'Continuities and transformations in social relationships from childhood to adulthood'. In W.W. Hartup, & Z. Rubin (Eds.), *Relationships and development* (pp. 95-110). Hillsdale, N.J.: Lawrence Erlbaum Associates Inc.

Whiting, B.B., & Whiting, J.W.M. (1975) *Children of six cultures*. Cambridge, Mass.: Harvard University Press.

Wong, M.M., & Csikzentmihalyi, M. (1991) 'Affiliation motivation and daily experience: Some issues on gender differences'. *Journal of Personality and Social Psychology*, 60, 154-164.

Youniss, J. (1980) *Parents and peers in social development: A Piaget-Sullivan perspective*. Chicago: University of Chicago Press.

Youniss, J., & Smollar, J. (1986) *Adolescent relations with mothers, fathers and friends*. Chicago: University of Chicago Press.

24.   Peer Relations and Later Personal Adjustment: Are Low-Accepted Children at Risk?

Jeffrey G. Parker and Steven R. Asher

In this review, we examine the oft-made claim that peer-relationship difficulties in childhood predict serious adjustment problems in later life. The article begins with a framework for conceptualizing and assessing children's peer difficulties and with a discussion of conceptual and methodological issues in longitudinal risk research. Following this, three indexes of problematic peer relationships (acceptance, aggressiveness, and shyness/withdrawal) are evaluated as predictors of three later outcomes (dropping out of school, criminality, and psychopathology). The relation between peer difficulties and later maladjustment is examined in terms of both the consistency and strength of prediction. A review and analysis of the literature indicates general support for the hypothesis that children with poor peer adjustment are at risk for later life difficulties. Support is clearest for the outcomes of dropping out and criminality. It is also clearest for low acceptance and aggressiveness as predictors, whereas a link between shyness/withdrawal and later maladjustment has not yet been adequately tested. The article concludes with a critical discussion of the implicit models that have guided past research in this area and a set of recommendations for the next generation of research on the risk hypothesis.

There are striking individual differences in the extent to which children are accepted by their peers. In the extreme, some children are well regarded by all and enjoy many friendships, whereas others are nearly universally disliked and have no friends. In this review, we consider the implication of variability in acceptance or in acceptance-relevant behavior (aggression and shyness/withdrawal) for children's subsequent personal adjustment in three domains: dropping out of school, juvenile and adult criminality, and adult psychopathology. Our goal is to evaluate the empirical support for the premise that poorly accepted children stand a greater chance than others of developing later life difficulties and, therefore, should be considered a group of children at risk. This premise is widespread in the social development literature. Indeed, it serves as the explicit rationale for attempts to delineate the social skills that ensure adequate peer acceptance (see Hartup, 1983; Putallaz & Gottman, 1981, 1983), for attempts to design effective interventions to aid unpopular children (see Asher & Renshaw, 1981; Combs & Slaby, 1977; J. C. Conger & Keane, 1981; Foster & Ritchey, 1979; Hops, 1982; Ladd & Mize, 1983; Wanlass & Prinz, 1982), and for appeals for social skills training in schools (e.g., Johnson & Johnson, 1981; Stocking, Arezzo, & Leavitt, 1980). The risk premise can also be found in several introductory child development

Jeffrey G. Parker and Steven R. Asher: 'Peer Relations and Later Personal Adjustment: Are Low-Accepted Children at Risk?' *PSYCHOLOGICAL BULLETIN* (1987), 102, No. 3, pp. 357-389. Copyright © 1987 by the American Psychological Association, Inc. Reprinted by permission.

textbooks (e.g., Fitch, 1985; E. Hall, Perlmutter, & Lamb, 1982; Kopp & Krakow, 1982; Shaffer, 1985; Skolnick, 1986) and in books on friendship intended for nonspecialists (e.g., Duck, 1983). Yet the empirical basis for the risk premise has not been adequately evaluated to date.

Studies suggesting a link between problematic childhood peer relationships and adult maladjustment have accumulated slowly but more or less continuously since the early 1930s. However, widespread acceptance of the premise that low-accepted children are at risk is relatively recent and accompanies a rise in theoretical and empirical interest in children's peer relationships generally (Hartup, 1983; Parke & Asher, 1983). An emergent theme in this broader literature is the conviction that peer interaction plays indispensable multiple causal roles in the socialization of social competence. As Johnson (1980) wrote, "Experiences with peers are not superficial luxuries to be enjoyed by some students and not by others. Student-student relationships are an absolute necessity for healthy cognitive and social development and socialization" (p. 125).

This "necessities-not-luxuries" conviction derives in part from rediscovery of the theories of Piaget (1932), Mead (1934), and Sullivan (1953), each of whom accorded child-child interaction a central place in facilitating children's development (see Damon, 1977; Denzin, 1977; Flavell, 1977; Rest, 1983; Selman, 1979; Shantz, 1983; Youniss, 1980). It also gains appeal because of empirical work demonstrating the positive influence of peer interaction on the socialization of aggressive impulses (see Hartup, 1978) and on cognitive (e.g., Rardin & Moan, 1971), social-cognitive (see Shantz, 1983), linguistic (see Bates, 1975), sex role (e.g., Fagot, 1977), and moral (e.g., Berndt, McCartney, Caparulo, & Moore, 1983-1984) development.

If peers contribute substantially to the socialization of social competence, it follows that low-accepted children might become more vulnerable to later life problems. Specifically, because low-accepted children experience limited opportunities for positive peer interaction, it follows that they would be relatively deprived of opportunities to learn normal, adaptive modes of social conduct and social cognition. Furthermore, because academic pursuit takes place in a social context, poor peer relationships might undermine academic progress as well. It is this line of reasoning that has made recent peer-relationships researchers so receptive to the premise that low-accepted children are at risk.

However, the notion that peers contribute to socialization and, hence, directly to children's vulnerability to later problems need not be accepted to accept the premise that low acceptance might foretell later disorder. Indeed, an alternative view of the link between early peer rejection and later outcomes is that some continuously present behavioral process, underlying pathology, or deficit is directly or indirectly responsible for problematic peer relationships in childhood and for later adult maladaptive functioning. According to this perspective, problems with peers act as correlated "lead indicators" of future adjustment status. In fact, until very recently, it was common for authors to suggest that the form of childhood peer disturbance may even tell something about the form of the eventual disturbed adult outcome. For example, in the literature on schizophrenia, it was long suggested that schizophrenia ought to be preceded by social withdrawal and shyness in childhood because extreme withdrawal is an element of chronic adult schizophrenia (e.g., Fish, 1971; Kohn & Clausen, 1955).

The need for an adequate review

The premise that poorly accepted children are at risk is widespread in the literature and has at times been stated in bold and dramatic terms. Duck (1983), for example, wrote that it is quite clear from available data that

> the socially withdrawn, socially incompetent and aggressive child soon becomes the socially inept adult social casualty. For example, the most famous mass murderers of almost every country (e.g., Christie, the Black Panther, Blue Beard, the Michigan Murderer, the Boston Strangler, and others) have invariably been found to have had abnormal social experiences in childhood . . . . They are usually found to have been loners, quiet types and unsociable people, often dominated by selfish parents, or hounded by thoughtless classmates. If friendmaking had been properly learned — or if they had been helped to learn — their violent, destructive and unusual personalities may have turned out in a more rewarding and acceptable form. (p. 115)

Yet, despite the widespread acceptance of such views and despite their role in motivating social skills research and intervention programs, there has not yet been a thorough evaluation of the research relating peer relationships in childhood to later adjustment. Although several excellent reviews exist in the risk literature (e.g., Garmezy, 1974; Kohlberg, LaCross, & Ricks, 1972; Lavin, 1965; Loeber, 1982; Loeber & Dishion, 1983; Offer & Cross, 1969; Robins, 1972), these do not specifically concern prediction from peer-relationships measures. Instead, they concern a variety of predictors, ranging from prenatal and birth complications to intelligence scores. As a consequence, issues specific to prediction from peer-relationships measures necessarily receive limited consideration.

In the absence of a more focused but comprehensive review, most proponents of the at-risk premise simply cite uncritically a common litany of illustrative studies. Putallaz and Gottman (1983) aptly criticized this approach. Following a paragraph in which they reference the typically cited studies (e.g., Cowen, Pederson, Babijian, Izzo, & Trost, 1973; M. Roff, 1963; M. Roff, Sells, & Golden, 1972; Ullmann, 1957), they commented,

> Some variation of the previous paragraph can be found in the introduction of almost all published work in the area of children's peer acceptance. In fact this paragraph appears a perfunctory necessity; variations involve a fresh writing approach or an obscure study to support known, or identify new negative consequences. The paragraph itself has become so perfunctory that its premise is rarely, if ever, challenged.

(Putallaz & Gottman, 1983, pp.8-9)

One result of such a cursory treatment is that studies that vary widely in methodological adequacy are often given equal consideration. Yet, as we shall discuss, there are good reasons for preferring certain designs and samples over others. Accordingly, before examining the existing literature on how peer acceptance relates to various indexes of later maladjustment, we first outline several methodological and conceptual issues essential to assessing peer-relationships adjustment and designing long-term risk research.

Methodological and conceptual issues in assessing children's peer difficulties

Labeling a low-accepted child as at risk for later maladjustment presupposes that there are dimensions of adaptive-maladaptive peer relationships, that these dimensions can be reliably and accurately assessed, and that children can be meaningfully classified. Several comprehensive reviews of assessment of children's peer relationships already exist (see Asher & Hymel, 1981; Berndt, 1984; Hymel, 1983; Hymel & Rubin, 1985; Ladd, 1985), and these efforts need not be duplicated here. In this section, we consider two critical distinctions regarding the conceptualization and measurement of children's difficulties in peer relationships. Using these two distinctions, we organize existing peer-relationships measures. These distinctions also help guide our subsequent discussion of the risk research literature.

Distinction 1: "Is the child liked?" versus "What is the child like?"

In discussions of acceptance and later risk, it is difficult to resist treating findings from sociometric measures, such as the number of friendship choices a child receives, as interchangeable with findings from measures of behavior, such as aggressiveness or shyness/withdrawal, that are relevant to status. Indeed, children of differing status levels, measured sociometrically, do have differing behavioral profiles; for example, many sociometrically rejected children are likely to be aggressive (Coie, Dodge, & Coppotelli, 1982; McGuire, 1973). Thus, the two kinds of measures are likely to yield partially overlapping groups. Nonetheless, the distinction between sociometric measures of peer acceptance and assessments of social behavior is an important one and should be preserved. Measures of peer acceptance are indexes of the collective attraction of a group of children toward one member. They address the question "Is the child liked?" By contrast, reports about children's behavior address the question "What is the child like?" Although children's behavior (what they are like) influences their peers' attraction toward them (how much they are liked), correlations between measures of acceptance and any given behavior are rarely high and depend partly on the age of the child, the setting, and the history of the group (Dodge, 1983; Hartup, 1983; Putallaz & Gottman, 1983). Moreover, a child's level of acceptance may be influenced by a number of nonbehavioral characteristics, such as the child's physical attractiveness (e.g., Langlois & Stephan, 1981). Therefore, knowledge of a child's characteristic behavioral style can only suggest that child's level of acceptance, and findings from studies identifying children by one type of measure may not generalize to children identified by the other type of measure.

Distinction 2: Peer-based versus teacher-based assessment

Related to the issue of what is assessed is the issue of who is rendering the assessment. In the risk literature, a child's peer adjustment has been assessed by surveying members of his or her peer group or through the reports of teachers who know the child and his or her peer group well. Although both approaches are common, distinguishing them is important because peers and teachers are not entirely redundant sources of information concerning peer adjustment.

With regard to behavior, teacher judgments correlate moderately with peer judgments, with better correspondence for some children (extremely deviant children) than for others (less deviant children) and for some behavioral dimensions (e.g., aggressiveness) than for others (e.g., withdrawal). (See Hymel & Rubin, 1985; Ledingham & Younger, 1985.) Thus, although there is general agreement between the two sources, there is also a great deal of nonoverlap. This nonshared variance stems partly from the sources' differing experiences with various types of behavior. For example, compared with peers, teachers are less likely to see instances of aggression, rough-and-tumble play, and gross motor activity (Ledingham & Younger, 1985). It may also result from differential sensitivity to various behavioral dimensions. For example, there is evidence that aggression is a salient dimension to children at all ages, but shyness/withdrawal may be less salient to younger children than to older children (Ledingham & Younger, 1985).

The opinions of peers and teachers can often be disparate when judgments of acceptance are involved. Correlations between peer sociometric scores and teachers' acceptance judgments rarely exceed .60 and generally are closer to .40 or .50 (e.g., Green, Forehand, Beck, & Vosk, 1980; Kleck & DeJong, 1981; La Greca, 1981; Milich, Landau, Kilby, & Whitten, 1982). The difficulty, of course, lies in the accuracy of teacher judgments, because peer sociometric measures, when appropriately worded, are face-valid measures of how much children like one another. The validity of teacher estimates of acceptance is susceptible to a number of threats. Teachers may be heavily biased by their knowledge of the child's academic success (Lerner & Lerner, 1977) or, under some circumstances, by the child's sex and social class (Gronlund, 1959). Further, as Hymel (1983) noted, teachers and peers may hold differing expectations of what constitutes appropriate and inappropriate behavior; and teachers lack access to all incidents or contexts of peer interaction and, therefore, may be unable to observe certain types of interaction that may be important in judging levels of acceptance.

This raises the issue of how peer- and teacher-based assessments of peer acceptance should be weighted and combined in our review. Clearly, teacher assessments cannot ordinarily replace peer-based assessments as a primary source of data on the predictive risk of poor peer acceptance. However, in the absence of an abundance of well-designed studies using peer-based assessments, studies using teacher-based assessments can be informative in corroborating evidence of risk or in suggesting potential directions of findings in otherwise unresearched areas. Teacher ratings of acceptance, therefore, warrant consideration, despite some of their limitations.

A typology of peer-adjustment indexes

The distinction between acceptance and behavior and the distinction between peer- and teacher-based assessments suggest a fourfold typology of peer-adjustment indexes, which we use in considering the risk research literature. The four types of measures are peer measures of acceptance/rejection, teacher measures of acceptance/rejection, peer measures of status-related behavior, and teacher measures of status-related behavior.

Peer measures of acceptance/rejection. In the risk literature, peer measures of acceptance/rejection include positive and negative sociometric nomination measures.[1]

Positive nomination measures involve soliciting children's friendship or companionship choices. The number of choices a child receives (often standardized within classrooms) constitutes his or her level of acceptance. Negative nomination measures involve asking children to name the children they dislike. The number of negative nominations that a child receives constitutes his or her level of rejection.

An issue that arises with the use of sociometric data is classification. Until recently, researchers tended to view status in the peer group unidimensionally, as a continuum of popularity (number of positive nominations) or preference (number of positive nominations minus the number of negative nominations). However, the repeated finding that the number of positive nominations a child receives is fairly independent of the number of negative nominations he or she receives (e.g., Goldman, Corsini, & de Urioste, 1980; Gottman, 1977; Hartup, Glazer, & Charlesworth, 1967) has led recently to the development of several multidimensional schemes for classifying children in terms of their peer acceptance (see Coie *et al.*, 1982; Newcomb & Bukowski, 1983; Peery, 1979). These schemes separate two previously confounded but conceptually different types of low-accepted children: rejected children who are openly disliked (i.e., few positive and many negative nominations) and neglected children who do not have friends but are not unduly disliked (i.e., few positive or negative nominations). This distinction between rejected and neglected children has appeared in the risk literature only once (Kupersmidt, 1983). This is a serious omission given that research, most of it recent, has shown its utility. Rejected children are more aggressive and disruptive in behavior (Coie *et al.*, 1982; Coie & Kupersmidt, 1983; Dodge, Coie, & Brakke, 1982; Dodge, Schlundt, Schocken, & Delugach, 1983), are more stable in status over time (Coie & Dodge, 1983; Coie & Kupersmidt, 1983; Newcomb & Bukowski, 1983), report greater feelings of loneliness and social dissatisfaction (Asher & Wheeler, 1985), and experience greater academic difficulties (Green, Vosk, Forehand, & Beck, 1981; Muma, 1968; Porterfield & Schlichting, 1961). Neglected children, by contrast, experience no more of these problems than average-status children, although there is some evidence that they tend to be somewhat shy and less interactive (Coie *et al.*, 1982; Dodge, 1983; Dodge *et al.*, 1982; Ladd, Price, & Hart, in press).

Teacher measures of acceptance / rejection. The teacher measures of acceptance/rejection used in risk research have involved mostly ad hoc, single-item measures that are part of broader measures of adjustment. Typically, these are simply teachers' responses to questions asking them to check their agreement or disagreement with such statements as "This child fails to get along with other children" (Janes & Hesselbrock, 1978) or to rate their pupils' acceptance, popularity, rejection, or isolation (e.g., Amble, 1967; Bower, Shellhammer, & Daily, 1960; Cohen, 1982). A concern with almost all of these ad hoc measures is that very little information exists on their psychometric properties.

In addition, investigators have sometimes attempted to infer a child's level of acceptance secondarily, from teachers' structured or unstructured comments in the annual or semiannual progress reports maintained by school personnel (e.g., Conger & Miller, 1966; Warnken & Siess, 1965) or from the notes of caseworkers' interviews with the teachers of children referred to child guidance clinics (e.g., Robins, 1966; M. Roff, 1963). Procedures in such instances range from simple comment tallies (e.g., Conger &

Miller, 1966) to complex systems for weighting and dimensionalizing teacher comments (e.g., Watt & Lubensky, 1976).

A central concern with inferring acceptance level from teachers' spontaneous comments in cumulative school files is that in most cases, data in cumulative school files are cryptic, unstandardized, and nonsystematic. Among other things, this makes it difficult to interpret the absence of references to peer problems. Should one assume, for example, that a child is not unpopular if his or her files contain no comments indicating unpopularity? Further, teachers' judgments may be influenced by comments that are already part of the student's file. Similar questions of reliability and validity arise when assessments are derived from comments in child guidance clinic files (see Garmezy, 1974).

Peer measures of behavior. Included in this category are behavioral nomination measures (e.g., Coie *et al.*, 1982; Havighurst, Bowman, Liddle, Matthews, & Pierce, 1962; Kuhlen & Collister, 1952; Ledingham, Younger, Schwanzman, & Bergeron, 1982; Pekarik, Prinz, Liebert, Weintraub, & Neale, 1976; West & Farrington, 1973) that require children to nominate one another for behavioral vignettes, such as "This person fights a lot." For each child, a score is computed from the number of mentions received for that item. This score is sometimes combined with the child's scores on similar items to yield an overall index of aggressiveness, sociability, or withdrawal (e.g., Ledingham *et al.*, 1982; Pekarik *et al.*, 1976). Other investigators prefer to analyze data at the item level on the grounds that more global scores can obscure important distinctions between subtypes of behavior (e.g., Coie *et al.*, 1982).

Another approach to peer assessment of behavior involves Class Play assessments (Bower & Lamben, 1961). Class Play techniques require children to cast one another for roles in a hypothetical class play. The assumption here is that the roles typically ascribed to a given child by classmates reveal how the peer group perceives that child. Initial research with the Class Play measure (e.g., Cowen *et al.*, 1973; Lambert, 1972) posed something of a problem for the fourfold typology proposed here. Traditionally, 20 to 30 roles were provided with either positive connotations (e.g., "someone who is smart") or negative connotations (e.g., "a bully who picks on smaller boys and girls"). A score was then derived for each child on the basis of the absolute or proportionate number of nominations for positive or negative roles. Used in this way, then, Class Play scores measured general peer reputation rather than specific behavioral or personality characteristics. However, recent revisions and uses of the Class Play (Asarnow, 1982; King & Young, 1981; Masten, Morison, & Pellegrini, 1985) have moved away from using the measure as an omnibus measure of reputation and toward using the measure to assess children's perceptions of one another's behavioral style (e.g., aggressiveness, sociability, and withdrawal). Throughout this review, wherever investigators have treated Class Play assessments as global assessments of peer regard, we treat the findings as relevant to acceptance rather than behavioral style. On the other hand, when investigators have preserved the behavioral information contained in the Class Play assessments, we treat the measure as a peer-based assessment of aggression or shyness/withdrawal, as appropriate.

Teacher measures of behavior. The final category includes measures that require teachers to assess children's behavior with peers, particularly their aggressiveness and shyness/withdrawal. The practice of using teachers' ratings to assess children's behavior dates at least as far back as G. Stanley Hall (1904), and there now exist a number of relatively standardized measures of behavior for which reliability and validity data are available (see Michelson, Foster, & Richey, 1981). Unfortunately, none of the more standardized behavioral batteries have been used in longitudinal studies predicting adult adjustment. Measures that have been used instead include a troublesomeness scale developed by West and Farrington (1973); the Pupil Behavior Rating Scale, developed by Bower and Lambert (1961); and the Behavioral Description Chart, developed by Havighurst *et al.* (1962). The last two measures yield scores for both aggressiveness and withdrawal. In addition, teachers have been asked to nominate their most aggressive pupils (Feldhusen, Thurston, & Benning, 1973) or to make judgments about aggression or withdrawal on checklists (Janes, Hesselbrock, Myers, & Penniman, 1979; Mednick & Schulsinger, 1970). There have also been attempts to determine a child's aggressiveness or shyness/withdrawal from teachers' comments in cumulative school files (e.g., J. J. Conger & Miller, 1966; Janes & Hesselbrock, 1978). Very little is known about the internal reliability and validity of most teacher measures of behavior used in risk research. However, some authors have presented evidence of adequate interrater agreement (Watt & Lubensky, 1976) or test-retest reliability (Havighurst *et al.*, 1962).

Methodological and conceptual issues in longitudinal research and prediction

A second set of methodological and conceptual issues that guide our review focuses on how longitudinal data are collected and interpreted.

Follow-back versus follow-up data analyses

Two types of research designs are represented in the literature to be reviewed.[2] The first type, so-called *follow-back designs*, begin by selecting a sample of adults who are deviant on some adjustment outcome (e.g., schizophrenia) and a second sample of adults, who are free from disorder, and then examine available childhood school or clinic records to determine the aspects of childhood functioning that are associated with adult problems. Such studies, for example, ask whether a disproportionately greater number of schizophrenic than normal adults were shy/withdrawn in childhood. The second type, so-called *follow-up designs*, begin by selecting groups of children who differ in acceptance or behavior and then compare their subsequent adjustment. Such studies, for example, assess the numbers of shy and not-shy children who eventually become schizophrenic.

Follow-back designs offer several advantages over follow-up designs, mostly having to do with their relative ease, economy, and flexibility of data collection. (See Garmezy, 1974; Garmezy & Devine, 1977, for relevant discussions.) They suffer, however, from the limitation of relying on childhood data that were not originally collected for the purpose of testing hypotheses about long-term risk — data that may be disappointingly crude and of unknown reliability and validity (see Garmezy, 1974). Even more important, compared with follow-up designs, they are constrained in the type of prediction claims that can be made when significant findings emerge. As Kohlberg *et al.* (1972) and others (Garmezy, 1974; Robins, 1972) have pointed out, follow-back designs, although useful for suggesting connections between adult and child behavior, ordinarily cannot provide data interpretable in terms of predictive risk; that is, children with a certain level of low acceptance, when compared with children with higher levels of acceptance, have an increased probability of developing later problems. Such probabilistic predictions can come only from follow-up designs that document the incidence of a particular disorder in target and comparison samples.

In a related way, it is important to be cautious in assuming that follow-up findings will parallel follow-back findings. It is quite possible, for example, for the majority of adult schizophrenics to show a history of low acceptance without a high percentage of low-accepted children developing schizophrenia (see Garmezy, 1974; Kohlberg *et al.*, 1972). Under such circumstances, one would have learned something about the etiology of schizophrenia, but that knowledge would be of little utility for screening for risk. This possibility is familiar to most life history psychopathologists, but it has rarely been acknowledged in the peer-acceptance literature dealing with risk, in which authors often generalize freely across follow-back and follow-up studies.

A further point is that a design that assesses children and then follows them over time to determine outcome does not ensure that data will be analyzed in ways that yield statements of probabilistic prediction. For example, in their well-known study, Cowen *et al.* (1973) collected Class Play data on third graders and 11 to 13 years later determined which children later appeared in a psychiatric treatment register. Rather than examining the incidence of later psychiatric treatment among children with and without problematic Class Play scores, they compared the Class Play scores of register subjects with those of nonregister subjects, as a follow-back researcher might do. As their study illustrates, it is more appropriate to talk of follow-back versus follow-up *data analyses* rather than *designs*, and we use this approach throughout this review.

Predictive accuracy

As we have noted, a number of students of social competence explicitly or implicitly view low acceptance as causally related to later maladjustment. Others have implied that low acceptance should be viewed not as causal but as a lead indicator for later disorder that may prove valuable for screening purposes. If one assumes the former, then any amount of later outcome variance that is explained by childhood acceptance — no matter how small — is interesting as long as the finding is stable. But if one is primarily interested in low acceptance for its screening and diagnostic value, then one needs to be concerned with its predictive accuracy, that is, its sensitivity, specificity, and efficacy.[3] These important issues have not been addressed in characterizations of the risk hypothesis to date.

Sensitivity in the present context refers to the extent to which some index of low acceptance results in few, if any, so-called *false negative predictions* (i.e., few children destined for disorder escape detection; see Loeber & Dishion, 1983; Monahan, 1982). In other words, sensitivity is reduced to the extent that high- or average-accepted children develop disorder. *Specificity* refers to the extent to which an index of low acceptance results in few, if any, so-called *false positive predictions* (i.e., few children who are not at risk are labeled at risk). Specificity, then, is reduced to the extent that large numbers of low-accepted children do not develop disorder.

Efficacy, a more omnibus measure of predictive accuracy, is concerned with the total number of correct predictions in the prediction table (i.e., valid positives and valid negatives). Several indexes of predictive efficacy exist. Unfortunately, most of these do not take into account the number of correct identifications by chance alone or are not comparable across different studies because of base-rate differences and differences in selection ratios (see Loeber & Dishion, 1983). The index that Loeber and Dishion recommended is the index of relative improvement over chance (RIOC). It expresses the difference between the observed percentage of correct identifications (valid positives and negatives) and the expected percentage based on chance, as a function of the range between the maximum possible percentage correct and the percentage correct on the basis of chance alone given the base rate and the selection ratio. (See Loeber & Dishion, 1983, for the computational formula.)[4]

Of course, the constructs of predictive sensitivity, specificity, and efficacy are meaningful only with respect to follow-up data analyses, that is, situations in which outcome is a dependent rather than an independent variable.

Clinic versus high-risk versus school samples

A final consideration is the type of sample studied and the impact of sample choice on the generalizability and interpretation of findings. The two most common types of samples in the risk literature are samples of children who have been referred to clinics for evaluation or therapy and samples of unselected schoolchildren. In addition, a few studies have involved samples of children who are the offspring of psychiatrically disturbed parents, typically schizophrenics.

The school sample has the potential for the widest generalizability of findings. Because the only criterion for inclusion in such a sample is attendance at a school at the time of childhood assessment, such a sample is representative of the vast majority of children. Disadvantages of school samples, however, are that the severe disorders, especially severe psychopathology, occur infrequently, and very large samples are needed. For this reason, in the area of psychopathology, school-based studies of low-accepted children, especially follow-up studies, are virtually nonexistent. School samples, however, have been used in the prediction of problematic outcomes with higher base rates, such as dropping out and delinquency.

In contrast to school samples, samples composed of children of schizophrenic parents or parents with other diagnosed severe disorders promise a much higher incidence of later psychological disorder and for this reason are usually referred to as *high-risk samples*. At the same time, they are much less representative because the vast majority of children, including most low-accepted children, do not have severely disordered parents. The question of generalizability applies to clinic samples as well, because for various reasons most disordered adults are never seen at clinics in childhood. The danger, then, is that findings from the study of clinic populations will hold true only for a select group of disordered individuals — those whose premorbid adjustment was severe enough to result in referral, those whose socioeconomic circumstances made such services possible, or both. Further, boys are referred to clinics almost four times as often as girls (Cass & Thomas, 1979), meaning that much more is learned about the life histories of low-accepted boys than about those of girls.

A further point concerns the heterogeneity of each sample. School samples manifest the widest range of variability with regard to acceptance and acceptance-relevant behavior. Therefore, any comparison of high- and low-accepted schoolchildren will be not only very powerful but also straightforwardly interpretable. This is not necessarily the case with clinic or high-risk samples. Children whose parents have severe psychiatric disturbances are less socially skilled and accepted among their peers than children with psychiatrically healthy parents (see Watt, Anthony, Wynne, & Rolf, 1984). Children referred to clinics, too, are less socially skilled and have poorer peer adjustment, lower achievement, and lower self-esteem than nonreferred children (e.g., Achenbach & Edelbrock, 1981; de Apodaca & Cowen, 1982). Accordingly, both samples are relatively homogenous and include few well-adjusted children. Finding follow-up or follow-back differences within such samples may be very difficult given their attenuated range. If most children in these samples have peer-relationship problems, it is unlikely that peer-relationships problems will readily differentiate children who develop later disorder from those who do not. This can lead to the mistaken impression that peer-relationships problems are not highly predictive of later adjustment.

Overview of the literature review

The preceding discussion suggests that the optimal risk study from the point of view of this review is one based on a school sample and yielding follow-up data. Further, if the focus is on acceptance (as opposed to behavior), then peer-based assessments are preferable to teacher-based assessments. In fact, as will be seen, most existing studies fail to meet one or another of these requirements, and several studies do not meet any of them. Therefore, much of the existing literature is far from optimal. Still, there is value in a comprehensive review. To be more restrictive would omit from review many of the most frequently cited studies in this area, thereby missing an opportunity to place these studies in their proper perspective. In addition, the existing literature, even with some of its limitations, can suggest whether further longitudinal efforts and expenditures will ultimately prove fruitful. At the same time, it is important to give differential weight where possible to those studies that meet or come close to meeting requirements for an optimal study in this area.

In the section that follows, we review research on the relation between early peer relationships and later life adjustment, bringing to bear the methodological and conceptual issues discussed thus far. Thus, within each major life outcome to be reviewed, we make several distinctions. First, we distinguish studies that address whether the child is liked (i.e., acceptance) from those that address what the child is like (i.e., behavioral style). With respect to the latter, we distinguish two types of behavioral orientation, aggressiveness and shyness/withdrawal. Aggressiveness is an important behavioral dimension to study because it has been found to be a major determinant of peer rejection in childhood. (See Coie, Dodge, & Kupersmidt, in press, for a review.) Shyness/withdrawal is of significance because, in extreme forms, it may be an antecedent of peer rejection (see Rubin, 1985) and because there is evidence that withdrawal can be the consequence of peer rejection (Dodge, 1983). In either case, shyness/withdrawal, like aggression, can be seen as providing an index of children's peer-adjustment difficulties.[5]

Second, we distinguish assessments based on peer judgments from those based on the judgments of teachers, and we distinguish follow-up from follow-back analyses. Third, we specify whether findings are based on school, clinic, or high-risk samples. After reviewing research on each outcome, we introduce and examine the issue of predictive accuracy.

Two considerations guided our selection of studies for inclusion and exclusion. First, because we were specifically concerned with how early peer adjustment relates to later dropping out of school, juvenile and adult crime, and adult psychopathology, we excluded studies in which the stability of acceptance or acceptance-relevant behavior was the focus, for example, studies that examined the consistency of aggression from childhood to adulthood (e.g., Lefkowitz, Eron, Walder, & Huesmann, 1977; see Olweus, 1979, and Parke & Slaby, 1983, for recent reviews of that literature). Second, we limited our focus to the prediction of outcomes that have their onset in adolescence, young adulthood, or beyond. This focus excludes a small but promising set of studies devoted to the prediction of maladjustment in childhood from measures taken in the preschool period (e.g., Forness, Guthrie, & Hall, 1976; Kohn & Rosman, 1972; Lambert & Nicoll, 1977; Rubin, Daniels-Beirness, & Bream, 1984; Turner & Boulter, 1981).

Dropping out of school

By most estimates, about one in five children in the United States who enter the school system leave prior to graduation, about one third of these before eighth grade (Weiner, 1980). Students who drop out give various reasons for doing so. In some cases, they leave reluctantly because of economic or family hardships, serious illness, pregnancy, or the desire to marry (Bowman & Matthews, 1960; Snepp, 1953). However, such "involuntary dropouts probably make up only a very small proportion of all dropouts; more often than not, dropping out probably represents a flight from what is perceived as an unduly frustrating setting (Elliott & Voss, 1974; Lichter, Rapien, Siepert, & Sklansky, 1962). About one third of all dropouts can be classified as educationally handicapped, and their dropping out can be considered an understandable reaction to frustrations with educational tasks (Elliott & Voss, 1974). But the majority of dropouts are average or above average in intelligence, suggesting that most have sufficient ability to graduate (Elliott & Voss, 1974; Weiner, 1980). To explain dropping out among this group of more capable pupils, educators and counselors have long suggested that the motivation lies in the frustrations of past and present poor social adjustment (e.g., Berston, 1960; Elliott & Voss, 1974; Liddle, 1962; Sando, 1952; Snepp, 1953).

What makes dropping out particularly interesting when compared with other indexes of later academic maladjustment is that dropping out, to the extent that it is undertaken voluntarily and represents a flight from something unpleasant, is an unambiguous rebuke of the school's academic and social setting. In contrast, low grades, grade retention, or achievement test scores are evaluations imposed on an individual by a social system. They are important to predict because, like dropping out, they in turn predict future interpersonal and occupational success. But, compared with dropping out, the measures are more ambiguous reflections of subjective distress.

Table 1 contains a list of studies that relate earlier peer-relationship difficulties to later dropout status. The studies are grouped by peer-difficulty index (low acceptance vs. behavioral style) and source of assessment (peers vs. teachers). For each study, the table notes whether the analyses were follow-back or follow-up; whether the sample was school, clinic, or high risk; and whether the findings support the risk hypothesis. An over view of Table 1 reveals several interesting patterns. First, 37 of the 39 entries in Table 1 involve samples of schoolchildren; the 2 exceptions are Janes *et al.* (1979) and D. P. Morris, Soroker, and Burruss (1954), who conducted follow-up investigations of children referred to child guidance clinics. As will be seen, this very high proportion of school samples compares very favorably to the proportions in the criminality and psychopathology areas, in which researchers have relied much more heavily on clinic or high-risk samples. With respect to analyses, 14 entries in Table 1, or about 1 out of every 3 entries, involve follow-up as opposed to follow-back data. More important, 10 entries involve a school sample and follow-up data. The distribution of these 10 entries is instructive in view of the fact that these entries have the potential to be the most informative. Of these 10 entries, 7 involve assessments of acceptance as opposed to behavior; the remaining 3 involve assessments of aggressiveness. Significantly, then, the existing literature on shyness/withdrawal and later dropping out does not include a single entry that might be described as optimal in terms of sample and type of longitudinal design. It is worth noting, too, that of the 7 entries that deal with acceptance and involve school samples and follow-up data, 5 also involve assessments based on peer as opposed to teacher reports. This is encouraging in the light of the methodological and conceptual advantages of peer-based assessments of acceptance.

Several additional general features of the existing literature in this area deserve comment. The typical study in Table 1 is based on peer-relationship assessments made in 5th or 6th grade and assessments of dropout status using school records 6 or 7 years later, when most children would be expected to have reached 12th grade or to have graduated. A few studies involve peer-relationships assessments at earlier (Feldhusen, Thurston, & Benning, 1971, 1973; Lambert, 1972) or later ages or at both Amble, 1967; Bowman & Matthews, 1960; Kuhlen & Collister, 1952; Ullmann, 1957) or dropping-out assessments as early as 9th grade (Barclay, 1966; Lambert, 1972). Most studies include both sexes, although results are not always presented separately (Amble, 1967; Bowman & Matthews, 1960; Kupersmidt, 1983), and one study involves only boys (Janes *et al.*, 1979). In general, there is an absence of efforts to distinguish intellectually capable dropouts from less capable dropouts. This is a limitation because, as implied earlier, it is plausible that these are decidedly different phenomena, with potentially different relations with earlier peer acceptance.

Table 1   **Studies predicting later dropping out of school grouped by indicator (acceptance and behavioral style) and assessment source (peers and teachers)**

Study	Analysis	Sample Type	Sex	Age (years)	Results
		Acceptance			
Peer assessed					
Kuhlen & Collister (1952)	FB	School	M	11	Support
	FB	School	F	11	Support
	FB	School	M	14	No support
	FB	School	F	14	No support
Lambert (1972)	FB	School	M + F	7, 10	Support[a]
Ullmann (1957)	FB	School	M	14	Support
	FB	School	F	14	Support
Bowman & Matthews (1960)	FB	School	M + F	11	No support
	FB	School	M + F	14	Support
Gronlund & Holmlund (1958)	FU	School	M	11	Support
	FU	School	F	11	Support
Barclay (1966)	FU	School	M	10-14	Support
	FU	School	F	10-14	Support
Kupersmidt (1983)	FU	School	M + F	10	Support
Teacher assessed					
Amble (1967)	FB	School	M	14	Support
	FB	School	F	14	Support
Barclay (1966)	FU	School	M	10-14	Support
	FU	School	F	10-14	Support
Jane, Hesselbrock, Myers, & Penniman (1979)	FU	Clinic	M	4-15	Support
		Behavioral style: aggressiveness			
Peer assessed					
Kuhlen & Collister (1952)	FB	School	M	11	No support
	FB	School	F	11	No support
	FB	School	M	14	Support
	FB	School	F	14	No support
Bowman & Matthews (1960)	FB	School	M + F	11	No support
	FB	School	M + F	14	Support

Note FB = follow-back; FU = follow-up; M = male; F = female.
[a] The criterion was a composite of dropping out of school, remedial placement, referral, and academic probation.

Table 1 **Studies predicting later dropping out of school grouped by indicator (acceptance and behavioral style) and assessment source (peers and teachers)   (cont)**

| Study | Analysis | Sample | | | Results |
		Type	Sex	Age (years)	
		Behavioral style: aggressiveness *(continued)*			
Peer assessed					
Havighurst, Bowman, Liddle, Matthews, & Pierce (1962)	FU	School	M + F	11-12	Support
Kupersmidt (1983)	FU	School	M + F	10	No support[b]
Teacher assessed					
Bowman & Matthews (1960)	FB	School	M + F	11	No support
	FB	School	M + F	14	Support
Lambert (1972)	FB	School	M + F	10	Support[a]
Feldhusen, Thurston, & Benning (1973)	FU	School	M + F	8, 11, 14	Support
Janes, Hesselbrock, Myers, & Penniman (1979)	FU	Clinic	M	4-15	No support
		Behavioral style: shyness/withdrawal			
Peer assessed					
Bowman & Matthews (1960)	FB	School	M + F	11	No support
	FB	School	M + F	14	Support
Teacher assessed					
Bowman & Matthews (1960)	FB	School	M + F	11	No support
	FB	School	M + F	14	Support
Lambert (1972)	FB	School	M + F	10	Support[a]
D.P. Morris, Soroker, & Burruss (1954)	FU	Clinic	M + F	3-15	No support[c]
Janes, Hesselbrock, Myers, & Penniman (1979)	FU	Clinic	M	4-15	No support

Note. FB = follow-back; FU = follow-up; M = male; F = female.
[a] The criterion was a composite of dropping out of school, remedial placement, referral, and academic probabion.
[b] The criterion was a composite of dropping out of school, truancy, and grade retention.
[c] There was no control group.

Acceptance

In this section, as in later sections, we first consider follow-back analyses and then consider follow-up analyses. Every follow-back study (Amble, 1967; Bowman & Matthews, 1960; Kuhlen & Collister, 1952; Lambert, 1972; Ullmann, 1957) has found some evidence that high school dropouts have more problematic peer-acceptance histories than do high school graduates, and this is true regardless of the operationalization of acceptance (teacher or peer based). What these follow-back studies typically report is that dropouts have significantly lower mean levels of earlier acceptance than do graduates. Amble (1967), however, provided data on the actual proportion of dropouts with problematic levels of peer acceptance. Calculations from Amble's data indicate that 46% of later male dropouts and 14% of later female dropouts were described by ninth-grade teachers as "rejected" or "barely tolerated" by peers. These figures compare with 7% and 4% of male and female graduates, respectively.

Unfortunately, there is little specific agreement across follow-back studies on the age or ages at which it is possible to distinguish dropouts and graduates in terms of acceptance. Kuhlen and Collister (1952) reported lower sixth-grade but not ninth-grade sociometric scores for dropouts of both sexes relative to graduates. In contrast, Bowman and Matthews (1960) reported that dropouts of both sexes have lower sociometric scores than graduates in ninth grade but not in sixth grade. Ullman (1957) and Amble (1967) also found evidence of lower ninth-grade acceptance among later dropouts, but neither author examined acceptance at any earlier ages. Lambert (1972) found Class Play differences in both second and fifth grades, but it is not clear whether her study is comparable with these others because Lambert selected her subjects not just on the basis of dropout status but also on the basis of any of a number of other negative academic outcomes. Interestingly, Kuhlen and Collister (1952) reported that among boys, the relation between dropping out and sixth-grade low acceptance is especially strong when status is derived solely from the nominations of other boys, suggesting that what is most important for sixth-grade students is being accepted by peers of their own gender, rather than being accepted by peers more generally. This was not true in ninth grade, however, and no other researchers have made such a comparison.

Follow-up analyses address the question of whether low-accepted children show a tendency to drop out in greater numbers than do accepted children. In an early examination of this issue, Gronlund and Holmlund (1958) compared the rate of dropping out among low-accepted sixth-grade children with the rate among same-age, high-accepted children of comparable intelligence. They reported that the incidence of later dropping out among low-accepted boys was 54%, or about 2½ times that among high-accepted boys (19%). Among low-accepted girls, the incidence of later dropping out (35%) was over 8 times that among high-accepted girls (4%).

In a later study, Barclay (1966) found that low-accepted boys and girls were roughly two to three times more likely to subsequently drop out than were other children, regardless whether teachers or peers were used to assess acceptance. In fact, when peer and teacher judgments were combined into composite measure of acceptance, low-accepted boys and girls were four to five times more likely to later drop out than were other children.

More recently, Janes and her colleagues (Janes et al., 1979; C. L. Janes, personal communication, May 31, 1983), working with a clinic rather than a school sample, found that 25% of boys whom teachers identified as "failing to get along with other children" later dropped out of school, an incidence twice high as that among boys with no indication of peer problems (12.6%).

Together, these studies provide support for the premise that both teacher-based and peer-based assessments of low peer status foretell later dropping out. But, partly because these studies predated recent concern for subclassifying unpopular children, no attempt was made to differentiate rejected children from neglected children. In a recent study, Kupersmidt (1983) addressed this important issue. Kupersmidt followed for 6 years a group of 112 fifth graders for whom positive and negative sociometric data were available and noted instances of dropping out, truancy, and grade retention. Kupersmidt identified 24 reject children and 20 neglected children and compared their incidence of dropping out with that of 21 average children and 27 popular children. Of the rejected children, 30% subsequently dropped out. By comparison, only 21% of the average children, 10% of the neglected children, and 4% of the popular children later dropped out. Overall, these differences in proportions were only marginally significant, perhaps because of the small sample sizes. But the fact that rejected children showed an elevated dropout rate, whereas neglected children did not, and the fact that other analyses indicated a similar pattern in relation to later grade retention prompted Kupersmidt to suggest that perhaps only the rejected subset of low-accepted children is really at risk.

Kupersmidt's (1983) follow-up analysis is noteworthy in another respect. For the most part, other work in this area has paid scant attention to whether the relation between peer acceptance and later dropping out could be due to other confounding variables, especially academic achievement. Kupersmidt conducted a separate multiple regression analysis of children's academic adjustment (a weighted composite of dropping out plus grade retention and truancy) and their earlier social preference scores (positive minus negative sociometric scores), controlling for sex, race, earlier grade point average, and behavioral reputation. The important result of this analysis was that despite controlling for early achievement, peer status accounted for significant amounts of the variance in later academic adjustment. Whether this implies that earlier studies would have obtained a similarly robust relation with similar controls is not clear because grade retention and truancy — and not just dropping out — could lead to high maladjustment scores for this analysis in Kupersmidt's study.

Behavioral style

Follow-back comparisons consistently indicate that dropouts receive higher teacher and peer ratings of both aggressiveness and withdrawal when they enter high school (ninth grade) than do graduates (Bowman & Matthews, 1960; Kuhlen & Collister 1952, Lambert, 1972). Nonetheless, several issues cloud the interpretation of this relation and stand in the way of any firm conclusions in this regard. First, differences in behavior that are apparent at ninth grade typically are not apparent at earlier ages, especially differences in aggression as reported by peers (e.g., Bowman & Matthews, 1960; Kuhlen & Collister, 1952). This is so even when differences in sixth-grade acceptance are evident (Kuhlen & Collister, 1952). Second, because only mean scores have been used in such comparisons, it is impossible to know precisely the proportion of dropouts with aggressive or withdrawn backgrounds early in school or the extent to which the two groups overlap in numbers of highly aggressive or withdrawn individuals. Nor is it possible in studies that include measures of both aggression and withdrawal (e.g., Kuhlen & Collister, 1952) to tell whether the same individuals are responsible for the higher mean scores on both measures (see Ledingham & Schwartzman's, 1984, discussion of aggressive-withdrawn children) or whether some later dropouts show aggressive backgrounds whereas others show withdrawal. Third, when boys and girls are considered separately, there is no evidence suggesting that female dropouts are any more aggressive or any more shy/withdrawn than female graduates (Kuhlen & Collister, 1952).

Even more ambiguity surrounds potential follow-up links between behavioral style and later dropping out. Follow-up analyses of guidance clinic samples have not resulted in predictability for either aggressive (Janes et al., 1979) or shy/withdrawn behavior (Janes et al., 1979; D. P. Morris et al., 1954) in childhood. Whether shyness/withdrawal would predict dropping out in school samples is not known because no such study has ever been conducted. But aggressiveness has been studied in school samples in at least three investigations, with somewhat contradictory results. Havighurst et al. (1962) reported that nearly two thirds of youngsters with high sixth- and seventh-grade peer-nominated aggressiveness scores drop out, compared with about one fourth of all remaining children and one sixth of children with very low aggressiveness scores. Subsequently, Feldhusen et al. (1973) found that teacher-nominated aggressive children were six times as likely to later drop out as a group of matched nonaggressive controls. These rather impressive findings are in contrast to Kupersmidt's (1983) more recent report that a child's reputation among peers for starting fights does not contribute significantly to the prediction of later academic maladjustment after controlling for acceptance, sex, race, and academic achievement. Because academic maladjustment in Kupersmidt's case meant more than dropping out *per se* (see above), interpretation of this disparate result is unclear. But Kupersmidt's finding clearly points out that more systematic research into the follow-up links between dropping out and aggression is needed before firm conclusions can be drawn.

To summarize this section, there appears to be very good evidence that the decision to drop out of school in adolescence often follows an earlier period of poor peer adjustment in middle childhood and early adolescence. The evidence for this comes from the several follow-back analyses that have been conducted in this area. These studies indicate a link between drop out status and barometers of earlier peer-relationship difficulties of every type (peer and teacher measures of acceptance, aggressiveness, or shyness/withdrawal). More significant from the standpoint of risk and primary prevention is the generally clear evidence in the existing literature of a predictive, or follow-up, link between peer-relationship adjustment and later dropout status. Children who were poorly accepted by their peers were found to be more likely to drop out of school than children who were better accepted. This was true whether acceptance was assessed sociometrically or based on teacher judgment. Aggression, too, appeared to predict later dropping out, although here the predictive link did not appear as consistently as it did for acceptance level. Much less can be said about the link between shyness/withdrawal and later dropping out. This relation has not been adequately examined.

Juvenile and adult crime

Juvenile crime, or delinquency, remains a critical social problem in most Western societies, and concern over the problem of delinquency continues to motivate interest in description and especially in prediction (see Achenbach, 1982; Elliott & Voss, 1974; Loeber & Dishion, 1983; Rutter & Garmezy, 1983; Van Dusen & Mednick, 1983). In considering risk and prediction, it is important to appreciate the myriad ways in which delinquency and delinquent acts may be operationalized:

> Delinquent acts themselves may range from major crimes against persons and property (assault, theft) to relatively minor misdemeanors (public intoxication, reckless driving), and they also include behavior that is illegal only by virtue of the subject's youth (purchasing liquor, leaving home). The outcomes of delinquency are as variable as the behaviors that define it. The perpetrator of a delinquent act may be brought before a court and either adjudged delinquent or not, he may come to the attention of some agency (police, clinic, school) that responds in a nonadjudicating manner, he may be detected by persons that do not refer him to any agency, or he may go completely undetected. These categories have been formally labeled by Carr (1950, p. 90) as "adjudged," "alleged," "agency" "detected" and "legal" delinquency, respectively. (Weiner 1970, p. 289)

There are obvious problems with treating all delinquents alike for prediction purposes. It is one task to predict serious acts against people, such as assault; it is quite another to predict relatively minor acts, such as running away or vandalism, which self-report data indicate are committed by a majority of boys at some stage in their development (Farrington, 1973; Shepherd, 1978). Similarly, factors that predict juvenile offenders' being brought before a court (alleged delinquency), for example, may not predict offenders who go undetected (legal delinquency) because a host of extraneous factors (e.g., intelligence, race, socioeconomic status, and geographic area) can determine both who is detected and the disposition of a case.

Relatedly, juvenile offenders show differing commitments to a criminal way of life. Most studies indicate that about one fourth to one third of boys and 1 in 13 to 1 in 16 girls are officially declared delinquent (Rutter & Garmezy, 1983). However, only about one half of all such delinquents become repeat offenders, and the vast majority of all delinquents, including repeat offenders, do not continue their criminal careers into young adulthood (Farrington, 1979; West & Farrington, 1977). Again, factors that predict which individuals will engage in one-time criminal activity may not predict which individuals will become repeat offenders or offenders who continue their criminal activities into adulthood, and vice versa. Furthermore, it is important to recognize that the ability to predict juvenile crime, even juvenile crime that persists into adulthood, does not ensure excellent prediction of adult criminal activity because some individuals do not commit their first crime until adulthood.

Table 2 includes studies relating earlier peer-relationship difficulties to later juvenile or adult crime. The studies are grouped, once again, by peer-difficulty index (acceptance and behavioral style) and source of assessment (peers and teachers). For each entry, the table contains the operationalization of delinquency or adult crime, the type of analysis (follow-back or follow-up), the characteristics of the sample (type, sex , and age), and whether the findings support the risk hypothesis. An overview shows that most entries (38 of 54) involve samples of schoolchildren. Two entries involve high-risk samples, and the number of entries based on clinic samples (14) is substantial relative to the corresponding number in the dropout area. Regardless of their origin, samples are almost always exclusively made up of boys and usually involve individuals between 8 and 10 years old. Most research in this area has yielded follow-up rather than follow-back data (40 of 54 entries). Further, from the point of view of entries with optimal characteristics, there are 27 entries based on follow-up data from school samples. The vast majority of these (19) pertain to aggressiveness. Of the remaining entries, 6 pertain to acceptance (notably, all 6 of these involve peer-based assessments), and only 2 examine shyness/withdrawal. Two additional features of the literature are worth noting: (a) The studies vary considerably in how criminality is operationalized (legal, detected, agency, alleged, or adjudicated), and (b) only a few authors have attempted to differentially predict severe and minor offenses (Havighurst et al., 1962; Magnussen, Stattin, & Duner, 1983), to predict repeat offenders (Magnussen et al., 1983; Mulligan, Douglas, Hammond, & Tizard, 1963), or to predict adult offenders (Janes et al., 1979; Magnussen et al., 1983; M. Roff, 1961).

Acceptance

Acceptance has been studied relatively infrequently in relation to later juvenile or adult crime. As a consequence, it is difficult to make fine-grained methodological and conceptual comparisons among studies and findings, such as comparisons among differing types of samples, sources of assessment, or operationalizations of juvenile crime. Acknowledging this limitation, the available follow-back evidence nonetheless supports the view that offending adolescents or young adults are indeed often individuals with a history of pervasive and persistent peer rejection. J. J. Conger and Miller (1966), who studied teachers' ratings and comments in the school records of delinquents, and M. Roff (1961), who studied the child guidance clinic files of servicemen with dishonorable discharges, both reported more signs of peer dislike and fewer signs of peer liking in the backgrounds of offenders. In J. J. Conger and Miller's data, differences in acceptance were apparent at a very early age, grew more apparent over time, and remained even after differences in intelligence, socioeconomic status, and several other possible confounding variables were controlled for. M. Roff (1961), too, found differences, despite controlling for differences in intelligence.

More important, several follow-up analyses have linked poor peer acceptance to later juvenile or adult criminality in the predictive sense. Data from M. Roff (1975) and M. Roff et al. (1972) indicate that the chances for children with very low sociometric preference scores to become delinquent prior to age 14 are 1½ to 2 times greater than those of other children, depending on the sex of the child (differences are less dramatic among girls) and the geographic location of the school (differences are less dramatic in schools located in severely economically depressed areas). In fact, these data show that in most schools the risk of later delinquency for both boys and girls increases more or less monotonically with decreasing peer status. Likewise, J. D. Roff and Wirt (1984), using a sample that partially overlapped with M. Roff et al.'s reported an inverse relation between level of preference and risk of delinquency at any age, regardless of the sex of the child or the location of the school. Other evidence suggests that clinic boys described by teachers as failing to get along with peers are markedly more likely than other referred boys to come in contact with police or to be arrested as young adults and somewhat more likely to be convicted and incarcerated (Janes et al., 1979; C. L. Janes, personal communication, May 31, 1983). The percentages of poorly accepted children with later criminal records in these studies range from about 10% among girls in J. D. Roff and Wirt's study to over 50% among boys in Janes et al.'s study.

These findings, then, provide general support for the risk hypothesis, but several unresolved issues remain. Not all studies have found that low acceptance is linked to later juvenile or adult criminality; at least two studies have found no links or only weak links (Kupersmidt, 1983; West & Farrington, 1973). Thus, we need to understand more fully the circumstances under which predictability will occur. Unfortunately, because so few studies have been conducted and because successful and unsuccessful studies differ in many respects, this issue is difficult to resolve. The source of assessment and type of sample do not appear to be factors because predictive links have been found with both teacher judgments (Janes et al., 1979) and peer judgments (J. D. Roff & Wirt, 1984) and in both school (J. D. Roff & Wirt, 1984) and clinic (Janes et al., 1979) samples. On the other hand, the wording of the sociometric test may be important. For example, West and Farrington (1973) had children nominate other children whom they would like to have as friends. As West and Farrington (1973) acknowledged, "Different results might have been obtained if boys had been asked to name those who were their friends rather than those who they would like to have as friends" (p. 107). Alternatively, Kupersmidt's failure to find strong differences in risk may have been partly due to a comparatively small sample size, her not examining predictability separately by sex, or both.

Another interesting possibility is that successful prediction depends to a large extent on whether actively disliked (i.e., rejected) children are differentiated from children who are not particularly liked but not particularly disliked either (i.e., neglected children). By identifying children with extremely low sociometric preference scores, M. Roff et al. (1972) and J. D. Roff and Wirt (1984) focused on low-accepted children who were by definition high in disliking and low in liking, that is, rejected. These investigators' relative success in prediction can be contrasted with the relative lack of success of West and Farrington (1977), who used only positive nominations and, therefore, confounded disliked and nondisliked low-accepted children. In this regard, it is noteworthy that Kupersmidt (1983) found that although there was no strong overall association between peer status and later delinquency, sociometrically rejected children nonetheless were more likely to later come in contact with police and juvenile courts than were sociometrically neglected children.

Table 2 **Studies predicting later juvenile and adult crime grouped by indicator (acceptance and behavioral style) and assessment source (peers and teachers).**

Study	Criterion	Analysis	Sample Type	Sex	Age (years)	Results
			Type	Sex	Age (years)	

Study	Criterion	Analysis	Type	Sex	Age (years)	Results
Acceptance						
Peer assessed						
M. Roff, Sells, & Golden (1972)	JC (agency)	FU	School	M	8-10	Support
M. Roff (1975)	JC (agency)	FU	School	F	8-10	Support
J.D. Roff & Wirt (1984)	JC (agency)	FU	School	M	8-10	Support
				F	8-10	Support
West & Farrington (1973)	JC (alleged)	FU	School	M	8	No support
Kupersmidt (1983)	JC (detected)	FU	School	M + F	10	No support
Teacher assessed						
J.J. Conger & Miller (1966)	JC (alleged)	FB	School	M	8	Support
				M	11	Support
M. Roff (1961)	AC (adjudicated)	FB	Clinic	M	Unspecified	Support
Janes, Hesselbrock, Myers & Penniman (1979)	AC (detected)	FU	Clinic	M	4-15	Support
	AC (arrested)	FU	Clinic	M	4-15	Support
	AC (convicted)	FU	Clinic	M	4-15	No Support
	AC (jailed)	FU	Clinic	M	4-15	No Support
Behavioral style: aggressiveness						
Peer assessed						
Havighurst, Bowman, Liddle, Matthews, & Pierce (1962)	JC (detected)	FU	School	M	11	Support
West & Farrington (1973)	JC (alleged)	FU	School	M	8	Support
Farrington (1978)	JC (adjudicated)	FU	School	M	8	Support
Kupersmidt (1983)	JC (detected)	FU	School	M + F	10	Support
Teacher assessed						
Mulligan, Douglas, Hammond, & Tizard (1963)	JC (adjudicated)	FB	School	M + F	13	Support
	JC (persistent)	FB	School	M + F	13	Support
J.J. Conger & Miller (1966)	JC (alleged)	FB	School	M	8	Support
				M	11	Support
Kirkegaard-Sørensen & Mednick (1977)	AC (convicted)	FB	School	M	10-20	Support
			High risk	M	10-20	Support
Farrington (1978)	JC (self-report)	FB	School	M	8-10	Support

Note JC = Juvenile crime; AC = adult crime; FU = follow-up; FB = follow-back; M = male; F = female

Table 2 **Studies predicting later juvenile and adult crime grouped by indicator (acceptance and behavioural style) and assessment source (peers and teachers) (cont)**

Study	Criterion	Analysis	Sample Type	Sex	Age (years)	Results

Behavioral style: aggressiveness *(continued)*

Teacher assessed

Study	Criterion	Analysis	Type	Sex	Age (years)	Results
Magnussen, Stattin, & Duner (1983)	JC (detected)	FU	School	M	10	Support
	JC (severe)	FU	School	M	10	Support
	JC (persistent)	FU	School	M	10	Support
	AC (detected)	FU	School	M	10	Support
	AC (severe)	FU	School	M	10	Support
	AC (persistent)	FU	School	M	10	Support
Robins (1966)	AC (sociopathy)	FU	Clinic	M + F	Unspecified	Support
West & Farrington (1973)	JC (alleged)	FU	School	M	8	Support
				M	10	Support
Ensminger, Kellam, & Rubin (1983)	JC (self-report)	FU	School	M	6	Support
				F	6	No support
Feldhusen, Thurston, & Benning (1973)	JC (detected)	FU	School	M + F	8, 11, 14	Support
	JC (alleged)	FU	School	M + F	8, 11, 14	Support
	JC (adjudicated)	FU	School	M + F	8, 11, 14	Support
J.D. Roff & Wirt (1984)	JC (agency)	FU	School	M	8-10	Support
				F	8-10	Support
Janes, Hesselbrock, Myers & Penniman (1979)	AC (detected)	FU	Clinic	M	4-15	No support
	AC (arrested)	FU	Clinic	M	4-15	No support
	AC (convicted)	FU	Clinic	M	4-15	No support
	AC (jailed)	FU	Clinic	M	4-15	No support

Behavioral style: shyness/withdrawal

Peer assessed

None

Teacher assessed

Study	Criterion	Analysis	Type	Sex	Age (years)	Results
J.J. Conger & Miller (1966)	JC (adjudicated)	FB	School	M	8	No support
				M	11	No support
Kirkegaard-Sørensen & Mednick (1977)	AC (convicted)	FB	School	M	10-20	Support
			High risk	M	10-20	No support
Ensminger, Kellam, & Rubin (1983)	JC (self-report)	FU	School	M	6	No support
				F	6	No support
Janes, Hesselbrock, Myers & Penniman (1979)	AC (detected)	FU	Clinic	M	4-15	No support
	AC (arrested)	FU	Clinic	M	4-15	No support
	AC (convicted)	FU	Clinic	M	4-15	No support
	AC (jailed)	FU	Clinic	M	4-15	No support

Note. JC = juvenile crime; AC = adult crime; FU = follow-up; FB = follow-back; M = male; F = female.

In addition, it is not clear whether socioeconomic status affects the relation between acceptance and later criminal activity. Early evidence on this point was provided by M. Roff *et al.* (1972), who found that in economically deprived areas, popular boys had as high an incidence of later delinquency as did low-accepted boys. They interpreted their findings as support for theories of delinquency that place emphasis on inequities in the larger social structure (e.g., Cloward & Ohlin, 1961; A. K. Cohen, 1955; Merton, 1957; Miller, 1958). However, socioeconomic-level differences in predictability from status have not been found in recent investigations (J. D. Roff & Wirt, 1984).

Finally, the extent to which the findings characterize both severe and minor or one-time and persistent offending is not known. In fact, differences in the way criminality is operationalized may help explain some discrepancies in findings across studies. Kupersmidt's (1983) definition was much more inclusive than M. Roff *et al.'s* (1972). (It included police contact as well as agency/court contact.) This raises the possibility that predictability was weakened by the fact that a number of children were labeled delinquent in her study for relatively minor mischief.

Behavioral style

The lower portion of Table 2 contains studies relating earlier aggressive or shy/withdrawn behavioral style to later crime. With regard to aggressiveness, Table 2 shows a clear and consistent tendency across at least three follow-back studies for teachers to describe future juvenile or adult offenders as more aggressive than future nonoffenders (J. J. Conger & Miller, 1966; Kirkegaard-Sørensen & Mednick, 1977; Mulligan *et al.*, 1963). In fact, such differences have been found as early as 8 years of age, the earliest age at which they have been examined (J. J. Conger & Miller, 1966). Moreover, the tendency for offenders to show a history of aggressiveness seems fairly robust, insofar as these studies differ notably in their sample types and their operationalizations of offense and in how carefully they control for possible confounding variables. When comparisons have been made, the proportions of juvenile or adult offenders with markedly aggressive backgrounds have ranged from 23% to 45%, with higher proportions associated with persistent offending (Mulligan *et al.*, 1963). These proportions are between 8% and 10% among nonoffenders.

More important, Table 2 also indicates frequent follow-up links between both teacher-rated and peer-rated childhood aggressiveness and later juvenile offenses, especially among boys. For example, Magnussen *et al.* (1983) reported a monotonic positive relation between aggressiveness at ages 10 to 13 and later police contact such that 50% of the very aggressive boys had at least one offense, compared with only 5% of the very unaggressive boys. Further, nonaggressive boys in their sample seldom, if ever, had more than one later offense, compared with over 20% of the very aggressive boys. When only serious offenses are considered, 1 out of every 4 of the one-third most aggressive boys had offenses, compared with fewer than 1 in 16 of all the remaining boys and fewer than 1 in 50 of the one-third least aggressive boys.

As another example, Feldhusen *et al.* (1973) reported that teacher-identified aggressive boys and girls in their sample were about twice as likely as nonaggressive children to have later police contact (47.9% vs. 22.3%), were about 7 times as likely to later appear in juvenile court (23.9% vs. 3.1%), and were nearly 10 times as likely to have a later conviction (9.9% vs. 1%). Similarly, Havighurst *et al.* (1962) reported that 83% of the boys with peer reputations at 11 years for aggressive behavior later committed serious to very serious juvenile offenses, compared with 16% of the nonaggressive boys. Other authors who have reported links between either teacher- or peer-rated aggressiveness and later delinquency include West and Farrington (1973), Farrington (1978), Kupersmidt (1983), J. D. Roff and Wirt (1984), and Ensminger, Kellam, and Rubin (1983). The last study is notable in that differential prediction was possible from assessments made as early as 6 years of age, at least among boys.

What is more, Magnussen *et al.'s* (1983) recent study indicates that aggressiveness in a school sample predicts criminal activity beyond the juvenile period, in young adulthood. Of the boys in their sample who fell in the top third in aggressiveness, 30% had police or court contacts of some sort after age 18, compared with only about 13% of all the remaining boys and 9.9% of the boys in the bottom third in aggressiveness. When only serious offenses are considered, 14% of the aggressive boys had at least one adult offense, compared with less than 2% of all the remaining boys. This is a significant finding because two prior attempts to link aggressiveness to adult criminality relied exclusively on clinic samples and produced different results. Janes *et al.* (1979) found no link between aggression and postjuvenile police contact (to age 28) among clinic-referred boys, whereas Robins (1966) demonstrated that aggressiveness at the time of a child's referral to a guidance clinic predicted sociopathy in adulthood. Specifically, Robins (1966) found that the nearly one third of her sample of clinic boys and girls with indications of excessive physical aggressiveness showed a higher incidence of later diagnosed sociopathy relative to clinic children in general. A component of sociopathy, of course, is that the individual shows a history of *repeat* offending, which may help explain why Robins (1966) was able to find predictability, whereas Janes *et al.* were not.

The finding that aggressiveness in early childhood bears a regular, robust relation, at least in school samples, to later juvenile and adult crime accords with other evidence indicating a consistency between early and later antisocial behavior in general (e.g., Craig & Glick, 1963; Mitchell & Rosa, 1981; Robins, 1966; Wadsworth, 1979). This is not surprising because it is common for aggressive children to show other forms of socially disapproved behavior in childhood (e.g., temper tantrums, defiance, and "immoderation") and adolescence (e.g., vandalism, theft, drug use, and truancy; Achenbach & Edelbrock, 1981; Quay, 1979). But the distinction between aggressiveness and other behaviors that are sometimes labeled antisocial is important because some forms of antisocial behavior have more to do with relationships with institutional authority (e.g., truancy, defiance, and drug use) than with peer relationships *per se*. Indeed, many years ago, Hewitt and Jenkins (1946) pointed out that some antisocial individuals have adequate relationships with peers. Researchers testing the risk hypothesis need to be sensitive to this distinction.

What evidence is there that aggression on its own carries with it an increased risk of juvenile or adult offending? Moore, Chamberlain, and Mukai (1979) studied the overlap in delinquency prediction between aggressive children who do not steal and children who steal but are not aggressive. They reported that aggressiveness on its own carried no increased risk for later delinquency. However, aggressiveness in their study was defined in relation to family members, not peers. J. D. Roff and Wirt (1984) studied the separate contributions of peer-directed aggression and antisocial behavior to later criminality. Using path analysis, they reported that childhood aggression contributes directly to so-called "predelinquent" behavior (stealing, running away, trouble with the law, lying, and truancy), although only among male subjects.

A final and related issue concerns the relative predictive power of aggressive behavior versus poor peer acceptance. In studies that have included both indexes, criminal behavior has been found to relate only to low acceptance (Janes et al., 1979), only to aggressiveness (Kupersmidt, 1983; West & Farrington, 1973), or to both (J. J. Conger & Miller, 1966; J. D. Roff & Wirt, 1984). J. D. Roff and Wirt recently examined this issue in a different way: They examined the extent to which aggressiveness predicts later offending in a sample of disliked children (low peer-preference scores). They reported a low but significantly positive correlation between aggressiveness and later delinquency for both disliked boys and disliked girls. That is, for both boys and girls, the added knowledge that a disliked child was aggressive made it more certain that the child was at risk for criminal behavior. J. D. Roff and Wirt's data could be used to do the complementary analysis — whether acceptance predicts beyond the knowledge that the child was aggressive. This type of analysis has not been made in research to date.

The question of whether shyness/withdrawal relates to later criminality is interesting in the light of the fact that many factor-analytic models of delinquency continue to identify a type of passive, neurotic delinquent described as anxious, shy, seclusive, sensitive, and timid (e.g., Quay, 1979), and this nosological distinction has now been incorporated into the American Psychiatric Association's (1980) official diagnostic manual (*Diagnostic and Statistical Manual of Mental Disorders*). From Table 2, it is clear that juvenile and adult offenders are generally not any more shy/withdrawn as children than nonoffenders, at least according to teachers (J. J. Conger & Miller, 1966; Kirkegaard-Sørensen & Mednick, 1977; Mulligan et al., 1963; Robins, 1966). This is so regardless of controls for intelligence and other potential confounding variables and regardless of how stringent the operationalization of offending is. Furthermore, it is clear from the few follow-up studies that have been conducted that unless they are also aggressive, children identified by teachers as shy/withdrawn are not more likely to commit later crimes than are other children (Ensminger et al., 1983; Janes et al., 1979). None of these studies, however, systematically examined shyness/withdrawal in girls, and most excluded girls from their samples entirely. There is increasing evidence that shyness/withdrawal may be more of a developmental problem for girls than for boys (Dodge & Feldman, in press; Rutter & Garmezy, 1983); therefore, analyses of the role of shyness/withdrawal are needed for each gender separately.

To summarize this section on criminality, except for shyness/withdrawal, the evidence for a link between early peer-relationships disturbance and later criminality is generally very good. The follow-back studies reviewed show that the backgrounds of criminals of all types show a history of aggressiveness and poor peer regard that in some cases extends as far back as the point of the child's entry into formal schooling.

As for whether peer-relationships problems can, in the follow-up sense, predict future crime, the evidence for aggressiveness is strongly supportive; the evidence for low acceptance *per se* is somewhat mixed, though also generally supportive. In a sense, then, the pattern in this area is just the reverse of that found with regard to dropping out, for which acceptance *per se* was more consistently related to later outcome than was aggressiveness. Prediction from low-acceptance measures may improve as more studies begin to distinguish children who are actively disliked (rejected) from children who are simply ignored (neglected) and control more carefully the mediating effects of socioeconomic status.

Adult psychopathology

The serious personal and societal costs of adult psychological disorder need not be detailed here. Clearly, the demonstration of a reliable relation between early peer adjustment and later psychological disorder would be of considerable value in the process of early mental health screening and primary prevention. Nonetheless, within the risk literature, psychopathology has been studied much less adequately than has either dropping out or criminality. Table 3 is a list of existing studies in which earlier peer-relationships difficulties and later psychopathology were examined. It includes with each entry the particular criterion of adult psychopathology used. Most criteria are diagnostic categories, such as neurosis, conduct disorder, alcoholism, and especially psychosis/schizophrenia. Other, less frequently used criteria include global mental health adjustment ratings done by researchers and simple archival measures of psychiatric service usage or psychiatric hospitalization. Note that Table 3 indicates a marked preponderance of clinic or high-risk samples (40 of 48 entries). As a result, very few entries (3) in Table 3 involve school samples and follow-up data. This is particularly true for shyness/withdrawal, for which all existing follow-up data are based entirely on nonschool samples.

Acceptance

Four decades ago, Friedlander (1945) observed that the childhood of hospitalized adult psychotics tends to be characterized by poor adjustment to peers and few friends. Friedlander's data are anecdotal, based on impressions culled from teachers' comments in child guidance clinic records and with no comparison with a control group. But, as Table 3 indicates, subsequent, more systematic, follow-back analyses of teachers' comments uniformly support this impression for both child clinic samples (Flemming & Ricks, 1970; Frazee, 1953; Ricks & Berry, 1970; M. Roff, 1957, 1960, 1963) and school samples (Warnken & Siess, 1965). For example, M. Roff (1957, 1960, 1963) studied teachers' comments in the child guidance clinic records of various samples of psychotic, neurotic, and well-adjusted servicemen. For M. Roff (1957, 1960, 1963) poor peer adjustment consisted of pervasive, persistent, and openly hostile peer-group regard. It did not apply to children who were not particularly liked but also not particularly disliked (i.e., servicemen who had been neglected but not rejected as children). M. Roff (1957, 1960, 1963) reported the striking finding that 65% of psychotic servicemen and 51% and 69% in two samples of neurotic servicemen had poor peer adjustment in childhood, compared with 25%, 13%, and 22%, respectively, of controls.

A well-known study by Cowen *et al.* (1973) suggests that peer-assessed as well as teacher-assessed acceptance relates to later mental health problems. Cowen *et al.* examined information from the Monroe County Psychiatric Register to learn whether children studied 11 to 13 years earlier had subsequently received mental health services. Cowen *et al.* found that individuals with mental health problems had received more negative Class Play nominations from peers in third grade. In fact, later problems were more strongly related to negative Class Play scores than to third-grade teacher ratings of adjustment or to indexes of physical health, intellectual potential, academic performance, self-esteem, and anxiety.

Indeed, some evidence suggests that even within a population of disordered adults, individuals with differing degrees of psychopathology show differing levels of premorbid peer acceptance: Rolf, Knight, and Wertheim (1976) found a positive correlation ($r =$ .39) between summary ratings of early peer adjustment and later clinical judgments of a favorable schizophrenic prognosis. This is an impressive finding given that peer acceptance has an attenuated range within disordered populations.

That psychologically troubled people have histories of poor peer acceptance seems to be in little doubt from follow-back studies. Two limitations, however, deserve mention. Most follow-back studies have included only male subjects, and in those that have included both sexes, no systematic attempt was made to analyze results separately (see Table 3). Whether a follow-back relation also holds for female subjects is generally unknown. Likewise, very little attention has been paid to developmental issues within samples. Samples sometimes have included assessments made as early as 6 years of age, but because follow-back comparisons have never been studied as a function of age of assessment, it is still not possible to specify the age at which differences become apparent or the ages at which differences are greatest.

A second set of studies in Table 3 (Janes & Hesselbrock, 1978; Janes *et al.*, 1979; John, Mednick, & Schulsinger, 1982; Robins, 1966; J. D. Roff & Wirt, 1984) indicates whether low acceptance relates to adult psychopathology in the follow-up, or prospective, sense. Most of these studies were with special populations of children (clinic children or children of schizophrenic parents). Most used ad hoc teacher measures of acceptance of unknown reliability or validity. Also, most were carried out by investigators primarily concerned with other, larger issues of prediction. As a group, then, these studies are not particularly well suited to answering questions regarding peer acceptance and later psychopathology.

Table 3 **Studies predicting adult psychopathology grouped by indicator (acceptance and behavioral style) and assessment source (peers and teachers)**

Study	Criterion	Analysis	Type	Sex	Age (years)	Results
			Sample			
Acceptance						
Peer assessed						
Cowen, Pederson, Babijian, Izzo, & Trost (1973)	Receiving psychiatric services	FB	School	M + F	8	Support
J.D. Roff & Wirt (1984)	Hospitalization	FU	School	M	8-10	Support
				F	8-10	Support
Teacher assessed						
Warnken & Siess (1965)	Schizophrenia	FB	School	M	Unspecified	Support
M. Roff (1957, 1960)	Neurosis	FB	Clinic	M	Unspecified	Support
M. Roff (1963)	Psychosis	FB	Clinic	M	Unspecified	Support
Friedlander (1945)	Hospitalization	FB	Clinic	M + F	Unspecified	Support[a]
Frazee (1953)	Schizophrenia	FB	Clinic	M	5-16	Support
Judge Baker studies (Flemming & Ricks, 1970; Ricks & Berry, 1970)	Schizophrenia	FB	Clinic	M	13 (mean)	Support
	Conduct disorder	FB	Clinic	M	13 (mean)	Support
	Alcoholism	FB	Clinic	M	13 (mean)	No Support
Rolf, Knight, & Wertheim (1976)	Schizophrenia prognosis	FB	Clinic	M	11 (mean)	Support
Janes & Hesselbrock (1978)	Adjustment rating	FU	Clinic	M + F	4-15	Support
Janes, Hesselbrock, Myers & Penniman (1979)	Hospitalization	FU	Clinic	M	4-15	Support
Robins (1966)	Schizophrenia	FU	Clinic	M + F	Unspecified	No support
	Neurosis	FU	Clinic	M + F	Unspecified	No support
	Alcoholism	FU	Clinic	M + F	Unspecified	No support
John, Mednick, & Schulsinger (1982)	Schizophrenia	FU	High risk	M	9-20	Support
				F	9-20	Support
	Borderline schizophrenia	FU	High risk	M	9-20	Support
				F	9-20	No support
Behavioral style: aggressiveness						
Peer assessed						
Havighurst, Bowman, Liddle, Matthews, & Pierce (1962)	Adjustment rating	FB	School	M	11	Support
	Adjustment rating	FB	School	F	11	No support
		FU	School	M + F	11	Support

Note. FB = follow-back; FU = follow-up; M = male; F = female.
[a] No control group.

409

Table 3 **Studies predicting adult psychopathology grouped by indicator (acceptance and behavioral style) and assessment source (peers and teachers) (cont)**

Study	Criterion	Analysis	Sample Type	Sex	Age (years)	Results
			Sample			

Study	Criterion	Analysis	Type	Sex	Age (years)	Results

<table>
<tr><th>Study</th><th>Criterion</th><th>Analysis</th><th>Type</th><th>Sex</th><th>Age (years)</th><th>Results</th></tr>
<tr><td colspan="7">Behavioral style: aggressiveness (continued)</td></tr>
<tr><td colspan="7">Teacher assessed</td></tr>
<tr><td>Frazee (1953)</td><td>Schizophrenia</td><td>FB</td><td>Clinic</td><td>M</td><td>5-16</td><td>No support</td></tr>
<tr><td>Judge Baker studies (Flemming & Ricks, 1970; Ricks & Berry, 1970)</td><td>Schizophrenia</td><td>FB</td><td>Clinic</td><td>M</td><td>13 (mean)</td><td>Support</td></tr>
<tr><td>Janes, Hesselbrock, Myers & Penniman (1979)</td><td>Hospitalization</td><td>FU</td><td>Clinic</td><td>M</td><td>4-15</td><td>No Support</td></tr>
<tr><td>Janes & Hesselbrock (1978)</td><td>Adjustment rating</td><td>FU</td><td>Clinic</td><td>M</td><td>4-15</td><td>Support</td></tr>
<tr><td>Robins (1966)</td><td>Schizophrenia
Neurosis
Alcoholism</td><td>FU
FU
FU</td><td>Clinic
Clinic
Clinic</td><td>M + F
M + F
M + F</td><td>Unspecified
Unspecified
Unspecified</td><td>No support
No support
No support</td></tr>
<tr><td colspan="7">Behavioral style: shyness/withdrawal</td></tr>
<tr><td colspan="7">Peer assessed</td></tr>
<tr><td colspan="7">None</td></tr>
<tr><td colspan="7">Teacher assessed</td></tr>
<tr><td>Warnken & Siess (1965)</td><td>Schizophrenia</td><td>FB</td><td>School</td><td>M</td><td>Unspecified</td><td>Support</td></tr>
<tr><td>Frazee (1953)</td><td>Schizophrenia</td><td>FB</td><td>Clinic</td><td>M</td><td>5-16</td><td>Support</td></tr>
<tr><td>Robins (1966)</td><td>Schizophrenia</td><td>FB</td><td>Clinic</td><td>M + F</td><td>Unspecified</td><td>No support</td></tr>
<tr><td>Judge Baker studies (Flemming & Ricks, 1970; Ricks & Berry, 1970)</td><td>Schizophrenia</td><td>FB</td><td>Clinic</td><td>M</td><td>13 (mean)</td><td>Supports</td></tr>
<tr><td>D.P. Morris, Soroker, & Burruss (1954)</td><td>Adjustment rating</td><td>FU</td><td>Clinic</td><td>M + F</td><td>3-15</td><td>No support[a]</td></tr>
<tr><td>Michael, Morris, & Soroker (1957)</td><td>Schizophrenia</td><td>FU</td><td>Clinic</td><td>M</td><td>2-18</td><td>No support</td></tr>
<tr><td>Janes & Hesselbrock (1978)</td><td>Adjustment rating</td><td>FU</td><td>Clinic</td><td>M</td><td>4-15</td><td>No support</td></tr>
<tr><td></td><td></td><td></td><td></td><td>F</td><td>4-15</td><td>Support</td></tr>
<tr><td>Janes, Hesselbrock, Myers & Penniman (1979)</td><td>Hospitalization</td><td>FU</td><td>Clinic</td><td>M</td><td>4-15</td><td>No support</td></tr>
<tr><td>Robins (1966)</td><td>Alcoholism
Schizophrenia
Neurosis</td><td>FU
FU
FU</td><td>Clinic
Clinic
Clinic</td><td>M + F
M + F
M + F</td><td>Unspecified
Unspecified
Unspecified</td><td>No support
No support
No support</td></tr>
<tr><td>John, Mednick, & Schulsinger (1982)</td><td>Schizophrenia</td><td>FU</td><td>High risk</td><td>M
F</td><td>9-20
9-20</td><td>No support
No support</td></tr>
<tr><td></td><td>Borderline schizophrenia</td><td>FU</td><td>High risk</td><td>M
F</td><td>9-20
9-20</td><td>No support
Support</td></tr>
</table>

Note. FB = follow-back; FU = follow-up; M = male; F = female.
[a] No control group.

Perhaps as a result, follow-up findings concerning low acceptance and risk have been mixed and generally inconclusive. For example, data from Robins (1966) indicate that clinic children who had "difficulties with contemporaries" had no greater incidence of later psychosis, neurosis, or alcoholism than did other clinic children. Yet Janes *et al.* (1979) reported that clinic boys and girls whose teachers indicated that they "fail to get along with other children" had significantly poorer mental health ratings as adults than did other clinic children. Moreover the Janes *et al.* data indicate that a failure to get along with peers according to teachers also predicted subsequent psychiatric hospitalization among boys. (They did not examine the incidence among girls.) In a third study, John *et al.* (1982) examined prediction in a high-risk sample of children born to severely schizophrenic mothers and reported that an indication by the teacher that a child had difficulty making friends and was lonely and rejected differentially predicted later schizophrenia versus borderline schizophrenia versus nonschizophrenic disorders.

A study by J. D. Roff and Wirt (1984) is an important exception to both the tendency to study special populations and the tendency to use simple teacher measures. As part of a study described in detail earlier, in connection with delinquency and adult crime, J. D. Roff and Wirt used statewide public psychiatric hospitalization records to detect the incidence of later psychiatric disorder among a subset ($n = 2,453$) of the longitudinal cases first assessed by M. Roff *et al.* (1972). J. D. Roff and Wirt found a significant but very low negative correlation between childhood sociometric status and later hospitalization both for boys ($r = -.17$) and for girls ($r = -.10$). Perhaps stronger effects would have been obtained had J. D. Roff and Wirt compared the most unpopular children with all others rather than correlating adjustment with the entire range of sociometric status.

Behavioral style

The expectation that childhood shyness/withdrawal relates to adult psychiatric impairment has a long history within the literature on life history psychopathology. This expectation is based in part on a presumed continuity between childhood and adult disorder — a point noted in the introduction to this review (also see Garmezy, 1974; Kohlberg *et al.*, 1972). It is also based on the conclusions of authors conducting retrospective interview studies of preschizophrenic behavior (e.g., Birren, 1944; Bower *et al.*, 1960; Kohn & Clausen, 1955; Schofield & Balian, 1959). Consistent with this expectation, follow-back comparisons have sometimes found that shyness or withdrawal is more characteristic of the backgrounds of schizophrenic than non-schizophrenic adults. For example, Warnken and Siess (1965), in an analysis of teachers' comments in cumulative school records, found that the terms *shy* and *withdrawn* appear much more regularly in the records of schizophrenics than nonschizophrenics. Similarly, Frazee (1953) found that shy, listless behavior was characteristic of the histories of 78% of the 23 schizophrenic adults whom she studied, compared with 44% of the 23 controls. To this, Ricks and Berry (1970) added that it is the schizophrenics with the most severe prognosis who showed the most severe forms of withdrawal; milder forms of shyness/withdrawal are associated with less chronicity. Also, Barthell and Holmes (1968) presented findings from a content analysis of high school yearbooks to suggest that the withdrawal of preschizophrenics is social; that is, Barthell and Holmes's data indicate that preschizophrenics do not avoid activities of all kinds, only activities that require regular, cooperative contact with other people (e.g., they were more likely to be library aides than members of student government or members of special-interest clubs).

It has yet to be consistently established, however, that shyness or withdrawal in childhood can predict later psychiatric disorder in the follow-up sense, although only clinic and high-risk samples have been studied. Several follow-up analyses have found an absence of predictability (Janes et al., 1979; Michael, Morris, & Soroker, 1957; D. P. Morris et al., 1954; Robins, 1966). Two studies, however, suggest a relation. Janes and Hesselbrock (1978) found that an indication from teachers that a child was shy or withdrawn was related to lower mental health ratings made later by psychiatrists. This was true only for girls, however. In another study, John et al. (1982) found that among girls (but not boys) with schizophrenic parents, an indication from the teacher that the child was "shy, reserved, and silent" was related to increased risk of later schizophrenia or borderline schizophrenia, relative to nonschizophrenic forms of disorder.

Further, if we take a second look at the follow-back comparisons discussed above, several problems are apparent. No study used peer-assessed shyness or withdrawal. Those based on clinic samples generally did not include information on how shyness or withdrawal was assessed (e.g., Flemming & Ricks, 1970; Frazee, 1953; Ricks & Berry, 1970). It is particularly critical for clinic studies to include information on how shyness/withdrawal is operationalized, because analyses of clinic case files allow enormous latitude in coding and interpretation. Studies using school samples have generally been better at stating measurement criteria but have sometimes used measures of questionable reliability and validity (e.g., Barthell & Holmes, 1968, assessed withdrawal by using activities reported in high school yearbooks).

A second concern is that not all follow-back analyses have found evidence of greater shyness or withdrawal in the backgrounds of schizophrenics relative to controls (Robins, 1966) or of chronic schizophrenics relative to schizophrenics with more favorable prognoses (Rolf et al., 1976). Yet there are no obvious differences that help explain the discrepancies between these latter studies and the studies finding relations discussed above.

The second aspect of behavioral style that is of interest here is aggressiveness. Some of those follow-back analyses that indicate that emotionally disturbed adults show a history of greater shyness/withdrawal also indicate that many impaired adults show histories of aggressiveness (Flemming & Ricks, 1970; Ricks & Berry, 1970). Moreover, other studies also indicate a follow-back link between later disorder and earlier aggressiveness toward peers (Havighurst et al., 1962; Robins, 1966). Accordingly, a simple characterization of the predisordered individual that emphasizes only shyness/withdrawal seems incomplete. Perhaps, as Ledingham and Schwartzman (1984) recently argued, shyness/withdrawal is most problematic when individuals also show deviant levels of aggressive behavior.

Follow-up analyses, too, provide evidence of a predictive link between early aggressiveness and later psychopathology. In a school study, Havighurst *et al.* (1962) followed 411 sixth-grade boys and girls for 9 years and reported a modest but significant negative correlation ($r = -.24$) between earlier peer nominations for aggressiveness and "initial adult adjustment." Poor initial adult adjustment meant poor mental health as judged by interviewers, as well as signs of irresponsibility, an unstable marriage, poor work relationships, or criminal activity. It was, thus, a global measure of psychosocial impairment in young adulthood rather than a diagnosis of a specific disorder.

In clinic or high-risk samples, in which teachers report on aggression, some follow-up analyses indicate risk, whereas others do not. Janes and Hesselbrock (1978) reported that clinic girls whose teachers indicated at the time of their referral that they were frequently involved in fighting did not later have notably poorer mental health as young adults (as judged through psychiatric interviews) than did nonaggressive clinic girls. Aggressive clinic boys did have poorer later mental health than did nonaggressive boys, but these apparent differences disappeared after socioeconomic and intelligence differences were controlled for. Moreover, aggressive boys were not different from nonaggressive boys in terms of their risk for later psychiatric hospitalization. (No similar comparison was made for girls.)

Using specific psychiatric diagnoses rather than global indicants of psychopathology, Robins (1966), in her sample of clinic boys and girls, found that those with indications of excessive physical aggression were not at elevated risk for later schizophrenia, neurosis, or alcoholism. Interestingly, although aggression alone was not predictive, successful prediction was possible from a general category of antisocial behavior that included truancy, theft, and aggression. A link between generalized antisocial behavior and later psychopathology has also been reported in other follow-up studies of clinic children (H. H. Morris, Escoll, & Wexler, 1956; Pritchard & Graham, 1966). Future work should carefully compare the risk of children who fight but are not otherwise antisocial, children who fight and are generally antisocial, and children who do not fight but nonetheless engage in such behaviors as lying and stealing.

Overall, then, very little can be safely concluded regarding the link between behavioral orientation toward peers and later psychopathology; the literature here, like that pertaining to acceptance *per se*, is largely incomplete and conflicting. In addition to the insufficient number of follow-up studies, one problem that plagues this literature is the almost total absence of work with school samples. This is unfortunate because greater individual variation in shyness/withdrawal or aggressiveness that occurs in school samples might allow more powerful tests of the risk hypothesis. Also, as we shall discuss later, there is a need — not only with behavioral style but also with acceptance — to differentiate the type of mental health outcome being investigated. More differentiated assessment of outcomes may result in stronger relations between early peer problems and later mental health difficulties. In the meantime, it can be said that some evidence suggests a link between behavior style and later psychopathology and that further, more carefully designed research is needed.

Predictive accuracy

In this section, we examine the predictive accuracy of measures of poor peer adjustment in terms of predictive efficacy, specificity, and sensitivity. Here we restrict the focus to those follow-up studies that have yielded significant relations between early peer-group maladjustment and later outcomes. These significant follow-up findings are presented in Table 4, grouped by type of peer-difficulty index (acceptance and behavioral style) and source of assessment (teachers and peers). Only follow-up findings are included because, as noted earlier, the constructs of efficacy, specificity, and sensitivity are meaningful only with regard to follow-up findings. Furthermore, Table 4 includes only significant findings because the vast majority of the reports yielding nonsignificant findings do not present the data needed (percentages and sample sizes) for calculating RIOC. It is important, then, to avoid drawing conclusions from Table 4 about the average level of accuracy in the general literature because nonsignificant findings could not be included. Instead, our goal is to demonstrate the value of doing an RIOC analysis by presenting a picture of the magnitude of the accuracy of prediction in instances in which prediction was possible.

For each entry in Table 4, column 4 contains the percentages of children in the focal group (i.e., low accepted, aggressive, or shy/withdrawn) who ultimately showed maladjustment (dropping out, criminality, or adult psychopathology). These percentages indicate the specificity of peer relationships as a predictor. When these percentages are large, few false positive errors of prediction occurred, and poor peer relationships was a relatively specific predictor of maladjustment. When these percentages are small, there were many false positives; that is, using the criterion of poor peer-group adjustment led to an overselection of children as at risk.

Column 5 contains the percentages of nonfocal, or remaining, children who eventually experienced negative outcomes. These percentages reveal the predictive sensitivity of measures of poor peer relationships. When sensitivity is good, few false negative errors of prediction occurred, and the percentage of nonfocal children who developed maladjustment was small. When poor peer relationships is a relatively insensitive predictor, many children destined for disorder escaped detection, and the percentage of nonfocal children with later maladjustment was large.

On the basis of these percentages, we calculated the values of Loeber and Dishion's (1983) RIOC index. These values are presented in column 6 of Table 4. Recall that RIOC is a summary measure of the efficacy of prediction based on the number of correct and incorrect predictions. It is somewhat distinct from specificity and sensitivity, which indicate the extent to which certain types of prediction errors occur. RIOC can be interpreted as the extent to which the observed accuracy approaches its theoretical maximum, after correcting for chance.

Table 4   Predictive sensitivity, specificity, and efficacy of significant follow-up findings

Study	Outcome	N	% disordered		RIOC	Source
			Focal	Remaining		
Acceptance						
Peer assessed						
M. Roff, Sells, & Golden (1972)	JC (agency)	1,729 (male)	25.30	9.90	10.48	Table 25
M. Roff (1975)	JC (agency)	6,676 (female)	11.40	6.96	4.72	Figure 2
J.D. Roff & Wirt (1984)	JC (agency)	1,224 (male)	35.30	17.78	33.03	Table 2
		1,224 (female)	10.34	6.14	24.39	Table 3
Gronlund & Holmlund (1958)	Dropping out	55 (male)	54.20	19.40	44.10	Table 2
		47 (female)	36.00	4.50	78.50	Table 2
Barclay (1966)	Dropping out	308 (female)	15.40	7.60	16.55	Table 1
		356 (male)	13.80	4.10	42.86	Table 1
Teacher assessed						
Barclay (1966)	Dropping out	380 (female)	20.80	6.90	28.85	Table 1
		356 (male)	13.40	4.60	33.33	Table 1
Janes, Hesselbrock, Myers, & Pennimann (1979)	Dropping out	127 (male)	25.00	12.60	23.45	Personal communication
	AC (detected)	138 (male)	53.30	34.60	22.00	"
	AC (arrest)	135 (male)	34.10	14.30	31.42	"
	Psychiatric hospitalization	137 (male)	8.90	0.00	100.00	"
Behavioral style: aggressiveness						
Peer assessed						
Havighurst, Bowman, Liddle, Matthews, & Pierce (1962)	Dropping out	352	57.00	26.30	37.50	Table 15
	JC (detected)	242 (male)	83.30	15.60	78.99	Table 19
West & Farrington (1973)	JC (alleged)	353 (male)	37.50	13.90	25.30	Appendix A
Teacher assessed						
Feldhusen, Thurston, & Benning (1973)	Dropping out	384	18.20	3.00	42.13	p. 346
	JC (detected)	384	47.90	22.30	36.36	p. 344
	JC (alleged)	384	23.90	3.10	76.87	p. 344
	JC (adjudicated)	384	9.90	1.00	79.63	p. 344
Magnussen, Stattin, & Duner (1983)	JC (detected)	412 (male)	35.30	10.70	45.82	Table 16.3
	JC (severe)	412 (male)	26.00	5.70	56.02	Table 16.3
	JC (persistent)	412 (male)	22.70	2.70	73.60	Table 16.3
	AC (detected)	412 (male)	30.00	13.00	32.37	Table 16.5
	AC (severe)	412 (male)	14.00	1.90	70.00	Table 16.5
	AC (persistent)	412 (male)	18.00	5.30	46.03	Table 16.5
West & Farrington (1973)	JC (alleged)	411 (male)	41.00	13.80	32.14	App. A (8yrs)
		411 (male)	38.40	14.70	27.97	App. A (10 yrs)
		411 (male)	38.10	11.90	41.61	App. A (8 + 10 yrs)

Note RIOC = relative improvement over chance; JC = juvenile crime; AC = adult crime

Table 4   Predictive sensitivity, specificity, and efficacy of significant follow-up findings (cont)

| Study | Outcome | N | % disordered | | | |
			Focal	Remaining	RIOC	Source
	Behavioral style: shyness/withdrawal					
Peer assessed						
None						
Teacher assessed						
None						

Note. RIOC = relative improvement over chance; JC = juvenile crime; AC = adult crime.

To calculate RIOC and the percentages in columns 4 and 5, one needs dichotomous predictor (i.e., focal vs. nonfocal) and outcome (i.e., maladjusted vs. nonmaladjusted) variables. This requirement could not be met if original reports did not contain contingency tables or their equivalent in the text (e.g., correlational analyses would not suffice). Six instances of this problem occurred even when significant relations were obtained (Ensminger *et al.*, 1983; Janes & Hesselbrock, 1978; John *et al.*, 1982; Kupersmidt, 1983; Robins, 1966; J. D. Roff & Wirt, 1984); therefore, six significant findings that appear in Tables 1–3 do not appear in Table 4. A number of other significant findings involved polytomous or continuous predictor variables (e.g., five levels of sociometric status in M. Roff *et al.'s* 1972 study). This posed a solvable problem. Here, following Loeber and Dishion (1983), we created dichotomous groups by setting cutting scores to obtain the optimal RIOC value. We adopted this procedure for approximately one third of the findings in Table 4.

A noteworthy feature of Table 4 is the absence of entries pertaining to the predictive accuracy of shyness/withdrawal. This reflects the important fact that despite several attempts, shyness/withdrawal has not been shown to predict either dropping out or juvenile or adult criminality and has been found to be linked to later psychopathology in only 2 of 14 comparisons (see Table 3). These two exceptions — female subjects in Janes and Hesselbrock's (1978) study and female subjects in John *et al.'s* (1982) study — do not appear in Table 4 because of insufficient detail about incidence. Therefore, the discussion of predictive accuracy that follows applies only to peer and teacher measures of low acceptance and aggressiveness.

The information in Table 4 can be used to address several important questions about the strength of prediction in instances in which predictive relations have been found. These include the accuracy of overall prediction, the differential predictive accuracy of various peer-relationship measures, the differential predictability to various outcomes, and potential interactions between peer-relationship measures and later outcomes with regard to predictability.

With respect to the overall accuracy of prediction, the 30 entries in the RIOC column of Table 4 yield an average value of 43.2, and several entries have values greater than 70. An RIOC value of 43.2 indicates an improvement over chance accuracy that is about 43% of its theoretical maximum given the base rate and the selection ratio. RIOC values much greater than 40 to 50 are difficult to obtain with single predictor variables (Loeber & Dishion, 1983). Certainly, accuracy much closer to chance might have been found. The typical pattern of errors of prediction is also informative. On the average, 30% of focal children experienced negative outcomes as adults, but 70% did not (column 4) On the average, only 10.5% of nonfocal children had documented problems as adults (column 5). Together, these percentages indicate that measures of poor peer adjustment are particularly accurate at identifying those children who are actually destined for difficulties but tend to select many children who are not actually at risk (i.e., sensitivity is high, but specificity is low).

These overall values mask a slight imbalance, however, between acceptance and aggression in terms of accuracy. If we consider just the 16 entries that concern aggressiveness, the average RIOC increases slightly (to 50.3). If we consider only the 14 entries that involve acceptance, RIOC drops off notably (to 25.5). Aggression and acceptance show the same pattern, however, of sensitivity and specificity: Few children destined for difficulties escape detection (column 5 means are 10.6% for aggression and 10.3% for acceptance), but most children with poor peer adjustment do not develop difficulties (see column 4).

Dropping out and criminality seem equally well predicted by early peer-adjustment measures (mean RIOCs = 40.5 and 41.5, respectively). Only one finding in Table 4 includes information about predictability of adult psychopathology (Janes *et al.*, 1979), making comparisons with other outcomes questionable. However, in this single case, predictive efficacy was perfect (RIOC = 100).

A final issue of interest concerns the relative predictive accuracy of peer- and teacher-based assessments. Most teacher measures in Table 4 are measures of aggression rather than acceptance (13 vs. 6), and most peer measures are measures of acceptance rather than aggression (8 vs. 3). When peers and teachers are compared for acceptance and aggression separately, there do not appear to be large differences in accuracy between peers and teachers. The average RIOC value for teacher measures of aggression is 50.8, whereas the average RIOC for peer measures of aggression is 47.3. Similarly, the average RIOC for teacher measures of acceptance is 39.8, whereas the average RIOC for peer measures of acceptance is 31.8.

In view of such symmetry in predictive accuracy, it might be tempting to conclude that teacher-based assessments are as good as or even preferable to peer-based ones because the two alternatives seem equally efficacious and because teacher data are more economical to collect. To draw such a conclusion, however, is to ignore the important caveat noted earlier in this article regarding the as-yet-unproved validity of virtually all teacher measures used in the risk literature to date. Perhaps the safest conclusion is that teacher approaches seem to corroborate the level of predictive accuracy attained by peer-based approaches.[6]

Conclusions

In the introduction, we noted that the belief that low-accepted children constitute a population at risk is widespread in both the popular and professional literature on social development and that it is essential to assess whether this assertion has empirical support. At this point, we are in a position to offer certain conclusions regarding this at-risk premise.

With regard to follow-back comparisons, our review indicates that it is indeed not difficult to find differences suggesting greater childhood peer-relationship difficulties for maladjusted individuals. Depending on the type of analysis, group differences existed either in childhood average acceptance, aggressiveness, or shyness/withdrawal or in the proportion of individuals labeled low accepted, aggressive, or shy/withdrawn. With regard to proportions, from 28% to 70% of disordered adults showed a history of problematic peer relationships (see Tables 1–3). Differences were found in every outcome area considered. In fact, they were sometimes observed even in comparisons of disordered and nondisordered adults referred to clinics as children. It is particularly impressive that peer-relationship differences emerged here as well given that children referred to clinics are a relatively homogeneous population.

Follow-back analyses may indicate that maladjusted adults had peer-relationship difficulties sometime in childhood, but, as we have discussed, this does not by itself indicate that a child's poor peer relationships are predictive of later disturbance. When we look across all outcomes and measures, it is clear that general support for the risk hypothesis emerges from follow-up analyses even as specific points of some disagreement or uncertainty become apparent. Clearly, the number of instances of predictability far outstrips the number of instances of nonpredictability. In fact, Table 4 contains 30 significant follow-up findings that document links between early peer relationships and later life problems.

Our review, then, should provide some reassurance to such researchers as Putallaz and Gottman (1983), who, as we have noted, have expressed concern that the at-risk view is being popularized without an adequate analysis of its empirical basis. At the same time, although our review provides support for the risk hypothesis, it also suggests that the risk premise must be significantly qualified in three heretofore unacknowledged ways. First, predictability varies as a function of the type of peer-relationships measure considered. To begin with, low acceptance and aggressiveness are more consistent predictors of later negative outcomes than is shyness/withdrawal. In fact, we found very little evidence linking shyness/withdrawal to later negative outcomes in the follow-up sense. Follow-back differences in shyness/withdrawal, on the other hand, were frequent. Thus, it does appear that a sizable number of individuals headed for disorder go through a period of shyness/withdrawal. However, shyness/withdrawal has not yet been demonstrated to be predictive of later maladjustment.

The fact that shy or withdrawn children do not appear to be at risk for later difficulty is interesting given the importance that clinicians and parents attach to such behavior as an index of peer difficulty (e.g., Achenbach & Edelbrock, 1981; Evans & Wilson, 1982). A number of years ago, Kohlberg et al. (1972) suggested that shyness/withdrawal was unlike aggressiveness and low peer acceptance in that shyness/withdrawal was episodic, not cumulative in nature, and lacked a developmental-adaptational basis. They argued that for this reason, predictions based on shyness/withdrawal could never be as precise as predictions based on either aggressiveness or poor peer relationships themselves. Although our conclusions are consistent with Kohlberg *et al.*'s formulation, an alternative explanation may lie in the methodological rigor with which shyness/withdrawal has been operationalized and studied to date. Recall from the discussion of Tables 1 through 3 that shyness/withdrawal has almost always been studied by using nonschool samples and follow-back methods of data analysis. Thus, from an interpretation and generalizability standpoint, most existing research on this issue is of questionable utility. Indeed, inspection of Tables 1 through 3 reveals only one study (Ensminger *et al.*, 1983; see Table 2) that examines shyness/withdrawal and meets our criteria for an optimal study (i.e., school sample and follow-up data). Thus, it is perhaps fairest to say that the ideal study of shyness/withdrawal has not yet been done and that firm conclusions about this aspect of the literature would be premature.

Further evidence of variation in predictability as a function of type of peer index is that acceptance and aggressiveness show somewhat different relations to later dropping out and criminality. Low acceptance was more predictive of later dropping out than of criminality. On the other hand, aggressiveness was more predictive of later criminality than of dropping out. One cautionary note is that the less consistent predictor in each case is also the one that has been studied less often, and for both outcomes, acceptance and aggressiveness are not independent of the source of assessment (teacher vs. peers) and the type of sample (school vs. clinic). Nevertheless, the pattern is intriguing and suggests different pathways to different outcomes.

The second qualifying conclusion from our review is that although predictive efficacy was high overall, peer-relationship measures of all types tended to show the same pattern of errors of prediction; namely, they tended to make few false negative errors but many false positive errors. In other words, indexes of peer-relationship problems were relatively sensitive to those children who would ultimately show problematic outcomes but at the same time tended to select many children who were not actually at risk. As a practical matter, both the direction and the degree of prediction error that is acceptable depend on why children are being selected. If children are being selected for intervention and if one's concern is to avoid intervening with children not actually in need of treatment (e.g., to avoid the iatrogenic effects of labeling), then a large number of false positive errors is a concern. But, if potential iatrogenic effects can be anticipated and avoided and if the planned intervention might be helpful to all children, there would be little reason to fear overselection.

The final qualification concerns differences in predicted outcomes. Specifically, the risk premise appears to be on surer ground with regard to dropping out and criminality than it is for adult psychopathology. One explanation of this difference may be methodological. The literature regarding psychopathology is on the whole the least sophisticated methodologically: It includes the greatest reliance on nonschool samples and the greatest use of teacher ratings with unknown psychometric properties. But the possibility remains that peer difficulties are indeed more strongly predictive of later dropping out and criminality than of the kinds of mental health outcomes studied thus far. Research in this area has either focused on schizophrenia or has obtained some general indicator of an individual's mental health status (e.g., global ratings or indications of receiving mental health services). Kohlberg et al. (1972) noted the challenge that schizophrenia presents to prediction and pointed out the discontinuity between schizophrenia and other disordered outcomes from a prediction standpoint:

> Delinquency, character disorders, neuroses, and learning failures can readily be interpreted as due to retardation in cognitive and social development or to social learning of maladaptive values and behaviors . . . the differences between these disorders and normal personality patterns can be viewed as matters of degree only. However, it is extremely difficult to look at schizophrenic behavior in these terms. The core phenomena of schizophrenia — apathy, emotional withdrawal, and thought disorder — appear to be qualitatively different from normal behavior, from other forms of maladjustment, and from the early behavior of the patient himself. (p. 1262)

We concur with Kohlberg et al. Furthermore, what seems needed is a broadening of the kinds of mental health outcomes that are studied in relation to peer-relationship problems in children. It seems plausible, for example, that children without social support from peers would, over the long term, be at risk for feelings of extreme loneliness or even depression. Or, insofar as peer relationship, especially friendships, provide valuable support during times of life stress, it also makes sense that individuals with peer-relationship problems would be at risk for stress-related difficulties, such as various psychosomatic disturbances (e.g., hypertension, ulcers, and chronic headaches). In the long run, however, the ability to specify such links will require a clearer, more explicit, and more comprehensive conceptualization of the nature of the relation between peer relationships and adjustment than there has been in the past — a conceptualization that indicates not only how various forms of peer-relationships disturbance relate to various later disordered outcomes but also why. Toward this end, in the next, concluding section, we discuss the two implicit models that have guided risk research to date and suggest several important ways in which both models are limited. We conclude with a discussion of critical components that any new model of the risk premise must contain. Our goal is to give direction to the next generation of risk studies.

Toward the next generation of risk research

Current models and their limitations

At the beginning of this article, we noted that researchers who have done work on the risk premise have proceeded from one of two implicit models. The first model, shown at the top of Figure 1, might be termed a causal model and stems from the growing evidence that peer interaction ordinarily plays multiple indispensable roles in the socialization of social, cognitive, and moral development — the necessity-not-luxury view of peer interaction that we outlined earlier. Here the assumption seems to be that because they are excluded from normal patterns of peer interaction, low-accepted children are also systematically excluded from normal socialization experiences and deprived of important sources of support. As a result, these children become more extreme and more idiosyncratic in their modes of thought and behavior over time and are made more vulnerable to stress and breakdown.

The alternative belief, shown at the bottom of Figure 1, might be termed an incidental model because it makes no assumption that peer-relationship problems cause later maladjustment. Instead, this model assumes that early forms of the disorders that will emerge fully in adulthood have a negative influence on interpersonal relationships in childhood. Accordingly, in this view it is the early forms of disorder that are responsible for both the early disturbances in peer-group adjustment and the ultimate maladaptive outcomes. Put differently, the assumption is that peer-relationship problems are tangential and epiphenomenal to later maladjustment, though potentially useful for screening purposes. There is no assumption that poor peer relationships make any independent contribution to later maladjustment and no prediction that children who are rejected by peers for reasons other than underlying disorder will have later maladjustment.

These two models lead to somewhat different research objectives. Research conducted from an incidental perspective focuses on the relative predictive utility of poor peer relationships, compared with other potential diagnostic measures, such as neurological functioning, adjustment to parents or teachers, or academic success. Studies of this type (e.g., John *et al.*, 1982; West & Farrington, 1973) typically sample a broad range of childhood variables in the hope of finding a small subset that is highly predictive of a specific adult outcome of interest (e.g., schizophrenia). By contrast, research from a causal perspective (e.g., Feldhusen *et al.*, 1973; Havighurst *et al.*, 1962; Kupersmidt, 1983) focuses on a more circumscribed set of childhood peer-adjustment variables but includes a broader array of potential adult outcomes in the hope of finding those that are related to earlier peer functioning. Otherwise, the two models focus on the same three classes of variables: characteristics of the child (i.e., the child's deviant behavior), characteristics of the child's social relationships (i.e., the child's peer acceptance), and the child's eventual adult adjustment status (e.g., dropping out, criminality, and psychopathology).

In our view, both models are deficient in terms of the range of issues they consider and the sophistication with which they reason about both the nature of peer-relationships disturbance and the course and etiology of deviant development. The extreme incidental model seemingly denies the very real possibility that the experience of peer rejection, especially prolonged peer rejection, leads a child to view the world and him- or herself negatively (see Dodge & Feldman, in press; Hymel & Franke, 1985). Ongoing rejection by peers must negatively affect many aspects of the child's subsequent social, academic, affective, and moral development. Perhaps it is appropriate to think of peer-relationship disturbances as incidental to outcomes that are relatively chronic and include a large genetic or biological component, such as schizophrenia; but it seems to us ill-advised to ignore the potential contribution of peer rejection to such developmental-adaptational outcomes as dropping out and delinquency.

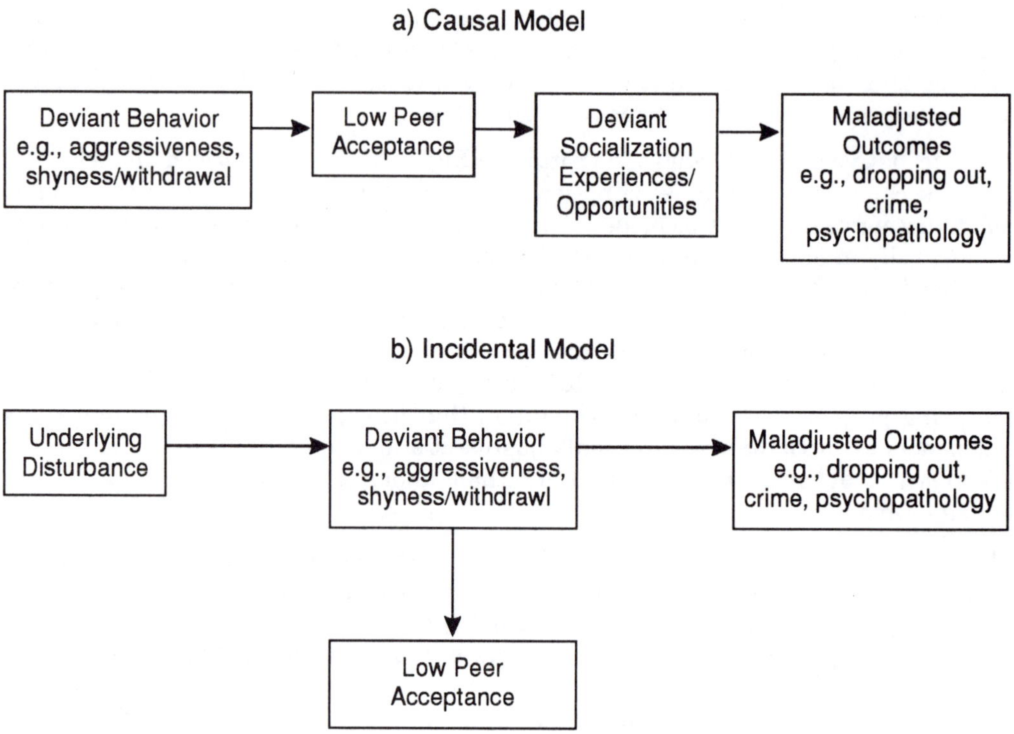

a) Causal Model

b) Incidental Model

Figure 1 **Implicit models concerning the link between peer-relationship problems and later maladjustment**

Alternatively, an extreme causal view ignores the fact that factors that antedate poor interpersonal relationships continue to play a role in subsequent outcomes. It seems likely that factors that contribute to poor peer adjustment also continue to shape the course and nature of subsequent adjustment. For example, there is evidence that some types of low-accepted children are biased to interpret the ambiguous behavioral cues of other children as hostile provocations (see Dodge & Feldman, in press). The initial evidence is that this bias can be the cause of poor peer relationships, not just their consequence (Richard, 1985, cited in Dodge & Feldman, in press). One could argue that low-accepted youngsters who are prone toward making hostile attributions would be more likely than other low-accepted youngsters to exhibit paranoid modes of thought as adults.

In our view, what is needed is a more comprehensive model of the link between peer relationships and later maladjustment. This model must be more inclusive than either of the simple, linear models that appear in Figure 1, allowing for feedback among the causes of low acceptance, the consequences of low acceptance, and the course of later maladjustment. In addition, it must allow for different pathways to maladjustment and account for why some children with peer-relationship problems develop later problems, whereas others do not. We are not, of course, the first to suggest the need for such a model. Indeed, promising groundwork for such a model appears in several recent thoughtful reviews of the literature on familial origins of social competence (e.g., Putallaz & Heflin, in press; Rubin, Le Mare, & Lollis, in press). It is not within the scope or aims of this review to elaborate these emerging models. Indeed, we believe that a prerequisite to any final model is future research that assesses children's behavioral functioning, peer adjustment, and later adult adjustment in a more sophisticated manner and incorporates in its design and analyses broader questions of development and risk. Toward this end, we close with eight recommendations for future research in this area. The first four recommendations pertain to our concern that the child's behavioral functioning, the nature of the child's social relations, and the child's eventual adjustment be studied in a more differentiated and integrated manner. The fifth recommendation is a call for more sensitivity to developmental factors in research designs, and the sixth suggests consideration of the child's perspective on his or her peer adjustment. The remaining two recommendations pertain to hypothesized causal links between early peer disturbance and later outcomes: The seventh is a call for more process-oriented research, and the eighth suggests that hypothesized causal links be tested experimentally. Together, these recommendations present our view of the minimum set of key methodological and assessment features to be included in future research on the at-risk premise.

The child's behavioral functioning

An important goal for future research is to gain a picture of the child's behavioral functioning that is more comprehensive than what has emerged from risk research to date. Better prediction (and explanation) should be possible as one gains a more differentiated and multifaceted view of the child's typical social exchanges.

If aggressiveness and shyness/withdrawal are to continue to be used to predict later problematic outcomes — and they should be — then these constructs should be assessed in a more differentiated manner than has been typical in past risk research. To begin with, the terms *shy* and *withdrawn* have been treated in the existing literature as interchangeable descriptors. *Shyness* usually implies nonassertive behavior and infrequent interaction. To the extent that the term *withdrawal* is used to describe this same constellation of behavior, then using the two terms interchangeably is appropriate. But there are other, more extreme types of behavior that can sometimes lead a child to be labeled as withdrawn, including being anxious, apprehensive, or nonresponsive or even exhibiting bizarre, autistic thought and behavior. Children who are unresponsive and avoidant or who display unusual types of behavior are likely to be far more aversive to peers than are children who simply are nonassertive and interact infrequently. The two subgroups would not be expected to show the same pattern of later adjustment. Treating shy/withdrawn children as a homogenous group, therefore, may obscure important risk differences. Recent evidence on the behavioral correlates of sociometric status suggests the value of distinguishing shy from withdrawn behavior. The former tends not to be correlated with acceptance or rejection (Coie *et al.*, 1982), whereas the latter does not appear to be, at least among older children (Hymel & Rubin, 1985).

Assessment of aggressiveness also requires sensitivity to variations in typical form and function. As Bierman (1986) pointed out, "Aggression is a general class of behaviors, not all of which are socially unacceptable" (p. 160). The acceptability of aggressive behaviors may be influenced by whether the act is instrumental (i.e., impersonal and directed toward obtaining some object or territory) or hostile (i.e., person directed and designed to harm; see Hartup, 1974) and by whether the act is provoked or unprovoked (Lesser, 1959). Moreover, a child who engages in aggressive acts but, in general, displays a range of socially, athletically, and academically competent behaviors may be evaluated differently from an aggressive child who generally behaves in an unskilled, unfriendly manner (Bierman, 1986). Further, it is important that interpersonal aggression be distinguished from impulsive, distractible, hyperactive behavior. This distinction has often been overlooked, both within and outside the long-term-risk area. Research within the past decade suggests that subgroups of children who show one or both of these problems can be reliably identified (e.g., Pelham & Bender, 1982; Prinz, Connor, & Wilson, 1981). These groups of children will probably follow differing developmental-adaptational trajectories.

Apart from aggression and shy or withdrawn behavior, many behavioral tendencies play a role in peer rejection and, hence, may prove to be predictive of later personal maladjustment. One set of such behaviors has just been suggested — impulsive, hyperactive behaviors. Other potential sets include bossy and demanding behaviors and behaviors indicative of general untrustworthiness (i.e., cheating, lying, breaking confidences, and stealing). Although this list could easily be expanded on an ad hoc basis, the challenge lies in selecting behaviors for future research through some systematic means. Asher and Williams (1987) offered a heuristic framework for considering the types of positive and negative behaviors that lead to peer acceptance and rejection. They suggested that children and probably adults attend to a set of implicit core questions as they choose their friends and associates. These core questions are (a) Is this child fun to be with? (b) Is this child trustworthy? (c) Do we influence each other in ways I like? (d) Does this child facilitate and not undermine my goals? (e) Is this child similar to me? (f) Does this child make me feel good about myself? Asher and Williams hypothesized that children implicitly evaluate another child's behavior in relation to these core questions. Behaviors that lead others to answer no to one or more of these implicit core questions will decrease the likelihood of a child's acceptance or increase the likelihood of a child's rejection. For example, aggression is a strong correlate of rejection because it leads other children to conclude that the child is not fun to be with (Question a), is not trustworthy (Question b), and attempts to have influence in unacceptable ways (Question c).

Thinking about core relationship questions might serve as a point of departure for considering behaviors to include in long-term-adjustment research. For example, the question "Is this child fun to be with?" suggests that in addition to aggressiveness, a child's sense of humor, resourcefulness, and bossiness should be assessed. With respect to bossiness, it is noteworthy that Watt and his co-workers (Lewine, Watt, Prentky & Fryer, 1978, 1980; Watt, 1978; Watt & Lubensky, 1976; Watt, Stolorow, Lubensky, & McClelland, 1970) conducted a number of careful comparisons of the school records of preschizophrenic and control children and reported that the comments of teachers in the annual reports of preschizophrenics suggested that they were more disagreeable than control subjects.

Similarly, the question "Is this child trustworthy?" suggests that a child's honesty, reliability, and loyalty would be important to assess in long-term-risk projects. Support for this suggestion comes from West and Farrington (1973), who found that the boys considered the most dishonest by their peers were more likely to become delinquent.

"Do we influence each other in ways I like?" suggests the utility of assessments of cooperation, responsivity, dominance, and rigidity. Cooperativeness is also suggested by the question "Does this child facilitate and not undermine my goals?", as are such behaviors as helpfulness, disruptiveness, and impulsiveness. The question "Is this child similar to me?" suggests the relevance of respect for peer and adult conventions. Finally, the question "Does this child make me feel good about myself?" suggests such qualities as supportiveness and responsivity.

This framework and the accompanying behaviors are meant to be illustrative. The primary point here is that the process of considering the behaviors to include in future research should be systematic, not ad hoc. Another point suggested by the framework is that in addition to studying negative behaviors, one should pay attention to a broad range of positive social skills.

Nature of the child's social relationships

The second assessment objective is to compile a more complete mosaic of the child's social relationships. This involves a more differentiated assessment of classroom relationships and necessitates moving outside the boundaries of the classroom to assess other social relationships.

Rejected versus neglected status. In considering the assessment and conceptualization of peer-relationships difficulties, we noted the distinction between children who are actively disliked by peers (i.e., rejected children) and children who are not liked but not especially disliked either (i.e., neglected children). Because most of the risk literature predates concern for this distinction, actual attempts to examine the possible long-term significance of this distinction have been extremely rare — the single exception being Kupersmidt's (1983) study. Recall that Kupersmidt compared rejected and neglected children with each other and with children with average or high peer acceptance and found that rejected, not neglected, children were the most at risk for grade retention, dropping out, and delinquency. Clearly, more studies in which children of different ages are sub-classified into different status groups are needed for studying the long-term outcomes associated with various types of low peer status. Indeed, it may even be possible for researchers to reanalyze existing data sets that contain both positive and negative nomination data (e.g., Havighurst *et al.*, 1962; M. Roff *et al.*, 1972) by making use of this approach.[7]

Acceptance versus friendship. A current distinction in the peer-relationships literature (Asher & Hymel, 1981; Furman & Robbins, 1985) that has not received attention in past risk research but may be important for understanding differences in eventual adjustment is the distinction between getting along well in one's peer group (i.e., peer acceptance) and forming close emotional ties to one or a few age-mates (i.e., having friends). It is possible to have no friends and yet be generally well accepted by the peer group and, conversely, to maintain friendships despite generally low peer-group regard.

The skills involved in getting along well in a group and those involved in forming and maintaining a close friendship may not entirely overlap (Berndt, 1984; Parker, 1987), nor should one assume that group acceptance and having a friendship play the same roles in children's lives. Furman and Robbins (1985) cogently argued that friendships serve certain needs in children's lives (e.g., affection, intimacy, reliable alliance, and enhancement of worth), whereas group acceptance serves others (e.g., providing a sense of inclusion). Following this line of reasoning, we might expect the long-term implications of difficulties in each domain to be different.

Extraclassroom friendships. At all ages but especially as children get older they form friendships beyond the boundaries of their classrooms (Epstein, 1986). Students may have friends in other classes whom they see only at lunchtime or recess or during extracurricular activities. They may have friends in their neighborhood whom they see only after school or on weekends or vacations, or they may have friends in their church, scouting organization, or soccer team. Because acceptance is typically assessed only among classmates, it is possible that some children identified as unpopular do, in fact, have friends in other settings. Such children would not be expected to show the same elevated incidence of later disorder as children with low acceptance in all settings. They would, in effect, be "six-hour unpopular children" — analogous to "six-hour retarded children" (Hobbs, 1975), who function poorly in academic settings but do satisfactory at home or in the community. From a psychometric standpoint, the inclusion of these "pseudorejected" children in the prediction equation is of concern because it may depress the level of prediction that would otherwise be possible. Although longitudinal evidence is lacking, Schmuck (1966) found that unpopular children who also have a few friends outside the classroom show poorer concurrent academic adjustment than unpopular children with more nonclass friends.

Nonpeer social relationships. The quality of a child's extraclassroom, nonpeer relationships also may play a role in whether low peer acceptance is related to later maladjustment. Children's parents, siblings, grandparents, and other family members may serve as emotional buffers when school-peer relationships are not going well (Cohn, Lohrmann, & Patterson, 1985; Furman & Buhrmester, 1985). Even pets may play some role in providing emotional support (Bryant, 1985). In addition to providing emotional support, these other relationships provide alternative sources for the acquisition of social skills. By attending to the child's relationships with these various individuals, one should be able to reduce the number of false positive errors of prediction without concomitantly increasing the number of false negative errors.

Integrating sociometric and behavioral assessment

We began this review by making a distinction between the question "Is the child liked?" and the question "What is the child like?" Answering these questions involves sociometric and behavioral assessment, respectively. Unfortunately, within the risk literature, most studies contain information on sociometric status or behavioral style but rarely both. Even when both types of information are collected, the data are rarely used to evaluate interactions between status and behavioral effects or to learn whether one effect remains when the other is statistically controlled.

Several researchers have recently called for attention to sub-groups of peer-rejected children, subgroups that would be defined on the basis of behavioral style (Bierman, 1986; Coie & Koeppl, in press; Rubin *et al.*, in press). For example, Coie and Koeppl argued that rejected children who are aggressive or disruptive may be less responsive than other subgroups to existing intervention approaches.

Rubin *et al.* (in press) also called for attention to subgroups of rejected children, especially withdrawn rejected children. Rubin *et al.* (in press) hypothesized that these children may be at particular risk for internalizing problems (Achenbach & Edelbrock, 1981), such as low self-esteem, loneliness, or depression. Rubin *et al.'s* (in press) view was that focusing on particular subgroups of rejected children leads to more plausible conceptual links between particular peer-relationship problems in childhood and particular adjustment difficulties in adulthood.

Two recent studies of children's loneliness (Parkhurst & Asher, 1987; Williams & Asher, 1987) lend support to the idea of focusing on subgroups of rejected children. Rejected children who were described by peers as "easy to push around" (Parkhurst & Asher, 1987) or as "timid and hangs back" (Williams & Asher, 1987) were particularly lonely, compared both with average-status children and with aggressive-rejected children. These findings have implications for the types of adjustment outcomes that different rejected subgroups might experience. Certainly, the results are consistent with the hypothesis that withdrawn-rejected children are at risk for internalizing problems (Rubin *et al.*, in press). The data also show the potential predictive power that may result from combining sociometric and behavioral information.

The child's eventual adult adjustment

We also recommend that future risk research aim for a more comprehensive portrait of the child's later life functioning. The vast majority of existing research is focused on dropping out, juvenile or adult criminality, or adult psychopathology because problems in any of these areas are significant and because these three areas are the focus of considerable public, private, and institutional concern. But there are other important outcomes that might be profitably considered in the future. We have already discussed how attention to internalizing disorders — such as depression, psychosomatic illness, or low self-esteem — may help bring the predictability of psychopathological outcomes closer to the level now possible for dropping out and criminality. And we have noted that examination of such outcomes might also improve the level of predictability possible from shyness/withdrawal. We add here three more adjustment outcomes worthy of greater attention in the risk literature.

The first is marital adjustment. Insofar as poor childhood peer relationships result from social skills deficits and insofar as these deficits persist, it is plausible that children with peer-relationships problems will be less likely than other children to marry or, if married, more likely to experience repeated difficulties and repeated divorce. There is currently some isolated evidence to support this supposition (Havighurst *et al.*, 1962; Robins, 1966).

Another potentially significant outcome is occupational adjustment. It is not difficult to imagine that children who have problems getting along with classmates might later have problems getting along with co-workers and supervisors. Thus, we might expect low-accepted children to fare relatively poorly in later interviews for jobs, to be less satisfied with their jobs, and to evidence poorer performance and attendance records. Again, some isolated evidence currently supports this view (Havighurst *et al.*, 1962; Janes *et al.*, 1979; Robins, 1966).

The potential link between early low acceptance and later suicidal behavior also deserves attention. Much of the literature on child or adult suicide emphasizes the contributing role of interpersonal difficulties or social isolation (e.g., Anderson, 1981; Grob, Klien, & Eisen, 1983; Haim, 1974; Jacobs, 1971; Schaffer & Fisher, 1981; Stengel, 1974; Trout, 1980). Despite oft-made claims, however, the question of whether there is a link between early peer-relationship difficulties and later suicidal behavior is far from settled. The existing literature is based on interviews with suicide attempters (e.g., Schrut, 1968; Topal & Reznikoff, 1982) or, in the case of completed suicide, on interviews with relatives of the victim (e.g., *Schaffer*, 1974), on victims' suicide notes (Jacobs, 1971), or on "psychological autopsies" done by coroners or caseworkers (e.g., Jan-Tausch, cited in Trout, 1980). The available literature is entirely retrospective and rarely quantitative. Whether measures of acceptance and behavior obtained in childhood bear any follow-back or follow-up relation to suicidal behavior later in life remains to be seen.

Finally, it is worth noting that proponents of the risk hypothesis have rarely made strong claims for predictability of specific outcomes. Instead, they have tended to assert that problematic peer relationships represent an important nonspecific predictor of later disorder (e.g., Kohlberg *et al.*, 1972). This suggests two further possibilities. First, perhaps we should be asking how accurately poor peer relationships foretell disturbance of any type, not just specific negative outcomes. Very few studies have examined this question directly or even permitted such a determination from the data presented. Second, perhaps we should ask whether peer-relationship difficulties in childhood are most predictive of multiple negative outcomes; that is, they may be most predictive of that subset of later disordered individuals who experience disorder in two or more areas of personal adjustment (e.g., academic, societal, or psychiatric). Kupersmidt's (1983) finding that sociometrically rejected children had more cumulative problems (dropping out, grade retention, truancy and juvenile court contacts) than sociometrically average, neglected, and popular children is consistent with this possibility, although the alternative explanation is that her cumulative problems index is a more reliable index of problems than is any single item that goes into the variable.

Developmental considerations

The literature on friendship expectations (e.g., Berndt, 1986; Bigelow, 1977; Furman & Bierman, 1984; Reisman & Shorr, 1978) indicates that the qualities that children value in a peer change with age. For example, issues of trustworthiness do not become salient until preadolescence; therefore, measures of honesty and dishonesty might not predict later outcomes as well in early childhood as they do later on. Similarly, Gottman and Mettetal (1987) recently argued that with age, the significant context for social interaction with age-mates changes in accordance with the salient developmental goals of the period. In their view, the salient social context in early childhood is coordinated, dyadic play, because it is this context that offers the most opportunities for emotional and cognitive growth. Later, in middle childhood, the most significant opportunities for affective and cognitive growth take place in the context of interaction within the larger same-sex peer group. Building on Gottman and Mettetal's formulation, one could argue that a behavioral style that disrupts dyadic interaction might become predictive of later maladjustment at an earlier age than would a behavioral style that interferes with a child's ability to get along in a larger group of peers. Likewise, Rubin (1985) argued that certain behavioral orientations become problematic for children only over time. Writing about withdrawn, solitary behavior, Rubin (1985) commented,

> In the early years, solitary activity is quite normal; consequently there is little reason for solitary players to be singled out as displaying behaviors deviant from age-group play norms. However, in the middle years of childhood, individuals who continue to choose to remain alone in situations that strongly "pull for" social interaction, may become increasingly noteworthy; consequently, their deviance from social play norms may result in the establishment of negative peer reputations and peer rejection. (p. 128)

These possibilities illustrate that the relation between specific behavioral characteristics and later outcomes may vary with age. Risk researchers have selected their samples on the basis of accessibility and convenience, without offering strong conceptual arguments for choosing to study one age over another. Indeed, except for guidance clinic studies, almost all studies have involved populations of fifth or sixth graders. Researchers who have used guidance clinic samples have had populations with broad age ranges but have not been particularly concerned with developmental trends.

In addition, researchers should more systematically examine the separate and combined effects of age of peer rejection and length of time of peer rejection on subsequent adjustment. The questions to be addressed include the following: At what point in development does low acceptance become predictive of later disorder? Is predictability better at some ages as opposed to others or for different behaviors at different ages? Addressing these questions will require, among other things, that assessment of peer acceptance be done at much younger ages than has been typical. Historically, one obstacle to very early assessment of peer acceptance was the poor reliability of sociometric-nomination measures with very young children. This should no longer be an obstacle, given the recent development and standardization of reliable sociometric rating scales (Asher, Singleton, Tinsley, & Hymel, 1979) and paired comparison techniques (A. S. Cohen & Van Tassel, 1978; Vaughn & Waters, 1981) for use with preschoolers.

The child's perspective

The child's perceptions and beliefs about his or her peer relationships have been ignored in the risk literature. The child's perspective may be useful in helping researchers understand the links between peer relationships and later adjustment and predict which children will develop problems (Hymel & Franke, 1985). Children's perceptions of others' views toward them are often not veridical (Ausubel, 1955; Goslin, 1962). Intuitively, we might expect children who are cognizant of their negative peer adjustment to show a pattern of later adjustment different from that of children who are equally unpopular but unaware of it. (For relevant data, see Schmuck, 1966.)

Important, too, is the child's degree of concern for peer-group acceptance. As a rule, throughout middle childhood, children express considerable concern for getting along with classmates and being included in group activities and group discussion (Buhrmester, 1982; Sebald, 1981). At the same time, however, they also express concern over doing well academically, their family relationships, their health and safety, and their future (Buhrmester, 1982). Different children weigh these concerns differently. Peer rejection must be an emotional experience qualitatively different for the low-accepted child who cares about acceptance from what it is for the low-accepted child who is not especially concerned with being accepted. For the child concerned with acceptance, the experience of rejection could have opposite effects. On one hand, it may have immediate deleterious effects on social cognition, self-image, and self-esteem that negatively affect long-term adjustment. On the other hand, concerns about acceptance could have a salutary effect on long-term adjustment by motivating action to avoid rejection in the future. Perhaps the long-term adjustment of low-accepted children who are motivated to improve their status is as adequate as that of children who are generally well accepted in the first place. These alternative possibilities suggest that the role of children's perspectives on their own rejection could prove to be complex but certainly informative.

Process-oriented research

Researchers who have assumed causal links between early peer relationships and later adjustment have concentrated primarily on documenting the degree of predictability and all but overlooked attention to the mechanisms through which low acceptance brings about its hypothesized effects. Consider the school-dropout literature. A consistent finding is that children who are poorly accepted by their peers are more likely to drop out. Yet authors who have reported these findings have rarely offered an explanation of why this relation holds. One possibility is that the experience of being unpopular actually leads children to do poorly academically and, therefore, to drop out. Because students often study together for tests, collaborate on homework, and informally tutor one another, unpopular students may miss important opportunities to learn school material and may suffer academically. Furthermore, because school is likely to be a stressful experience for children who are rejected, they may not be as able to concentrate on their reading material and lectures. An alternate possibility is that for low-accepted children, schools are aversive, with few of the social rewards that constitute much of school's holding power for adolescents. To go to school each day without looking forward to seeing anyone or participating in group activities might give sufficient cause for dropping out, regardless of academic achievement. Unless researchers explicitly attend to process in their assessments, designs, and analyses, there is little basis for choosing among such post hoc explanations as these and little hope of developing such explanations further.

Experimental tests of the risk hypothesis

Follow-back and follow-up methodologies, even when ideally executed, are correlational, making it impossible to confidently infer causal relations between peer-relationship disturbances and later maladjustment. As a final recommendation, we suggest that such relations should be tested experimentally by intervening with children with peer-relationship problems and learning whether improvement in peer adjustment leads to long-term gains in personal adjustment. Such tests are now possible because of advances in intervention methods with children who are poorly accepted by their peers. Several studies have found that cognitively based social skills training programs can produce significant gains in the sociometric status of children who are among the least liked children in their classroom. (See Ladd & Asher, 1985, for a recent review.) Indeed, in the only study in which long-term follow-up data were gathered, Oden and Asher (1977) found that teaching children social interaction concepts (participation, communication, cooperation, and validation-support) led to gains in acceptance that were not only maintained but increased at a 1-year follow-up. If poor peer relationships place children at risk for long-term difficulties, children for whom intervention is successful should experience fewer subsequent adjustment difficulties than low-accepted children not included in the intervention effort.

The challenge ahead

From the preceding discussion, it is obvious that future research into the at-risk hypothesis will differ from past research in its underlying rationale and in its approach to data collection and analysis. The generation of a new, coherent explanation of the relation between poor peer relationships in childhood and later maladjustment is a particularly demanding challenge, one that sits at the interface of developmental and clinical psychology and demands a productive interplay between empirical research and theory construction. The available data reviewed in this paper clearly provide a foundation for taking this ambitious step.

Acknowledgement

The research and writing of this article was supported by a university fellowship from the University of Illinois to the first author, by National Institute of Child Health and Human Development Research Grant HD05951 to the second author, and by National Institute of Child Health and Human Development Training Grant HD07205.

This article benefited greatly from our lengthy and thought-provoking discussions with Kenneth A. Dodge. We would also like to acknowledge Gary W. Ladd, Gladys A. Williams, and three anonymous reviewers for their very helpful comments.

Notes

1. The rating-scale sociometric measure (e.g., Asher, Singleton, Tinsley, & Hymel, 1979; Roistacher, 1974; Semler, 1960), although widely used in recent research on peer relations (see Asher & Hymel, 1981; Hymel & Rubin, 1985), has not been used at all in the risk literature. For this measure, children are provided with a list of classmates' names and are asked to indicate how much they like or would like to play with or work with each person. A Likert-like scale, usually ranging from *don't like to* (1) to *like to a lot* (5), is provided. A

child's acceptance score consists of his or her average received rating. Rating scales offer certain distinct advantages over nomination measures. First, rating scales provide an indication of a child's attitude toward every other child rather than just toward those peers he or she nominates. As a result, a child's acceptance status is based on a considerably larger number of data points than is status based on nominations alone. An additional advantage to rating scales over nomination measures is that they exhibit relatively higher test–retest stability, especially with very young children.

2. Not included in this review are studies with retrospective interview designs. Such studies, like follow-back studies, begin with normal and deviant adults and attempt to gain an understanding of childhood functioning. Unlike follow-back studies, however, retrospective studies do not make use of acceptance or behavioral data collected when the subject was a child. Instead, they rely on the recollections of the subject or his or her close associates. The inherent unreliability of retrospective data are well documented (see Garmezy, 1974; Kohlberg, LaCross, & Ricks, 1972; Yarrow, Campbell, & Burton, 1970). Therefore, any portrait of childhood functioning based wholly or partly on retrospective accounts is likely to be inaccurate, if not outright misleading.

3. We are indebted to Kenneth A. Dodge for calling our attention to the relevance of the sensitivity and specificity constructs.

4. Interestingly, because RIOC is a measure of relative predictive accuracy and is independent of the base rate, it is possible for RIOC accuracy to be very high while specificity remains low. (See, e.g., the Janes, Hesselbrock, Myers, & Penniman, 1979, entry in Table 4.) Likewise, because RIOC is also independent of the selection ratio, it is possible for RIOC to be high while sensitivity is low. The converse is not true, however. If either sensitivity or specifically is high or if both are high, RIOC cannot be low. The three indexes are related but not wholly redundant indexes of predictive accuracy.

5. Clearly, other types of behavioral orientations toward peers are important to study. Virtually all the existing research, however, has been focused on aggression or shyness/withdrawal. See the last section of this article for recommendations on other behavioral dimensions to study.

6. Looking ahead, we suggest that when using teacher measures, researchers would do well to explicitly train teachers to observe children's behavioral style to avoid the ambiguity that currently surrounds the validity of teacher ratings (Coie, Dodge, & Kupersmidt, in press). The current practice of having teachers rate behavior without much preparation or time for focused observations seems unnecessarily handicapping.

7. A concern that is sometimes raised regarding the assessment of neglected and rejected status is the use of negative (dislike) nominations with some populations of children. Available data suggest that asking children to nominate children whom they dislike does not pose ethical problems (see Havyren & Hymel, 1983). Nonetheless, alternative multi-dimensional classification systems that do not require negative nominations are available (Asher & Dodge, 1986) and might be exploited for this purpose.

References

Achenbach, T.M. (1982) *Developmental psychopathology* (2nd ed.). New York: Wiley.

Achenbach, T.M., & Edelbrock, C.S. (1981) 'Behavioral problems and competencies reported by parents of normal and disturbed children aged four through sixteen'. *Monographs of the Society for Research in Child Development*, 46 (1, Serial No. 188).

Amble, B.R. (1967)'Teacher evaluations of student behavior and school dropouts'. *Journal of Educational Research*, 60, 53-58.

American Psychiatric Association. (1980) *Diagnostic and statistical manual of mental disorders* (3rd ed.). Washington, DC: Author.

Anderson, D.R. (1981) 'Diagnosis and prediction of suicidal risk among adolescents'. In C.F. Wells & I.R. Stuart (Eds.), *Self-destructive behavior in children and adolescents* (pp.45-61). New York: Van Nostrand Reinhold.

Asarnow, J.R. (1982, August) *Children with peer problems: Sequential and non-sequential analysis of behavior*. Paper presented at the annual convention of the American Psychological Association, Washington, DC.

Asher, S.R., & Dodge, K.A. (1986) 'Identifying children who are rejected by their peers'. *Developmental Psychology*, 22, 444-449.

Asher, S.R., & Hymel, S. (1981) 'Children's social competence in peer relations: Sociometric and behavioral assessment'. In J.D. Wine & M.D. Smye (Eds.), *Social competence* (pp. 125-157). New York: Guilford.

Asher, S.R., & Renshaw, P.D. (1981) 'Children without friends: Social knowledge and social-skill training'. In S.R. Asher & J.M. Gottman (Eds.), *The development of children's friendships* (pp.273-296). New York: Cambridge University Press.

Asher, S.R., Singleton, L., Tinsley, B.R., & Hymel, S. (1979) 'A reliable sociometric measure for preschool children'. *Developmental Psychology*, 15, 443-444.

Asher, S.R., & Wheeler, V.A. (1985) 'Children's loneliness: A comparison of rejected and neglected peer status'. *Journal of Consulting and Clinical Psychology*, 53, 500-505.

Asher, S.R., & Williams, G.A. (1987) 'Helping children without friends in home and school contexts'. In *Children's social development: Information for teachers and parents* (pp. 1-26). Urbana, IL: ERIC Clearinghouse on Elementary and Early Childhood Education.

Ausubel, D.P. (1955) 'Socioempathy as a function of sociometric status in an adolescent group'. *Human Relations*, 8, 75-84.

Barclay, J.R. (1966) 'Sociometric choices and teacher ratings as predictors of school dropout'. *Journal of Social Psychology*, 4, 40-45.

Barthell, C.N., & Holmes, D.S. (1968) 'High school yearbooks: A non-reactive measure of social isolation in graduates who later became schizophrenic'. *Journal of Abnormal Psychology*, 73, 313-316.

Bates, E. (1975) 'Peer relations and the acquisition of language'. In M. Lewis & L. Rosenblum (Eds.), *Friendships and peer relations* (pp. 259-292). New York: Wiley.

Berndt, T.J. (1984) 'Sociometric, social-cognitive, and behavioral measures for the study of friendship and popularity'. In T. Field, J.L. Roopnarine, & M. Segal (Eds.), *Friendships in normal and handicapped children* (pp. 31 -52). Norwood, NJ: Ablex.

Berndt, T.J. (1986) 'Children's comments about their friendships'. In M. Perlmutter (Ed.), *Cognitive perspectives on children's social and behavioral development* (pp. 189-212). Hillsdale, NJ: Erlbaum.

Berndt, T.J., McCartney, K.A., Caparulo, B.K., & Moore, A.M. (1983-1984) 'The effects of group discussions on children's moral decisions'. *Social Cognition*, 2, 343-360.

Berston, H.M. (1960) 'The school dropout problem'. *Clearing House* , 35, 207-210.

Bierman, K.L. (1986) 'The relation between social aggression and peer rejection in middle childhood'. In R. J. Prinz (Ed.), *Advances in behavioral assessment of children and families* (Vol. 2, pp. 151-178). Greenwich, CT: JAI Press.

Bigelow, B.J. (1977) 'Children's friendship expectations: A cognitive developmental study'. *Child Development*, 48, 246-253.

Birren, J.C. (1944) 'Psychological examinations of children who later became psychotic'. *Journal of Abnormal and Social Psychology*, 39, 84-96.

Bower, E.M., & Lambert, N.M. (1961) *A process for in-school screening of emotionally handicapped children*. Princeton, NJ: Educational Testing Service.

Bower, E.M., Shellhammer, T.A, & Daily, J.M. (1960) 'School characteristics of male adolescents who later become schizophrenic'. *American Journal of Orthopsychiatry*, 30, 712-729.

Bowman, D.H., & Matthews, C.V. (1960) *Motivations of youth for leaving school* (Project No. 200). Washington, DC: U.S. Office of Education Cooperative Research Program.

Bryant, B.K. (1985)'The neighborhood walk: Sources of support in middle childhood'. *Monographs of the Society for Research in Child Development*, 50 (3, Serial No. 210).

Buhrmester, D. (1982) *Children's Concerns Inventory*. Unpublished manuscript, University of California, Los Angeles.

Cass, L.K., & Thomas, C.B. (1979) *Childhood pathology and later adjustment; The question of prediction*. New York: Wiley.

Cloward, R.A., & Ohlin, L.E. (1961) *Delinquency and opportunity*. London: Routledge.

Cohen, A.K. (1955) *Delinquent boys: The culture of the gang*. New York: Free Press of Glencoe.

Cohen, A.S., & Van Tassel, E. (1978) 'A paired-comparison sociometric test for preschool groups'. *Applied Psychological Measurement*, 2, 31-41.

Cohen, E. (1982, May) *The relationship among measures of social competence in children*. Paper presented at the annual meetings of the Western Psychological Association, Sacramento, CA.

Cohn, D.A., Lohrmann, B.C., & Patterson, C.J. (1985, April) *Social networks and loneliness in children*. Paper presented at the biennial meetings of the Society for Research in Child Development, Toronto, Ontario, Canada.

Coie, J.D., & Dodge, K.A. (1983) 'Continuities and changes in children's social status: A five-year longitudinal study'. *Merrill-Palmer Quarterly*, 29, 261-282.

Coie, J.D., Dodge, K.A., & Coppotelli, H. (1982) 'Dimensions and types of social status: A cross-age perspective'. *Developmental Psychology*, 18, 557-570.

Coie, J.D., Dodge, K.A., & Kupersmidt, J. (in press) 'Peer group behavior and social status'. In S.R. Asher & J.D. Coie (Eds.), *Peer rejection in childhood*. New York: Cambridge University Press.

Coie, J.D., & Koeppl, G.K. (in press) 'Adapting intervention to the problems of aggressive and disruptive rejected children'. In S. R. Asher & J. D. Coie (Eds.), *Peer rejection in childhood*. New York: Cambridge University Press.

Coie, J.D., & Kupersmidt, J.B. (1983) 'A behavioral analysis of emerging social status in boys' groups'. *Child Development*, 54, 1400-1416.

Combs, M.L., & Slaby, D.A. (1977) 'Social skills training with children'. In B.B. Lahey & A.E. Kazdin (Eds.), *Advances in clinical child psychology* (Vol, 1, pp. 161-201). New York: Plenum Press.

Conger, J.C., & Keane, S.P. (1981) 'Social skills intervention in the treatment of isolated or withdrawn children'. *Psychological Bulletin*, 90, 478-495.

Conger, J.J., & Miller, W.C. (1966) *Personality, social class, and delinquency*. New York: Wiley.

Cowen, E.L., Pederson, A., Babijian, H., Izzo, L.D., & Trost, M.A. (1973) 'Long-term follow-up of early detected vulnerable children'. *Journal of Consulting and Clinical Psychology*, 41, 438-446.

Craig, M.M., & Glick, S.J. (1963) 'Ten years experience with the Glueck Social Prediction Table'. *Crime and Delinquency*, 9, 249-261.

Damon, W. (1977) 'The social world of the child'. San Francisco: Jossey-Bass.

de Apodaca, R.F., & Cowen, E.L. (1982) 'A comparative study of the self-esteem, sociometric status, and insight of referred and nonreferred school children'. *Psychology in the Schools*, 19, 394-401.

Denzin, N.K. (1977) *Childhood socialization*. San Francisco: Jossey Bass.

Dodge, K.A. (1983) 'Behavioral antecedents of peer social status'. *Child Development*, 54, 1386-1389.

Dodge, K.A., Coie, J.D., & Brakke, N.D. (1982) 'Behavior patterns of socially rejected and neglected preadolescents: The roles of social approach and aggression'. *Journal of Abnormal Child Psychology*, 10, 389-409.

Dodge, K.A., & Feldman, E. (in press) 'Issues in social cognition and sociometric status'. In S.R. Asher & J.D. Coie (Eds.), *Peer rejection in childhood*. New York: Cambridge University Press.

Dodge, K.A., Schlundt, D.C., Schocken, I., & Delugach, J.D. (1983) 'Social competence and children's sociometric status: The role of peer group entry strategies'. *Merrill-Palmer Quarterly*, 29, 309-336.

Duck, S. (1983) *Friends, for life: The psychology of close relationships*. New York: St. Martin's Press.

Elliott, D.S., & Voss, H.L. (1974) *Delinquency and dropout*. Lexington, MA: Lexington Books.

Ensminger, M.C., Kellam, S.G., & Rubin, B.R. (1983) 'School and family origins of delinquency: Comparisons by sex'. In K.T. Van Dusen & S. A. Mednick (Eds.), *Prospective studies of crime and delinquency* (pp.73-97). Hingham, MA: Kluwer-Nijhoff.

Epstein, J.L. (1986) 'Choice of friends over the life-span: Developmental and environmental influences'. In E.C. Mueller & C.R. Cooper (Eds.), *Process and outcome in peer relationships* (pp. 129-160). New York: Academic Press.

Evans, I.M., & Wilson, F. (1982) 'The reliability of target behavior selection in behavioral assessment'. *Behavioral Assessment*, 5, 15-32.

Fagot, B.I. (1977) 'Consequences of moderate cross-gender behavior in preschool children'. *Child Development*, 48, 902-907.

Farrington, D.P. (1973) 'Self-reports of delinquent behavior: Predictive and stable?' *Journal of Criminal Law and Criminology*, 64. 99-110.

Farrington, D.P. (1978) 'The family background of aggressive youths'. In L. Hersov, M. Berger, & D. Schaffer (Eds.), *Aggression and antisocial behavior in childhood and adolescence*. Oxford, England: Pergamon.

Farrington, D.P. (1979) 'Longitudinal research on crime and delinquency'. In N. Morris & M. Toney (Eds.), *Criminal justice: An annual review of research* (Vol. 1, pp. 171-200). Chicago: University of Chicago Press.

Feldhusen, J.F., Thurston, J.R., & Benning, J.J. (1971) 'Aggressive classroom behavior and school achievement'. *Journal of Special Education*, 4, 431-439.

Feldhusen, J.F., Thurston, J.R., & Benning, J.J. (1973) 'A longitudinal study of delinquency and other aspects of children's behavior'. *International Journal of Criminology and Penology*, 1, 341-351.

Fish, B. (1971) 'Contributions of developmental research to a theory of schizophrenia'. In J. Hellmuth (Ed.), *Exceptional infant: Studies in abnormalities* (Vol. 2, pp. 473-482). New York: Brunner/Mazel.

Fitch, S.K. (1985) *The science of child development*. Homewood, IL: Dorsey Press.

Flavell, J.H. (1977) *Cognitive development*. Englewood Cliffs, NJ: Prentice-Hall.

Flemming, D., & Ricks, D. F. (1970) 'Emotions of children before schizophrenia and before character disorder'. In M. Roff & D.F. Ricks (Eds.), *Life history research in psychopathology* (Vol. 1, pp. 240-264). Minneapolis: University of Minnesota Press.

Forness, S.R., Guthrie, D., & Hall, R.J. (1976) 'Follow-up of high risk children identified in kindergarten through direct classroom observation'. *Psychology in the Schools*, 13, 45-49.

Foster, S.L., & Ritchey, W.L. (1979) 'Issues in the assessment of social competence in children'. *Journal of Applied Behavioral Analysis*, 12, 625-638.

Frazee, H.E. (1953) 'Children who later became schizophrenic'. *Smith College Studies in Social Work*, 23, 125-149.

Friedlander, D. (1945) 'Personality development of twenty-seven children who later became psychotic'. *Journal of Abnormal Social Psychology*, 40, 330-335.

Furman, W., & Bierman, K.L. (1984) 'Children's conceptions of friendship: A multimethod study of developmental changes'. *Developmental Psychology*, 20, 925-931.

Furman, W., & Buhrmester, D. (1985) 'Children's perceptions of the qualities of sibling relationships'. *Child Development*, 56, 448-461.

Furman, W., & Robbins, P. (1985) 'What's the point: Issues in the selection of treatment objectives'. In B.H. Schneider, K.H. Rubin, & J.E. Ledingham (Eds.), *Children's peer relations: Issues in assessment and intervention* (pp.41-56). New York: Springer-Verlag.

Garmezy, N. (1974) 'Children at risk: The search for antecedents of schizophrenia: Part 1. Conceptual models and research methods'. *Schizophrenia Bulletin*, 1, 14-89.

Garmezy, N., & Devine, V.T. (1977) 'Longitudinal versus cross-sectional research in the study of children at risk for psychopathology'. In J.S. Strauss, H. Babigian, & M. Roff (Eds.), *The origins and course of psychopathology* (pp.193-222). New York: Plenum Press.

Goldman, J.A., Corsini, D.A., & de Urioste, R. (1980) 'Implications of positive and negative sociometric status for assessing the social competence of young children'. *Journal of Applied Developmental Psychology*, 1, 209-220.

Goslin, D.A. (1962) 'Accuracy of self-perception and social acceptance'. *Sociometry*, 25, 283-296.

Gottman, J.M. (1977) 'Toward a definition of social isolation in children'. *Child Development*, 48, 513-517.

Gottman, J.M., & Mettetal, G. (1987) 'Speculations about social and affective development: Friendship and acquaintanceship through adolescence'. In J.M. Gottman & J.G. Parker (Eds.), *Conversations of friends: Speculations on affective development* (pp. 192-237). New York: Cambridge University Press.

Green, K.D., Forehand, R., Beck, S.J., & Vosk, B. (1980) 'An assessment of the relationship among measures of children's social competence and children's academic achievement'. *Child Development*, 51, 1149-1156.

Green, K.D., Vosk, R., Forehand, R., & Beck, S.J. (1981) 'An examination of the differences among sociometrically identified, accepted, rejected, and neglected children'. *Child Study Journal*, 11, 117-124.

Grob, M.L., Klien, A.A., & Eisen, S.U. (1983) 'The role of the high school professional in identifying and managing adolescent suicidal behavior'. *Journal of Youth and Adolescence*, 12, 163-173.

Gronlund, N.E. (1959) *Sociometry in the classroom.* New York: Harper.

Gronlund, N.E., & Holmlund, W. S. (1958) 'The value of elementary school sociometric status scores for predicting pupils' adjustment in high school'. *Educational Administration and Supervision*, 44, 225-260.

Haim, A. (1974) *Adolescent suicide.* New York: International Universities Press.

Hall, E., Perlmutter, M., & Lamb, M.E. (1982) *Child psychology today.* New York: Random House.

Hall, G.S. (1904) *Adolescence: Its psychology and its relation to physiology, anthropology, sociology, sex, crime, religion, and education.* New York: Appleton.

Hartup, W.W. (1974) 'Aggression in childhood: Developmental perspectives'. *American Psychologist*, 29, 336-341.

Hartup, W.W. (1978) 'Children and their friends'. In H. McGurk (Ed.), *Issues in childhood social development* (pp. 130-170). London: Methuen.

Hartup, W.W. (1983) 'Peer relations'. In E.M. Hetherington (Ed.), *Handbook of child psychology* (Vol. 4): *Socialization, personality, and social development* (pp. 103-198). New York: Wiley.

Hartup, W.W., Glazer, J.A., & Charlesworth, R. (1967) 'Peer reinforcement and sociometric status'. *Child Development*, 38, 1017-1024

Havighurst, R.J., Bowman, P.H.. Liddle, G.P., Matthews, C.V., & Pierce, J.V. (1962) *Growing up in River City.* New York: Wiley.

Havyren, M., & Hymel, S. (1983) 'Ethical issues in sociometric testing. The impact of sociometric measures on interactive behavior'. *Developmental Psychology*, 20, 844-849.

Hewitt, L.E. & Jenkins, R.L. (1946) *Fundamental patterns of maladjustment: The dynamics of their origins.* Springfield, IL: Charles C Thomas.

Hobbs, N. (Ed.). (1975) *Issues in the classification of children.* San Francisco: Jossey-Bass.

Hops, H. (1982) 'Social skills training for socially withdrawn/isolated children'. In P. Karoly & J. Steffen (Eds.), *Improving children's competence* (Vol. 1, p. 39-102). Lexington, MA: Lexington Books.

Hymel, S. (1983) 'Preschool children's peer relations: Issues in sociometric assessment'. *Merrill-Palmer Quarterly*, 29, 237-260.

Hymel, S., & Franke, S. (1985) 'Children's peer relations: Assessing self-perceptions'. In B.H. Schneider, K.H. Rubin, & J.E. Ledingham (Eds.), *Children's peer relations: Issues in assessment and intervention* (pp. 75-91). New York: Springer-Verlag.

Hymel, S., & Rubin. K.H. (1985) 'Children with peer relationship and social skills problems: Conceptual, methodological, and developmental issues'. In G.J. Whitehurst (Ed.), *Annuals of child development* (Vol. 2, pp. 251-297). Greenwich, CT: JAI Press.

Jacobs, J. (1971) *Adolescent suicide*. New York: Wiley-Interscience.

Janes, C.L., & Hesselbrock, V.M. (1978) 'Problem children's adult adjustment predicted from teachers' ratings'. *American Journal of Orthopsychiatry*, 48, 300-309.

Janes, C.L., Hesselbrock, V.M., Myers, D.G., & Penniman, J.H. (1979) 'Problem boys in young adulthood: Teachers' ratings and twelve-year follow-up'. *Journal of Youth and Adolescence*, 8, 453-472

John, R.S., Mednick, S.A., & Schulsinger, F. (1982) 'Teacher reports as a predictor of schizophrenia and borderline schizophrenia: A Bayesian decision analysis'. *Journal of Abnormal Psychology*, 6, 399-413.

Johnson, D.W. (1980) 'Group processes: Influences of student-student interaction on school outcomes'. In J.H. McMillan (Ed.), *Social psychology of school learning* (pp. 123-168). New York: Academic Press.

Johnson, D.W., & Johnson, R.T. (1981, September) 'Peers: The key to healthy development and socialization'. *Character*, pp. 1-8.

King, C.A., & Young, R.D. (1981) 'Peer popularity and peer communication patterns: Hyperactive versus active but normal boys'. *Journal of Abnormal Child Psychology*, 9, 465-482.

Kirkegaard-Sørensen, L., & Mednick, S.A. (1977) 'A prospective study of predictors of criminality: 4. School behavior'. In S. Mednick & K.O. Christianson (Eds.), *Biosocial bases of criminal behavior* (pp. 255-266). New York: Gardner Press.

Kleck, R.E., & DeJong, W. (1981) 'Adults' estimates of the sociometric status of handicapped and nonhandicapped children'. *Psychological Reports*, 49, 951-954.

Kohlberg, L., LaCross, I., Ricks, D. (1972) 'The predictability of adult mental health from childhood behavior'. In B. B. Wolman (Ed.). *Manual of child psychopathology* (pp. 1217- 1284). New York: McGraw-Hill.

Kohn, M., & Clausen, J. (1955) 'Social isolation and schizophrenia'. *American Sociological Review*, 20, 265-273.

Kohn, M., & Rosman, B.L. (1972) 'A social competence scale and symptom checklist for the preschool child: Factor dimensions, their cross-instrument generality, and longitudinal persistence'. *Developmental Psychology*, 6, 430-444.

Kopp, C.B., & Krakow, J.B. (Eds.). (1982) *The child: Development in a social context*. Reading, MA: Addison-Wesley.

Kuhlen, R., & Collister, E.G. (1952) 'Sociometric status of sixth- and ninth-graders who fail to finish high school'. *Educational and Psychological Measurement*, 12, 632-637.

Kupersmidt, J. B. (1983, April) 'Predicting delinquency and academic problems from childhood peer status'. In J. D. Coie (Chair), *Strategies for identifying children at social risk: Longitudinal correlates and consequences*. Symposium conducted at the biennial meeting of the Society for Research in Child Development, Detroit, MI.

Ladd, G.W. (1985) 'Documenting the effects of social skills training with children: Process and outcome assessment'. In B.H. Schneider, K.H. Rubin, & J.E. Ledingham (Eds.), *Children's peer relations: Issues in assessment and intervention* (pp. 243-271). New York: Springer-Verlag.

Ladd, G.W., & Asher, S.R. (1985) 'Social skills training and children's peer relations'. In L. L'Abate & M. Milan (Eds.), *Handbook of social skills training and research* (pp. 219-244). New York: Wiley.

Ladd, G.W., & Mize, J. (1983) 'A cognitive-social learning model of social-skill training'. *Psychological Review*. 90, 127-157.

Ladd, G.W., Price, J.M., & Hart, C.H. (in press) 'Preschooler's behavioral orientation and patterns of peer contact: Predictive of peer status?' In S.R. Asher & J.D. Coie (Eds.), *Peer rejection in childhood*. New York: Cambridge University Press.

La Greca, A.M. (1981) 'Peer acceptance: The correspondence between children's sociometric scores and teacher's ratings of peer interactions'. *Journal of Abnormal Child Psychology*, 9, 167-178.

Lambert, N.A. (1972) 'Intellectual and nonintellectual predictors of high school status'. *Journal of Scholastic Psychology*, 6, 247-259.

Lambert, N.A., & Nicoll, R.C. (1977) 'Conceptual model for nonintellectual behavior and its relationship to early reading achievement'. *Journal of Educational Psychology*, 69, 481-490.

Langlois, J.H., & Stephan, C.W. (1981) 'Beauty and the beast: The role of physical attractiveness in the development of peer relations and social behavior'. In S. Brehm, S. Kassin, & F. Gibbons (Eds.), *Developmental social psychology: Theory and research*. New York: Oxford University Press.

Lavin, D.E. (1965) *The prediction of academic performance*. New York: Sage.

Ledingham, J.E., & Schwartzman, A. (1984) 'A 3-year follow-up of aggressive and withdrawn behavior in childhood: Preliminary findings'. *Journal of Abnormal Child Psychology*, 12, 157-168.

Ledingham, J.E., & Younger, A.J. (1985) 'The influence of evaluator on assessments of children's social skills'. In B.H. Schneider, K.H. Rubin, J.E. Ledingham (Eds.), *Children's peer relations: Issues in assessment and intervention* (pp. 111-124). New York: Springer-Verlag.

Ledingham, J.E., Younger, A.J., Schwartzman, A., & Bergeron, G. (1982) 'Agreement among teacher, peer, and self-rating of children's aggression, withdrawal, and likeability'. *Journal of Abnormal Child Psychology*, 10, 363-372.

Lefkowitz, M.M., Eron, L.D., Walder, L.Q, & Huesmann, L.R. (1977) *Growing up to be violent*. New York: Pergamon Press.

Lerner, R.M., & Lerner, J.V. (1977) 'Effects of age, sex, and physical attractiveness on child-peer relations, academic performance, and elementary school adjustment'. *Developmental Psychology*, 13, 585-590.

Lesser, G.S. (1959) 'The relationship between various forms of aggression and popularity among lower-class children'. *Journal of Educational Psychology,* 50, 20-25.

Lewine, R.J., Watt, N.E., Prentky, R.A., & Fryer, J.H. (1978) 'Childhood behavior in schizophrenia, personality disorder, depression, and neurosis'. *British Journal of Psychiatry*, 132. 347-357.

Lewine, R.J, Watt, N.E., Prentky, R.A., & Fryer, J.H. (1980) 'Childhood social competence in functionally disordered psychiatric patients and normals'. *Journal of Abnormal Psychology*, 89, 132-138.

Lichter, S.O., Rapien, E.B., Siepert, F.M., & Sklansky, M.A. (1962) *The drop-outs*. New York: Free Press.

Liddle, G.P. (1962) 'Psychological factors involved in dropping out of school'. *High School Journal*, 45, 276-280.

Loeber, R. (1982) 'The stability of antisocial and delinquent behavior: A review'. *Child Development*, 53, 1431-1446.

Loeber, R., & Dishion, T. (1983) 'Early predictors of male delinquency: A review'. *Psychological Bulletin*, 94, 68-99.

Magnussen, D., Stattin, H., & Duner, A. (1983) 'Aggression and criminality in a longitudinal perspective'. In K.T. Van Dusen & S.R. Mednick (Eds.), *Prospective studies of crime and delinquency* (pp. 277-301) Hingham, MA: Kluwer-Nijhoff.

Masten, A.S., Morison, P., & Pelligrini, D.S. (1985) 'A revised Class Play method of peer assessment'. *Developmental Psychology*, 21, 523-533.

McGuire, J.M. (1973) 'Aggression and sociometric status with pre-school children'. *Sociometry*, 36, 542-549.

Mead, G.H. (1934) *Mind, self, and society*. Chicago: University of Chicago Press.

Mednick, S.A., & Schulsinger, F. (1970) 'Factors related to breakdown in children at high risk for schizophrenia'. In M. Roff & D.F. Ricks (Eds.), *Life history research in psychopathology* (Vol. 1, pp. 51 -93). Minneapolis: University of Minnesota Press.

Merton, R.K. (1957) *Social theory and social structure*. New York: Free Press of Glencoe.

Michael, C.M., Morris, D.P., & Soroker, E. (1957) 'Follow-up studies of shy, withdrawn children II: Relative incidence of schizophrenia'. *American Journal of Orthopsychiatry*, 27, 331-337.

Michelson, L., Foster, S.L., & Richey, W.L. (1981) 'Social-skills assessment of children'. In B.B. Lahey & A.E. Kazdin (Eds.), *Advances in clinical child psychology* (Vol. 4, pp. 119-165). New York: Plenum Press.

Milich, R., Landau, S., Kilby, G., & Whitten, P. (1982) 'Preschool peer perceptions of the behavior of hyperactive and aggressive children'. *Journal of Abnormal Child Psychology*, 10, 497-510.

Miller, W.B. (1958) 'Lower class culture as a generating milieu of gang delinquency'. *Journal of Social Issues*, 14(3), 5-19.

Mitchell, M., & Rosa, P. (1981) 'Boyhood behavioral problems as a precursor to criminality: A fifteen year follow-up study'. *Journal of Child Psychology and Psychiatry*, 22, 19-33.

Monahan, J. (1982) 'Childhood predictors of adult criminal behavior'. In F.N. Dutile, C.H. Foust, & D.R. Webster (Eds.), *Early childhood intervention and juvenile delinquency* (pp. 11-21). Lexington, MA: Lexington Books.

Moore, D.R., Chamberlain, P., & Mukai, L.H. (1979) 'Children at risk for delinquency: A follow-up comparison of aggressive children and children who steal'. *Journal of Abnormal Child Psychology*, 7, 345-355.

Morris, D.P., Soroker, E., & Burruss, G. (1954) 'Follow-up studies of shy, withdrawn, children — I: Evaluation of later adjustment'. *American Journal of Orthopsychiatry*, 24, 743-754.

Morris, H.H., Escoll, P.J., & Wexler, R. (1956) 'Aggressive behavior disorders of childhood: A follow-up study'. *American Journal of Psychiatry*, 112, 991-997.

Mulligan, G., Douglas, J.W.B., Hammond, W.A., & Tizard, J. (1963) 'Delinquency and symptoms of maladjustment: The findings of a longitudinal study'. *Proceedings of the Royal Society of Medicine*, 56, 183-186.

Muma, J.R. (1968) 'Peer evaluation and academic achievement in performance classes'. *Personnel and Guidance Journal*, 46, 580-585.

Newcomb, A.F., & Bukowski, W.M. (1983) 'Social impact and social preference as determinants of children's peer group status'. *Developmental Psychology*, 19, 856-867.

Oden, S., & Asher, S.R. (1977) 'Coaching children in social skills for friendship making'. *Child Development*, 48, 495-506.

Offer, D.R., & Cross, L.A. (1969) 'Behavioral antecedents of adult schizophrenia'. *Archives of General Psychiatry*, 21, 267-283.

Olweus, D. (1979) 'Stability of aggressive reaction patterns in males: A review'. *Psychological Bulletin*, 86, 852-875.

Parke, R.D., & Asher, S.R. (1983) 'Social and personality development'. In M.R. Rosenweig & L. W. Porter (Eds.), *Annual review of psychology* (Vol. 34, pp. 465-509). Palo Alto, CA: Annual Reviews.

Parke, R.D., & Slaby, R.G. (1983) 'The development of aggression'. In E.M. Hetherington (Ed.), *Handbook of child psychology* (Vol. 4): *Socialization, personality, and social development* (pp. 547-642). New York: Wiley.

Parker, J.G. (1987) 'Becoming friends: Conversational skills for friendship formation in young children'. In J. M. Gottman & J. G. Parker (Eds.), *Conversations of friends: Speculations of affective development* (pp. 103-138). New York: Cambridge University Press.

Parkhurst, J.T., & Asher, S.R. (1987, April) *The social concerns of aggressive-rejected children*. Paper presented at the biennial meetings of the Society for Research in Child Development, Baltimore, MD.

Peery, J.C. (1979) 'Popular, amiable, isolated, rejected: A reconceptualization of sociometric status in preschool children'. *Child Development*, 50, 1231-1234.

Pekarik, E., Prinz, R., Liebert, D., Weintraub, S., & Neale, J.M. (1976) 'The Pupil Evaluation Inventory: A sociometric technique for assessing children's social behavior'. *Journal of Abnormal Child Psychology*, 4, 83-97.

Pelham, W.E., & Bender, M.E. (1982) 'Peer relationships in hyperactive children: Descriptions and treatment'. In K.D. Gadgow & I. Bialer (Eds.), *Advances in learning and behavioral disabilities* (Vol. 1, pp. 365-436). Greenwich, CT: JAI Press.

Piaget, J. (1932) *The moral judgment of the child.* New York: Free Press of Glencoe.

Porterfield, O.V., & Schlichting, H.F. (1961) 'Peer status and reading achievement'. *Journal of Educational Research*, 54, 291-297.

Prinz, R.J., Connor, P.A., & Wilson, C.C. (1981) 'Hyperactive and aggressive behaviors in childhood: Intertwined dimensions'. *Journal of Abnormal Child Psychology*, 9, 191-202.

Pritchard, M., & Graham, P. (1966) 'An investigation of a group of patients who have attended both the child and adult departments of the same psychiatric hospital'. *British Journal of Psychiatry*, 112, 603-612.

Putallaz, M., & Gottman, J.M. (1981) 'Social skills and group acceptance'. In S.R. Asher & J.M. Gottman (Eds.), *The development of children's friendships* (pp. 116-149). New York: Cambridge University Press.

Putallaz, M., & Gottman, J.M. (1983) 'Social relationship problems in children: An approach to intervention'. In B.B. Lahey & A.E. Kazdin (Eds.), *Advances in clinical child psychology* (Vol. 6, pp. 1-39). New York: Plenum Press.

Putallaz, M., & Heflin, A.H. (in press) 'Parent-child interaction'. In S.R. Asher & J.D. Coie (Eds.), *Peer rejection in childhood*. New York: Cambridge University Press.

Quay, H. C. (1979) 'Classification'. In H.C. Quay & J.S. Werry (Eds.), *Psychopathological disorders of childhood* (2nd ed.). New York: Wiley.

Rardin, D.R., & Moan, C.E. (1971) 'Peer interaction and cognitive development'. *Child Development*, 42, 1685-1699.

Reisman, J.M., & Shorr, S.I. (1978) 'Friendship claims and expectations among children and adults'. *Child Development*, 48, 1685-1699.

Rest, J.R. (1983) 'Moral development'. In J.H. Flavell & E.M. Markman (Eds.), *Handbook of child psychology* (Vol. 3): *Cognitive development* (pp.556-629). New York: Wiley.

Ricks, D.F., & Berry, J.C. (1970) 'Family and symptom patterns that precede schizophrenia'. In M. Roff & D.F. Ricks (Eds.), *Life history research in psychopathology* (Vol. 1, pp. 31-39). Minneapolis: University of Minnesota Press.

Robins, L.N. (1966) *Deviant children grown up*. Baltimore, MD: Williams & Wilkins.

Robins, L.N. (1972) 'Follow-up studies of behavior disorders in children'. In H.C. Quay & J.S. Weery (Eds.), *Psychopathological disorders of childhood* (pp.415-450). New York: Wiley.

Roff, J.D., & Wirt, D. (1984) 'Childhood aggression and social adjustment as antecedents of delinquency'. *Journal of Abnormal Child Psychology*, 12, 111-126.

Roff, M. (1957) *Preservice personality problems and subsequent adjustments to military service: The prediction of psychoneurotic reactions* (U.S. Air Force School of Aviation Medical Report, No. 57-136). Colorado Springs, CO: U.S. Air Force School of Aviation.

Roff, M. (1960) 'Relations between certain preservice factors and psychoneurosis during military duty'. *Armed Forces Medical Journal*, 11, 152-160.

Roff, M. (1961) 'Childhood social interactions and young adult bad conduct'. *Journal of Abnormal Social Psychology*, 63, 333-337.

Roff, M. (1963) 'Childhood social interactions and young adult psychosis'. *Journal of Clinical Psychology*, 19, 152-157.

Roff, M. (1975) 'Juvenile delinquency in girls: A study of a recent sample'. In R.D. Wirt, G. Winokur, & M. Roff (Eds.), *Life history research in psychopathology* (Vol. 4, pp. 135- 151). Minneapolis: University of Minnesota Press.

Roff, M., Sells, S.B., & Golden, M.M. (1972) *Social adjustment and personality development in children*. Minneapolis: University of Minnesota Press.

Roistacher, R.C. (1974) 'A microeconomic model of sociometric choice'. *Sociometry*, 37, 219-238.

Rolf, J.E., Knight, R., & Wertheim, E. (1976) 'Disturbed preschizophrenics: Childhood symptoms in relation to adult outcomes'. *Journal of Nervous and Mental Disease*, 162, 274-279.

Rubin, K.H. (1985) 'Socially withdrawn children: An "at risk" population?' In B.H. Schneider, K.H. Rubin, & J.E. Ledingham (Eds.) *Peer relations and social skills in childhood* (Vol. 2): *Issues in assessment and training* (pp.125-139). New York: Springer-Verlag.

Rubin, K.H., Daniels-Beirness, T., & Bream, L. (1984) 'Social isolation and social problem solving: A longitudinal study'. *Journal of Consulting and Clinical Psychology*, 52, 17-25.

Rubin, K.H., Le Mare, L.J., & Lollis. S. (in press) 'Social withdrawal in childhood: Developmental pathways to rejection'. In S.R. Asher & J.D. Coie (Eds.), *Peer rejection in childhood*. New York: Cambridge University Press.

Rutter, M., & Garmezy, N. (1983) 'Developmental psychopathology'. In E.M. Hetherington (Ed.), *Handbook of child psychology* (Vol, 4): *Socialization, personality, and social development* (pp. 775-912). New York: Wiley.

Sando, R.F. (1952) 'How to make and utilize follow-up studies of school leavers'. *Bulletin of the National Association of Secondary School Principals*, 36, 67-75.

Schaffer, D. (1974) 'Suicide in childhood and adolescence'. *Journal of Child Psychology and Psychiatry*, 15, 275-291.

Schaffer, D., & Fisher P. (1981) 'Suicide in children and young adolescents'. In C.F. Wells & I.R. Stuart (Eds.), *Self-destructive behaviour in children and adolescents* (pp. 75-104). New York: Van Nostrand Reinhold.

Schmuck, R. (1966) 'Some aspects of classroom social climate'. *Psychology in the Schools*, 3, 59-65.

Schofield, W., & Balian, L. (1959) 'A comparative study of the personal histories of schizophrenic and nonpsychiatric patients'. *Journal of Abnormal and Social Psychology*, 59, 216-225.

Schrut, A. (1968) 'Some typical patterns in the behavior and background of adolescent girls who attempt suicide'. *American Journal of Psychiatry*, 125, 69-74.

Sebald, H. (1981) 'Adolescents' concept of popularity and unpopularity, comparing 1960 with 1976'. *Adolescence*, 16, 23-30.

Selman, R.I. (1979) *The growth of interpersonal understanding*. New York: Academic Press.

Semler, I.J. (1960) 'Relationships among several measures of pupil adjustment'. *Journal of Educational Psychology*, 51, 60-64.

Shaffer, D.R. (1985) *Developmental psychology*. Monterey, CA: Brooks/Cole.

Shantz, C.U. (1983) 'Social cognition'. In J.H. Flavell & E.M. Markman (Eds.), *Handbook of child psychology* (Vol. 3): *Cognitive development* (pp.495-555). New York: Wiley.

Shepherd, M. (1978) 'Epidemiology and clinical psychiatry'. *British Journal of Psychiatry*, 133, 289-298.

Skolnick, A.A. (1986) *The psychology of human development*. New York: Harcourt, Brace, Jovanovich.

Snepp, D.W. (1953) 'Why they drop out: 8 clues to greater holding power'. *Clearing House,* 27, 492-497.

Stengel, E. (1974) *Suicide and attempted suicide* (2nd ed.). Baltimore, MD: Penguin.

Stocking, S.H., Arezzo, D., & Leavitt, S. (1980) *Helping kids make friends*. Allen, TX: Argus Communications.

Sullivan, H.S. (1953) *The interpersonal theory of psychiatry*. New York: Norton.

Topal, P., & Reznikoff, M. (1982) 'Perceived peer and family relationships, hopelessness, and locus of control as factors in adolescent suicide attempts'. *Suicide and Life- Threatening Behavior,* 12, 141-150.

Trout, D.L. (1980) 'The role of social isolation in suicide'. *Suicide and Life-Threatening Behavior,* 10, 10-23.

Turner, R.R., & Boulter, L. (1981, August) *Predicting social competence: The validity of the PIPS*. Paper presented at the annual convention of the American Psychological Association, Los Angeles, CA.

Ullmann, C.A. (1957) 'Teachers, peers, and tests as predictions of adjustment'. *Journal of Educational Psychology,* 48, 257-267.

Van Dusen, K.T., & Mednick, S.A. (Eds.). (1983) *Prospective studies of crime and delinquency*. Hingham, MA: Kluwer-Nijhoff.

Vaughn, B.E., & Waters, E. (1981) 'Attention structure, sociometric status, and dominance: Interrelations, behavior correlates, and relationships to social competence'. *Developmental Psychology,* 17, 275-288.

Wadsworth, M. (1979) *Roots of delinquency*. Oxford, England: Martin Robertson.

Wanlass, R.L., & Prinz, R.J. (1982) 'Methodological issues in conceptualizing and treating childhood social isolation'. *Psychological Bulletin,* 92, 39-55.

Warnken, R.G., & Siess, T.F. (1965) 'The use of the cumulative record in the prediction of behavior'. *Personnel and Guidance Journal,* 31, 231-237.

Watt, N.E. (1978) 'Patterns of childhood social development in adult schizophrenics'. *Archives of General Psychiatry,* 35, 160-165.

Watt, N.E., Anthony, E.J., Wynne, L.C., & Rolf, J.E. (1984) *Children at risk for schizophrenia: A longitudinal perspective*. New York: Cambridge University Press.

Watt, N.E., & Lubensky, A. (1976) 'Childhood roots of schizophrenia'. *Journal of Consulting and Clinical Psychology,* 44, 363-375.

Watt, N.E., Stolorow, R.D., Lubensky, A.W., & McClelland, D.C. (1970) 'School adjustment and behavior of children hospitalized for schizophrenia as adults'. *American Journal of Orthopsychiatry,* 40, 637-657.

Weiner, I.P. (1970) *Psychological disturbance in adolescence*. New York: Wiley-Interscience.

Weiner, I.P. (1980) 'Psychopathology in adolescence'. In J. Adelson (Ed.), *Handbook of adolescent psychology* (pp. 447-471). New York: Wiley.

West, D.J., & Farrington, D.P. (1973) *Who becomes delinquent?* London: Heinemann.

West, D.J., & Farrington, D.P. (1977) *The delinquent way of life*. London: Heinemann.

Williams, G.A., & Asher, S.R. (1987, April) *Peer and self-perceptions of peer rejected children: Issues in classification and subgrouping*. Paper presented at the biennial meetings of the Society for Research in Child Development, Baltimore, MD.

Yarrow, L.J., Campbell, J.D., & Burton, R.V. (1970) 'Recollections of childhood: A study of the retrospective method'. *Monographs of the Society for Research in Child Development*, 35 (5, Serial No. 138).

Youniss, J.E. (1980) *Parents and peers in social development: A Sullivan-Piaget perspective*. Chicago: University of Chicago Press.

25.   Having Friends, Keeping Friends, Making Friends, and Being Liked by Peers in the Classroom: Predictors of Children's Early School Adjustment?

Gary W. Ladd

The potential role that children's classroom peer relations play in their school adjustment was investigated during the first 2 months of kindergarten and the remainder of the school year. Measures of 125 children's classroom peer relationships were obtained on 3 occasions: at school entrance, after 2 months of school, and at the end of the school year. Measures of school adjustment, including children's school perceptions, anxiety, avoidance, and performance, were obtained during the second and third assessment occasions. After controlling mental age, sex, and preschool experience, measures of children's classroom peer relationships were used to forecast later school adjustment. Results indicated that children with a larger number of classroom friends during school entrance developed more favorable school perceptions by the second month, and those who maintained these relationships liked school better as the year progressed. Making new friends in the classroom was associated with gains in school performance, and early peer rejection forecasted less favorable school perceptions, higher levels of school avoidance, and lower performance levels over the school year.

Schools are among the most pervasive socialization contexts in our culture, and among the most influential for shaping the course of human development over the life span. Yet as much as 20% to 30% of the school-age population (Achenbach & Edelbrock, 1981; Rubin & Balow, 1978) experience substantial adjustment problems in the classroom and thus are at risk for a variety of interpersonal, emotional, and career difficulties in later life (see Cowen, Pedersen, Bagigian, Izzo, & Trost, 1973; Kohlberg, LaCrosse, & Ricks, 1972, Ladd & Asher, 1985; Parker & Asher, 1987). Many school adjustment problems appear to have lasting or cumulative effects; problems that arise early in children's school careers are often perpetuated by social-psychological factors (e.g., reputational bias, self-fulfilling prophesies) or are exacerbated when nascent difficulties undermine later progress (see Butler, Marsh, Sheppard, & Sheppard, 1985; Coie & Dodge, 1983; Horn & Packard, 1985; Perry, Guidubaldi, & Kehle, 1971). Given the pervasiveness of this problem, and the potential costs to both the individual and society, further research is needed on the precursors of school adjustment. In particular, there is a need to study early school adaptation and to identify factors that forecast children's adjustment to new school environments (e.g., entrance into grade school).

Gary W. Ladd: 'Having Friends, Keeping Friends, Making Friends, and Being Liked by Peers in the Classroom: Predictors of Children's Early School Adjustment?' *CHILD DEVELOPMENT* (1990), Vol. 61, pp. 1081-1100. Copyright © by the Society for Research in Child Development, Inc. All rights reserved.

As children begin school, they must cope with many new demands; often they must meet new academic challenges, negotiate new school buildings and classrooms, learn new school and teacher expectations, and gain acceptance into a new peer group (see Bogat, Jones, & Jason, 1980; Ladd & Price, 1987). Moreover, as children progress through the school year, they must negotiate an increasingly complex array of interpersonal and cognitive tasks. Recent theories of early school adjustment (see Ladd 1989) suggest that the degree to which children adapt to these challenges and become comfortable and successful in the new school environment is partly dependent on the degree of support they receive from teachers, parents and classmates.

Of these potential sources of support, children's relationships with classmates may be among the most important. Previous research shows that peer relations in the class room are a major concern to children as they enter and progress through the primary grades (Levine, 1966; Rakieten, 1961), and that the quality of children's peer relations in grade school forecasts school avoidance, disruption, and failure during adolescence (Parker & Asher, 1987; Roff, Sells, & Golden 1972). It may be the case that the types of relationships children form with peers in the classroom function as a source of stress or support and shape the course of early school adaptation. For example, Berndt and Perry (1986) have shown that grade school and junior high children view their friends in school as a source of support, and studies by Asher and colleagues (e.g., Asher, Hymel, & Renshaw, 1984; Asher & Wheeler, 1985) reveal that grade schoolers who are rejected by their classmates feel lonely in school. Little is known, however, about the adaptive significance of peers as children begin grade school and cope with new academic and social challenges.

Preliminary evidence concerning the potential contributions of classmates to children's early school adjustment can be found in a recent study by Ladd and Price (1987). These investigators found that children who began kindergarten with familiar classmates became more accepted and less rejected by their classmates at both the beginning and the end of the school year. Also, children who had a larger number of familiar peers in their new classrooms tended to develop positive attitudes toward school and displayed lower levels of school avoidance at the beginning of the school year (as indexed by absences and requests to see the school nurse).

Although these findings are intriguing, they leave many important questions unanswered. The Ladd and Price (1987) investigation of children's peer relationships in the new school environment was limited to an assessment of the number of "familiar" peers present in children's classrooms at the beginning of the school year. Consequently, other important features of children's relationships with classmates in kindergarten and their potential contributions to school adjustment remain unexplored.

The purpose of this investigation was to further explore the potential role that children's classroom peer relations play in their school adjustment during both the first 2 months of kindergarten (late August to late October) and over the balance of the school year (from October to May). Because classrooms are a peer *group* context, it was deemed important to consider factors such as the network of interpersonal ties (e.g., friendships) and the social status (i.e., peer acceptance vs. rejection) children developed among classmates.

448

During the first weeks of school, friendships may be an important source of support for young children. School entrance, which requires negotiating a novel physical and interpersonal environment, can be stressful for young children, especially when it must be negotiated in the absence of parents or other attachment figures. During this period, close ties with classmates (e.g., friendships) may serve as a "secure base" from which to explore and cope with novel surroundings and demands (see Ispa, 1981; Ladd & Price, 1987; Schwarz, 1972). Moreover, the stress or "strangeness" of new classrooms may be reduced by the number of friends or acquaintances children find in this setting. To explore this possibility, we assessed the number of close friends, "other" (secondary) friends, and acquaintances present in children's classrooms as they began school in late August. Higher levels of school adjustment were anticipated for children whose classrooms contained many familiar peers (i.e., classmates children had known prior to school entrance), especially during the early months of the school year (i.e., when novelty or "strangeness" was greatest). Moreover, it was reasoned that the number of friends (i.e., close relationships) available to children in the classroom would provide greater support than the number of acquaintances and thus forecast higher levels of adjustment by the second month of school (late October).

By the second month of school, children have had the opportunity to sustain or lose prior friendships and to form new ones. Moreover, sufficient time has passed for children to develop social reputations among classmates. These developments may determine, in part, the course of children's school adjustment over the remainder of the school year. Children who have few friends, either because they have failed to maintain prior friendships or because they have not succeeded in forming new ones, may be deprived of a context that fosters skill development (see Howes, 1983, 1988) and fulfills affective needs (Howes, 1988). Over time, this type of deprivation might be expected to reduce children's interest, involvement, and performance in school. Based on this logic, we measured the number of friendships children maintained during the first 2 months of the school year as an index of the degree to which they stayed friends with classmates they had known prior to kindergarten. We also measured the number of new friends each child developed during the first 2 months of school. It was anticipated that these two measures (i.e., the ability to maintain and develop new friends) would be positively related to changes in school adjustment over the school year.

Another aspect of children's classroom peer relations that may influence early adaptation is their peer status among classmates. Recent theory and research suggest that children's friendships (dyadic relations) and peer status (group relations) refer to different phenomena that may serve both separate and overlapping functions in child development and socialization (see Berndt & Ladd, 1989; Buhrmester & Furman, 1986; Bukowski & Hoza, 1989; Ladd, 1988). Although friends appear to be an important source of companionship and emotional support in the classroom (e.g., Berndt & Perry, 1986), children's social position in the peer group may affect other aspects of their school experience, including their access to play opportunities and partners (see Ladd, Price, & Hart, in press), achievement (Krappman, 1985), feelings of belongingness or loneliness (Asher *et al.*, 1984; Asher & Wheeler, 1985), and perceptions of interpersonal competence (Bukowski & Hoza, 1989). In short, we anticipated that the support or stress associated with early classroom peer acceptance or rejection would also forecast changes in adjustment over the course of the school year. Specifically, children who experienced lower levels of peer acceptance by the second month of kindergarten were expected to become less involved in school, develop more negative school perceptions, and decline in school performance.

All of the above measures of children's classroom peer relationships were used to forecast their school adjustment in new kindergarten classrooms. Although the concept of school adjustment is not well defined in the literature, it is used here to refer to the outcome(s) of children's attempts to adapt to the demands of the school environment (for further treatment of this concept, see Ladd, 1989). As children enter grade school, a potentially important indicator of their adjustment is the degree to which they become comfortable and involved in new classrooms and succeed at academic tasks (Bogat *et al.*, 1980; Ladd & Price, 1987). Presumably, children who like school and become involved in classroom activities are more likely to profit from their educational experiences. Conversely, negative attitudes toward school, or an inclination to avoid or withdraw from the school environment, may disrupt children's progress.

The measures used to tap these potential adjustment outcomes were organized into three categories, including: *(a)* children's perceptions of school and various aspects of the school environment (i.e., school liking; attitudes toward teachers and learning activities), *(b)* children's school involvement (i.e., manifest anxiety and school avoidance), and *(c)* children's school performance (i.e., attentional and task-related behaviors; academic "readiness"). Each of the measures employed within these three categories was administered during the second month of school (October) and at the end of the school year (May). Thus, using the peer relationship predictors, it was possible to forecast early school adjustment (October) as well as potential changes in school adjustment over the course of the school year (October to May).

Finally, although the purpose of this study was to identify features of children's classroom peer relations that may affect their school adjustment, alternative directions of effect were also considered. It is possible that children's school adjustment, or the degree to which they adapt to the school environment, affects the scope and quality of their relationships with classmates. Bidirectional relations may also be plausible. For example, while negative school perceptions may foster dislike of classmates or disrupt friendships, poor peer relations in the classroom may cause children to dislike and avoid school. These alternative hypotheses were also examined with the measures obtained during October and May of the school year but were not considered when examining the role of prior friendships during school entrance. (The hypothesis that early school adjustment determined the number or form of friendships children had developed prior to kindergarten is not tenable.)

Method

Sample and timeline

The subjects were 125 children from eight kindergarten classrooms in four Midwestern schools. The sample consisted of 53 children (28 males, 25 females) who participated in a prior investigation of the transition to grade school (Ladd & Price, 1987) and 72 of their grademates (38 males, 34 females) who completed kindergarten during the same school year. The entire sample consisted of 66 males and 59 females with a mean age of 64.2 months (SD = 3.7).

The children in this sample came from predominantly white, middle-class families, and all were attending kindergarten for the first time in "new" school buildings and classrooms. Parental consent was obtained to assess children's peer relationships and school adjustment on three occasions: at school entrance (late August), after 2 months of school (late October), and at the end of the school year (late April and early May).

Procedures, instrumentation, and measures

School Entrance

Demographic and school experience data

Questionnaires were mailed to children's parents at the beginning of the school year. Measures of children's chronological age, gender, and prior school experience were obtained from these questionnaires. Estimates of prior school experience were calculated by counting the total number of days (5-8-hour time blocks) constituting each reported period of preschool attendance. Adjustments were made for factors such as extended absences and number and length of class sessions each week.

Identification of prior friendships

A roster of children's kindergarten classmates was included in the questionnaire, and parents were asked to designate the type of relationship their child had with each classmate prior to school entrance (i.e., close friend, friend, acquaintance, unfamiliar peer) and the estimated duration of each friendship or acquaintanceship (in months). Instructions about how to classify children's relationships and estimate durations were provided with the roster. For example, companions with whom children displayed shared positive affect, preferred most as playmates, and associated with most often were defined as close friends (see Howes, 1983, 1988; Ladd & Golter, 1988).

Although parent reports of children's friendships are known to be reliable and accurate (Ladd & Emerson, 1984; Ladd & Golter, 1988; Ladd & Price, 1987), a 3 (relationship type) x 2 (sex of child) ANOVA was performed on the duration scores to determine whether parents discriminated among the types of relationships included on the roster. Significant effects were obtained only for relationship type, $F = 22.57, p < .001$. Post-hoc tests (Newman Keuls; $p < .05$) revealed that close friendships ($M = 25.5$ months) were estimated to have significantly longer durations than secondary friendships ($M = 15.4$), which in turn were estimated to have significantly longer durations than acquaintanceships ($M = 8.5$).

Scores for the number of close friends, "other" friends, and acquaintances in children's classrooms as they began school were created by summing the number of classmates parents had assigned to each relationship category on the roster. Proportion scores were created to control for class size, but because variation in class size was small (range = 16–22), similar distributions were obtained.

The First 2 Months

Mental age

The Peabody Picture Vocabulary Test (PPVT; Dunn & Dunn, 1981) was individually administered to subjects in a private location by a trained examiner during the first 2 months of school. The PPVT yields a reliable mental age score that correlates well with other aptitude measures.

Classroom friendships and peer status

Trained graduate assistants conducted individual friendship and sociometric interviews with children's classmates during late October in a private location. During the interview, each child was shown a randomly ordered display of classmates' photographs, and was asked to name each peer. Liking nominations (see Asher, Singleton, Tinsley, & Hymel, 1979) were obtained by asking the child to designate up to three preferred classmates ("someone you like to play with at school") and three disliked classmates ("someone you don't like to play with at school"). Acceptance ratings were also obtained but are not reported in this article. An unlimited number of friendship nominations were gathered by asking children to point to the pictures of their best friends. Teachers were asked, during late October, to circle the names of the subject's best friends on a class roster.

Peer and teacher friendship nominations were used to identify children's classroom friends during the second month of school. Classroom friends were those classmates who were: (a) nominated by the subject as a best friend and who, in turn, nominated the subject as a best friend during the peer sociometric interviews, and (b) nominated by the teacher as the subject's friend on the class roster. Friendships defined in this manner were compared to those parents had identified at school entrance (i.e., both close and "other" friendships) to determine the number of prior friendships that had been maintained and the number of new friendships that had been formed during the first 2 months of school. The score for maintained friendships was the number of classmates who were identified as the subject's friends at both times of assessment, and the score for new friendships was the number of previously unfamiliar classmates who were classified as the subject's friends at the second time of assessment.

Liking and disliking nominations were used to measure children's peer status during the second month of school. A social preference score was calculated for each child by subtracting the standardized positive nomination scores from their negative counterparts (see Coie, Dodge, & Coppotelli, 1982).

Early school adjustment

Early school adjustment data were gathered from teachers, children, observers, and parents during the first 2 months of school. Teachers completed the Preschool Behavior Questionnaire (PBQ; Behar, 1977) and the California Preschool Social Competence Scale (CPSC; Levine, Elzey, & Lewis, 1969), which were administered in counterbalanced order during late October. The PBQ includes measures of anxious-fearful and hyperactive-distractible classroom behaviors and yields reliable and valid scores with preschool and kindergarten children (Rubin & Clark, 1982; Rubin

& Daniels-Bierness, 1983). Similarly, a subscale of the CPSC (e.g., task mastery) produces scores for academic task competence that are both internally consistent and moderately stable with preschool and kindergarten children (Ladd & Price, 1987).

Teachers also used a daily log to record children's absences and the number of times they requested to visit the school nurse during the first 2 months of the school year. A measure of children's school readiness, the Metropolitan Readiness Test — Form P (MRT; Harcourt Brace & Jovanovich), was group administered by teachers in each classroom during late October.

Seven trained observers and a reliability judge gathered data on children's classroom behaviors during 15–30-min free-play periods scheduled two to three times per week during the first 2 months of school. Among the codes employed, five were used to document children's anxious behaviors (see Ladd & Price, 1987; Rubin, 1984), including: (a) immobile — unoccupied and displays no movement; (b) rocking — back-and-forth rocking motion in either a standing or sitting position; (c) shuffling — repetitive foot movements while standing; (d) sucking — fingers in mouth; and (e) automanipulation — excessive, repetitive manipulation of hair or body parts. Children were observed for 60 scans in a predetermined random order using a modified scan-sampling scheme (see Ladd, 1983; Ladd & Price, 1987). Observers first located a target child, focused 1–2 sec on his or her behavior, and then coded it into mutually exclusive categories, including those described above. Observers conducted 15%–20% of their observations on a scan-by-scan basis with a reliability judge, and kappas calculated between each observer and judge on the observed behaviors did not fall below .82 at each time of assessment.

Ratings of school avoidance during the first 2 months of school were obtained from parents. Included in the parent questionnaire were four statements describing potential forms of school avoidance (e.g., "In the morning, before school, how often has your child expressed concern or hesitation about going to school?"), and parents were asked to rate each statement on a scale of 1 (seldom occurs) to 5 (frequently occurs).

School anxiety and avoidance. — From the teacher, observer, and parent data, two measures of manifest anxiety and three measures of school avoidance were derived. Measures of children's classroom anxiety were the sum of teacher's ratings on the anxious-fearful subscale of the Preschool Behavior Questionnaire, and the total number of scans in which observers coded one of the five types of anxious behaviors. The school avoidance measures included the number of absences and the number of nurse requests recorded for each child, and the sum of the parent's ratings of school avoidance.

School perceptions. — Three measures of children's school-related perceptions were derived from the School Sentiment Inventory (SSI, Bogat *et al.*, 1980; Ladd & Price, 1987). Children were individually interviewed on an additional occasion in late October to complete a 32-item version of the SSI (see Ladd & Price, 1987). Interviewers read each item aloud and asked children to respond either "yes" or "no." Items with homogeneous content and high factor loadings on the same dimension in principal components analyses were grouped into subscales termed perceived teacher support (e.g., "My teacher listens to what I say"), attitudes toward school activities (e.g., "I like to sing songs in school"), and school liking (e.g., "School is fun"). Each subscale contained a minimum of six items (range = 6–8 items), and all four measures had moderately high levels of internal consistency (Kuder-Richardson, 20 reliability coefficients exceeded .82).

Academic behavior and achievement. — Measures of children's school performance were obtained from three sources. Ratings of children's academic behaviors were obtained from teachers on the task mastery subscale of the California Preschool Social Competence scale, and the hyperactive-distractible subscale of the Preschool Behavior Questionnaire. Children's total stanine score on the Metropolitan Readiness Test was used as a measure of school readiness or achievement.

The End of the School Year

The instruments employed to assess children's classroom peer relations and school adjustment during the first 2 months of school were readministered at the end of the school year using the same procedures and examiners. Data from the peer and teacher sociometric instruments, PBQ, CPSC, MRT (Form Q), SSI, and school avoidance questionnaire were gathered during late April and early May. Data on children's absences, nurse requests, and anxious behaviors in the classroom were collected during the final 2 months of the school year.

Measures of children's classroom friendships at the end of the school year were created using procedures similar to those employed during the second month of school. The score for maintained friendships was number of classmates who were identified as the subject's friends in August, October, and May, and the score for new friendships was the number of classmates who were identified as friends in May but not at the outset or the second month of school.

Results

Creation of School Adjustment Composites

A series of correlational and principal components analyses were employed to estimate communality among the respective measures and form composite scores. These analyses were first performed on the measures obtained during the second month of school (early school adjustment indices) and then applied to those obtained at the end of the school year (end-of-school adjustment indices).

In general, the results of these analyses indicated that conceptually related measures of school adjustment (i.e., measures of school perceptions, involvement, and performance) were moderately positively correlated and, by the end of the school year, achieved moderate loadings on the same factor in principal components analyses. Correlations between measures within the same domain were higher than those for measures across domains at both times of assessment, and relations among the measures within each domain were stronger at the end of the school year than at the beginning (see Table 1). One exception to this pattern was that the five school involvement measures factored into two subscales, one containing the two anxiety measures, and the other containing the three avoidance measures. Of the two sets of measures, the avoidance indices evidenced greater convergence and discriminability (from the anxiety measures). Stability coefficients were also calculated for each of the school adjustment measures by correlating scores obtained for each measure in October and May. These coefficients range from .74 (Task Mastery) to .34 (School Liking and Parent-reported School Avoidance), and are reported in Table 1.

Table 1 **School adjustment measures: correlations within domain and stability coefficients**

Domain/Measure	Second Month				End of Year					Stability
	PS	TS	SA	SL	PS	TS	SA	SL		
School perceptions:										
Teacher support............			.10	.31			.50	.66		.48
School activities............				.31				.54		.43
School liking..............										.34
	AF	AB	ABS	NR	PSA	AF	AB	ABS	NR	PSA
School involvement:										
Anxious-fearful		.22	.32	.37	.19		.33	.24	.26	.10	.57
Anxious behavior...........			−.01	.01	.03			.23	.21	.08	.55
Absences..................				.71	.37				.78	.52	.39
Nurse requests.............					.40					.54	.50
Parent — school avoid........											.34
	TM	HD	SR			TM	HD	SR		
Academic behavior and achievement:										
Task mastery		−.52	.50				.60	.65			.74
Hyperactive-distractible			−.22					−.39			.57
School readiness............											.59

Note. — Correlations greater than + .15 or less than −.15 are significant ($p < .05$).

Based on these findings, four composite school adjustment measures were created by standardizing and summing the scores obtained from measures that loaded on the same factor. These composites were termed *school perceptions* (the three subscales of the SSI), *school anxiety* (the PBQ and observationally derived anxiety measures), *school avoidance* (the absence, nurse request, and parent-report measures), and *school performance* (the CPSC task mastery, PBQ hyperactive-distractible, and MRT measures). Correlations among these measures were moderate in magnitude for both the October (−.32 to .19) and May (−.31 to .46) assessment occasions.

Having Friends and Acquaintances in New Classrooms

A series of correlational and hierarchical regression analyses were employed to determine whether early school adjustment and changes in school adjustment over the school year could be forecasted from children's attributes (i.e., mental age, gender, preschool experience) and prior relationships with classmates at school entrance (i.e., number of acquaintances, "other" friends, and close friends in new classrooms). Because none of these predictors could reasonably be viewed as potential consequences of children's adjustment to school entrance, analyses designed to explore alternative directions of effect (e.g., attempting to predict either child attributes or previously established peer relationships from early school adjustment) were not attempted.

Scores for the predictors were correlated in order to detect potential multicollinearity. Because the obtained values were small to moderate in magnitude (see Table 2), all of the predictors were retained. Next, each school adjustment composite was regressed separately on the child attribute and classroom peer relations predictors. Separate analyses were also performed using raw scores versus proportion scores for each of the friendship predictor measures. However, because the findings were nearly identical, only the results for the raw score measures are reported here. Scores for children's mental age, gender, and preschool experience were entered on the first through third steps of the analysis, respectively, to examine differences attributable to child attributes and to control for their effects on subsequent predictors. The measures of children's relationships with classmates at school entrance (i.e., acquaintances, "other" friends, and close friends) were entered on the fourth through sixth steps of the analysis. This order of entry reflects the logical priority of the predictors (e.g., the adaptive value of close friendships was hypothesized to outweigh that offered by less intimate ties). Finally, variables representing each child attribute x peer relations interaction were alternately entered on the final step of the analyses (see Cohen & Cohen, 1975; Ladd & Price, 1987). The format of the analyses used to forecast changes in adjustment from October to May was similar, except that one of the four composite scores obtained in October was entered on the first step of each equation and corresponding values obtained in May served as the criterion. Results for the regression analyses are presented in Table 3. (Interaction terms, unless significant, are not listed in Tables 3–6 in order to save space.)

School perceptions

The overall regressions performed on children's early school perceptions and change-in-school perceptions were significant. Results indicated that, after controlling for all three child attributes, both number of "other" friends and the number of close friends in new classrooms forecast favorable school perceptions in the second month of kindergarten. However, in forecasting changes in school perceptions, only prior preschool experience emerged as a significant predictor.

School anxiety and avoidance

The overall regression analyses performed on both the early school anxiety and avoidance composites were not significant, and none of the investigated predictors achieved significance in the analysis performed on the residualized anxiety or avoidance composites.

Table 2   Correlations among predictors and criteria

Measures	MA	GND	PE	ACQ	OFR	CFR	Composite (October)				Composite (May)			
							PER	ANX	AVD	SPF	PER	ANX	AVD	SPF
MA........		−.16	−.03	.03	.21	.22	.21	−.11	−.06	.31	.11	−.13	−.14	.35
GND			.10	.08	.07	−.10	.01	.09	.11	.02	.10	.04	.16	.05
PE				−.01	.09	.01	.06	−.18	.03	.25	.17	.15	−.11	.12
ACQ.......					.30	.09	.18	.12	−.15	.13	.18	.09	−.04	.14
OFR.......						.32	.25	.01	−.12	.16	.26	.09	−.07	.15
CFR.......							.29	−.14	−.06	.15	.15	−.08	−.12	.15

Measures	MFR1	NFR1	PREF1	PER	ANX	AVD	SPF	PER	ANX	AVD	SPF
MA........	.25	.20	.32								
GND	.01	.05	.11								
PE	.04	−.12	−.10								
MFR1		.22	.39	.33	−.16	−.17	.28	.39	−.17	−.22	.28
MFR2	.51	.55	.46	.35	−.23	−.24	.25	.49	−.31	−.25	.39
NFR1......	.22		.51	.26	−.19	−.27	.09	.30	−.18	−.20	.25
NFR2......	.13	.30		.17	−.01	−.08	.04	.44	−.19	−.25	.18
PREF1.....				.33	−.37	−.17	.20	.36	−.29	−.34	.38
PREF2.....	.44	.40	.62	.31	−.22	−.16	.18	.55	−.32	−.38	.42

Note. — MA = mental age; GND = gender; PE = preschool experience; ACQ = number of acquaintances; OFR = number of other friends; CFR = number of close friends; MFR1 = number of maintained friends in October; MFR2 = number of maintained friends in May; NFR1 = number of new friends in October; NFR2 = number of new friends in May; PREF1 = social preference in October; PREF2 = social preference in May; PER = school perceptions; ANX = school anxiety; ACD = school avoidance; SPF = school performance. Correlations greater than .15 and less than −.15 are significant ($p < .05$).

School performance

The investigated predictors accounted for a significant amount of variation in both early school performance and changes in school performance. Children with higher mental age scores and greater preschool experience received higher school performance scores in the second month of school, and mental age also forecasted performance gains across the school year.

Table 3   Regression analyses: predicting early school adjustment and changes in school adjustment from children's attributes and prior acquaintanceships and friendships with classmates

Predictors	Perceptions			Anxiety			Avoidance			Performance		
	Rsq	Rinc	B	Rsq	Rinc	B	Rsq	Rinc	B	Rsq	Rinc	B
Early school adjustment (October):												
MA	.05	.05	.15	.02	.02	−.10	.00	.00	−.05	.10	.10**	.31**
GND	.05	.00	.02	.03	.01	.09	.01	.01	.12	.10	.00	.04
PE	.05	.00	.06	.05	.02	.13	.02	.01	.05	.16	.06**	.24**
ACQ	.07	.02	.12	.06	.01	.09	.03	.01	−.10	.16	.00	.06
OFR	.11	.04**	.18*	.06	.00	.01	.03	.00	−.04	.16	.00	.00
CFR	.15**	.04	.21**	.07	.01	−.13	.03	.00	.00	.17**	.01	.06
Change in school adjustment:												
PRE	.28	.28**	.49**	.33	.33**	.55**	.12	.12**	.32**	.36	.36**	.53**
MA	.29	.01	−.01	.33	.00	−.08	.13	.01	−.07	.38	.02*	.18*
GND	.30	.01	.10	.33	.00	−.06	.14	.01	.13	.38	.00	.07
PE	.32	.02*	.16*	.34	.01	.06	.16	.02	−.14	.39	.01	.00
ACQ	.32	.00	.04	.34	.00	.02	.16	.00	.00	.39	.00	.06
OFR	.34	.02	.14	.35	.01	.12	.16	.00	.00	.39	.00	.00
CFR	.34**	.00	−.04	.35**	.00	−.03	.17**	.01	−.08	.39**	.00	.03

Note.— PRE = various school adjustment composites measured in October; MA = mental age; GND = gender; PE = preschool experience; ACQ = number of acquaintances; OFR = number of other friends; CFR = number of close friends; Rsq = squared multiple correlation; Rinc = increment to the squared multiple correlation; B = standardized regression weight.

* $p < .05.$
** $p < .01.$

Keeping Friends and Making Friends During the School Year

Additional correlational and regression analyses were employed to examine the following hypotheses concerning the relation between children's classroom friendships and their school adjustment: *(a)* the maintenance of prior friendships and formation of new ones during the early months of school fosters adaptation, or gains in adjustment over the school year, and *(b)* early school adaptation forecasts changes in friendship maintenance and formation over the course of the school year.

Predicting changes in school adjustment

Small to moderate correlations were found among the predictors for both October and May of the school year (also reported in Table 2). To predict changes in school adjustment, four hierarchical regression analyses were performed, one for each of the school adjustment composites. Specifically, scores for the child attribute measures (mental age, gender, preschool experience) and the number of maintained and new friends (October) were used to predict each end-of-the-year adjustment composite (May), after first entering the corresponding adjustment composite that was assessed in October. Findings are shown in Table 4.

Table 4 **Regression analyses: predicting changes in school adjustment from children's attributes and their maintained and new friendships in the classroom**

| | Change in School Adjustment | | | | | | | | | | | |
| | Perceptions | | | Anxiety | | | Avoidance | | | Performance | | |
Predictors	Rsq	Rinc	B	Rsq	Rinc	B	Rsq	Rinc	B	Rsq	Rinc	B
PRE	.28	.28**	.49**	.33	.33**	.55**	.12	.12**	.32**	.36	.35**	.53**
MA	.29	.01	−.01	.33	.00	−.08	.13	.01	−.07	.38	.02*	.18*
GND	.30	.01	.10	.33	.00	−.06	.14	.01	.13	.38	.00	.07
PE	.32	.02*	.16*	.34	.01	.06	.16	.02	−.14	.39	.01	.00
MFR1	.38	.06**	.24**	.34	.00	−.07	.18	.02	−.13	.40	.01	.08
NFR1	.39**	.01	.12	.34**	.00	−.03	.19**	.01	−.12	.43**	.03*	.18*

Note.— PRE = various school adjustment composites measured in October; MA = mental age; GND = gender; PE = preschool excperience; MFR1 = number of maintained friends in October; NFR1 = number of new friends in October; Rsq = squared multiple correlation; Rinc = increment to the squared multiple correlation; B = standardized regression weight.

* $p < .05$.
** $p < .01$.

School perceptions. — Together, the investigated predictors accounted for a significant proportion of the variance in the residual school perception scores. Results indicated that children who had more extensive preschool experience, and those who tended to maintain prior friendships during the first two months of kindergarten, developed more favorable school perceptions over the course of the year. Scores for maintained friendships made a significant contribution regardless of whether they were entered before or after the new friendships variable.

School anxiety and avoidance. — None of the targeted child attributes or friendship variables were found to enhance the prediction of changes in school anxiety or avoidance.

School performance. — The overall regression equation performed on this composite was significant. Gains in performance were forecasted by children's mental age and the number of new friendships formed during the first 2 months of kindergarten. Scores for new friendships made a significant contribution regardless of whether they were entered before or after those obtained for maintained friendships.

Predicting changes in classroom friendships

A similar design was used to construct the regression analyses used to predict changes in children's maintained and new friendships. For example, scores for the child attribute measures and the initial school perception composite (October) were used to predict scores for maintained friends (May) after first entering scores for maintained friends (October) in the equation. The same format was used to predict changes in new friendships. The results for these analyses are presented in Table 5.

Table 5 **Regression analyses: predicting changes in children's maintained and new classroom friendships from early school adjustment**

	Perceptions			Anxiety			Avoidance			Performance		
Predictors	Rsq	Rinc	B	Rsq	Rinc	B	Rsq	Rinc	B	Rsq	Rinc	B
Change in maintained friendships:												
MFR1	.25	.25**	.42**	.25	.25**	.42**	.25	.25**	.42**	.25	.25**	.42**
MA.................	.27	.02	.12	.27	.02	.12	.27	.02	.12	.27	.02	.12
GND	.28	.01	.11	.28	.01	.11	.28	.01	.11	.28	.01	.11
PE	.30	.02	.13	.30	.02	.13	.30	.02	.13	.30	.02	.13
PERC1	.33	.03*	.18*									
ANX1...............				.32	.02	−.15						
AVD1...............							.33	.03*	−.17*			
SPF1										.31	.01	.12
Change in new friendships:												
NFR1...............	.05	.05*	.20*	.05	.05*	.23*	.05	.05*	.23*	.05	.05*	.23*
MA.................	.05	.00	−.03	.05	.00	−.01	.05	.00	−.01	.05	.00	−.01
GND	.05	.00	−.03	.05	.00	−.03	.05	.00	−.03	.05	.00	−.03
PE	.05	.00	.07	.05	.00	.07	.05	.00	.07	.05	.00	.07
PERC1	.06	.01	.12									
ANX1...............				.05	.00	.00						
AVD1...............							.05	.00	.00			
SPF1										.05	.00	.00

Note.— MA = mental age; GND = gender; PE = preschool experience; MFR1 = number of maintained friends in October; NFR1 = number of new friends in October; PERC1 = school perceptions; ANX1 = school anxiety; AVD1 = school avoidance; SPF1 = school performance; Rsq = squared multiple correlation; Rinc = increment to the squared multiple correlation; B = standardized regression weight.

* $p < .05$
** $p < .01$.

Maintained friendships. — Although the overall regression equations were significant for all four analyses, the findings revealed that only two of the investigated school adjustment composites significantly enhanced the accuracy of predicting the residual maintained friendship scores. Specifically, children with more favorable school perceptions in October tended to maintain more of their prior friendships over the school year. Also, children who displayed lower levels of school avoidance in the first 2 months of school tended to retain more of their prior friends during the school year.

New friendships. — No significant relationships were found between the investigated school adjustment composites, measured in October, and changes in children's new friendships over the course of the school year.

Peer Status in the Classroom

Analyses identical to those described in the prior section were used to determine whether (*a*) early peer status (October) forecasted changes in school adjustment, and (*b*) early school adjustment (October) predicted changes in children's peer status over the school year. The resulting correlations are shown in Table 2, and regression findings are presented in Table 6.

Table 6 **Regression analyses: predicting changes in children's school adjustment from their early peer status and changes in peer status from early school adjustment**

Predictors	Perceptions			Anxiety			Avoidance			Performance		
	Rsq	Rinc	B	Rsq	Rinc	B	Rsq	Rinc	B	Rsq	Rinc	B
Change in school adjustment:												
PRE...............	.28	.28**	.47**	.33	.33**	.52**	.12	.12**	.27**	.36	.36**	.52**
MA................	.29	.01	−.05	.33	.00	−.00	.13	.01	−.00	.38	.02*	.16*
GND	.30	.01	.08	.33	.00	−.02	.14	.01	.13	.38	.00	.05
PE	.32	.02*	.12*	.34	.01	.05	.16	.02	−.15	.39	.01	.03
PREF1.............	.35**	.03*	.20	.34**	.00	−.04	.26**	.10**	−.35**	.45**	.06**	.27**
Change in peer status:												
PREF1.............	.38	.38**	.58**	.38	.38**	.63**	.38	.38**	.61**	.38	.38**	.61**
MA................	.38	.00	.00	.38	.00	.02	.38	.00	.00	.38	.38**	.00
GND	.38	.00	.00	.38	.00	−.01	.38	.00	.00	.38	.00	−.00
PE	.39	.01	.09	.39	.01	.08	.39	.01	.09	.39	.01	.07
PERC1	.40**	.01	.12									
ANX1.............				.39**	.00	.00						
AVD1.............							.40**	.01	−.08			
SPF1										.39**	.00	.06

Note.— PRE = corresponding school adjustment composites measured in October; MA = mental age; GND = gender; PE = preschool experience; PREF1 = social preference score in October; PERC1 = school perceptions; ANX1 = school anxiety; AVD1 = school avoidance; SPF1 = school performance; Rsq = squared multiple correlation; Rinc = increment to the squared multiple correlation; B = standardized regression weight.

* *p* < .05.
** *p* < .01.

Predicting changes in school adjustment

F tests performed on the overall regression equations were significant for all four analyses. Beyond the contributions of the targeted child attributes (these are described in prior sections), early classroom peer status (October) emerged as a significant predictor of all but the residual school anxiety composites. Lower peer status in October forecasted less favorable school perceptions, higher levels of school avoidance, and lower performance levels over the course of the school year.

Supplementary analyses were conducted in which the two friendship measures (i.e., the number of maintained and new friendships in October) were entered into the regression equations prior to the classroom peer status measure. These analyses were employed because there was a moderate relation between the friendship and peer status measures (see Table 2), and it was of interest to determine whether early peer status made a contribution to school adjustment, independent of that found for children's classroom friendships. Results indicated that, after both friendship measures had been taken into account, early peer status continued to make a significant contribution to changes in school perceptions, avoidance, and performance (all F values for the increment $> 3.78, p < .05$).

Predicting changes in peer status

After the investigated child attributes were taken into account, none of the early school adjustment composites (October) contributed significantly to the prediction of residual peer status scores. The results of these analyses are shown in Table 6.

Differences in school adjustment for peer status groups

In light of these findings, additional analyses were undertaken to explore the potential role of peer rejection in children's school adjustment. First, children in the sample were assigned to one of four sociometric categories (i.e., popular, average, neglected, or rejected) using the classification scheme developed by Coie *et al.*, 1982). Children who did not fit one of these categories were considered unclassifiable, and excluded from further analyses. This yielded a sample of 22 popular, 34 average, 15 neglected, and 18 rejected children. Second, a series of one-way analyses of covariance were conducted on the four school adjustment composites, with status groups as levels of the independent variable and changes in school adjustment (scores for the May composite adjusted for its October counterpart) as the dependent variable in each analysis (gender was initially included as a factor but was excluded because it consistently produced nonsignificant effects). Finally, post hoc tests (Newman-Keuls, $p < .05$) were used to determine significant differences between means.

A significant effect for group was obtained in all four analyses, and means and adjusted means are shown for each criterion in Table 7. The findings reveal that, after controlling for initial adaptation to kindergarten, rejected children had significantly less favorable school perceptions, significantly higher levels of school avoidance, and significantly lower levels of school performance than did popular, average, and neglected children.

Table 7   Means, adjusted means, and standard deviations for peer status groups on the four school adjustment composites

	Popular (n = 22)		Average (n = 34)		Neglected (n = 15)		Rejected (n = 18)	
	M	SD	M	SD	M	SD	M	SD
Perceptions:								
October	1.04	1.97	.03	2.00	.37	2.50	−1.49	1.67
May	.86	2.56	.54	1.86	.70	2.53	−2.20	2.39
Adjusted	.36*		.52*		.51*		−1.49	
Anxiety:								
October	−.65	.70	−.47	1.04	.57	1.39	1.48	2.31
May	−.44	.82	−.50	.90	−.22	1.04	1.39	2.66
Adjusted	.11		−.06		−.43		.61	
Avoidance:								
October	−.19	.75	−.47	1.36	.44	2.02	.95	1.96
May	−.40	.76	−.67	1.17	−.42	1.07	1.27	1.80
Adjusted	−.36*		−.59*		−.46*		1.17	
Performance:								
October	.36	1.49	−.07	1.25	.60	1.56	−.74	2.20
May	.45	1.19	.37	1.36	.61	1.22	−1.70	1.53
Adjusted	.30*		.42*		.34*		−1.32	

Note.— Means without an asterisk differ significantly from those with an asterisk. An adjusted mean is the average of the residual composite scores, which are created by partialing scores obtained in October from their counterparts obtained in May.

Discussion

This study was conducted to further our understanding of early school adaptation and, in particular, to examine the relation between children's classroom peer relations and their school adjustment as they entered and completed their first year of grade school. Two overarching hypotheses representing differing directions of effect were investigated. The first hypothesis was based on a model of early school adaptation in which children's personal attributes (i.e., formative experiences and personal characteristics children "bring" to school) and their relationships with classmates are seen as important determinants of early school adaptation (see Ladd, 1989, Ladd & Price, 1987). An alternative view, and the basis for the second hypothesis, was that children's success in adjusting to new school environments determines the quality of their classroom peer relationships. Children who have poor academic skills, or who feel anxious in new classrooms and wish to avoid this context, may have difficulty making friends and becoming accepted by classmates.

Although evidence consistent with both of these hypotheses was obtained, the majority of findings were consistent with the premise that early classroom peer relations are a precursor of later school adjustment. Consequently, these findings and their potential implications are considered prior to the discussion of alternative hypotheses.

One inference we may draw from the present findings is that the potential benefits or risks children derive from classmates may depend on the types of relationships they access or establish in the classroom. We may also infer from these findings that the adaptive value of particular child attributes or classroom peer relationships varies depending on the type of school adjustment that is forecasted. Consequently, it is important to consider how the various types of peer relationships may influence specific forms of school adjustment.

Prior friendships may serve as an important familiarization function as children enter school. Children who enter classrooms that contain many prior friends may find the new school environment less "strange" and more accommodating. Prior friendships provide a shared history and a common basis for future interactions and, therefore, a context for immediate companionship, conversation, and play. Close friendships, which often have a firm foundation in mutually rewarding exchanges (Hartup, 1989), may be especially adaptive or supportive in this regard. Our findings suggest that access to close friendships during school entrance may be especially important in the formation of positive school perceptions. Scores on this predictor forecasted children's early attitudes toward school *after* the contributions of their acquaintances and secondary classroom friendships had been taken into account.

Although it would appear that having friends in new classrooms encourages children to develop more favorable attitudes toward school, the same cannot be said for other domains of school adjustment. The number of prior friendships, either close or secondary, failed to predict children's levels of anxiety avoidance, or performance by the second month of school. Perhaps children's prior friendships affect how they think and feel about school more than how they behave toward it, or succeed at school related tasks.

Our findings also suggest that the potential benefits of prior friendships may be fleeting, unless these relationships are maintained in the school setting. Although the presence of prior friendships at school entrance failed to predict changes in school adjustment over the school year, the number of prior friendships that were *maintained* did forecast gains in children's in school perceptions. One interpretation of this finding is that stable friendships become an important source of emotional support as children cope with ever-increasing school demands. Howes (1988) has argued that maintained friendships function as "peer attachments" for young children and foster feelings of safety and security. Parker and Gottman (1989) also emphasize the emotional significance of early friendships. In their view, developments that emerge in stable friendships, such as complex fantasy play, allow children to explore their emotions (e.g., fears, anxieties) and cope with everyday frustrations. Another potential interpretation is that prior friendships, when maintained beyond school entrance, become "close" relationships in the school context. By retaining ties with prior friends, children may surround themselves with a network of rewarding exchanges, or natural communities of reinforcement. Were this the case, children who maintain their prior friendships may be more likely to view school as a rewarding environment.

We also found evidence to suggest that children who formed more new friendships in their classrooms tended to gain in school performance over the course of the year.

Perhaps by making friends with previously unfamiliar peers in the classroom, children not only established new bases for support, but also integrated themselves into the academic milieu in a way that fostered learning and achievement. In kindergarten classrooms, children often perform academic tasks in dyads and small groups, and are encouraged to work cooperatively with classmates. Perhaps children who expanded their friendship network to include new classmates found companions with similar academic skills and interests and had a wider choice of peers to turn to for help seeking and other forms of academic collaboration. Moreover, as Bronfenbrenner (1979) has argued, children's learning and competence is enhanced when they are permitted to undertake new tasks in the company of familiar persons. By making new friends in the classroom, children may have reduced the number of "unknown bystanders" and created a more familiar or supportive learning environment.

In addition to classroom friendships, we also sought to examine the potential adaptive significance of children's early peer status among classmates. Measures of children's peer status represent the collective sentiment of group members toward specific class members. We reasoned that early peer rejection, or becoming disliked by many classmates early in the school year, might function as a stressor in the school environment and, therefore, interfere with children's subsequent school adjustment. Consistent with this logic, findings from this investigation revealed that early peer rejection predicted less favorable school attitudes, increasing school avoidance, and lower levels of performance over the course of kindergarten.

Perhaps further research on the types of experiences that rejected children face in school will add to our understanding of this finding. Recent research has shown that young children who are rejected by classmates tend to feel lonely in school (Cassidy & Asher, 1989) and are rebuffed more often when attempting to enter play groups (Howes, 1988). Moreover, young children who are rejected early in the school year appear to have difficulty finding play partners at later points in time, and spend more time wandering from activity to activity in search of companions (Ladd, Price, & Hart, in press). In view of this growing body of evidence, and in light of the present findings, we are inclined to think that experiences such as these do not bode well for children's school adjustment, and may well foster negative school attitudes, discourage school attendance, undermine achievement, and so on.

It is also important to recognize that several of the child attributes investigated here were predictive of children's early school adjustment and/or changes in their school adjustment during kindergarten. It would appear that children's mental age and their prior school experience are potential contributors to their early school performance. By the second month of school, children with higher mental age scores and greater preschool experience tended to receive higher ratings from teachers for academic behaviors and readiness. Mental age, but not prior school experience, also forecasted gains in school performance across the year. Whereas children's mental maturity may underlie both their initial readiness for kindergarten and subsequent progress during the year (see Stevenson, Parker, Wilkinson, Hegion, & Fish, 1976; Worland, Weeks, & Janes, 1984), these data suggest that prior school experience may not be as strong a determinant of later progress.

The duration of children's preschool experience was not predictive of their early school perceptions, but did forecast changes in school perceptions. Specifically, children with more preschool experience tended to develop more favorable views of school and the school environment during kindergarten. Of the four adjustment composites, children's school perceptions were the least stable over the school year, suggesting that early school perceptions may be shaped by different factors than those formed by the end of the school year. Perhaps as the year progressed, children with greater preschool experience found it easier to adapt to kindergarten routines, and developed more "realistic" and positive views of school.

Overall, these findings are consistent with the view that early school adjustment is partly a function of the attributes and experiences that children "bring" to new classrooms, and partly a function of the types of relationships children experience as they cope with these settings. Although it was possible to forecast some aspects of children's school adjustment from their personal attributes and experiences, features of their relationships with classmates often enhanced the accuracy of these predictions. That is, children's classroom peer relationships tended to add to the prediction of school adjustment, above and beyond that which could be accounted for by their personal attributes and experiences. Furthermore, features of children's classroom peer relationships forecasted both their adjustment during the early weeks of kindergarten and changes in their adjustment during the school year. The fact that *changes* in children's school adjustment were predicted by these variables lends support to the hypothesis that children's personal attributes, their prior experiences, and their relationships with classmates affect their adaptational progress over the course of the school year.

This pattern of results, along with the absence of significant interaction terms, is consistent with an additive or "compensatory" model of school adjustment (see Garmezy, Mastern, & Tellegen, 1984; Ladd, 1989). An additive model implies that, in addition to any predictability offered by particular child attribute(s), environmental supports or stressors (e.g., stressful or supportive relationships with classmates) may make independent contributions to school adjustment. In other words, an attribute that places a child at risk for early school maladjustment may be: (a) partially offset (compensated for) by supportive features of the school environment, or (b) exacerbated by accompanying stressors. Similarly, child attributes that increase the likelihood of school adjustment may be enhanced or mitigated by supportive or stressful features of the school environment.

Although more limited in scope, we also obtained evidence consistent with the hypothesis that children's success in adjusting to the new school environment may affect their relationships with classmates. Specifically, children who developed unfavorable perceptions of school or who evidenced higher levels of school avoidance by October were less likely to maintain their prior friendships over the school year. One explanation for these findings is that poor school adjustment, particularly the tendency to avoid school, may reduce children's opportunities to nurture and maintain their relationships with classmates. Children who tend to be absent from school, or prefer to spend time in the nurse's office may be less available to their classroom friends as play and learning partners. Negative attitudes toward school may compound this problem especially if one's prior friends view school in a positive light.

Another potential explanation for these findings is that children who have trouble adjusting to school may be less mature than their classmates and, therefore, less skilled at maintaining their friendships. Although mental age was controlled for in the analyses used to explore this question, various forms of social maturity were not measured and may underlie both children's early school adjustment difficulties and their eventual loss of friendships. Ladd and Price (1987), for example, found that children who tended to associate primarily with younger companions during preschool were more likely to develop negative attitudes toward kindergarten.

In conclusion, the results of this investigation offer limited support for *both* of our initial hypotheses and imply that children's classroom peer relations and their early school adjustment may be reciprocally or "transactionally" related (see Sameroff & Chandler, 1975). However, the largest share of these findings are consistent with the first hypothesis and suggest that, along with specific child attributes, features of children's classroom peer relationships foster school adjustment. Although not all forms and features of children's peer relationships were studied here, several of those investigated did emerge as significant predictors of one or more forms of school adjustment. In particular, the extensivity and form of children's friendship ties in the classroom, including the number of prior friends enrolled in the same classroom, the extent to which these relationships were maintained, and the degree to which children formed new friendships, were found to forecast higher levels of school adjustment. In addition, acceptance by one's classmates early in the school year was associated with changes in most of the school adjustment measures studied here. Rejected children, in particular, appear to be at risk for school adjustment problems.

Although subject to replication and elaboration, these findings may have important implications for educators, and may be especially relevant to policies concerning the composition of kindergarten classrooms in new school buildings and the facilitation of children's ties with classmates during the early weeks of school. In planning the peer composition of kindergarten classrooms, school administrators may wish to consider grouping children so as to maximize contact with prior friends. Moreover, teachers may wish to experiment with techniques designed to help children maintain existing friendships and form new ones, and for preventing early peer rejection in the classroom (e.g., see Mize & Ladd, in press).

This study was funded in part by a grant from the Foundation for Child Development to Gary W. Ladd. The author would like to thank the children, parents, and school personnel who made this study possible. I am grateful to Beckie Golter, Craig Hart, Joseph Price, Emily Wadsworth, and Linda Wark for their efforts in coordinating various aspects of this study, and to Chris Graves, Avery Goldstein, Scott Hammer, Vemon Maas, Jaci Miller, Colet McKnight, Judy Stevenson, Margie Story, and Till Strand for their assistance with data collection and compilation.

References

Achenbach, T.M., & Edelbrock, C.S. (1981) 'Behavioral problems and competencies reported by parents of normal and disturbed children aged four through sixteen'. *Monographs of the Society for Research in Child Development*, 46 (1, Serial No. 188).

Asher, S.R., Hymel, S., & Renshaw, P.D. (1984) 'Loneliness in children'. *Child Development*, 55, 1457-1464.

Asher, S.R., Singleton, L.C., Tinsley, B.R., & Hymel, S. (1979) 'A reliable sociometric measure for preschool children'. *Developmental Psychology*, 15, 443-444.

Asher, S.R., & Wheeler, V.A. (1985) 'Children's loneliness: A comparison of rejected and neglected peer status'. *Journal of Consulting and Clinical Psychology*, 53, 500-505.

Behar, L. (1977) 'The preschool behavior questionnaire'. *Journal of Abnormal Psychology*, 5, 265-275.

Berndt, T.J., & Ladd, G.W. (1989) *Peer relationships in child development*. New York: Wiley.

Berndt, T.J., & Perry, T.B. (1986) 'Children's perceptions of friendships as supportive relationships'. *Developmental Psychology*, 22, 640-648.

Bogat, G.A., Jones, J.W., & Jason, L.A. (1980) 'School transitions: Preventive intervention following an elementary school closing'. *Journal of Community Psychology*, 8, 343-352.

Bronfenbrenner, U. (1979) *The ecology of human development*. Cambridge, MA: Harvard University Press.

Buhrmester, D., & Furman, W. (1986) 'The changing functions of friends in childhood: A neo-Sullivanian perspective'. In V.J. Derlega & B.A. Winstead (Eds.), *Friendship and social interaction* (pp. 41-62). New York: Springer-Verlag.

Bukowski, W., & Hoza, B. (1989) 'Popularity and friendship: Issues in theory, measurement, and outcome'. In T.J. Berndt & G.W. Ladd (Eds.), *Peer relationships in child development* (pp. 15-45). New York: Wiley.

Cassidy, J., & Asher, S.R. (1989, April) *Loneliness and peer relations in young children*. Paper presented at the biennial meetings of the Society for Research in Child Development, Kansas City.

Cohen, J., & Cohen, P. (1975) *Applied multiple regression analysis for the behavioral sciences*. Hillsdale, NJ: Erlbaum.

Coie, J., & Dodge, K.A. (1983) 'Continuities and changes in children's social status: A five-year longitudinal study'. *Merrill-Palmer Quarterly*, 29, 261-281.

Coie, J.D., Dodge, K.A., & Coppotelli, H. (1982) 'Dimensions and types of social status: A cross-age perspective'. *Developmental Psychology*, 18, 557-570.

Cowen, E.L., Pedersen, A., Bagigian, H., Izzo, L.D., & Trost, M.A. (1973) 'Long-term follow-up of early detected vulnerable children'. *Journal of Consulting and Clinical Psychology*, 41, 438-446.

Dunn, L.M., & Dunn, L.M. (1981) *Peabody Picture Vocabulary Test — revised: Manual for forms L and M*. Circle Pines, MN: American Guidance Service.

Garmezy, N., Masten, A., & Tellegen, A. (1984) 'The study of stress and competence in children: A building block for developmental psychopathology'. *Child Development*, 5,, 97-111.

Hartup, W.W. (1989) 'Behavioral manifestations of children's friendships'. In T.J. Berndt & G.W. Ladd (Eds.), *Peer relationships in child development* (pp. 46-70). New York: Wiley.

Horn, W.F., & Packard, T. (1985) 'Early identification of learning problems: A meta-analysis'. *Journal of Educational Psychology*, 77, 597-607.

Howes, C. (1983) 'Patterns of friendship'. *Child Development*, 54, 1041-1053.

Howes, C. (1988) 'Peer interaction of young children'. *Monographs of the Society for Research in Child Development*, 53, (1, Serial No. 217).

Ispa, J. (1981) 'Peer support among Soviet daycare toddlers'. *International Journal of Behavioral Development*, 4, 255-269.

Kohlberg, L., LaCrosse, J., & Ricks, D. (1972) 'The predictability of adult mental health from childhood'. In B. Wolman (Ed.), *Manual of child psychopathology* (pp. 1217-1283. New York: McGraw-Hill.

Krappman, L. (1985) 'The structure of peer relationships and possible effects on school achievement'. In R.A. Hinde, A.N. Perret-Clermont, & J. Stevenson-Hinde (Eds.), *Social relationships and cognitive development* (pp. 149-166). Oxford: Clarendon.

Ladd, G.W. (1983) 'Social networks of popular, average, and rejected children in school settings'. *Merrill-Palmer Quarterly*, 29, 283-307.

Ladd, G.W. (1988) 'Friendship patterns and peer status during early and middle childhood'. *Journal of Developmental and Behavioral Pediatrics*, 9, 229-238.

Ladd, G.W. (1989) 'Children's social competence and social supports: Precursors of early school adjustment?' In B.H. Schneider, G. Attili, J. Nadel, & R. Weissberg (Eds.), *Social competence in developmental perspective* (pp. 277-291). Amsterdam: Kluwer Academic Publishers.

Ladd, G.W. & Asher, S.R. (1985) 'Social skill training and children's peer relations'. In L. L'Abate & M. Milan (Eds.), *Handbook of social skills training and research* (pp. 219-244). New York: Wiley.

Ladd, G.W., & Emerson, E.S. (1984) 'Shared knowledge in children's friendship'. *Developmental Psychology*, 20, 932-940.

Ladd, G.W., & Golter B.S. (1988) 'Parent's initiation and monitoring of children's peer contacts: Predictive of children's peer relations in nonschool and school settings?' *Developmental Psychology*, 24, 109-117.

Ladd, G.W., & Price, J.M. (1987) 'Predicting children's social and school adjustment following the transition from preschool to kindergarten'. *Child Development*, 58, 1168-1189.

Ladd, G.W., Price, J.M., & Hart, C.H. (1988) 'Predicting preschoolers' peer status from their playground behaviors'. *Child Development*, 59, 986-992.

Ladd, G.W., Price, J.M., & Hart, C. (in press) 'Preschoolers' behavioral orientations and patterns of peer contact: Predictive of peer status?' In S.R. Asher & J.D. Coie (Eds.), *Peer rejection in childhood: Origins, maintenance, and intervention*. Cambridge: Cambridge University Press.

Levine, M. (1966) 'Residential change and school adjustments'. *Mental Health Journal*, 2, 61-69.

Levine, S., Elzey, F.F., & Lewis, M. (1969) *California Preschool Social Competence Scale*. Palo Alto, CA: Consulting Psychologists Press.

Mize, J., & Ladd, G.W. (in press) 'Toward the development of successful social skill training for preschool children'. In S.R. Asher & J.D. Coie (Eds.), *Peer rejection in childhood*. New York: Cambridge University Press.

Parker, J.G., & Asher, S.R. (1987) 'Peer acceptance and later interpersonal adjustment: Are low-accepted children at risk?' *Psychological Bulletin*, 102, 357-389.

Parker, J.G., & Gottman, J.M. (1989) 'Social and emotional development in a relational context: Friendship interaction from early childhood to adolescence'. In T.J. Berndt & G.W. Ladd (Eds.), *Peer relationships in child development* (pp. 95-131). New York: Wiley.

Perry, J.D., Guidubaldi, J., & Kehle, T.J. (1971) 'Kindergarten competencies as predictors of third-grade classroom behavior and achievement'. *Journal of Educational Psychology*, 4, 443-450.

Rakieten, H. (1961) *The reactions of mobile elementary school children to various elementary school induction and orientation procedures*. Unpublished doctoral dissertation, Teachers College, Columbia University.

Roff, M., Sells, S., & Golden, M. (1972) *Social adjustment and personality development in children*. Minneapolis: University of Minnesota Press.

Rubin, K.H. (1984) *Relations between peer and teacher ratings of social competence*. Unpublished manuscript, University of Waterloo.

Rubin, R.A., & Balow, B. (1978) 'Prevalence of teacher-identified behavior problems'. *Exceptional Children*, 45, 102-111.

Rubin, K.H., & Clark, M.L. (1982) 'Preschool teachers' ratings of behavioral problems: Observational, sociometric, and social-cognitive correlates'. *Journal of Abnormal Psychology*, 11, 273-286.

Rubin, K.H., & Daniels-Bierness, T. (1983) 'Concurrent and predictive correlates of sociometric status in kindergarten and grade one children'. *Merrill-Palmer Quarterly*, 29, 279-282.

Sameroff, A.J., & Chandler, M.J. (1975) 'Reproductive risk and the continuum of caretaking casualty'. In F.D. Horowitz, M. Hetherington, S. Scarr-Salapatek, & G. Siegel (Eds.), *Review of child development research* (Vol. 4, pp. 187-244). Chicago: University of Chicago Press.

Schwarz, J.C. (1972) 'Effects of peer familiarity on the behavior of preschoolers in a novel situation'. *Journal of Personality and Social Psychology*, 24, 276-284.

Stevenson, H.W., Parker, T., Wilkinson, A., Hegion, A., & Fish, E. (1976) 'Longitudinal study of individual differences in cognitive development and scholastic development'. *Journal of Educational Psychology*, 68, 377-400.

Worland, J., Weeks, D.G., & Janes, C.L. (1984) 'Intelligence, classroom behavior, and academic achievement in children of high and low risk for psychopathology: A structural equation analysis'. *Journal of Abnormal Child Psychology*, 12, 437-454.

26. Improving the Social Behavior and Peer Acceptance of Rejected Boys: Effects of Social Skill Training With Instructions and Prohibitions

Karen Linn Bierman, Cindy L. Miller and Sally D. Stabb

Thirty-two boys who were rejected by their peers in Grades 1–3 were identified on the basis of negative sociometric nominations and negative social behavior. They were randomly assigned to one of four treatment conditions: (a) instructions to promote positive social behavior, (b) prohibitions to reduce negative social behavior, (c) a combination of instructions and prohibitions, or (d) no treatment. Interventions were applied during 10 half-hour school play sessions. Behavioral observations and peer and teacher ratings were collected prior to treatment, immediately after treatment, and at a follow-up assessment 6 weeks after treatment. Additional peer and teacher ratings were collected at a 1-year follow-up. Prohibitions combined with a response cost for negative behaviors resulted in immediate and stable declines in negative behavior and led to temporary increases in positive responses received from peers. Instructions and the reinforcement of specific social skills promoted sustained positive peer interactions 6 weeks after treatment. Only the combination of instructions and prohibitions led to improved sociometric ratings from nontarget treatment partners.

Peer-rejected grade school children are often disruptive and aggressive socially (Coie & Dodge, 1983). Relative to their peer-accepted or peer-neglected classmates, rejected children are more likely to experience continued social problems, poor school adjustment, loneliness, and poor adult mental health (Ladd & Asher, 1985). Although social skill training may improve the social adjustment of some unaccepted children, the effectiveness of such training for rejected children who show high rates of inappropriate and aversive social behaviors has not yet been established.

In social skill training programs, instructions, modeling, and discussions are used to teach children prosocial skill concepts such as participation, cooperation, and communication. Supervised peer interactions and supportive feedback then provide opportunities to rehearse target skills (Ladd & Mize, 1983). When used with children who show low pretreatment rates of target skills, skill training often leads to increased skill performance and, consequently, to more positive peer responses and increased peer acceptance (Bierman, 1986; Bierman & Furman, 1984; Ladd, 1981).

Investigators have suggested that skill training may also benefit children who exhibit high rates of negative social behavior by teaching them to use nonaversive behavioral

Karen Linn Bierman, Cindy L. Miller and Sally D. Stabb: 'Improving the Social Behavior and Peer Acceptance of Rejected Boys: Effects of Social Skill Training With Instructions and Prohibitons'. *JOURNAL OF CONSULTING AND CLINICAL PSYCHOLOGY* (1987), Vol. 55, No. 2, pp. 194-200. Copyright © 1987 by the American Psychological Association.

strategies to solve conflicts and to acquire interpersonal attention and influence (Combs & Slaby, 1977). However, when Coie and Krehbiel (1984) used skill training with socially rejected children, they observed no changes in classroom behavior and only partial improvements in sociometric ratings. Perhaps skill training programs would be more effective with rejected children if the negative behaviors of these children were targeted directly.

In skill training programs, children may be asked to consider negative as well as positive examples of skill performance, and negative behaviors may be identified for modification during feedback sessions. However, direct behavioral prohibitions or specific consequences for negative behaviors are often not included (Coie & Krehbiel, 1984; Ladd, 1981). Although gradual skill acquisition may lead to gradual decreases in negative behavior, direct procedures such as time-out or response cost contingent on the performance of specific negative behaviors should produce immediate reductions in these behaviors (Brown & Elliott, 1965). Reduced rates of negative behaviors alone will not necessarily lead to increased prosocial interaction or to improved peer acceptance (Drabman & Lahey, 1974: Drabman, Spitalnik, & Spitalnik, 1974) but might facilitate further skill training. Indeed, instructions combined with prohibitions may produce different and complementary effects, with instructions and reinforcement increasing prosocial behaviors and prohibitions and response cost procedures decreasing negative behaviors.

The present study compared the effects of positive instructions and negative prohibitions in a social skill training program for socially negative, peer-rejected boys. Disliked first-, second-, and third-grade boys who showed high levels of negative social behavior during pretreatment observations were randomly assigned to one of four conditions: (a) instructions and coaching in positive behaviors, (b) prohibitions and response cost for negative behaviors, (c) a combination of instructions and prohibitions, or (d) no treatment. Interventions were implemented during 10 half-hour, supervised, small group play sessions, and treatment effects were assessed using behavioral observations and peer and teacher ratings.

On the basis of previous research, it was postulated that instructions and coaching would increase children's positive behavior and perhaps, over time, lead to decreased negative behavior. In contrast, prohibitions and response cost procedures were expected to produce immediate decreases in negative behavior. The combination of instructions and prohibitions was expected to be the most effective treatment for this target population, producing both increases in socially skillful behavior and decreases in negative social behavior. Improved peer acceptance was expected only for boys who received this combined treatment.

Method

Subjects

Subjects were 32 boys in Grades 1–3 (mean age = 7 years, 7 months; range = 6 years, 1 month – 10 years, 1 month). They were selected from a sample of 198 boys from four schools serving a rural, predominantly white, middle- to working-class population who received parental permission to participate in the study (out of a total sample of 260 boys invited to participate in the study). Subjects were selected in a two-step process. First, the 2–3 boys who received the most negative peer nominations in each of the 21 classrooms were observed in a playgroup setting (described in the following section). Of these 50 rejected boys, the 32 boys who displayed the highest levels of negative peer interaction, were retained as target subjects. Additionally, 72 boys who scored below the median of their class in negative nominations were randomly selected to serve as treatment partners.

Measures

Behavioral observations. Each target boy was observed for 8 min during each of two 15-min small group play sessions, providing a total of 16 min of observational data for each subject during each assessment period. The play groups included male classmates who had received parental permission to participate; each group included 5–12 boys ($M = 9$). In one session the boys constructed a group poster using felt pens and in the other they played with army men. Two observers were present at each session and watched each target boy for 1 min at a time, alternating between 6 s of observing and 6 s of recording behaviors. Additionally 2–3 randomly selected nontarget classmates were observed for 1 min each during each play group. These observations were combined to provide 16 min of normative observational data for each group.

Coding categories for play included (a) a *positive* designation, which comprised helping, sharing, and cooperative play and questions, praise, and the offering of suggestions, guidance or invitations; (b) a *negative* designation, which comprised verbal or physical aggression, disapproval of others, disagreement, threats, quarrels, noncompliance, and whining; (c) a *neutral* designation, which comprised all other talking and play behavior such as neutral statements, directives, and jokes: and (d) a *no-interaction* designation, which was coded if no peer interaction occurred during the 6-s interval. An interaction category was coded as *initiated* when the target child directed the behavior toward a peer and as *received* when a peer directed the behavior toward the target child.

Two undergraduate assistants, naive to the purpose of the study and to the status of the boys, were trained as observers. The first author served as trainer and established estimates of interrater reliability. Observers coded videotapes of children's play groups until they reached a reliability criterion of .80, then coded recess interactions for practice prior to data collection. Throughout data collection, periodic checks on interrater reliability were made, and when necessary, booster training sessions were conducted. Interrater reliability was collected for 28% of all observations. Kappa coefficients were computed separately for each behavioral category on an interval by interval basis and ranged from .92 to .80, with a mean of .86.

Aggression ratings. Peer ratings of aggression were made with an abridged version of the Pupil Evaluation Inventory (PEI; Pekarik, Prinz, Liebert, Weintraub, & Neale, 1976) that included 24 behavioral descriptors, including 10 descriptors for aggressive behavior. Boys were given each descriptor and were asked to nominate corresponding classmate names.[1] The total number of aggressive nominations received by each boy was divided by the number of raters and standardized within each class.

Teacher ratings of aggression were made on the PEI and on the Abbreviated Teacher Rating Scale (ATRS; Conners, 1969), which consists of 10 items that describe disruptive classroom behaviors. On both of these scales, teachers gave each boy in their class a 0–3-point rating for each behavioral description (0 = *not at all characteristic* to 3 = *very characteristic*). Total teacher PEI and ATRS scores were standardized within each class.

Sociometric status. Boys rated each classmate on a 5-point scale according to how much they liked to play with that classmate (1= *not at all, never* to 5 = *very much, all the time*). Boys also nominated up to 3 classmates they especially liked and up to 3 classmates they did not like. Play ratings and positive and negative nominations were totalled, divided by the number of raters, and standardized within each class. Additionally, partner sociometric ratings were computed separately to represent the play ratings and positive and negative nominations given to each target boy by the 3 peers who served as his treatment partners.

Procedure

Assessment. Each boy participating in the study was interviewed individually by an undergraduate student who was naive to the status of the boy and to the purpose of the study. The boy was shown a roster of participating classmates and was asked to name each one. The interviewer then read aloud each PEI item, asking the boy to name any class mates on the roster who fit the description. The interviewer then requested up to three (but at least one) positive and negative nominations from the roster and also acquired play ratings for each boy on the roster. Teacher rating measures were distributed at the time of these child interviews and were collected 2 weeks later. Identical procedures were followed prior to treatment, immediately after treatment, and at a follow-up period 6 weeks after treatment. Additionally, at 1 year after treatment peer and teacher ratings were again collected to measure the social adjustment of target boys after they had made transitions to new classrooms.

On the basis of the initial sociometric interviews, the 2–3 boys who received the most negative nominations in each class were observed for 16 min each during two play group sessions with male classmates. The 32 boys who had the highest negative behavioral scores (for both initiated and received interactions) were selected as target subjects. Posttreatment and follow-up play group sessions were identical to the pretreatment sessions.

Treatment. Within each school, boys were randomly assigned to one of four treatment conditions: (a) instructions, (b) prohibitions, (c) instructions and prohibitions, or (d) no treatment. Each of the treatment conditions consisted of 10 half-hour sessions during which a target child engaged in a series of cooperative tasks with nontarget classmates. Three nontarget classmates rotated as peer partners during treatment: one for the first 5 sessions, two for the next 4 sessions, and all three for the last session. The procedure of rotating partners and gradually increasing the size of the treatment group was designed to enhance the generalization of treatment effects to the naturalistic peer group. An adult coach was present at all treatment sessions to facilitate skill acquisition according to treatment condition.

In the instructions condition, the adult began each session with a brief discussion, describing a target skill and eliciting behavioral examples from the group. The target skills were (a) questioning others (for information, clarification, and invitation), (b) helping (by giving support and suggestions) and cooperating in play, and (c) sharing (by sharing materials and taking turns). These skills were selected on the basis of developmental research linking them to social acceptance during the early grade school years (cf. Hartup, 1983) and on the basis of their inclusion in previous successful coaching programs (Ladd, 1981; Oden & Asher, 1977). Two activities designed to promote practice of specific target skills were then conducted, with brief pre- and postactivity skill reviews led by the adult coach. Activities included cooperative art projects, guessing games, constructive activities with blocks and clay, audiotaped interviews, playing with army men, and hide-and-seek. As the children played, the coach praised skill performance and rewarded each skillful behavior by labeling the behavior and placing a token in a cup marked with the child's name. (Although token reinforcement in not usually a part of skill training, it was included here to balance the use of tokens in the prohibition condition.)

In the prohibition condition, the coach presented a set of rules to control the children's negative behavior during the sessions: no fighting or arguing, no yelling, no being mean, no whining or bad temper. Each session included the same cooperative activities used in the instruction condition. However, no instructions in specific skills were provided and no specific skills were rewarded. Instead, the coach provided nonspecific praise and delivered tokens on a random schedule as long as the children engaged in cooperative activities without violating any of the rules (e.g., "Good work, you're not breaking any rules"). Whenever a child violated one of the rules, the coach removed their cup for one min., temporarily removing the ability to earn tokens. Using this modification of the Foxx and Shapiro (1978) "time-out ribbon" technique, it was possible to levy a response cost for negative behaviors without reducing the amount of peer interaction.

In the combined condition, the coach both instructed the children in the target skills and discussed the prohibitive rules. As in the instruction condition, pre- and postactivity reviews were used to provide children with feedback about their target skill performance, and the coach delivered praise and tokens whenever children demonstrated target skills. As in the prohibition condition, the coach also stressed the rules and removed a child's cup and ability to earn tokens for one min contingent on negative behavior. In all conditions, tokens were exchanged for a small snack at the end of each session.[2]

Results

Pretreatment scores

The mean pretreatment standard scores of the target children were examined on each dependent measure to determine the level of pretreatment deviance. As a group, the target children revealed high standard scores on peer aggression ratings ($M = .87$), on negative nominations ($M = 1.11$), on teacher aggression ratings ($M = .87$), and on teacher ATRS scores ($M = .64$). Additionally, the target children revealed low standard scores on positive nominations ($M = -.91$) and play ratings ($M = -79$). Generally, this sample fell in the upper 25% on aggression and peer rejection measures and in the lower 25% on peer acceptance measures. When compared with their nontarget peers, target boys initiated and received 3.5 times as many negative behaviors during pretreatment observations.

Because target children were randomly assigned to treatment groups, no significant pretreatment differences were expected. However, a series of 2 (Instructions) x 2 (Prohibitions) analyses of variance (ANOVAS) conducted on the pretreatment dependent variables revealed two significant differences. Prior to treatment, boys in the prohibition condition received fewer negative behaviors from peers during play group observation sessions than boys in the other treatment conditions, $F(1, 28) = 4.92$, $p < .05$, $M = 6.67$ versus $M = 10.38$, and boys in the instruction condition received higher negative nomination scores than boys in the no treatment condition, $F(1, 28) = 7.89$, $p < .01$, $M = 1.33$ versus $M = .77$.

To control for these group differences, pretreatment variables were used as covariates in the analyses of posttreatment and follow-up scores.[3]

The main effects of each treatment strategy (instructions and prohibitions) were of major interest in this study; therefore, a 2 x 2 (Instructions x Prohibitions) analytic design was used. It was assumed that effects attributable to the combination of these treatment strategies (beyond the main effects of each strategy) would be reflected in significant interaction effects. Initially, multivariate analyses of variance (MANCOVAS) were conducted on measures representing positive interactions, negative interactions, aggression ratings, and sociometric measures. Effects that were significant at a $p < .10$ level were explored further with ANCOVAS.

Behavioral observations

Posttreatment assessment. A 2 x 2 (Instruction x Prohibitions) MANCOVA was conducted on posttreatment observations of initiated and received positive behavior, with pretreatment values serving as covariates. This analysis resulted in an effect for prohibitions that approached significance ($p < .07$). Univariate ANCOVAS revealed that boys in the prohibition condition received more positive responses from peers than did boys in the instruction only or the no treatment condition (see Table 1).

A MANCOVA on posttreatment observations of negative initiated and received behaviors (in which pretreatment values served as covariates) revealed a main effect for prohibitions, $F(2, 25) = 3.85$, $p < .05$. Subsequent ANCOVAS showed that boys who received prohibitions initiated fewer negative behaviors after treatment than boys who did not receive prohibitions (see Table 1). No significant treatment effects emerged for negative received behavior.

Follow-up assessment. Follow-up observations of positive initiated and received behavior were then subjected to a MANCOVA that revealed an effect for instructions that approached significance, ($p < .08$). Six weeks after treatment, instructed boys received more positive peer responses than noninstructed boys and tended to initiate more positive behaviors (see Table 2).

Table 1   Means and standard deviations of behavioral effects of prohibitions across time

Behavior	Pretreatment		Posttreatment		Follow-up		$F(1,27)$
	P	NP	P	NP	P	NP	
Positive initiated							
M	8.80	6.13	6.38	4.25	6.25	4.25	
SD	3.36	2.50	4.82	3.72	4.01	2.75	
Positive received							
M	2.13	2.63	3.38*	1.63*	1.87	1.75	6.46*
SD	1.20	2.47	2.47	1.31	2.06	1.65	
Negative initiated							
M	10.56	11.75	5.81*	13.06*[a]	4.31*	8.56*[b]	6.09*
SD	4.75	5.01	4.51	9.74	4.01	6.22	5.92*
Negative received							
M	6.69	10.38	3.94	7.69	3.56	5.84	
SD	4.42	4.89	2.79	6.89	3.25	5.31	

Note. P = prohibitions; NP = no prohibitions.
[a]This test of difference between posttreatment means corresponds to an F value of 6.09.
[b]This test of difference between follow-up means corresponds to an F value of 5.92.
* $p < .05$.

The MANCOVA on negative initiated and received behavior at follow-up revealed a significant interaction effect for instructions and prohibitions, $F(2,25) = 2.77, p < .05$. Subsequent ANCOVAS and Duncan post hoc comparisons revealed that boys who received instructions, prohibitions, or the combination of instructions and prohibitions initiated fewer negative behaviors than boys who received no treatment (Ms = 5.26, 4.64, and 3.63 vs. M = 12.23, respectively). Additionally, instructed boys received fewer negative behaviors than noninstructed boys (see Table 2).

Pattern of change. Next, changes over time within each condition were examined. Standardized scores were computed to represent children's total positive interactions (initiated plus received) and total negative interactions (initiated plus received). Then, paired t tests were computed to examine change in positive and negative interactions from pretreatment to follow-up within each treatment condition. As shown in Table 3, boys in the three treatment conditions maintained the same level of positive interactions at the follow-up assessment that they had shown prior to treatment within .5 of a standard deviation of the normative mean. In contrast, boys in the no treatment condition experienced significant declines in positive interactions and decreased from a normative level of positive interactions to a level of 1.5 standard deviations below the norm.

Table 2   **Means and standard deviations of behavioral effects of instructions across time**

Behavior	Pretreatment		Posttreatment		Follow-up		F(1,27)
	I	NI	I	NI	I	NI	
Positive initiated							
M	5.94	6.06	5.31	5.31	6.31*	4.19*	3.14*
SD	3.19	2.72	4.84	3.80	4.11	2.54	
Positive received							
M	2.19	2.56	2.31	2.69	2.50**	1.12**	4.66**
SD	1.76	2.13	2.24	2.09	2.00	1.41	
Negative initiated							
M	12.25	10.06	8.88	10.00	5.19*	7.69*	3.63*
SD	5.71	3.64	7.06	9.63	4.65	6.28	
Negative received							
M	9.50	7.56	7.19	4.44	3.31**	6.19**	4.05**
SD	5.11	4.76	5.13	5.69	3.03	5.31	

Note. I = instructions; NI = no instructions.
* $p < .10$. ** $p < .05$.

An examination of negative interactions revealed an opposite pattern of change. Boys in the three treatment conditions showed significant decreases in negative interactions from very high pretreatment levels to follow-up levels within 1 standard deviation of the norm. Boys who received no treatment, however, experienced no improvements in their negative interactions and remained over 4 standard deviations above the normative mean at the follow-up assessment (see Table 3).

Aggression ratings

Posttreatment aggression ratings, available from three sources (peer PEI, teacher PEI, and teacher ATRS scores), were subjected to a 2 x 2 MANCOVA. Pretreatment values on these variables served as covariates. This analysis revealed a significant Instructions x Prohibitions interaction, $F(3, 23) = 4.19$, $p < .01$. Univariate ANCOVAS revealed a similar interaction effect on peer PEI aggression ratings, $F(1, 25) = 14.75$, $p < .001$. Boys who received either the combined treatment or no treatment had lower peer aggression ratings immediately after treatment than did boys who received prohibitions or instructions alone ($Ms = .56$ and .50 vs. $Ms = 1.28$ and 1.64, respectively); however, between groups differences were not significant according to Duncan post hoc comparisons. The MANCOVA on aggression ratings 6 weeks after treatment resulted in no significant effects.

Table 3   Changes in mean standardized scores for positive and negative interactions by condition

Condition	Pretreatment	Posttreatment	Follow-up	$T(7)$
Positive interactions				
Instructions only	−.45	−1.49	−.32	−.18
Prohibitions only	−.54	.04	−.81	.39
Instructions & prohibitions	.09	.77	.44	−.42
No treatment	.54	−.50	−1.58	4.21*
Negative interactions				
Instructions only	5.63	5.35	.87	3.78*
Prohibitions only	2.73	1.28	.47	4.07*
Instructions & prohibitions	4.66	1.28	.87	3.34*
No treatment	4.91	4.30	4.75	.11

Note. T values represent changes from pretreatment to follow-up. Positive interactions include initiated and received behaviors; negative interactions include initiated and received negative behaviors. Standard scores based on comparisons with normative observations.

* $p < .01$.

Sociometric ratings

Classroom ratings. A MANCOVA conducted on boys' posttreatment play ratings, positive nominations, and negative nominations (in which pretreatment values on these variables served as covariates) revealed no significant effects. A similar MANCOVA on boys' 6-week follow-up classroom sociometric ratings revealed no treatment effects. (Sociometric ratings given to the boys by the peers who served as treatment partners were examined separately.)

Partner ratings. Peer partner ratings were not available for boys in the no treatment condition or for 2 subjects in the coaching alone condition (one peer moved from the school and two others moved to different classrooms). A series of one-way ANCOVAS were conducted on the posttreatment and follow-up partner ratings of other boys to evaluate differences between the treatment conditions.

These analyses revealed a significant effect for condition on negative nominations received from partners at the posttreatment assessment, $F(2, 18) = 3.93$, $p < .05$, and at the follow-up assessment $F(2, 18) = 5.01$, $p < .05$. Duncan post hoc comparisons revealed that boys who received a combination of instructions and prohibitions received fewer negative nominations immediately after treatment than did boys who received prohibitions alone *(M* = 1.04 vs. *M* = 2.21, $p < .05$), whereas the scores of boys who received instructions alone were intermediate in value *(M* = 1.46). By follow-up, boys who received the combined treatment received fewer negative nominations from their treatment partners than boys who received either instructions or prohibitions alone *(M* = .77 vs. *M*s = 2.03 and 1.82, respectively, $p < .05$).

The T tests examining within-group patterns of change revealed that boys in the combined condition received significantly fewer negative nominations from their treatment partners at posttreatment and follow-up compared with pretreatment assessment (Ms = 1.00 and .75 vs. M = 1.75, $T[7]$ = −2.39, $p < .05$). In contrast, boys who received instructions or prohibitions alone showed no change in the number of negative nominations received from their treatment partners (all $ps > .10$).

One-year follow-up. Teacher and peer aggression and sociometric ratings were collected 1 year after treatment in the new classrooms of all but 3 of the target boys. (Two boys in the no treatment condition and 1 boy in the prohibition condition had moved out of the school district.) The MANCOVAs conducted on these measures revealed no significant effects on either aggression ratings or sociometric ratings.

Discussion

Instructions and prohibitions had different and complementary effects on the social interactions of peer-rejected boys. Boys who received prohibitions and were levied a response cost for negative behaviors during small group play sessions with nontarget classmates initiated fewer negative behaviors during large group interactions immediately after and 6 weeks after the intervention. These boys also received more positive behavior from their peers immediately after treatment but not 6 weeks later. Prohibitions did not affect the level of negative behavior that target boys received from peers. In contrast, instructions and rewards for specific positive behaviors produced less immediate but more stable behavioral improvements. By the follow-up assessment, instructed boys were initiating and receiving fewer negative behaviors than noninstructed boys. Instructed boys were also initiating and receiving more positive peer interaction than noninstructed boys, primarily because boys who received no treatment experienced steady declines in positive peer interactions over time. The primary behavioral advantage of combining prohibitions with instructions was additive; boys who received the combined program showed immediate posttreatment decreases in negative initiations, later decreases in negative peer responses, and stable positive peer interactions.

Improving the social behavior of rejected boys is easier than improving their reputations or increasing peer acceptance. In spite of the reductions in negative behavior observed for treated boys during naturalistic peer group interactions, teacher and peer aggression ratings showed no stable improvements. Additionally, peer acceptance measured by positive nominations, negative nominations, and play ratings received from male classmates revealed no treatment effects. The only increases in peer acceptance were documented for boys who received the combination of instructions and prohibitions. Compared with their own pretreatment scores and with the scores received by boys in other treatment conditions, boys who received the combined program received fewer negative nominations (at posttreatment and at follow-up) from the classmates who served as their treatment partners.

The failure to increase peer acceptance despite observed reductions in negative behavior and increases in skillful behavior is not uncommon (Bierman & Furman, 1984; Drabman & Lahey, 1974; La Greca & Santogrossi, 1980). Perhaps, in such cases, target children do not generalize behavioral improvements to naturalistic settings or fail to maintain behavioral improvements over a long enough period of time to affect peer preferences. In the present study, the age of the target boys may have reduced the likelihood of generalization across situations and time. That is, boys targeted in this program were younger than boys targeted in previous coaching programs (Grades 1-3 compared with Grades 3–6). The younger boys were selected because research has suggested that aggressive behavior becomes stable and predictive by age 6 (Gersten, Langner, Eisenberg, Simcha-Faga, & McCarthy, 1976), and we hypothesized that negative behavior patterns and reputations would be more easily changed before they became well-established. However, perhaps younger boys are less able to generalize the skill concepts and behavioral principles to new untrained situations than older boys who generally have more well-developed cognitive capacities for using rules to guide their own behavior.

In contrast to this possibility, previous research has suggested that children may generalize behavioral improvements to naturalistic peer interactions and, nonetheless, fail to improve peer ratings (Bierman & Furman, 1984). In this case, the lack of generalized improvement may reflect the rigidity of peer expectations and stereotypes. Rejected children may find it particularly difficult to escape negative reputations unless active measures are taken to change peer attitudes. Previous research has suggested that working cooperatively with disliked classmates under environmental contingencies that support positive interactions may increase positive peer responding (Bierman, 1986). Indeed, in the combined condition of the present study, peer partners did become less rejecting of the target children with whom they worked. Perhaps a larger program that involves controlled interactions with more classmates will lead to greater sociometric improvements. Alternatively, instructions and prohibitions applied in small groups might be followed by larger classroom programs, such as Teams-Games-Tournaments or Jigsaw Classroom, which use interdependent tasks and superordinate goals to increase cooperation and positive interaction among all classmates (Blaney, Stephan, Rosenfield, Aronson, & Sikes, 1977; DeVries & Slavin, 1976).

One unexpected finding of this study was that boys selected on the basis of negative nominations and observed negative behavior did not show lower than average levels of positive peer interactions prior to treatment. However, intervention appeared necessary to prevent the significant declines in positive interactions over time that were experienced by nontreated boys. Although some theorists have suggested that aggressive behavior is often the result of social skill deficits (e.g., children behave aggressively because they lack the social problem-solving skills, self-control skills, or prosocial interaction skills to behave adaptively), the reverse may sometimes be true. That is, children who have learned to behave in a negative or egocentric fashion may alienate peers and may therefore have gradually fewer opportunities to engage in positive peer interactions over time. For these children, the positive effect of social skill training may not be the promotion of skill acquisition but rather the provision of structured opportunities that elicit, reward, and maintain positive peer interactions.

The results of this study highlight the importance of both social behavior and sociometric status in the evaluation of treatment of children with poor peer relations. Children's negative interpersonal behavior appears to be fairly responsive to environmental control. Increasing peer acceptance is more difficult, perhaps due to limited generalization of behavior changes or to stable negative peer expectations. In this study, only the provision of structured opportunities for interaction between target children and nontarget classmates during which both prohibitions and instructions were implemented resulted in both behavioral and sociometric improvements. Further research may clarify the relations among social skill deficits, aggressive behavior, and peer rejection and may identify alternative procedures to strengthen the impact of school-based interventions on the social adjustment of socially negative, peer-rejected children.

This research was supported by a Scholars in Mental Health of Children grant awarded by the W.T. Grant Foundation to the first author. Appreciation is expressed to Robin Blair, Debbie Kycko, Nancy Micci, Annette Miller, Penny Pearson, and Kathy Aumiller for their assistance in data collection. We are also extremely grateful to the students and faculty at Ferguson, Park Forest, and Radio Park Elementary Schools in State College, Pennyslvania and at Bellefonte and Marion-Walker Elementary Schools in Bellefonte, Pennsylvania for their participation in and support of this project.

Notes

1. Nine items were deleted from the original PEI on the basis of lower factor loadings in the Pekarik, Prinz, Liebert, Weintraub, and Neale (1976) study and to enable repeated assessments with young elementary children. Pilot testing suggested little difference between aggression ratings based on this abridged version of the PEI and ratings based on the original 35-item version.

2. Copies of the coding manual and the intervention manual may be obtained from the first author.

3. In only a chance number of cases (1 out of 20 variables) was a test of the null hypothesis concerning the homogeneity of regression coefficients significant, indicating that, in general, this basic condition necessary for the analysis of covariance was met.

References

Bierman, K.L. (1986) 'Process of change during social skills training with preadolescents and its relation to treatment outcome'. *Child Development*, 57, 230-240.

Bierman, K.L., & Furman, W. (1984). The effects of social skills training and peer involvement on the social adjustment of preadolescents'. *Child Development*, 55, 151-162.

Blaney, N.T., Stephan, S., Rosenfield, D., Aronson, E., & Sikes, J. (1977) 'Interdependence in the classroom: A field study'. *Journal of Educational Psychology*, 69, 121-128.

Brown, P., & Elliott, R. (1965) 'Control of aggression in a nursery school class'. *Journal of Experimental Child Psychology*, 2, 103-107.

Coie, J.D., & Dodge, K.A. (1983) 'Continuities and changes in children's social status: A five-year longitudinal study'. *Merrill-Palmer Quarterly*, 29, 261-282.

Coie, J.D., & Krehbiel, G. (1984) 'Effects of academic tutoring on the social status of low-achieving, socially rejected children'. *Child Development*, 55, 1465-1478.

Combs, M.L., & Slaby, D.A. (1977) 'Social skills training with children'. In B. Lahey & A. Kazdin (Eds.), *Advances in clinical child psychology* (Vol. 1, pp. 161-201). New York: Plenum Press.

Conners, C. (1969) 'A teacher rating scale for use in drug studies with children'. *American Journal of Psychiatry*, 126, 152-156.

DeVries, D.L., & Slavin, R.E. (1976) *Teams-games-tournament: A final report on the research* (Tech. Rep. No. 217). Baltimore, MD: Johns Hopkins University, Center for Social Organization of the Schools.

Drabman, R.S., & Lahey, B.B. (1974) 'Feedback in classroom behavior modification: Effects on the target and her classmates'. *Journal of Applied Behavior Analysis*, 7, 591-598.

Drabman, R., Spitalnick, R., & Spitalnick, K. (1974) 'Sociometric and disruptive behavior as a function of four types of token reinforcement programs'. *Journal of Applied Behavior Analysis*, 7, 93-101.

Foxx, R.M., & Shapiro, S.T. (1978) 'The timeout ribbon: A nonexclusionary timeout procedure'. *Journal of Applied Behavior Analysis*, 11, 125-136.

Gersten, J.C., Langner, T.S., Eisenberg, J.C., Simcha-Faga, O., & McCarthy, E.D. (1976) 'Stability and change in types of behavioural disturbance of children and adolescents'. *Journal of Abnormal Child Psychology*, 4, 111-127.

Hartup, W.W. (1983) 'Peer relations'. In E.M. Hetherington (Ed.), *Handbook of child psychology: Vol. 4. Socialization, personality, and social development* (pp. 103-196). New York: Wiley.

Ladd, G. (1981) 'Effectiveness of social learning and method for enhancing children's social interaction and peer acceptance'. *Child Development*, 52, 171-178.

Ladd, G.W., & Asher, S.R. (1985) 'Social skill training and children's peer relations: Current issues in research and practice'. In L. L'Abate & M. Milan (Eds.), *Handbook of social skill training* (pp. 219-244). New York: Wiley.

Ladd, G.W., & Mize, J. (1983) 'A cognitive-social learning model of social skill training'. *Psychological Review*, 90, 127-157.

LaGreca, A.M., & Santogrossi, D.A. (1980) 'Social skills training with elementary school students: A behavioral group approach'. *Journal of Consulting and Clinical Psychology*, 48, 220-227.

Oden, S., & Asher, S.R. (1977) 'Coaching children in social skills'. *Child Development*, 48, 495-506.

Pekarik, E.G., Prinz, R.J., Liebert, D.E., Weintraub, S., & Neale, J.M. (1976) 'The Pupil Evaluation Inventory. A sociometric technique for assessing children's social behavior'. *Journal of Abnormal Child Psychology*, 4, 83-97.

Adolescence

The articles appearing in this section cover two main topics: internal conflict generated in the process of identity formation, and the logical abilities of adolescents.

Adolescence was seen by Erik Erikson as a period dominated by concerns with constructing a coherent identity, or view of the self. Erikson maintained that during the lifespan, individuals go through eight stages of psychosocial development, each being characterised by a key concern with associated internal conflicts. The greater intellectual maturity of the adolescent, coupled with the increased self-consciousness brought about by puberty and feelings of urgency about the future, make for more intense internal conflicts than in earlier periods. The chapter by Erikson provides a summary of his ideas on the genesis of internal conflict in the pursuit of an identity. The article by Harter and Monsour takes a closer look at the nature of internal conflicts in the adolescent years, and how these are influenced by general cognitive changes.

Adolescence also represents the final stage in Piaget's theory of cognitive development, culminating in the emergence of 'formal operations'. The individual can now engage in formal, abstract reasoning, of the sort encountered in scientific testing of hypotheses and deductive reasoning. Recently, investigators have challenged Piaget's assertion that formal operations develop spontaneously, and are widely used in solving problems. The articles by Markovitz and Vachon and by Linn explore various ways in which the content of a problem influences the use of formal reasoning in the adolescent years.

27.   The Life Cycle: Epigenesis of Identity

Erik H. Erikson

Adolescence

As technological advances put more and more time between early school life and the young person's final access to specialized work, the stage of adolescing becomes an even more marked and conscious period and, as it has always been in some cultures in some periods, almost a way of life between childhood and adulthood. Thus in the later school years young people, beset with the physiological revolution of their genital maturation and the uncertainty of the adult roles ahead, seem much concerned with faddish attempts at establishing an adolescent subculture with what looks like a final rather than a transitory or, in fact, initial identity formation. They are sometimes morbidly, often curiously, preoccupied with what they appear to be in the eyes of others as compared with what they feel they are, and with the question of how to connect the roles and skills cultivated earlier with the ideal prototypes of the day. In their search for a new sense of continuity and sameness, which must now include sexual maturity, some adolescents have to come to grips again with crises of earlier years before they can install lasting idols and ideals as guardians of a final identity. They need, above all, a moratorium for the integration of the identity elements ascribed in the foregoing to the childhood stages: only that now a larger unit, vague in its outline and yet immediate in its demands, replaces the childhood milieu — "society." A review of these elements is also a list of adolescent problems.

If the earliest stage bequeathed to the identity crisis is an important need for trust in oneself and in others, then clearly the adolescent looks most fervently for men and ideas to have *faith* in, which also means men and ideas in whose service it would seem worth while to prove oneself trustworthy. At the same time, however, the adolescent fears a foolish, all too trusting commitment, and will, paradoxically, express his need for faith in loud and cynical mistrust.

If the second stage established the necessity of being defined by what one can *will* freely, then the adolescent now looks for an opportunity to decide with free assent on one of the available or unavoidable avenues of duty and service, and at the same time is mortally afraid of being forced into activities in which he would feel exposed to ridicule or self-doubt. This, too, can lead to a paradox, namely, that he would rather act shamelessly in the eyes of his elders, out of free choice, than be forced into activities which would be shameful in his own eyes or in those of his peers.

If an unlimited *imagination* as to what one *might* become is the heritage of the play age, then the adolescent's willingness to put his trust in those peers and leading, or misleading, elders who will give imaginative, if not illusory, scope to his aspirations is only too obvious. By the same token, he objects violently to all "pedantic" limitations

Erik H. Erikson: Extracts from 'The Life Cycle: Epigenesis of Identity' in *IDENTITY: YOUTH AND CRISIS* (Faber and Faber Limited, 1968). pp. 128-141.

on his self-images and will be ready to settle by loud accusation all his guiltiness over the excessiveness of his ambition.

Finally, if the desire to make something work, and to make it work well, is the gain of the school age, then the choice of an occupation assumes a significance beyond the question of remuneration and status. It is for this reason that some adolescents prefer not to work at all for a while rather than be forced into an otherwise promising career which would offer success without the satisfaction of functioning with unique excellence.

In any given period in history, then, that part of youth will have the most affirmatively exciting time of it which finds itself in the wave of a technological, economic, or ideological trend seemingly promising all that youthful vitality could ask for.

Adolescence, therefore, is least "stormy" in that segment of youth which is gifted and well trained in the pursuit of expanding technological trends, and thus able to identify with new roles of competency and invention and to accept a more implicit ideological outlook. Where this is not given, the adolescent mind becomes a more explicitly ideological one, by which we mean one searching for some inspiring unification of tradition or anticipated techniques, ideas, and ideals. And, indeed, it is the ideological potential of a society which speaks most clearly to the adolescent who is so eager to be affirmed by peers, to be confirmed by teachers, and to be inspired by worth-while "ways of life." On the other hand, should a young person feel that the environment tries to deprive him too radically of all the forms of expression which permit him to develop and integrate the next step, he may resist with the wild strength encountered in animals who are suddenly forced to defend their lives. For, indeed, in the social jungle of human existence there is no feeling of being alive without a sense of identity.

Having come this far, I would like to give one example (and I consider it representative in structure) of the individual way in which a young person, given some leeway, may utilize a traditional way of life for dealing with a remnant of negative identity. I had known Jill before her puberty, when she was rather obese and showed many "oral" traits of voracity and dependency while she also was a tomboy and bitterly envious of her brothers and in rivalry with them. But she was intelligent and always had an air about her (as did her mother) which seemed to promise that things would turn out all right. And, indeed, she straightened out and up, became very attractive, an easy leader in any group, and, to many, a model of young girlhood. As a clinician, I watched and wondered what she would do with that voraciousness and with the rivalry which she had displayed earlier. Could it be that such things are simply absorbed in fortuitous growth?

Then one autumn in her late teens, Jill did not return to college from the ranch out West where she had spent the summer. She had asked her parents to let her stay. Simply out of liberality and confidence, they granted her this moratorium and returned East.

That winter Jill specialized in taking care of newborn colts, and would get up at any time during a winter night to bottle feed the most needy animals. Having apparently acquired a certain satisfaction within herself, as well as astonished recognition from the cowboys, she returned home and reassumed her place. I felt that she had found and hung on to an opportunity to do actively and for others what she had always yearned to have done for her, as she had once demonstrated by overeating: she had learned to feed needy young mouths. But she did so in a context which, in turning passive into active, also turned a former symptom into a social act.

One might say that she turned "maternal" but it was a maternalism such as cowboys must and do display; and, of course, she did it all in jeans. This brought recognition "from man to man" as well as from man to woman, and beyond that the confirmation of her optimism, that is, her feeling that something could be done that felt like her, was useful and worth while, and was in line with an ideological trend where it still made immediate practical sense.

Such self-chosen "therapies" depend, of course, on the leeway given in the right spirit at the right time, and this depends on a great variety of circumstances. I intend to publish similar fragments from the lives of children in greater detail at some future date; let this example stand for the countless observations in everyday life, where the resourcefulness of young people proves itself when the conditions are right.

The estrangement of this stage is *identity confusion*, which will be elaborated in clinical and biographic detail in the next chapter. For the moment, we will accept Biff's formulation in Arthur Miller's *Death of a Salesman*: "I just can't take hold, Mom, I can't take hold of some kind of a life." Where such a dilemma is based on a strong previous doubt of one's ethnic and sexual identity, or where role confusion joins a hopelessness of long standing, delinquent and "borderline" psychotic episodes are not uncommon. Youth after youth bewildered by the incapacity to assume a role forced on him by the inexorable standardization of American adolescence, runs away in one form or another, dropping out of school, leaving jobs, staying out all night, or withdrawing into bizarre and inaccessible moods. Once "delinquent," his greatest need and often his only salvation is the refusal on the part of older friends, advisers, and judiciary personnel to type him further by pat diagnoses and social judgments which ignore the special dynamic conditions of adolescence. It is here, as we shall see in greater detail, that the concept of identity confusion is of practical clinical value, for if they are diagnosed and treated correctly, seemingly psychotic and criminal incidents do not have the same fatal significance which they may have at other ages.

In general it is the inability to settle on an occupational identity which most disturbs young people. To keep themselves together they temporarily overidentify with the heroes of cliques and crowds to the point of an apparently complete loss of individuality. Yet in this stage not even "falling in love" is entirely, or even primarily, a sexual matter. To a considerable extent adolescent love is an attempt to arrive at a definition of one's identity by projecting one's diffused self-image on another and by seeing it thus reflected and gradually clarified. This is why so much of young love is conversation. On the other hand, clarification can also be sought by destructive means. Young people can become remarkably clannish, intolerant, and cruel in their exclusion of others who are "different," in skin color or cultural background, in tastes and gifts, and often in entirely petty aspects of dress and gesture arbitrarily selected as the signs of an in-grouper or out-grouper. It is important to understand in principle (which does not mean to condone in all of its manifestations) that such intolerance may be, for a while, a necessary

489

defense against a sense of identity loss. This is unavoidable at a time of life when the body changes its proportions radically, when genital puberty floods body and imagination with all manner of impulses, when intimacy with the other sex approaches and is, on occasion, forced on the young person, and when the immediate future confronts one with too many conflicting possibilities and choices. Adolescents not only help one another temporarily through such discomfort by forming cliques and stereotyping themselves, their ideals, and their enemies; they also insistently test each other's capacity for sustaining loyalties in the midst of inevitable conflicts of values.

The readiness for such testing helps to explain the appeal of simple and cruel totalitarian doctrines among the youth of such countries and classes as have lost or are losing their group identities — feudal, agrarian, tribal, or national. The democracies are faced with the job of winning these grim youths by convincingly demonstrating to them — by living it — that a democratic identity can be strong and yet tolerant, judicious and still determined. But industrial democracy poses special problems in that it insists on self-made identities ready to grasp many chances and ready to adjust to the changing necessities of booms and busts, of peace and war, of migration and determined sedentary life. Democracy, therefore, must present its adolescents with ideals which can be shared by young people of many backgrounds, and which emphasize autonomy in the form of independence and initiative in the form of constructive work. These promises, however, are not easy to fulfill in increasingly complex and centralized systems of industrial, economic, and political organization, systems which increasingly neglect the "self-made" ideology still flaunted in oratory. This is hard on many young Americans because their whole upbringing has made the development of a self-reliant personality dependent on a certain degree of choice, a sustained hope for an individual chance, and a firm commitment to the freedom of self-realization.

We are speaking here not merely of high privileges and lofty ideals but of psychological necessities. For the social institution which is the guardian of identity *is* what we have called *ideology*. One may see in ideology also the imagery of an aristocracy in its widest possible sense, which connotes that within a defined world image and a given course of history the best people will come to rule and rule will develop the best in people. In order not to become cynically or apathetically lost, young people must somehow be able to convince themselves that those who succeed in their anticipated adult world thereby shoulder the obligation of being best. For it is through their ideology that social systems enter into the fiber of the next generation and attempt to absorb into their lifeblood the rejuvenative power of youth. Adolescence is thus a vital regenerator in the process of social evolution, for youth can offer its loyalties and energies both to the conservation of that which continues to feel true and to the revolutionary correction of that which has lost its regenerative significance.

We can study the identity crisis also in the lives of creative individuals who could resolve it for themselves only by offering to their contemporaries a new model of resolution such as that expressed in works of art or in original deeds, and who furthermore are eager to tell us all about it in diaries, letters, and self-representations. And even as the neuroses of a given period reflect the ever-present inner chaos of man's existence in a new way, the creative crises point to the period's unique solutions.

We will in the next chapter present in greater detail what we have learned of these specialized individual crises. But there is a third manifestation of the remnants of infantilism and adolescence in man: it is the pooling of the individual crises in transitory upheavals amounting to collective "hysterias." Where there are voluble leaders their creative crises and the latent crises of their followers can be at least studied with the help of our assumptions — and of their writings. More elusive are spontaneous group developments not attributable to a leader. And it will, at any rate, not be helpful to call mass irrationalities by clinical names. It would be impossible to diagnose clinically how much hysteria is present in a young nun participating in an epidemic of convulsive spells or how much perverse "sadism" in a young Nazi commanded to participate in massive parades or in mass killings. So we can point only most tentatively to certain similarities between individual crises and group behavior in order to indicate that in a given period of history they are in an obscure contact with each other.

But before we submerge ourselves in the clinical and biographic evidence for what we call identity confusion, we will take a look beyond the identity crisis. The words "beyond identity," of course, could be understood in two ways, both essential for the problem. They could mean that there is more to man's core than identity, that there is in fact in each individual an "I," an observing center of awareness and of volition, which can transcend and must survive the *psychosocial identity* which is our concern in this book. In some ways, as we will see, a sometimes precocious self-transcendence seems to be felt strongly in a transient manner in youth, as if a pure identity had to be kept free from psychosocial encroachment. And yet no man (except a man aflame and dying like Keats, who could speak of identity in words which secured him immediate fame) can transcend himself in youth. We will speak later of the transcendence of identity. In the following "beyond identity" means life after adolescence and the uses of identity and, indeed, the return of some forms of identity crisis in the later stages of the life cycle.

Beyond identity

The first of these is the crisis of *intimacy*. It is only when identity formation is well on its way that true intimacy — which is really a counterpointing as well as a fusing of identities — is possible. Sexual intimacy is only part of what I have in mind, for it is obvious that sexual intimacies often precede the capacity to develop a true and mutual psychosocial intimacy with another person, be it in friendship, in erotic encounters, or in joint inspiration. The youth who is not sure of his identity shies away from interpersonal intimacy or throws himself into acts of intimacy which are "promiscuous" without true fusion or real self-abandon.

Where a youth does not accomplish such intimate relationships with others — and, I would add, with his own inner resources — in late adolescence or early adulthood, he may settle for highly stereotyped interpersonal relations and come to retain a deep *sense of isolation*. If the times favor an impersonal kind of interpersonal pattern, a man can go far, very far, in life and yet harbor a severe character problem doubly painful because he will never feel really himself, although everyone says he is "somebody."

The counterpart of intimacy is *distantiation:* the readiness to repudiate, isolate, and, if necessary, destroy those forces and people whose essence seems dangerous to one's own.

Thus, the lasting consequence of the need for distantiation is the readiness to fortify one's territory of intimacy and solidarity and to view all outsiders with a fanatic "overvaluation of small differences" between the familiar and the foreign. Such prejudices can be utilized and exploited in politics and in war and secure the loyal self-sacrifice and the readiness to kill from the strongest and the best. A remnant of adolescent danger is to be found where intimate, competitive, and combative relations are experienced with and against the selfsame people. But as the areas of adult responsibility are gradually delineated, as the competitive encounter, the erotic bond, and merciless enmity are differentiated from each other, they eventually become subject to that *ethical sense* which is the mark of the adult and which takes over from the ideological conviction of adolescence and the moralism of childhood.

Freud was once asked what he thought a normal person should be able to do well. The questioner probably expected a complicated, "deep" answer. But Freud simply said, "*Lieben und arbeiten*" ("to love and to work"). It pays to ponder on this simple formula; it grows deeper as you think about it. For when Freud said "love," he meant the generosity of intimacy as well as genital love; when he said love and work, he meant a general work productiveness which would not preoccupy the individual to the extent that he might lose his right or capacity to be a sexual and a loving being.

Psychoanalysis has emphasized *genitality* as one of the developmental conditions for full maturity. Genitality consists in the capacity to develop orgastic potency which is more than the discharge of sex products in the sense of Kinsey's "outlets." It combines the ripening of intimate sexual mutuality with full genital sensitivity and with a capacity for discharge of tension from the whole body. This is a rather concrete way of saying something about a process which we ready do not yet quite understand. But the experience of the climactic mutuality of orgasm clearly provides a supreme example of the mutual regulation of complicated patterns and in some way appeases the hostilities and the potential rages caused by the daily evidence of the oppositeness of male and female, of fact and fancy, of love and hate, of work and play. Such experience makes sexuality less obsessive and sadistic control of the partner superfluous.

Before such genital maturity is reached, much of sexual life is of the self-seeking, identity-hungry kind; each partner is really trying only to reach himself. Or it remains a kind of genital combat in which each tries to defeat the other. All this remains as part of adult sexuality, but it is gradually absorbed as the differences between the sexes become a full polarization within a joint life style. For the previously established vital strengths have helped to make the two sexes first become similar in consciousness, language, and ethics in order to then permit them to be maturely different.

Man, in addition to erotic attractions has developed a selectivity of "love" which serves the need for a new and shared identity. If the estrangement typical for this stage is *isolation,* that is, the incapacity to take chances with one's identity by sharing true intimacy, such inhibition is often reinforced by a fear of the outcome of intimacy: offspring — and care. Love as mutual devotion, however, overcomes the antagonisms inherent in sexual and functional polarization, and is the vital strength of young adulthood. It is the guardian of that elusive and yet all-pervasive power of cultural and personal style which binds into a "way of life" the affiliations of competition and co-operation, production and procreation.

If we should continue the game of "I am" formulations "beyond identity" we should have to change the tune. For now the increment of identity is based on the formula *"We* are what we love."

EVOLUTION has made man a teaching as well as a learning animal, for dependency and maturity are reciprocal: mature man needs to be needed, and maturity is guided by the nature of that which must be cared for. *Generativity,* then, is primarily the concern for establishing and guiding the next generation. There are of course, people who, from misfortune or because of special and genuine gifts in other directions, do not apply this drive to offspring of their own, but to other forms of altruistic concern and creativity which many absorb their kind of parental drive. And indeed, the concept of generativity is meant to include productivity and creativity, neither of which, however, can replace it as designations of a crisis in development. For the ability to lose oneself in the meeting of bodies and minds leads to a gradual expansion of ego-interests and to a libidinal investment in that which is being generated. Where such enrichment fails altogether, regression to an obsessive need for pseudointimacy takes place, often with a pervading *sense of stagnation,* boredom, and interpersonal impoverishment. Individuals, then, often begin to indulge themselves as if they were their own — or one another's — one and only child; and where conditions favor it, early invalidism, physical or psychological, becomes the vehicle of self-concern. On the other hand, the mere fact of having or even wanting children does not "achieve" generativity. Some young parents suffer, it seems, from a retardation in the ability to develop true care. The reasons are often to be found in early childhood impressions; in faulty identifications with parents; in excessive self-love based on a too strenuously self-made personality; and in the lack of some faith, some "belief in the species", which would make a child appear to be a welcome trust. The very nature of generativity, however, suggests that its most circumscribed pathology must now be sought in the next generation, that is, in the form of those unavoidable estrangements which we have listed for childhood and youth and which may appear in aggravated form as a result of a generative failure on the part of the parents.

As to the institutions which reinforce generativity and safeguard it, one can only say that *all* institutions by their very nature codify the ethics of generative succession. Generativity is itself a driving power in human organization. And the stages of childhood and adulthood are a system of generation and regeneration to which institutions such as shared households and divided labor strive to give continuity. Thus the basic strengths enumerated here and the essentials of an organized human community have evolved together as an attempt to establish a set of proven methods and a fund of traditional reassurance which enables each generation to meet the needs of the next in relative independence from personal differences and changing conditions.

IN THE aging person who has taken care of things and people and has adapted himself to the triumphs and disappointments of being, by necessity, the originator of others and the generator of things and ideas — only in him the fruit of the seven stages gradually ripens. I know no better word for it than *integrity*. Lacking a clear definition, I shall point to a few attributes of this stage of mind. It is the ego's accrued assurance of its proclivity for order and meaning — an emotional integration faithful to the image-bearers of the past and ready to take, and eventually to renounce, leadership in the present. It is the acceptance of one's one and only life cycle and of the people who have become significant to it as something that had to be and that, by necessity, permitted of no substitutions. It thus means a new and different love of one's parents, free of the wish that they should have been different, and an acceptance of the fact that one's life is one's own responsibility. It is a sense of comradeship with men and women of distant times and of different pursuits who have created orders and objects and sayings conveying human dignity and love. Although aware of the relativity of all the various life styles which have given meaning to human striving, the possessor of integrity is ready to defend the dignity of his own life style against all physical and economic threats. For he knows that an individual life is the accidental coincidence of but one life cycle with but one segment of history, and that for him all human integrity stands and falls with the one style of integrity of which he partakes.

Clinical and anthropological evidence suggest that the lack or loss of this accrued ego integration is signified by *disgust* and by *despair:* fate is not accepted as the frame of life, death not as its finite boundary. Despair expresses the feeling that time is short, too short for the attempt to start another life and to try out alternate roads to integrity. Such a despair is often hidden behind a show of disgust, a misanthropy, or a chronic contemptuous displeasure with particular institutions and particular people — a disgust and a displeasure which, where not allied with the vision of a superior life, only signify the individual's contempt of himself.

A meaningful old age, then, preceding a possible terminal senility, serves the need for that integrated heritage which gives indispensable perspective to the life cycle. Strength here takes the form of that detached yet active concern with life bounded by death, which we call *wisdom* in its many connotations from ripened "wits" to accumulated knowledge, mature judgment, and inclusive understanding. Not that each man can evolve wisdom for himself. For most, a living *tradition* provides the essence of it. But the end of the cycle also evokes "ultimate concerns" for what chance man may have to transcend the limitations of his identity and his often tragic or bitterly tragicomic engagement in his one and only life cycle within the sequence of generations. Yet great philosophical and religious systems dealing with ultimate individuation seem to have remained responsibly related to the cultures and civilizations of their times. Seeking transcendence by renunciation, they yet remain ethically concerned with the "maintenance of the world." By the same token, a civilization can be measured by the meaning which it gives to the full cycle of life, for such meaning, or the lack of it, cannot fail to reach into the beginnings of the next generation, and thus into the chances of others to meet ultimate questions with some clarity and strength.

TO WHATEVER abyss ultimate concerns may lead individual men, man as a psychosocial creature will face, toward the end of his life, a new edition of an identity crisis which we may state in the words "I am what survives of me." From the stages of life, then, such dispositions as faith, will power, purposefulness, competence, fidelity, love, care, wisdom — all criteria of vital individual strength — also flow into the life of institutions. Without them, institutions wilt; but without the spirit of institutions pervading the patterns of care and love, instruction and training, no strength could emerge from the sequence of generations.

Psychosocial strength, we conclude, depends on a total process which regulates individual life cycles, the sequence of generations, and the structure of society simultaneously: for all three have evolved together.

28. Developmental Analysis of Conflict Caused by Opposing Attributes in the Adolescent Self-Portrait

Susan Harter and Ann Monsour

The differentiation of the self was examined in 7th, 9th and 11th graders who generated self-descriptors for the following 4 different roles: self in the classroom, with friends, with parents, and in romantic relationships. The findings revealed that the self becomes increasingly differentiated into role-related multiple selves with age. A central focus was on intrapsychic and affective consequences of opposing role-related self-attributes (e.g., outgoing vs. shy, cheerful vs. depressed). Contradictions and conflict were lowest in early adolescence, peaked in middle adolescence, and then began to decline in later adolescence. From a neo-Piagetian perspective, though the young adolescent can construct single abstractions about the self, he or she cannot yet simultaneously compare these abstractions in order to experience opposing attributes. During midadolescence, one develops the ability to compare but not resolve contradictory self-attributes. In later adolescence, the capacity to coordinate, resolve, and normalize seemingly contradictory attributes emerges, reducing the experience of conflict within one's self-theory.

Within the developmental literature, there is considerable evidence that the self becomes more differentiated with age (Damon & Hart, 1982; Harter, 1983, 1990b; Livesly & Bromley, 1973; Montemayor & Eisen, 1977; Mullener & Laird, 1971; Rosenberg, 1986; Secord & Peevers, 1974). Not only are more categories of self-description added to one's repertoire, but the range of trait labels and abstractions becomes expanded with development. The number of discriminable domains across which one can evaluate the self also increases. In fact, the field has undergone a general theoretical orientation in its current emphasis on the multidimensional nature of the self-concept (see Harter, 1985, 1986b, 1990a; Marsh, 1986).

Additional support for the increasing differentiation of the self-concept during adolescence can be found in recent studies documenting how self-descriptions vary across different social roles or contexts (Gecas, 1972; Griffin, Chassin, & Young, 1981; Harter, 1986a; Hart, 1988; .Rosenberg, 1986; Smollar & Youniss, 1985). These studies reveal differences in self-attributes depending on whether one is describing the self in one's role with father, mother, close friends, romantic partners, or classmates, as well as one's role as student, employee, and athlete. For example one's self with parents may be open, depressed, or sarcastic; with friends, the self may be caring, cheerful, or rowdy; and with a romantic partner, the self may be fun-loving, self-conscious, or flirtatious.

Two broad classes of determinants have generally been invoked to account for the developmental shift toward the proliferation of role-related selves during adolescence.

Susan Harter and Ann Monsour: 'Developmental Analysis of Conflict Caused by Opposing Attributes in the Adolescent Self-Portrait'. *DEVELOPMENTAL PSYCHOLOGY* (1992), Vol. 28, No. 2. pp 251-260. Copyright © 1992 by the American Psychological Association, Inc. Reprinted by permission.

Cognitive-structural advances permit the adolescent to make greater differentiations among such role-related attributes (see Fischer, 1980; Fischer & Lamborn, 1989; Harter, 1983, 1986a, 1990b; Keating, 1990). Second, socialization pressures during adolescence force the individual to differentiate the self vis-à-vis social roles, given the different expectations of the various significant others within different social contexts. As Erikson (1959, 1968) cogently observed, the period of adolescence brings with it the formidable task of establishing familial, ideological, friendship, occupational, and romantic/sexual roles or identities and differentiating one's various selves accordingly. More recent theorists have emphasized the adolescent's need to develop autonomy as he or she seeks to redefine the self in contexts that are separate from his or her parents (see Grotevant & Cooper, 1983,1986; Hill & Holmbeck, 1986; Steinberg, 1990). Rosenberg's (1986) observations of the "barometric self" during adolescence highlight the fact that different people in different roles will have varying impressions of the self, resulting in feedback that causes one to view the self as highly mutable.

Although the research to date has provided descriptive accounts of the differentiation of various selves during adolescence, less attention has been devoted to either developmental differences within the period of adolescence or to the experiential and affective consequences of this proliferation of selves. Interestingly, William James (1892) alluded to the potential incompatibility of the various roles one must necessarily assume in his reference to the "conflict of the different Me's" (p.185). However, existing studies have not explored the extent to which opposing role-related attributes cause phenomenological conflict in the developing adolescent.

Thus, the present research addresses the following questions. First, to what extent do role-specific self-descriptions (the self with parents, friends, and romantic others and the self in the classroom) become increasingly differentiated during adolescence? Do role-related attributes merely differ across these contexts, or do some attributes represent opposites that are judged incompatible? If opposing attributes do emerge, do they produce an experience of intrapsychic conflict? Moreover, is such conflict accompanied by distress in the form of negative affective reactions or confusion?

The general expectation of conflict and distress can be derived from the adult self literature that is replete with theories emphasizing the need to integrate multiple attributes into a theory of one's personality that is coherent and unified (Allport, 1955, 1961; Epstein, 1973; Horney, 1950; Jung, 1928; Kelly, 1955; Lecky, 1945; Maslow, 1961; Rogers, 1950). Epstein (1973) has argued by analogy that the self-theory, like any comprehensive scientific theory, must meet certain criteria including parsimony, usefulness, testability, and internal consistency. As is the case with any formal theory, one's self-theory will be threatened by postulates in the theory that appear contradictory. Thus, given the developmental task of differentiating role-related self-attributes during adolescence, the integration of these diverse self-representations may pose a particular challenge.

The purpose of this study was to examine these processes at the following three developmental levels: early, middle, and late adolescence (7th, 9th, and 11th grades, respectively). On the basis of the cognitive-developmental and socialization perspectives described, two general developmental hypotheses are advanced: (a)

Attributes associated with four roles (self with parents, self with friends, self as student, and self with romantic other) should become increasingly differentiated over the course of adolescence. That is, there should be less overlap in role-related attributes with increasing grade level. (b) A different developmental pattern is predicted for opposing as well as conflicting attributes, namely that they should peak in middle adolescence.

Fischer's (1980) cognitive-developmental theory provides a framework for predicting developmental differences, because he distinguishes several levels within formal operational thought. At the first level of single abstractions, which emerge in early adolescence, one can construct abstractions about the self (e.g., outgoing, self-conscious, obnoxious, empathic, cheerful, and depressed). However, one does not yet have the cognitive ability to simultaneously compare these abstractions to one another. As a result, young adolescents should tend not to detect or be concerned over self-attributes that are potential opposites (e.g., cheerful and depressed).

The cognitive skills necessary to compare such abstractions, what Fischer called "abstract mapping," do not emerge until middle adolescence. With the advent of the ability to relate attributes to each other, the individual can now evaluate the postulates of one's self-theory from the standpoint of whether they are internally consistent. However, at this stage, the adolescent does not yet have the cognitive skills to resolve such contradictions. As a result, opposing self-attributes (e.g., outgoing vs. self-conscious, obnoxious vs. empathic, and cheerful vs. depressed) become very salient as well as conflictual and distressing.

Conflict should begin to diminish, according to Fischer's theory, in later adolescence with the emergence of "abstract systems." This new cognitive level brings with it the ability to integrate single abstractions into compatible higher order abstractions about the self. For example, cheerful and depressive attributes can be combined into the higher order abstraction of "moody." The older adolescent can also resolve potentially contradictory attributes across roles by asserting that he or she is flexible or adaptive across roles or contexts, thereby subsuming apparent inconsistencies under more generalized abstractions about the self. Thus, more advanced cognitive skills allow the older adolescent to cognitively coordinate and resolve seemingly contradictory self-attributes.

A secondary goal of the present research was to examine the structure of the adolescent self-portrait from the standpoint of the valence of central and peripheral constructs. In discussing the self-theory, Kelly (1955) and others have suggested the fruitfulness of determining which attributes are more important or at the core of one's personality and which appear to be less important or peripheral. We predicted that one's positive attributes would assume more importance, whereas one's negative attributes would be relegated to the periphery of one's self-portrait. This prediction was based on previous theorizing and findings within the attributional literature revealing that, as a mechanism to protect and enhance the self, individuals are more likely to emphasize and take credit for their successes than their failures (see Greenwald, 1980; Harter, 1985, 1986b).

We developed a new procedure to test these hypotheses. Subjects were first asked to describe what they were like with parents, with friends, in the classroom, and in romantic relationships and to indicate whether each attribute was a positive or negative feature of the self. Subjects then created a picture of their personality by spatially arranging their self-descriptions within a large circle that had a core circle for the most important attributes, an adjacent concentric circle for less important attributes, and an outer ring for the least important aspects of the self.

Subjects then examined the entire array of self-descriptions and identified any they considered to be opposites (e.g., smart vs. dumb, friendly vs. mean, shy vs. outgoing, and cheerful vs. depressed). To assess intrapsychic conflict between opposing attributes, subjects next indicated whether any of the opposites identified were clashing, fighting, struggling, "at war," or in conflict with each other; subjects next provided a verbal description and responded to a checklist of potential emotional reactions. In this manner, we could determine whether any of the opposites were a cause of phenomenological conflict within the self or whether they could comfortably coexist without causing an experience of inner tension.

Method

Subjects

There were a total of 30 boys and 34 girls drawn from middle, junior high, and senior high schools in the Denver, Colorado area. The 7th-grade sample consisted of 10 boys and 14 girls (*M* age = 13 years, 2 months) . The 9th-grade sample comprised 10 boys and 10 girls (*M* age = 15 years, 1 month). The 11th-grade sample consisted of 10 boys and 10 girls (mean age = 17 years, 2 months). Subjects were from middle- and upper-middle-class families. The racial composition was predominantly White with 2 Hispanic subjects at each grade level. All subjects were individually seen in our University of Denver laboratory. The task was divided into several subsections.

Self-report of role-related attributes. Each subject was presented with four sheets, one for each of four roles. At the top of each sheet was the heading "What I am Like With (my Parents)" (or, alternatively, "my Friends," "in the Classroom," and "in Romantic Relationships," for the other three roles). Six sentence stems were presented on each page (e.g., I am ——— with my parents), and the subject was asked to generate six descriptors, if possible. They were told that these descriptors could be similar or different across roles. Subjects were encouraged to include negative as well as positive attributes ("Nobody's perfect," and "Everybody has something about themselves they may not like or may want to change"). Next to each sentence was a plus and a minus, which the subject used to indicate whether the attribute was positive or negative. Subjects were free to complete one set of descriptors before moving to another or to alternate between different roles, whichever they preferred.

Self-portrait display. After completing the self-descriptors in each role, the key word (or words) of each was transferred onto a gummed label that the subject placed in one of three circles on the large self-portrait sheet. The subject was then asked to put the most important descriptors in the smallest center circle (labeled *most important),* to put less important descriptors in the next concentric circle (labeled *less important),* and to put the least important descriptors in the outer circle (labeled *least important).*

Inquiry about opposites. After all of the self-descriptors had been positioned in the appropriate circles, the subject was asked to look at all of the self-attributes and see if any of them seemed liked they were the opposites of one another. For any pairs of opposites identified, either the experimenter or the subject drew a line connecting the two opposites.

Inquiry about clashes or conflict. For each pair of opposites identified, the subject was asked to think about whether the two attributes were fighting, clashing, disagreeing, at war, or in conflict with each other. All of these descriptions were included in order to best communicate what we meant by the experience of conflict. For those opposites experienced as conflicting, arrowheads were placed on each end of the line connecting the two attributes. All subjects were systematically asked to explain why each of the conflicting attributes clashed. A systematic inquiry to determine why certain nonclashing attributes did not produce conflict was conducted with 75% of the subjects.

Affective responses to conflict. Finally, each subject was given an emotion checklist and asked to indicate which emotions he or she felt about clashing as well as nonclashing opposites. We focused only on potential negative reactions. The emotions included the following: guilty, embarrassed, mad at myself, ashamed, unhappy, pressured, mad, sad, bothered, frustrated, worried or nervous, depressed, upset, and no special feeling. More cognitive reactions (e.g., mixed-up or confused) were also included.

Results

Overlap of attributes across roles

It was predicted that there should be increasing differentiation in role-related attributes (i.e., less overlap across roles) with age. As can be seen in Table 1, for three of the combinations (e.g., self with parents vs. self with friends, self with parents vs. self in the classroom, and self with friends vs. self in the classroom) there was a systematic tendency for overlap to decrease over the period of adolescence. Separate, one-way analyses of variance (ANOVAs) across the three developmental levels revealed that each of these differences was significant: parents versus friends, $F(2, 58) = 3.40, p < .05$; parents versus classroom, $F(2, 58) = 7.37, p < .001$; and friends versus classroom $F(2, 58) = 2.78, p < .05$. For each comparison, using Dunn tests, there was significantly more overlap for the 7th graders than either the 9th or 11th graders ($ps < .05$). There were no significant decreases in the overlap for romantic relationships and the other three roles because, even in 7th grade, overlap was minimal ($Ms = .15-.10$).

Table 1   Proportion of attributes overlapping across roles by grade

Role	7		9		11	
	M	*SD*	*M*	*SD*	*M*	*SD*
Parent vs. friends	0.38	0.19	0.23	0.18	0.17	0.09
Parents vs. classroom	0.31	0.20	0.10	0.09	0.06	0.04
Friends vs. classroom	0.29	0.17	0.18	0.12	0.11	0.08

Prototypical example of opposites that do and do not conflict

Figure 1 represents a prototypical example of the major features of a ninth-grade female adolescent self-portrait. In this protocol several opposites were identified, most of which were conflicting. Thus, clashes were reported between being smart at school and being fun-loving with friends, being happy with friends and being depressed with family, being caring with family and being inconsiderate with friends, being talkative as well as being nervous in romantic relationships, and being attentive and being lazy in school.

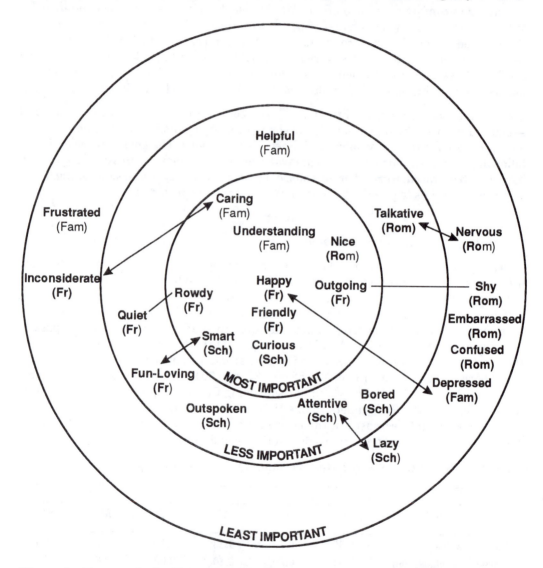

Figure 1 Prototypical self-portrait by a 9th-grade girl. (Fam = family; Rom = romantic relationships; Fr = friends; Sch = school)

For the conflict between the ninth-grade female adolescent in school and her friends, she stated the following: "When you are with your friends, you tend to do things that you want, you mess around and have fun, at school, you have to be more serious which lets you be smart." In the example of being happy with friends versus being depressed with her family at home, she noted that "I really think of myself as a happy person, and I want to be that way with everyone because I think that's my true self, but I get depressed with my family and it bugs me because that's not what I want to be like." In the example of the conflict between being talkative and being nervous within romantic relationships, the subject described, with some exasperation, that "I hate the fact that I get so nervous. I wish I wasn't so inhibited! The real me is talkative; I just want to be natural."

Other subjects described the conflict in very dynamic terms (e.g., " You don't want to act this way but then something uncaring comes out in you, you try to stop it, you have to fight it all the time!"). Another subject described it as "I want to be polite, I try to, but then the opposite feelings just overpower me." Another 15-year-old girl exclaimed, "I really think of myself as friendly and open-armed to people, but the way the other girls act, they force me to become an introvert, even though I know I'm really not. It really bothers me and sometimes the only way to handle it is to become immune to yourself." Another ninth-grade girl exclaimed about her self-portrait: "It's not right, it should all fit together into one piece."

Equally compelling were the examples for why opposites were not clashing or in conflict. Many explanations involved reference to the fact that people act differently in different situations. Specific examples included the following: "Well, you are nice to your friends and then mean to people who don't treat you nicely"; It's just that I am real open with my family, but I tend to be shy with kids my age"; "Sometimes it's fun to be rowdy but at other times you just want to be in a quiet mood, you really need to do both with really good friends"; "It's just that you are different with different people; you can't always be the same person and you shouldn't be"; "Usually I am happy with my friends, but sometimes I get angry, everyone has to get angry sometimes, and that's how I am." One 13-year-old girl, on being asked why her opposing attributes did not clash, exlaimed, "That's a really stupid question, I don't fight with myself!" For the most part, subjects reporting that opposites did not clash gave relatively brief descriptions, suggesting that they felt no particular need to justify the lack of conflict. Opposing traits could comfortably coexist within the self and did not appear to command much of their attention.

In order to examine the hypothesis that the prevalence of opposites, as well as of conflict, would peak during middle adolescence, we examined the following four indexes: number of opposites, number of conflicts, percentage of opposites in conflict, and percentage of subjects reporting that at least one opposite caused conflict. As can be seen in Figure 2, for each of these four indexes, there is a dramatic increase from 7th to 9th grade and then a smaller, but systematic, decrease between the 9th and 11th grades.

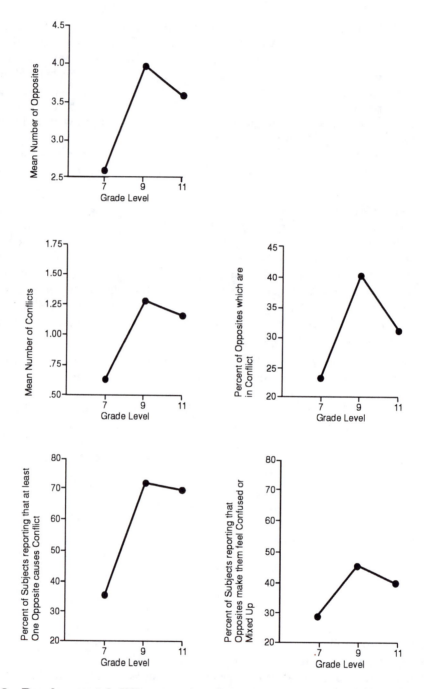

Figure 2 Developmental differences in adolescents' perceptions of opposing and conflicting self-attributes

Separate Grade (3) x Gender (2) ANOVAs were performed for each of the four indexes. For the index labeled *number of opposites perceived*, the grade effect was significant, $F(2, 58) = 13.77, p < .05$; multiple comparisons reveal that the primary difference was between the 7th ($M = 2.54, SD = 1.77$) and 9th ($M = 3.95, SD = 2.41$) graders ($p < .06$). A significant main effect for gender, $F(1, 58) = 18.07, p < .05$, was due to the fact that girls ($M = 3.74, SD = 1.74$) identified more opposite attributes than did boys ($M = 2.77$, $SD = 1.01$).

An examination of the protocols revealed that at the 7th-grade level, there were more potential opposites that went undetected in comparison with the 9th- and 11th-grade levels. Examples not identified as opposites in the 7th graders' self-portraits included being talkative as well as shy in romantic relationships, being uptight with family but carefree with friends, being caring as well as insensitive with friends, being quiet as well as talkative in school, being serious as well as goofy in romantic relationships, being a good student as well as getting in trouble at school, being understanding and unfair with friends, feeling pressured but also safe in romantic relationships, and being active as well as lazy in school. It was not possible, however, to calculate a reliable or valid numerical index of potential opposites that went undetected, given that we did not confront subjects with these possible contradictions.

For the index labeled *number of opposites in conflict* the main effect for grade was again significant, $F(2, 58) = 13.78, p < .05$; multiple comparisons revealed that the 7th graders ($M = 0.62, SD = 0.51$) were significantly different ($ps < .05$) from both the 9th ($M = 1.35$, $SD = 0.93$) and 11th ($M = 1.20, SD = 0.88$) graders. As with the number of opposites, gender differences were also revealed, indicating that girls reported significantly more conflicting opposites ($M = 1.29, SD = 0.56$) than did boys ($M = 0.73, SD = 0.41$).

We next examined the index labeled *percentage of opposites in conflict* because the grade-related increase in the number of clashes could partially be explained by the increase in the number of opposite attributes reported. The pattern (see Figure 2) was similar, with 7th graders with the lowest percentage ($M = 23.0\%, SD = 21.3$), 9th graders with the highest percentage ($M = 42.0\%, SD = 31.4$), and the 11th graders in between ($M = 32.2\%, SD = 21.5$); the main effect for grade approached significance, $F(2, 58) = 13.28, p < .075$, as did the effect for gender, $F(1, 58) = 12.64, p < .10$, with girls ($M = 39.1\%, SD = 20.4$) reporting more conflict than boys ($M = 25.0\%, SD = 18.2$).

The differences in the index labeled *percentage of subjects reporting at least one opposite in conflict* were also found to be significant, $\chi^2 (N = 2) = 7.72, p < .02$, due to the fact that fully 62.5% of the 7th graders reported no conflict, whereas only 21% of the 9th graders and 30% of the 11th graders reported no conflict.

Subjects' explanation of conflict

A content analysis was performed on the reasons given by adolescents for why opposing attributes were experienced as conflictual. Two broad but conceptually similar types of explanations emerged and could reliably be rated by two independent judges (82.6% agreement). Attributes were perceived as conflicting if there was a conflict between one's overt behavior and one's intentions or if there was a conflict between incompatible intentions. Moreover, 97% of all explanations for conflict fell within these two broad categories. Examples included the following: "You want to be thoughtful with your friends, but something uncaring comes out in you. You try to stop it, you fight it all the time"; "I know I should be attentive in school, I should try harder, because I get pressure from my father, but I act lazy, and do what I want instead of what I should do"; "I hate being shy and so embarrassed on a date, I don't like it, I wish I could be easygoing, natural, I wish I wasn't so inhibited"; "I know I am being mean with my family, and I could help it, but I don't feel like it cause part of me wants to be mean, and the other part wants to be nice"; "I'm really close with my family and then fun-loving with my friends, but it seems like my family is working against my friends, and I'm afraid I'll get in trouble with both."

Subjects' explanations for why opposites did not conflict. We systematically queried 70% of the 7th graders, 80% of the 9th graders, and 85% of the 11th graders about the reasons for every pair of opposites that did not conflict and performed a content analysis of the types of reasons given for nonconflict between opposites. The vast majority (87%) of explanations could be categorized into one of two broad categories that reflected either (a) differentiation or separation of the two attributes or (b) attempts at integrating, normalizing, and ascribing value to such opposites. Examples of differentiation or separation over time or situation included the following: "I'm outgoing with people that are my friends and quiet with people that I don't know"; "I can be lazy at school, but also energetic but since they never happen at the same time, they never clash." Examples of attempts at integration, normalization, and ascription of value of opposites included the following: "Yea, I can be both depressed and cheerful because I am a moody person"; "Sometimes you're happy and sometimes you're depressed, those are just two separate sides of me that are normal, you have to take the good with the bad"; "I can be talkative with friends and quiet with friends, they complement each other, its good to be able to be both ways." Examples of differentiation or separation declined with grade level (7th graders = 86%, 9th graders = 50%, and 11th graders = 23%), whereas examples of integration, normalization, and value increased with grade level (7th graders = 0%, 9th graders = 31%, and 11th graders = 65%) with differences that were quite significant, $\chi^2 = 14.96$, $df = 2$, $p < .001$.

Affective reactions to conflicting and nonconflicting opposing attributes. Another index of the potential distress caused by opposing attributes that were judged to be conflicting was the degree of negative affect aroused. We compared the mean percentage of conflicting and nonconflicting opposites that produced at least one of the negative affects versus "no special feeling." A Valence (negative affect vs. no special feeling) x Conflict (presence vs. absence) x Grade x Gender ANOVA (with valence and conflict as repeated measures) revealed one significant effect, a striking interaction between valence of the affect and conflict, $F(1, 21) = 24.97$, $p < .001$. Subjects were much more likely to report negative affects in response to conflicting self-attributes ($M = 89.1\%$, $SD = 42.3$) than to nonconflicting opposites ($M = 27.2\%$, $SD = 22.7$). Conversely, subjects were much more likely to report no special feeling in response to their nonconflicting ($M = 72.1\%$, $SD = 43.0$) than to their conflicting opposites ($M = 11.1\%$, $SD = 0.14$). These findings provide converging evidence for the validity of subjects' judgments concerning the presence or absence of conflict, although the affect ratings were not independent of the conflict judgments.

In analyzing the 15 specific indexes of distress, only the more cognitive type of reaction, confused or mixed-up (see Figure 2) resulted in developmental differences. A greater percentage of 9th graders (48%) reported these reactions in comparison with the 7th graders (29%) or the 11th graders (40%). The difference between the 7th and 9th graders was significant ($p < .05$).

Valence of attributes judged most, less, and least important

It was predicted that subjects would be more likely to place their positive attributes at the core of the self-portrait, whereas negative attributes would be relegated to the periphery of least important characteristics (see Figure 1). The findings for all subjects strongly confirmed this pattern, as revealed in Figure 3. The vast majority of self-attributes judged to be most important were positive ($M = 76.2\%$, $SD = 19.3$) with only a few negative ($M = 10.0\%$, $SD = 12.2$) and mixed ($M = 15.0\%$, $SD = 12.3$) attributes (both positive and negative) at the core of the self. As can be seen in Figure 3, there is a systematic decline in positive attributes as one moves toward the periphery of the self, whereas the number of negative attributes increases. A Valence (positive, negative, or mixed) x Self-Diagram Position (center, middle, or outer circle) x Grade x Gender ANOVA (with valence and position as repeated measures) revealed one effect, a highly significant interaction, $F(4, 236) = 71.78$, $p < .001$.

Discussion

The findings provide clear support for developmental changes in role-related self-attributes over the course of adolescence. One such shift involves the greater differentiation of selves associated with the varying social roles that the adolescent must come to adopt. Socialization pressures to develop different selves in different social contexts (Grotevant & Cooper, 1983, 1986; Erikson, 1959, 1968; Hill & Holmbeck, 1986; Rosenberg, 1986) as well as cognitive-developmental advances that allow for a more differentiated sense of self (Fischer,1980; Fischer & Lamborn, 1989; Harter, l983, 1986a, 1990b) should conspire to produce a proliferation of role-related selves.

The findings supported this hypothesis in that for three role-related comparisons — self with parent versus self with friends, self with parent versus self in the classroom, and self with friends versus self in the classroom — there was a systematic and significant linear decrease in the proportion of overlapping attributes across grade level. Thus, with regard to spontaneously generated attributes, adolescents' role-related selves become increasingly differentiated as they move through this developmental period. Interestingly, the comparisons involving one's self in romantic relationships seem to be the first to be differentiated, because even in early adolescence (seventh grade) there was already little overlap between one's attributes in this particular role and those in the other three roles.

A major purpose was to examine the experiential consequences of this age-related proliferation of selves, namely the phenomenological conflict provoked by the identification of contradictory role-related self attributes. The increasing differentiation of selves between 7th and 9th grades may well contribute to the increase in opposing attributes and conflict reported by the 9th graders. However, the suggested grade-related curvi-linear relationship, revealing that opposing and conflicting attributes peak in middle adolescence and then begin to decline in late adolescence, cannot be a direct function of the degree of differentiation (i.e., that more differentiation inevitably leads to more opposition and conflict between attributes), because role-related selves are the most differentiated in the 11th grade. Thus, one needs an alternative explanation for why conflict among highly differentiated role-related selves seems to decline in later adolescence.

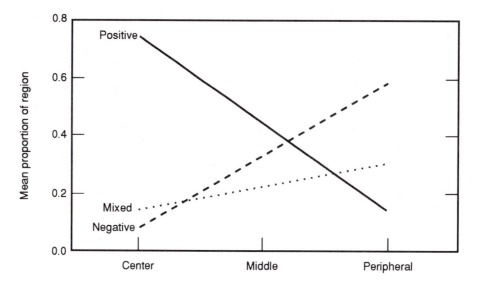

Figure 3   Mean proportion of each self-portrait region occupied by positive, negative, and mixed valence attributes

The hypothesis that opposing as well as conflicting attributes should not appear with great frequency among young adolescents, should peak for those in midadolescence, and should finally begin to decline in later adolescence was supported. For five converging measures (number of opposing attributes, number of opposing attributes that were in conflict, percentage of opposing attributes in conflict, percentage of subjects reporting that at least one opposite caused conflict, and the percentage of subjects reporting that opposing self-attributes made them feel confused or mixed up), the lowest scores were obtained for 7th graders, scores peaked for 9th graders, and scores began to decline for 11th graders. This pattern has now been replicated in a subsequent study (Harter & Carlson, 1988) that included both 11th and 12th graders, in which an even greater drop among older adolescents was found. Moreover, the meaningfulness of the distinction between opposing attributes that do and do not provoke conflict was bolstered by subjects' descriptions as well as by the finding that opposing attributes in conflict produced significantly more negative affective reactions, whereas nonconflicting opposites were far more likely to result in no special feeling. (Although our focus was on the potential for negative emotions, interesting questions for future research include whether positive emotional reactions ever accompany the report of opposing attributes and whether the pattern reported here might have been different had we added positive affects.)

Fischer's cognitive–developmental theory provided one framework for predicting the suggested curvilinear relationship, because it identifies several substages within adolescence. Traditional Piagetian theory cannot provide an explanation for the findings because it postulates only one major shift at adolescence, the emergence of formal operations (Piaget, 1960). Fischer's neo-Piagetian framework, in contrast, predicts that certain features of the self-portrait will change as one moves through substages of formal operational thought.

Our youngest adolescents can be characterized as being at Fischer's first level of formal operational thought, "single abstractions," allowing one to construct rudimentary, abstract self-descriptors (e.g., cheerful, depressed, outgoing, or shy). However, they do not yet have the ability to simultaneously compare these abstractions to one another, and therefore they tend not to detect or to be concerned over self-attributes that are potential opposites (e.g., outgoing vs. shy). Those opposites that were detected typically produced no conflict because they were separated in time or by situation.

During middle adolescence, the cognitive skills necessary to compare abstractions, namely "abstract mappings," begin to emerge. This particular substage, therefore, should usher in the initial press to integrate one's multiple attributes into a theory of one's personality that is coherent, unified, and internally consistent. However, the emergence of such abstract mapping abilities represents a double-edged sword: Although the adolescent can now compare opposing self-attributes, he or she does not yet have sufficient cognitive control over these budding skills to integrate seemingly contradictory postulates within the self-system. As a result, the adolescent should experience opposing attributes as contradictions within the self-theory that provoke conflict and distress. Thus, although socialization pressures promote the continued differentiation of role-related selves, the cognitive skills available during midadolescence do not yet equip one to consolidate these selves into an integrated self-theory.

Consolidation should be more possible in later adolescence with the emergence of "abstract systems," according to Fischer's theory. The findings revealed small but systematic decreases between the 9th and 11th grades for all indexes, including opposing attributes, conflict, and confusion. From a cognitive–developmental perspective, abstract system should allow one to integrate or resolve seeming contradictions within the self-theory. The specific reasons most often given by older subjects for why opposites did not conflict involved strategies that integrated, normalized, or found value in the seeming inconsistency, namely that it was understandable or desirable to act differently in different social situations.

Therefore, the pattern suggests that one is particularly vulnerable during middle adolescence, when conflict and distress are at their peak with regard to contradictions within the self. At this developmental juncture, there would appear to be competing forces, namely socialization pressure to differentiate the self into multiple roles while the cognitive apparatus is pressing for integration. The tension created can well be conceptualized as one form of "storm and stress." Although there are those (e.g. Offer, Ostrow, & Howard, 1981) who have taken the position that the prevalence of adolescent storm and stress has been vastly overemphasized, the issue needs to be addressed in terms of the specific type of stress as well as the specific period of adolescence. Those attempting to refute the storm and stress hypothesis have focused primarily on the fact that the self-evaluations of most adolescents are not overwhelmingly negative (Offer *et al.*,1981) nor do most engage in major conflict with their parents on larger issues and values (Hill & Holmbeck 1986; Steinberg, 1990). However, these studies have not involved conflict within the self-system. That is, they do not address the fact that the internal canvas on which the self-portrait is painted must accommodate a crowd of proliferating persona whose characteristics are not necessarily compatible.

The more recent literature reveals that during adolescence there are numerous potentially contradictory selves clamoring for expression (see Harter, 1990a). There are various forms of ideal selves that may conflict with one's real self (see Glick & Zigler, 1985; Harter, 1986b; Higgins, 1987). These conflicts can be distressing (Higgins, 1987), as well as motivating, as in the case of discrepancies between one's positive or desired selves and one's negative, feared, or possible selves (Markus & Nurius, 1986). The responses of the adolescents in this study attest to the fact that they typically experience conflict between their present behavioral selves and the desired selves that they wish or are motivated to become. In addition, there were numerous spontaneous references to confusion about which behaviors represent one's real or true self. It is understandable that the need to create multiple selves would usher in concern over which is the "real me," a preoccupation that we have recently documented (Harter & Lee, 1989), as have others (Broughton, 1981: Rosenberg, 1979; Selman, 1980). The fact that the adolescent necessarily encounters different people in various roles and contexts that have different impressions of the self adds to the perplexity over which is one's true self (Rosenberg, 1986). In his metaphoric reference to the "barometric self-concept," Rosenberg focused primarily on how factors associated with socialization lead to the volatility of the self-concept, whereas in our own reference to the "self as chameleon" (Harter,1988) we have addressed the adolescent's difficulty in cognitively coordinating disparate self-perceptions. Both perspectives contribute to an understanding of why internal conflict is provoked by multiple selves, particularly during midadolescence.

It should be noted that we are making reference here to multiple selves as a normative-developmental phenomenon, not to pathological manifestations that are captured by the clinical diagnosis of multiple personality disorder (see Braun, 1988: Kluft, 1987; Putnam, 1989). This relatively rare disorder is characterized by the existence, within the person, of at least two distinct personalities or personality fragments that alternately take full control of the person's cognitions, emotions, and behavior (Diagnostic and Statistical Manual of Mental Disorders, 3rd. ed., American Psychiatric Association, 1987). In resorting to the defense mechanism of dissociation, there is little or often no awareness or coconsciousness on the part of some personalities for other personalities. Rather, there is fragmentation, as well as amnesia for certain personalities, and in some cases fugue states (see also Fine, 1988; Fink, 1988; Franklin, 1988). Often, when alternative personalities are acknowledged, there is the strong sense that the other person is "not me" (Fink, 1988).

In contrast, what we have referred to as multiple selves in the adolescent repertoire are consciously experienced contradictions between one's behaviors and one's conflicting ideals or intentions. During the period of middle adolescence, in particular, our subjects revealed that, in contrast to fragmentation and dissociation, they are very much aware of these contradictions and are highly motivated to resolve them. One such strategy may be revealed in subjects' placement of attributes within their self-portrait. Positive characteristics were afforded greater centrality as the most important or core constructs in one's personality, whereas less desirable attributes were relegated to the periphery of the self as relatively unimportant. Such a positivity bias allows one to protect the self, while at the same time to preserve all of one's attributes as part of a single personality. Similar strategies (e.g., taking credit for one's successes while downplaying responsibility for one's failures) have been identified in the attributional literature as mechanisms for self-protection and self-enhancement (Greenwald, 1980; Harter, 1985, 1986b). Of interest was the finding that those few subjects who did not adopt such a strategy, but identified negative attributes at the core of the self, reported lower global self-esteem.

Finally, although the focus of this study was on normative, developmental changes during adolescence, the findings revealed unpredicted gender differences. Although the developmental trajectory was similar for male subjects and female subjects, girls detected more contradictory self-attributes and reported more conflict than did boys at every grade level. Moreover, these gender differences have now been replicated in two subsequent studies (Harter & Brèsnick, 1990; Harter & Carlson, 1988). Because these differences were not hypothesized, we can only speculate on their interpretation, turning to socialization rather than cognitive-developmental theory. We have been drawn to Gilligan's (1982) analysis of gender differences as a possible framework within which to interpret this pattern. Gilligan suggested that the socialization of the girl involves far more embeddedness within the family, as well as more involvement and concern with relationships. The boy in contrast, forges a path of independence and autonomy in which the logic of his moral and social decisions takes precedence over an affective, empathic response to others with whom one has formed emotional bonds.

In extrapolating from these observations, it may well be that in an effort to maintain the multiple relationships that girls are developing during adolescence, and to create harmony among these necessarily differentiated roles, opposing attributes within the self become particularly salient as well as problematic. Boys, on the other hand, can move more facilely among their different roles and multiple selves if such roles are logically viewed as more independent of one another. Such an interpretation also assumes that for girls, the self is more likely to be defined in terms of relationships, and thus the relational network impinges more strongly on the self (see Jordan, 1991; Miller, 1986). This speculative analysis deserves more systematic attention, as does the study of individual differences within each gender, in order to determine the particular psychosocial precursors responsible for the degree of contradiction and conflict experienced within the self.

The research reported here was supported by Grant HD 09613 from National Institute of Child Health and Human Development, awarded to Susan Harter. This study was based on the doctoral dissertation of Ann Monsour. An earlier version of this article was presented at the Society for Research in Child Development meetings in Detroit, Michigan, in 1985.

References

Allport, G.W. (1955) *Becoming: Basic considerations for a psychology of personality*. New Haven, CT: Yale University Press.

Allport, G.W. (1961) *Pattern and growth in personality* New York: Holt, Reinhart & Winston.

American Psychiatric Association. (1987) *Diagnostic and statistical manual of mental disorders* (3rd ed.). Washington, DC: Author.

Braun, B. (1988) 'The BASK model of dissociation: Clinical applications.' *Dissociation,* 1, 16-23.

Broughton, J. (1981) 'The divided self in adolescence.' *Human Development,* 24, 13-32.

Damon, W., & Hart, D. (1982) 'The development of self-understanding from infancy through adolescence.' *Child Development,* 53, 841-864.

Epstein, S. (1973) 'The self-concept revisited or a theory of a theory.' *American Psychologist,* 28, 405-416.

Erikson, E. (1959) 'Identity and the life cycle.' *Psychological Issues,* 1, 18-164.

Erikson, E. (1968) *Identity, youth and crisis.* New York: Norton.

Fine, C.G. (1988) 'Thoughts on the cognitive perceptual substrates of multiple personality disorder.' *Dissociation,* 1, 5-10.

Fink, D.L. (1988) 'The core self: A developmental perspective on the dissociative disorders.' *Dissociation,* 1, 43-47.

Fischer, K.W. (1980) 'A theory of cognitive development: The control and construction of hierarchies of skills.' *Psychological Review,* 87, 477-531.

Fischer, K.W., & Lamborn, S. (1989) 'Mechanisms of variation in developmental levels: Cognitive and emotional transitions during adolescence.' In A. de Ribaupierre (Ed.), *Transition mechanisms in child development: The longitudinal perspective* (pp. 37-61). Cambridge, England: Cambridge University Press.

Franklin, J. (1988) 'Diagnosis of covert and subtle forms of multiple personality disorder through dissociative signs.' *Dissociation,* 1, 27-33.

Gecas, V. (1972) 'Parental behavior and contextual variations in adolescent self-esteem.' *Sociometry,* 35, 332-345.

Gilligan, C. (1982) *In a different voice.* Cambridge, MA: Harvard University Press.

Glick, M., & Zigler, E. (1985) 'Self-image: A cognitive-developmental approach.' In R. Leahy (Ed.), *The development of the self* (pp. 1-59). San Diego, CA: Academic Press.

Greenwald, A.G. (1980) 'The totalitarian ego: Fabrication and revision of personal history.' *American Psychologist,* 7, 603-618.

Griffin, N., Chassin, L., & Young, R.D. (1981) 'Measurement of global self-concept versus multiple role-specific self-concepts in adolescents.' *Adolescence,* 16, 49-56.

Grotevant, H.D., & Cooper, C.R. (1983) *Adolescent development in the family: New Directions for Child Development.* San Francisco: Jossey-Bass.

Grotevant, H.D., & Cooper, C.R. (Eds.). (1986) 'Individuation in family relationships.' *Human Development, 29,* 83-100.

Hart, D. (1988) 'The adolescent self-concept in social context.' In D.K. Lapsley & F.C. Power, (Eds.), *Self, ego, and identity* (pp.71-90). New York: Springer-Verlag.

Harter, S. (1983) 'Developmental perspectives on the self-system.' In M. Hetherington (Ed.), *Handbook of child psychology, 4: Socialization, personality, and social development* (pp. 275-386). New York: Wiley.

Harter, S. (1985) 'Competence as a dimension of self-evaluation: Toward a comprehensive model of self-worth.' In R. Leahy (Ed.), *The development of the self,* (pp. 55-122). San Diego, CA: Academic Press.

Harter, S. (1986a) 'Cognitive-developmental processes in the integration of concepts about emotion and the self.' *Social Cognition, 4,* 119-151.

Harter, S. (1986b) 'Processes underlying the construction, maintenance and enhancement of the self-concept in children.' In J. Suls & A. Greenwald (Eds.), *Psychological perspectives on the self, 3* (pp. 137-181). Hillsdale, NJ: Erlbaum.

Harter, S. (1988) 'Developmental and dynamic changes in the nature of the self-concept: Implications for child psychotherapy.' In S. Shirk (Ed.), *Cognitive development and child psychotherapy* (pp. 119-160). New York: Plenum Press.

Harter, S. (1990a) 'Causes, correlates and the functional role of global self-worth: A life-span perspective.' In J. Kolligian and R. Sternberg (Eds.), *Perceptions of competence and incompetence across the lifespan* (pp. 67-97). New Haven, CT: Yale University Press.

Harter, S. (1990b) 'Issues in the assessment of the self-concept of children and adolescents.' In A. La Greca (Ed.), *Childhood assessment: Through the eyes of a child* (pp. 292-325). Needham Heights, MA: Allyn and Bacon.

Harter, S., & Bresnick, S. (1990) *Developmental and gender differences in the conflict caused by opposing attributes within the adolescent self.* Unpublished manuscript, University of Colorado at Denver, Denver.

Harter, S., & Carlson, J. (1988) *Developmental differences during adolescence in opposing self-attributes.* Unpublished manuscript, University of Denver, Colorado.

Harter, S., & Lee, L. (1989, April) *Manifestations of true and false selves in early adolescence.* Society for Research in Child Development presentation, Kansas City, MO.

Higgins, E.T. (1987) 'Self-discrepancy: A theory relating self and affect.' *Psychological Review, 94,* 319-340.

Hill, J.P., & Holmbeck, G.N. (1986) 'Attachment and autonomy during adolescence.' In G.J. Whitehurst (Ed.), *Annals of child development (Vol. 3,* pp.145-189). Greenwich, CT: JAI Press.

Horney, K. (1950) *Neurosis and human growth.* New York: Norton.

James, W. (1892) *Psychology: The briefer course.* New York: Holt, Rinehart & Winston.

Jordan, J. (1991) 'The relational self: A new perspective for understanding women's development.' In G. Goethals & J. Strauss (Eds.), *The self: An interdisciplinary approach* (pp. 136-149). New York: Springer-Verlag.

Jung, C.G. (1928) *Two essays on analytical psychology.* New York: Dodd, Mead.

Keating, D.P. (1990) 'Cognitive processes in adolescence.' In S. Feldman & G. Elliot (Eds.), *At the threshold: The developing adolescent* (pp. 54-89). Cambridge, MA: Harvard University Press.

Kelly, G.A. (1955) *The psychology of personal constructs.* New York: Norton.

Kluft, R.P. (1987) 'First-rank symptoms as a diagnostic clue to multiple personality disorder.' *American Journal of Psychiatry,* 144, 293-298.

Lecky, P. (1945) *Self-consistency: A theory of personality* New York: Island Press.

Livesley, W.J., & Bromley, D. B. (1973) *Person perception in childhood and adolescence.* New York: Wiley.

Markus, H., & Nurius, P. (1986) 'Possible selves.' *American Psychologist,* 41, 954-969.

Marsh, H.W. (1986) 'Global self-esteem: Its relation to specific facets of self-concept and their importance.' *Journal of Personality and Social Psychology,* 51, 1224-1236.

Maslow, A.H. (1961) 'Peak-experiences as acute identity-experiences.' *American Journal of Psychoanalysis,* 21, 254-260.

Miller, J.B. (1986) *Toward a new psychology of women.* Boston: Beacon Press.

Montemayor, R., & Eisen, M. (1977) 'The development of self-conceptions from childhood to adolescence.' *Developmental Psychology,* 13, 314-319.

Mullener, N., & Laird, J.D. (1971) 'Some developmental changes in the organization of self-evaluations.' *Developmental Psychology,* 5, 233-236.

Offer, D.M., Ostrow. E., & Howard, D. I. (1981) *The adolescent: A psychological portrait.* New York: Basic Books.

Piaget, J. (1960) *The psychology of intelligence.* Patterson, NJ: Littlefield, Adams.

Putnam, F.W. (1989) *Diagnosis and treatment of multiple personality disorder.* New York: Guilford Press.

Rogers, C.R. (1950) 'The significance of the self-regarding attitudes and perceptions.' In M.L. Reymert (Ed.), *Feelings and emotions: The Mooseheart symposium* (pp. 78-99). New York: McGraw-Hill.

Rosenberg, M. (1979) *Conceiving the self.* New York: Basic Books.

Rosenberg, M. (1986) 'Self-concept from middle childhood through adolescence.' In J. Suls and A.G. Greenwald (Eds.), *Psychological perspective on the self* (Vol. 3, pp.182-205). Hillsdale, NJ: Erlbaum.

Secord, P., & Peevers, B. (1974) 'The development of person concepts.' In T. Mischel (Ed.), *Understanding other persons* (pp. 117-142). Oxford, England: Blackwell.

Selman, R. (1980) *The growth of interpersonal understanding.* San Diego, CA: Academic Press.

Smollar, J., & Youniss, J. (1985) 'Adolescent self-concept development.' In R.L. Leahy (Ed.), *The development of self* (pp. 247-266). San Diego, CA: Academic Press.

Steinberg, L. (1990) 'Autonomy, conflict, and harmony in the family.' In S.S. Feldman & G.R. Elliot (Eds.), *At the threshold: The developing adolescent* (pp. 255-276). Cambridge, MA: Harvard University Press.

29. Conditional Reasoning, Representation, and Level of Abstraction

Henry Markovits and Robert Vachon

This study examined the idea that (a) reasoning involves construction of mental representations (models) of premises and that (b) there is a developmental progression in the ability of subjects to reason with models containing concrete and abstract elements. Experiment 1 found that for 13- and 16-year-old subjects, reasoning with abstract content was more difficult than with concrete content. Younger subjects appeared to rely more on concrete representations that used real-world knowledge than on more general abstract representations. Experiment 2 explored order effects in the presentation of concrete and abstract problems. Abstract followed by concrete problems led to reduced concrete-problem performance for high school students but did not affect performance for university students. These results support the hypotheses and suggest that development of formal reasoning abilities goes through 2 levels.

The Piagetian analysis of deductive reasoning can be taken to imply the development of a capacity to make cognitive judgments that are relatively independent of the immediate material content of deductive reasoning problems. Piaget (1983/1987b) characterized formal thought as a period in which reality is "subordinated to systems of necessary connections" (p. 5). This definition implies that a formal reasoner should be capable of producing deductive arguments that reflect the logical relationships between given premises and that are relatively free of contextual variability that does not affect these relationships. However, research into human reasoning has consistently found that content significantly influences the way that people derive conclusions (Johnson-Laird, Legrenzi, & Legrenzi, 1972; Markovits, 1986; Markovits & Vachon, 1989; O'Brien, Costa, & Overton, 1986; Overton, Ward, Black, Noveck, & O'Brien, 1987). Such results have led to the abandonment of the notion of cross-domain generality (Piaget, 1972) and to the search for processes that can explicitly integrate contextual influences within the scope of the formal operational model (Byrnes, 1988a; Overton, 1990; Piaget, 1981/1987a). These results have also led to attempts to incorporate meaning systems into models of deductive logic (Piaget & Garcia, 1986; Piéraut-Le Bonniec, 1980). Nonetheless, it can be argued that the nature of development as conceived by Piagetian theory involves processes such as reflective abstraction (Piaget, 1987) that should converge toward a logic that is progressively less context dependent (Borel, 1987). One of the major challenges for this approach to reasoning is to specify processes that can integrate contextual variability into the description of formal deductive thinking while maintaining the idea that cognitive development tends toward capacities that are more impervious to such variability.

Henry Markovits and Robert Vachon: 'Conditional Reasoning, Representation, and Level of Abstraction'. *DEVELOPMENTAL PSYCHOLOGY* (1990), Vol. 26, No. 6. pp 942-951. Copyright © 1990 by the American Psychological Association, Inc. Reprinted by permission.

A series of studies (Byrnes & Overton, 1986; Markovits, Schleifer, & Fortier, 1989; Markovits & Vachon, 1989; O'Brien & Overton, 1980, 1982; Overton *et al.*, 1987) indicated that the ability to reason consistently on a variety of conditional reasoning tasks does not appear until early adolescence and that any content effects must be superimposed on this basic competence. Overton's competence-moderator-performance model (Overton, 1985; Overton & Newman, 1982) specifically incorporates this idea by suggesting that an underlying level of formal competence must be attained before other factors, such as context, can operate to facilitate propositional reasoning. In the present study, we attempted to extend this model by suggesting a specific mechanism by which content effects in conditional reasoning may be understood and to propose a developmental sequence that tends toward a reasoning process that is relatively insensitive to content variation.

One approach to understanding the way in which content might affect reasoning involves the amalgamation of two distinct notions that are drawn from very different paradigms. Johnson-Laird (1983) recently introduced the idea that one of the basic processes underlying reasoning may involve the construction by the subject of a "mental model." This requires the generation of an internal representation of the premises. The characteristics of such a model determine to a large extent the conclusions at which people may arrive. In the context of conditional reasoning tasks that require subjects to reason from a given conditional relation of the form "If P then Q," one critical aspect of any representation of the premises appears to involve the incorporation of relations of the form "If A then Q" (where A is any term that is different from P) into the model (Johnson-Laird, 1983; Markovits, 1984, 1985, 1988; Rumain, Connell, & Braine, 1983) or into an alternate model of the premises.

It would be useful at this point to give an example of how such a process might work (for this, we have adapted Johnson-Laird's, 1983, description of syllogistic inference, pp. 94-125). Let us suppose that the following problem (which is an example of the affirmation of the consequent) is presented: "If it rains, then the street outside will be wet. The street outside is wet." The first step in the reasoning process would involve the creation of a model of the major premise. There are two possible ways of doing this; these are presented schematically as Models 1 and 2:

Model 1   It rains ——— street wet

Model 2   It rains ——— street wet

Street cleaned ——— street wet

Model 2 contains an alternative of the form "If A then Q" (if the street is cleaned, then the street will be wet). The second step involves adding the information contained in the second premise to the model of the major premise (i.e. The street is wet) while attempting to take into account the different ways that this might be done. If we use the convention that underlining a term indicates that it is to be considered true, then Model 1 generates the following representation:

It rains ——— street is wet.

There is only one possible conclusion from this (i.e., It has rained), which is obtained by reading backward through the causal relation. This response corresponds to a biconditional interpretation of the if–then relation (i.e. the model implies that the street is wet if and only if it has rained). However, Model 2 leads to three possible representations:

It rains ———— street wet

Street cleaned ———— street wet

It rains ———— street wet

Street cleaned ———— street wet

It rains ———— street wet

Street cleaned ———— street wet

These three representations lead to three possible conclusions: (a) it has rained; (b) the street has been cleaned; or (c) it has rained and the street has been cleaned. Thus, subjects starting from Model 2 have the possibility of reaching the (logically correct) answer (i.e., that it is not certain that it has rained) if they are able to generate at least the first two of the three possible representations. It must be noted that a similar analysis would be made for problems involving the negation of the antecedent ("If P then Q, P is false), for which the logically correct answer is also that there is no certain conclusion (both the affirmation of the consequent and the negation of the antecedent are indeterminate forms).

Explicitly incorporating a representational component of the kind suggested by Johnson-Laird (1983; see also Overton, 1990; Russell, 1987) provides an elegant explanation for content effects because varying the specific "If P then Q" relation would conceivably affect the probability that a subject would generate a model that includes an "If A then Q" relation. Many different mechanisms could have such effects, from "invited inferences" (Geis & Zwicky, 1971) to various pragmatic schemas (Cheng & Holyoak, 1985) and contextual effects (Byrne, 1989).

This approach thus supposes that correctly reasoning with a given "If P then Q" relation requires that subjects generate a model (or models) that includes an "If A then Q" relation. The second part of our analysis attempted to examine the problem of how and why people generate such additional relations in the context of problems in which these are not explicitly present. To do this, we used the Piagetian analysis of the role and developmental pattern of "the possible" (Piaget, 1981/1987a). According to this analysis, there is a developmental progression in the extent to which children and adolescents can extrapolate from a given situation to possible outcomes or configurations. Generally speaking, younger children appear to be more constrained by the specific parameters of a given situation and tend to generate possibilities that are determined either by direct analogy with what is visible or by anticipating possible outcomes that are directly attainable. The two final forms interest us particularly: The third level is characterized by the generation of specific examples, which are inferred with respect to the characteristics of the problem and represent a subset of many other possibilities. The fourth level is determined by the realization that possibilities may exist despite the subjects' inability to specify their exact form.

Our general approach assumed that someone who is presented with an "If P then Q" proposition must spontaneously generate an alternate relation of the form "If A then Q" to correctly resolve the problems requiring uncertainty responses (indeterminate forms). Without perceptual support, neither direct analogy nor anticipating possible outcomes would permit this, implying that younger children should tend to produce biconditional responses to these problems, which is what is generally observed. However, the third-level strategy should enable production of alternate possibilities if the "If P then Q" relation is such that it permits generation of specific examples, (i.e., by use of subjects' real-world knowledge). This implies the corollary construction of a model using referents to specific, concrete elements. People who are able to function at the fourth level could be expected to generate alternate possibilities that are not necessarily well defined, and could thus do this in the context of models that do not use such referents in their construction. Thus, children and adolescents should initially perform better with conditional reasoning problems for which the specific content easily permits accessing appropriate alternate relations by use of real-world knowledge, whereas the ability to consistently resolve problems that do not permit such access should be a later development and should be associated with a corresponding representational component. In this context, it is important to specify that both of the proposed modes require the ability to reason on the basis of propositions and are thus formal operational in the Piagetian sense. The term *concrete* here refers to the referents of the propositions and does not imply the necessity for the kind of direct perceptual support that characterizes concrete operational thought.

The purpose of this study was thus two-fold. First, we wished to examine the prediction that the spontaneous production of uncertainty responses to the indeterminate logical forms, affirmation of the consequent and negation of the antecedent, would be easier for conditional propositions with content for which real-world knowledge should permit generation of specific "If A then Q" relations than for problems without such content. It must be noted that studies of problems of inclusion (Bucci, 1978) and the selection task (Overton *et al.*, 1987) have provided indirect support for this conclusion. However, there does not appear to be a systematic study of this distinction for conditional syllogisms. The second aim of the present study was to attempt to examine age differences in the relation between the generation of representations of conditional relations of varying degrees of access to appropriate possibilities and performance on reasoning problems.

Experiment 1

This initial experiment examined two specific questions. The first concerned expected performance on the indeterminate logical forms, affirmation of the consequent and negation of the antecedent. It was hypothesized that there would be poorer performance on conditional reasoning problems with content that did not easily permit generation of "If A then Q" relations by accessing real-world knowledge than on problems with content that did permit such access. Three content types were used to test this hypothesis: (a) concrete terms such that generating alternate possibilities of the form

"A implies Q" was facilitated *(many alternatives)*; (b) concrete terms such that generating alternate possibilities was considered less probable (*few alternatives*); and (c) terms with two elements that involved nonsense words so that real-world knowledge would not provide any specific alternates (no alternatives). The few-alternatives problems were included to provide an intermediate level between the many-alternatives and the no-alternatives contents. Few-alternatives problems were found by Bucci (1978) to be more difficult on class inclusion tasks that are similar to conditional syllogisms. It was predicted that many-alternatives problems would yield the most successful reasoning performance, followed by few-alternatives and no-alternatives problems.

The second question concerned the relation between the ability to generate spontaneous representations of if–then relations that included alternate possibilities of the form "A implies Q," and reasoning performance. Short scenarios (modeled after Markovits, 1984) were included that presented subjects with an "If P then Q" relation (these relations were different from, but modeled after, those used in the reasoning problems). Subjects were informed that "Q was true" and were asked to imagine the possible reason for this. These scenarios were designed to provide a measure of the spontaneous tendency of subjects to generate a representation of the premises that included alternate possibilities, in a situation that did not require reasoning. Globally, it was predicted that subjects who spontaneously indicated that something other than "P" could have been the reason would perform better on the reasoning problems. More specifically, the model proposed here implies that younger adolescents would rely primarily on real-world knowledge (the Level 3 strategy) in attempting to solve conditional reasoning problems. Thus, these subjects should show consistent relations between reasoning performance and the ability to generate other possibilities in the many-alternatives scenario; such relations would explicitly suggest the use of a Level 3 strategy.

Method

Subjects. A total of 168 French-speaking middle-class boys from a private high school in Montreal were examined. Of these, 98 were in the 2nd year of high school (mean age = 13 years, 4 months) and 70 were in the 5th year of high school (mean age = 16 years, 1 month).

Material. Test booklets written in French and containing six items were constructed. Each of the three conditional reasoning problems were presented (one per page) in the following format: At the top of each page was written "Suppose that it is true that: followed by a statement in the form "If P then Q.' Four multiple-choice questions were then presented. These were in the following form:

A) If P is true, then you can say that:

   a) you are certain that Q is true.

   b) you are certain that Q is false.

   c) you are not certain whether Q is true or not.

The four multiple-choice questions corresponded to the logical forms "P is true" (modus ponens; MP), "P is false" (negation of the antecedent; NA), "Q is true" (affirmation of the consequent; AC), and "Q is false" (modus tollens; MT).

The three representational scenarios were presented in the following form:

> France and Brigitte are talking about trees. France is certain that _if one cuts down a tree, the tree will fall down._ Last week, Brigitte saw a tree that had fallen down. Can you imagine what could have made the tree fall down?

All three of the scenarios were presented on the same page. The if–then statements used for the reasoning problems were taken from one of two sets of three relations (the if–then statements used in the scenarios were always taken from the set not used for the reasoning problems). These were as follows:

Set 1

    (a) If a rock is thrown through a window, the window will break. (many alternatives)

    (b) If one cuts down a tree, the tree will fall down. (few alternatives)

    (c) If one fretres, the puyge will fall. (no alternatives)

Set 2

    (a) If an object is put into boiling water, the object will become hot. (many alternatives)

    (b) If a myopic person puts on glasses, they will see well. (few alternatives)

    (c) If one fruitines, then the motiyou will be stained. (no alternatives)

For each of the two sets, the first item was designed to have concrete content such that it should be easy to find specific examples of the form "If A then Q" (other ways of breaking windows or heating objects). The second item had concrete referents but presented more difficulties in generating possibilities. The third item had nonsense referents that did not permit generation of specific real-world possibilities.

For half of the booklets, the reasoning problems used the first set of relations and the scenarios used the second set. This was reversed for the other half of the booklets. In addition, the scenarios preceded the reasoning problems in half of the booklets and followed them in the other half. The order of the three reasoning problems and the three scenarios were systematically varied. Finally, the order of the four questions asked on each reasoning problem was also varied.

Procedure. Test booklets were given to entire classes of students. No time limit was imposed, and subjects were asked to respond to their own satisfaction.

Results

We were initially interested in subjects' performance on the reasoning problems. Table 1 gives the mean number of correct responses for the four logical forms by problem type (many alternatives, few alternatives, and no alternatives) and age level. A 4 (logical form) x 3 (problem type) x 2 (age) analysis of variance (ANOVA) with repeated measures of logical form and problem type was performed. This analysis indicated significant main effects of problem type, $F(2, 163) = 5.41, p < .01$, logical form, $F(3, 162) = 81.46, p < .001$, and age, $F(1, 164) = 6.55, p < .02$. In addition, there was a significant Problem Type x Logical Form interaction, $F(6, 159) = 5.22, p < .001$. The performance of the older subjects was globally better than that of the younger subjects. In addition, analysis of contrast variables indicated that there were more correct uncertainty responses on the ACs with many-alternatives problems than on those with few-alternatives problems, $F(1, 164) = 13.84, p < .01$, and more on the latter than on those with no alternatives, $F(1, 164) = 4.10, p < .01$. There were fewer correct responses on MTs with many-alternatives problems than on those with few alternatives, $F(1, 164) = 10.58, p < .01$, or with no alternatives, $F(1, 164) = 6.14, p < .001$. No other differences were significant. It is of interest to note that the percentage of correct responses on two indeterminate forms (AC and NA) combined was 30.5%, 37.9%, and 47.0% for the no-alternatives, few-alternatives, and many-alternatives problems, respectively.

Table 1   **Mean number of correct responses by problem type on the four logical forms**

Age	Many alternatives				Few alternatives				No alternatives			
	MP	MT	AC	NA	MP	MT	AC	NA	MP	MT	AC	NA
13 years	0.86	0.77	0.54	0.34	0.86	0.87	0.41	0.31	0.89	0.84	0.30	0.23
16 years	0.93	0.83	0.58	0.44	0.94	0.94	0.44	0.37	0.93	0.93	0.39	0.33

Note. MP = modus ponens; MT = modus tollens; AC = affirmation of the consequent; NA = negation of the antecedent.

A second analysis concerned performance on the three scenarios. Subjects generated one of four types of response: (a) repetition of the previously stated antecedent, (b) an enumeration of one or more specific possibilities, (c) statements that some unspecified effect other than the antecedent term was possible, or (d) statements that there was no way of knowing the true antecedent of the observed effect. Subjects who only repeated the stated antecedent term were given a score of 0. All other responses were taken to indicate that subjects spontaneously recognized that the stated antecedent was not the only possible reason for the effect (a score of 1 was thus given for any of the other responses). The percentages of subjects among the 13-year-olds who gave some form of alternate relation were 48%, 31%, and 26% for the many-alternatives, low-alternatives, and no-alternatives scenarios, respectively. The corresponding percentages were 40%, 31%, and 23% among the 16-year-olds. A 3 (scenario type) x 2 (age) ANOVA with repeated measures on scenario type was performed. This indicated a significant main effect of scenario type, $F(2, 165) = 12.47, p < .001$. Analysis of contrast variables showed that there were more uncertainty responses on the many-alternatives scenarios than on the low-alternative scenarios, $F(1, 166) = 11.52, p < .001$. There was no significant difference between the low-alternatives and the no alternatives scenarios.

The relation between performance on the scenarios and on the reasoning problems was subsequently examined. Table 2 presents the correlations between scenarios and reasoning problems for both age levels. Inspection of this table reveals some interesting patterns. First, it is useful to note that there are two major types of correlations that can be observed here. As initially hypothesized, there were generally positive correlations between performance on the scenarios and the number of correct responses generated on the two invalid forms (forms AC and NA, for which the logically correct response is uncertainty). However, for the two valid forms MP and MT (for which there is a logically valid conclusion), the observed correlations were either very small or negative. For the 13-year-olds, there was a consistent relation observed between performance on the high-alternatives scenario and on the three forms of reasoning problems. The relation between scenario performance and reasoning was more variable for the other two scenario types. For the 16-year-olds, the pattern was quite different. The relation between performance on the scenarios and reasoning was much more mixed, with fewer significant correlations. There was, however, a somewhat clearer relation between performance on the no-alternatives scenario and on the corresponding reasoning problem than that observed for the 13-year-olds.

Finally, a separate analysis determined that the order of presentation of the scenarios and the reasoning problems did not affect performance on the latter.

Table 2   Pearson correlations between performance on the three scenarios and on the three reasoning problems

Age/scenario	Many alternatives (MA)				Few alternatives (FC)				No alternatives (NA)			
	MP	MT	AC	NA	MP	MT	AC	NA	MP	MT	AC	NA
13 years												
MA	−.02	−.24*	.40*	.27*	−.13	−.29*	.20*	.25*	.02	−.07	.27*	.24*
FC	−.05	−.10	.21*	.18	−.29*	−.26*	.03	.08	.10	.11	.30*	.21*
NA	.10	−.39*	.26*	−.26	−.29*	−.25	.13	.12	.01	.07	.18	.06
16 years												
MA	−.11	−.02	.27*	.15	−.18	.08	.15	.10	.00	−.11	.13	.05
FC	−.05	−.02	.13	.20	.10	.17	.02	.05	.07	−.05	.10	.11
NA	.02	.16	.25*	.13	−.16	.01	.20	.07	−.25*	.02	.20	.34*

Note. MP = modus ponens; MT = modus tollens; AC = affirmation of the consequent; NA = negation of the antecedent.
*p < .05.

Discussion

These results provide some support for our basic hypotheses. First, the proportion of correct uncertainty responses to the logical forms AC and NA was greater on the high-alternatives problems, for which generation of real-world possibilities was facilitated, than on the few-alternatives problems, for which generation of real-world possibilities was restricted, although this difference was significant only for the AC form. The same difference was found between few-alternatives and no-alternatives problems. In addition, there was an interesting developmental pattern in the relationship between specific scenarios and reasoning problems. For the youngest subjects, performance on all three types of reasoning problems was most clearly related to performance on the many-alternatives scenario. For the older subjects, the relationship was more complex, with generally lower correlations.

These results are consistent with the idea that younger subjects often approach reasoning problems of the type used here by attempting to construct problem representations mostly on the basis of real-world knowledge. These results do not indicate the strategy used by the older subjects. However, within our general framework, they suggest the possibility that these subjects may have used a mixture of strategies involving both real-world knowledge and a more abstract representation.

One final point must be discussed. The obtained correlations between scenarios and reasoning indicate that there is a low or negative relation between performance on the former and the level of correct responding to the two valid logical forms MP and MT. A similar phenomenon has been noted in studies that presented subjects with explicit relations in the form "If A then Q" (contramands), for which higher levels of incorrect uncertainty responses have been found for MT when presented with a contramand (Byrnes & Overton, 1986; Markovits, 1985; Rumain, Connell, & Braine, 1983). There is some evidence that this phenomenon is associated with a developmental progression in reasoning performance (Byrnes & Overton, 1986; O'Brien & Overton, 1982; see also Byrnes, 1988b, for one explanation of this). We will come back to this problem later.

Experiment 2

Experiment 1 provided support for our hypotheses. Both our overall framework and the results of Experiment 1 suggest that subjects may have available two different strategies for constructing models of premises. One of these relies on real-world knowledge, and the other is more abstract in form. It is possible that subjects who receive an abstract problem (and who would presumably be encouraged to use a more abstract representation) tend to use the same form of processing in a subsequent problem (i.e., they would be less likely to use real-world knowledge in attempting to solve the latter). Thus, younger subjects who are presumably more dependent on real-world knowledge in solving reasoning problems should do less well on subsequent concrete problems (in the indeterminate forms) than they are capable of doing. Inversely, these subjects should perform better on concrete problems when given these initially. Older subjects who are able to use consistently a Level 4 strategy (generating possibilities that do not depend on real-world knowledge) should be much less affected by order of presentation because such a strategy can be successfully transferred from abstract to concrete contents. Thus, the relative order of presentation of concrete and abstract problems should affect reasoning performance on the indeterminate forms with concrete problems for younger subjects but not for older subjects who are able to consistently use a Level 4 strategy.

The main aim of this study was to explore the effect of order of presentation of concrete and more abstract items. In this context, item variability was examined along a more explicit concrete–abstract dimension. The few-alternatives contents were replaced with "If P then Q" relations for which Q is a concrete term but for which P is a relatively abstract term. Previous research has indicated that subjects should respond to reasoning problems containing mixed relations of this kind better than to abstract problems and less well than to many-alternatives problems (Markovits, 1986). The inclusion of these problems should better permit examination of the interaction between abstract and concrete modeling. The relation between the representation scenarios and reasoning problems was also reexamined in a form that would eliminate any possible interactions between the various scenarios. Thus, subjects were presented with a single representational scenario that was varied in content. Finally, a sample of university students was added to the age groups used in the first study in order to examine responses of subjects who were presumably at a more abstract stage of processing. We purposefully chose subjects with a computer-science major, who would be expected to be capable of a relatively high level of such functioning (i.e., subjects able to consistently use a Level 4 strategy).

Method

Subjects. A total of 407 subjects were examined. Of these, 118 (53 boys and 64 girls) were in the 2nd year of high school (mean age = 14 years, 3 months) and 139 (71 boys and 68 girls) were in the 5th year of high school (average age = 17 years, 3 months) at a middle-class French-speaking high school in the Montreal area. The remaining 150 subjects (127 men and 23 women) were university students at the Université du Québec à Montréal (mean age = 29 years) recruited mainly from undergraduate computer-science classes.

Material. Test booklets containing three reasoning problems and one representation scenario were constructed. All of the booklets were in French. The basic format was identical to that used in Study 1 except that there was only one representation scenario per booklet. There were two sets of conditional relations in the form "P implies Q" used in the study, each of which consisted of (a) a concrete relation for which examples of "A implies Q" could be produced (corresponding to the many-alternatives problems of the previous study), (b) an intermediate relation for which the Q term was concrete but the P term was more abstract, (c) an abstract relation for which both P and Q were nonsense terms (corresponding to the low-alternatives problems of the previous study). It must be noted that the concrete-to-abstract dimension refers only to the direct referents of the two main terms in the propositions; in all cases, the implication is clearly expressed in ordinary language. The relations were as follows:

Set 1

    (a) If a rock hits a glass, the glass will break. (concrete)

    (b) If a proton explodes, the temperature will rise. (intermediate)

    (c) If one makes a frolix, a trinom will be produced. (abstract)

Set 2

    (a) If Christian has homework, he will be in a bad mood. (concrete)

    (b) If one mixes thorium with silex, there will be a fire. (intermediate)

    (c) If one fruitines, there will be a motiyou. (abstract)

In all of the booklets, the three reasoning problems were together and were preceded or followed by a single representation scenario. In half of the booklets, the reasoning problems were presented in order from concrete to intermediate to abstract (direct order). In the other half, the order was inverted (inverted order). Half of the problems used the first series and the other half used the second series. In half of the booklets, the representation scenario preceded the reasoning problems; in the other half, it came after. The representation scenario was varied systematically in content among the three forms (concrete, intermediate, and abstract) and was always taken from a different set than the reasoning problems.

Procedure. Test booklets were given to entire classes of students. No time limit was imposed and subjects were asked to respond to their own satisfaction.

Results

Our initial analysis concerned the proportion of correct responses to the logical reasoning problems as a function of age and order of presentation. These results are summarized in Table 3. A 4 (logical form) x 3 (problem type) x 3 (age) x 2 (order of presentation) ANOVA with repeated measures of logical form and problem type was performed. This indicated significant main effects for logical form, $F(3, 399) = 109.70$, $p < .001$, problem type, $F(2, 400) = 12.13$, $p < .001$, and age, $F(2, 401) = 112.88$, $p < .001$. In addition, there were significant interactions involving Problem Type x Order, $F(2, 400) = 6.10$, $p < .01$, Logical Form x Age, $F(6, 396) = 9.59$, $p < .001$, Problem Type x Order, $F(6, 396) = 15.70$, $p < .001$, Logical Form x Age x Order, $F(6, 396) = 2.62$, $p < .02$, and Logical Form x Problem Type x Order, $F(6, 396) = 4.67$, $p < .001$.

To simplify the analysis, scores were combined on the two indeterminate forms (AC and NA) and on the two determinate forms (MP and MT). First, a 3 (problem type) x 3 (age) x 2 (order of presentation) ANOVA with repeated measures on problem type was performed on the indeterminate forms. This indicated significant main effects of problem type, $F(2, 400) = 34.97$, $p < .001$, age, $F(2, 401) = 83.90$, $p < .001$, and order, $F(1, 401) = 9.27$, $p < .01$. In addition, there were significant interactions involving Problem Type x Order, $F(2, 400) = 6.20$, $p < .01$, and Age x Order, $F(2, 401) = 4.14$, $p < .02$. To clarify these results, Newman-Keuls post hoc comparisons were performed. Overall differences among the problem types indicated that performance on the concrete problems was better than that observed on the intermediate problems, which was

Table 3 **Mean number of correct responses by problem type on the four logical forms**

Age/order	Concrete				Intermediate				Abstract			
	MP	MT	AC	NA	MP	MT	AC	NA	MP	MT	AC	NA
14												
Direct	0.76	0.57	0.33	0.59	0.81	0.57	0.45	0.41	0.84	0.66	0.36	0.28
Inverted	0.87	0.68	0.27	0.40	0.83	0.62	0.22	0.37	0.80	0.73	0.28	0.25
16												
Direct	0.66	0.51	0.52	0.68	0.89	0.65	0.49	0.59	0.86	0.63	0.32	0.31
Inverted	0.86	0.76	0.34	0.40	0.91	0.71	0.28	0.29	0.87	0.81	0.32	0.18
Adult												
Direct	0.86	0.72	0.86	0.94	0.94	0.77	0.82	0.77	0.94	0.71	0.72	0.56
Inverted	0.85	0.68	0.83	0.90	0.89	0.66	0.82	0.80	0.86	0.68	0.72	0.76

Note. MP = modus ponens; MT = modus tollens; AC = affirmation of the consequent; NA = negation of the antecedent.

superior to that obtained on the abstract problems. There was, in addition, a clear developmental effect, with adults doing better across the three problem types than the 17-year-olds, who performed better than the 14-year-olds.

Subsequently, the Age x Order interaction was examined. This indicated that both the 14- and 17-year-olds did better on the indeterminate forms when given the concrete problems first and less well when given the abstract problem first. Adults showed no difference between the two forms of presentation. In addition, the overall developmental difference varied with order of presentation. For the direct order, performance was significantly better among 17-year-olds than among 14-year-olds, both of whom performed less well than adults. However, when the abstract problem was presented first, there was no difference in performance between 14- and 17-year-olds, although both performed less well than the adults.

Finally, the Problem Type x Order interaction was examined. This indicated that overall, performance on the concrete and intermediate problems was superior when subjects were presented with the concrete problems first. The abstract problems showed no effect of order. In addition, the overall differences among the problem types varied with order of presentation. When the concrete problems were presented first, performance on the concrete and on intermediate problems were both superior to that on the abstract problem. When the abstract problems were presented first, no significant difference was observed among the three problem types.

A second analysis was performed using the combined scores on the determinate logical forms (MP and MT). A 3 (problem type) x 3 (age) x 2 (order of presentation) ANOVA with repeated measures on problem type was performed. This indicated a significant main effect of problem type, $F(2, 400) = 4.03$, $p < .02$, and significant interactions involving Problem Type x Order, $F(2, 400) = 4.77, p < .01$, and Age x Order, $F(2, 401) = 3.50, p < .05$. A post hoc comparison of differences among problem types indicated that there was no single significant difference among the three types. Examination of the Age x Order interaction indicated that for both the 14- and 17-year-olds, performance was worse on the two valid forms when the concrete problems were presented first. The opposite effect was found with the adults, for whom the concrete first presentation produced better overall performance. Finally, examination of the Problem Type x Order interaction showed that the effect of order of presentation was concentrated on the concrete problems. Subjects did worse on the concrete problems when given these problems first, and they did correspondingly better when receiving the abstract problems first.

Final analyses concerned performance on the representational scenarios and on the reasoning problems. The percentages of subjects giving alternate possibilities on the concrete, intermediate, and abstract scenarios were 51%, 22%, and 36%, respectively, for 14-year-olds; 69%, 27%, and 36% for 17-year-olds; and 80%, 65%, and 34% for adult subjects. A 3 (age) x 3 (scenario type) ANOVA was performed. This indicated significant main effects for age, $F(2, 398) = 10.86, p < .001$, and scenario type, $F(2, 398) = 20.23, p < .001$, in addition to a significant Age x Scenario Type interaction, $F(4, 398) = 3.44, p < .01$. Post hoc analyses indicated that adult subjects gave alternative possibility responses more often than the younger subjects and that the concrete scenarios produced more such responses overall. For both 14- and 17-year-olds, there was no significant difference between abstract and intermediate scenarios, whereas for adult subjects, intermediate scenarios produced higher levels of alternative responding than did abstract ones.

Table 4 indicates correlations between performance on the scenarios and reasoning performance across all three grade levels. It must be noted that because only one scenario was presented per booklet, the numbers are small and the interpretation correspondingly difficult. Nonetheless, inspection of Table 4 reveals a fairly similar pattern to that obtained in Study 1. The youngest subjects show a fairly clear relation between performance on the concrete scenario and performance on all three reasoning problems, whereas for the older subjects, the correlations are weaker and more dispersed.

A final analysis examined the effects of the order of presentation of the scenarios and the reasoning problems on the latter. A 3 (age) x 2 (scenario order) x 3 (problem type) ANOVA with repeated measures on problem type was performed on the combined scores for the two indeterminate forms (AC and NA). This indicated a significant Age x Scenario Order interaction, $F(2,401) = 4.93, p < .01$. Post hoc comparisons indicated that both 14- and 17-year-olds performed less well on the reasoning problems when they received the scenarios first, whereas the adults performed better in the same condition. A second ANOVA was then performed on the combined scores for the two determinate forms (MP and MT). This indicated a significant Problem Type x Scenario Order interaction, $F(2, 400) = 4.98, p < .01$. Post hoc analyses indicated that no single difference was significant.

Table 4   **Pearson correlations between performance on the three scenarios and on the three reasoning problems**

Age/scenario	Concrete (CON)				Intermediate (INT)				Abstract (ABS)			
	MP	MT	AC	NA	MP	MT	AC	NA	MP	MT	AC	NA
14 years												
CON	−.23	−.43*	.14	.37*	−.27	−.32*	.28*	.51*	−.23	−.28	.33*	.29
INT	−.07	−.31	.21	.24	−.34*	−.21	.27	.27	−.28	−.08	.33*	.18
ABS	.08	−.07	.13	.06	−.47*	.01	.18	.08	−.36*	−.37*	.15	.53*
17 years												
CON	−.04	−.08	.12	.16	−.08	−.11	.15	.23	−.08	−.19	−.01	.26
INT	.02	−.20	.14	.50*	−.11	−.35	.42*	.50*	.02	−.32*	.24	.31*
ABS	−.21	−.08	.14	.35*	−.43	−.37*	.30	.18	−.37*	−.28	.05	.21
Adult												
CON	−.07	−.13	.24	.15	−.13	−.02	.17	.27*	.08	−.10	.19	.29*
INT	−.18	−.15	.26	.36*	−.01	−.12	.33*	.28	−.06	.14	.21	.04
ABS	−.08	−.29	.23	.23	.19	−.12	−.03	.05	.11	.21	.15	.28

Note. MP = modus ponens; MT = modus tollens; AC = affirmation of the consequent; NA = negation of the antecedent.
* *p* <.05.

Discussion

The results of this study provide clear support for our hypothesis that there are order effects that vary with developmental level. For the indeterminate forms AC and NA, reasoning performance decreased among 14- and 17-year olds when an abstract problem was presented first, as predicted. The adults in this study showed no such effect. Inspection of Figure 1 provides a synthesis of the patterns of interactions and the corresponding age variations of performance on the indeterminate forms. For both the 14- and 17-year-olds, the same overall pattern is observed. First, performance on the indeterminate forms when content was abstract remained invariantly low irrespective of order of presentation. However, there was a clear improvement on both the concrete and intermediate problems when the concrete problem was presented first, although this was not the case when the abstract problem was presented first. This effect was somewhat restricted for the youngest children but was clearly present for the 17-year-olds.

For the determinate forms MP and MT, the 14- and 17-year olds did better when the abstract problem was presented initially, whereas the adults did worse in this condition. In this case, the interaction between age and order of presentation exists, but the effects are inversed. Such a result is similar to the negative correlations obtained between the scenarios and the valid forms and implies that whatever processes improve performance on the invalid forms also result in diminished performance on the valid forms.

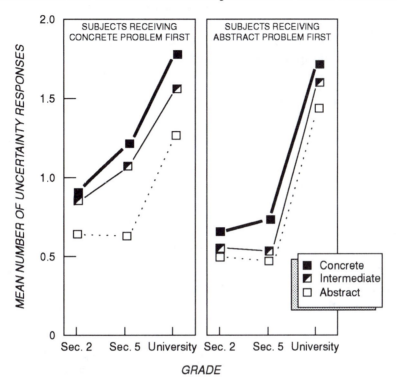

Figure 1   **Mean number of combined uncertainty responses on the affirmation of the consequent and the negation of the antecedent for concrete, intermediate, and abstract problems for subjects receiving concrete problems first and for those receiving abstract problems first, by age. (Sec = secondary)**

These results indicate that 14- and 17-year-olds attempt to solve abstract reasoning problems in a way that leads them to be less efficient in solving concrete problems than they would normally be. In addition, they appear to attempt to solve concrete problems in a way that has little effect on their performance with more abstract problems. On the other hand, these results indicate that adults with experience in abstract reasoning attempt to solve abstract problems in a way that does not affect their efficiency in solving concrete problems. In this context, it is also interesting to note that for 13- and 17-year-olds, performance on intermediate problems was closer to that found on concrete problems when subjects receive the latter first. On the other hand, when these subjects received abstract problems first, performance on intermediate problems more closely resembled that on abstract problems. This is consistent with the idea that there may be a tendency to transfer modes of representation from an initial problem to a subsequent one.

Finally, the correlations between performance on the representational scenarios and on the reasoning problems confirms the overall patterns found in Experiment 1. There is a generally positive relation between the capacity to generate alternate possibilities with a variety of contents and reasoning performance on the indeterminate forms (AC and NA) with differing contents. There are generally low or negative relations between this capacity and performance on the determinate forms (MP and MT). The age-related results are also consistent with the notion that younger children generate possibilities primarily by reference to real-world knowledge, whereas older subjects show a more mixed, and somewhat less clear, pattern of relationships between representation and reasoning. This latter point is somewhat problematic for our present approach because a stronger relation would ideally be expected between performance on the abstract scenarios and on the abstract reasoning problems among older subjects. The results of Experiment 1 did in fact tend toward this expectation, but the present results do not. The formulation of the question in the representation scenarios ("Can you imagine what could have made . . .") may have prompted subjects to search for specific examples and may not have encouraged more generalized forms of alternate possibilities. If this was the case, then the lower correlations obtained among older subjects would be consistent with the idea that these subjects use specific counterexamples less frequently than do subjects in solving reasoning problems. This idea, however, remains to be verified.

Finally, the effect of the order of presentation of the representation scenarios and the reasoning problems indicates that 14- and 17-year-olds do less well on the indeterminate forms when they receive the scenarios first, whereas adults do better in the same condition. This effect remains to be explained. However, the observed age difference does reinforce the idea that the adults in this study approached reasoning problems in a qualitatively different way than did the adolescents.

Conclusion

The results of these two studies provide support for the idea that there is a representational component in conditional reasoning, one that undergoes some developmental change. They also indicate that there may be a qualitative difference in the way that reasoning problems with concrete and abstract referents are processed. Although there may be several ways of interpreting such results, they are all consistent with the general approach we have taken here.

The major distinction that can be established here concerns reasoning with conditional propositions of the form "If P then Q" containing referents that are of two differing types: (a) concrete terms such that specific counterexamples of the form "If P then Q" can be generated using real-world knowledge and (b) abstract forms for which this is not the case. Our results indicate that problems of the first type are successfully resolved at an earlier age than are problems of the second type. Particularly interesting is the finding that there is an interaction between the two forms and that this interaction appears to be age-related. This pattern of results is consistent with our basic framework, which supposes that reasoners generate a mental model of the premises and suggests the following developmental progression: Younger children tend to generate models that involve specific representations of the premises and, within this context, have a beginning capacity to spontaneously generate alternate possibilities by using real-world knowledge. Older children generate alternate possibilities by using real-world knowledge. Older children use this strategy often and with growing success and are also more capable of using more abstract representations of premises. When they use abstract representations, they are much less able to generate appropriate possibilities because real-world knowledge is less useful in this context. Advanced adult reasoners appear to be able to use abstract representations and to successfully generate alternate possibilities in this context. This sequence provides a framework with which the observed interactions can be understood. Younger subjects perform optimally on concrete problems when they attempt to use real-world knowledge to generate possibilities. However, when they attempt to transfer a more abstract mode of functioning to a concrete problem, they are not able to generate appropriate information and their performance decreases. The greater relative decrease in performance among the 17-year-olds is consistent with the idea that these subjects are more at ease with abstract representations and that they transfer more easily (although they cannot yet generate possibilities easily in this context). Advanced reasoners, on the other hand, appear quite successful in generating abstract possibilities. However, when they transfer from a more concrete mode of representation to abstract problems, they are somewhat less successful, presumably because they transfer a tendency to use real-world knowledge on the latter.

The mental-models framework also provides a possible context for understanding the negative correlations between performance on the scenarios and reasoning performance on MT. As mentioned earlier, a similar phenomenon has been observed both developmentally and in studies using explicit contramands. Suppose the following problem: "If it rains, then the street will be wet. The street is not wet." As stated in the introduction, subjects can create two basic types of models. Some subjects will tend to generate the following model:

It rains ——— street wet

Incorporating the information that the street is not wet leads only to one possible result (underlined terms are to be considered false):

It rains ——— street wet,

from which the logically correct conclusion, "it has not rained," can be read off. However, other subjects (including those who are able to benefit from an explicit contramand) may generate the following model:

It rains ——— street wet

Street cleaned ——— street wet

Incorporating the information that the street is not wet can be done in two possible ways. The first is sequential and leads to the following models:

It rains ——— street wet

Street cleaned ——— street wet

It rains ——— street wet

Street cleaned ——— street wet

The second is simultaneous and leads to the following:

It rains ———— street wet

Street cleaned ———— street wet

Of course, only the last model is the logically correct one. However, subjects generating the two sequential models would erroneously respond that it is not certain whether or not it has rained. The sequential strategy would presumably take less processing capacity and would thus conceivably be found most often among younger formal reasoners. This might explain why children who are beginning to reason well with propositions and those who require contramands to do so, make this particular error. It is interesting to note that the distinction between sequential and simultaneous processing mirrors, on the formal propositional level, the Piagetian distinction between intermediate and concrete operational reasoners. It must be noted, however, that such an explanation remains highly speculative and requires empirical verification.

Another interesting characteristic of this model involves the way in which content effects can be incorporated. For subjects who are operating in a concrete mode when attempting to resolve conditional reasoning problems, it is assumed that spontaneous generation of the alternate relations required to correctly resolve such problems depends, at least partly, on the use of real-world knowledge. The specific nature of the conditional relations in question may thus determine the probability that alternate relations will indeed be generated, by such mechanisms as invited inferences (Geis & Zwicky, 1971), pragmatic reasoning schemas (Cheng & Holyoak, 1985), contextual effects (Byrne, 1989), or familiarity (Markovits, 1986; Overton et al., 1987). Such content effects would clearly require the basic ability to generate the requisite possibilities in optimal conditions in line with Overton's competence-moderator-performance model (Overton, 1985). Note that in this perspective, the influence of any such moderator variables would depend on the kind of representation used by the subject, and it would be predicted that subjects using an abstract mode would be less susceptible to such influences.

Finally, and as a corollary to the last point, the notion that formal reasoning tends toward processes that reduce content effects is retained here as the end-point of the proposed developmental sequence. In the present context, abstract representations for which indeterminate possibilities that are not dependent on specific problem characteristics (and are therefore less content dependent) are generated would produce reasoning that would be relatively impervious to content effects. Note that it is not claimed that subjects who are able to produce such models will do so all of the time, simply that they are capable of doing so. There is no evidence to indicate that subjects capable of such abstract formal reasoning will not use concrete modes when encouraged to do so. Finally, it must be repeated that the adults in this study were from a population selected as having a high level of abstract performance. The available evidence suggests that such performance levels would not generalize to a larger population of the same age.

The combination of a Piagetian developmental approach and the mental-models theory thus appears to provide a useful framework for understanding several aspects of conditional reasoning. However, it must be repeated that the results of this study can be interpreted in other contexts and that much future work remains before such an approach can be considered to have a solid theoretical and empirical base.

Portions of this article were presented at the annual meeting of the Jean Piaget Society, Philadelphia, June 1, 1988. Preparation of this article was supported by grants from the Quebec Ministry of Education (Fonds Pour la Formation de Chercheurs et l' Aide à la Recherche) and the Natural Sciences and Engineering Research Council of Canada to Henry Markovits.

We would like to thank the teachers and students of the Collège des Eudistes and the Ecole Secondaire St-Léonard for their assistance. We would also like to thank the anonymous reviewers for their very useful comments and criticisms.

References

Borel, M.-J. (1987) 'Piaget's natural logic.' In B. Inhelder, D. de Caprona, & A. Cornu-Wells (Eds.), *Piaget today* (pp. 65-77). Hillsdale, NJ: Erlbaum.

Byrne, R.M.J. (1989) 'Suppressing valid inferences with conditionals.' *Cognition,* 31, 61-83.

Byrnes, J.P. (1988a) 'Formal operations: A systematic reformulation.' *Developmental Review* 8, 66-87.

Byrnes, J.P. (1988b) 'What's left is closer to right.' *Developmental Review,* 8, 385-392.

Byrne, J. P., & Overton, W.F. (1986) 'Reasoning about certainty and uncertainty in concrete, causal, and propositional contexts.' *Developmental Psychology,* 22, 793-799.

Bucci, W. (1978) 'The interpretation of universal affirmative propositions.' *Cognition,* 6, 55-77.

Cheng, P. W., & Holyoak, K.J. (1985) 'Pragmatic reasoning schemas.' *Cognitive Psychology,* 17, 391-416.

Geis, M.L., & Zwicky, A.M. (1971) 'On invited inferences.' *Linguistic Inquiry,* 2, 561-566.

Johnson-Laird, P.N (1983) *Mental models.* Cambridge, MA: Harvard University Press.

Johnson-Laird, P.N, Legrenzi, P., & Legrenzi, M. (1972) 'Reasoning and a sense of reality.' *British Journal of Psychology,* 63, 395-400.

Markovits, H. (1984) 'Awareness of the "possible" as a mediator of formal thinking in conditional reasoning problems.' *British Journal* of *Psychology,* 75, 367-376.

Markovits, H. (1985) 'Incorrect conditional reasoning among adults: Competence or performance?' *British Journal of Psychology,* 76, 241-247.

Markovits, H. (1986) 'Familiarity effects in conditional reasoning.' *Journal of Educational Psychology,* 78, 492-494.

Markovits, H. (1988) 'Conditional reasoning, representation, and empirical evidence on a concrete task.' *Quarterly Journal of Experimental Psychology,* 40A, 483-495.

Markovits, H., Schleifer, M., & Fortier, L. (1989) 'The development of elementary deductive reasoning in young children.' *Developmental Psychology,* 25, 787-793.

Markovits, H. & Vachon, R. (1989) 'Reasoning with contrary-to-fact propositions.' *Journal of Experimental Child Psychology,* 47, 398-412.

O'Brien, D.P., Costa, G. & Overton, W.F. (1986) 'Evaluations of causal and conditional hypotheses.' *Quarterly Journal of Experimental Psychology,* 38A, 493-512.

O'Brien, D.P., & Overton, W.F. (1980) 'Conditional reasoning following contradictory evidence: A developmental analysis.' *Journal of Experimental Child Psychology, 30,* 44-61.

O'Brien, D.P., & Overton, W.F. (1982) 'Conditional reasoning and the competence-performance issue: A developmental analysis of a training task.' *Journal of Experimental Child Psychology, 34,* 274-290.

Overton, W.F. (1985) 'Scientific methodologies and the competence-moderator-performance issue.' In E. Neimark, R. DeLisi, & J. Newman (Eds.), *Moderators of competence* (pp. 15-41). Hillsdale, NJ: Erlbaum.

Overton, W.F. (1990) 'Competence and procedures: Constraints on the development of logical reasoning.' In W.F. Overton (Ed.), *Reasoning, necessity and logic: Developmental perspectives* (pp. 1-34). Hillsdale. NJ: Erlbaum.

Overton, W.F. & Newman, J.L. (1982) 'Cognitive development: A competence-activation/utilization approach.' In T. M. Field, A. Huston, H.C. Quay, L. Troll, & G.E. Finley (Eds.), *Review of human development.* New York: Wiley.

Overton, W.F. Ward, S.L., Black, J., Noveck, I.A., & O'Brien, D.P. (1987) 'Form and content in the development of deductive reasoning.' *Developmental Psychology, 23,* 22-30.

Piaget, J. (1972) 'Intellectual evolution from adolescence to adulthood.' *Human Development, 15,* 1-12.

Piaget, J. (1977) *Recherches sur l'abstraction réfléchissante: I. Abstraction des relations logico-mathématiques* [Research on reflective abstraction: I. Abstraction of logico-mathematical relations]. Paris: Presses Universitaires de France.

Piaget, J. (1987a) *Possibility and necessity Vol. 1. The role of possibility in cognitive development* (H. Feider, Trans.). Minneapolis: University of Minnesota Press. (Original work published 1981)

Piaget, J. (1987b) *Possibility and necessity: Vol. 2. The role of necessity in cognitive development* (H. Feider, Trans.). Minneapolis: University of Minnesota Press. (Original work published 1983)

Piaget, J., & Garcia, R. (1986) *Vers une logique des significations* [Toward a logic of meaning]. Geneva, Switzerland: Murionde.

Piéraut-Le Bonniec, G. (1980) *The development of modal reasoning.* San Diego, CA: Academic Press.

Rumain, B., Connell, J., & Braine, M.D.S. (1983) 'Conversational comprehension processes are responsible for reasoning fallacies in children as well as adults.' *Developmental Psychology, 19,* 471-481.

Russell, J. (1987) 'Rule-following, mental models, and the developmental view'. In M. Chapman & R.A. Dixon (Eds.), *Meaning and the growth of understanding* (pp. 23-48). New York: Springer-Verlag.

30. Content, Context, and Process in Reasoning During Adolescence: Selecting a Model

Marcia C. Linn

Models of how reasoning occurs and develops shape thinking and research about adolescent cognition. Four models of historical, current, or potential interest are considered in this paper. For each model, the role of content, context, and process information is delineated. In a subsequent section, some research results concerned with content and context influences are summarized. The usefulness of these models for interpreting the research results forms the focus of the final section.

This paper emphasizes cognitive models and cognitive research results. Models primarily emphasizing social, personality, or physiological factors, for example, are not represented. Cognitive models can have implications for these factors, however. For example, Damon and Hart (1982) demonstrate the role of cognitive models of self concept in interpreting the development of self esteem.

Inhelder and Piaget's (1958) book initiated serious interest in the period of adolescence and described a model of reasoning which has had profound influence on research. What is referred to as the Piagetian model in Table 1 emphasizes the role of process knowledge in adolescent reasoning. Process knowledge is knowledge of logical strategies such as the combinatorial strategy or the proportionality strategy. Inhelder and Piaget (1958) emphasized the structure of logical reasoning and the difficulty of altering the speed or course of the development of reasoning. They hypothesized that certain strategies, which underlie reasoning, develop during adolescence and lead to qualitative changes in reasoning performance. Unfortunately, the period of adolescence was of less interest to Piaget than Piaget has been to researchers of adolescent reasoning.

In contrast to the Piagetian model, the mental ability model of reasoning focuses on the gradual acquisition of a broad range of knowledge. Characterized by the work of Cattell (1971) this approach focuses on individual differences. Work on aptitude treatment interactions reflect this perspective (e.g., Cronbach & Snow, 1977). Constructs such as fluid and crystallized ability as well as cognitive style and ego control have been measured. Adolescence has received limited attention as a special period from those following the mental ability model.

Recently, those following the mental ability model have extended their interests to include information processing analysis of mental ability tasks (e.g., Snow, Federico, & Montague, 1980; Sternberg, 1977). This approach offers considerable promise for characterizing the nature of intelligence. Snow and his co-workers for example, (e.g., Kyllonen, Woltz, & Lohman, 1982; Kyllonen, Lohman, & Snow, 1982) suggest that

Marcia C. Linn: 'Content, Context, and Process in Reasoning During Adolescence: Selecting a Model'. *JOURNAL OF EARLY ADOLESCENCE* (1983), Vol. 3, Nos. 1-2, pp. 63-82. Copyright © 1983 by Marcia C. Linn. Reprinted by permission of Sage Publications, Inc.

"flexibility" in strategy selection characterizes expert performance on mental ability tests.

There are several reasons why adolescence has not been studied separately by those following the mental ability model. First, life span research (e.g., Baltes, 1963) has been fraught with methodological problems. Second, researchers have found it difficult to measure the same abilities at different ages. For example, in a meta-analysis of gender differences in spatial ability, Linn and Peterson[1] found that measures, such as paper folding, used in adolescence had no clear counterpart in tests for younger children. Thus, most researchers have focused on college age individuals when building models of mental ability.

Recently, models of reasoning performance have emerged from a field called cognitive science (Larkin, McDermott, Simon & Simon, 1980; Simon, 1980). Cognitive science represents a collaboration of cognitive psychology and computer science. A common methodology in this field is to build a computer simulation of performance and then modify the simulation based on input from the performance of individuals being simulated. These researchers have focused primarily on content or subject matter knowledge and on how that knowledge is stored and retrieved from memory. A popular approach has been to contrast skilled and unskilled performance on complex tasks, such as physics problem solving, to clarify reasoning processes (e.g., Heller and Reif)[2].

A fourth category of models of reasoning performance comes from philosophy of science. Although models from philosophy of science have, as yet, received little attention, they have tremendous potential (Carey & Block, 1982; Linn and Siegel, in press). This potential lies in the focus of philosophers of science on persistence and *change* in reasoning performance. Very little theoretical or empirical work has addressed how reasoning changes, yet understanding change in reasoning is essential for fostering effective reasoning. Models from philosophy of science can also aid understanding because they often emphasize context influences on reasoning which are minimized in other models. The societal context, for example the context of religious beliefs can have tremendous impact on the reasoning of groups of scientists. Similarly, context has impact on the reasoning of individuals (e.g., Mishler, 1979). Philosophy of science offers models for change in scientists' collective ideas which may have implications for changes in individuals' ideas.

Table 1   Models of reasoning performance during adolescence and adulthood

Model	Focus	Emphasis	Methodology
Piagetian	processes or strategies which govern reasoning	underlying logical structure	clinical interviews using apparatus
Mental Ability	acquisition of a variety of abilities	general ability	mental testing
Cognitive Science	acquisition and structuring of knowledge	knowledge organization	simulations of skilled and unskilled performance
Philosophy of Science	change in scientific ideas over time	factors influencing change	case studies

These four models are characteristic of those used by cognitive researchers to investigate reasoning during adolescence. The labels chosen are somewhat arbitrary, others might choose them differently. For example Keating refers to the psychometric model which closely parallels the mental ability model and the information processing model of which the cognitive science model is a part. The important point is that models place different emphasis on content or subject matter knowledge, on context or beliefs, and on processes or strategies. The emphasis determines how researchers choose problems to study. Thus, those following Piaget have tended to focus on the emergence of logical strategies while those from cognitive science have tended to contrast the character of subject matter knowledge for subjects who are skilled in a narrow subject matter domain with those who are unskilled.

Recent research on adolescent reasoning has examined the assumptions of the Piagetian model and suggested the potential of the other models by showing the importance of content and context in reasoning. The next section describes some of the research findings emphasizing content and context influences on adolescent reasoning. These studies suggest why researchers are turning to new models of reasoning performance.

Research results

Research suggesting that investigators place greater emphasis on content and context influences on adolescent reasoning has recently emerged. Three examples illustrate the sort of findings models of reasoning during adolescence might need to explain.

Effects of subject matter knowledge on reasoning: the Wason selection task

Wason first described the selection task in the literature in 1966. As described below, subsequent researchers have found that this difficult logical task is facilitated when translated to certain types of familiar subject matter (e.g., Griggs & Cox, 1982; Johnson-Laird, Legrenzi & Legrenzi, 1972). This task illustrates the complex nature of subject matter knowledge influences on reasoning.

The selection task, which has also been referred to as the four card problem, typically features four cards lying on a table. The participant is told that each has a letter on one side, and a number on the other; the visible symbols are "A," "B," "2" and "3." The participant is then asked to test the truth of the following rule: "If there is an A on one side of the card then there is a 2 on the other side of the card."

The participant must decide which card or cards need necessarily be turned over, in order to discover whether the rule is true or false. The correct answer is the "A" and the "3" since only a card with an A on one side and a number that is *not* 2 on the other could disprove the rule. Typically, subjects choose either the "A" alone or the "A" and the "2."

This response was originally explained as a motivation to verify, rather than falsify, the rule (see Wason & Johnson-Laird, 1972). Subsequently, manipulations of the rule statement revealed that these responses may simply reflect a tendency to match responses to the card named in the rule. That is, if the rule is stated with a negative consequent, e.g., "If there is an A on one side of the card then there is *not* a 2 on the other side of the card," the matching choices (A and 2) are chosen more frequently (and are also logically correct). Far more subjects give the correct solution on the rule with the negative consequent than on the same rule with an affirmative consequent. This finding, however, does not explain why close to 95% of the respondents get the affirmative version of the task wrong.

A long series of studies evaluated what was referred to as the "thematic materials effect" in the selection task. These studies employed rules using subject matter which might facilitate performance such as transportation to towns (e.g., if I went to Dover I went by train) and values for postage stamps (e.g., if the envelope is unsealed the letter has a 12 pence stamp). As Griggs (in press) summarizes, some of these versions facilitated performance while others did not. For example, those familiar with the postal regulation in England concerning unsealed envelopes performed better on that version of the selection task than they did on the abstract version.

Recently, researchers have identified a class of problems with subject matter which facilitates reasoning performance (Cox & Griggs, in press; D'Andrade[3]; Griggs & Cox, 1982). An example from Griggs and Cox (1982) involves the legal drinking age in Florida. The rule subjects investigated was:" If a person is drinking beer, then the person must be over 19." The subjects were told to imagine that they were police officers responsible for ensuring that the regulation was followed. Four cards, representing information about four possible people sitting at a table, were presented. They were labeled "DRINKING BEER," "DRINKING COKE," "16 YEARS OF AGE," and "22 YEARS OF AGE." The task was to select those people (cards) that definitely needed to be turned over to determine whether or not they were violating the rule. Seventy-four percent of Griggs and Cox's respondents made the correct selection for this problem, while not one did so for the abstract problem using letters and numbers.

Griggs and Cox (1982) used a memory cuing explanation to interpret these results (see also Manktelow & Evans, 1979). Griggs and Cox argued that performance is facilitated by content which permits the respondent to recall past experience with the content of the task, with the relationship (rule) in the problem, and with a counterexample to the rule. Further research is underway to clarify the role of subject matter knowledge in performance on the selection task.

Thus, some forms of subject matter knowledge must be represented in our models of reasoning performance. From these studies of the selection task, one might hypothesize that a representation of the structure of knowledge of alcoholic beverage consumption for the drinking age problem would be sufficient to understand reasoning performance on that problem. Our other research findings broaden this view.

The role of subject matter knowledge in reasoning: predicting displaced volume

Another example of how subject matter knowledge influences complex problem solving involves a task called predicting displaced volume. In this task, illustrated in Figure 1, subjects are told that there are two metal blocks, both of which sink when immersed in water. They are asked to predict which of the two blocks will displace the most liquid when immersed in water. A typical student (referred to as John) responded as illustrated in Figure 1. What alternative conception is John using to predict which of the two metal blocks will make the water go up higher?

John's responses indicate that his alternative conception is "The greater the weight of the solid immersed in water, the more liquid it will displace." Thus, John uses what we refer to as the weight conception for predicting how much water will be displaced. For a more detailed discussion of this task, and the alternative conceptions used by subjects, see Linn and Pulos (1983).

Another typical student, referred to as Susan, responded as shown in Figure 2. Susan's conception is more complex than John's. Essentially, Susan's conception is: "If the blocks differ in size, then the bigger one makes the water go up higher, and if the size of the blocks is the same, then the heavier one makes the water go up higher." Linn and Pulos (1983) frequently found this response among twelve- to sixteen-year-old adolescents; in fact, less than one-third of the 778 twelve- to sixteen-year-olds studied, used the correct volume-only rule.

These examples illustrate that learners generate alternative conceptions for reasoning problems rather than simply giving wrong answers. John's and Susan's responses to the predicting displaced volume task, tell us how they used subject matter knowledge to solve the problem.

Generally, students are consistent in their responses. The responses of Susan and John represent consistent alternative conceptions for predicting displaced volume (alternatives to the correct answer that the volume of the block is the only factor which influences how much liquid is displaced) which Linn and Pulos (1983) find occur regularly.

Why do learners have alternative conceptions for predicting displaced volume? In general, their knowledge about weight contributes to their performance: they expect weight to be influential when it is not. Weight is often a variable in other domains. Individuals solving predicting displaced volume may use an improper analogy and expect that weight is important in predicting displaced volume because it is also important in how far an object moves when hit by another object or how much one's toe hurts when something is dropped on it. Thus, individuals may have knowledge about the role of weight which they consider relevant to this situation.

Is it easy to alter the students' ideas concerning the role of weight in predicting displaced volume? If teachers demonstrate that weight is not a variable in this situation, do most students accept this pronouncement and move on to the next task? Evidently not. Predicting displaced volume is a topic in most science curricula in 7th and 8th grade, yet over 50 percent of 12th grade respondents to this task use an incorrect alternative conception which involves weight in some respect (Linn & Pulos, 1983).

Furthermore, when we investigated the role of instruction, we found that many participants failed to learn the volume rule when taught. We demonstrated how much water was displaced by solids of varying size and weight during about ten minutes of instruction for subjects who initially used a weight based alternative conception for solving predicting displaced volume (Pulos, de Benedictis, Linn, Sullivan, & Clement, 1982). In general, subjects made only slight gains in performance following this instruction.

One subject, when confronted with a contradiction to the weight conception responded: "Humm, the water went up the same in both the containers even though one of those cubes weighs more than the other. You must have *magic* water." This subject felt that the experimenter was being tricky and using water that did not have the usual properties. The subject believed that weight was an important factor and was willing to suggest that the experimenter was using magic water in order to defend the role of weight in predicting displaced volume.

Clearly subject matter knowledge influences performance and is somewhat resistant to change. It should be noted that tenacious defense of erroneous ideas has proven valuable in the history of science (Lakatos, 1972), so tenacious defense of ideas concerning a scientific phenomena may not be totally inappropriate. However, in predicting displaced volume, weight does not determine displacement. This view needs to be remediated, perhaps after the subject tenaciously and creatively defends it.

Figure 1   John's response to the water glass puzzle

1. BLOCKS *A* AND *B* ARE THE SAME SIZE. BLOCK *B* WEIGHS MORE THAN BLOCK *A*.

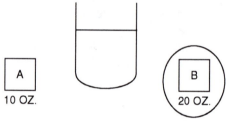

WHICH BLOCK WILL MAKE THE WATER GO UP HIGHER?

BLOCK *A*

BLOCK *B*

BOTH THE SAME

2. BLOCKS *D* IS LARGER THAN BLOCK *C*. BLOCK *C* WEIGHS MORE THAN BLOCK *D*.

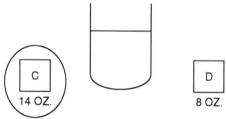

WHICH BLOCK WILL MAKE THE WATER GO UP HIGHER?

BLOCK *C*

BLOCK *D*

This study illustrates that subject matter knowledge influences reasoning. Many researchers have identified alternative conceptions which govern scientific reasoning (e.g., McClosky, Carramazza, & Green, 1980; Viennot, 1979). Models of reasoning performance which incorporate both prevalent alternative conceptions and the propensity of alternative conceptions to resist change, will foster understanding of adolescent reasoning.

Figure 2   Susan's response to the water glass puzzle

1. BLOCKS *A* AND *B* ARE THE SAME SIZE. BLOCK *B* WEIGHS MORE THAN BLOCK *A*.

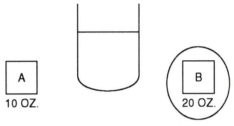

WHICH BLOCK WILL MAKE THE WATER GO UP HIGHER?

BLOCK *A*

BLOCK *B*

BOTH THE SAME

2. BLOCKS *D* IS LARGER THAN BLOCK *C*. BLOCK *C* WEIGHS MORE THAN BLOCK *D*.

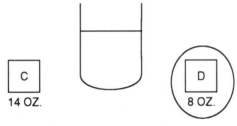

WHICH BLOCK WILL MAKE THE WATER GO UP HIGHER?

BLOCK *C*

BLOCK *D*

BOTH THE SAME

The role of context in reasoning: an example from reasoning about advertisements

A summary of results reported by Linn, de Benedictis, and Delucchi (1982) of how adolescents reason about advertisements, illustrates how the reasoning context might influence performance. We studied adolescent reasoning about advertising because we wished to investigate a prevalent reasoning problem. Since adolescents view over

20,000 advertisements annually we felt this was an area where adolescent reasoning was frequently required.

We investigated how reasoners respond to advertisements displaying product tests. The reasoning context may influence performance. For example, reasoners may accept the message in the ad because too much effort is required to refute it or to generate alternatives (e.g., Shugan, 1980; Wright, 1975). Simon (1969) suggested that individuals "satisfice" rather than "optimize" in this sort of complex context. That is, reasoners may accept their less than optimal reasoning as satisfactory, given the circumstances. For example, Shor (1980, p. 61) remarks, "Still another means of pre-scientific irrationalism in daily life is known as 'brand name' loyalty. People become totemistically allied to a commercial product...." Reasoners' ideas about how advertisements are generated, about their ability to avoid persuasion combined with their limited information contradicting the message, may create a context of uncritical acceptance of commercial messages.

One characteristic of the reasoning context concerns how adolescents view advertisements. In a study of adolescent reasoning about advertising, Linn, *et al.*, (1982) found that adolescents were extremely skeptical of advertisers and of the methods advertisers use to substantiate ad claims (See Figure 3). Almost two-thirds (62%) expect that advertisers often or always lie or cheat.

Another aspect of the reasoning context concerns beliefs about produce tests. Adolescents generally believe that tests reported by advertisers are unfair. Responses to "How do advertisers get the results they want?" fell into four categories. About 27 percent said advertisers lie by not doing a test at all or by testing but fabricating the results (e.g., "they switch labels on products"), about 61 percent said advertisers do unfair testing, and about 19 percent said advertisers do many tests and pick supporting results. Thus, over three-quarters (88%) of adolescents think advertisers lie or do unfair tests.

Adolescents' views of advertisements are consistent with surveys of adolescent attitudes toward advertisers (e.g., Moschis & Churchill, 1979), and with Elkind's (1967, 1968) observations that adolescents are skeptical of social and political systems. They also reflect Lewis' (1981) findings that between 7th and 12th grade adolescents increase in awareness of "vested interests" in social and political groups and in cautious treatment of information reflecting vested interests.

How do adolescents reason about advertisements, given the context in which their reasoning takes place? In spite of their skepticism, adolescents tend to believe the claims in ads they view (See Figure 4). When Linn *et al* (1982) asked adolescents whether they believed the claims in three ads over half the subjects said they did. Furthermore 43% of the subjects said they believed the ad because it said the product was effective. In contrast, only 9 percent expressed the general skepticism reported above, while 33 percent named a specific flaw in the ad. Thus close to half of adolescents interviewed believe ads, basing their belief on the results in the ads, which is consistent with other evidence that adolescents focus on results rather than procedures (Tschirgi, 1980; Linn, 1978). This finding is consistent with the notion that reasoners accept the message in the advertising context because too much effort is required to refute it. Adolescents appear to give up on trying to find the possible misleading aspects of ads, possibly because they consider the task too difficult.

To test the strength of this acceptance, Linn *et al* (1982) pointed out possible procedural flaws in the ads. When presented with this information, an average of 86 percent of adolescents agreed that the procedures used by the advertisers could be unfair or misleading. Thus, adolescents recognize misleading procedures when probed, but they do not mention them spontaneously when asked whether they believe a product claim.

Figure 3   Skepticism of advertisers

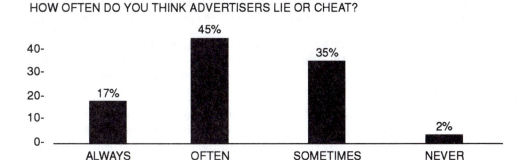

After the procedural flaws had been pointed out, Linn *et al* (1982) asked whether the participants believed the ads in light of these potential problems. A surprisingly high percentage (41%) said they still believed the ads and an average of 37 percent said they would buy the advertised product, in spite of these potential flaws in the procedures used to test the product (Figure 4).

Adolescents, when reasoning about advertisements seem to respond to the elements of the reasoning context by accepting the messages of advertisers. Adolescents' extreme skepticism of advertisers (e.g., "advertisers always lie and cheat") may accompany suspension of critical thought due to the difficulty of detecting lies. Adolescents seem to expect advertisers to be devious, but not to expect that they can recognize this deviousness. Thus, the context of adolescent reasoning about advertisements includes extreme skepticism which may interfere with logical analysis of the advertisers' message.

Adolescents may fail to act on their criticism of ads because they lack an alternative to advertising as a source of brand information, or because they have no information to *contradict* that presented in the ad. Ads may fill an "information void" for adolescents who lack experience with many brands. Adolescents appear to have the ability to criticize ads, but, when viewing an ad, they tend to accept it. These findings suggest the importance of the reasoning context when interpreting reasoning performance.

Linn *et al.* (1982) contrasted the scientific context with the advertising context by asking adolescents to design experiments about Bending Rods and about Shampoo effectiveness. They used the standard procedure for Bending Rods based on Inhelder and Piaget (1958) and a similar procedure for Shampoo reported in Linn *et al.* 1982).

Two main results emerged. First, there was little relationship between performance on Shampoo and performance on Bending Rods, suggesting the influence of reasoning context. Second, the tests designed for Shampoo reflected a lack of rigor in three ways: (a) participants did not use all the opportunities to test the shampoo, (b) although they were instructed to design tests relevant to their own hair characteristics, only one third of the tests designed by participants were unconfounded and relevant; (c) although participants were able to choose as many subjects for their tests as they wished without penalty, most indicated they would use fewer than 25 subjects per test (See Figure 5).

These results suggest that adolescents do not fully comprehend the value of repeated experimentation. In general, they do not take advantage of the opportunity to design many tests or use large numbers of subjects. Tversky and Kahneman (1974) report similar results for adults.

These results also suggest that adolescents when confronted with an advertisement, have difficulty designing tests relevant to their own interests. Consistent with Linn (1977) many choose to design tests that make a big difference in the outcome. Consistent with Tschirgi (1980) some prefer to replicate the positive outcome reported in an advertisement. Adolescents seem to lose track of the purpose of their tests, choosing to make sure the test shows a big difference or to test the advertiser's claim rather than gathering information relevant to their own decision (Linn, Delucchi, & de Benedictis, 1982).

The reasoning context seems to influence reasoning performance. Adolescents' skepticism seems to be so extreme that they fail even to consider information they could refute. Adolescents' concepts of evidence, when reasoning about advertisements, differ substantially from those described for formal reasoning. In general, adolescents appear to make decisions based on limited information and to seek only a limited amount of information when given the opportunity to gather evidence for a decision. Adolescents' reasoning about advertisements appears expedient rather than thoughtful consistent with Simon's notion of "satificing" (e.g., Simon, 1969) and may result in acceptance of misleading claims. Such expediency may stem from the belief that advertisers are too devious to understand.

Interpreting research results using models of reasoning performance

How do the four models of reasoning deal with the content and context effects described above? Since research is generally governed by a particular model, results from studies reflecting one model may not be interpretable from another perspective. A useful educational model, however, should shed light on findings which are educationally relevant, such as those described above.

As noted above, the Piagetian model pays limited attention to content and context effects. Piagetian theory focuses on strategy acquisiton. Acquisition is insufficient to explain the inconsistencies in performance on tasks such as Shampoo and Bending Rods which require the same strategy. Given that most reasoners appear to use the formal reasoning strategies on some problems, one could argue that the strategies are acquired but not used in all situations (e.g., Linn, Clement, & Pulos, in press; Flavell & Wohlwill, 1969). In contrast, Wason (in press) has argued that the strategies cannot be separated from content and treated as separate entities, as Piaget has hypothesized. Suppose that the formal strategies are acquired but not used in all situations, then what explains performance?

Figure 4   Percentage of adolescents who believe the results of test reported in ads

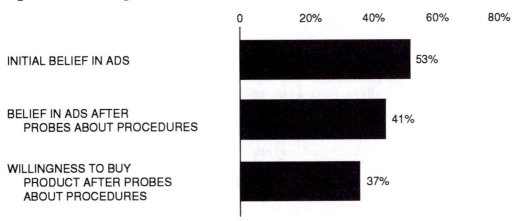

As Siegel (in press) has argued, advances in reasoning, once the logical strategies of formal reasoning have been acquired, cannot result from enhanced logic. Formal operations is the zenith of logical stages. The strategies characterizing formal reasoning also characterize the reasoning of scientists. The formal reasoning stage is as thoroughly logical as a stage can be. Thus, researchers must focus on other factors to explain the performance of reasoners who have achieved formal reasoning.

Turning to the mental abilities model, it is clear that this model, before the influence of information processing approaches, says more about who reasons at a given level than about how individuals reason. The mental abilities model does emphasize subject matter knowledge in crystallized ability tests. Whereas analysis of the aptitude characteristics of reasoners displaying particular types of reasoning could prove useful, thus far payoff has been limited (e.g., Cloutier & Goldsmith, 1976; Linn, Pulos & Gans, 1981; Linn & Swiney, 1981). As Hill notes, this has also been a problem in social psychological investigations. Ford (1982) is an exhaustive investigation of social competence illustrates the shortcomings of the mental ability model. There appears to be a level of analysis problem in that the precision of the aptitude measures is insufficient to differentiate among responses on tasks such as controlling variables or social competence. In addition, this approach makes it difficult to identify precise explanations for observed relationships. A high correlation indicates that two measures require the same process but does not clearly indicate what that process is. Thus, Linn and Kyllonen (1981) identified an aspect of cognitive style which they called familiar field, and showed that it contributed variance to measures of scientific reasoning such as predicting displaced volume (Linn & Pulos, 1983), but this information was not sufficient to clarify what familiar field actually measured.

In contrast, the information processing approach reflected in the work of Sternberg (1977, 1981), Snow and his co-workers (e.g., Kyllonen, Lohman & Snow, 1982), and Keating offers promise for understanding the processes involved in performance on mental ability tests. This direction offers possibilities for understanding the nature of intelligence. In particular, flexible switching from one distinct solution procedure to another in solving a series of mental ability items appears to characterize performance (e.g., Kyllonen, *et al.*, 1982). These findings tell us what processes underlie performance on mental test items and can be combined with research on broader facets of performance (such as subject matter knowledge), to enhance our understanding of the development of reasoning.

In contrast to the Piagetian model and the mental ability model, the cognitive science model focuses specifically on subject matter knowledge, how it is represented and how it is retrieved. Researchers using the cognitive science model, by emphasizing subject matter knowledge, have gained insight into performance on the selection task. As Griggs and Cox (1982) and D'Andrade (1982) illustrate, examination of how subject matter knowledge about the selection task is represented and recalled, reveals why some versions are more difficult than others. Research on predicting displaced volume also suggests the usefulness of the cognitive science approach of focusing on subject matter knowledge. This approach provides methodology for researchers to state precise hypotheses about reasoning (using models) and to examine these hypotheses.

Figure 5   Quality of experiments designed by 7th and 8th graders to test shampoo

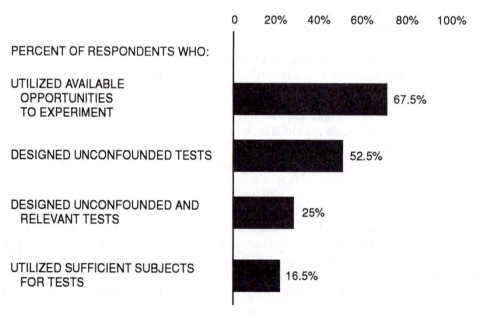

The cognitive science model focuses on content and offers approaches for understanding how subject matter knowledge representation influences reasoning. The models employed by cognitive scientists have tended to represent knowledge at a given point in time, rather than to represent how knowledge changes. Researchers have contrasted skilled and novice performance more than they have modeled change from novice to skilled performance. This approach depends dramatically on how knowledge is represented. Advances in methods for modeling knowledge are helping us understand how content or subject matter knowledge influences reasoning.

Two types of findings in the research studies described above suggest ways that models from philosophy of science might be incorporated into models from cognitive science. One finding concerns the role of context in reasoning performance, for example the role of context in reasoning about advertising. Another finding concerns persistence and change in ideas. As research on predicting displaced volume illustrates, reasoners persist with ideas in spite of contradiction and, when they do change, may change from one conception like the weight rule to a totally different conception, like the volume rule.

Philosophers of science have focused on the role of societal context in reasoning. The societal context profoundly influences the development and acceptance of scientific ideas. Consider ideas about motion that emerged during the Renaissance. At this time, Aristotle's ideas were challenged by Galileo. This challenge reached the very core of current societal values. Aristotle believed that everything moved to its specific fulfillment. (Note, however, that Aristotle did *not* impute will to objects, only a destiny; Artistotle's view of causality was largely teleological.) Objects, according to Aristotle, are simultaneously pushed and pulled to their destinations. In contrast, Galileo expressed what has been called a "clockwork" notion, suggesting that once the world was set in motion, it operated according to its own autonomous laws. Galileo set out to uncover the laws governing movements. Galileo's notion that the universe operated according to autonomous laws was considered heretical within the societal context. Galileo's ideas about motion were challenged largely because of their relationship to current societal values.

Philosophers of science such as Kuhn (1972), Hanson (1961) and Lakatos (1972) have proposed models to explain how societal context influences the collective reasoning of scientists. These models might also help researchers understand how societal context influences the reasoning of individuals.

Both persistence with erroneous ideas and sudden change to new ideas characterize the history of science and therefore interest philosophers of science. Philosopher of science Lakatos (1972) offers some especially thought provoking ideas relevant to these issues.

Lakatos refers to ideas about a particular phenomenon or concept as a research program. A research program is a series of theories. Two characteristics of research programs as described by Lakatos seem useful. One is the distinction between the "protective belt" of ideas and the "hard core" of ideas. The other is the distinction between a "progressing" and a "degenerating" research program. The hard core consists of unquestioned assumptions which are not challengeable by data. The protective belt is differentiated from the hard core in that it consists of ideas which change as often as necessary, responding to data. A scientific research program is a series of theories with the same hard core of ideas and differing protective belts. A *progressing* research program is a series of theories that predicts novel facts. A *degenerating* research program does not predict new facts.

Persistence is clearly useful for advancing knowledge. If reasoners changed all their ideas after each contradiction, they would gain little insight into a problem. Persistence, even with wrong ideas, leads to refinements of ideas which ultimately prove useful. Lakatos' distinction between the "hard core" of ideas and the "protective belt" of ideas clarifies how persistence fosters understanding. Scientists, when confronted with data that contradict their viewpoint, change the protective belt so that the hard core can remain unchanged. Thus, Lakatos differentiates the ideas in the hard core, which are immune to data, from ideas in the protective belt, which are responsive to data.

In the research on predicting displaced volume, the subject who mentioned the magic water could be seen as protecting a hard core idea. For this subject, the weight rule appeared to be a hard core idea. This subject, when confronted with a contradiction to the rule, sought to alter the protective belt to protect the hard core. In this case protective belt ideas concerning the nature of water, and the nature of experimenters, were altered to protect the idea about how weight influences displacement.

An example of a hard core idea in the history of science would be Kepler's idea that the orbit of Mars must be circular. Kepler accepted Aristotle's pronouncement that planets exhibit "perfect motion" which was circular motion. Kepler developed a procedure called the method of area for verifying an orbit. Using this method, Kepler found that his calculations did not conform to observations of the position of Mars. Rather than question the shape of the orbit of Mars, since that was part of his hard core of ideas, Kepler came to doubt his method of area. In this example, the hard core of ideas influenced how new information was incorporated into a conceptualization. Further, Kepler refined his method of area because it made erroneous predictions. By pursuing his hard core idea of perfect motion, Kepler refined his notions about measuring planetary motion. Thus pursuing a hard core idea may advance knowledge even though that hard core idea is later changed because the research program is degenerating.

Creative and tenacious protection of the hard core results in development of more powerful ideas. If reasoners can be perceived as having research programs, the development of their reasoning can be evaluated by examining the development of their research programs. One can assess how reasoners protect their hard core. One can document the tenacity with which the hard core is defended and the creativity with which the hard core is protected. Such protection occurs, it appears, when reasoners confronted with anomalies — experimental results incompatible with their theories — creatively alter the protective belt such that the anomaly becomes positive evidence for the hard core.

Eventually even creative persistence in defending the hard core fails to predict novel facts. Lakatos characterizes change in the hard core as cataclysmic change.

Degenerating research programs have inadequate hard cores and fail to predict novel facts. They are completely replaced by new research programs, which are new series of theories attached to new hard cores. Similarly, reasoners in the predicting displaced volume research, when they do change their views, often change from a weight rule to a volume rule, dropping weight altogether. Thus, Lakatos provides a perspective on both persistence and change in scientific ideas which is congruent with research on persistence and change in ideas held by adolescents.

Conclusions

Content and context effects influence reasoning in dramatic ways. Their influence needs to be represented in models of reasoning performance. Process knowledge as described by Inhelder and Piaget (1958) may be necessary for sophisticated reasoning but not sufficient. Models from information processing, cognitive science, and philosophy of science offer promising perspectives on reasoning performance.

Although the process influences on reasoning described by Piaget cannot be ignored, they may need to be reconceptualized to include a role for content and context influences. One view is that many or most adolescents have acquired the process knowledge inherent in formal reasoning. Another view is that the process knowledge of formal reasoning does not exist independent of content; process knowledge therefore is a type of subject matter knowledge associated with a particular problem. Using either perspective, researchers might incorporate process knowledge into a knowledge representation for a particular problem.

Perhaps the most pressing problem in research on reasoning concerns how it changes. As the myriad of unsuccessful training studies attest (e.g., Linn, 1980), teaching formal reasoning as a generalized process is difficult. In addition, presenting contradictions as was done in the predicting displaced volume training does not have complete success. Reasoners' ideas do persist. Following Lakatos, we may surmise that reasoners alter their protective belts as in the "magic water" example, while protecting their hard core ideas. We need a deeper understanding of the process of change which philosophy of science, with its concern with persistence, may bring us.

One reason that ideas persist is that they are alternative conceptions of phenomena rather than random ideas. Reasoners such as mature scientists may still hold "alternative conceptualizations" for certain phenomena. Di Sessa (1981), for example, provides evidence that sophisticated scientists often apply what he calls "naive physics" to everyday non-textbook problems. Physicists often have difficulty explaining the forces on a yo-yo, when the yo-yo is laid on the table and the string is pulled horizontally. Similarly, physicists and other mature reasoners frequently display "naive physics" when asked to indicate what happens to the motor of a vacuum cleaner when its air intake valve is blocked. Thus, many reasoners may have alternative conceptualizations of problems from physics and other problems.

From Lakatos' perspective, these alternative conceptions form a persistent hard core. Efforts to teach individuals to change to a new hard core will not succeed immediately. Reasoners will protect their hard core. One implication of Lakatos' view is that educators could benefit from recognizing that reasoners may need many contradictions to their ideas before they change their hard core. Further, such lengthy processes may lead to better understood and more generalizable ideas in the long run. Thus, rather than becoming frustrated when learners fail to accept new ideas, educators could examine how learners adjust to new ideas.

If we view learners as having hard core ideas, it becomes apparent that educators would benefit from knowing alternative conceptions likely to be hard core ideas in their particular subject matter area. For example, curriculum people could design effective contradictions to these conceptions for teachers and explain to teachers that learners will be slow to give up their conceptions. Curricula might even reassure teachers by explaining that the slow process of changing conceptions, although seemingly frustrating to the instructor has advantages for the learner and ultimately, for the instructor. Thus, one direction for new research is to identify alternative conceptions in important subject matter areas, areas such as smoking, alcoholism, or obesity seem especially timely, and to characterize how reasoners will respond to these contradictions.

Thus content, context, and process influences on reasoning need to be incorporated into models or adolescent reasoning performance. Both models from cognitive science and models from philosophy of science offer promise. Simon (1980) referred to cognitive science as a revolution in thinking about reasoning performance. Combining recent advances in philosophy of science with models from cognitive science promises to enhance the revolutionary forces.

This material is based upon research supported by the National Science Foundation under grant numbers 81-12631 and 79-19494. Any opinions, findings and conclusions, or recommendations expressed in this publication are those of the author and do not necessarily reflect the views of the National Science Foundation.

Philosophers Harvey Siegel and Nick Burbules provided opportunities for discussion of how models from philosophy of science might inform psychological researchers; their encouragement and contributions have been invaluable. In addition, this paper draws on experiments conducted by the Adolescent Reasoning Project, helpful discussions with staff members including Kevin Delucchi, Tina de Benedictis, and Steven Pulos are gratefully acknowledged.

Reference notes

1. Linn, M. C. & Petersen, A. C. *The emergence of gender differences in spatial ability: A metaanalysis.* Paper presented at the AERA Special Interest Group on Research on Women in Education, Mid-Year Conference, November, 1982.

2. Heller, J. I. & Reif, F. *Cognitive mechanisms: Facilitating human Problem solving in physics: Empirical validation of a prescriptive model.* Paper presented at the annual meeting of the American Educational Research Association, New York, March, 1982.

3. D'Andrade. R. *Reason versus logic.* Talk for Symposium on the Ecology of Cognition: Biological, Cultural, and Historical Perspectives, Greensboro, North Carolina, April, 1982.

References

Baltes, P. B. (1968) 'Longitudinal and cross-sectional sequences in study of age and generation effects.' *Human Development*, 11, 145-171.

Carey, S. & Block, N. (1982) *NSE-NIE project,* Massachusetts Institute of Technology.

Cattell, R. B. (1971) *Abilities: Their structure, growth, and action.* Boston: Houghton Mifflin.

Cloutier, R., & Goldschmid, M. (1976) 'Individual differences in the development of formal reasoning.' *Child Development,* 47, 1097-1102.

Cox, J. R., & Griggs, R. A. 'The effects of experience on performance in Wason's selection task.' *Mem. Cog.,* in press.

Cronbach, L. J., & Snow, R. E. (1977) *Aptitude Treatment Interactions.* New York: Irvington.

Damon, W., & Hart, D. (1982) 'The development of self-understanding from infancy through adolescence.' *Child Development,* 53, 841- 864.

Elkind, D. (1968) 'Cognitive development in adolescence.' In J. F. Adams (Ed.), *Understanding adolescence.* Boston: Allyn & Bacon.

Elkind, D. (1967) 'Egocentrism in adolescence.' *Child Development,* 38, 1025-1034.

Flavell, J. H., & Wohlwill, J. F. (1969) 'Formal and functional aspects of cognitive development.' In D. Elkind & J. Flavell (Eds.), *Studies in Cognitive Development: Essays in Honor of Jean Piaget.* New York: Oxford University Press.

Ford, M. E. (1982) 'Social cognition and social competence in adolescence.' *Developmental Psychology,* 18, 323-340.

Griggs, R. A. 'The role of problem content in the selection task and THOG problem.' In J.St.B.T. Evans (Ed.), *Thinking and Reasoning: Psychological Approaches.* London, Routledge & Kegan Paul, in press.

Griggs, R. A., & Cox, J. R. (1982) 'The elusive thematic-materials effect in Wason's selection task.' *British Journal of Psychology,* 73, 407-420.

Hanson, N. R. (1961) *Patterns of Discovery. An Inquiry Into the Conceptual Foundations of Science.* Cambridge, England: Cambridge University Press.

Inhelder, B., & Piaget, J. (1958) *The Growth of Logical Thinking from Childhood to Adolescence.* New York: Basic Books.

Johnson-Laird, P. N., Legrenzi, P., & Legrenzi, M. (1972) 'Reasoning and a sense of reality.' *British Journal of Psychology,* 63, 395-400.

Kuhn, T. S. (1972) *The Structure of Scientific Revolutions,* (2nd Edition, enlarged). Chicago: University of Chicago Press.

Kyllonen, P. C., Lohman, P. F., & Snow, R. E. (1982) *Effects of aptitudes, strategy training and task facets on spatial task performance,* School of Education, Stanford University.

Kyllonen, P. C., Woltz, D. J., & Lohman, D. F. (1982) *Models of strategy and strategy-shifting in spatial visualization performance.* Tech. Report 17, Aptitude Research Project, School of Education, Stanford University.

Lakatos, I. (1972) 'Falsification and the methodology of scientific research programmes.' In I. Lakatos & A. Musgrave (Eds.), *Criticism and the Growth of Knowledge.* Cambridge, England: Cambridge University Press.

Larkin, J., McDermott, J., Simon, D. P., & Simon, H. A. (1980) 'Expert and novice performance in solving physics problems.' *Science,* 208, 1335-1342.

Lewis, C. (1981) 'How adolescents approach decisions: Changes over grades seven to twelve and policy implications.' *Child Development,* 52, 538-544.

Linn, M. C. (1978) 'Cognitive style, training, and formal thought.' *Child Development,* 49, 874-877.

Linn, M. C. (1977) 'Scientific reasoning: Influences on task performance and response categorization.' *Science Education*, 61, 357-369.

Linn, M. C. (1980) 'Teaching children to control variables: Some investigations using free choice experiences.' In S. Modgil and C. Modgil (Eds.), *Toward a theory of psychological development within the Piagetian framework,* London: National Foundation for Educational Research.

Linn, M. C., Clement, C., & Pulos, S. M. 'Is it formal if it's not physics? The influence of laboratory and naturalistic content on formal reasoning.' *Journal of Research in Science Teaching,* in press.

Linn, M. C., de Benedictis, T., & Delucchi, K. (1982) 'Adolescent reasoning about advertisements: Preliminary investigations.' *Child Development,* 53, 1599-1613.

Linn, M. C., Delucchi, K., & de Benedictis, T. (1982) *Adolescent reasoning about advertisements: Relevance of product claims.* Adolescent Reasoning Project Report, ARP-A-8. Lawrence Hall of Science, Berkeley, CA.

Linn, M. C., & Kyllonen, P. (1981) 'The field dependence-independence construct: Some one, or none.' *Journal of Educational Psychology,* 73, 261-273.

Linn, M. C., & Pulos, S. (1983) 'Male-female differences in predicting displaced volume: Strategy usage, aptitude relationships and experience influences.' *Journal of Educational Psychology,* 75, 86-96.

Linn, M. C., Pulos, S., & Gans, A. (1981) 'Correlates of formal reasoning: Content and problem effects.' *Journal of Research in Science Teaching,* 18, 435-447.

Linn, M. C., & Siegel, H.' Post-formal reasoning: A progressing research program.' In M. Commons (Ed.), *Models of Post Formal Reasoning,* Praeger Publishers, in press.

Linn, M. C. & Swiney, J. (1981) 'Individual differences in formal thought: Role of expectations and aptitudes.' *Journal of Educational Psychology,* 73, 274-286.

Manktelow, K. I., and Evans, J.St.B.T. (1979) 'Facilitation of reasoning by realism: Effect or non-effect?' *British Journal of Psychology,* 70, 477-88.

McCloskey, M., Carramazza, A., & Green, B. (1980) 'Curvilinear motion in the absence of external forces: Naive beliefs about the motion of objects.' *Science,* 210, 1139-1141.

Mishler. E. G. (1979) 'Meaning in context: Is there any other kind?' *Harvard Educational Review,* 49 (1), 1-19.

Moschis, G. P., & Churchill, G. A. (1979) 'An analysis of the adolescent consumer.' *Journal of Marketing*, 43, 40-48.

Pulos, S., de Benedictis, T., Linn, M. C., Sullivan, P., & Clement, C. (1982) 'Predicting displaced volume: A training study.' *Journal of Early Adolescence,* 2, 61-74.

Shor, I. (1980) *Critical Teaching and Everyday Life.* Boston, MA: South End Press.

Shugan, S . M. (1980) 'The cost of thinking . *Journal of Consumer Research,* 7, 99-111.

Siegel, H. (1982) 'On the parallel between Piagetian cognitive development and the history of science.' *Philosophy of the Society Sciences,* in press.

Simon, H. A. (1980) 'The behavioral and social sciences.' *Science,* 209 72-78.

Simon, H. A. (1969) *The Sciences of the Artificial.* Cambridge, MA: M.I.T. Press.

Snow, R. E., Federico, P. A., & Montague, W. (Eds.). (1980) *Aptitude, learning and instruction: Cognitive process analysis* (Vol . 1) . Hillsdale, N.J.: Erlbaum.

Sternberg, R. J. (1981) 'Intelligence and nonentrenchment.' *Journal of Educational Psychology,* 73, 1-16.

Sternberg, R. J. (1977) *Intelligence, information processing, and analogical reasoning: The componential analysis of human abilities.* Hillsdale, N.J.: Lawrence Erlbaum Associates.

Tschirgi, J. E. (1980) 'Sensible reasoning; A hypothesis about hypotheses.' *Child Development,* 51, 1-10.

Tversky, A., & Kanneman, D. (1974) 'Judgment under uncertainty: Heuristics and biases.' *Science,* 185, 1124- 1131.

Viennot, L. (1979) 'Spontaneous reasoning in elementary dynamics.' *European Journal of Science Education,* 1, 205-221.

Wason, P. C. 'Realism and rationality in the selection task.' In J.St.B.T. Evans (Ed.), *Thinking and reasoning.* London: Routledge and Kegan Paul, in press.

Wason, P. C., & Johnson-Laird, P. N. (1972) *Psychology of Reasoning: Structure and Content.* Cambridge, MA: Harvard University Press.

Wright, P. (1975) 'Consumer choice strategies: Simplifying vs. optimizing.' *Journal of Marketing Research,* 12, 60-68.

Appendix

31.   A Statistics Primer
James D. Demetre

Statistics: overview and aims

Statistical analysis of data generated by studies is a crucial tool in helping the researcher make sense of his/her findings. For example, if we embark upon a study to find out whether young girls adapt better to primary school or to a hospital ward than young boys, we need to do two things. First, we need to define what we mean by "better" and by "adapt"; and then establish what kinds of behaviour and attitudes we will study. This kind of issue falls under *Methodology*. Second, we need to define how much overall difference should exist between boys and girls in order for us to be confident that these differences are real and not due to random factors that give the impression that one group does better than the other. This issue falls under *Statistical Analysis*.

The aim of the following seven sections is to provide an elementary knowledge of statistics. The techniques to which the reader will be introduced are widely used by researchers in many disciplines but are by no means exhaustive. The main objective is to offer an appreciation of why statistical procedures are important, and to enable the reader to acquire some sense of how they work. Some mathematical formulae will be encountered but these do not need to be memorised. The emphasis is on acquiring some basic understanding of what these formulae allow us to do.

1. Making sense of data

Most studies in child development involve collecting data. Essentially, aspects of children's behaviour and mental activity are made meaningful when expressed in numerical terms. Investigations are usually conducted in order to answer more or less circumscribed questions, or to test particular scientific hypotheses.

For example, our investigations may seek to discover whether violence on TV affects young children's behaviour and attitudes. A little reflection will reveal that a proper study of this question will require us to resort to some kind of quantitative analysis. We may ask a number of different versions of this question but each will require quantification:

a) Are children who watch some violent TV *more often* aggressive than children who watch no violent TV? (This involves a comparison of frequencies of aggressive behaviour in two groups of children.)

b) Are children who watch some violent TV *more likely* to be physically aggressive in the playground than children who watch no violent TV? (This involves a comparison of frequencies of children showing physical aggression in two groups of children.)

c)   Are children who watch some violent TV *more strongly aggressive* than children who watch no violent TV? (This involves a comparison of some kind of aggression score in two groups of children.)

Descriptive and inferential statistics

When we talk of statistics the term can have two uses. In everyday language, as well as in media and government reports, we refer to statistics in a *descriptive* way. For example, we may say that rates of violent crime have increased over the past 12 months, or that infant mortality figures have gone down. These statements depend essentially on someone comparing at least two numbers: these are the descriptive statistics used. Often, however, the data are fairly complex and we cannot adequately describe a situation with only two numbers. We then have to resort to various strategies for capturing a complex situation to render it meaningful. This can be achieved either through the way we represent data (e.g. the use of summary tables and various kinds of charts and diagrams), or by calculating summary measures such as averages. For now, the *description of data* will be our focus.

In the remainder of this primer we shall focus on *inferential statistics*. This is an umbrella term for various kinds of statistical tests that help us to draw inferences. Inferential statistics allow us to establish the extent to which a given pattern of data is not due simply to random events (i.e. due to chance). For example, supposing we do a study on TV violence and find that out of 50 children who are 'heavy viewers', 35 are rated as being aggressive by teachers, compared to 27 out of 50 children who are 'light viewers'. What inferences can we draw? Some people will be tempted to conclude that TV violence does have a negative effect, while others would say the numbers do not differ enough to warrant this conclusion. The point is, how much should the numbers differ to merit the conclusion that TV violence has an effect? Even if there were *no effect* of violent TV (so that in theory the two numbers should be exactly the same), it is extremely unlikely that the two numbers would be identical. Statistical tests allow us to come to grips with this problem of random influences. Let us now turn to descriptive statistics.

Representing data

When we wish to present all our data in a summary form we can choose various methods of representation. If our data are in the form of frequencies (number of events, e.g. number of people), we can illustrate our data in Tables, Bar Charts or Pie Charts. The advantage of using charts is that it allows the reader to form a very rapid impression of the data. The main disadvantage of using charts, however, is that they may take up a lot of space or become very complex when the data involve more than one dimension (what statisticians call *factor*). This may defeat the object of providing easy access to the reader. In one's own work it is important to think carefully about the best method of representing data: **it is pointless representing the same set of data using more than one method of representation.**

When dealing with data in the form of scores we can usefully represent the data as a **histogram**. Histograms involve carving up the scores into categories defined by an appropriate interval size. The values of these intervals are represented on the *x axis* (also known as the *abscissa*). The number of individuals with scores falling within each interval is then represented on the *y axis* (also known as the *ordinate*). Histograms allow us to represent the *frequency distribution* of a given set of scores (how often certain scores or ranges of score occur). Frequency distributions have very important implications for some statistical tests.

There are no hard and fast rules as to the exact size and number of intervals to be used when constructing a histogram. Generally, it is best to limit these to between 10 and 20 intervals. If there are many empty intervals (with no individual having a score corresponding to these intervals), it is likely that too many intervals/too small an interval size has been used.

Examples of data representation

Age	Severity of injury			
	Fatal	Serious	Slight	Total
0-4	96	1246	6408	7750
5-7	79	1663	7088	8830
8-11	104	2619	11308	14031
12-15	161	3437	13698	17296
All children	440	8965	38502	47907

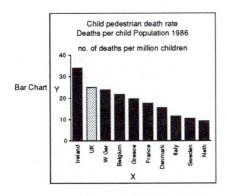

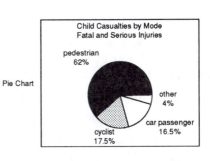

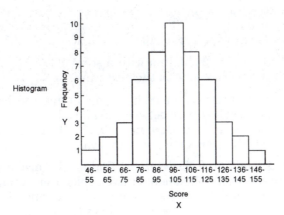

Summary descriptive statistics

Another way of making sense of data is to compute a few measures that provide a summary description of the data. The most commonly used is 'the average' (which statisticians call the *mean*). For example, you may find that on average 5-year-olds can remember 6 names that they have heard in a story, and 7-year-olds can remember 7.5 names. Taking the mean provides a very quick, if imprecise, summary of the scores of the two groups. The alternative is to construct two separate histograms, which may leave one guessing as to 'the average' in any case.

Of course, if there is a lot of variablity in a given group's scores the mean may give a misleading impression. Various summary statistics attempt to provide an index of 'the average' (what statisticians call a *measure of central tendency*) and an index of variability (what statisticians call a *measure of dispersion*).

Measures of central tendency

Three different measures are widely used: the mean; the median; and the mode. The *mean* is simply the total of a given set of scores divided by the number of scores (the everyday 'average'). Mathematically, this is represented as $\Sigma x / N$ (where Σ = sum; x = individual score; N = number of scores).

The advantage of the mean is that it takes each individual's score into account, and is especially useful if there are not too many outliers:

4, 6, 5, 3, 8*, 12*, 0*, 4, 5, 6, 3, 4, 5

When there are several outliers, or even one extreme outlier, the mean will give a very distorted picture. For example, let's look at the vocabulary size of a group of autistic and a group of normal children:

Autistic: 20, 23, 300*, 15, 17, 19, 18, 12, 25, 20 (mean = 46.9).

Normal: 50, 30, 40, 45, 29, 43, 53, 34, 45, 35 (mean = 40.4).

In this particular case the *median* would be a better measure of central tendency. The median is the middle score. To calculate the median, we first need to order (rank) each group's scores in ascending order:

Autistic: Score:12, 15, 17, 18, 19, 20, 20, 23, 25, 300

Rank: 1, 2, 3, 4, 5, 6.5, 6.5, 8, 9, 10

When there are *tied* scores (the 2 children with a score of 20), we assign the *average* rank to these (6 + 7)/2, then proceed with the next rank (8).

The median score is the one that has the middle rank: in this case between rank 5 and rank 6. Thus, our median is somewhere between 19 and 20. By convention we can take the mean of these two scores and our median is 19.5: half the scores in the group fall below this value, and half the scores fall above this value.

When there is an odd number of observations finding the median is a little easier because there is no need to take the mean of two ranks. For example, if we have 11 scores the score with a rank of 6 would be the mid-point. The general formula for finding out at which rank the median lies is (N + 1) /2 (where N=number of scores).

The mean and the median are the most widely used measures of central tendency. One other measure that is sometimes useful is the *mode*: this is simply the score with the highest frequency. In the above example the mode = 20. Generally speaking, the mode is only useful if a fairly high proportion of individuals have the same score.

Measures of dispersion: the standard deviation

As noted previously, measures of central tendency (mean, median and mode) are inadequate as useful summary measures because they do not take into account the degree of variablity in a set of scores. A number of measures of dispersion are used, but the most useful is the standard deviation and we shall focus on this. The problem of variability can be illustrated by the findings from two different studies on the effects of TV viewing:

Frequency of aggressive acts by children

Violent Viewing	Non-Violent Viewing
Study 1	
3	2
10	6
6	1
0	0
12	2
11	0
8	1
1	8
12	3
7	0
M = 7	M = 2.3
Study 2	
7	1
6	3
5	2
5	3
6	2
8	3
10	2
9	3
8	3
6	1
M = 7	M = 2.3

In study 2, the means (M) appear to be more representative of the totality of individual measures than they do in study 1.

$$\text{S.D.} = \sqrt{\Sigma\,(X-M)^2/(N-1)}$$

Steps in the calculation of the standard deviation

1. Subtract the mean from every individual score (X), ignoring the sign of the difference $(X-M)$.

2. Square each of these difference scores $(X-M)^2$.

3. Sum these squared difference scores $\Sigma\,(X-M)^2$.

4. Divide this sum by the number of scores you have minus 1. $\Sigma\,(X-M)^2/(N-1)$.

5. Obtain the square root of this number. $\sqrt{\Sigma\,(X-M)^2/(N-1)}$

2. Introduction to inferential statistics

Studies in developmental psychology be they in the form of systematic observations, experiments or case studies, require us to compare and contrast measures. For example, do 5-year-olds show more impulsive behaviour than 7-year-olds? When investigating such differences inferential statistics help to answer the question: do these collections of numbers *really differ from each other*?

Populations and samples

A limitation confronted by all investigators is that they wish to address questions or hypotheses (see below) concerning *populations of individuals*, but can only do so by investigating *samples* of individuals drawn from the population. For example, if a cell biologist is interested in the characteristics of cancerous cells he cannot hope to study every single cancer cell on earth (the population of cancer cells), so a sample of such cells has to be selected. The cell biologist may decide to select 100 cancerous cells from a given organ in order to compare and contrast them with 100 healthy cells from the same organ. Thus, the biologist has drawn *two samples of cells* in order to answer questions about the *general population* of that kind of cell.

Clearly, our biologist would be very upset if you were to suggest to her/him that any conclusions drawn can only be applied to the samples that were studied. Research would be quite pointless if we could not generalise (at least provisionally) from samples to populations.

The same limitation confronts an investigator of child development, with arguably greater force, as we may expect greater individual variation in children's behaviour and abilities than is to be found among different cancer cells.

There are two ways of dealing with the problem of *generalising* results. First, by using random sampling or other methods that increase the chances that our samples are representative of the general population: we then apply inferential statistics to determine whether apparent differences between the samples can be explained by chance variations (due to sampling errors). Second, major findings that pass this test as *being significant* are accepted as true only on a provisional basis, pending *replication* of results by other investigators.

Hypotheses

Most studies (especially experimental studies) are undertaken to test specific hypotheses (e.g. autistic children are less capable at understanding others' feelings than other mentally handicapped children). Our study may use two samples of children: a sample of autistic children, and say, a sample of children with Down's Syndrome. Our *working hypothesis* is that our *independent variable* (in this case autistic versus Down's Syndrome) will have an effect on our *dependent variable* (what we are measuring — in this case ability to understand other people's feelings). Other examples of *independent variables* might include: age, gender, family size; and other examples of *dependent variables* could be: I.Q., memory span, frequency of aggressive behaviour.

Statistical tests assess whether *the opposite of our working hypothesis*, known as the *null hypothesis*, can be rejected. In other words, if our working hypothesis is correct, then there should only be a small probability that any differences found between autistic and Down's Syndrome children can be explained by chance.

Probability

In order to understand the use of inferential tests we need to have some idea about probability. A probability is a value expressing the likelihood of a given event, and ranges from 0 (an impossible event) to 1 (an absolute certainty). A probability is simply the proportion of occasions that a given event should occur. For example, when tossing an ordinary unbiased coin there are two events: heads or tails. Either of these can occur: by chance we would expect the coin to show a head half the time, and a tail half the time; i.e. the probability (p) of a head is 0.50, and the probability of a tail is also 0.50. What is the p of pulling a playing card with a heart from a full deck of cards? What is the p of pulling a red 7 from a full deck of cards? (Hint: multiply the two probabilities).

We can best illustrate the use of inferential statistics by using coin tossing as an example. Supposing that our working hypothesis is that the coins used in Joe's Casino are biased. The null hypothesis is that the coins are not biased. If our working hypothesis is correct, we would expect the coins to produce a disproportionate number of heads or tails. If the null hypothesis is correct, we would expect a roughly equal proportion of heads and tails. But what does 'roughly equal' actually mean?

For example, Joe's coins produce the following after 3 tosses each:

    COIN 1: H H H
    COIN 2: T T T
    COIN 3: H H T

Can we infer that coin 1 is biased toward heads and coin 2 biased toward tails? Let us look at the *chance* probability of obtaining more heads or tails, even with an *ordinary* coin:

With 3 tosses, there are 8 possible outcomes:

```
H H H
H H T
H T H
H T T
T H H
T H T
T T H
T T T
```

Out of 8 events, 4 involve more heads than tails. Therefore with 3 tosses of the coin we would expect that about half the time more heads than tails, i.e. $p = 0.50$. Out of 8 events, 1 produces all heads. Therefore the chance probability of throwing 3 heads in a row = 0.125. How impressive is this as evidence of biased coins? Clearly, the lower the probability of this occurring by chance, the more confident we can be that the coins really are biased and different from the normal.

Analysing the data from a study is very similar in principle to our finding out whether a coin is biased or not. We can work out a probability associated with random differences: if this probability is very low, then the more confidence we have that our results are not due to chance.

Statistical significance

By convention we say that a result is statistically significant if the probability that it arose by chance is 0.05 or less. Thus, if a statistical analysis reveals that there is only a 0.05 probability of your findings resulting from chance, we take this as preliminary evidence that the null hypothesis is wrong and that the working hypothesis is right. The lower the p value, the higher the significance level.

Examples of notation for significance levels:

$p < 0.05$ (p of null hypothesis is less than 0.05, or 1 in 20).

$p > 0.10$ (p of null hypothesis is greater than 0.10, or 1 in 10 — too high for us to be confident that our working hypothesis is correct).

$p < 0.01$ (p of null hypothesis is 0.01 or 1 in 100 — highly significant).

3. The sign test

In comparing two or more conditions we need to know the extent to which differences can be attributed to chance. Another way of stating this is that we must determine how confident we can be that the observed differences between our samples are a true characteristic of the underlying population.

Levels of significance

This is the term used to refer to the probability that differences between conditions arise by chance. In most research the minimum significance level accepted is 0.05. In journal articles you will often see statements such as: "The difference between the two methods of instruction proved to be significant ($p < 0.05$)." This means that the probability is less than 1 in 20 and that the observed differences in the two methods of instruction arose by chance.

The Null Hypothesis

This states that there is no true difference between conditions. Statistical tests are essentially a test of the Null Hypothesis. A significance level of $p < 0.05$ means there is less than 1 in 20 chance that the Null Hypothesis is correct.

The Working (or Alternative) Hypothesis

This states that there is a real difference between conditions. If the probability of the Null Hypothesis being correct is only 0.05, then the probability of the Working or Alternative Hypothesis being correct is 0.95.

How do we determine significance level? The binomial distribution

Some statistical tests rely on the binomial distribution for assessing the significance level of differences between two sets of measures. The binomial distribution specifies the probabilities with which certain combinations of events occur. For example, if you have tossed a coin 3 times, what is the probability of obtaining 3 heads? To find out, you need to work out all the possible outcomes from these 3 tosses. How many of these involve 2 heads and 1 tail? The binomial distribution is simply the probability of obtaining various combinations of two events (e.g. 7 heads and 3 tails; 10 boys with autism and 1 girl with autism; 8 children showing less fear on the ward after a parental visit and 2 children showing more fear).

The sign test

This test is based on the binomial distribution and is the simplest statistical test for comparing scores available. It can only be used when we have *pairs* of scores (either the same subjects going through the 2 different conditions or matched subjects). The collection of signs of differences (+, −) between the two conditions is assessed in the same way that the collection of heads and tails was used in the example above. For instance, if we ran an experiment with 12 children and compared their behaviour after viewing violent TV and then viewing non-violent TV, we may find that 10 of them were more aggressive after violent TV (10 +) and 2 of them were less aggressive after violent TV (2 −). Like the heads and tails example, we would expect the number of minuses and the number of pluses to be about equal if there were no differences between conditions. Is 10 out of 12 statistically significant?

Frequency of aggressive acts following TV viewing

Subject	Violent TV	Non-Violent TV	Difference
John	10	7	
Mary	4	5	
Paul	5	2	
Peter	6	1	
Walter	3	4	
Rashid	9	7	
Saul	8	4	
Maya	6	2	
June	7	6	
Lola	8	2	
Margo	4	1	
Angela	3	2	

Steps

1. Work out the sign of the difference between the 2 conditions for each child.

2. Determine which sign has the lowest frequency of occurrence (X).

3. Determine the number of individuals with a positive or negative difference score (N). Ignore all individuals where the difference in scores = 0.

4. Consult the sign test table to find out the significance level.

One-tailed and two-tailed tests of significance

For some research purposes the working hypothesis is very specific in its predictions and states the direction of differences between two conditions (e.g. children will be more aggressive when they watch violent TV than when they watch non-violent TV). In this case a one-tailed test of significance is appropriate. For some research purposes, especially research of an exploratory nature, the working hypothesis is more general (e.g. are there any differences in effectiveness between two currently used teaching methods?) In this case the direction of difference is not specified, and a tougher criterion of significance, called two-tailed, is required.

One-tailed test: Let us look at this more closely. In the case of the specific (called *directional*) hypothesis, it is similar to predicting that there will be more heads than tails in a sample of coin tosses. If we have 3 tosses of a coin, we have the following possibilities:

    H H H
    H H T
    H T H
    T H H
    T T H
    T H T

H T T
T T T

In 4 out of the 8 possibilities, there are more heads than tails. Hence, there is a probability of 0.5 of obtaining more heads than tails when we toss a coin 3 times. A similar situation holds with our study of children watching different kinds of TV. Out of 3 children, the probability that most of the children produce more aggression following violent than following non-violent TV is 4 out of 8, which equals 0.5:

+ + +
+ + −
+ − +
− + +
− − +
− + −
+ − −
− − −

where + equals a child showing more aggression following violent TV; − equals a child showing more aggression following non-violent TV.

Two-tailed test: With a more general, non-directional hypothesis, this is like predicting that there will be *either* more heads than tails, or that there will be more tails than heads. With 3 tosses of a coin, 8 out of 8 possibilities support this prediction. Hence, there is a probability of 1 (absolute certainty) of obtaining either more heads or more tails. A similar situation holds with a study of 3 children whose performance following two different kinds of teaching method is analysed. The working hypothesis will then be that there are either more +s (a child does better following method 1) or more −s (a child does better following method 2). Again, the probability of this prediction being correct is (absolute certainty).

Comparing one-tailed and two-tailed tests: In the examples above the one-tailed tests indicated that there was a 0.5 probability of the null hypothesis being correct. In other words, if we manage to get more heads than tails, or more children showing more aggression to violent than non-violent TV, we should not be satisfied with the result. Given the sample sizes used (3 tosses of a coin, 3 children), random factors alone would produce the result that we are interested in. The two-tailed tests indicated that chance factors alone are guaranteed to produce the result that we are interested in ($p = 1$).

Non-directional working hypotheses are always exactly twice as likely as directional hypotheses to produce a result that seems to be correct. To correct for this, two-tailed tests of significance expect more extreme deviations from chance than do one-tailed tests. Any given result in a one-tailed test (e.g. $p < 0.05$) has exactly twice this likelihood in a two-tailed test, so we double the probability of the null hypothesis being correct ($p < 0.10$, which is not significant).

Using the table to determine significance level

First go to the column labelled N and find the appropriate number. If your x value is equal to or lower than the value in a given column, then your result is significant at that level.

N	Level of significance for one-tailed test				
	0.05	0.025	0.01	0.005	0.0005
	Level of significance for two-tailed test				
	0.10	0.05	0.02	0.01	0.001
5	0	—	—	—	—
6	0	0	—	—	—
7	0	0	0	—	—
8	1	0	0	0	—
9	1	1	0	0	—
10	1	1	0	0	—
11	2	1	1	0	0
12	2	2	1	1	0
13	3	2	1	1	0
14	3	2	2	1	0
15	3	3	2	2	1
16	4	3	2	2	1
17	4	4	3	2	1
18	5	4	3	3	1
19	5	4	4	3	2
20	5	5	4	3	2
25	7	7	6	5	4
30	10	9	8	7	5
35	12	11	10	9	7

4. The normal distribution

The normal distribution characterises a number of biological variables such as height and weight of a population. A number of psychologists also believe that certain psychological variables such as intelligence and personality are also normally distributed, and this is reflected in the way they produce their intelligence tests and personality inventories.

The normal distribution is illustrated in Figure 1. It has a number of properties which have made it especially useful both for inferential and descriptive purposes.

Figure 1   The normal distribution.

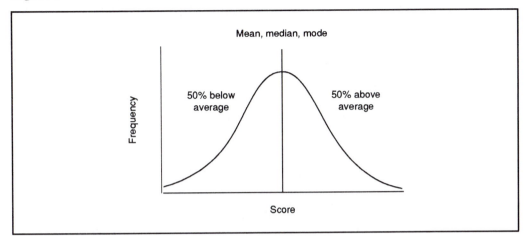

Some properties of the normal distribution

1. The curve is symmetrical about the mean. From this it is clear that low scores at a certain distance below the mean are as probable as high scores at the same distance above the mean. Thus, the more extreme the value of a score (either extremely low or extremely high), the lower its probability of occurrence. So, if the average height of adult males is 5′ 10", we would expect as many to be 6′ 10" as are 4′ 10".

2. Because of this symmetry all three measures of central tendency — the mean, median and mode — are equal.

3. One particularly useful property is that the probability of a given score can be worked out with reference to the standard deviation. This property is illustrated in Figure 2. The distance between the mean and the first standard deviation above the mean covers 0.3413 (34.13%) of the observations; the distance between the first standard deviation and the second standard deviation covers a further 0.1359 (13.59%) of the observations. The distance between the mean and 3.5 standard deviations covers almost all the observations falling within a given half of the distribution.

Figure 2   Percentage area covered by successive standard deviations.

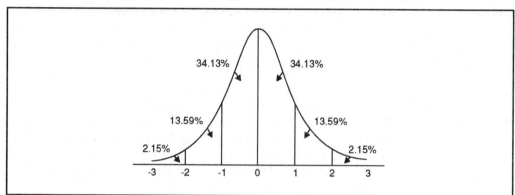

If a vocabulary test is administered to children, and we know that scores on this test are distributed normally and have a mean of 100 and a standard deviation of 15, we would know that:

a)   0.3413 of the children will have scores between 100 and 115.

b)   Only about 0.02 of the children will have scores above 130.

c)   About 0.16 of the children will have scores below 85.

The z test

We often find ourselves concerned with the performance of an individual child. For example, we may be worried that a particular child is falling behind in his/her vocabulary attainments. In our attempts to identify and remedy the child's problem, we may first want some indication of the magnitude of the problem. One way of looking at this is how the child performs relative to other children.

Because there is a precise relation between number of standard deviations away from the mean and probability, we can work out how untypical our child is by expressing his/her score on a standard vocabulary test in terms of the standard deviation:

$$z = X - M / \text{S.D.}$$

Let us say our child obtains a score of 75 on a test with a mean of 100 and a standard deviation of 20.

$$z = 75 - 100 / 20 = -25/20 = -1.25$$

In other words, this girl is 1.25 standard deviations below the mean on this test. Statisticians have worked out the exact probabilities associated with different Z scores (see Table 1).

The proportion of children who have a score more extreme than his/hers can be worked out by looking in column (C) in Table 1. This indicates that 0.1056 of children have more extreme scores than him/her.

In some cases we would want to use this information inferentially. For example, if we have done a serious case study of a child with a rare disorder and we need to examine whether she is different from children without the disorder, we would want to apply the principles of testing for statistical significance. In this case we would only be confident that our clinical case was significantly different from other children if the probability value in column (C) is 0.05 or less.

Standard scores

The z score computed above is also very useful if we want to compare children's performance on tests or other variables that have different means and standard deviations. For example, if a particular child obtains 105 on a vocabulary test and 70 on an arithmetic test, and these tests have different means and standard deviations, the "raw" scores cannot be compared easily.

If for the vocabulary test, $M = 100$, S.D. = 10; and for the arithmetic test, $M = 60$, S.D. = 5, then the child's standard score on the vocabulary test is:

$$105 - 100/10 = +5/10 = + 0.50$$

and on the arithmetic test:

$$70 - 60/5 = +10/5 = +2.0$$

This child appears to do better on the arithmetic test than on the vocabulary test, though he/she is above average on both. If we consult the table, it is clear that his/her arithmetic performance is significantly above average ($z = 2$, $p < 0.023$).

Table 1   Proportions of area under the normal curve

(A) z	(B) area between mean and z	(C) area beyond z	(A) z	(B) area between mean and z	(C) area beyond z	(A) z	(B) area between mean and z	(C) area beyond z
0.00	.0000	.5000	0.15	.0596	.4404	0.30	.1179	.3821
0.01	.0040	.4960	0.16	.0636	.4364	0.31	.1217	.3783
0.02	.0080	.4920	0.17	.0675	.4325	0.32	.1255	.3745
0.03	.0120	.4880	0.18	.0714	.4286	0.33	.1293	.3707
0.04	.0160	.4840	0.19	.0753	.4247	0.34	.1331	.3669
0.05	.0199	.4801	0.20	.0793	.4207	0.35	.1368	.3632
0.06	.0239	.4761	0.21	.0832	.4168	0.36	.1406	.3594
0.07	.0279	.4721	0.22	.0871	.4129	0.37	.1443	.3557
0.08	.0319	.4681	0.23	.0910	.4090	0.38	.1480	.3520
0.09	.0359	.4641	0.24	.0948	.4052	0.39	.1517	.3483
0.10	.0398	.4602	0.25	.0987	.4013	0.40	.1554	.3446
0.11	.0438	.4562	0.26	.1026	.3974	0.41	.1591	.3409
0.12	.0478	.4522	0.27	.1064	.3936	0.42	.1628	.3372
0.13	.0517	.4483	0.28	.1103	.3897	0.43	.1664	.3336
0.14	.0557	.4443	0.29	.1141	.3859	0.44	.1700	.3300

Table 1   Proportions of area under the normal curve (cont)

(A) z	(B) area between mean and z	(C) area beyond z	(A) z	(B) area between mean and z	(C) area beyond z	(A) z	(B) area between mean and z	(C) area beyond z
0.45	.1736	.3264	0.90	.3159	.1841	1.35	.4115	.0885
0.46	.1772	.3228	0.91	.3186	.1814	1.36	.4131	.0869
0.47	.1808	.3192	0.92	.3212	.1788	1.37	.4147	.0853
0.48	.1844	.3156	0.93	.3238	.1762	1.38	.4162	.0838
0.49	.1879	.3121	0.94	.3264	.1736	1.39	.4177	.0823
0.50	.1915	.3085	0.95	.3289	.1711	1.40	.4192	.0808
0.51	.1950	.3050	0.96	.3315	.1685	1.41	.4207	.0793
0.52	.1985	.3015	0.97	.3340	.1660	1.42	.4222	.0778
0.53	.2019	.2981	0.98	.3365	.1635	1.43	.4236	.0764
0.54	.2054	.2946	0.99	.3389	.1611	1.44	.4251	.0749
0.55	.2088	.2912	1.00	.3413	.1587	1.45	.4265	.0735
0.56	.2123	.2877	1.01	.3438	.1562	1.46	.4279	.0721
0.57	.2157	.2843	1.02	.3461	.1539	1.47	.4292	.0708
0.58	.2191	.2810	1.03	.3485	.1515	1.48	.4306	.0694
0.59	.2224	.2776	1.04	.3508	.1492	1.49	.4319	.0681
0.60	.2257	.2743	1.05	.3531	.1469	1.50	.4332	.0668
0.61	.2291	.2709	1.06	.3554	.1446	1.51	.4345	.0655
0.62	.2324	.2676	1.07	.3577	.1423	1.52	.4357	.0643
0.63	.2357	.2643	1.08	.3599	.1401	1.53	.4370	.0630
0.64	.2389	.2611	1.09	.3621	.1379	1.54	.4382	.0618
0.65	.2422	.2578	1.10	.3643	.1357	1.55	.4394	.0606
0.66	.2454	.2546	1.11	.3665	.1335	1.56	.4406	.0594
0.67	.2486	.2514	1.12	.3686	.1314	1.57	.4418	.0582
0.68	.2517	.2483	1.13	.3708	.1292	1.58	.4429	.0571
0.69	.2549	.2451	1.14	.3729	.1271	1.59	.4441	.0559
0.70	.2580	.2420	1.15	.3749	.1251	1.60	.4452	.0548
0.71	.2611	.2389	1.16	.3770	.1230	1.61	.4463	.0537
0.72	.2642	.2358	1.17	.3790	.1210	1.62	.4474	.0526
0.73	.2673	.2327	1.18	.3810	.1190	1.63	.4484	.0516
0.74	.2704	.2296	1.19	.3830	.1170	1.64	.4495	.0505
0.75	.2734	.2266	1.20	.3849	.1151	1.65	.4505	.0495
0.76	.2764	.2236	1.21	.3869	.1131	1.66	.4515	.0485
0.77	.2794	.2206	1.22	.3888	.1112	1.67	.4525	.0475
0.78	.2823	.2177	1.23	.3907	.1093	1.68	.4535	.0465
0.79	.2852	.2148	1.24	.3925	.1075	1.69	.4545	.0455
0.80	.2881	.2119	1.25	.3944	.1056	1.70	.4554	.0444
0.81	.2910	.2090	1.26	.3962	.1038	1.71	.4564	.0436
0.82	.2939	.2061	1.27	.3980	.1020	1.72	.4573	.0427
0.83	.2967	.2033	1.28	.3997	.1003	1.73	.4582	.0418
0.84	.2995	.2005	1.29	.4015	.0985	1.74	.4591	.0409
0.85	.3023	.1977	1.30	.4032	.0968	1.75	.4599	.0401
0.86	.3051	.1949	1.31	.4049	.0951	1.76	.4608	.0392
0.87	.3078	.1922	1.32	.4066	.0934	1.77	.4616	.0384
0.88	.3106	.1894	1.33	.4082	.0918	1.78	.4625	.0375
0.89	.3133	.1867	1.34	.4099	.0901	1.79	.4633	.0367

Table 1   Proportions of area under the normal curve (cont)

(A)	(B)	(C)	(A)	(B)	(C)	(A)	(B)	(C)
z	area between mean and z	area beyond z	z	area between mean and z	area beyond z	z	area between mean and z	area beyond z
1.80	.4641	.0359	2.25	.4878	.0122	2.70	.4965	.0035
1.81	.4649	.0351	2.26	.4881	.0119	2.71	.4966	.0034
1.82	.4656	.0344	2.27	.4884	.0116	2.72	.4967	.0033
1.83	.4664	.0336	2.28	.4887	.0113	2.73	.4968	.0032
1.84	.4671	.0329	2.29	.4890	.0110	2.74	.4969	.0031
1.85	.4678	.0322	2.30	.4893	.0107	2.75	.4970	.0030
1.86	.4686	.0314	2.31	.4896	.0104	2.76	.4971	.0029
1.87	.4693	.0307	2.32	.4898	.0102	2.77	.4972	.0028
1.88	.4699	.0301	2.33	.4901	.0099	2.78	.4973	.0027
1.89	.4706	.0294	2.34	.4904	.0096	2.79	.4974	.0026
1.90	.4713	.0287	2.35	.4906	.0094	2.80	.4974	.0026
1.91	.4719	.0281	2.36	.4909	.0091	2.81	.4975	.0025
1.92	.4726	.0274	2.37	.4911	.0089	2.82	.4976	.0024
1.93	.4732	.0268	2.38	.4913	.0087	2.83	.4977	.0023
1.94	.4738	.0262	2.39	.4916	.0084	2.84	.4977	.0023
1.95	.4744	.0256	2.40	.4918	.0082	2.85	.4978	.0022
1.96	.4750	.0250	2.41	.4920	.0080	2.86	.4979	.0021
1.97	.4756	.0244	2.42	.4922	.0078	2.87	.4979	.0021
1.98	.4761	.0239	2.43	.4925	.0075	2.88	.4980	.0020
1.99	.4767	.0233	2.44	.4927	.0073	2.89	.4981	.0019
2.00	.4772	.0228	2.45	.4929	.0071	2.90	.4981	.0019
2.01	.4778	.0222	2.46	.4931	.0069	2.91	.4982	.0018
2.02	.4783	.0217	2.47	.4932	.0068	2.92	.4982	.0018
2.03	.4788	.0212	2.48	.4934	.0066	2.93	.4983	.0017
2.04	.4793	.0207	2.49	.4936	.0064	2.94	.4984	.0016
2.05	.4798	.0202	2.50	.4938	.0062	2.95	.4984	.0016
2.06	.4803	.0197	2.51	.4940	.0060	2.96	.4985	.0015
2.07	.4808	.0192	2.52	.4941	.0059	2.97	.4985	.0015
2.08	.4812	.0188	2.53	.4943	.0057	2.98	.4986	.0014
2.09	.4817	.0183	2.54	.4945	.0055	2.99	.4986	.0014
2.10	.4821	.0179	2.55	.4946	.0054	3.00	.4987	.0013
2.11	.4826	.0174	2.56	.4948	.0052	3.01	.4987	.0013
2.12	.4830	.0170	2.57	.4949	.0051	3.02	.4987	.0013
2.13	.4834	.0166	2.58	.4951	.0049	3.03	.4988	.0012
2.14	.4838	.0162	2.59	.4952	.0048	3.04	.4988	.0012
2.15	.4842	.0158	2.60	.4953	.0047	3.05	.4989	.0011
2.16	.4846	.0154	2.61	.4955	.0045	3.06	.4989	.0011
2.17	.4850	.0150	2.62	.4956	.0044	3.07	.4989	.0011
2.18	.4854	.0144	2.63	.4957	.0043	3.08	.4990	.0010
2.19	.4857	.0143	2.64	.4959	.0041	3.09	.4990	.0010
2.20	.4861	.0139	2.65	.4960	.0040	3.10	.4990	.0010
2.21	.4844	.0136	2.66	.4961	.0039	3.11	.4991	.0009
2.22	.4868	.0132	2.67	.4962	.0038	3.12	.4991	.0009
2.23	.4871	.0129	2.68	.4963	.0037	3.13	.4991	.0009
2.24	.4875	.0125	2.69	.4964	.0036	3.14	.4992	.0008

Table 1   Proportions of area under the normal curve (cont)

(A) z	(B) area between mean and z	(C) area beyond z
3.15	.4992	.0008
3.16	.4992	.0008
3.17	.4992	.0008
3.18	.4993	.0007
3.19	.4993	.0007
3.20	.4993	.0007
3.21	.4993	.0007
3.22	.4994	.0006
3.23	.4994	.0006
3.24	.4994	.0006
3.25	.4994	.0006
3.30	.4995	.0006
3.35	.4996	.0004
3.40	.4997	.0003
3.45	.4997	.0003
3.50	.4998	.0002
3.60	.4998	.0002
3.70	.4999	.0001
3.80	.4999	.0001
3.90	.49996	.00000
4.00	.49997	.00000

5. The t test

The t test is used for the same purpose as the sign test: to establish whether two conditions differ significantly from one another. The main difference between the two tests is that the t test takes into account the size of the difference between pairs of scores as well as the sign of the difference. Because the t test takes into account more information (sign of difference and size of difference), it is a more powerful statistical test for detecting statistical significance.

This means that when there is a true difference between conditions in the population at large, analysis of a data sample with a t test will sometimes detect this (i.e. give a statistically significant result), even when analysis with a sign test will not. For example, in a sample of 10 children we may find that 8 of the children show a huge difference in scores, doing much better on condition A; and 2 of the children do very slightly better on condition B. The sign test does not take into account the fact that in this example the 2 cases that contradict the majority trend actually produce a smaller difference between conditions than the other 8 cases. The sign test would produce a non-significant result. By contrast, the t test would take into account the fact that on average the scores in condition A are much higher than in condition B.

When there is a choice the t test is always the preferred test to use in comparing two conditions because it is so much more powerful than the sign test.

When to use the t test

The t test is designed to be used with data that are normally distributed (remember the bell-shaped curve). In fact as long as the data are fairly symmetrical around the median and mean, and scores further from the mean (either lower or higher) are progressively rarer, then this condition is satisfied. It is also important that the standard deviations of the two sets of numbers do not differ too much from each other.

Let us put these two pieces of information together to see what the t test is actually testing. Figure 3 below shows a situation where we have two distributions of scores, with one set being higher than the other set. Notice that there are overlaps between the two distributions but it is clear that the two sets of scores come from different distributions. The t test is a statistical technique for finding out whether the two conditions produce scores that differ in the way shown in this figure – i.e. whether the two sets of scores come from two distinct distributions.

The bigger the difference between the two means and the smaller the spread of scores (the standard deviation) within each set of scores, the greater the likelihood that the two sets of scores come from separate distributions. The t value calculated for the t test is essentially the ratio of how different the means are to how much variablity (or spread) there is in the data. As this value gets bigger, the more confident we are that the two sets of scores really do come from different distributions. Obviously, if you have two sets of normally distributed scores there is always the possibility that by chance they will seem to come from different distributions when in fact they come from one distribution. As with all statistical tests, we need to establish the probability (significance level) of obtaining a t value of a given size.

Figure 3

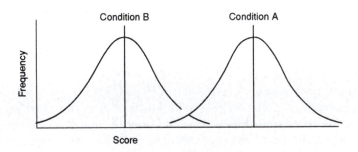

Calculating the t value

$$t = \frac{M1 - M2}{S.E.d} = \frac{M1 - M2}{S.D.\,d/\sqrt{N}}$$

where $M1$ = mean of first set of scores.

$M2$ = mean of second set of scores.

S.D. d = standard deviation of the difference between pairs of scores (condition 1 – condition 2, or condition 2 – condition 1).

S.E. d = standard error of difference scores (see below for explanation of standard error).

In this formula, as the difference between the means increases and the standard deviation decreases, the size of the t value increases.

Why do we divide the difference in means by the standard error of difference scores? The standard deviation of difference scores tells us how much inconsistency there is in the difference between the two conditions. If there is truly a significant difference between the two sets of scores, then the size and direction of the difference should be consistent. With reference to Figure 3, the greater the spread in scores within conditions A and B, the greater the spread in difference scores for individuals. We divide the S.D. by $\sqrt{N}$ (this gives us the standard error of the *difference* scores) to give a greater weighting to differences in means that involve larger samples. In general, any given size of mean difference is more probable the fewer the difference scores used to calculate the means. This is a bit like our previous coin-tossing examples: by chance, we get more extreme results (e.g. all heads) when we toss a coin 5 times than when we toss it 10 times.

A worked example

Subject	Score on Task X	Score on Task Y	d
1	3	5	2
2	8	11	3
3	8	10	2
4	9	11	2
5	7	9	2
6	10	12	2
7	12	13	1
8	3	4	1
9	9	11	2
10	2	4	2
11	9	11	2
12	9	8	-1
13	10	9	-1
14	9	8	-1

$$M1\ (X) = 7.71$$

$$M2\ (Y) = 9$$

$$S.D.\ d = 1.28$$

$$S.E.\ d = 1.28\ /\ \sqrt{14} = 1.28/3.74 = 0.36$$

$$t = \frac{9 - 7.71}{0.34} = 3.79$$

Testing for significance

Once the t value has been calculated for your data, you then need to find out whether it is significant. The table below presents critical t values for one- and two-tailed levels of significance.

1. Work out the degrees of freedom (d.f.) in your data. When using the t test on repeated measurements (as in our case), d.f. = number of individuals − 1. For our worked example with 14 children, d.f. = 13.
2. Go down the column marked d.f. and find the appropriate d.f. for your analysis. For our worked example, we go to 13.
3. Check to see whether your t value is equal to or greater than the critical values listed. We obtained a t value of 3.79 in our worked example. If we decided at the outset on a one-tailed test (we predicted that the children would do better on task Y than on task X), then our value is certainly significant at the $p < 0.05$ level (critical value needed is at least 1.771). We can now check whether it is significant at a higher level. In fact our value is greater than that needed for $p < 0.005$, but not quite high enough for $p\ 0.0005$. We conclude that children do perform significantly better on task Y than on task X ($t = 3.79$, 13 d.f., one-tailed $p < 0.005$).

	\multicolumn{6}{c}{Level of significance for one-tailed test}
	.10	.05	.025	.01	.005	.0005
df	\multicolumn{6}{c}{Level of significance for two-tailed test}
	.20	.10	.05	.02	.01	.001
1	3.078	6.314	12.706	31.821	63.657	636.619
2	1.886	2.920	4.303	6.965	9.925	31.598
3	1.638	2.353	3.182	4.541	5.841	12.941
4	1.533	2.132	2.776	3.747	4.604	8.610
5	1.475	2.015	2.571	3.365	4.032	6.859
6	1.440	1.943	2.447	3.143	3.707	5.959
7	1.415	1.895	2.365	2.998	3.499	5.405
8	1.397	1.860	2.306	2.896	3.355	5.041
9	1.383	1.833	2.262	2.821	3.250	4.781
10	1.372	1.812	2.228	2.764	3.169	4.587

df	Level of significance for one-tailed test					
	.10	.05	.025	.01	.005	.0005
	Level of significance for two-tailed test					
	.20	.10	.05	.02	.01	.001
11	1.363	1.796	2.201	2.718	3.106	4.437
12	1.356	1.782	2.179	2.681	3.055	4.318
13	1.350	1.771	2.160	2.650	3.012	4.221
14	1.345	1.761	2.145	2.624	2.977	4.140
15	1.341	1.753	2.131	2.602	2.947	4.073
16	1.337	1.746	2.120	2.583	2.921	4.015
17	1.333	1.740	2.110	2.567	2.898	3.965
18	1.330	1.734	2.101	2.552	2.878	3.922
19	1.328	1.729	2.093	2.539	2.861	3.883
20	1.325	1.725	2.086	2.528	2.845	3.850
21	1.323	1.721	2.080	2.518	2.831	3.819
22	1.321	1.717	2.074	2.508	2.819	3.792
23	1.319	1.714	2.069	2.500	2.807	3.767
24	1.318	1.711	2.064	2.492	2.797	3.745
25	1.316	1.708	2.060	2.485	2.787	3.725
26	1.315	1.706	2.056	2.479	2.779	3.707
27	1.314	1.703	2.052	2.473	2.771	3.690
28	1.313	1.701	2.048	2.467	2.763	3.674
29	1.311	1.699	2.045	2.462	2.756	3.659
30	1.310	1.697	2.042	2.457	2.750	3.646

6. Correlation coefficients: Spearman's Rho

So far we have focused on assessing differences between conditions in terms of one measured variable (e.g. whether TV viewing affects frequency of aggressive behaviour). In experimental studies we systematically vary one variable (e.g. TV programmes viewed) and measure its effects on another variable (aggressive behaviour). This allows us to make inferences about the causal relations between the two variables.

However, in many instances we have to resort to non-experimental methods for assessing links between two variables. For example, we may want to know whether there is a link between parents' use of positive remarks to their child and the child's tendency to co-operate with peers in nursery school. Clearly, it would be impractical to manipulate experimentally the parent's behaviour over a lengthy period. Instead, we look at the relationship between parental positive remarks and children's co-operative activity with peers. If the two variables are positively related, we would expect parents who use a relatively high frequency of positive remarks to have children who produce a relatively high frequency of co-operative activity (see Table 2).

Table 2 **Frequencies of positive parental remarks and child co-operative activity.**

Positive remarks (X)	Co-operative activity (Y)
20	7
8	3
11	4
25	8
1	1
9	3
10	4

If we convert these scores into ranks, we can begin to obtain some idea of how closely related are the two variables. The smaller the difference in ranks, the more positive is the relationship between the two variables (see Table 3).

Table 3 **Frequencies and ranks of positive parental remarks and child's co-operative activity.**

Score X	Rank X	Score Y	Rank Y	Diff
20	6	7	6	0
8	2	2	2	0
11	5	5	5	0
25	7	8	7	0
1	1	1	1	0
9	3	3	3	0
10	4	4	4	0

The example above would yield a perfect positive correlation since the ranks for the two variables are identical. Of course, in reality, relationships between variables are rarely perfect and various statistical tests are used to assess the significance of the relationship between two variables.

We may have a situation where the relationship between two variables is significantly negative. In this case, high scores on variable X would be associated with low scores on variable Y (see Table 4).

Table 4 **Frequencies and ranks of positive parental remarks and child co-operative activity.**

Score X	Rank X	Score Y	Rank Y	Diff
20	6	2	2	4
8	2	7	6	4
11	5	3	3	2
25	7	1	1	6
1	1	8	7	6
9	3	5	5	2
10	4	4	4	0

Steps in the calculation of Spearman's Rho

Correlations based on similarity in ranks can be obtained using a special formula. It is important to know that the value of the correlations obtained using this formula can range from −1 to +1. −1 signifies a perfect negative correlation (see Table 4); 0 signifies no correlation; +1 signifies a perfect positive correlation (see Table 3). The Null Hypthesis is that there is no correlation between variables so that the correlation is not significantly different from 0.

Formula

$$rho = 1 - \frac{6\,\Sigma D^2}{N(N^2 - 1)}$$

1. Rank each of the two variables. If you have more than one instance of the same score in a given set, then remember to use the appropriate average rank (see notes on ranking scores from the section 'Making sense of data').

2. D (difference): subtract the rank of one variable from that of the other (the sign of the difference is unimportant).

3. D^2 : square each of these differences.

4. $6\,\Sigma D^2$: sum the squared differences, and multiply by 6.

5. $N(N^2 - 1)$: multiply the number of pairs by the number of pairs squared, minus 1.

6. Divide step 4 by step 5.

7. 1 – value obtained in step 6.

8. Consult the table of critical values to establish whether the observed correlation is significant. Note that in order for your obtained correlation to be significant at a given level, it has to be equal to, or greater than, the value shown in the table. One-tailed tests of significance apply only when the direction of correlation is predicted in advance (e.g. a predicted negative correlation). Notice how (as with all statistics) as the number of cases increases (sample size), the smaller the correlation value required for significance.

Thinking about this curious formula

If there are no differences in ranks between the two variables (i.e. perfect alignment of ranks), then $6\ \Sigma D^2$ will be equal to 0, as will be the whole of the right-hand side of the formula. 1 minus 0 produces 1: a perfect positive correlation.

If the differences between the two variables are at a maximum, then the right-hand side of the formula will be equal to 2. 1 minus 2 = −1: a perfect negative correlation.

It is important to appreciate that a significant correlation does not necessarily mean that X causes Y. This is because we have not manipulated variable X to see its effect on Y. It is possible that Y causes X (e.g. co-operative children receive more positive remarks from their parents). It is also possible that a 'third variable' accounts for the correlation between X and Y (e.g. children who receive a lot of positive remarks may tend to be first-born or only children), and these may be more co-operative with peers. Thus, in this case, the correlation between positive parental remarks and co-operative behaviour does not reflect a causal linkage between the two variables.

Another, more graphic example of a 'third variable' giving rise to a correlation is as follows: there may be a correlation between the number of guards fainting on duty at Buckingham Palace and the softness of the tarmac on the road surface. This does not mean that one of these variables causes the other. Rather, both may be caused by a third variable: air temperature.

Plots of X and Y showing different correlations.

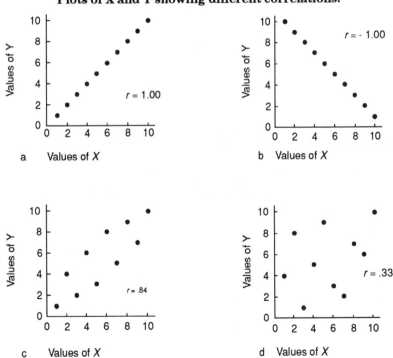

581

Critical values of Spearman's Rho

n*	Level of significance for one-tailed test			
	.05	.025	.01	.005
	Level of significance for two-tailed test			
	.10	.05	.02	.01
5	.900	1.000	1.000	—
6	.829	.886	.943	1.000
7	.714	.786	.893	.929
8	.643	.738	.833	.881
9	.600	.683	.783	.833
10	.564	.648	.746	.794
12	.506	.591	.712	.777
14	.456	.544	.645	.715
16	.425	.506	.601	.665
18	.399	.475	.564	.625
20	.377	.450	.534	.591
22	.359	.428	.508	.562
24	.343	.409	.485	.537
26	.329	.392	.465	.515
28	.317	.377	.448	.496
30	.306	.364	.432	.478

* n = number of pairs

7. Chi Square: a test for analysing associations between categorical variables

In testing the relationship between two variables we often wish to establish whether two sets of categories are related. For example, in assessing the relationship between cigarette smoking and lung cancer we can devise a test with 4 categories: smokers who have cancer; smokers who do not have cancer; non-smokers who have cancer; non-smokers who do not have cancer. In this case we will have what statisticians call a 2 x 2 contingency table (2 categories for the smoking variable x 2 categories for the cancer variable).

In this example we would expect proportionately more smokers to have cancer than non-smokers if there is truly an association between cigarette smoking and lung cancer.

	Cancer	No Cancer	
Smokers	25	15	40
Non-Smokers	11	24	35
	36	39	75

We can see from the above data that a greater proportion of smokers than non-smokers develop cancer. But can we reject the Null Hypothesis? To do this, we need to establish to what extent this distribution of frequencies is beyond what would be expected by chance.

Expected (chance) frequencies

In the above example there are 40 smokers out of a total of 75 people, and 36 people with cancer, out of a total of 75 people. By chance, we would expect 40/75 (p smokers) x 36/75 (p of people with cancer) x 75 people to be smokers and have cancer. This totals to 0.53 x 0.48 x 75 = 19.1. We can work out the expected frequencies for each of the 4 entries (cells) in the above contingency table.

The simplest way of calculating the expected frequencies is to multiply the *marginal totals* that correspond to a given cell, then divide by the grand total. For example, for the cell containing smokers with cancer the corresponding marginal totals are 36 (number of people with cancer) and 40 (number of people who smoke). If we multiply these two marginal totals, and divide by the grand total of 75, we will obtain the number of people expected to be both smokers and have cancer by chance.

Chi Square

$$X^2 = \Sigma \ \frac{(O - E)^2}{E}$$

Where O = observed frequency.

E = expected frequency.

We compute this for each of the 4 cells, and sum.

The greater the value of chi square, the more the frequencies in the different cells differ from chance. However, we need to assess whether the value obtained is statistically significant. This can be established by consulting the Chi Square Table below. This table contains the critical values that chi square must reach before an association between categorical variables is deemed significant. The probabilities in the table have been calculated by statisticians using an extension of the ideas behind the binomial distribution discussed previously.

Notes on the formula

1. $O - E$. Here we are simply determining how far away from expected levels (Null Hypothesis) our observations are deviating.

2. Why square? This is a technique that gives even greater weight to larger deviations from expected frequencies.

3. We divide by E to make this deviation proportionate. For example, for a cell where $O = 20$ and $E = 5$, the difference of 15 is far more extreme than where $O = 50$ and $E = 35$.

Chi square table

v. \ P.	0.99	0.95	0.05	0.01
1	0.0002	0.004	3.84	6.64
2	0.020	0.103	5.99	9.21
3	0.115	0.35	7.82	11.34
4	0.30	0.71	9.49	13.28
5	0.55	1.14	11.07	15.09
6	0.87	1.64	12.59	16.81
7	1.24	2.17	14.07	18.48
8	1.65	2.73	15.51	20.09
9	2.09	3.32	16.92	21.67
10	2.56	3.94	18.31	23.21
11	3.05	4.58	19.68	24.72
12	3.57	5.23	21.03	26.22
13	4.11	5.89	22.36	27.69
14	4.66	6.57	23.68	29.14
15	5.23	7.26	25.00	30.58

Using the table

1. Work out the degrees of freedom in your contingency table. Degrees of freedom = (number of rows, minus 1) x (number of columns, minus 1). In our cancer x smoking example, we have (2 rows minus 1) x (2 columns minus 1) = 1 degree of freedom.

2. Locate the appropriate degrees of freedom in the table under v. In our case, we begin with the first row where $v. = 1$.

3. Go along this row and look for a value that is equal to, or smaller than, your own chi square value. If this value is significant at $p < 0.05$, then check to see whether it is also significant at $p < 0.01$.